The New Zealand
Bed & Breakfast Book
2009

PUBLISHED BY...

Moonshine Press

P.O. Box 6843
Wellington
New Zealand
Tel: +64 4 385-2615
Fax: +64 4 385-2694
Web: www.bnb.co.nz
Email: info@bnb.co.nz

© Moonshine Press, 2008

ISBN 978-0-9582569-4-2

Cover illustration *Afternoon Corner of the Garden,* a watercolour by Jane Smith, courtesy of Millwood Gallery, Wellington

Welcome to this edition of The Bed & Breakfast Book. Bed & Breakfast in New Zealand means a warm welcome and a unique holiday experience. Most B&B accommodation is in private homes with a sprinkling of guesthouses and small hotels. Each listing in the guide has been written by the host themselves and you will discover their warmth and personality through their writing. The New Zealand Bed & Breakfast Book is not just an accommodation guide – it is an introduction to a uniquely New Zealand holiday experience. The best holidays are often remembered by the friends one makes. How many of us have loved a country because of one or two memorable individuals we encountered? For the traveller who wants to experience the real New Zealand and get to know its people, bed and breakfast offers an opportunity to do just that. We recommend you don't try to travel too far in one day. Take time to enjoy the company of your hosts and other local people. You will find New Zealand hosts friendly and generous, and eager to share their local knowledge with you.

We have carefully inspected every property;

B&B Approved; All B&Bs in The Bed & Breakfast Book have been inspected on joining. They conform to the Schedule of Standards following. As important as the requirement of meeting a physical standard, we expect that all of our properties will offer excellent hospitality. Some hosts who are members of associations or marketing groups, which also undertake inspections, have chosen to display the logos below.

The **@home NEW ZEALAND** logo represents the largest organisation of hosted accommodation providers in New Zealand. It assures you of a warm welcome from friendly, helpful hosts. Accommodations displaying this logo are regularly assessed every two years and have met the quality standards set by the Association.

Qualmark™ is New Zealand tourism's official mark of quality. All Qualmark™ licenced accommodation listed in this directory means they have been independently assessed as professional and trustworthy, so you can book and buy with confidence. They will meet your essential requirements of cleanliness, safety, security and comfort; and offer a range and quality of services appropriate to their star grade.

Heritage Inns; A collection of luxury historic hosted character bed and breakfast lodges across NZ, are superior and often recommended by tourists. Our B&Bs have knowledgeable and friendly hosts. Our luxury accommodation ranges from the quiet honeymoon lodge in boutique romantic locations to central city accommodation - rivaling superior apartments, hotels or motels. Alternatively, enjoy the genuine NZ experience of an idyllic farmstay, lodge or luxury country B&B.

Superior Inns; Superior Inns of New Zealand properties are specially selected. All offer a true bed and breakfast experience, highlights of your visit to New Zealand. The specially selected bed and breakfast properties offer spacious bedrooms with bathrooms, luxury fittings, private guest lounges, fabulous delectable breakfasts and a chance to meet other visitors or be on your own. Our hosts can organise airport pickups, rental cars, restaurant bookings, honeymoon packages and short stay options.

Finding your way around
We travel from north to south listing the towns as we come to them. In addition, we've divided New Zealand into geographical regions, a map of which is included at the start of each chapter. In some regions, such as Southland, our listings take a detour off the north to south route, and follow their nose - it will soon become obvious.

Happy Travelling
The B&B Book Team

Our Guarantee

Hosts in The New Zealand Bed & Breakfast Book are committed to offering quality hospitality. If you receive hospitality which is less than you expected please discuss your concerns with your hosts at the time. If you are not satisfied you should contact the publishers who will take up the matter with the hosts. If you are still not satisfied the publishers will refund their assessment of a fair proportion of the tariff you paid.

Your comments

We welcome your views on The Bed & Breakfast Book and the hosts you meet.
Please visit our website **www.bnb.co.nz** or write to us at,
PO Box 6843, Wellington, New Zealand.

Comment Forms

Please help us to maintain our high standards by sending us comments about where you stayed. Guest Comments forms are available from your hosts.

- You may submit your comment on our website **www.bnb.co.nz**

- Or your hosts will give you a comment form.

- Or simply cut one from the back of the book.

- Each comment returned will be in our ongoing monthly draw for a free night's B&B.

- Each person staying can submit a comment for an increased chance of success.

- Guest comments are displayed on the hosts' pages at **www.bnb.co.nz**

About Bed & Breakfast

Our B&Bs range from homely to luxurious, but you can always be assured of generous hospitality.

Types of accommodation
Traditional B&B
Generally small owner-occupied home accommodation usually with private guest living and dining areas.
Homestay
A homestay is a B&B where you share the family's living area.
Farmstay
Country accommodation, usually on a working farm.
Self-contained
Separate self-contained accommodation, with kitchen and living/dining room. Breakfast provisions usually provided at least for the first night.
Separate/suite
Similar to self-contained but without kitchen facilities. Living/dining facilities may be limited.

Bathrooms
Ensuite and private bathrooms are for your use exclusively.
Guests share bathroom means you will be sharing with other guests.
Family share means you will be sharing with the family.

Tariff
The prices listed are in New Zealand dollars and include GST. Prices listed are subject to change, and any change to listed prices will be stated at time of booking. Some hosts offer a discount for children - this applies to age 12 or under unless otherwise stated. Most of our B&Bs will accept credit cards.

Reservations
We recommend you contact your hosts well in advance to be sure of confirming your accommodation. Most hosts require a deposit so make sure you understand their cancellation policy. Please let your hosts know if you have to cancel, they will have spent time preparing for you. You may also book accommodation through some travel agents or via specialised B&B reservation services.

Breakfast & Dinner
Breakfast is included in the tariff, with each host offering their own menu. You'll be surprised at the range of delicious breakfasts available, many using local produce. If you would like dinner most hosts require 24 hours notice.

Smoking
Most of our B&Bs are non-smoking, but smoking is permitted outside. Listings displaying the no smoking logo do not permit smoking anywhere on the property. B&Bs which have a smoking area inside mention this in their text.

Accessibility
     Certified as being wheelchair accessible.

Schedule of Standards

General
Friendly, warm greeting at door by host
Local tourism and transport information available to guests
Property appearance neat and tidy, internally and externally
Absolute cleanliness of the home in all areas used by the guests
Absolute cleanliness of kitchen, refrigerator and food storage areas
Gate or roadside identification of property
Protective clothing and footwear available for farmstay guests
Hosts accept responsibility to comply with local body bylaws
Host will be present to welcome and farewell guests
Hosts' pets and young children mentioned in listing
Smoke alarms in each guest bedroom and above each landing
Evacuation advice card displayed in each bedroom (recommended)
Working torch beside every bed
Suitable fire extinguisher in kitchen and on landing of each upper floor (recommended)
Fire blanket in kitchen (recommended)

Hosts accept responsibility to comply with applicable laws and regulations
Fire safety laws and requirements
Insurances
Swimming and spa pool regulations
Other laws impacting on operation of a B&B

Bedrooms
Each bedroom solely dedicated to guests with...
Bed heating
Heating
Light controlled from the bed
Wardrobe space with variety of hangers
Drawers
Good quality floor covering
Mirror
Power point near a mirror
Waste paper basket
Drinking glasses
Clean pillows with additional available
No Host family items stored in the room
Night light for guidance to w.c. if not adjacent to bedroom
Blinds or curtains on all windows where appropriate
Good quality mattresses in sound condition on a sound base
Clean bedding appropriate to the climate, with extra availabl

Bathroom & toilet facilities
At least one bathroom adequately ventilated and equipped with...
Bath or shower
Wash handbasin and mirror
Covered wastebasket in bathroom
Extra toilet roll
Lock on bathroom and toilet doors
Electric razor point if bedrooms are without a suitable power point
Soap, towels, bathmat, facecloths, fresh for each new guest
Towels changed or dried daily for guests staying more than one night
Sufficient bathroom and toilet facilities to serve family and guests

New Zealand and Regions

Northland

Whangarei

Auckland

Coromandel

Bay of Plenty

Waikato, King Country

Tauranga

Hamilton

Rotorua

Gisborne

Gisborne

Taranaki, Wanganui,
Ruapehu, Rangitikei

New Plymouth

Napier

Manawatu, Horowhenua

Nelson, Golden Bay

Hawkes Bay

Palmerston North

Wairarapa

Masterton

Nelson

Blenheim

Wellington

West Coast

Greymouth

Marlborough

Canterbury

Christchurch

Timaru

South Canterbury,
North Otago

Queenstown

Dunedin

Otago, North Catlins

Invercargill

Southland,
South Catlins

Stewart Island

Contents

Introduction _____ 2
New Zealand Regions Map _____ 6

North Island
Northland _____ 8
Auckland _____ 50
Waikato, King Country _____ 99
Coromandel _____ 116
Bay of Plenty _____ 138
Gisborne, East Coast _____ 186
Taranaki, Wanganui, Ruapehu, Rangitikei _____ 190
Hawkes Bay _____ 206
Manawatu, Horowhenua _____ 228
Wairarapa _____ 236
Wellington _____ 243

South Island
Marlborough _____ 281
Nelson, Golden Bay _____ 298
West Coast _____ 332
Canterbury _____ 354
South Canterbury, North Otago _____ 413
Otago, North Catlins _____ 433
Southland, South Catlins _____ 478

Index _____ 497

Northland

Houhora *44 km N of Kaitaia*
Houhora Lodge & Homestay *Homestay*

Jacqui & Bruce Malcolm
3994 Far North Road,
Houhora,
RD 4,
Kaitaia

Tel (09) 409 7884
or 021 926 992
Fax (09) 409 7801
houhora.homestay@xtra.co.nz
www.topstay.co.nz

Double/Twin $130-$180
Single $100-$110
(Full breakfast)
Dinner $45 by arrangement
Visa MC accepted
Children welcome
3 King/Twin 3 Single (3 bdrm)
Bathrooms: 2 Ensuite 1 Private

We have fled our largest city with Max our Hunterway cross dog to live on the shores of Houhora Harbour, and look forward to sharing this special part of New Zealand with you. Come and enjoy remote coastal walks, shell-collecting, Cape Reinga, 90 Mile Beach and other attractions. We can arrange 4x4 trips, sport or game fishing and provide relaxed and quality accommodation on your return. Home-made bread, home-grown fruit, home-pressed olive oil, vegetables and eggs. Email, internet, fax and laundry facilities available.

Cape Karikari - Whatuwhiwhi *30 km SE of Kaitaia*
Riviera Lodge *Luxury B&B Apartment with Kitchen Luxury B&B*

Lisa Wright
69a Whatuwhiwhi Road,
RD 3, Cape Karikari, Kaitaia

Tel (09) 406 7128 or 027 284 6380
021 277 2510
(06) 752 3989
riviera.lodge@xtra.co.nz
www.rivieralodge.co.nz

Double/Twin $130-$200
Single $130-$200
(Continental breakfast)
Children over 1yr $40
High rate 21 December-28 Feb
including public holidays
Visa MC accepted
Children welcome
1 Queen 1 Single (1 bdrm)
Bathrooms: 1 Ensuite Shower

Riviera Lodge is a Luxury B&B/semi self contained unit nestled on the edge of Doubtless Bay set alongside native bush, 15 minutes off Highway 10 Whatuwhiwhi, Cape Karikari. Recreational activities: rock fishing, diving, swimming, also fishing trips arranged.Walk to Perihipi Bay,handy to Matai Bay, Rangiputa and Tokerau beach.Just minutes to Carrington Resort which has a 18 hole golf course, winery and restaurant.Close to dairy & cafe etc; We at Riviera Lodge welcomes you to the winterless north.

Coopers Beach *4 km N of Mangonui*
Doubtless Bay Lodge *B&B*

Barbara & Ian Easterbrook
33 Cable Bay Block Road,
Coopers Beach,
Mangonui

Tel (09) 406 1661
or 021 824 571
Fax (09) 406 1662
enquiries@doubtlessbaylodge.co.nz
www.doubtlessbaylodge.co.nz

Double/Twin $90-$120
Single $70-$85
(Full breakfast)
Children $25
Visa MC Eftpos accepted
Children welcome
3 Queen 1 Twin (4 bdrm)
Bathrooms: 4 Ensuite

Enjoy your breakfast on the balcony or in the dining room and experience the panoramic views over Doubtless Bay and surrounding countryside. Short walk to the golden sands of Coopers Beach and local shops. Each room has its own ensuite, Sky TV, fridge, tea/coffee making facilities. Guest laundry and barbeque available. Cape Reinga tours, fishing trips and golf games can be arranged. Visit the many historic places, isolated beaches and local wineries in the area. Let us help you make this the perfect holiday destination.

Kaitaia - Pamapuria *10 km S of Kaitaia*
Plane Tree Lodge *B&B Homestay Cottage with Kitchen*

Rosemary & Mike Wright
Pamapuria,
RD2,
Kaitaia,
Northland

Tel (09) 408 0995
Fax (09) 408 0959
reservationsplanetreelodge@xtra.co.nz
www.plane-tree-lodge.net.nz

Double/Twin $150-$185
Single $100-$135
(Special breakfast)
Children negotiable
2 s/c cottages sleep 4 & 6 $180-$220
Visa MC accepted
Children welcome
5 Queen 2 Twin (7 bdrm)
Bathrooms: 2 Ensuite 2 Private

Rosemary, Mike, Polly & Jenna, (their golden retrievers), welcome you to Northland, where summer lingers longer. Experience the beauty & tranquility of subtropical NZ. Enjoy the difference of receiving great hospitality in a quiet, peaceful rural setting with large relaxing gardens. Your friendly knowledgable hosts love helping to plan your activities or adventures from their architectually designed home. Relax in the evening with a spa & complementary glass of wine, & wake each morning to birdsong & the aroma of a delicious breakfast.

Ahipara *15 km W of Kaitaia*

Beachfront *Luxury Apartment with Kitchen Self contained and serviced*

Paul and Jenny Steele
14 Kotare Street,
Ahipara
0551

Tel (09) 409 4007
or 021 227 3376
Fax (09) 409 4007
pauljenny@beachfront.net.nz
www.beachfront.net.nz

Double/Twin $150-$350
Single $120-$300
(Full breakfast)
Dinner $60 pp by arrangement
Breakfast extra
Visa MC Eftpos accepted
Children and pets welcome
4 King 2 Double/Twin (4 bdrm)
Bathrooms: 4 Ensuite
All bedrooms ensuite

Upmarket absolute water front self-contained seviced, private apartments. A studio covered patio with a 2nd bedroom option. A two bedroom apartment with balconies. All bedrooms ensuite - wireless broadband -surf views from every pillow Paul and Jenny are 5th generatiion New Zealanders and have a cat called Sunshine who is not allowed in the apartments.

~

Kerikeri *3 km E of Kerikeri*

Matariki Orchard *B&B Homestay*

Alison & David Bridgman
14 Pa Road,
Kerikeri,
Bay of Islands

Tel (09) 407 7577
or 027 408 0621
Fax (09) 407 7593
matarikihomestay@xtra.co.nz
www.kerikeri.co.nz/matariki

Double/Twin $160-$180
Single $100
(Full breakfast)
Children negotiable
Visa MC accepted
Pet free home
Children welcome
1 King 1 Queen 2 Single (3 bdrm)
Bathrooms: 1 Ensuite 1 Private 1 Guest share

We welcome guests to our home large garden swimming pool and subtropical orchard.Are walking distance to historic area[oldest buildings]and 3k to township.Retired farmers and David a local tour operator for 9yrs loves to help with where to go and what to do Walks and beaches close by. We are 5th generation New Zealanders and have been home hosting for 17yrs our wealth of knowledge has been enjoyed by guests. No pets or children can arrange tour bookings. Phone for directions.

Kerikeri - Okaihau *12 km W of Kerikeri*
Clotworthy Farmstay *B&B Farmstay*

Shennett & Neville Clotworthy
914 Wiroa Road,
RD 1,
Okaihau,
Bay of Islands

Tel (09) 401 9371
or 0274 941 759
Fax (09) 401 9371

Double/Twin $90
Single $65
(Full breakfast)
Dinner $25 by arrangement
Visa MC accepted
1 Queen 2 Single (2 bdrm)
Bathrooms: 1 Guest share

We farm cattle, sheep and horses on our 310 acres. There are panoramic views of the Bay of Islands area from our home 1000 feet above sea level. Of 1840s pioneering descent, our interests are travel, farming, genealogy and equestrian activities. We have an extensive library on Northland history and families. Directions: SH10 take Wiroa/Airport Road at the Kerikeri intersection. 9km on the right OR SH1, take Kerikeri Road just south of Okaihau. We are fourth house on the left, past the golf course (8km).

Kerikeri *10 km N of Kerikeri Central*
Kerikeri Inlet View *B&B Homestay Farmstay*

Trish & Ryan Daniells
99C Furness Road,
RD 3,
Kerikeri

Tel (09) 407 7477
Fax (09) 407 7478
kerikeri_inlet_view@hotmail.com

Double/Twin $95
Single $50
(Full breakfast)
Children $15
Dinner $18 by arrangement
Backpackers $15 (no breakfast or water view)
Visa MC accepted
Children and pets welcome
1 Queen 2 Double/Twin
2 Single (3 bdrm)
Bathrooms: 1 Ensuite 1 Private 1 Guest share

We welcome you to our spacious home on top of our 1100 acre beef and sheep farm. Enjoy the superb views of the Kerikeri Inlet and the Bay of Islands while you relax in our spa pool. Join us for breakfast consisting of seasonal fruit, homemade bread and butter, free-range chook eggs, and our own sausages, before exploring the many attractions around Kerikeri. Backpackers has private lockable bedrooms, lounge, kitchen/laundry. Note: please phone first for detailed directions. We can speak Japanese.

Kerikeri *2 km W of Kerikeri*
Palm View *Luxury B&B*
Judy & Tony Pratt
8 Kotare Heights,
Kerikeri,
Bay of Islands

Tel (09) 407 6883
or 021 0245 0615
palmview@xtra.co.nz
www.palmview.co.nz

Double/Twin $205-$320
Single $195-$300
(Full breakfast)
Dinner by arrangement
Visa MC accepted
Not suitable for children
1 King/Twin 2 King (3 bdrm)
Bathrooms: 3 Ensuite

Judy and Tony welcome you to Palm View House which was built and opened in 2007. This is a place to unwind and relax in our acre of garden, planted with many native and English shrubs.Our 3 spacious luxury bedrooms with ensuites containing heated towel rails/floors,bathrobes, toiletries, hairdryers. Bedrooms have, fridges, TV, electric blankets, iron and ironing board, coffee and tea making facilities, also enjoy spectacular inlet views .We are 2 ks from Kerikeri township where you will find many cafes, restaurants and many attraction.

Kerikeri *20 km N of Paihia*
Glenfalloch *B&B Homestay*
Keith
48 Landing Road,
Kerikeri

Tel (09) 407 5471
Fax (09) 407 5473
glenfall@ihug.co.nz
www.kerikeri-accommodation.co.nz

Double/Twin $90-$115
Single $80-$90
(Full breakfast)
Children $25
Dinner $30pp by arrangement
Visa MC accepted
Children welcome
1 King 1 Queen 1 Double/Twin
1 Single (3 bdrm)
Bathrooms: 2 Ensuite 1 Private

Venture down Glenfalloch's driveway to our secluded bed and breakfast, nestled in a garden paradise. Enjoy the hospitality of Keith. Relax in the spa and swimming pool and on teh decks, or for the energetic there is lawn tennis. Glenfalloch is just 500 metres from Kerikeri's Stone Store and Kemp Mission House, and adjacent to the lovely Rainbow Falls walking track. Kerikeri is unique and offers some good golf courses within short distances, lovely shops and excellent restaurants.

Paihia *7 km N of Paihia*
Lily Pond Estate B&B (Est 1989) *B&B*

Allwyn & Graeme Sutherland
725B Puketona Road,
Paihia
Lily Pond Estate sign at gate

Tel (09) 402 7041

Double/Twin $105
Single $60
(Full breakfast)
1 Double/Twin 1 Twin
1 Single (3 bdrm)
Bathrooms: 1 Private 1 Guest share

Drive in through an avenue of mature Liquid Amber trees to our comfortable timber home on our 5 acre country estate growing citrus and pip fruit. The guest wing has views of the fountain, bird aviary, small lake and black swan with the double and twin rooms having private verandah access. Fresh orange juice, fruit and home-made jams are served at breakfast. We are born New Zealanders, and will gladly share our Bay of Island knowledge to make your visit most memorable.

Paihia *1.5 km S of Paihia*
Te Haumi House *B&B Homestay*

Enid & Ernie Walker
12 Seaview Road,
Paihia

Tel (09) 402 8046
Fax (09) 402 8046
enidanderniewalker@xtra.co.nz
www.bnb.co.nz/tehaumihouse.html

Double/Twin up to $100
Single up to $70
(Continental breakfast)
Visa MC accepted
Pet free home
Not suitable for children
2 Queen 1 Single (2 bdrm)
Bathrooms: 1 Guest share
1 Family share

Millennium Sunrise. Welcome to our modern waterfront home, set amongst subtropical gardens with expansive harbour views, just minutes from tourist activities and town centre. Guests enjoy privacy through a clever split-level design. Buffet breakfast with a choice of dining room, garden deck or courtyard. Ample off-street parking and courtesy pick up from bus available. Descendants of early settlers, we have a good knowledge of local history. Ernie is a Masonic Lodge member.

Paihia *0.5 km SE of Wharf*

Craicor Accommodation *Luxury Apartment with Kitchen*

Garth Craig & Anne Corbett
49 Kings Road, Paihia
P.O.Box 15, Paihia

Tel (09) 402 7882
Fax (09) 402 7883
craicor@actrix.gen.nz
www.craicor-accom.co.nz

Double/Twin $160
Single $120
(Optional continental breakfast
by arrangement $7.50pp)
Visa MC Amex accepted
Not suitable for children
2 King 2 Single (2 bdrm)
Bathrooms: 2 Ensuite

The perfect spot for those seeking a quiet, sunny and central location. Discover the Garden Suite and Tree House. Self-contained modern apartments nestled in a garden setting with trees that almost hug you, native birds and sea views. Each apartment has ensuite bathroom, fully equipped kitchen for self-catering, super king bed, TV, insect screens and is tastefully decorated to reflect the natural colours of the surroundings. Safe off-street parking, all within a 5 minute stroll to the waterfront, restaurants and town centre.

Paihia *0.5 km N of Paihia Central*

Marlin House *Luxury B&B Apartment with Kitchen*

George & Marie-Claire Houry
15 Bayview Road,
Paihia,
Bay of Islands

Tel (09) 402 8550
or 021 882 169
Fax (09) 402 6770
marlinhouse@xtra.co.nz

Double/Twin $180
Single $150
(Special breakfast)
Laundry $10
Visa MC accepted
1 King 1 Queen 1 Twin (3 bdrm)
Bathrooms: 3 Ensuite

Marlin House is a large comfortable colonial-style house with spacious luxury accommodation in 3 self-contained ensuites with fridge microwave and TV, all with seperate entrances onto decks with seating overlooking the bay. Ample off-road parking is available. Situated in a quiet tree-clad spot above Paihia with beautiful sea views and only 4 minutes easy walk to the beach shops and restaurants. Special breakfasts with home-baking. Benny the cat is outside (minimum 2 night stay).

Paihia *0.2 km S of wharf*

Chalet Romantica *B&B & Apartment with Kitchen*
Ed & Inge Amsler
Bedggood Close, Paihia/Bay of Islands, 0200

Tel (09) 402 8270
or 027 226 6400
Fax (09) 402 8278
info-chalet@xtra.co.nz
www.chaletromantica.homestead.com/accom1.html

Double/Twin $135-$210
Single $125-$210
(Continental breakfast)
Children $15 when sharing room with parents
Apartments $155-$255, breakfast $15pp
Visa MC Eftpos accepted
Children welcome
2 King/Twin 1 Queen (3 bdrm)
Bathrooms: 2 Ensuite 1 Private

Spoil yourself and experience the magic of Chalet Romantica. Each room has its own balcony with superb seaviews, quality furnishings and fittings, wireless internet, crisp linen and extra comfy beds. Central town location within a stroll to shops, wharf, restaurants etc. In house pool, spa, gym and laundry facilities.

For our B&B guests a gourmet breakfast is served in stunning conservatory overlooking the Bay. We'd love to welcome you and to share our slice of paradise with you!

Paihia *0.5 km NW of Paihia*
Windermere *B&B Apartment with Kitchen*

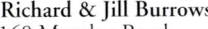

Richard & Jill Burrows
168 Marsden Road,
Paihia,
Bay of Islands

Tel (09) 402 8696
or 021 115 7436
Fax (09) 402 5095
windermere@igrin.co.nz
www.windermere.co.nz

Double/Twin $120-$220
Single $100-$180
(Continental breakfast)
Children $25
Extra adult $50
Visa MC accepted
2 Queen 2 Single (2 bdrm)
Bathrooms: 2 Ensuite

Windermere is a large modern family home set in a bush setting and yet located right on one of the best beaches in the Bay of Islands. Superior accommodation is provided with suites having their own ensuite and kitchen facilities. For longer stays 1 suite has its own laundry, dryer and fully equipped kitchen. The other suite has microwave and fridge only. Each suite has its own decks where you can sit and enjoy the view enhanced by spectacular sunsets. Sky TV. Outdoor Spa.

Paihia *6 km W of Paihia*
Appledore Lodge *Luxury B&B Separate Suite*
Cottage with Kitchen

Janet & Jim Pugh
624, Puketona Road,
Paihia, Bay of Islands

Tel (09) 402 8007
or 021 165 0072
Fax (09) 402 8007
appledorelodge@xtra.co.nz
www.appledorelodge.co.nz

Double/Twin $170-$260
Single $140-$190
(Continental breakfast)
Minimum 2 nights occupancy
Visa MC Amex accepted
Not suitable for children under 12
2 King/Twin 1 Queen
1 Double/Twin (4 bdrm)
Bathrooms: 4 Ensuite

Miniature waterfalls and rapids await your discovery as the Waitangi River gently tumbles past your bedroom window. Tranquillity & peace is here to rediscover with our spellbinding riverside setting where you can fish for trout or stroll the riverbank. Set in two acres all our accommodation have magnificent views up & down the river, are self-contained with ensuite & private decks where Janet's special home made breakfast basket is provided for your enjoyment. Janet, Jim & Misty our golden retriever look forward to meeting you.

Paihia *0.2 km N of Paihia-Central*
Allegra House *B&B Apartment with Kitchen*
Heinz & Brita Marti
39 Bayview Road,
Paihia,
Bay of Islands

Tel (09) 402 7932
or 027 470 1137
Fax (09) 402 7930
allegrahouse@xtra.co.nz
www.allegra.co.nz

Double/Twin $135-$210
Single $135-$210
(Continental breakfast)
Children negotiable
Apartment $175-$240
Visa MC accepted
1 King/Twin 1 King
1 Queen (3 bdrm)
Bathrooms: 3 Ensuite

Allegra House, our spacious, modern home is centrally located, just up the hill from Paihia's wharf, shops and restaurants. Spectacular views from all rooms. B&B rooms have ensuite bathroom, tea/coffee making facilities, fridge, TV and balcony. Self catering apartment with separate bedroom, large bathroom, fully equipped kitchen and spacious lounge opening onto a large balcony. Each room has its own air conditioning and the whole house is smokefree. BBQ, laundry facilities and internet access. Plenty of good local information.

Paihia *7 km N of Paihia*
Quilters Rest *B&B Separate Suite*
Sue & Andy Brown
41 Retreat Road,
Paihia,
Bay of Islands

Tel (09) 402 6047
or 021 164 7483
a.s.brown@xtra.co.nz

Double/Twin $120-$180
(Special breakfast)
Visa MC accepted
Pet free home
Not suitable for children
1 Queen (1 bdrm)

Bathrooms: 1 Ensuite

Enjoy the peace and tranquility at our private located home. Set in 3 acres of English style gardens, situated in beautiful countryside. Minutes from the waterfront of Paihia and within easy reach of all that the Bay of Islands and Northland offers. Relax by the pool and spa, for your exclusive use or just watch the sunset. A slice of paradise in your private suite with husband and wife hosts discretely on hand, devoted to making your stay completely memorable. Resident horse called 'Bear'.

Paihia *0.5 km SW of Post Office*
Decks of Paihia *Luxury B&B*
Philip & Wendy Hopkinson
69 School Road,
Paihia,
Bay of Islands

Tel (09) 402 6146
or 021 278 7558
Fax (09) 402 6147
info@decksofpaihia.com
www.decksofpaihia.com

Double/Twin $165-$220
(Continental breakfast)
Visa MC accepted
Not suitable for children
3 King/Twin (3 bdrm)
Bathrooms: 3 Ensuite
Stylish tile & granite bathrooms

Recently constructed contemporary home incorporating 3 guest suites with private ensuite bathrooms. Quiet peaceful central Paihia location. Stylish modern furnishings provide a very comfortable interior with generous living spaces. All guest suites open onto secluded deck areas overlooking the swimming pool offering ample sun drenched outdoor living space. Philip and Wendy are experienced operators in the hospitality industry, and offer an extensive knowledge of Northland. Philip has strong links to the area - his great grandfather Patrick McGovern was Russel's police constable during the 1880s.

Paihia *1 km N of Paihia Central*
Admiral's View Lodge *B&B Separate Suite Apartment with Kitchen*
Deb & Mark Yarrall
2 MacMurray Road,
Paihia,
Bay of Islands

Tel (09) 402 6236
Fax (09) 402 6237
admiralsviewlodge@ihug.co.nz
www.admiralsviewlodge.co.nz

Double/Twin $95-$245
(Breakfast by arrangement)
Children welcome in apartments and
twin studios
Apartments $195-$275
Visa MC Diners Amex Eftpos accepted
Pet free home Children welcome
4 King 6 Queen 2 Double/Twin
6 Twin 11 Single (11 bdrm)
Bathrooms: 11 Ensuite

Relax at our Qualmark rated 4+ star lodge in a quiet location. Sea views (most units), sunny terraces. 2 spacious Apartments, 7 Luxury studios, 2 with spa baths, plus our popular Garden studios. Meander along to the beach, restaurants/cafes & activities, take the ferry to Romantic Russell or soak up historic Waitangi. Meet our children - Guy and Anna - and our friendly cat, Eva. Sky TV; airconditioning (most units); high speed internet; Dvd players, activity booking service; Free bikes & tennis; Guest BBQs; Filtered water.

Paihia *1 km S of Paihia Central*
All View Lodge *B&B*

Robyn & Peter Rhodes
30 H Sullivans Road,
Paihia,
Bay of Islands

Tel (09) 402 8606
Fax (09) 402 8607
allviewlodge@xtra.co.nz

Double/Twin $220-$250
(Full breakfast)
2 day min stay may apply
during peak season.
3 Queen 2 Single (3 bdrm)
Bathrooms: 1 Ensuite 1 Private

Absolute beachfront, 5 min stroll along beach to cafes and tourist pier. We have 2 suites, 1x1 bedroom and a 1x2 bedroom, both with ensuites, lg walk-in showers, spacious lounge/dining areas and private patios. 1 suite has a 2 person bath. Guests full laundry and kitchen adjacent to both suites. Private beach access. Superb uninterrupted sea and island views, complimentary kayaks, start of coastal walking track. No traffic noise. Warm friendly hosts, generous full breakfast and evening meals available.

Paihia *3 km N of Paihia Central*
Fallsview B&B *B&B Homestay*

Midge & Bob Turner
4 Fallsview Road,
Haruru,
Paihia
RD 1

Tel (09) 402 7871
or 027 200 9523
turnerfallsview@xtra.co.nz
www.fallsview.co.nz

Double/Twin $120
Single $70
(Full breakfast)
1 Double/Twin 1 Single (3 bdrm)
Bathrooms: 1 Guest share, seperate
toilet. Large bathroom with shower
and bath for guests use only

A modern apartment with comfortable beds, large sunny lounge with fridge, microwave, stereo, TV, tea coffee facilities and access to pretty garden. Off street parking. Breakfast upstairs with glorious country views and glimpse of the Haruru Falls. Our boxer dog is a big softy.

Paihia *8 km E of Paihia*
Morepork Riverside Lodge *B&B Homestay*

Paul & Barbara
846 Puketona Road,
Paihia, Bay of Islands

Tel (09) 402 5577
or 021 986 687
Fax (09) 402 5575
enquiries@moreporklodge.co.nz
www.moreporklodge.co.nz

Double/Twin $130-$170
Single $100-$140
(Full breakfast)
May not suit younger children,
please enquire before booking
Gourmet evening meals
by arrangement
Visa MC accepted
2 King 1 Single (2 bdrm)
Bathrooms: 2 Ensuite

We offer friendly B&B/Homestay accommodation set in four acres of native bush and gardens on the Waitangi River. Private bush walk with many NZ birds, including Moreporks. Meet our friendly goats and personable cat, Kactus. We'll happily advise you on local attractions and places to dine. If you'd like to join us for a gourmet evening meal, we can swap stories. Rain-water from our reservoir is UV sterilized/filtered. NZ born hosts. Both rooms have: Private Deck, Ensuite (one with Spa bath), TV/DVD, Sofa, Tea/Coffee, Refrigerator, Wireless Broadband.

Paihia - Opua *5 km S of Paihia*
Rose Cottage *B&B Separate Suite*

Pat & Don Jansen
37A Oromahoe Road,
Opua
0200,
Bay of Islands

Tel (09) 402 8099
Fax (09) 402 8096
rosecottageopua@paradise.net.nz
www.bnb.co.nz/rosecottageopua.html

Full breakfast
Pet free home
Not suitable for children
1 Queen 1 Double/Twin (2 bdrm)
Bathrooms: 1 Private

Welcome to our home set in peaceful surroundings and overlooking picturesque upper harbour,bush and rural views.Guest rooms are comfortable and sunny opening onto a private deck area. The guest wing has private entrance, tea/coffee facilities, fridge, T.V and microwave. Hosting one party at a time is ideally suited for groups of 2,3 or 4 guests. We have hosted since 1987 and our knowledge of local history and other activities can help to make your stay memorable.Minimum booking 2 nights.

Paihia - Opua *0.3 km E of Opua*
Sinclair B&B *B&B Homestay Apartment with Kitchen*

Margaret Sinclair
7 Franklin Street,
Opua

Tel (09) 402 8285
Fax (09) 402 8285
bbopua@clear.net.nz

Double/Twin $80-$100
Single $50
(Continental breakfast)
Self-contained flat $120 double
$10 single
Children welcome
1 Double/Twin 2 Single (2 bdrm)
Bathrooms: 1 Private 1 Family share
Shower and toilet in apartment

Welcome to my lovely home above Opua Harbour. Enjoy panoramic views of water and boat activities - always something happening. Tourist activities are nearby. You may like to wander in my garden - my big interest. Downstairs is a 2 roomed unit with separate shower, toilet and private deck with stunning views. Take the Whangarei - Paihia road. Turn right for Opua - Russel Ferry. This is Franklin Street. My house is clearly visible on the seaward side.

Paihia - Opua *5 km S of Paihia*
Seascape *B&B Homestay Self-contained Flat*

Vanessa & Frank Leadley
17 English Bay Road,
Opua,
Bay of Islands

Tel (09) 402 7650
or 027 475 6793
Fax (09) 402 7650
frankandvanessa@leadley.co.nz

Double/Twin $140-$160
Single $100-$120
(Special breakfast)
Self-contained flat $140-$160
Visa MC accepted
1 Queen (1 bdrm)
Bathrooms: 1 Ensuite

Photo Taken From House

Seascape is on a tranquil bush-clad ridge. Enjoy spectacular views, stroll through bush to the coastal walk-way, enjoy our beautifully landscaped garden, experience the many activities in the Bay, or relax on your deck. We are keen NZ and international travellers. Other interests include music, art, gardening, boating, and Rotary. Our fully self-contained flat has queen bed, TV, laundry, kitchen, BBQ, own entrance and deck. You are welcome to join us for breakfast or to look after yourselves. 2 night minimum preferred.

Paihia - Opua *5 km S of Paihia*
Pt Veronica Lodge *B&B Homestay*
Audrey & John McKiernan
39 Point Veronica Drive,
Opua,
Bay of Islands

Tel (09) 402 5579
Fax (09) 402 5579
stay@ptveronicalodge.co.nz
www.ptveronicalodge.co.nz

Double/Twin $160-$220
Single $160-$200
(Full breakfast)
Visa MC accepted
Not suitable for children
1 King/Twin 1 Queen (2 bdrm)
Bathrooms: 2 Ensuite

On the coast between Paihia and Opua located above the coastal track with views towards Paihia and Russell. A special place, peaceful, romantic, restful, with bush and coastal walks. We invite you to soak in the spa or rest on the decks. Bedrooms are air conditioned with views over an inlet. Shops, Cafe's and restaurants are within 10 minutes drive. An ideal base to explore the Bay of Islands and Northland. Audrey, John and our friendly dogs, Bonnie & Clyde, welcome you.

Paihia - Opua *5 km S of Paihia*
Waterview Lodge *B&B Separate Suite Apartment with Kitchen Cottage with Kitchen*
Antionette & Jess Cherrington
14 Franklin Street, Opua,
Bay of Islands 0290

Tel (09) 402 7595
Fax (09) 402 7596
info@waterviewlodge.co.nz
www.waterviewlodge.com

Double/Twin $140-$230
Single $100-$140
(Full breakfast)
Children $20 Dinner $40-$50
Studio $150 Garden unit $150-$200,
Cottage $180-$300
Visa MC Eftpos accepted
Children welcome
3 King 3 Queen 1 Double/Twin
1 Twin 5 Single (8 bdrm)
Bathrooms: 3 Ensuite 2 Private
Bath in cottage

Overlooking the picturesque Port of Opua, Waterview Lodge is a quality accommodation establishment. The Harbour and River Suites have expansive sea views of Opua. quality linen, ensuite, TV, CD, telephone, fridge and tea making facilities. Breakfasts are complimentary with the suites. The 3 bedroom cottage is a charming residence capturing sun and sea views. The 2 bedroom Garden unit is located next to the garden suite. We enjoy living at Waterview Lodge with our son Oliver aged 13, and two little dogs Amy and Milly.

Russell - Matauwhi Bay *1 km E of Russell*

Ounuwhao B&B *B&B Separate Suite Cottage with Kitchen Seperate Suite*
Marilyn Nicklin
16 Hope Avenue, Matauwhi Bay, Russell
The Heart of the Bay of Islands

Tel (09) 403 7310 or 027 414 1310   Fax (09) 403 8310
thenicklins@xtra.co.nz   www.bedandbreakfastbayofislands.co.nz

Double $250-$350 Single $160-$200 (Full breakfast)
Children under 12 $45
Self-contained & garden suite double $280-$350   Visa MC accepted
2 King 4 Queen 3 Twin 2 Single (7 bdrm)
Bathrooms: 5 Ensuite 2 Private

Welcome to historic Russell, the Heart of the Bay of Islands and the first settled area of NZ. Take a step back into a bygone era and spend some time with us in our delightful, nostalgic, immaculately restored Victorian villa (Circa 1894).

Enjoy your own large guest lounge; tea/coffee and biscuits always available, with open fire in the cooler months, and wrap-around verandahs for you to relax and take in the warm sea breezes. Each of our four queen rooms have traditional wallpapers and paintwork,

with hand-made patchwork quilts and fresh flowers to create a lovingly detailed, traditional romantic interior. Breakfast is served in our farmhouse kitchen around the large kauri dining table or alfresco on the verandah if you wish. It is an all home-made affair; from the freshly baked fruit and nut bread, to the yummy daily special and the jam conserves.

Our self-contained cottage is set in park-like grounds for your privacy and enjoyment: with two double bedrooms, it is ideal for a family or two couples travelling together. It has a large lounge overlooking the reserve and out into the bay, a sunroom and fully self-contained kitchen. Wonderful for people looking for that special place for peace and time-out. Maximum four persons. Breakfast is available if required. Complimentary afternoon tea on arrival. Laundry service available.

We look forward to meeting you soon. Our homes are SMOKE-FREE. We are closed June and July. EXPERIENCE OUR HISTORIC B&B. ENJOY A WORLD OF DIFFERENCE

Russell *0.1 km W of Russell Central*
Te Manaaki *Apartment with Kitchen Cottage with Kitchen*

Sharyn & Dudley Smith
2 Robertson Road,
Russell 0242
PO Box 203,
Russell 0242

Tel (09) 403 7200
or (021) 972 171
Fax (09) 403 7537
info@temanaaki.co.nz
www.temanaaki.co.nz

Double/Twin $150-$280
Single $150-$280
(Full breakfast)
Children $20
Visa MC accepted
Children welcome
2 King 1 Twin (2 bdrm)
Bathrooms: 2 Ensuite

Te Manaaki overlooks the picturesque harbour and village of historic Russell with its delightful seaside restaurants, shops and wharf a gentle stroll away. Magnificent harbour, bush and village views are a feature of guests private accommodation. The Villa is an attractively appointed sunny spacious deluxe unit set in its own grounds and adjacent to the main house. The Studio is a self-contained suite-styled apartment on the ground floor of our new modern home. Both units have mini-kitchen facilities, Sky TV & off-street parking.

Russell *1 km NW of Russell Central*
Arapohue House *B&B*

Bradley & Vivienne Morrison
9 Wellington Street,
Russell,
Bay of Islands

Tel 09 403 8109
or 027 272 8881
021 943 484
Fax (09) 403 8107
arapohuehouse@xtra.co.nz
www.arapohuehouse.com

Double/Twin $160-$220
Single $150-$165
(Full breakfast)
Visa MC Eftpos accepted
Pet free home
Not suitable for children
2 Queen (2 bdrm)
Bathrooms: 2 Ensuite all ensuite

This beautiful old bungalow has been rebuilt recently. Only 200 metres from Russell Beach, it is an easy leisurely, level walk to all the fine restaurants and coffee houses. Historic Russell, with it's museum and craft shops, offers natural history with nature walks, and beautiful beaches. We can organise any trips you wish, or alternately, you are welcome to spend time in our beautiful garden with a great book. All bedrooms have tea & coffee facilities, digital radio clocks, hair dryers & colour TV.

Russell - Te Wahapu *7 km S of Russell*

Bay of Island Cottages *B&B Cottage with Kitchen*
Jenny & Peter Sharpe
92B Te Wahapu Road, RD 1, Russell
Tel (09) 403 7757 or 0800 274 727
enquires@bayofislandscottages.co.nz
www.bayofislandscottages.co.nz/

Double/Twin $200-$250 Single $170-$220
(Special breakfast)
Dinner $45pp by arrangement
Visa MC accepted
1 King/Twin 3 Queen 2 Single (4 bdrm)
Bathrooms: 4 Ensuite

At the end of a private road which winds down to the water are four charming and stylish cottages. Their position makes them ideal for a summer holiday in the north, a romantic honeymoon or weekend. Here you can spend time in peace and privacy enjoying the sun, fresh air and views over the bay just below.

Each special cottage is secluded within the garden and has a wide sunny terrace to make the most of the outdoors. The artistically furnished interiors include a spacious lounge/bedroom, a well equipped kitchenette and ensuite. For your comfort there are top quality beds and bedding, cotton sheets, soft robes and towels. For your enjoyment there are books, magazines, TV, fresh flowers and home baking.

Breakfast is a special event with fine china, linen and silver. Each morning guests gather around our big table to share experiences, good food and conversation. Where possible the cafe style fare is from our own organic garden with free range eggs and local specialities.

Historic Russell is just seven minutes away by car and we can help you with maps and suggestions for local walks and sightseeing trips. For a quiet day at home our dinghy is on the beach ready for fishing or a leisurely paddle out in the bay.

Russell - Okiato *9 km S of Russell*
Aimeo Cottage *B&B Cottage with Kitchen Studio unit with mini-kitchen*

Annie Hormann
26 Okiato Point Road,
Russell

Tel (09) 403 7494
or 027 27 22 393
aimeo@xtra.co.nz
www.bay-of-islands.co.nz/aimeo

Double/Twin $160-$180
Single $150-$170
(Special breakfast)
Children $25
Visa MC accepted
Children welcome
2 King/Twin 1 King
1 Single (2 bdrm)
Bathrooms: 1 Ensuite 1 Private

A quiet place to relax. We have sailed half way around the world to find this beautiful quiet place in the heart of the Bay of Islands and would be happy to share this with you for a while. Aimeo is built on the hill of Okiato Point, which is the site of NZ's first capital. 8 km to Russell, once known as the hell hole of the Pacific, now home to an international comunity, with many historic buildings, an interesting museum and art galleries.

Russell *1 km E of Russell*
Lesley's *B&B*
Lesley Coleman
1 Pomare Road,
Russell, Northland

Tel (09) 403 7099
or 021 108 0369
three.gs@xtra.co.nz
www.Lesleys.co.nz

Double/Twin $140-$170
Single $110-$140
(Special breakfast)
Children $30
Dinner by arrangement.
2 nights minimum
Visa MC accepted
Children welcome
1 Queen 2 Single (2 bdrm)
Bathrooms: 1 Private with clawfoot bath,
shower and toilet

Walk beside a palm cluster to our secluded home inspired by living in Greece. See Matauwhi Bay and overseas yachts from the deck. Enjoy breakfast (with organic emphasis) and eggs from our hens in the cosy guest conservatory. Our guest room has its own entrance and tea/coffee making facilities. Lesley's original artwork is on the walls and the private bathroom features a clawfoot bath. Guestbook comments: " We came exhausted and left refreshed!" "Awesome waffles." Billy the terrier lives here too. Welcome.

Russell *0.5 km N of Russell*

La Veduta *Homestay*
Danielle & Dino Fossi
11 Gould Street,
Russell,
Bay of Islands

Tel (09) 403 8299
Fax (09) 403 8299
laveduta@xtra.co.nz
www.laveduta.co.nz

Double/Twin $180
Single $150-$180
(Full breakfast)
King-size rooms $220-$250
Visa MC accepted
1 King/Twin 1 King 1 Queen
2 Double/Twin (5 bdrm)
Bathrooms: 3 Ensuite 2 Private

La Veduta. Enjoy our mix of traditional European culture in the midst of the beautiful Bay of Islands. Historic heartland of New Zealand. La Veduta is the perfect pied a terre for your Northland holiday. We offer our guests a warm welcome and personalised service. All our bedrooms are individually styled, offering full sea view. A delicious cooked breakfast is served on the balcony. We can arrange tours and activities. Restaurants, beach, ferries handy. French and Italian spoken. Complimentary afternoon tea.

≈

Russell *0.4 km N of Russell Central*

A Place in the Sun *B&B Separate Suite Apartment with Kitchen*
Pip & Oliver Campbell
57 Upper Wellington Street,
Russell 0202, Bay of Islands

Tel (09) 403 7615
Fax (09) 403 7610
BayView_Russell@paradise.net.nz
www.aplaceinthesun.co.nz

Double/Twin $135-$185
Single $125-$165
(Breakfast by arrangement)
Children by arrangement
Group of 4 $260-$295
(two ensuites plus studio)
Visa MC accepted
Pet free home
2 Queen 1 Double/Twin (3 bdrm)
Bathrooms: 2 Ensuite

Our special place, Romantic Russell, this retired Kiwi sailing couple's 'perfect anchorage'. Two queen bedroom en-suite apartments, Fern or BayView, (separate entrances often combined for four guests). B&B or self-catering options. Ranchsliders open to patio and garden(no stairs).T.Vs Barbecue. Great views overlooking Russell village and the Bay.Sunny, peaceful setting bordering bush reserve (kiwi habitat). Uncrowded beaches, heritage trails, brilliant night sky, cleaner air!. Ideal for relaxing holidays, honeymoons. All cruises depart Russell. Explore or simply unwind. A different world. It's Paradise.

Russell *0.2 km N of Russell Central*
Villa Russell *Luxury B&B*
Sue & Steve Western
2 Little Queen Street,
Russell,
Bay of Islands

Tel (09) 403 8845
or 027 492 8912
Fax (09) 403 8845
info@villarussell.co.nz
www.kingfishercharters.co.nz

Double/Twin $185-$320
(Full breakfast)
Rollaway bed available,
suitable for children up to 6 years
Visa MC accepted
1 King/Twin 2 Queen (3 bdrm)
Bathrooms: 3 Ensuite

Enjoy a welcoming visit to Villa Russell, 2 minutes from the beach and Russell's restaurants. Relax with magnificent views of the bay and wharf from the deck of our beautifully restored 1910 Villa, or from one of two spacious suites in the new guest cottage. A short walk takes you to a surf beach or up the historic Flagstaff Hill. Off-street parking provided. Charters on our 11.6 metre yacht Kingfisher may also be arranged to sail the Bay of Islands. Friendly family dog.

~

Russell - Te Wahapu *7 km S of Russell*
A Tranquil Place *B&B*
Susanne and Uwe
14 Major Bridge Drive,
off Te Wahapu Road,
Russell
0242

Tel (09) 403 7588
or 021 403 976
Fax (09) 403 7588
TranquilPlace@xtra.co.nz
www.atranquilplace.co.nz

Double/Twin $160-$195
Single $130-$160
(Special breakfast)
Dinner by arrangement
Visa MC accepted
1 Queen (1 bdrm)
Bathrooms: 1 Ensuite

Our cosy home is nestled in native bush on Te Wahapu peninsula opposite historic Russell. You can access the secluded beach via a footpath next to the house and may use our rowing dinghy. Otherwise just relax on our spacious deck, go for a walk, enjoy romantic Russell or join a coach or boat trip to explore the further environment. We speak German and we love sailing, golfing & travelling, have been living in Asia for more than 10 years.

Russell - Okiato *9 km SW of Russell*
Pipiroa Bay Homestay and Garden *B&B Apartment with Kitchen*
Paula & Gary Franklin
348 Aucks Road, Russell, 0272

Tel (09) 403 8856
or 027 295 3640
Fax 09 403 8856
gpfranklin@xtra.co.nz
www.bay-of-islands.co.nz/accomm/
pipiroa.html

Double/Twin $120-$150
Single $80-$120 (Full breakfast)
Children $20 for each child
Dinner $30pp includes glass of wine
Waterbased activities from $20pp
Visa MC accepted
Pet free home
Children and pets welcome
2 Queen 1 Double/Twin
2 Single (4 bdrm)
Bathrooms: 2 Ensuite 1 Guest share

Nestled in the hillside, overlooking historically significant Pipiroa Bay, at Okiato Point, handy to Russell, Opua and Paihia, our warm north facing purpose built homestay bed and breakfast will delight you. As kiwis, with years of sailing experience in the Bay of Islands, we will ensure you enjoy the best the Bay can offer. Choose from our self contained apartment and bed and breakfast suite and savour our delicious breakfast using fresh produce from the garden. Other meals by arrangement.

Russell *0.4 km N of Russell village centre*
Russell Bay Lodge *Luxury B&B*
Aom & Dave Metcalfe
71 Wellington Street,
Russell
0202

Tel (09) 403 7376
or 027 417 3310
Fax (09) 403 7376
info@russellbay.co.nz
www.russellbay.co.nz

Double/Twin $150-$295
(Continental breakfast provisions)
Visa MC accepted
Pet free home
Not suitable for children
2 King (2 bdrm)

Bathrooms: 2 Ensuite

Romantic Russell, luxury accommodation, fabulous bay views. Contemporary Russell Bay Lodge has an idyllic location overlooking Russell and it's beautiful harbour. Just a short walk to waterfront cafes, shops and al fresco dining. The purpose designed accommodation offers king suites with mini kitchen, lounge area with TV/DVD/CD/Wifi, own entrance and own patio area. We provide a sumptuous breakfast basket each day. Select from a wide range of local activities, then later relax on the main balcony soaking up possibly the best sea views in Russell!

Russell *0.1 km E of Information Centre*
The White House *Luxury B&B Guest House*

Emma & Steve Jury
7 Church Street,
Russell
0202

Tel (09) 403 7676
or 021 241 1010
info@thewhitehouserussell.com
www.thewhitehouserussell.com

Double/Twin $195-$275
Single $175.50-$247.50
(Full breakfast)
Visa MC Eftpos accepted
Not suitable for children under 12
(3 bdrm)
Bathrooms: 3 Ensuite

Come and have a truly unique stay with us in one of NZ's oldest houses (circa 1840) ideally situated in the heart of Russell. A beautifully restored villa with plenty of character. She features 3 well appointed rooms with super-king size beds and fresh new ensuites along with guest lounge and full kitchen. Indulge in absolute luxury, with a dip in the spa pool, read a book on the shaded sundeck or wander to the waterfront. 12 midday check-out, free WiFi & SKY TV.

Pakaraka *15 km NW of Pahia/ Kerikeri/Kaikohe*

Jarvis Family Farmstay & Equestrian Centre *B&B Farmstay*
Frederika & Douglas Jarvis
State Highway 1, Pakaraka, RD 2 Ohaeawai, Bay of Islands

Tel (09) 405 9606 or 021 259 1120   Fax (09) 405 9607
baystay@igrin.co.nz   www.nzbaystay.com

Double/Twin $120-$130 Single $60-$70
(Continental breakfast)
Children half price up to 9 years
Dinner $30 by arrangement
Discount for longer stays
Visa MC accepted Pets welcome
2 Queen 2 Double/Twin 1 Twin (3 bdrm)
Bathrooms: 3 Private spa bathroom

The middle of everywhere en route SH 1. A gateway for touring North & West coasts and the Bay of Islands. Giant Kauri tree forest, swim with the dolphins, diving & fishing, Ngawha hot springs and pools, golf and Culture North Night Theatre.

Share the sunset at our homely, pet friendly Farmstay, with Winnie the Pooh sign at our gate. There's Winston our Great Dane and Piglet (they live with us) and outside Tigger n' Eeyore too.

Book a ride at Charlies Stables or stroll on the (30 aker) parkland to visit the horses and ponies. While the Patron can prepare a dinner party in his kitchen. Breakfast includes home made conserves, an orchard bowl of fruitfullness,(parsley scrambled eggs a 'speciality').Al fresco dining on the deck with local wine and a crackling log chiminea.

Our fabulous subtropical palm and water garden is a bird lovers 'Bay of Islands' haven.Queen-size honeymoon 4 poster bed suite and Scottish room."Les Routiers" (UK) recommended.

Holiday bach and swimming pool planned for summer seasonclick on www.nzbaystay.com for Northland weather rerports.

Kohukohu *80 km S of Kaitaia*
Harbour Views Guest House *B&B Homestay*

Jacky Kelly & Bill Thomson
32B Rakautapu Road,
Kohukohu,
Northland

Tel (09) 405 5815
Fax (09) 405 5865

Double/Twin $120
Single $75
(Full breakfast)
Dinner $25
Not suitable for children
1 Queen 2 Single (2 bdrm)

Bathrooms: 1 Private

Historic Kohukohu, now a friendly and charming village, is situated on the north side of the Hokianga Harbour. Our beautifully restored kauri home is set in 2 acres of gardens and trees and commands a spectacular view of the harbour. The guest rooms, opening on to a sunny verandah, are in a private wing of the house. Meals are prepared using home-grown produce in season. We are interested in, and knowledgeable about, the history and geography of the area. We have a cat.

Opononi *6 km W of Opononi*
Koutu Lodge *B&B Homestay*

Tony and Sylvia Stockman
Koutu Loop Road,
Opononi,
RD 3,
Kaikohe

Tel (09) 405 8882
Fax (09) 405 8893
koutulodgebnb@xtra.co.nz
www.waireboulders.co.nz/
koutulodge

Double/Twin $90-$110
Single $70 (Full breakfast)
Visa MC accepted
1 King 1 Queen
1 Double/Twin (3 bdrm)
Bathrooms: 2 Ensuite 1 Private

Situated on Koutu Point overlook-ing the beautiful Hokianga Harbour, our home has views both rural and sea. Two rooms have private entrances, decks, and ensuites, and are very comfortable. We are a friendly, relaxed Kiwi couple, and our aim is to provide a memorable stay in the true B&B tradition. Stay a while and enjoy everything the historic Hokianga has to offer. Koutu Loop Rd is 4.3 kms north of Opononi then left 2.3 kms on tar seal to Lodge on right.

Opononi *57 km W of Kaikohe*
Opononi Dolphin Lodge *B&B Separate Suite*
Sue & John Reynard
Corner of SH12 & Fairlie Crescent,
Opononi

Tel (09) 405 8451
or 021 064 4050
Fax (09) 405 8451
opononidolphinlodge@xtra.co.nz

Double/Twin $75-$105
Single $65-$95
(Continental breakfast)
1x Self Contained unit -
Sleeps 6
Visa MC accepted
1 Queen 1 Double/Twin
1 Twin 1 Single (3 bdrm)
Bathrooms: 2 Ensuite
1 Private 1 Guest share

Situated on the corner of Fairlie Crescent and SH12, opposite a beach reserve on the edge of the pristine Hokianga Harbour. Our sunsets are breathtaking. 20 minutes from "Tane Mahuta" the largest kauri tree in the world. Step outside for picture postcard views of beautiful blue beconing waters and huge sand dunes. Visit the boulders, sand board, walking tracks, boating, great fishing, local crafts. Come, enjoy the friendly hospitality. The West Coast Diamond in the North awaits you.

Omapere *55 km W of Kaikohe*
Harbourside Bed & Breakfast *B&B*
Joy & Garth Coulter
State Highway 12,
1 Pioneer Walk,
Omapere

Tel (09) 405 8246
harboursidebnb@xtra.co.nz

Double/Twin $95-$105
Single $70-$80
(Continental breakfast)
Visa MC accepted
1 Queen 2 Single (2 bdrm)
Bathrooms: 2 Ensuite

Our beachfront home on corner State Highway 12 and Pioneer Walk overlooking the Hokianga Harbour is within walking distance of restaurants and bars. Both rooms have ensuites, tea making facilities, refrigerators and TV with separate entrances onto private decks to relax and enjoy superb views. We're close to the Waipoua Forest, West Coast beaches, sand hills and historic Rawene. We have an interest in farming, forestry and education. Stay and share our home and cat. Also available self catering flat.

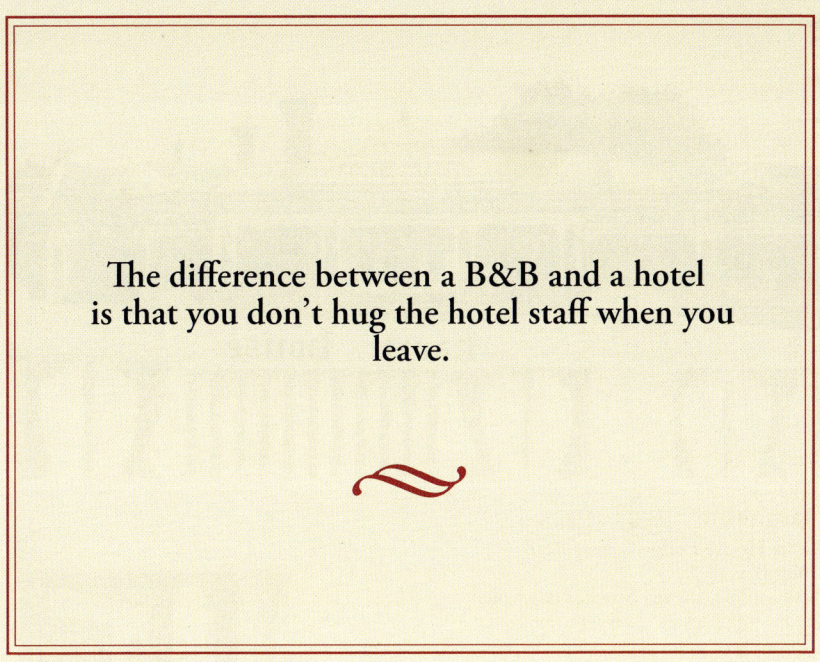

The difference between a B&B and a hotel
is that you don't hug the hotel staff when you
leave.

Omapere *60 km W of Kaikohe*
Hokianga Haven Omapere Beachfront *B&B Separate Suite*

Heather Randerson
226 State Highway 12,
Omapere,
Hokianga

Tel (09) 405 8285
or 021 393 973
Fax ((09) 405 8285
tikanga2000@xtra.co.nz
www.hokiangahaven.co.nz

Double/Twin $150-$180
Single $120-150
(Continental breakfast)
Two night minimum stay Oct-March
Visa MC accepted
1 Super King (1 bdrm)
Bathrooms: 1 Private

Snuggled into this peaceful private, beachfront location, our comfortable home embraces the continuously inspiring seascape of the dramatic harbour entrance and magnificent dune. Simply relaxing in this harbourside haven is revitalizing. Local artists, forest walks, horse riding, harbour cruising, fishing, river and coastal swimming are some of the natural delights to be enjoyed in this historic area. Enjoy light filled, spacious self contained facility with direct beach access. Our dog Saab is a willing walking companion. Range of healing therapies available..

Dargaville *1.5 km S of Dargaville*
Kauri House Lodge *Luxury B&B*
Doug Blaxall
PO Box 382, Bowen Street, Dargaville

Tel (09) 439 8082 or 027 454 7769
Fax (09) 439 8082
kaurihouselodge@orcon.net.nz

Double/Twin $225-$300
Single $200 (Full breakfast)
Visa MC accepted
1 King/Twin 2 King (3 bdrm)
Bathrooms: 3 Ensuite

Kauri House Lodge sits high above Dargaville amongst mature trees. The 1880s villa retains all it's unique charm, style and grace with original kauri panelling and period antiques in all rooms.

Start your day woken by native birds, walk through extensive landscaped grounds or read in our library. In summer enjoy a dip in the large swimming pool. In winter our billiard room log fire is a cosy spot to relax for the evening.

Join Doug to explore beautiful mature native bush on the nearby farm overlooking the Wairoa River and Kaipara Harbour. The area offers many activities including deserted white sand beaches, fresh water lakes, river tours, horse treks, bush walks and restaurants.

THE MOST COMMON COMMENT IN OUR VISITOR BOOK: "SAVE THE BEST TO LAST".

I have been hosting Bed & Breakfast for over 30 years,

"Perfect Accommodation, good host, these things make holidays worthwhile" - Frank & Annie, Holland

"Fantastic house and timber furniture, best we've seen" - Gary & Trish, Australia

Dargaville *2 km E of Dargaville*
Awakino Point Boutique Motel *Separate Suite Apartment with Kitchen*

B&B Approved

June & Mick
State Highway 14,
Dargaville
PO Box 168,
Dargaville

Tel (09) 439 7870
or 027 451 9474
027 479 2126
awakinopoint@xtra.co.nz
www.awakinopoint.co.nz

Double/Twin $100-$125
(Special breakfast)
Extra person $25 each
Visa MC Amex accepted
3 Queen 4 Twin (5 bdrm)
Bathrooms: 3 Ensuite

Unique property set on its own acreage surrounded by attractive gardens.Just 2 mins drive from Dargaville on SH14 (The Whangarei Road) The best features of a NZ motel and a b&b have been amalgamated to give our guests the best of both worlds. You will enjoy your own 1 or 2 b/rm self-contained suite with private bathroom, friendly service and an attractive breakfast each morning.Guest laundry & BBQ available. Smoke-free Indoors.

Dargaville - Bayly's Beach *12 km W of Dargaville*
Ocean View *Cottage No Kitchen*

B&B Approved

Paula & John Powell
7 Oceanview Terrace,
Baylys Beach, RD 7,
Dargaville

Tel (09) 439 6256
or 021 0400 511
baylys@win.co.nz
www.bnb.co.nz/oceanview.html

Double/Twin $120
Single $80
(Continental breakfast provisions)
Children under 5 free,
5-15yrs $10
Extra adult $20
Visa MC accepted
Children welcome
1 Double/Twin 1 Single (1 bdrm)
Bathrooms: 1 Ensuite

Just off the trail, this expansive west coast beach is a wonderful place to relax. With a glimpse of the beach, your cottage is 1 minute walk to the beach and clifftop walkways. Locally enjoy the Funky Fish Cafe, 18-hole golf,astronomy adventures and more. Kai Iwi Lakes and Waipoua Forests are an easy day trip. Enjoy your sunny, comfortable cottage and breakfast at your leisure (provided in cottage). Internet and laundry available. With our 2 children, sleepy cat and delightful Jack Russell, we welcome you.

Dargaville *2 km S of Dargaville*
Turiwiri B&B *B&B*

Bruce & Jennifer Crawford
Turiwiri RAPID 6775,
State Highway 12,
Dargaville
0374

Tel (09) 439 6003
Fax (09) 439 6003
crawford@igrin.co.nz

Double/Twin $80
Single $40
(Continental breakfast)
2 Queen (2 bdrm)
Bathrooms: 1 Guest share
Seperate Toilet

We enjoy sharing our local knowledge with guests in our modern, 1 level home. Excellent parking for vehicles and an expansive garden in the midst of our 37 acre working farmlet.Tarrif includes Continental Breakfast. Our family of 3 grown children all live away from home. Interests include family, farming, Rotary International, gardening (especially Heritage Roses) and Big Game fishing. We have Meg, a Jack Russell house dog, that loves everyone and Rosie our house cat.

~

Dargaville - Tangowahine *25 km N of Dargaville*
Tangowahine Farmstay *Farmstay Separate Suite Cottage with Kitchen*

Pauline & Hugh Rose
1078 Tangowahine Valley Road,
RD 2 Dargaville

Tel (09) 439 1570
or 027 439 1570
027 439 1572
Fax (09) 439 5253
holiday@tangowahine.co.nz
www.tangowahine.co.nz

Double/Twin $135-$210
Single $120-$180
(Full breakfast)
Dinner $45 by arrangement
Visa MC accepted
1 King/Twin 1 King 3 Queen
4 Twin 1 Single (4 bdrm)
Bathrooms: 2 Ensuite
1 Private 1 Guest share

Tangowahine is a peaceful, private retreat on a working beef/sheep farm. Purpose built facility includes self-contained Taraire Cottage and studio en-suite, and features kauri walks, waterfalls and abundant bird life. Bush spas adjacent to cottage and garden spa near studio en-suite are chemical free, filled fresh each time. Northland's mild climate means Tangowahine is an all season destination and its central location provides proximity to kauri forests, New Zealand's longest driveable beach and many more. Numerous farm pets. Friendly assistance with Northland directions and attractions.

Matakohe *9 km S of Matakohe*
Petite Provence *B&B Homestay*
Linda & Guy Bucchi
703C Tinopai Road,
RD 1,
Matakohe,
New Zealand

Tel (09) 431 7552
Fax (09) 431 7552
petite-provence@clear.net.nz
www.petiteprovence.co.nz

Double/Twin $145
Single $100
(Continental breakfast)
Dinner $40 by arrangement
Visa MC accepted
2 King/Twin 1 King
2 Queen (3 bdrm)
Bathrooms: 2 Ensuite 1 Private

Ten minutes from Matakohe Kauri museum, Petite Provence is set on 7 hectares of rolling farmland. All rooms (insect screens) open onto a covered deck with panoramic and distant water views. Relaxing and peaceful atmosphere. Delicious evening meals, mediterranean, vegetarian, local cuisine. Guy is French, Linda a New Zealander. Our home in France was also a Bed & Breakfast. Loopy is our outside dog. Directions: From Matakohe museum drive 2 kms towards Tinopai, turn left into Tinopai road, drive 7kms. Roadside sign on left.

❀

Paparoa *7 km W of Paparoa*
Palm House *B&B Cottage with Kitchen*
Jenny & Hector MacKinnon
Pahi,
RD 1,
Paparoa

Tel (09) 431 6689
palmhouse@paradise.net.nz

Double/Twin $120
Single $75
(Full breakfast)
Children $55
Dinner $35
Garden cottage $120
Visa MC accepted
Children welcome
2 King/Twin 2 Queen (3 bdrm)
Bathrooms: 1 Ensuite 1 Guest share

Hector & Jenny will welcome you to Palm House with delicious home baking and good Kiwi/Scottish hospitality. Enjoy the tranquillity of beautiful Pahi and the Arapoa River. Visit the famous Morton Bay Fig Tree, wander the tide line, kayak the picturesque river or try your luck at fishing. Situated just 13kms from the famous Matakohe Museum, and en route to the spectacular Kauri Forest. Signposted on the main State Highway 12, travel 7km down Pahi Road and reach Palm House.

Paparoa *1 km E of Paparoa*
The Old Post Office Guesthouse *B&B Guest House*

B&B
Approved

Janice Booth
Corner of State Highway 12 &
Oakleigh Road,
PO Box 79,
Paparoa

Tel (09) 431 6444
paparoa.jan@xtra.co.nz

Double/Twin $100-$110
Single $55-$55
(Continental breakfast)
Dinner $30 - 3 courses
2 bedroom suite from $200 (sleeps 5)
Visa MC accepted
Children welcome
2 Queen 1 Double/Twin
2 Twin 4 Single (6 bdrm)
Bathrooms: 1 Ensuite 4 Private

From the moment you step inside you will succumb to the character and charm of this lovely old historic building (circa 1903), with delightful cottage garden and rural backdrop. Enjoy our true Kiwi hospitality, cuisine and homely atmosphere with separate guests lounges and free tea/coffee. Dinner by prior arrangement. Local restaurants Th/F/Sat/Sun only. Spend a day at the world famous Matakohe Kauri Museum only 8km away or if, like us, you enjoy the outdoors, our kayaks are available to explore the nearby Kaipara Harbour.

Whangarei *12 km SW of Whangarei*
Owaitokamotu *B&B Homestay*

B&B
Approved

Minnie & George Whitehead
727 Otaika Valley Road,
Otaika,
Whangarei

Tel (09) 434 7554
Fax (09) 434 7554
minniegeorge@xtra.co.nz

Double/Twin $85-$100
Single $65 (Full breakfast)
Dinner $25 by arrangement
Children and pets welcome
2 King/Twin 2 Queen (3 bdrm)
Bathrooms: 2 Guest share

Come, enjoy the tranquility of Owaitokamotu, place of water. Magnificent rocks of all shapes and sizes, pristine bush, rambling walks, set in 10 acres, easy contour. Created gardens, featuring ponds, bridges, archways, windmill, 1850s style shanty and more. Home wheelchair friendly. All bedrooms private access from exterior. TV, tea/coffee facilities. Join us for 3 course evening meal, $25 by arrangement. Restaurants nearby. Interests: travel, wood carving, our garden. Smoke-free indoors. Laundry facilities available. Warm welcome awaits you.

Whangarei *17 km E of Whangarei*
Parua House *B&B Homestay Farmstay*
Pat & Peter Heaslip
1113 Whangarei Heads Road, Parua Bay,
RD 4, Whangarei 0174

Tel (09) 436 5855 or 021 0250 4389
paruahomestay@clear.net.nz
www.paruahomestay.homestead.com

Double/Twin $150-$175 Single $90-$110 (Full breakfast)
Children half price Dinner $35 Visa MC accepted
2 Queen 1 Twin (3 bdrm)
Bathrooms: 2 Ensuite 1 Private

Parua House is a classical colonial house, built in 1883, comfortably restored and occupying an elevated site with panoramic views of Parua Bay and the Whangarei Harbour.

The property covers 29 hectares of farmland including 2 protected reserves, which are rich in native trees (including kauri) and birds.Guests are welcome to explore the farm and bush, milk the jersey cow, explore the olive grove and sub-tropical orchard, or just relax in the spa pool on the veranda. We are an environmentally friendly homestay. A safe swimming beach adjoins the farm, with a short walk to the fishing jetty; 2 marinas and an excellent golf course are just 2 minutes away.

Our wide interests include photography, patchwork quilting and horticulture.(Cats and an outside corgi)The house is attractively appointed with antique furniture and a rare collection of spinning wheels.

Awake to home-baked bread and freshly squeezed orange juice. Dine in elegant surroundings with generous helpings of home produce with our own eggs, home grown vegetables, olives and sub-tropical fruit (home-made ice cream a speciality). Pre-meal drinks and wine are provided to add to the bonhomie of an evening around a large French oak refectory table. As featured on TV's "Ansett NZ Time of Your Life" and "Corban's Taste NZ".

Whangarei *25 km SE of Whangarei*
Vealbrook B&B *B&B Homestay*

Bob & Pre Sturge
2013 McLeod Bay,
Whangarei Heads, RD 4,
Whangarei Heads Road, Whangarei

Tel (09) 434 0098
Fax (09) 434 0098
pretoria@clear.net.nz
www.vealbrook.co.nz

Double/Twin $100 Single $85
(Full breakfast)
Children $15 Dinner $25
Self-contained unit $130
Children welcome
1 King 1 Queen 1 Double/Twin
1 Twin 3 Single (3 bdrm)
Bathrooms: 1 Ensuite 1 Guest share
1 Family share (1 bath & 2 showers
& toilets)

Stunning harbour views. Coastal scenic walks. Mountains to climb. 20 metres to the beach. Safe swimming, snorkelling, kayaking, good fishing at jetty. Local dairy nearby. Pine Golf Course 15 minutes away. Surfing ocean beach. Pleasant drive round beautiful ocean bays. The house is arranged with antique furniture. Antique lace garments on display. For breakfast enjoy Bob's home-made marmalades jellies. Freshly picked fruit and fruit juice. Vegetables, subtropical fruits. Dinner supplied on request. Pre-meal drinks. Enjoy warmth and friendliness of your hosts.

Whangarei - Onerahi *9 km SE of Whangarei*
Channel Vista *B&B Apartment with Kitchen Cottage with Kitchen*

Braia & Paul Larsen
254 Beach Road,
Onerahi,
Whangarei

Tel (09) 436 5529
or 027 448 8507
021 124 2800
Fax (09) 436 5529
channelvista@igrin.co.nz
www.bnbwhangarei.co.nz

Double/Twin $160 (Full breakfast)
Visa MC accepted
Children welcome
2 Queen (2 bdrm)
Bathrooms: 2 Ensuite

Channel Vista is situated on the shores of Whangarei Harbour. We have 2 self-contained units each with their own private decks where you can relax and watch boats go by. Laundry, fax and email facilities available. Local shopping centre only 3 minutes away, 5 minute walk along waterfront to top restaurant. Sports facilities eg, golf, diving, game fishing, bowls etc nearby. We are one hour from the Bay of Islands, so it is a good place to base yourself for your Northland holiday.

Whangarei - Taiharuru *25 km E of Whangarei*
Tidesong *B&B Homestay Apartment with Kitchen*

Ros & Hugh Cole-Baker
Beasley Road,
Taiharuru Estuary,
Whangarei

Tel (09) 436 1959
or 027 636 5888
stay@tidesong.co.nz
www.tidesong.co.nz

Double/Twin $100-$120
Single $80-$85
(Full breakfast)
Dinner $30-$35
Visa MC accepted
Children welcome
3 Queen 1 Single (3 bdrm)
Bathrooms: 2 Ensuite

From Whangarei drive east for 25 minutes to Taiharuru Estuary. Comfortable secluded accommodation in a separate upstairs flat. Full breakfast with extra home-cooked meals available. Safe kayaking and other boating from our jetty. Large garden with bush tracks and outdoor games. Close to fishing, shellfish, varied birdlife,and great walks on surf beaches and spectacular ridges. Relax afterwards in the gas-fired outdoor garden bath. Members of Northland Sustainable Tourism Charter Project. We look forward to showing you warm and friendly Northland hospitality.

Whangarei *7 km N of Whangarei City*
Lotus Lodge *B&B Farmstay Self Contained Studio (double)*

Keith & Jill Clarke
58 Great North Road,
Springs Flat,
Kamo,
Whangarei

Tel (09) 435 2294
Fax (09) 435 2294
lotuslodge@clear.net.nz

Double/Twin $100-$140
Single $65-$80
(Continental breakfast)
Dinner by arrangement
2 Double/Twin 1 Twin (3 bdrm)
Bathrooms: 1 Guest share

We invite you to share in our 200 acres of paradise. 2 minutes from Kamo, 5 minutes to golf course. Experience moving cattle/sheep with farm dog Del, view native bush, find amazing limestone rocks,laze in the quietness of the garden, or read in the lounge. Make this your stop for seeing the north - beaches, fishing, diving, kauri forests, shopping, all in a days outing. Our interests: gardening, classic cars, travel, art and people.

Whangarei - Glenbervie *9 km NE of Whangarei*
Totara lodge Homestay *Luxury B&B Homestay*

John and Sue Hobden
252 Ngunguru Road Glenbervie,
RD3 Whangarei, 0173

Tel (09) 437 6269
Fax (09) 437 6249
info@totaralodgehomestay.co.nz
www.totaralodgehomestay.co.nz

Double/Twin $185
Single $160
(Full breakfast)
Dinner $45 by prior arrangement
Visa MC accepted
Pet free home
Not suitable for children under 15
2 Queen (2 bdrm)
Bathrooms: 2 Ensuite

A warm welcome awaits you at Totara Lodge where you can relax in the peaceful Glenbervie countryside. We feature tastefully decorated rooms throughout with luxurious queen size bedrooms for guests, which include tea/coffee making facilites, TV/DVDs, ensuites and private patios.A delicious breakfast is served offering fresh seasonal produce. Join us for dinner which is available by prior arrangement.Take some time out to explore the surrounding area which offers numerous recreational facilities set in scenic locations around Whangarei and the Tutukaka coast.

Whangarei - Mount Tiger *18 km E of Whangarei*
Eden House *B&B Homestay*

Richard & Carole Harris
510 Owhiwa Rd, Parua Bay, R.D. 1
Onerahi, Whangarei

Tel (09) 436 1938 or 027 366 4272
eden@igrin.co.nz
www.edenhomestay.co.nz

Double/Twin $140 Single $90
(Full breakfast)
Children $60. No charge for a baby
sharing the room. Dinner Per person,
$40 /30 /25 - three/ two/ one
course. Wine and drinks list available.
Complimentary beverages. Visa MC
accepted Children and pets welcome
1 King/Twin 2 Queen (3 bdrm)
Bathrooms: 1 Ensuite 1 Private
1 Family share Luxury en suite or
private bathroom.

Relax in a spacious luxury bedroom with a deck overlooking stunning views to the distant Pacific Ocean. Try the adventure of a theme cuisine, a delicious Bhutanese or Pacific dishes, and ambience. Nightime tranquillity is broken only by the cry of an occasional owl. Amenities include, petanque, swimming pool, two lounges, TV/DVD/library, laundry and email. 11 acres of private native bush with creek and peaceful glade. Handy to scenic beaches, walks, sports. Only twenty minutes to charming Whangarei. Pets and children welcome by arrangement.

Whangarei *5 km N of Whangarei*
Brantome Villa Fine Country Boutique Bed & Breakfast
Luxury B&B Homestay Boutique
Valerie & Roger Bloomfield
454 Crane Road, RD 1, Whangarei

Tel (09) 435 2088
or 021 512 006
Fax (09) 435 2089
relax@brantomevilla.co.nz
www.brantomevilla.co.nz

Double/Twin $190-$245
Single $190
(Full breakfast)
Dinner (main & dessert) $50pp
by arrangement -
Visa MC accepted
Pet free home
Not suitable for children
1 King 1 Queen (2 bdrm)
Bathrooms: 2 Ensuite

Welcome to our special place 'Brantome Villa' our sunny colonial-style home which is now an upmarket boutique B&B. California King & Queen beds, both rooms have ensuites & private entrance (no stairs) A/C, luxury beds & linen etc. Awake to bird song & trees wispering in this beautiful country setting. 2 hours north of Auckland or 10 mins north of Whangarei, perfect base for seeing Northland. Cat in garden. SH1, turn left at Apotu Rd left again Crane Rd, 2k on left.

Whangarei Heads *28 km SE of Whangarei*
Bantry *B&B Homestay*
Karel & Robin Lieffering
Little Munro Bay,
RD 4,
Whangarei Heads

Tel (09) 434 0751
robinl@igrin.co.nz

Double/Twin $120
Single $60
(Full breakfast)
Children under 12 half price
Dinner $35
Children and pets welcome
1 Queen 2 Single (2 bdrm)
Bathrooms: 1 Private 1 Guest share

We are a semi-retired couple. We speak Dutch, French, German, Japanese and we like to laugh. Our unusual home with some natural rock interior walls is on the edge of a safe swimming beach, and bush reserve with walking tracks and several good fishing spots. A photographically fascinating area with wonderful views of coastal mountains. Guests have own entrance and sitting room all with sea views. Enjoyable food and NZ wine. Phone, fax, email us for reservations and directions. One party bookings only.

Ruakaka - Bream Bay *30 km S of Whangarei*

Island View Lodge *Luxury B&B Homestay Farmstay Separate Suite Apartment with Kitchen*

Joyce & Vince Roberts
34 Doctors Hill Road, Waipu, Ruakaka

Tel (09) 432 7842 or 027 441 9585
021 419 515 Fax (09) 432 7847
robertsb.b@xtra.co.nz
www.breambayfarmstay.co.nz

Double/Twin $100-$150 Single $60-$80 (Full breakfast)
Children $30 Dinner $30
Visa MC accepted
Children and pets welcome
2 Queen 2 Double/Twin (3 bdrm)
Bathrooms: 3 Ensuite 3 Private

Come stressed, leave refreshed.

Spectacular is the only words to describe the sea views from this brand new home built especially for the discerning travelers. The main suite has its own kitchen & laundry with large lounge area. We have air con/heat pumps plus under floor heating for your comfort.

Have a swim in the heated lap pool or relax in the spa after having a game of pool in the games room.

Beautiful beaches, golf course, racetrack where Vince trains our racehorses and good restaurants are a short drive from our home. Meals include our home grown lamb.

As ex dairy farmers with grown up family of four, we have enjoyed hosting B&B for 16 years, other interests include travel, golf & gardening.

We look forward to meeting you and helping make your holiday enjoyable.

Indoor heated lap pool and spa, Pool table. Horse treks can be arranged.

Ruakaka *30 km S of Whangarei*
Waterview Bream Bay *B&B Farmstay Cottage with Kitchen*

B&B
Approved

Gayle & Rodney McPhee
34 Doctors Hill Road,
Waipu,
Ruakaka

Tel (09) 433 0050
Fax (09) 433 0050
rodneyandgaylesb.b@xtra.co.nz

Double/Twin $80
Single $50
(Full breakfast provisions)
Children $20 Dinner $25
Children and pets welcome
2 Queen 2 Single (3 bdrm)
Bathrooms: 1 Private 1 Family share

Waterview B & B offers a self-contained unit with panoramic sea and rural views. Our property has large gardens and children are welcome. Cot available. Large area for parking boats and wash down facility availble. Boat ramps are within 10mins away at Marsden Cove. Beautiful beaches, golf course, race track and restaurants are only a few minutes away. We look forward to meeting with you.

Waipu Cove *10 km S of Waipu*
labonte@xtra.co.nz *Homestay Farmstay Apartment with Kitchen*

B&B
Approved

Andre & Robin La Bonte
PO Box 60,
Waipu,
Northland

Tel (09) 432 0645
Fax (09) 432 0645
labonte@xtra.co.nz

Double/Twin $100
Single $50
(Continental breakfast)
Dinner $20 by arrangement
Visa MC accepted
1 King 1 Queen 2 Double/Twin
2 Single (3 bdrm)
Bathrooms: 2 Private

Sleep to the sound of the ocean in a separate studio apartment or in guest bedrooms on our 36 acre seaside property. Explore our limestone rock formations or just sit and relax under the mature trees that grace our shoreline. The beach at Waipu Cove is a 10 minute walk along the sea. We are a licensed fish farm, graze cattle, have flea-free cats and an outside dog. We are ocean and coastal engineers who enjoy hosting guests from around the world. American spoken.

Waipu Cove *8 km SE of Waipu*
Flower Haven *B&B Self-contained Downstairs Flat*

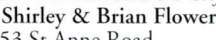

Shirley & Brian Flower
53 St Anne Road,
Waipu Cove,
RD 2,
Waipu 0582

Tel (09) 432 0421
bnb@flowerhaven.com
www.flowerhaven.com

Double/Twin $120-$140
(Continental breakfast)
Pet free home
Not suitable for children
2 Double/Twin (2 bdrm)
Bathrooms: 1 Private

Flower Haven is elevated with awesome coastal views, being developed as a garden retreat. The accommodation has separate access. Kitchen includes stove, microwave, fridge/freezer, washing machine, TV, radio. Linen, duvets, blankets and bath towels provided. Reduced tariff if continental breakfast not required. Our interests are gardening, genealogy and meeting people. Near bird sanctuary, museums, golf, horse treks, fishing, caving, walking tracks, oil refinery. 5 minutes walk to restaurant, shop, surf beach, rocks. Whangarei 35 minutes, Auckland 1 1/2 hours. Visit our website for more details.

Waipu Cove *9 km SE of Waipu*
Melody Lodge *B&B Homestay*

Melody Gard
996 Cove Road,
Waipu,
Northland 0582

Tel (09) 432 0939
Fax (09) 432 0939
melody@melodylodge.co.nz
www.melodylodge.co.nz

Double/Twin $100-$130
Single $80-$110
(Continental breakfast)
Not suitable for children
1 King/Twin 1 Queen
2 Single (3 bdrm)
Bathrooms: 1 Ensuite 1 Guest share

Situated between the popular beaches of Waipu Cove and Langs Beach, Melody Lodge overlooks the whole of Bream Bay. Stunning sea views from all rooms. Modern cedar house with garden and spectacular stand of native bush adjacent. Resident artist and cat. Attached Art Gallery features local artworks, exclusive screenprinted souvenirs and cards. Swim at Waipu, stroll Langs Beach, study birdlife, experience the bush, a round of golf, horseriding, kayaking, fishing. Bush, sea, music, art and good conversation... relax and enjoy it all from Melody Lodge.

Waipu Cove *6.5 km SE of Waipu*

The Stonehouse *Apartment with Kitchen, Cottage with Kitchen*
Backpackers welcome
Bob & Silvia Schmid
641 Cove Road,
Waipu

Tel (09) 432 0432
or 021 207 90 44
Fax (09) 432 0432
stonehousewaipu@xtra.co.nz
www.stonehousewaipu.co.nz

Double/Twin $90-$120
Single $80-$110
(Breakfast by arrangement)
Children $20
Visa MC accepted
Children and pets welcome
3 Queen 4 Single (4 bdrm)
Bathrooms: 2 Ensuite 1 Private

Get off the beaten track and relax in the selfcontained romantic Stonecottage or enjoy the privacy of the selfcontained cabin. Green pastures, giant Pohutukawa trees, Maori Pa site and the lagoon with distant Mt.Mannaia are your views. Explore the adjacent lagoon with its bird sanctuary in our canoes or dinghies. Take a stroll through the dunes, watch and listen to the waves breaking on the shore, have a swim in summer, light your log fire in winter. German and French spoken. Ideal for families .

Kaiwaka *19 km N of Wellsford*

Landfall Lodge *Homestay*
Adrienne & Arnold Atkinson
306 Oneriri Rd, RD 2,
Kaiwaka, 0573

Tel (09) 431 2706
or 021 036 8929
Fax (09) 431 2706
landfall-lodge@clear.net.nz
www.landfall-lodge.co.nz

Double/Twin $130
Single $85
(Continental breakfast)
Children by arrangement
Dinner by arrangement
Single party (2-4 persons) $215
Visa MC accepted
Pet free home Children welcome
1 King/Twin 1 Queen (2 bdrm)
Bathrooms: 1 Guest share Ensuite (Guest share if both rooms let)

Welcome to our modern home at the beginning of the Kauri Coast & almost half way between Auckland and the Bay of Islands. We offer excellent beds,comfortable rooms, great showers, sunny lounge/dining room. Enjoy the sunsets over a glass of wine before a superb dinner. The West Coast beaches, world famous Kauri Museum, Kauri forests, golf courses and charming Mangawhai beach and walks are within easy reach. Your hosts have completed an extensive circumnavigation, and have a keen interest in travel and people.

Auckland

Great Barrier Island →

Auckland

Auckland City

Silverdale

Whangaparaoa

Okura

Waiheke Island →

Coatesville

Albany

28

Riverhead

18

Greenhithe

Rangitoto Island

16

Hobsonville

Takapuna

Northcote Point

Bayswater

Devonport

Herne Bay

Auckland
Central

Mission Bay

St Heliers

Ponsonby

Grey Lynn

Parnell

Orakei

Ranui

Western Springs

Mt Eden

Remuera

Ellerslie

Howick

Titirangi

Hillsborough

Mangere Bridge

Mangere

1

Manukau City

Alfriston

Manurewa

Auckland
International
Airport

0 — Kilometres — 5
0 — Miles — 3

All our B&Bs are non-smoking
unless stated otherwise in the text.

Mangawhai Heads *.5 km SE of Mangawhai Heads*
Mangawhai Lodge - a room with a view Boutique B&B Inn
B&B Separate Suite s/c apartment
Jeannette Forde
4 Heather Street,
Mangawhai Heads 0505

Tel (09) 431 5311
info@seaviewlodge.co.nz
www.seaviewlodge.co.nz

Double/Twin $160-$250
Single $150-$185
(Special breakfast)
Children suit children 10 & over
Mid winter xmas dinner for groups
Visa MC Eftpos accepted
Pet free home
3 King/Twin 2 Queen
8 Single (5 bdrm)
Bathrooms: 3 Ensuite 2 Private
3 ensuite, 1 s/cont apartment, 1 guest suite

Midway between Auckland airport & the Bay of Islands Mangawhai Lodge offers the perfect beach destination for couples, groups, golfers & singles. Three stylish guest rooms, 1 luxury suite and 1 s/c apartment open to verandahs, seating and views of sea or garden. Two guests lounges offer a stylish, relaxing atmosphere with spectacular sea, and beach views. Championship Golf course adjacent, Off street parking. Enjoy beaches,walkways,bird sanctuary. Walk to cafes and shops. A sumptuous cooked/continental breakfast served. Complimentary internet access. For winter specials visit www.seaviewlodge.co.nz

Wellsford - Te Hana *6 km N of Wellsford*
The Retreat Historic Farmhouse *Farmstay*
Colleen & Tony Moore
Te Hana, RD 5, Wellsford 0975

Tel (09) 423 8547
enquiry@sheepfarmstay.com
www.sheepfarmstay.com

Double $100-$120
Single $65-$80 (Full breakfast)
Dinner $30pp by arrangement
Self-contained cottage $100
Visa MC Diners accepted
2 Queen 1 Double
1 Single (3 bdrm)
Bathrooms: 1 Ensuite 1 Private

Tony and Colleen welcome you to The Retreat, a spacious 1860s farmhouse built for a family with 12 children. Set well back from the road, the house is surrounded by an extensive landscaped garden, including a productive vegetable garden and orchard. Fresh produce from the garden is a feature in our home cooking.

Colleen is a spinner and weaver and our flock of sheep provides the raw material for the woollen goods that are hand-made and for sale from the studio. If you haven't got close up to a sheep this is your chance, as we always have friendly sheep to hand feed. We have hosted guests at The Retreat since 1988 and appreciate what you require.

We know New Zealand well, our families have lived in NZ for several generations and we have visited most places in our beautiful country, so if you have any questions on what to see or do, we are well equipped to provide the answers.

Also available is a self-contained cottage, close to the house, with the option of having meals with us, or self-catering.

The Retreat is very easy to find. Travelling North on SH1, we are 6km north of Wellsford, look for the Weaving Studio sign on your left. You will pass through Te Hana before arriving at The Retreat. Kaiwaka is 13km north of The Retreat.

Wellsford *6 km E of Wellsford*
Wisdome Cottage *Homestay Farmstay*

Peter and Sally Usher
196 Tomarata Valley Road,
Tomarata,
RD4 Wellsford

Tel (09) 423 9558
wisdome-cottage@paradise.net.nz

Double/Twin $130
Single $115
(Full breakfast)
Children negotiable
Delighted to provide
dinner by arrangement
Visa MC accepted
2 Queen (2 bdrm)
Bathrooms: 1 Ensuite 1 Private

Wisdome Cottage welcomes you for a relaxing and refreshing break in a deeply rural setting. Nestled amidst country gardens the cottage faithfully replicates a 17th century farmhouse, featuring beamed ceilings, open fires and hand crafted joinery. Barely an hour from Auckland, close to sensational beaches, bush walks and the Matakana wine country, the cottage is an ideal place to start or conclude Northland tours. Delicious dinners and local tours are also offered. Bicycles and kayaks available. Two children, one working dog, one idle cat!

Warkworth *0.5 km N of Warkworth*
Homewood Cottage *B&B Separate Suite*

Ina & Trevor Shaw
17 View Road,
Warkworth

Tel (09) 425 8667
or 021 11 48 760
Fax (09) 425 9610
ina.homewoodcottage@xtra.co.nz

Double/Twin $100-$100
(Special breakfast)
Visa MC accepted
1 Queen 1 Twin (2 bdrm)
Bathrooms: 2 Ensuite

Welcome to our home in a peaceful garden with views of Warkworth and the hills. The spacious rooms ensure privacy and quiet. The new beds are comfortable with electric blankets and quilts. Each room has TV, teamaking, own entrance, and car park. No cooking. Afternoon tea and substantial continental breakfast served. Ina is an artist who also enjoys walking, music and her guests. Restaurants are two minutes away, beaches vineyards and crafts close by. A smoke free home. View Rd. is off Hill St.

Warkworth - Sandspit *7 km E of Warkworth*

Belvedere Homestay *Homestay*

M & R Everett
38 Kanuka Road,
RD 2, Sandspit,
Warkworth

Tel (09) 425 7201 or Mobile 027 284 4771
or Mobile 027 343 0905
Fax (09) 425 7201
belvederehomestay@xtra.co.nz
www.belvederehomestay.co.nz

Double/Twin $150-$165
Single $110
(Special breakfast)
Dinner $50 pp
Visa MC accepted
Not suitable for children
2 Queen 1 Twin (3 bdrm)
Bathrooms: 1 Ensuite 2 Private

Sandspit the perfect stop to and from The Bay of Islands. Belvedere has 360 degree views, sea to countryside; it's awesome.

Relaxing decks, barbecue, garden, orchards, native birds and bush, peace and tranquillity with good parking. Air-conditioned, spa, games room, comfortable beds are all here for your comfort.

Many attractions are within 7km and Margaret's flair with cooking is a great way to relax after an adventurous day with pre-drinks, 2 course meal and wine. Have a warm and relaxing stay with Margaret & Ron.

SANDSPIT - "THE PERFECT STOP TO AND FROM THE BAY OF ISLANDS"

Warkworth *13 km E of Warkworth*
Maltby Homestay *B&B Self-contained unit*
Barbara & John Maltby
Omaha Orchards,
282 Point Wells Road,
RD 6,
Warkworth

Tel (09) 422 7415
Fax (09) 422 7419
jmaltby@clear.net.nz

Double/Twin $75-$95
Single $65-$75
(Full breakfast provisions)
Children & Extra guest $12
Dinner $15-$25 by arrangement
In-house accommodation
also available
1 Queen 1 Double/Twin (1 bdrm)
Bathrooms: 1 Ensuite

Our home and self-contained unit (built 1999) is set on 5 acres nestled beside the Whangateau Harbour. Relax in the extensive gardens and swim in the beautifully appointed pool. Nearby is Omaha Beach, golf course, tennis courts, restaurants, art and craft studios, pottery works, museum, Sheep World, Honey Centre and Kawau Island. This is some of the prettiest coastline in New Zealand. John and Barbara look forward to sharing their little slice of paradise with you.

Warkworth - Sandspit *10 km E of Warkworth*
Sea Breeze *Apartment with Kitchen*
Di & Robin Grant
14 Puriri Place,
RD 2,
Sandspit Heights,
Warkworth

Tel (09) 425 7220
or 021 65 7220
Fax (09) 425 7220
robindi.grant@xtra.co.nz
www.bnb.co.nz/seabreeze.html

Double/Twin $150
Single $120
(Continental breakfast)
Visa MC accepted
Not suitable for children
1 Queen (1 bdrm)
Bathrooms: 1 Ensuite

Sea Breeze is a self-contained luxury apartment with magnificent sea views and surrounding bush. Breakfast is provided in the kitchenette to be enjoyed at your leisure and a bed-settee in the lounge doubles for extra guests. There are easy bush walks to the beaches immediately below the property. Take a cruise to Kawau Island or visit the many vineyards, galleries and cafes. Your hosts have travelled extensively and now enjoy gardening and boating in their spare time. Phone/fax for directions.

Warkworth - Sandspit *6 km E of Warkworth*
Jacaranda House B&B *B&B Apartment with Kitchen*

Gillian Irons & Richard Bray
1186 Sandspit Road,
RD 2,
Warkworth

Tel (09) 422 2394
or 027 283 7772
jacarandahouse@xtra.co.nz
www.jacarandahouse.net.nz

Double/Twin $130
Single $110
(Continental breakfast)
 Not suitable for children
1 Queen (1 bdrm)
Bathrooms: 1 Ensuite 1 Private

We are on the Matakana Estuary, a short walk to the Sandspit Wharf, gateway to Kawau Island. A few minutes drive to restaurants, cafes, vineyards and pottery in the Matakana region. Enjoy your continental breakfast on our north facing deck with 180 degree view of the estuary, or enjoy the privacy of your self-contained unit. You will have your own ground level entrance, Sky TV and parking. Oscar, our house cat, is no bother.

Warkworth *4.5 km W of Warkworth*
Willow Lodge *B&B Homestay*
Colin Hilditch & Vicki Webster
541 Woodcocks Road,
RD 1,
Warkworth
0981

Tel (09) 425 7676
or 021 104 1807
021 064 5567
Fax (09) 425 7676
willow_lodge@xtra.co.nz

Double/Twin $110-$130
Single $80-$100
(Full breakfast)
Children $30
Dinner by arrangement
1 Queen 1 Double/Twin
2 Twin (4 bdrm)
Bathrooms: 1 Ensuite 2 Private

You've just found what you were looking for - peace and old world charm, 5 minutes drive from picturesque Warkworth (45 minutes from Auckland). Willow Lodge is nestled amid 2 acres of landscaped gardens. We offer in-house or semi-detached accommodation. Enjoy guest TV lounge, tea/coffee, BBQ all of which opens onto a private courtyard. Colin, Vicki and their dog Boss look forward to warmly welcoming you to their home. Much to explore, plenty to enjoy and treasured memories to be created.

Warkworth - Sandspit *10 km E of Warkworth*
Kotare Lodge *Luxury B&B Apartment with Kitchen*

Judy & Graeme Maker
5 Kotare Place,
RD 2,
Sandspit Heights,
Warkworth
0982

Tel (09) 425 7331
or 021 279 8116
Fax (09) 425 0311
makers@ihug.co.nz
www.sandspitkotarelodge.co.nz

Double/Twin $140-$180
Single $120-$150
(Continental breakfast)
Visa MC accepted
1 Queen 1 Twin (2 bdrm)
Bathrooms: 1 Private

Kotare Lodge has arguably the best views at Sandspit from Kawau Bay, Hauraki Gulf, Great Barrier, Little Barrier, the rural areas of Matakana and the inner harbour of Sandspit. Relax in your luxury self-contained apartment including swimming pool, Sky TV and spacious viewing decks. Enjoy bush walks to beaches, visit the many vineyards, galleries, cafes, restaurants, golf courses, Kawau Island ferry, all within a few minutes drive. Spend time cruising Kawau Bay and islands aboard our 54' Riviera launch (extra cost). The perfect stay.

Warkworth *70 km N of Auckland*
Warkworth Country House *B&B*

Perry & Jan Bathgate
18 Wilson Road,
RD 1
Warkworth,
0981

Tel (09) 422 2485
or 027 600 1510
Fax (09) 422 2485
p-jbathgate@xtra.co.nz
www.warkworthcountryhouse.co.nz

Double/Twin $120-$145
Single $95-$110
(Full breakfast)
Visa MC accepted
1 Queen 1 Twin (2 bdrm)
Bathrooms: 2 Ensuite

Warkworth Country House is 45 minutes north of Harbour bridge and situated in 2 acres of gardens and bush, surrounded by farmland. Each unit has ensuite with private entrance and patio, TV, tea/coffee, heater, electric blankets, radio and toiletries. Enjoy a full or continental breakfast in our dining room then visit one of the local places of interest. Warkworth township with its shops and restaurants is only 3 minutes drive away. You will always receive a warm and friendly welcome whenever you arrive. We love meeting new people and discussing various travel experiences. We will be happy to assist you in planning your travels around New Zealand over a glass of wine, tea or coffee in the comfort of our home.

Warkworth *1.8 km SE of Warkworth Information Centre*

RibbonWood B&B Apartment *B&B Apartment with Kitchen*

Berris & Alan Spicer
7 Thompson Road,
Warkworth, 0981

Tel (09) 422 2685
or 027 241 9986
Fax (09) 422 2684
berris@ribbonwoodwarkworth.co.nz
www.ribbonwoodwarkworth.co.nz

Double/Twin $120-$160
(Special breakfast)
Dinner From $18 p.p.
Extra person $30-60
Discount for 3+ night stay
Visa MC accepted
Pet free home
Children welcome
1 Queen 2 Single (2 bdrm)
Bathrooms: 1 Private Bath & shower

Where true NZ hospitality and special experience await! Enjoy every home comfort - your own entrance, patio, light and airy lounge dining kitchen, luxury bathroom, wifi internet access. Your choice to self-cater, enjoy quality home cooking or cafes within 3 minutes. Our delightful country setting offers peace, privacy, views. We're 45 minutes north of Auckland, next to the famous Parry Kauri Forest in historic Warkworth Village, on the door step to Matakana Wine Country. Modern, boutique, warm, welcoming ... we cater for 1 group only.

Warkworth - Matakana *5 km N of Matakana*

Takamatua Estate *Luxury B&B*
Michelle Amery & Harald Hermans
36 Schollum Road,
Matakana,
0948

Tel (09) 423 0232
or 021 517 504
stay@takamatua.co.nz
www.takamatua.co.nz

Double/Twin $180-$200
Single $140-$160
(Full breakfast)
Dinner by prior arrangement
Visa MC Eftpos accepted
2 King (2 bdrm)
Bathrooms: 1 Ensuite 1 Private

Takamatua, meaning 'Place of rest at the end of a long journey', is how you will come to remember this architecturally stunning lodge and extended family home. Set on 16 acres, with sweeping views over Ti Point, Omaha Beach, out to the Coromandel Peninsula. Within an hours drive of Auckland, surrounded by the wineries of Matakana, farmers markets and fine dining – this is paradise found. We have one dog and two cats.

Warkworth - Snells Beach *7 km E of Warkworth*
Heaven's Haven *B&B*

Beulah Heaven
23 Ariki Drive,
Snells Beach,
Warkworth
0920

Tel (09) 425 6545
or 021 289 5523
by.heaven@xtra.co.nz

Double/Twin $125
Single $75-$100
(Full breakfast)
Dinner $50 by arrangement
Visa MC accepted
Not suitable for children
1 Double/Twin 2 Twin (2 bdrm)
Bathrooms: 1 Ensuite 1 Guest share

Come and share this slice of Heaven in Snells Beach.Relax and enjoy the stunning golden sunrises and breath-taking crimson sunsets from this absolute beachfront property. No need to walk to the beach - you're on the beach here! Relax with a complimentary bottle of wine on arrival. Enjoy a delicious full breakfast with seasonal produce from the pristine Matakana Valley. Relax and soak up the views in the company of Sophie and Emma (our genteel dogs) or spend time visiting the boutique vineyards. cafes, art galleries or many walkways that dot this sparkling area. Sumptuous dinner by arrangement at $50 per head.

Puhoi *9 km N of Orewa*
Westwell Ho *B&B*

Fae & David England
34 Saleyards Road,
Puhoi,
0951

Tel (09) 422 0064
or 027 280 5795
Fax (09) 422 0064
dhengland@xtra.co.nz

Double/Twin $95-$115
Single $95
(Full breakfast)
Children $35
Visa MC Amex accepted
Children welcome
1 Queen 1 Double/Twin
1 Single (2 bdrm)
Bathrooms: 1 Ensuite 1 Private

We welcome you to our sunny colonial-style home in the lovely Puhoi Valley. We are only 2 minutes by car west of Main North Highway up a small road behind the old pub in this historic Puhoi Village. The homestead has wide verandahs around 3 sides where you can relax as you view the gardens and beautiful trees. Nearby are the fantastic Waiwera Thermal Pools, or you could hire a canoe and paddle down the Puhoi River to Wenderholm Beach and Park. Sky TV available.

Puhoi *18 km N of Orewa*

Our Farm-Park *B&B Farmstay*

Peter & Nichola(s) Rodgers
450 Krippner Rd, Puhoi, (postal) RD3,
Kaukapakapa, Auckland 1250

Tel (09) 422 0626 or 021 215 5165
Fax (09) 422 0626
ofp@friends.co.nz
www.friends.co.nz

Double/Twin $125-$195
Single $115-$150 (Special breakfast)
Children No charge
Dinner Taste-filled organic meals-
vegetarian available
Visa MC accepted
Children welcome
Non smokers only
1 Queen 1 Twin (2 bdrm)
Bathrooms: 1 Ensuite, bathroom solely for only guest family at one time

Farmstay, the gentle, organic way. Your family the only guests. No charge for International cuisine -- taste-filled organic meals, fresh baking. Children welcomed; We farm with kindness sheep, Belted Galloway cows with calves at foot, horses, ducks, poultry, providing milk, butter, yoghurt, ice-cream, cheeses. Come relax; sleep off 'jet-lag'. Comfortable beds. Panoramic views, fresh air, clean water. Share experiences over dinner. Farm fields, trees, streams, bird life, flora & fauna, private and secluded places. Gardeners will love it here. Use our library, email, business facilities....

Puhoi *9 km N of Orewa*

Puhoi Tudor Cottage *B&B or accommodation only*

Tina Chamberlin
80 Puhoi Road,
Puhoi,
Auckland 0951

Tel (09) 422 0130
or 0275 39 26 43
Fax (09) 422 0132
orewa@paradise.net.nz

Double/Twin $80-$150
Single $70-$90
(Full breakfast)
Children $35.00 pp
Dinner $20.00 pp
Visa MC accepted
Children welcome
1 Queen 1 Double/Twin
1 Single (3 bdrm)
Bathrooms: 1 Guest share

We welcome you to our English Tudor cottage situated in the heart of Puhoi's Historic Village and set on an acre of lovely gardens and peaceful surroundings. Located opposite Puhoi Museum, the quaint village church and next to the Puhoi River Canoes. Come enjoy our pet sheep, elderly dog Meg, and doves residing with us. Waiwera Hot pools and Wenderholm Regional Park are minutes away. We look forward to making your stay memorable, with comfortable rooms and good hearty meals. Private guest entrance.

Waiwera *6 km N of Orewa*
Estuary Cottage *B&B*
Jenny & Bob Kelly
15 Weranui Road
(PO Box 92)
Waiwera
0950

Tel (09) 426 2621
or 021 426 262
or 021 0247 0170
Fax (09) 426 2614
rj.kelly@ihug.co.nz

Double/Twin $110-$130
Single $80-$100
(Full breakfast)
Visa MC accepted
1 Queen 1 Single (1 bdrm)
Bathrooms: 1 Ensuite

A comfortable, centrally located B&B in the village of Waiwera - the beautiful Hibiscus Coast thermal area, with a safe scenic ocean beach, native bush covered hills, and world famous hot pools. Estuary Cottage - 'Owaimaru', is located on the tidal waters' edge, and offers quality accommodation with a stunning bedroom view, satellite television, tea & coffee making facilities, refrigerator, hot Spa pool, and a private en-suite. Our guests receive a generous discount to the nearby thermal pools.

Orewa *35 km N of Auckland Central*
Villa Orewa *Luxury B&B Homestay*
Sandra & Ian Burrow
264 Hibiscus Coast Highway,
Orewa,
Auckland

Tel (09) 426 3073
or 021 626 760 (Ian)
or 021 556 960 (Sandra)
Fax (09) 426 3053
rooms@villaorewa.co.nz
www.villaorewa.co.nz

Double/Twin $150-$225
(Full breakfast)
Dinner by arrangement
Visa MC accepted
1 King/Twin 2 Queen (3 bdrm)
Bathrooms: 3 Ensuite

W elcome to our beautifully appointed Mediterranean style home, with white-washed walls and blue vaulted roofs. A taste of the Greek Isles on beautiful Orewa Beach. Stay in 1 of our self-contained rooms, each with private balcony, and enjoy the panoramic beach and sea views, or socialise with us in our spacious living areas. Orewa offers a great range of activities and amenities; with cafes, restaurants, and shopping all within a short level walk. We are sure your stay will be enjoyable and memorable.

Orewa - Red Beach *5 km S of Orewa*
Hibiscus Hous*e B&B*

Judy & Brian Marsden
13A Marellen Drive, Red Beach,
Whangaparaoa - Hibiscus Coast

Tel (09) 427 6303
or 0274 492 025
or 0274 472 056
Fax (09) 427 6303
jb.marsden@clear.net.nz

Double/Twin $110
Single $85
(Continental breakfast)
Children Only 12 years or over.
Dinner $30 by prior arrangement
Pet free home
2 Queen 2 Twin (3 bdrm)
Bathrooms: 2 Ensuite 1 Private
Modern tile and glass with exellent showers.

We offer quality bed & breakfast, opposite a beach for the relaxing break you deserve, on route to Northland. Judy and Brian give friendly, personal hospitality in a very convenient location. Handy to shops, markets, cinema, beaches, golf courses and a leisure centre complex with heated swimming pool. Easy walks to surf, tennis and squash clubs. RSA 5 minutes away. Gulf Harbour Marina for ferries, fishing and sailing. Restaurants/bars/cafes for all tastes and occasions 5-15 minutes away. Sorry no pets. Children over 12 welcome. We have an outdoor spa pool available all year round.

Orewa *35 km N of Auckland*
Art & The Sea B&B *Apartment with Kitchen*

Vicki & John Lambert
12 Chelverton Terrace,
Red Beach,
Whangaparaoa,
Auckland 0932

Tel (09) 426 1060
or 021 426 107
vickilambert@actrix.co.nz
www.homeexchange.com ID#62402

Double/Twin $160-$180
Single $140-$160
(Full breakfast provisions)
Pet free home
Not suitable for children
1 Queen (1 bdrm)
Bathrooms: 1 Private Shower

Enjoy beautiful sea views and peace and quiet in this top-class cul-de-sac, where only a reserve separates you from beautiful Red Beach. Spread yourselves out in over 80sq.m. of exclusive use living area, with art, sky TV, stereo, books and games, well-equipped kitchen, washing machine, and patio with barbeque, table & chairs and sun-lounger. All this plus shops, golf courses, restaurants and tourist attractions while only 30mins north of Auckland city. To view living areas, visit www.homeexchange.com ID#62402.Breakfast provisions included.

Silverdale - Wainui *10.4 km W of Silverdale*
Ormond House *Luxury B&B*
Martin & Bridie Butler
470 Waitoki Road,
RD 1, Wainui,
Silverdale

Tel (09) 420 3317
or 021 048 5522
Fax (09) 420 3318
info@ormondhousenz.com
www.ormondhousenz.com

Double/Twin $130-$175
Single $90-$110
(Full breakfast)
Children $40 up to 13 yrs under 5 free
Visa MC Eftpos accepted
Pet free home
Children welcome
2 King 2 Queen 1 Single (4 bdrm)
Bathrooms: 4 Ensuite

Welcome to our large American style house on 4 acres with two hole 75 metre fairway with bunkers and pond. Set in the beautiful rolling hills of the Wainui Valley we are only 35 minutes from Auckland and are within easy reach of all major attractions in the Rodney District including beautiful Orewa Beach. Guests have access to the whole house including large conservatory, broadband is available. Your hosts Martin and Bridie are Irish, have travelled extensively and lived in Australia and Florida.

Whangaparaoa *4 km E of Orewa*
Duncansby by the Sea *B&B*
Kathy & Ken Grieve
72 Duncansby Road,
Whale Cove,
Stanmore Bay,
Whangaparaoa

Tel (09) 424 0025
or 027 200 9688
or 0274 422 278
Fax (09) 424 3607
duncansby@xtra.co.nz
www.duncansbybnb.co.nz

Double/Twin $120
Single $95
(Full breakfast)
Visa MC accepted
2 Queen (2 bdrm)
Bathrooms: 1 Ensuite 1 Private

Duncansby, our new home, offers relaxing panoramic sea views of the Hibiscus Coast. Located at Whale Cove between Red Beach and Stanmore Bay, our modern sunny well appointed rooms have own entrances, TV, decks, white linen, tea/coffee facilities. Paradise for golfers with 3 local courses including International Gulf Harbour Course with its boating marina. Bird watchers visit Tiritiri Island Bird Sanctuary, walk Shakespeare Park. Enjoy petanque, 9 superb beaches, excellent local restaurants and cafes. Only 35 minutes north of Auckland City, we welcome you.

Whangaparaoa *8 km E of Orewa*
Verdelais *Luxury B&B Homestay Boutique Wedding Venue*
Glenys and David Ferguson
36 Tindalls Bay Road, Tindalls Bay, Whangaparaoa

Tel (09) 424 7031 or 0210 414 322
Fax (09) 424 7031   glenys@verdelais.co.nz
www.verdelais.co.nz

Double/Twin $160-$205 Single $140-$160 (Full breakfast)
Visa MC accepted
1 King/Twin 2 Queen (3 bdrm)
Bathrooms: 2 Ensuite 1 Private

Verdelais is a luxury beachfront Bed and Breakfast and Boutique Wedding venue. It offers beauty, peace and comfort with genuine hospitality.

It is ideal for a weekend rest, a small wedding, local event, mini conference or a break in your journey. We have three rooms:- the Verdelais Suite is a garden suite with king size beds or twin beds, full bathroom with spa bath, private entrance and patio. The Coral and Aquarius Rooms have queen size beds, ensuites and spectacular views of the bay. All rooms have TV/DVDs, tea and coffee making facilities, home made cookies and reverse-cycle air-con. Sky and internet facilities are available in the comfort of our two lounge areas. We have ample and secure off-street parking.

Breakfast is a signature meal with seasonal vegetables and fruit home grown and freshly picked. Fresh eggs are laid daily by our four chooks. Dinner is served by request at our dining table or on the veranda taking in the view of the bay.

Alternatively there are a variety of international restaurants at nearby Manly Village.

Take a walk through our garden and down to the beach for a swim, there are three other safe beaches within easy walking distance. Verdelais is ideally situated near Gulf Harbour International Golf Course and Marina, Waiwera Thermal Pools, Ferry to city and islands and the wineries. There are so many other attractions in the locality too numerous to list. Timmy our tabby and Monty our golden lab are happy and friendly members of our family. We look forward to your stay with us.

Whangaparaoa *5 km E of Orewa*
Peone Place *B&B Homestay Apartment with Kitchen*

Parke & Elizabeth Horne
35 Surf Road,
Whangaparaoa,
0932

Tel (09) 424 1455
Fax (09) 424 1455
info@peone.co.nz
www.peone.co.nz

Double/Twin $120-$150
Single $30-$80
(Continental breakfast)
Children negotiable
Dinner by arrangement
Visa MC Eftpos accepted
Children welcome
2 King/Twin 1 Queen
3 Single (4 bdrm)
Bathrooms: 1 Private 1 Guest share

Welcome to our large, comfortable home, enjoy genuine, warm hospitality, wide sea views, & relax in our peaceful private garden with resident tuis. We have two double bedrooms and self-contained apartment.(Sleeps 5) Extended stay/group rates. Attractions include beaches, thermal pools, golf courses, indoor snowslope, walks & quality restaurants. Peone Place is an ideal base for trips to boutique wineries, colourful markets, distinctive galleries & potteries, & nearby beautiful islands including Tiritiri Matangi Bird sanctuary. Enquire for guest discounts, "Tiri" lunches & maps. Be at ease at Peones!

Silverdale - Waitoki *14.5 km SW of Silverdale*
Plover Lodge *B&B*

Michael & Pauline Tuckett
149 Ireland Road,
Waitoki,
R.D. 1,
Kaukapakapa
0871

Tel (09) 420 5282
ploverlodge@slingshot.co.nz
www.vianet.travel/visit/24426

Double/Twin $120
Single $80
(Full breakfast)
Visa MC accepted
Pet free home
Not suitable for children
1 Double/Twin (1 bdrm)
Bathrooms: 1 Ensuite

Magnificent sunsets can be seen from your own air-conditioned lounge overlooking a lush valley, only 12 minutes from Silverdaleís motorway exit and 35 minutes from Auckland Harbour Bridge. Come and relax on your own patio on this 7 acre property, meet the animals, or go for a stroll to Riverhead Forest and enjoy the spectacular views. Enjoy a delicious wholesome breakfast made with fresh home baked bread served in the separate dining room. Michael, Pauline and their 2 cats welcome you to their home.

Kumeu *26 km NW of Auckland*

Calico Lodge B&B *Countrystay B&B*

Kay & Kerry Hamilton
250 Matua Road, RD 1, Kumeu

Tel (09) 412 8167 or 0800 501 850 or 027 286 6064
bed@calicolodge.co.nz   www.calicolodge.co.nz

Double/Twin $150-$195 Single $130-$160
(Full breakfast)
Visa MC accepted
Pets welcome
1 King 2 Queen 2 Twin (4 bdrm)
Bathrooms: 2 Ensuite 2 Private
Bathroom amenities, heated, hairdryer, double spa bath.

Kerry and Kay, Zippy our little dog, 3 cats and tame sheep welcome you to Calico Lodge. Amidst the wineries, wedding venues, and cafes of Kumeu and Waimauku, near west coast beaches our modern home on 4 acres has beautiful trees and gardens.

Under an hour from Auckland Airport, Calico Lodge is an ideal base to start or end your New Zealand holiday.

Stay in the country and explore Auckland City and its sights only 26 kms away. Golf courses, 6 nearby are scenic and challenging. Hand made teddy bears and patchwork quilting (for sale) adorn the bedrooms and lounge in a separate guest wing.

Two minutes SH16, peace and stunning bush views complete the picture. We love to share our little piece of paradise.

At Calico Lodge we have free wireless broadband and a computer is available to check your email. Calico Lodge is endeavouring to be as eco friendly as possible. 100% New Zealand owned and operated.

Hobsonville *20 km NW of Auckland*
Eastview *B&B Homestay Separate Suite*

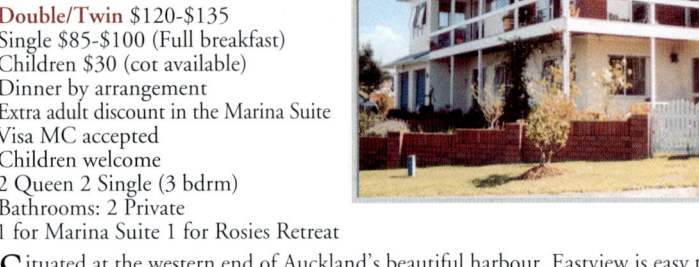

Joane & Don Clarke
2 Parkside Road,
Hobsonville, Auckland

Tel (09) 416 9254
or 027 437 3400
eastview@xtra.co.nz
www.eastview.co.nz

Double/Twin $120-$135
Single $85-$100 (Full breakfast)
Children $30 (cot available)
Dinner by arrangement
Extra adult discount in the Marina Suite
Visa MC accepted
Children welcome
2 Queen 2 Single (3 bdrm)
Bathrooms: 2 Private
1 for Marina Suite 1 for Rosies Retreat

Situated at the western end of Auckland's beautiful harbour. Eastview is easy to find from the airport or travel routes north and south. Well located for exploring Auckland. Panoramic water/city views. Near to Kumeu wine country (popular for weddings), superb beaches, rainforest clad hills, gannet colony. We offer many personal homely touches. 2 sunny accommodation areas. A 2 bedroomed suite, and a queen bedroom with private bathroom. A great place to relax after your trip or a day's sightseeing. Friendly small dog and cat.

Bethells Beach *15 km W of Swanson*
Bethells Beach Cottages - Natural Luxury for Humans Being
*Fully self contained Apartment and
2 Cottages - 1 celebration 10*

Trude & John Bethell-Paice
PO Box 95057, Swanson, Auckland

Tel (09) 810 9581
Fax (09) 810 8677
info@bethellsbeach.com
www.bethellsbeach.com

Double/Twin $250, $295, $350
(Special breakfast)
Children under 12 half price
Dinner 2 course $40pp
3 course $50pp
Breakfast $30pp
Visa MC accepted
Children welcome
3 Queen 2 Double/Twin
3 Single (4 bdrm)
Bathrooms: 3 Private

Love dances in the beauty of Nature. When you stay at Bethells Beach Cottages you become one with the elements. The sights and sounds of nature will awaken your passionate spirit and time will cease to exist. Whether walking the beach, relaxing in your cottage, or sitting in the Scandinavian hot tub watching the sun set you will know that love is everywhere but here it flows a little more easily.

Waitakere Ranges - Swanson *4 km W of Swanson*
Panorama Heights *B&B*
Allison & Paul Ingram
42 Kitewaho Road,
Swanson,
Waitakere City,
Auckland

Tel (09) 832 4777
or 0800 692 624 Outside Auckland
Booking
nzbnb4u@clear.net.nz
www.panoramaheights.co.nz

Double/Twin $160
Single $135
(Full breakfast)
Dinner by request
Visa MC accepted
2 Queen 1 Twin (3 bdrm)
Bathrooms: 3 Ensuite 1 Private

Paul & Allison invite you to vist and share our extremely special location high in the Waitakere Ranges with tranquility,privacy and magnificent panoramic views across Native Rainforest to Auckland City and Rangitoto Island beyond. Explore 250km walking/hiking trails in surrounding Regional Park, West Coast beaches(Piha,Karekare,Bethells, Muriwai) Wineries,2 Scenic Golf courses. Train to City is nearby. Excellent quality accommodation is here for you to Enjoy. Your hosts who reside nextdoor encourage relaxation while we spoil you. Please Phone/Email for Bookings/Directions.

Waitakere Ranges *15 km NW of Henderson*
Wairere Lodge *B&B Homestay*
Bob and Heather Harmes
351 Wairere Road,
Waitakere,
Auckland,
0782

Tel (09) 8109 467
info@wairerelodge.co.nz
www.wairerelodge.co.nz

Double/Twin $130-$150
Single $95-$105
(Full breakfast)
Dinner 3 courses $40,
2 courses $30, 1 course $20,
Wine and beer available to purchase
Visa MC accepted
2 Queen (2 bdrm)
Bathrooms: 1 Guest share

Heading north on northwestern motorway, take Lincoln Road turn off; second set of lights turn right into Universal Drive, 2 km to roundabout, straight through on to Swanson Road; 4 km; turn right into Waitakere Road; 3 km, over the railway overbridge, turn left into Bethells Road; 1/2 km right into Wairere Road.

Ranui *15 km W of Auckland*
The Garrett *B&B Homestay*
Alma & Rod Mackay
295 Swanson Road,
Waitakere City,
Auckland
0612

Tel (09) 833 6018
Fax (09) 833 6018
rodalmamacka@paradise.net.nz

Double/Twin $90
Single $60
(Continental breakfast)
2 King/Twin 1 King
2 Single (2 bdrm)
Bathrooms: 1 Ensuite

Just 15 minutes from Auckland City, 5 minutes from Henderson. The Garrett offers villa style accommodation with ensuite. Twin beds or king-size available. Accommodation for extra guests with folding beds on request; suitable for business people. High ceilings, period furniture and decor create a charming atmosphere in this delightful homestay, just minutes from Waitakere City. Attractions include wine trails, Art Out West - including Lopdell House Gallery, Waitakere Ranges, bush walks, Aratiki Centre, and golf courses. Westcity Shopping Centre, Lynn Mall and St Lukes.

≈

Ranui *15 km W of Auckland*
The Brushmakers Cottage *B&B Apartment with Kitchen*
Jeanette & Roger Brown
20 Clearview Heights,
Ranui, Waitakere City,
Auckland 0612

Tel (09) 833 8476 or 021 725 627
Fax (09) 833 8476
r.g.brown@xtra.co.nz

Double/Twin $90-$150
Single $75-$110
(Continental breakfast)
Dinner by arrangement
Extra guests $20
Not suitable for children
Non smokers only
3 Queen 1 Twin (4 bdrm)
Bathrooms: 1 Ensuite
2 Private 1 Family share

Choose between luxury self-contained apartment, featuring full kitchen, dishwasher, dining/lounge, TV/DVD, laundry, or traditional B&B. Backing onto a vineyard this peaceful location has views of both the Waitakere ranges and central Auckland. 10 minutes walk from train and bus stations and only 20 minutes drive from downtown Auckland. Close to both east and west coast beaches, gannet colony, golf courses, winery, cafes, restaurants and shopping malls. A great base for exploring Auckland. Ask about discounts. Some gluten-free food available.

Piha *20 km NW of Titirangi*
Piha Cottage *B&B Cottage with Kitchen*

Tracey & Steve Skidmore
PO Box 48,
Piha, Waitakere City,
Auckland

Tel (09) 812 8514
info@pihacottage.co.nz
www.pihacottage.co.nz

Double/Twin $120-$160
Single $110-$130
(Full breakfast provisions)
Children $30
Extra Adult $50
Visa MC accepted
Pet free home
Children welcome
1 Double/Twin 1 Single
Bathrooms: 1 Private

Leave the city behind. Beautiful Piha Cottage is hidden on a sunny, quiet bush setting, within easy walking distance of the surf beach and walking tracks. This spacious open plan home includes a kitchen, dining, living and sleeping areas. After a delicious self-serve breakfast (including waffles and maple syrup) go surfing, swimming or choose from one of Piha's outstanding walking tracks, through lush rainforest or along spectacular coastline. We, and our daughters, welcome you warmly and then allow you to enjoy the tranquility. Inquire about weekly rates.

Piha *25 km W of Henderson*
Westwood Cottage *Cottage with Kitchen*

Dianne & Don Sparrow
95 Glenesk Road,
Piha,
Auckland

Tel (09) 812 8203
Fax (09) 812 8203
westwoodcottage.piha@xtra.co.nz

Double/Twin $150
(Continental breakfast provisions)
Children $20
Visa MC accepted
Children welcome
1 Queen 1 Double/Twin (2 bdrm)
Bathrooms: 1 Private

Westwood Cottage offers a unique experience. Nestled in a secluded corner of our property, amongst beautiful bush overlooking Piha Valley. The Cottage is self-contained, open plan design, flowing on to a private deck. Full kitchen facilities with continental breakfast supplied. A cozy log fire for your enjoyment on cooler evenings. Off-road parking provided. Children 5 and over welcome. A short walk leads to Piha Surf Beach and bush walks include Kitekite Waterfall and Black Rock Dam. Forward book to avoid dissapointment.

Okura *20 km N of Auckland Central*
Okura B&B *B&B Separate Suite*

Judie & Ian Greig
20 Valerie Crescent,
Okura,
North Shore City,
Auckland

Tel (09) 473 0792
Fax (09) 473 1072
ibgreig@paradise.net.nz

Double/Twin $110
Single $85
(Full breakfast)
Visa MC accepted
1 Queen 1 Single (2 bdrm)
Bathrooms: 1 Private, own shower

Situated on Auckland's North Shore, Okura is a small settlement bounded by farmland and the Okura River, an estuary edged with native forest. If you like peace, quiet, with only bird song nearby, estuary and forest views, then this is for you. Accommodation includes your own, not shared, TV lounge, tea-making facilities, fridge, shower and toilet. Nearby is a wide variety of cafes, shops, beaches, walks, North Shore Stadium, Massey University and golf courses. Okura - one of Auckland's best kept secrets.

~

Okura - North Shore *20 km NE of Auckland Central*
Okura River Cottage *B&B Cottage with Kitchen*

Elizabeth & David Keay
12 Deborah Place,
Okura,
North Shore City

Tel (09) 473 6298
or 027 542 6699
okuracottage@xtra.co.nz
www.okuracottage.co.nz

Double/Twin $230
(Special breakfast)
1 Queen 1 Double/Twin (2 bdrm)
Bathrooms: 1 Ensuite 1 Private

Okura River Cottage is nestled alongside Auckland's prettiest river. The view from the cottage is stunning. Imagine waking up to sun streaming on calm waters and bush clad hills. Bird life is amazing. Swimming beaches minutes away with bush walks at your doorstep. Self contained top quality detached cottage. Scrumptious kiwi home baking awaits your arrival. Ideally situated for a first or last stop from the airport. We and our two Scottish Terriers extend a warm welcome to you at this beautiful tranquil place.

Auckland

Coatesville - Albany *7 km N of Albany*
Camperdown *B&B Farmstay*
Chris & David Hempleman
455 Coatesville/Riverhead Highway,
RD 3,
Albany,
Auckland

Tel (09) 415 9009
Fax (09) 415 9023
chris@camperdown.co.nz
www.camperdown.co.nz

Double/Twin $140
Single $100 (Full breakfast)
Children $50
Dinner $40
Children welcome
1 King/Twin 1 King
2 Queen 2 Single (5 bdrm)
Bathrooms: 2 Private 1 Guest share

We are only 20 minutes from Auckland City, relax in secluded tranquillity. Our home opens into beautiful gardens, native bush and stream offering the best of hospitality in a friendly relaxed atmosphere. On the farm we have sheep, cattle and pet lambs Our spacious guest areas consist of the entire upstairs. Guests may use our games room, play tennis on our superb court, row a boat on the lake, or just stroll by the stream. Camperdown is easy travelling to the main tourist route north.

Coatesville/Riverhead *30 km N of Auckland City*
Coatesville Lavender Hill *Luxury B&B Farmstay Bedroom/Ensuite/Dining/Lounge*
Tricia Henderson
11A Beacon Road,
Coatesville,
Auckland 0793

Tel (09) 412 5275
or (09) 412 5270
or 021 728 051
Fax (09) 412 5276
tricia@lavenderhill.co.nz
http://lavenderhill.co.nz

Double/Twin $150-$200
Single $100 (Full breakfast)
Dinner by arrangement to suit
BBQ facilities available
Visa MC Amex Eftpos accepted
Please provide credit card details
when confirming your booking
Not suitable for children
4 King/Twin (4 bdrm)
Bathrooms: 4 Ensuite Showers + mobility facilities

Luxury B&B farmstay accommodation in Coatesville/Riverhead; near Albany, Kumeu, Westgate. Superior Sealy beds, three rooms with ensuite, one room with separate mobility bathroom and ramp to outside. Set amongst the lavender beds, olive and lemon groves. Views to City and Riverhead Forest. Wireless broadband available.

Greenhithe *15 km N of Auckland*

Waiata Tui Lodge (The Song of the Tui) *B&B Homestay*

B&B
Approved

Therese & Ned Jujnovich

177 Upper Harbour Drive, Greenhithe, North Shore, Auckland,

Tel (09) 413 9270

therese.jujnovich@gmail.com   www.bnb.co.nz/waiata.html

Double/Twin $110-$120 Single $85 (Special breakfast)
Children negotiable
Dinner $35 - three course with wine
Visa MC Amex accepted
Pet free home
2 Queen 1 Twin 2 Single (3 bdrm)
Bathrooms: 2 Private 1 Guest share

A warm welcome to our haven. 8 acres of native forest and pasture only 15 minutes from NZ's largest city, yet so peaceful you could be in the heart of the countryside. A handy relaxing stay before your journey north. Spectacular views from over the kauri trees to the tranquil water below, with the distant Waitakere Ranges beyond.

Waken to tui song and the smell of freshly baked bread. A delicious healthy breakfast will be served: home-grown or local in-season fruit, various cereals, home-made yoghurt and spreads as well as a cooked breakfast, fruit juice, tea or coffee. From our large kauri breakfast table you can look out to the west and see the changing patterns of trees, water and tide. Perhaps a tui or a kereru (NZ's largest colourful pigeon) will stop for a drink at the birdbath on the adjoining deck.

You may like to walk in our lush rain forest with tree ferns and massive trees down to the waters edge or you can relax in the bush hammock. Do some bird watching or wander around our large garden usually bright with seasonal flowers. Swim in the pool during summer. Meet Harry, our friendly goat.

We have both travelled extensively overseas and within NZ and will be pleased to help you with your travel plans.

A Lockwood (solid-timber) home built for our family 30 years ago has been a homestay since 1987. Only minutes to North Harbour Stadium, North Shore Events Centre and east coast beaches. 5 minutes to Greenhithe Village & its quality restaurants.

Bayswater *5 km S of Takapuna*
Beresford B&B Homestay *B&B Homestay*
Lesley Brown & Gordon Storey
46A Beresford Street,
Bayswater,
North Shore,
0622

Tel (09) 445 3959
or 027 492 4462
beresfordhomestay@email.com
http://beresfordhomestay.awardspace.com

Double/Twin $100
Single $80
(Continental breakfast)
Dinner by arrangement $20-$30 pp
Full cooked breakfast available $10pp
Visa MC accepted
Not suitable for children
1 Queen (1 bdrm)
Bathrooms: 1 Private

We warmly welcome travellers from NZ and abroad to our comfortable, modern home in peaceful Bayswater, where you can relax and feel at home, but be within easy reach of all that Auckland has to offer. Easy walk to ferry, downtown Auckland 10 minute trip away. 5-10 minute drive to motorway, Devonport or Takapuna, restaurants and shopping. On bus route. Light, airy, upstairs bedroom, own TV lounge (or join us downstairs), tea & coffee making, internet, laundry, spa pool, scrumptious breakfast. One timid cat.

Devonport *1.5 km N of Devonport*
Ducks Crossing Cottage *B&B Homestay*
Gwenda & Peter Mark-Woods
58 Seabreeze Road,
Devonport,
Auckland

Tel (09) 445 8102
Fax (09) 445 8102
duckxing@splurge.net.nz

Double/Twin $100-$130
Single $70-$85
(Special breakfast)
Children $30
Pet free home
Children welcome
1 King/Twin 1 Queen
1 Single (3 bdrm)
Bathrooms: 1 Ensuite 2 Private

Welcome to our charming modern home in a garden setting. Peaceful, spacious, sunny bedrooms with television and clock radios. Tea, coffee and home-cooking available. We overlook Waitemata Golf Course and are 5 minutes from Narrow Neck Beach. Devonport Village, with cafes, restaurants and antique shops is 2 minutes by car or 15 minutes walk. Hosts are well travelled,informative and enjoy hospitality. Directions:airport door to door shuttle, or drive Route 26, Seabreeze Road, first house on left. Good off-street parking, courtesy ferry pick up on request.

Devonport *4 km N of Auckland Central*

Karin's Garden Villa *B&B Cottage with Kitchen Apartment*

Karin Loesch & Family
14 Sinclair Street, Devonport, Auckland 0624

Tel (09) 445 8689 Fax (09) 445 8689
stay@karinsvilla.com
www.karinsvilla.com

Double/Twin $155-$185
Single $95-$145
(Continental Breakfast)
Children $25
Self-contained cottage $195
Visa MC accepted
1 King/Twin 2 Double/Twin 3 Single (4 bdrm)
Bathrooms: 1 Ensuite 1 Private 1 Guest share

Tucked away at the end of a quiet cul-de-sac, Karin's Garden Villa - a Devonport dream - offers real home comfort with its light cosy rooms, easy relaxed atmosphere and the warmest of welcome from Karin and her family.

A beautifully restored spacious Victorian villa surrounded by large lawns and old fruit trees. Karin's Garden Villa has also been featured on NZ and Australian television advertising for its relaxed, peaceful setting. Just 5 minutes stroll from tree-lined Cheltenham Beach, sailing, golf, tennis, shops and restaurants and only a short drive or pleasant 10 minute walk past extinct volcanoes to the picturesque Devonport centre with its many attractions.

Your comfortable room offers separate private access through french doors, opening onto wide verandahs and cottage garden. And for those visitors wanting ultimate comfort and privacy, there is even a self-contained studio cottage with balcony and full kitchen facilities to rent. For longer stays enquire about our new open-plan private Garden Apartment (sleeps 2-4) in the heart of Devonport. Sit down to a nutritious breakfast in the sunny dining room with its large bay windows overlooking everflowering purple lavender and native gardens.

Feel free to use the kitchen, laundry and wireless broadband. Karin comes from Germany and she and her family have lived in Indonesia for a number of years. We have seen a lot of the world and enjoy meeting other travellers. Always happy to help you arrange island cruises, rental cars, bikes and tours.

Come as guests - leave as friends.

Devonport *0.25 km E of Devonport Township*
The Jasmine Cottage *B&B Cottage with kitchenette*

Joan & John Lewis
20 Buchanan Street,
Devonport,
Auckland

Tel (09) 445 8825
Fax (09) 445 8605
joanjohnlewis@xtra.co.nz
www.photoalbum.co.nz/jasmine/

Double/Twin $120
(Full breakfast)
1 Queen (1 bdrm)
Bathrooms: 1 Ensuite

Welcome to our cosy smoke-free quiet and private guest cottage. We are right in the heart of historic Devonport Village with all its attractions, cafes, beaches, golf course, scenic walks. The ferry to Auckland City and the Hauraki Gulf is 3 minutes walk away. A breakfast basket is delivered to your door and provides fruit juice, cereals, home made muesli and yoghurt, a platter of seasonal fruits, breads, jams, spreads, free-range eggs, breakfast teas and freshly brewed coffee. TV, fax.

Devonport *0.5 km N of Devonport*
Mahoe *B&B Apartment with Kitchen*

Judith & David Bern
15B King Edward Parade,
Devonport,
0624

Tel (09) 445 1515
or 027 291 3727
Fax (09) 445 1515
info@mahoe.co.nz
www.mahoe.co.nz

Double/Twin $160-$200
(Breakfast by arrangement)
Children by arrangement
Visa MC accepted
2 Queen 1 Double/Twin (3 bdrm)
Bathrooms: 1 Ensuite 1 Private

Mahoe is an old school house transported from Huntly in 1985. Situated on the Devonport waterfront up a driveway in a peaceful setting. The upstairs B&B has queen room with deck and double room with lounge. The bathroom is separate. Our B&B is suitable for one couple or 3 or 4 people who are family or friends. We can accommodate 3 couples by including the apartment, which has a separate entrance and is fully equipped.

Waiheke Island *1 km NE of oneroa*

Watermark Studio Apartments *Luxury studio apartments*

Jo Underwood
17 Tawa Street, Little Oneroa,
Waiheke Island, Auckland 1081

Tel (09) 372 2862
or 027 346 6117
info@watermarkwaiheke.com
http://watermarkwaiheke.com

Double/Twin $185-$260
Single $155-$260
(Breakfast by arrangement)
Dinner in village
Breakfast provisions
available on request
Visa MC Diners accepted
Not suitable for children
6 King/Twin 3 King (3 bdrm)
Bathrooms: 3 Ensuite

Jo, (and her 2 burmese cats), is your host at Watermark. Quiet location 300mtrs above beautiful beach. 3 private, self-contained studios face north. Floor to ceiling windows open onto private terraces maximising the lovely sea views from bed, living and terraces. TV/DVD/CD, wiresless internet, kingsize bed/kingtwin, radio,fridge,microwave/convectionoven/grill, en-suite, linen, robes, slippers, iron/ironingboard. BBQs, beach chairs, beach towels, penanque also available. 10 min scenic walk to more beaches, kayaking, village, shops, cafes, galleries etc. Stunning walks. Vineyards closeby.

Auckland - Herne Bay *2.5 km W of Auckland central*

Moana Vista *Luxury B&B Homestay Guest House*

Tim Kennedy & Matthew Moran
60 Hamilton Road,
Herne Bay,
Auckland

Tel (09) 376 5028
or 0800 213 761
Fax (09) 376 5025
info@moanavista.co.nz
www.moanavista.co.nz

Double/Twin $240-$350
Single $160-$240
(Full breakfast)
Visa MC Amex Eftpos accepted
Children welcome
2 Queen 1 Twin (3 bdrm)
Bathrooms: 2 Ensuite 1 Private

Just minutes stroll from the Waitmata Harbour, nestled in the exclusive enclave of Herne Bay. This charming, renovated 2 storey villa is owned and operated by your friendly hosts, Tim and Matthew. 2 of the upper rooms have lovely harbour views. All rooms have LCD TVs with sky digital, DVD players and complimentary wireless internet access. In the evening you can wander up the road to visit any one of the award winning Ponsonby restaurants.

Auckland - Ponsonby *3 km W of Auckland Central*
The Big Blue House *B&B*
Kate Prebble & Lynne Giddings
103 Garnet Road,
Westmere,
Auckland

Tel (09) 360 6384
or 0800 360 6384
or 021 884 662
kate-lynne@xtra.co.nz
www.thebigbluehouse.co.nz

Double/Twin $130-$160
Single $80-$140
(Continental breakfast)
Children $10
Dinner $50 by arrangment
Visa MC Eftpos accepted
Children welcome
2 King 3 Single (3 bdrm)
Bathrooms: 1 Ensuite 2 Family share

Kate and Lynne warmly invite you to enjoy our unique homelike environment close to Auckland's central city and harbour. Be greeted by our friendly cat and dog. Enjoy the luxury of spacious rooms with sea/hill views, TV, tea/coffee facilities, writing desk, electric blankets,heated towels and bathrobes. Generous continental breakfast. Luxuriate in our spa, splash in the pool. Take an easy stroll to the Auckland Zoo, Western Springs Stadium, cafes or seashore. Children welcome. Make yourself at home!

Auckland - Ponsonby *1.5 km W of Auckland Central*
Colonial Cottage *B&B Homestay*
Grae Glieu
35 Clarence Street,
Ponsonby,
Auckland
1034

Tel (09) 360 2820
Fax (09) 360 3436
bnb@colonial-cottage.com

Double/Twin $100-$120
Single $80-$100
(Special breakfast)
Dinner $25 by arrangement
Pet free home
1 King 1 Queen 1 Single (3 bdrm)
Bathrooms: 1 Guest share

Delightful olde-world charm with modern amenities to assure your comfort - accent on quality. Hospitable and relaxing. Quiet with green outlook. Close to Herne Bay and Ponsonby Road cafes and quality restaurants. Airport shuttle service door-to-door. Handy to public transport, city attractions and motorways. Smoke-free indoors. Alternative health therapies and massage available. Special dietary requirements catered for. Organic emphasis. Single party bookings available.

Auckland - Ponsonby *1 km NW of Auckland Central*
The Great Ponsonby Arthotel *B&B Hotel Guest House*
Sally James & Gerard Hill
30 Ponsonby Terrace, Ponsonby, Auckland 1011

Tel (09) 376 5989 or 0800 766 792
Fax (09) 376 5527
info@greatpons.co.nz
www.greatpons.co.nz

Double/Twin $180-$350
Single $180-$350 (Special breakfast)
Visa MC Diners Amex Eftpos accepted
Children and dogs welcome
6 King/Twin 5 Queen (11 bdrm)
Bathrooms: 11 Ensuite

Relax in a quiet, heritage, 1890's villa in the middle of cosmopolitan Auckland, just 2 minutes stroll to Ponsonby's vibrant cafes, restaurants, and galleries. Fifteen minutes by eco bus, five minutes by taxi to the waterfront or a 30 minute amble through Ponsonby's interesting streets. Close to Eden Park, the Zoo and all main attractions.

Wake up to an award winning breakfast in the lively dining room or al fresco on the balcony. Socialise and read in the large comfortable lounge, on your balcony, or relax with a glass of wine in the wisteria

covered courtyard.Each of our eleven individually designed guestrooms has original Pacific and New Zealand artworks that reflect the brightness of this part of the world.In the main house are villa rooms with queen beds. The courtyard and palm garden studios are roomier and have self catering facilities as well. An upstairs penthouse suite has expansive views from the deck out to the mountains.All rooms are non smoking, have opening windows, ipod docks and access to free wifi. A laptop and extensive guest library of New Zealand books, films and music is also available. Your hosts are knowledgeable about the area and are more than happy to help you with travel plans over a complimentary aperitif. We are committed to sustainability and we have two bikes for your enjoyment.

Auckland - Ponsonby *2 km W of Information centre*
Ponsonby Studio Loft *Luxury Separate Suite Apartment with Kitchen*

Chrissy and Reg Price
9 Picton Street,
Ponsonby, Auckland

Tel (09) 361 2461
or 021 637 908
or 021 336 640
info@ponsonbystudioloft.co.nz
www.ponsonbystudioloft.co.nz

Double/Twin $160 Single $160
(Breakfast by arrangement)
Children $30
Dinner Local cafes just up the road
Tarrif is for bed only
Visa MC Amex accepted
Pet free home
Children welcome
1 King 1 Double/Twin (1 bdrm)
Bathrooms: 1 Ensuite
Separate shower

We are 100m from the cafes and shops of Ponsonby yet nestled in a tree lined street of renovated 1900s wooden villas. The modern studio is completely separate and self-contained with kitchen however trying local cafes is the Ponsonby experience. There's a great outlook, but still a cosy, warm and private feeling. Subtropical gardens. King sized bed and luxury linen. Sky TV and free broadband. Ensuite bathroom and separate shower. Balcony with views. On city Link bus route. Special long stay and winter prices.

Auckland CBD *0.5 km E of Auckland CBD*
Braemar on Parliament Street *B&B*

Susan Sweetman
7 Parliament Street,
Auckland City Central,
1010

Tel (09) 377 5463
or 021 640 688
Fax (09) 377 3056
braemar@aucklandbedandbreakfast.com
www.aucklandbedandbreakfast.com

Double/Twin $205-$350
(Full breakfast)
Visa MC Diners Amex Eftpos accepted
Children and pets welcome
3 Queen 1 Double/Twin (4 bdrm)
Bathrooms: 1 Ensuite 1 Private 1 Guest share

A lovingly restored Edwardian townhouse in the Auckland CBD, Braemar provides comfortable, elegant accommodation to the discerning traveller. All upstairs bedrooms have posturepedic beds. All bathrooms have large claw foot baths. Complimentary toiletries, tea & coffee. Children welcome. Pets by prior arrangement. Toy poodles and cat live on site.

Auckland - Parnell *1.5 km NW of hotel*

Chalet Chevron *B&B Boutique Hotel*

Eileen Darwin & Mark Klaassen
14 Brighton Road, Parnell, Auckland

Tel (09) 309 0290 or 021 55 22 77
Fax (09) 373 5754
info@chaletchevron.com
www.chaletchevron.com

Double/Twin $165-$195
Single $90-$145 (Full breakfast)
Family room caters for 2 children;
foldout also available
Extra adult on foldout $45
Visa MC Eftpos accepted
Pet free home Children welcome
4 Queen 3 Double/Twin 4 Twin
6 Single (11 bdrm)
Bathrooms: 11 Ensuite Bath, shower
over bath, shower - all with toilet

Are you looking for the perfect city location for your hassle free holiday? Come and experience Chalet Chevron, "a great little hotel" "Thanks for 2 wonderful days we had a great time with you", Elad Luski, Israel. You will experience the answer to your accommodation success, beginning with a warm welcome. We guarantee you will be taken care of, you will find a cosy guest lounge, wireless internet, comfy beds, our famous continental and free range cooked breakfast - all topped off with a fantastic central location. Chalet Chevron is the perfect place to begin and end your day.

Auckland - Remuera *7 km E of Auckland Central*

Woodlands *B&B*

Jude & Roger Harwood
18 Waiatarua Road,
Remuera,
Auckland
1050

Tel (09) 524 6990
jude.harwood@xtra.co.nz
www.travelwise.co.nz

Double/Twin $145-$175
Single $125
(Special breakfast)
Children Not suitable
Visa MC accepted
Pet free home
Not suitable for children
1 King 1 Double/Twin
1 Twin 1 Single (3 bdrm)
Bathrooms: 1 Ensuite 1 Private

Guest book comments: "Absolutely purr-fect." "Very comfortable with stunning food." "A lovely oasis of calm with wonderful breakfasts." "Peaceful retreat with excellent breakfasts." Our breakfasts ARE special using seasonal fruit and produce. Relax by our heated swimming pool. Woodlands is very quiet, surrounded by native trees and palms and central to many places of interest. The 3 guest bedrooms have tea/coffee facilities, heated towel rails, swimming towels and colour TVs. Fridge. Safe off-street carparking. Arrive a guest - leave a friend.

Take time to enjoy your journey and the company of your hosts.

Auckland - Remuera *1.5 km E of Newmarket*

Green Oasis *B&B Homestay Apartment with Kitchen*

@ home NEW ZEALAND

B&B Approved

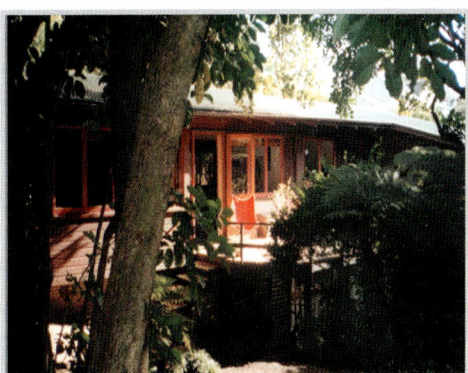

James & Joy Foote
25A Portland Road,
Remuera,
Auckland 1050

Tel (09) 520 1921
Fax (09) 522 9004
footes1@xtra.co.nz
www.babs.co.nz/greenoasis

Double/Twin $120
Single $80
(Full breakfast)
Children $65
Laundry, ironing - small charge by arrangement
Visa MC accepted
Children welcome
1 Queen 1 Single (2 bdrm)
Bathrooms: 1 Private

Green Oasis, a secluded, tranquil location in a much loved garden of native trees and ferns, 10 minutes to city centre. Close to the museum, antique & specialty shops, restaurants & cafes. An informal home of natural timbers, sunny decks where you will find us relaxed, welcoming and sensitive to your needs. Your accommodation, entered from a private garden, is self-contained with kitchen/dining room, tea/coffee making facilities, washing machine, TV. Special breakfast of seasonal and home-made taste sensations!

Auckland - Remuera *3 km E of Auckland Central*

Omahu Lodge *Luxury B&B*
Robyn & Ken Booth
33 Omahu Road, Remuera, Auckland 1050

Tel (09) 524 5648 or 021 954 333 or 027 475 4466
Fax (09) 524 5108
info@omahulodge.co.nz   www.omahulodge.co.nz

Double/Twin $195-$295 Single $160-$200
(Full breakfast)
Visa MC accepted
Pet free home   Not suitable for children
1 King/Twin 1 King 2 Queen 1 Twin 1 Single (4 bdrm)
Bathrooms: 4 Ensuite 1 Private
Plus luxurious separate bath suite

Omahu Lodge offers luxury Bed and Breakfast accommodation with total privacy in a peaceful residential setting. The Lodge is very spacious with beautifully appointed bedrooms all with ensuites, fine bed linen, heated towels, bathrobes, slippers, hair dryers, ironing and tea/coffee facilities. Rooms have views of Cornwall Park, Mt Hobson, Mt St John, the eastern suburbs or the pool and spa complex from the Poolside Suite. Relax with a complimentary drink and snacks in the large lounge amongst the antiques, in the separate entertainment room with a large plasma television, DVD and CD player or enjoy the solar heated pool, sauna or spa. Omahu Lodge is a boutique resort. The city centre and Auckland's renowned harbour are just 10 minutes away by car. Remuera, Parnell, Newmarket's exclusive shopping, restaurants, Epsom Showgrounds and public transport are easy walking distance. Walks in Cornwall Park, Mt Hobson and Mt St John add to the peaceful ambience of the suburban setting. A sumptuous breakfast is served in the conservatory overlooking the pool, on the patio beside the pool or room service is available. Dinner available by arrangement.

Auckland - Newmarket/Remuera

0.5 km N of Newmarket

Amerissit *B&B*
Barbara McKain
20 Buttle Street,
Remuera/Newmarket,
Auckland

Tel (09) 522 9297
or 027 284 4883
Fax (09) 522 9298
barbara@amerissit.co.nz
www.amerissit.co.nz

Double/Twin $185-$260
(Full breakfast)
Visa MC Diners Amex accepted
Pet free home
Children welcome
2 King 1 Queen (3 bdrm)
Bathrooms: 3 Ensuite One Spa Bath

Kia ora - welcomeAmerissit is an architecturally designed bed and breakfast offering luxury accommodation close to Newmarket in Remuera, Auckland, New Zealand. Located among prestigious streets in a quiet cul de sac, the emphasis is on privacy, peace and tranquility. This convenient location, close to central Auckland, is only minutes by car to the popular restaurants, bars, cafes, shopping, art galleries and museums of Auckland City plus the Viaduct Harbour, Parnell, Newmarket and Remuera.

Auckland - Grey Lynn *5 km W of Auckland Central*

Henry's *Luxury B&B Separate Suite*
Henry Boller & Anne Sadler
33 Peel Street,
Grey Lynn,
1022

Tel (09) 360 2700
or 027 210 2964
Fax (09) 360 2705
henrysonpeel@xtra.co.nz
www.henrysonpeel.co.nz

Double/Twin $180-$220
(Continental breakfast)
Visa MC accepted
1 King 1 Queen (2 bdrm)
Bathrooms: 2 Ensuite

Welcome to Henry's Boutique Accommodation. Our extensively renovated villa provides excellent facilities for the tourist, business person or simply a retreat for those wishing for some time out. Centrally situated, close to the heart of Auckland, Henry's is within short distances of all the most important sights and activities. The CBD and Ponsonby Road are just 2 - 5kms away. West Lynn shops with award winning bars and restaurants are within walking distance, Henry's overlooks Auckland harbour. Resident cat Thelma.

Auckland - Mt Eden *4 km N of Auckland Central*
811 Bed & Breakfast *B&B*
Bryan Condon & David Fitchew
811 Dominion Road,
Mt Eden,
Auckland
1003

Tel (09) 620 4284
Fax (09) 620 4286
811bnb@quicksilver.net.nz

Double/Twin $85
Single $55
(Full breakfast)
Children welcome
2 Double/Twin 1 Twin (3 bdrm)
Bathrooms: 2 Guest share

A ll are welcome at 811 Bed & Breakfast. Your hosts and their Irish water spaniels welcome you to their turn of the century home. Our home reflects years of collecting and living overseas. Located on Dominion Road (which is an extension of Queen Street city centre). The bus stop at the door, only 10 minutes to city and 20 minutes to airport, shuttle bus from airport. Easy walking to Balmoral shopping area (excellent restaurants). Our breakfast gives you a beaut start to your day.

Auckland - Mt Eden *2 km S of Auckland Central*
Bavaria B&B Hotel *B&B*
Ulrike & Rudolf
83 Valley Road,
Mt Eden, Auckland 1024

Tel (09) 638 9641
Fax (09) 638 9665
bavaria@xtra.co.nz
www.bavariabandbhotel.co.nz

Double/Twin $139-$145
Single $95-$99 (Full breakfast)
Children over 2 years $15
Extra adult $50
Please inquire about our reduced
rates from May-September
Visa MC Amex Eftpos accepted
Children welcome
1 King/Twin 4 Queen 2 Double/
Twin 2 Twin 2 Single (11 bdrm)
Bathrooms: 11 Ensuite

C harming small hotel in quiet, historic, residential surroundings, close to city with excellent connections to town, Mt. Eden summit with panoramic views easily accessible, immaculate quality rooms with ensuites, phones; wireless internet access available, guest computer in lounge, healthy breakfast buffet-style, complimentary tea/coffee/biscuits, sunny lounge and peaceful garden, good shopping, fine restaurants & cafes nearby, off-street parking, friendly and welcoming atmosphere. Ask us for advice on rental cars, tours etc.

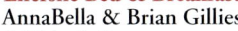

Auckland - Ellerslie *5 km SE of Auckland*
Ellerslie Bed & Breakfast Inn *Luxury B&B*

AnnaBella & Brian Gillies
6 Walpole Street,
Ellerslie,
Auckland

Tel (09) 589 1997
or 021 582 522
or 0800 589 199
Fax (09) 589 1994
info@ellersliebbi.co.nz
www.ellersliebbi.co.nz

Double/Twin $150-$180
Single $120-$150
(Full breakfast)
Visa MC accepted
Not suitable for children
2 Queen 1 Twin 2 Single (3 bdrm)
Bathrooms: 3 Ensuite

Some Guest Book comments - Welcome to EBBI which offers Wonderful Warm Hospitality - Great Facilities, Delicious full Breakfasts! & Situated midway between Airport and Auckland city. We are a quick walk - 8 minutes to train - bus- restaurants-shops! We have a Burmese cat "Purkins" We offer a truly fantastic start or finish to your NZ holiday! Plus - Free off street parking - Free Wireless (within reason) - Free computer to check emails. What more could you want? Phone AnnaBella now to reserve your room.

Auckland - Orakei/Okahu Bay *4.8 km E of Auckland Central*
Nautical Nook/Free Sailing *B&B Homestay*

Trish & Keith Janes & Irish Setter
23B Watene Crescent,
Orakei,
Auckland

Tel (09) 521 2544
or 0800 360 544
or 027 439 7116
nauticalnook@bigfoot.com
www.nauticalnook.com

Double/Twin $130-$151
Single $97-$119
(Full breakfast)
Visa MC accepted
Children welcome
1 King/Twin 2 Queen (3 bdrm)
Bathrooms: 2 Ensuite 1 Private

Friendly, relaxed beachside hospitality overlooking park/harbour, 4.8km from downtown. 100 metres from Okahu Bay. Gourmet breakfast. Stroll along picturesque promenade to Kelly Tarlton's Underwater World, Mission Bay beach and cafes. Bus at door to downtown, ferry terminal, museums and Vector Arena. Unwind for 2-3 day stopover. Complimentary sailing on the harbour on our 34' yacht. We have a wealth of local knowledge and international travel experience and can assist with sightseeing, travel planning. Welcome! Pay cash and deduct 7.5% off listed rates. Excellent website! Free Wireless Internet.

Auckland - Mission Bay *6 km E of Auckland Central*
Cockell Homestay *Homestay*

Jean & Bryan Cockell
41 Nihill Cresent,
Mission Bay,
Auckland

Tel (09) 528 3809
cockells@xtra.co.nz

Double/Twin $105
Single $85
(Full breakfast)
Dinner 30 by arrangement
Visa MC accepted
Pet free home
Not suitable for children
1 Double/Twin (1 bdrm)
Bathrooms: 1 Private

We warmly welcome you to our comfortable split level home. The upper level is for your exclusive use including a private lounge. 5 minutes walk to Mission Bay beach, cafes and restaurants and 10 minutes scenic car or bus ride to down town Auckland and ferry terminal for harbour and islands in the Gulf. We are retired and look forward to sharing our special part of Auckland with you. Please phone for directions or airport shuttle bus to our door. Please no smoking.

Auckland - Mission Bay *7 km E of Auckland CPO*
Whitmour *Luxury B&B*

Christine & Stephen Olsen
20 Cullwick Road,
Mission Bay,
Auckland

Tel (09) 528 1205
or 0274 791 000
stephenchristineolsen@gmail.com

Double/Twin $170-$190
Single $150-$170
(Full breakfast)
1 King (1 bdrm)
Bathrooms: 1 Ensuite

We welcome you to enjoy a relaxing stay at one of Auckland's most popular beaches, Mission Bay. Share a breakfast of homemade bread & muesli, seasonal fruits & berries, or traditional English cooked breakfast while enjoying a panoramic view of the Regional Park & harbour. Guests have their own lounge, with tea & coffee making facilities, opening onto a loggia that enjoys all day sun. Stroll to a number of beautiful beaches, including 10kms of wide, flat promenade that follows the seashore to downtown Auckland.

Auckland - St Heliers *10 km E of Auckland*
McPherson B&B *B&B*
Jill & Ron McPherson
102 Maskell Street,
St Heliers,
Auckland

Tel (09) 575 9738
Fax (09) 575 0051
ronjillmcpherson@xtra.co.nz

Double/Twin $120
Single $85
(Continental breakfast)
1 Queen 1 Twin (2 bdrm)
Bathrooms: 1 Private

Welcome to our modern home with off-street parking in a smoke-free environment. 1 group of guests is accommodated at a time. Having travelled extensively ourselves we are fully aware of tourists' needs. 8 minutes walk to St Heliers Bay beach, shops, restaurants, cafes, banks and post office. Picturesque 12 minutes drive along the Auckland waterfront past Kelly Tarlton's Antarctic and Underwater Encounter to downtown Auckland. Interests including all sports, gardening and Jill is a keen cross-stitch embroiderer. Not suitable for children/pets.

Auckland - St Heliers *12 km E of Auckland Central*
The Munro's *B&B Homestay*
Margaret and Don Munro
12 Emerson Street,
St Heliers,
Auckland
1071

Tel (09) 528 0459
Fax (09) 528 0459
dmlmunro@xtra.co.nz

Double/Twin $100-$120
Single $80-$90
(Full breakfast)
Dinner by arrangement
Pet free home
Not suitable for children
1 King/Twin 1 King (1 bdrm)
Bathrooms: 1 Ensuite

Our spacious guestroom has a king/twin comfortable bed(s), ensuite, tea/coffee, private entry, patio, off-street parking. Located only 2km from St Heliers Bay beach, shopping, restaurants & bistro's. A 10km scenic waterfront drive to CBD & Viaduct harbour. The airport is a 45min drive, or a taxi/shuttle bus will bring you to our door. Conveniently placed for accessing North & South motorways, transport to city by Bus or Railway. We are a retired Scottish couple who have lived in the tropics.

Auckland - Howick *2 km N of Howick*

French Lavender *B&B*
Michael & Barbara Davis
40 McCahill Views,
Howick,
Auckland

Tel (09) 535 4910
Fax (09) 535 4920
enquiries@frenchlavender.co.nz
www.frenchlavender.co.nz

Double/Twin $100
Single $80
(Continental breakfast)
Family rates available
Visa MC accepted
Children welcome
Non smokers only
1 Queen 2 Single (2 bdrm)
Bathrooms: 1 Guest share

Set in a quiet cul-de-sac, French Lavender is a modern two storey home with the guest rooms on the upper level, sharing a private balcony overlooking the garden and 180-degree views. The guest lounge provides a separate spot for relaxation, peace and quiet. Your hosts have travelled extensively, enjoy meeting people, visiting local restaurants as well as gardening and an occasional round of golf. Stroll in the garden; watch the birds and fish or make friends with our two cats.

Auckland - Titirangi *15 km W of Auckland Central*

Kaurigrove *B&B*
Gaby & Peter Wunderlich
120 Konini Road,
Titirangi,
Waitakere
0642
Auckland

Tel (09) 817 5608
or 027 275 0574
kaurigrove@yahoo.co.nz

Double/Twin $100-$110
Single $60-$65
(Continental breakfast)
Visa MC accepted
Children welcome
1 Queen 1 Single (2 bdrm)
Bathrooms: 1 Private

Welcome to our home! Kaurigrove offers a tranquil location amidst kauri trees in a park-like setting yet close to shops, cafes and restaurants. Situated at Titirangi, we are near Auckland's historic west coast with its magnificent beaches and vast native bush with a wonder-world of walking tracks. Gaby and Peter, your hosts of German background, are keen travellers themselves and are happy to introduce you to the highlights of Auckland and its surrounding areas. Non-smoking inside residence.

Auckland - Hillsborough *12 km S of city*

Mamreoak bnb *B&B*

Joyce Tan
78 Oakdale Road,
Hillsborough,
Auckland 1041

Tel (09) 624 0220
or (09) 624 6966
or 027 276 8398
Fax (09) 624 0227
info@mamreoak.co.nz
www.mamreoak.co.nz

Double/Twin $160-$225
Single $115-$150
(Continental breakfast)
Eftpos accepted
Pet free home
3 Queen 2 Double/Twin
2 Single (6 bdrm)
Bathrooms: 3 Ensuite 1 Guest share

Your hosts welcome you to their private haven- it's home but better. Mamre Oak Bed & Breakfast offers 6 queen, double and single bedrooms, including 1 very luxurious master bedroom with steam and massage bathroom facilities. Be mesmerized by the magnificent view of One Tree Hill while relaxing on the spacious balcony. All rooms are comfortably spacious and the solar-heated floor system keep your feet warm just like home, especially during those cold winter nights.

Auckland Airport - Mangere Bridge *14 km S of Auckland Central*

Mangere Bridge Homestay *Homestay*

Carol & Brian
1 Boyd Avenue,
Mangere Bridge,
Auckland

Tel (09) 636 6346
Fax (09) 636 6345
mangerebridgehomestay@xtra.co.nz

Double/Twin $100-$125
Single $80-$100
(Full breakfast)
Children $20, 12 & under
Dinner $30 by prior arrangement
2 King/Twin 1 Double/Twin
(3 bdrm)
Bathrooms: 3 Ensuite

We invite you to share our home, which is within ten minutes of Auckland Airport, an ideal location for your arrival or departure of New Zealand. We enjoy meeting people and look forward to making your stay an enjoyable one. We welcome you to join us for dinner by prior arrangement. Courtesy car to or from airport, bus and rail. Off street parking available. Handy to public transport. Short stroll to the waterfront. Please no smoking indoors. Our cat requests no pets. Inspection welcome.

Auckland Airport - Mangere *2 km N of Mangere*
Airport Homestay/B&B *B&B Homestay*

May Pepperell
288 Kirkbride Road,
Mangere,
Auckland

Tel (09) 275 6777
or 027 289 8200
Fax (09) 275 6728
marcia@venture.co.nz

Double/Twin $80
Single $50
(Continental breakfast)
Children $20
3 Single (2 bdrm)
Bathrooms: 1 Guest share

Clean comfortable home 5 minutes from airport but not on flight path. Easy walk to shops and restaurants. 10 minutes from shopping centres and Telstra Events Centre at Manukau. Aviation Golf Course near airport, also Villa Maria Winery. My interests are people, travel, Ladies' Probus and voluntary work. Beds have woollen underlays and electric blankets. There is a sunny terrace and fenced swimming pool. Courtesy car to/from airport at reasonable hour. Vehicles minded while you're away from $1 day. Bus stop very close.

~

Auckland Airport - Mangere *4 km N of Airport*
Airport Bed & Breakfast *B&B*

Laurel Blakey
1 Westney Road,
Corner of Kirkbride Road,
Mangere

Tel (09) 275 0533
Fax (09) 275 0968
airportbnb@xtra.co.nz
www.airportbnb.co.nz

Double/Twin $90-$120
Single $75-$105
(Continental breakfast)
Visa MC Diners Amex Eftpos accepted
1 King 3 Queen 5 Double/Twin
1 Twin 7 Single (10 bdrm)
Bathrooms: 4 Ensuite 3 Guest share

Just 5 minutes drive from Auckland Airport a friendly welcome and great value accommodation awaits. 10 quality rooms, 4 ensuites, central heating, large TV/Sky/dining room. Internet access, Wi Fi. 2 minutes walk to city bus stop - see Auckland by bus and ferry on the $11.00 day pass. Restaurants/takeaways nearby. Car, cycle and luggage storage. Rental cars and NZ wide sightseeing tours booked. Courtesy airport transfer (6.30am -8.45pm), free phone at airport, dial 28. Buffet breakfast, complimentary tea/coffee.

Auckland - Manukau *6.5 km NE of Manukau City*

Tanglewood *B&B Homestay*
Roseanne & Ian Devereux
5 Inchinnam Road,
Flat Bush,
Manukau City,
Auckland

Tel (09) 274 8280
Fax (09) 634 6896
tanglewood@clear.net.nz

Double/Twin $110
Single $70
(Full breakfast)
Children $15
Visa MC accepted
Children and pets welcome
1 King 2 Queen (3 bdrm)
Bathrooms: 1 Ensuite 1 Private
Garden loft has en suite

Our homely cottage, set in 2 acres is 20 minutes from the International airport. Wake up to birdsong in our garden loft which is separate from the house, with deck overlooking large peaceful gardens and ponds. There are two cosy rooms inside the house. We are 30 minutes from downtown Auckland, close to Botany Shopping Centre and good restaurants. Delicious home-cooked breakfast includes eggs from our free-range hens. We have a swimming pool and friendly dog, Daisy. We offer you warm and relaxed hospitality.

Auckland - Manukau *6.5 km NE of Manukau*

Calico Cottage *B&B*
Patty & Murray Glenie
7 Inchinnam Road,
Flat Bush,
Auckland

Tel (09) 274 8527
Fax (09) 274 8528
MG-PT@xtra.co.nz

Double/Twin $110
Single $85
(Full breakfast)
Children $15
Visa MC accepted
Children and pets welcome
1 Queen 1 Single (2 bdrm)
Bathrooms: 1 Ensuite

Welcome to Calico Cottage. We are on 2 acres with garden, paddocks, sheep, chickens - free range eggs, and 1 dog who lives outdoors. Peaceful and yet only 10 minutes from both Manukau City Centre and Botany Town Centre and 20 minutes from Auckland Airport. Transport to and from airport arranged if required. We have a double bedroom with new ensuite and a TV room adjoining for your own use. We look forward to your visit.

Auckland - Manurewa *2 km S of Manukau City*
Hillpark Homestay *B&B Homestay*

Katrine & Graham Paton
16 Collie Street,
Manurewa, Auckland 2102

Tel (09) 267 6847
or 021 207 2559
Fax (09) 267 8718
stay@hillpark.co.nz
www.hillpark.co.nz

Double/Twin $100
Single $60
(Full breakfast)
Children $20
Dinner $20 by arrangement
Visa MC accepted
Children welcome
1 Queen 4 Single (3 bdrm)
Bathrooms: 1 Ensuite 1 Guest share

Welcome to our sunny, spacious home and meet our friendly tonkinese cat. We are 15 minutes from Auckland Airport, 20 minutes from Auckland City centre, on the route south and the Pacific Coast Highway. Nearby are restaurants, Auckland Regional Botanic Gardens, TelstraClear Pacific Events Centre, Tipapa Events Centre, Manukau City Shopping Centre, Manukau Superclinic and Surgery Centre. Our interests include teaching, classical music, painting, gardening, photography, Christian activities, reading and travel. We are a smoke-free home. Directions: please phone or visit our website.

Auckland - Alfriston *10 km SE of Manukau City*
Top of the Hill Country Homestay *B&B Country Homestay*

Pat & Trevor Simpson
183 Fitzpatrick Road,
Brookby RD 1
Manurewa,
Auckland

Tel (09) 530 8576
Fax (09) 530 8576
topofthehill@wc.net.nz
www.topofthehill.co.nz

Double/Twin $120
Single $80
(Full breakfast)
Min 2 day stay, discounted 3 day
Visa MC accepted
Not suitable for children under 12
1 King/Twin 2 King (3 bdrm)
Bathrooms: 3 Ensuite

Be first to see the sunrise from our spacious well appointed home. High on the hill with breathtaking spectacular, landscape views to Auckland's sparking harbours and volcanoes. The guest wing has luxuriously large bedrooms, each with ensuite, plus floor to ceiling windows. Visit our friendly animals or just relax in the large lounge. We have a guest utility with cooking and laundry facilites. 25 mins to Auckland Airport and city, close to Clevedon, Tipapa Events Centre, Botanical Gardens, beaches & vineyards. Min 2 day stay. Discounted 3 days stays.

Clevedon *3 km S of Clevedon*
Karinya B & B *B&B Apartment with Kitchen*
Kevin & Judy Hanley
290 Clevedon Road,
RD 2,
Papakura,
Auckland

Tel (09) 292 9024
or 027 4759 317
Fax (09) 292 9025
hanley@xtra.co.nz
www.karinya.co.nz

Double/Twin $130-$160
Single $110-$110
(Continental breakfast provisions)
Lunch and dinner on request
Visa MC accepted
Pet free home
Children welcome
2 King 1 Single (2 bdrm)
Bathrooms: 2 Ensuite

Kevin and Judy invite you to stay in their guesthouse set in 30 acres in the Clevedon Valley. Separate from the main homestead giving total privacy. Relax and enjoy the peace and quiet of the rural lifestyle. A variety of wineries, cafes, beaches, bush walks, and golf courses nearby. Directions - Located on the Main Clevedon-Papakura Road 3km before Clevedon Village.Contact Kevin and Judy Hanley (09) 292 9024 or 027 4759 317

Kaiaua *4 km N of Kaiaua*
Kaiaua Seaside Lodge *B&B Lodge*
Fran Joseph & Denis Martinovich
1336 East Coast Road,
Kaiaua

Tel (09) 232 2696
or 027 274 0534
Fax (09) 232 2699
kaiaua_lodge@clear.net.nz
www.bluecastle.co.nz/
accommodation-316.htm

Double/Twin $100-$140
Single $75-$85
(Continental breakfast)
Children welcome
3 Queen 2 Single (5 bdrm)
Bathrooms: 2 Ensuite 1 Guest share

The Lodge is situated on the water's edge of The Seabird Coast, famous for its birdlife, Miranda Hot Springs, regional parks and fish 'n chips. Four km north of Kaiaua township, the Lodge features attractive beach gardens and panoramic views of the Coromandel. It is ideally positioned for leisurely seashore strolls or more active tramps in the Hunua Ranges. Boating and fishing facilities are available. En suite rooms are spacious and the separate guest lounge has a refrigerator and television.

Miranda *30 km SE of Bombay Hills Freeway*
Miranda Views B&B *B&B Cottage with Kitchen*

Millie & Wayne Taylor
1213 Miranda Road,
Miranda,
1872

Tel (09) 232 7800
or 027 4942 780
Fax (09) 232 7811
mill@xtra.co.nz

Double/Twin $145
Single $100
(Full breakfast provisions)
Children $30
Visa MC Eftpos accepted
Children welcome
1 Queen 3 Single (2 bdrm)
Bathrooms: 2 Guest share

Our lifestyle farm is situated in the beautiful Miranda Valley; less than an hours drive south from Auckland Airport. Enjoy the panoramic views of our lush valley, the Firth of Thames and Coromandel Ranges in the background. Relax and unwind in your own private chalet, take in views on your own balcony, stroll around our farm, visit some of our local attractions, or just watch abit of TV. We along with our daughter Ashley and our 2 spoilt cats and 1 friendly dog welcome you.

Papakura *1.5 km W of Papakura*
Campbell Clan House *B&B*

Colin & Anna Mieke Campbell
57 Rushgreen Avenue,
Pahurehure, Papakura

Tel (09) 298 8231
or 027 496 7754
Fax (09) 298 7792
colam@pl.net
www.campbellclan.co.nz

Double/Twin $130 Single $80
(Full breakfast)
Children negotiable
Dinner $30-$50 prior booking only
Discount for 3+ nights
Visa MC accepted
Pet free home
Children welcome
2 Queen 2 Single (3 bdrm)
Bathrooms: 2 Ensuite 1 Private

Our peaceful location is within walking distance of trains and buses, shopping centre and restaurants. We are 2 minutes from motorway north/south, 15 minutes from airport and enroute to Firth of Thames and the Coromandel. Our separate upstairs guest accommodation includes 3 double bedrooms, large comfortable lounge with tea/coffee, tourist information, TV and private balcony with lovely view. We are happy to assist with any holiday arrangements, car hire, transfers and offer internet and laundry facilities. Discount for 3 or more nights.

Drury *3 km E of Drury*
The Drury Homestead *B&B*
Carolyn & Ron Booker
349 Drury Hills Road, Drury, South Auckland

B&B
Approved

Tel (09) 294 9030 or 021 158 5061
Fax (09) 294 9035
druryhome@paradise.net.nz

Double/Twin $120 Single $90 (Full breakfast)
Children negotiable
3 Queen 1 Twin (4 bdrm)
Bathrooms: 3 Ensuite 1 Private

The Drury Homestead is a wonderful old colonial house, built in the 1860s and lovingly restored by your hosts Carolyn and Ron. With 4 beautifully decorated rooms to choose from where would you like to sleep?
Upstairs looking out over the creek and bush is The River Room with queen-size bed and en suite. Dunedin has magnificent views across the countryside, a queen bed and en suite. Cape Reinga has twin king-single beds and it's own bathroom with shower, toilet, vanity and claw-foot bath and oh what views from the bath!
Downstairs is The Lily Room, a self-contained studio with kitchen facilities , a queen size bed and en suite and own entrance and verandah. Ideal for a longer stay. We also have a cot and pull-out beds available for children.

We offer a discount for those staying 3 nights or more. We are situated on a rural block, minutes from the motorway, 35 minutes from Auckland CBD and 20 minutes from the airport. Set amidst paddocks with surrounding bush and a stream, the only noise you will hear are the birds and the sound of the tumbling stream. We love our lifestyle here and would like to make your stay in New Zealand a truely memorable one.

The guest lounge is the perfect retreat or somewhere you can get to know Ron!
Carolyn's breakfasts are famed for their fresh home-made ingredients and have received high praise. We value your time with us and look forward to welcoming you to our Homestead. Local restaurants are nearby in Drury. Family cat and dog.

Ramarama *7 km S of Drury*
Thistledown Lodge *B&B Homestay*

Sue & Archie McPherson
42 Coulston Road,
Ramarama,
Pukekohe,
RD 2

Tel (09) 238 1912
or 027 473 6313
inquiries@thistledownlodge.co.nz
www.thistledownlodge.co.nz

Double/Twin $140
Single $90
(Special breakfast)
Children negotiable
Dinner by arrangement
Visa MC accepted
Children welcome
1 King 2 Queen (3 bdrm)
Bathrooms: 3 Private

This peaceful country setting will be the perfect start or end to your holiday. Discover the secret of Archie's breakfasts which delight and surprise guests. The English-style country house has an idyllic setting down a leafy lane. Relax in quiet and spacious second floor bedrooms or unwind in the spa (jacuzzi) . Guest lounge/games room available. Easy to find from Ramarama motorway exit, secure off-street parking and just 25 minutes from Auckland Airport.

Please let us know
how you enjoyed your B&B experience.
Ask your host for a comment form
or leave a comment on www.bnb.co.nz.

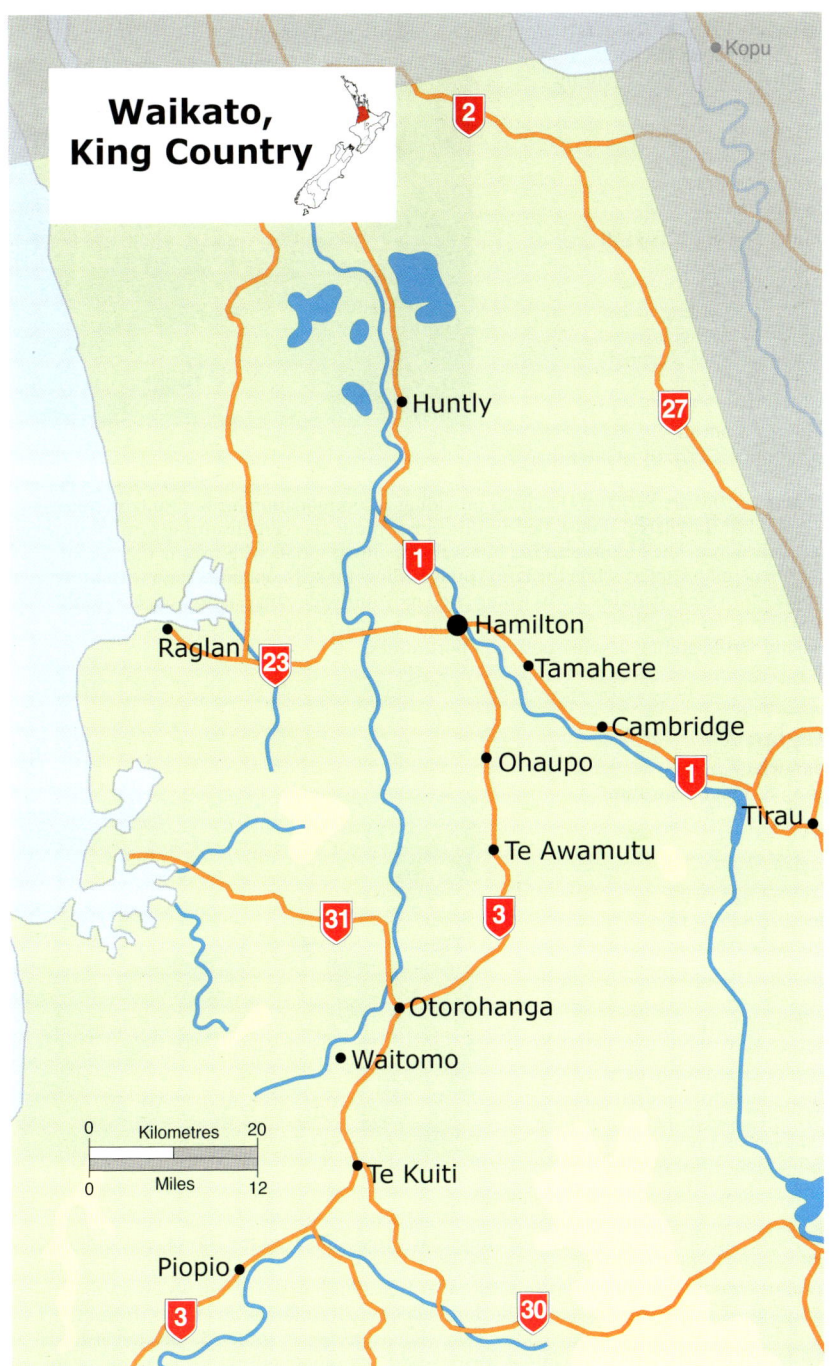

Waikato, King Country

Kopu

2

Huntly

27

1

Raglan
23
Hamilton
Tamahere

Cambridge
Ohaupo
1
Tirau

Te Awamutu

31
3

Otorohanga

Waitomo

0   Kilometres   20
0   Miles   12

Te Kuiti

Piopio
3
30

Huntly *4 km NW of Huntly*

Parnassus Farm & Garden *B&B Farmstay Cottage with Kitchen*

Sharon & David Payne
Te Ohaki Road, RD 1, Huntly

Tel (07) 828 8781
or 021 458 525
Fax (07) 828 8781
parnassus@xtra.co.nz
www.parnassus.co.nz

Double/Twin $120-$140
Single $70-$100
(Full breakfast)
Children according to age
Dinner by arrangement
Visa MC Eftpos accepted
Children welcome
2 King/Twin 2 Double/Twin
2 Single (3 bdrm)
Bathrooms: 3 Private 1 Guest share

For over 10 years Parnassus has been providing accommodation for both international and local travellers. Dinner, Bed and Breakfast is our speciality featuring farm & kitchen garden produce. The Homestead has two well-appointed rooms with private bathrooms and offers full breakfast while the farm cottages allow for self-contained stays with breakfast supplies provided. Families are welcome and enjoy our wide range of animals and birds. Parnassus is an hour from Auckland and central to many tourist destinations, bush & wetland walks, golfing & wine-tasting opportunities.

Raglan *20 km S of Raglan*

Matawha *Farmstay*

Jenny & Peter Thomson
61 Matawha Road,
RD 2,
Raglan

Tel (07) 825 6709
Fax (07) 825 6715
jennyt@wave.co.nz

Double/Twin $120
Single $60
(Full breakfast)
Dinner $20
Cash or cheque only please
Not suitable for children
1 King 1 Double/Twin
4 Single (3 bdrm)
Bathrooms: 1 Private
1 Guest share 1 Family share

We live on the west coast and our family has farmed this land for 100 years. Come and enjoy our private beach, expansive garden, home-grown vegetables, spa, 2 cats and the peace of no other buildings or people for miles. Take bush or mountain walks, a scenic drive, go surfing or fishing, or maybe find the hot-water beach! Auckland 2.5 hours, Hamilton 1 hour, Raglan 30 minutes. Directions - Take Hamilton/Raglan route 23, turn left at Bridal Veil Falls sign, right at Te Mata onto Ruapuke Rd, left onto Tuturimu Rd and follow to T-junction, straight ahead across to cattlestop - 61 Matawha Rd.

Hamilton *1.5 km E of Hamilton Central*
Matthews B&B *B&B Homestay*
Maureen & Graeme Matthews
24 Pearson Avenue,
Claudelands,
Hamilton

Tel (07) 855 4269
or 027 474 7758
Fax (07) 855 4269
mgm@xtra.co.nz
www.matthewsbnb.co.nz

Double/Twin $100-$140
Single $55-$75
(Full breakfast)
Children 1/2 price
Dinner $25
Pet free home
1 Double/Twin 1 Twin (2 bdrm)
Bathrooms: 1 Guest share
1 Family share

Welcome to our home 2 seconds off the city bypass on Routes 7 & 9 at Five Crossroads. We are adjacent to the Waikato Events Centre, Ruakura Research Station, handy to the university and only 3 minutes from central city. Our home is a lived-in comfortable home, warm in winter and cool in summer, with a pool available. We enjoy spending time with visitors from NZ and overseas. We have travelled extensively and enjoy helping to plan your holiday. Dinner by arrangement.

≈

Hamilton *3 km N of Hamilton Central*
Ebbett Homestay *B&B Homestay*
Glenys & John Ebbett
162 Beerescourt Road,
Hamilton

Tel (07) 849 2005
johnebbett@xtra.co.nz

Double/Twin $120
Single $85
(Full breakfast)
Dinner $30
Pet free home
Not suitable for children
2 Single (1 bdrm)
Bathrooms: 1 Private

Only minutes from town centre, our 17 year old home has a spectacular view of the Waikato River (New Zealand's longest) and easy access to Hamilton's popular river walk. We enjoy sharing travel anecdotes, but also respect our guests' wish for privacy. Your room has its own tea/coffee facility and private bathroom. Only 85 minutes from Auckland International Airport, we appeal to tourists arriving or departing New Zealand. Our interests include people, music, sport, travel, gardening and community. 15 years of happy hosting.

Hamilton *4 km S of Hamilton*
The Poplars *Homestay Home & Garden*

Lesley & Peter Ramsay
402 Matangi Road,
RD 4,
Hamilton

Tel (07) 829 5551
or 027 668 0985
pramsay@ihug.co.nz

Double/Twin $120
Single $90
(Full breakfast)
Dinner $40pp by arrangement
Visa MC accepted
Children and pets welcome
1 King 1 Twin (2 bdrm)
Bathrooms: 1 Private

Minutes from Hamilton, Mystery Creek and Cambridge, The Poplars offers a haven of peace and quiet. Set in a 3 acre garden with internationally acclaimed daffodils, 500 roses and water features. Guest rooms have tea and coffee making facilities, and TV. Solar heated swimming pool and spa are adjacent. Hosts Peter and Lesley, themselves seasoned travellers, offer you the charms of country living. A warm welcome shared with family pets awaits you. A unique place to stay Directions: Please phone.

Hamilton - Ohaupo *4 km SW of Hamilton*
Green Gables of Rukuhia *B&B*

Earl & Judi McWhirter
35 Rukuhia Road,
RD 2,
Ohaupo

Tel (07) 843 8511
or 021 583 462
Fax (07) 843 8514
judi.earl@clear.net.nz

Double/Twin $100-$130
Single $50-$65
(Continental breakfast)
Dinner by arrangement
Visa MC accepted
Children welcome
2 Double/Twin 1 Twin (2 bdrm)
Bathrooms: 1 Guest share

Warm, comfortable smoke-free family home in a quiet rural setting, close to Hamilton, Airport and field days (Mystery Creek). Free pick up/delivery airport, bus, train terminal all part of the friendly service. 5km to Vilagrad Winery; 2 minutes walk to Gostiona Restaurant. 2 storeyed house with guest bedrooms and lounge downstairs; dining and hosts upstairs. Continental breakfast with fresh home-baked bread. Judi lectures statistics, University of Waikato. Earl is a school teacher. Non-smokers preferred.

Hamilton 28 km S of Hamilton
Country Quarters Homestay *B&B Homestay*

Ngaere & Jack Waite
11 Corcoran Road,
Te Pahu,
Hamilton

Tel (07) 825 9727
graeme.waite@xtra.co.nz

Double/Twin $80-$100
Single $40-$50
(Full breakfast)
Children $10
Dinner $25
Visa MC Diners Amex Eftpos accepted
Children and pets welcome
1 Queen 1 Twin 3 Single (5 bdrm)
Bathrooms: 2 Guest share
Bathroom & Shower room

We welcome you to the peace and tranquillity of country life. Our place is central from Te Awamutu and Hamilton, located in the little farming community of Te Pahu, right under Mount Pirongia. We are in the middle of a block of chestnut trees and are quite secluded. Our home is very large and roomy and we have special facilities for the elderly person. Comfort and nice meals is what we offer you.

Hamilton - Tamahere *10 km S of Hamilton*
Lenvor B&B *B&B Homestay*

Lenora & Trevor Shelley
540E Oaklea Lane,
RD 3,
Tamahere,
Hamilton

Tel (07) 856 2027
Fax (07) 856 4173
lenvor@clear.net.nz

Double/Twin $110-$130
Single $70
(Full breakfast)
Children $10-$25
Dinner by arrangement
Children welcome
3 Queen 3 Single (4 bdrm)
Bathrooms: 1 Ensuite
2 Guest share 1 Family share

Lenora and Trevor warmly invite you to relax and to share the comfort of our home Lenvor, which is set in a rural area, down a country lane. Our 2 storeyed home has guest rooms and small lounge upstairs; dining, lounge and hosts downstairs. 10 minutes to Hamilton or Cambridge, 5 minutes to Mystery Creek or airport. Lenora's interests are floral art and cake icing. Trevor enjoys vintage cars. Centrally situated for day trips to Coromandel, Tauranga, Rotorua, Taupo and Waitomo Caves.

Hamilton *10 km E of Hamilton*
A&A Country Stay *Farmstay Cottage with Kitchen*
Ann & Alan Marsh
275 Vaile Road,
RD 4,
Hamilton 3284

Tel (07) 824 1908
or (07) 8241909
or 027 476 3014
aacountrystay@bordernet.co.nz

Double/Twin $140
Single $80
(Continental breakfast)
Children $20
Weekly rates for long-term stays
Visa MC accepted
Children and pets welcome
1 Queen 2 Single (2 bdrm)
Bathrooms: 1 Private

The Cottage is fully self-contained, 2 bedrooms, including laundry and Sky digital. Peaceful surroundings set in 2 acres of garden with a large pond. Sit, relax in privacy out on the veranda, have our ducks and doves visit you for that bit of bread while overlooking our 47 acres with sheep and cattle. Have a talk to our clydesdale (Sarah) and our miniature (Sha) who love people staying especially when they have apples in their hand. Two Jack Russells will also welcome you.

∼

Hamilton - Ohaupo *15 km S of Hamilton*
Ridge House *B&B*
Margaret Birtles & Matthew Harris
15 Great South Road,
Ohaupo 3803

Tel (07) 823 6555
Fax (07) 823 6550
m.a.birtles@xtra.co.nz

Double/Twin $85-$100
Single $65
(Continental breakfast)
Children $15
Dinner $20 by arrangement
Visa MC accepted
Children and pets welcome
2 Queen 1 Single (2 bdrm)
Bathrooms: 1 Ensuite 1 Guest share

We welcome you to come and visit our home with its wonderful lake and pastoral views. Our home is shared with our dog, Zoe, who loves to welcome visitors. We are just 6 minutes to Hamilton International Airport and can arrange pick up from there and car storage ($10). This is an ideal base for trips to Hamilton, Te Awamutu, Waitomo Caves, Cambridge, Rotorua and Tauranga. Mystery Creek (home of the Field Days) and popular golf courses are close by. Travel well.

Hamilton *12 km SW of Hamilton*
Uliveto Countrystay *Homestay Countrystay B&B*

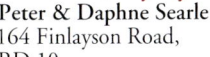

Peter & Daphne Searle
164 Finlayson Road,
RD 10,
Ngahinapouri,
Hamilton

Tel (07) 825 2116
or 027 200 5320
peedee@wave.co.nz
www.uliveto.co.nz

Double/Twin $120-$130
Single $90-$120
(Full breakfast)
Dinner by arrangement
Visa MC accepted
Not suitable for children
2 Queen (2 bdrm)
Bathrooms: 2 Ensuite Private ensuite

Come and enjoy the peace and tranquility of the beautiful countryside with us and our chocolate labrador, Bella. Wander in our olive grove and gardens or relax on your private deck. Hamilton City,the airport and National Fieldays are 20 minutes away.Nearby attractions include - Waitomo Caves,lavender farm, golf course, award winning winery, horse treks/tramping tracks on Mt Pirongia, Raglan beaches and cafes. To complete your day, share dinner and wine with us or relax in the guest lounge or our therapeutic spa.

Hamilton CBD *0.2 km N of Hamilton CBD*
Home Hospitality *B&B Homestay*
Diana & Fred Houtman
7A Hamilton Parade, Hamilton

Tel 07 838 1538
or 021 170 3210 (text only)
frediana@ihug.co.nz
www.accommodationinnewzealand.
co.nz//homehospitality

Double/Twin $120
Single $70
(Full breakfast)
Not suitable for children
Dinner $30 - advance notice required
Separate rate for special events,
please enquire
Pet free home
1 Queen 2 Single (2 bdrm)
Bathrooms: 1 Guest share

Comfortable self-contained accommodation in a quiet riverside cul-de-sac in the centre of Hamilton. Private sitting room for guests, with tea/coffee making facilities. Leave your car in our secure off-road parking area & walk to restaurants, shops, theatres, sports venues, conference centres - no parking hassles. A handy point from which to explore a large area of central NZ. Hosts are well travelled & enjoy meeting new people. Dutch spoken. Credit cards NOT accepted.

Hamilton - Whatawhata *10 km W of Hamilton*
Beaumere Lodge *B&B*
Isobel and Peter Wiren
10 Genevieve Way,
Highbrook, RD 9,
Whatawhata,
Hamilton

Tel (07) 829 8652
or 027 232 9149
Fax (07) 829 8652
beaumere@wave.co.nz

Double/Twin $100-$130
Single $60-$80 (Full breakfast)
Children by negotiation
Dinner & light meals by arrangement
No Eftpos/CC available
Children and pets welcome
1 Queen 1 Twin (2 bdrm)
Bathrooms: 1 Private
Seperate Spa-Bath & toilet

Wonderful country setting, magic views and sunsets over the Hakaramatas. Romantic fairy-lit gardens. Guest wing, own patio, spa. One-group bookings. Close Golf, Zoo, Tree Arboratum, Bridal Veil Falls, Raglan seaside resort 25 mins. Glowworm Caves 1 hour. En route Auckland-Waitomo-Taupo. Semi-retirees with a friendly cat, enjoy golf, bowls gardening, travel, and Isobel sings in a choir. Peter has lived in Japan and Korea so we are always delighted to help with language and travel plans. You are assured of a memorable stay.

Hamilton - Te Pahu *20 km W of Hamilton*
Harmony Hours Retreat and B&B *B&B Retreat*
Chrystene Hansen and Bill Bailey
1385 Te Pahu Road,
RD 5,
Hamilton, 3285

Tel (07) 825 9877
or 021 128 6083
relax@harmonyhours.co.nz
www.harmonyhours.co.nz

Double/Twin $120-$150
Single $100-$100
(Special breakfast)
Children up to 12years $50
Dinner by arrangement $25 pp
24 hour stay, all meals, healing
therapies available
Visa MC accepted
1 Queen 1 Single (1 bdrm)
Bathrooms: 1 Ensuite

Relax in this beautiful, spacious, upstairs room with lovely views of rural waikato including Mount Pirongia. Soak in the spa pool on your very own balcony under a night sky. Bill and Chrystene offer a relaxing experience and are negotiable with meal times. Meals are homegrown, sprayfree or organic. Enjoy our 2 acre block, which also has gardens an orchard and sheep. Muffy is our resident cat. Enquire with Chrystene for a massage/healing. 20 minutes to Hamilton, 30 to Raglan, 90 to Auckland Airport

Hamilton - Matangi *10 km SE of Hamilton*
Kowhai Lodge *B&B Homestay*

Sheila and John
81 Butcher Road,
RD 4,
Hamilton
3284

Tel (07) 829 6014
kowhai.lodge@yahoo.co.nz

Double/Twin $120
Single $85
(Full breakfast)
Dinner by arrangment
Pet free home
2 Queen 1 Twin (3 bdrm)
Bathrooms: 3 Ensuite

Sheila and John would like to welcome you to Kowhai Lodge, a new pet free home built in Matangi. Located 90 minutes from Auckland Airport and just 15 minutes from Hamilton city centre. A few minutes drive from State highway 1 & 1B, Matangi is centrally situated for Hamilton airport, Mystery Creek Event Centre and day trips to Rotorua, Tauranga or Waitomo Caves. Matangi is ideal for couples looking for the tranquility of the countryside in comfortable surroundings; rooms have tea/coffee making facilities and ensuites.

~

Hamilton *5 km N of Hamilton Central*
Saint Andrews B&B *B&B Homestay*

Ken and Patricia Scott
32 Madill Road,
Hamilton, 3200

Tel (07) 850 9978
or (07) 362 8245
patricia.scott@xtra.co.nz

Double/Twin $120
Single $80
(Full breakfast provisions)
Children welcome
Visa MC accepted
Pet free home
1 Queen 2 Twin (2 bdrm)
Bathrooms: 2 Private
Two separate bathrooms with bath and shower

Welcome to our friendly home in the quiet suburb of St. Andrews. Close to the beautiful Waikato River Walkway and the St. Andrews Golf Course (www.standrews.co.nz), you are a ten minute drive away from the city centre and an eighty minute drive from Auckland Airport. Attractions within the region include the famous Waitomo Caves, Rotorua and Raglan Surfers' Beach.

Cambridge *0.3 km N of Cambridge Central*
Park House *B&B*

Pat & Bill Hargreaves
70 Queen Street,
Cambridge

Tel (07) 827 6368
Fax (07) 827 4094
Park.House@xtra.co.nz
www.parkhouse.co.nz

Double/Twin up to $160
Single up to $160
(Full breakfast)
Visa MC Amex accepted
Not suitable for children
1 King/Twin 1 Queen (2 bdrm)
Bathrooms: 1 Ensuite 1 Private

Park House, circa 1920, is for guests of discernment who appreciate quality and comfort. For 20 years we have offered this superb setting for guests. Throughout this large home are antiques, traditional furniture, patchworks and stained glass windows creating an elegant and restful ambience. The guest lounge features an elaborately carved fireplace, fine art, library, TV and complimentary sherry. Bedrooms in separate wing upstairs ensues privacy. Unbeatable quiet location overlooking village green, 2 minute walk to restaurants, antique and craft shops.

Cambridge *5 km SW of Cambridge*
Birches *B&B Farmstay Cottage with Kitchen Farmhouse bed & breakfast or self contained cottage*

Sheri Mitchell & Hugh Jellie
263 Maungatautari Road,
PO Box 194, Cambridge

Tel (07) 827 6556
or 021 882 216
Fax (07) 827 3552
birchesbandb@xtra.co.nz
www.birches.co.nz

Double/Twin $120
Single $80 (Special breakfast)
Children by arrangement
Dinner by arrangement
Visa MC accepted
Children and pets welcome
1 Queen 1 Double/Twin
1 Single (2 bdrm)
Bathrooms: 1 Ensuite 1 Private

Our character farmhouse offers open fires, tennis, swimming pool and hottub in country garden amongst renown horse studs. Proximity to Lake Karapiro makes Birches an ideal base for lake users. Hugh, a veterinarian, and I are widely travelled. Olivia, 16 attends St Peter's Cambridge. We have farm pets and a cat. Cherry Tree Cottage is ideal for couples wanting privacy. The twin room in farmhouse has private bathroom with spa bath. We serve delicious farmhouse breakfasts alfresco or in dining room.

Cambridge *2 km S of Cambridge*
Glenelg *B&B Homestay*
Shirley & Ken Geary
6 Curnow Place,
Cambridge

Tel (07) 823 0084
Fax (07) 823 4279
glenelgbnb@ihug.co.nz
www.cambridge.co.nz

Double/Twin $110
Single $85
(Full breakfast)
Children $25
Dinner $25 by arrangement
Children and pets welcome
3 Queen 1 Twin (4 bdrm)
Bathrooms: 3 Ensuite 1 Private

Glenelg welcomes you to Cambridge to a new home with quality spacious accommodation warm quiet and private overlooking Waikato farmland, with plenty of off-street parking. Beds have electric blankets and woolrests. 200 rose bushes in the garden. 5 minutes to Lake Karapiro. Mystery Creek, where NZ National Field Days and many other functions are held is only 15 minutes away. Laundry facilities available. No smoking indoors please. Home away from home. For a brochure and directions please phone.

Cambridge *10 km N of Cambridge*
Dunfarmin *B&B Countrystay*
Jackie & Bob Clarke
46 Oaklea Lane, RD 3, Hamilton

Tel (07) 856 6643
or 027 611 5247
Fax (07) 856 6032
dunfarmin@wave.co.nz
http://Dunfarmin.co.nz

Double/Twin $110-$120
Single $60-$70 (Full breakfast)
Children $25 under 12 years
Dinner $25 by arrangement
Visa MC accepted
Children welcome
2 Queen 2 Single (3 bdrm)
Bathrooms: 1 Ensuite 1 Guest share

Welcome to our home built among chestnut trees in a rural area, We are situated mid-way between Cambridge and Hamilton, 2 minutes off Highway 1. 5 minutes away are the Hamilton Airport and Mystery Creek. Close by is the Waikato River with its lovely river walks and the paddle steamer and Hamilton Gardens. Cambridge has many cafes, restaurants, antique and craft shops. We are ex-farmers with alpacas, and Possum the cat.

Cambridge *2 km S of Cambridge*
Pamade B&B *B&B Cottage with Kitchen*
Paul & Marion Derikx
229 Shakespeare Street,
Cambridge - Leamington,
- opposite turn off to Karapiro Lake

Tel (07) 827 4916
or 021 261 7122
pamadebnb@slingshot.co.nz

Double $100-$120
Single up to $75
(Special breakfast)
Dinner by arrangement
1 King 1 Queen 1 Twin
4 Single (3 bdrm)
Bathrooms: 2 Ensuite 1 Private

Pamade is a character home, very comfortable with beautiful gardens. We are situated 2 minutes from central Cambridge with its wonderful selection of fascinating art, craft, boutique and antique shops, restaurants, stud farms and golf course. Just around the corner from Lake Karapiro, with its water skiing and rowing. Mystery Creek is only 10 minutes drive away. Self-contained unit plus large double room (ensuite and coffee and tea arrangements) with private exit. Ideal for longer stays. Great breakfast guaranteed. Dinner by prior arrangement.

~

Tirau *10 km S of Matamata*
Oraka Deer Park *Luxury B&B Homestay Farmstay Separate Suite*
Cottage with Kitchen
Linda & Ian Scott
71 Bayly Road, RD1, Tirau

Tel (07) 883 1382
Fax (07) 883 1384
oraka@xtra.co.nz
www.oraka-deer.co.nz

Double/Twin $90-$245
Single $90-$200
(Breakfast by arrangement)
Children welcome
Dinner by arrangement
Visa MC Amex accepted
Children and pets welcome
2 King 1 Double/Twin
1 Single (3 bdrm)
Bathrooms: 2 Ensuite Showers

Scott Family, Ian & Linda and twins Lani & Travis, Labrador Tilly and two burmese. This is a working deer farm, restaurant and tourist business. Lovely garden with mature trees & flower borders, swimming pool & spa, tennis & petanque. Private & peaceful green Waikato countryside.

Te Awamutu *4.5 km N of Te Awamutu*
Bleskie Farmstay *Farmstay*
Mrs R Bleskie & C Bleskie
Storey Road,
Te Awamutu

Tel (07) 871 3301
bleskie@xtra.co.nz

Double/Twin $115
Single $60
(Full breakfast)
Children $25
Dinner $25
Children and pets welcome
1 Double/Twin 8 Single (5 bdrm)
Bathrooms: 1 Ensuite 1 Guest share
1 Family share

The 85 acre farm, situated in beautiful country side with cattle, horses, pigs, poultry, sheep, goats and pets. A spacious home welcomes you with swimming pool and tennis court. Large guest rooms with doors to garden. Specials: horseback riding and gig rides for children and adults for $10 a ride. Raspberry picking in season and access to the milking of 500 dairy cows.

Te Awamutu *2 km S of Te Awamutu*
Leger Farm *B&B Farmstay*
Beverley & Peter Bryant
114 St Leger Road,
Te Awamutu

Tel (07) 871 6676
Fax (07) 871 6679

Double/Twin $125-$140
Single $85-$100
(Full breakfast)
Dinner $35
1 Queen 1 Double/Twin
1 Twin 3 Single (4 bdrm)
Bathrooms: 1 Ensuite
1 Private 1 Guest share

Leger Farm is a private residence with country living at its finest. The discerning leisure traveller seeking quality accommodation, in peaceful, relaxing surroundings, will find warm hospitality and every comfort here. Spacious bedrooms share stunning views of surrounding countryside. Each bedroom has its own balcony with garden vistas. We farm cattle and sheep, and are centrally based for visiting Waitomo Caves and black water rafting, Rotorua with its thermal activity and NZ's dramatic West Coast and ironstone sands. Golf course nearby for relaxation. Smoke-free home.

Otorohanga - Waitomo District *8 km NW of Otorohanga*

Meadowland *B&B Farmstay Cottage with Kitchen*

Jill & Tony Webber
746 State Highway 31,
RD 3,
Otorohanga

Tel (07) 873 7729
Fax (07) 873 7719
meadowland@xtra.co.nz

Double/Twin $100
Single $60
(Full breakfast)
Children $20
Visa MC accepted
Children welcome
2 Queen 1 Double/Twin
1 Twin 2 Single (5 bdrm)
Bathrooms: 1 Private 1 Guest share

Welcome to Meadowland. Our accommodation is: a self-contained unit which can sleep up to 6 - extra adults $25. 1 twin and 2 double bedrooms in homestead with guest shared bathroom and separate toilet. All beds have woolrests and electric blankets. We have a tennis court, swimming pool and spa pool on site. We are 5 minutes from the Otorohanga Kiwi House & Aviary, 20 minutes from Waitomo Caves area, 20 minutes to 3 golf courses. Non-smokers preferred. Subsequent nights $20 less.

～

Otorohanga - Waitomo District *10 km S of Otorohanga*

Redwood Lodge *Luxury B&B Homestay*

John & Georgina Owen
222 Puketawai Road,
RD 6,
Otorohanga

Tel (07) 873 6685
or 0275 411 905
Fax (07) 873 6694
welcome@redwood-lodge.co.nz
www.redwood-lodge.co.nz

Double/Twin $140-$170
Single $110-$130
(Full breakfast)
Children by arrangement
Visa MC accepted
1 King/Twin 3 Queen
2 Single (4 bdrm)
Bathrooms: 4 Ensuite

Only 10 minutes from Waitomo Caves, Redwood Lodge offers travellers affordable luxury in a tranquil setting. John & Georgina welcome you to their well-appointed and comfortable home offering 4 good-sized heated/air conditioned en-suite rooms, each provided with tea/coffee making facilities. Enjoy our 8 acres of parklike grounds (for company take our Irish Terrier with you) our guest lounge and games room with TV and pool table. A hot spa, sauna and in-ground swimming pool are all available to our guests.

Waikato Caves *9.7 km W of Waitomo Village*

Te Tiro *B&B Farmstay Cottage with Kitchen*

Rachel & Angus Stubbs
970 Caves Te Anga Road,
RD 8
Te Kuiti,

Tel (07) 878 6328
 Fax (07) 878 6328
tetiro@waitomocavesnz.com
www.waitomocavesnz.com

Double/Twin $110
Single $70
(Continental breakfast provisions)
Children $15 per person
Dinner by prior arrangment
Familys of 5 welcome,
we add extra mattress to loft
Visa MC accepted
Children and pets welcome
2 Queen 4 Single (2 bdrm)
Bathrooms: 2 Private with shower, toilet and washbasin.

Te Tiro (The View) welcomes you. Enjoy fantastic panoramic views of the central North Island and mountains. At night enjoy glowworms nestled in lush NZ bush only metres from your cottage. Situated on an established sheep farm with 350 acres of reserve bush. Our self-contained pioneer style cottages can accommodate up to 5 people in a cosy open plan room. Hosts Rachel and Angus have 30 years of tourism experience between them and would be happy to advise you on the wonders of Waitomo.

Waitomo Caves *16 km S of Otorohanga*

Waitomo Caves Guest Lodge *B&B Studio units each with own entrance*

Janet & Colin Beeston
7 Te Anga Road,
Waitomo Caves Village

Tel (07) 878 7641
or 0800 465 762
Fax (07) 878 7466
waitomocavesguestlodge@xtra.co.nz
www.waitomocavesguestlodge.co.nz

Double/Twin $100-$110
Single $75
(Continental breakfast)
Children up to 5yrs $10
5-10yrs $15, 10-15yrs $20
Extra adult $25
Visa MC Eftpos accepted
Children welcome
7 Queen 9 Single (8 bdrm)
Bathrooms: 7 Ensuite 1 Private There is a bath in the private bathroom

We are right in Waitomo Caves village, adjacent to a shop and 2 cafes, and an easy walking distance to the Museum/i-SITE, Glowworm Caves, adventure caving offices and other eating places. Our quality ensuite studio units are in a beautiful peaceful garden setting, with lovely views over the surrounding countryside. You can expect a warm welcome from Colin, Janet and Gypsy the family dog. We can give you knowledgeable advice, make bookings for local activities and help you with your itinerary.

Te Kuiti - Waitomo District *2 km N of Te Kuiti*
Simply the Best B&B *B&B Farmstay*

Margaret & Graeme Churstain
129 Gadsby Road,
RD 5,
Te Kuiti

Tel (07) 878 8191
or 027 666 9343
Fax (07) 878 5949
enquiry@simplythebestbnb.co.nz
www.simplythebestbnb.co.nz

Double/Twin $90
Single $50
(Continental breakfast)
Children negotiable
Dinner $30pp by arrangement
Pet - cats on property
2 Queen 1 Twin (3 bdrm)
Bathrooms: 1 Ensuite 1 Private
1 Guest share

Just 2.5hours from Auckland Airport our peaceful farmlet, signposted off SH3, northern end of Te Kuiti, we welcome you to 'Simply the Best' way to break a journey or to begin or end your New Zealand adventure. Happy to share our knowledge of the local area, Waitomo Caves, Blackwater rafting 10minutes away. Our comfortable 1 level home is unique for easy access from all rooms to decks overlooking stunning rural views. We offer secure parking, restaurants nearby, and 'above all' a place to remember.

Te Kuiti - Waitomo District *21 km W of Te Kuiti*
Tapanui Cottage *B&B Farmstay Cottage with Kitchen*

Craig and Sarah Fagan
1714 Oparure Rd, RD 5, Te Kuiti

Tel (07) 877 8498
or 027 251 1340
Fax (07) 877 8432
info@tapanui.co.nz
www.tapanui.co.nz

Double/Twin $250-$370
(Continental breakfast)
Visa MC accepted
Not suitable for children
Non smokers only
1 King 1 Queen (2 bdrm)
Bathrooms: 1 Private

Elegant secluded country retreat located near the renowned Waitomo Caves. Spacious self contained cottage set in quiet rolling hills amidst spectacular rock formations, on a 2500 acre working sheep and cattle farm. The cottage is fully equipped for self-catering. If you're planning a honeymoon, special anniversary or peaceful weekend the self contained cottage is perfect. Email and satellite broadband facilities are available at the homestead. 2.5hrs drive to Auckland International Airport. Exclusive single party occupancy. Minimum 2 nights stay. Guest welcome after 2pm. $250-$370 (2-4 persons)

Pio Pio - Waitomo District *19 km S of Te Kuiti*

Carmel Farm *B&B Homestay Farmstay*

Barbara & Leo Anselmi
1832 SH3, PO Box 93, Pio Pio

Tel (07) 877 8130 or 0800 877 813
Fax (07) 877 8130
Carmelfarms@xtra.co.nz

Double/Twin $120 Single $80 (Continental breakfast)
Dinner $25pp
Children and pets welcome
2 King/Twin 4 Single (4 bdrm)
Bathrooms: 1 Ensuite 1 Guest share

B&B Approved

Barbara and Leo Anselmi operate a 2000 acre sheep, beef and dairy farm. You will be welcomed into an established homestead set in a picturesque limestone valley.

You will be treated to delicious home-cooked meals and the warmth of our friendship.

Whether mustering mobs of cattle and sheep, viewing the milking of 550 Friesian cows, driving around the rolling hills on the 4 wheeled farm-bike, basking in the sun by the pool or enjoying the gardens, you will feel relaxed and rejuvenated. Whether you seek excitement or tranquility, Carmel Farm is the perfect retreat.

We are ideally located for you to explore many other attractions. We are adjacent to a beautiful 18 hole golf course which welcomes visitors. The property is a short distance from black water rafting and canoeing activities, The Lost World Cavern, and the famous Waitomo Caves. Nearby are bush walks, waterfalls, and the home of the rare kokako bird. The Mangaotaki stream is a mecca for the trout enthusiast. We can help to arrange activities for people of all ages and interests; from garden visits to horse riding. (P.S. In the TV lounge there is Sky for those all-important rugby matches.) Please let us know your preference.

We are 140km from Rotorua/Taupo. Directions: Travel 19km south of Te Kuiti on SH3 towards Piopio. Carmel Farm is on the right. We can arrange to pick up from Otorohanga, Te Kuiti or Waitomo, if required.

Coromandel Peninsula

Waiheke Island

Kuaotunu
Opito Bay
Coromandel

Whitianga
Hahei
Cooks Beach
Hot Water Beach

Beachlands

Whitford

Clevedon

Papakura

Tairua

Kaiaua

Te Puru

25

rury

Thames

Bombay

Whangamata

Mercer

2

Paeroa
Karangahake
Waihi

Waihi Beach

0   Kilometres   20
0   Miles   12

Paeroa - Karangahake *7 km S of Paeroa*

Karangahake Gold 'n Views B&B *Homestay Cottage with Kitchen*

Pamela and Nigel Blaikie
21 John Cotter Road,
Karangahake - RD 4, Paeroa 3674

Tel 0800 023 259 or 021 902 780
Fax (07) 862 6905
goldnviews@orcon.net.nz
www.goldnviewsbnb.co.nz

Double/Twin $130-$230
Single $90-$110
(Full breakfast)
Children under 12 years $30
Dinner $30 by arrangement
Cottage breakfast provisions available
Visa MC accepted
Pet free home Children welcome
1 Queen 2 Double/Twin
2 Twin 2 Single (5 bdrm)
Bathrooms: 1 Private 1 Guest share Cottage - shower. Home - bath & shower

Nestled beneath Mt. Karangahake among the stunning scenic views of the Karangahake Gorge, we (Pam and Nigel) welcome you to our peaceful location. Only minutes from the Ohinemuri winery, cafe, trout fishing, and the famous Windows walkway.Our homestay offers one double and one twin room. Our new Cedar wood self contained country cottage offers one bedroom, and one pull out setee.Our Ohinemuri historic cottage (self contained) offers two bedrooms and river views. It is located at 11 Moresby Street, next to the winery/restaurant.

Thames *8 km SE of Thames*

Wharfedale Farmstay *Homestay Farmstay Apartment with Kitchen*

Rosemary Burks
RD 1,
Kopu,
Thames

Tel (07) 868 8929
Fax (07) 868 8926
wharfedale@xtra.co.nz

Double/Twin $150
Single $100
(Full breakfast)
Children not suitable
Visa MC accepted
Not suitable for children
1 Double/Twin 2 Single (2 bdrm)
Bathrooms: 2 Private

For 17 years our guests have enjoyed the beauty of Wharfedale which has featured in Air NZ's "Airwaves" and Japan's "My Country" magazines. We invite you to share our idyllic lifestyle set in 9 acres of park-like paddocks and gardens, surrounded by native bush. Delight in private river swimming, abundant bird life. We enjoy wholefood and organically grown produce. There are cooking facilities in the studio apartment. Cool shade in summer and cozy log fires and electric blankets in winter. Golf club nearby.

Coromandel

Thames *3 km SE of Thames*
Corolight B&B *B&B Homestay*
Julia & Bob Bissett
108 Whitehead Way,
Parawai,
Thames
3500

Tel (07) 868 5538
Mobile 021 184 8334
Fax (07) 868 5537
juliabissett@clear.net.nz
www.corolight.co.nz

Double/Twin $130
Single $95
(Special breakfast)
Visa MC accepted
1 King/Twin 1 Queen (2 bdrm)
Bathrooms: 1 Guest share

Welcome to our elegant home where Julia, Bob and Amber (our Abyssinian cat) offer you warm hospitality. The upstairs guest lounge has TV, DVD and video, a kitchenette and a conservatory providing spectacular views and glorious sunsets. From this serene spot and central location visitors can enjoy Thames and its history with the rest of the Coromandel and its beauty spots within an hours reach. Corolight also provides natural therapy sessions, so why not pamper yourself while you stay. (View website)

Thames *6.4 km E of Thames*
Mountain Top B&B *Homestay*
Elizabeth McCracken & Allan Berry
452 Kauaeranga Valley Road,
RD 2,
Thames

Tel (07) 868 9662
Fax (07) 868 9662
nzh_mountain.top@xtra.co.nz

Double/Twin $115-$120
Single $80
(Full breakfast)
Children half price
Dinner $30-$35
Visa MC Diners Amex accepted
Children and pets welcome
1 Queen 2 Twin (2 bdrm)
Bathrooms: 1 Guest share

Allan and I grow mandarins, native trees and raise coloured sheep on a small organic farm. Our private, peaceful, guest wing with lounge, TV and extensive library has bedrooms and decks with superb views overlooking river, forest swimming pools and mountains. Nearby Forest Park has wonderful walking tracks. We have a productive, rambly garden, Jack Russell Roly, cat Priscilla. No cell phone coverage - best to phone mornings or evenings. We love entertaining and cooking for people, mostly from farm produce. Let's look after you.

Thames *8 km E of Thames*
Huia Lodge *B&B*
Celia & Murray Newby
589 Kauaeranga Valley Road,
Thames,

Tel (07) 868 6557
Fax (07) 868 6557
celian@wave.co.nz
www.thames-info.co.nz/HuiaLodge

Double/Twin $110
Single $75
(Full breakfast)
Extra person $40
Visa MC accepted
2 Queen 2 Single (2 bdrm)
Bathrooms: 2 Ensuite

B&B
Approved

Each unit has an ensuite and tea/coffee facilities. Relax and enjoy the tranquility of the valley, hike in the nearby Forest Park or circle the Peninsula to view the famous Coromandel scenery. We enjoy meeting travellers, love the rural lifestyle, grow fruit/vegetables, and enjoy the peace with our pet dog on our 3 acre paradise. Turn at BP corner (south end of township)into Banks Street then follow Parawai Road into the valley. We're 8km from BP. Just 1 1/2 hours from Auckland.

Thames *3 km S of Thames*
Totara Valley Barns *B&B*
Shona & Bruz MacGregor
65 Totara Valley Road,
RD 1,
Thames

Tel (07) 868 9730
or 027 310 3644
Fax (07) 868 9730
info@totarabarns.co.nz
www.totarabarns.co.nz

Double/Twin $135
Single $100
(Continental breakfast)
Dinner $35
Visa MC accepted
Not suitable for children
2 Queen (2 bdrm)
Bathrooms: 2 Ensuite

B&B
Approved

Unique, quality accommodation in a tranquil rural garden setting. 90 minutes south of Auckland Airport, Totara Barns is perfect as a relaxing getaway or as a base to explore the Coromandels exciting attractions. Separate guest accommodation with ensuites and spacious guest lounge. Enjoy the quiet surroundings, safe off-road parking, a generous continental breakfast and beautiful garden to unwind in at days end. Evening meal available using home-grown produce. Your local hosts, Shona and Bruz, assure you of true Kiwi hospitality.

Thames *2.5 km SE of Post Office*
The Heights *Luxury B&B*

Vicky & Phil English
300 Grafton Road,
Thames, 3500

Tel (07) 868 9925
or 0800 68 9925 (NZ)
or 0808 337 7020 (UK)
or 1800 557 671 (AUS)
info@theheights.co.nz
www.theheights.co.nz

Double/Twin $195-$225
Single $185-$210
(Full breakfast)
Dinner $50-$60 per person by pre-arrangement
Ariel premium non-alcoholic wines $25
Visa MC Diners Amex accepted
Not suitable for children
2 King (2 bdrm)
Bathrooms: 2 Ensuite

Photos can't do justice to the breathtaking panoramic views of sea, mountains and countryside at The Heights.

Relax in luxury with your own private deck or patio, king bed, ensuite, tea making, fridge, SKY TV, DVD, Internet, and all the special touches for a memorable stay. Hosts Vicky and Phil love sharing with you all the best spots to visit, and our friendly cats add to the welcome.

The 100 km of views from the deck from Te Moana are worth the short climb of stairs, while garden-view Te Koru features its own fireplace.

Only 1.5 hours from Auckland International Airport, take time to pamper yourself at The Heights.

Thames *5 km S of Thames*

Thorold Country House *Luxury Homestay Self-contained Garden Cottage*

Wendy & Gary
36 Ngati Maru Highway,
Kopu, Thames, 3578

Tel (07) 868 8480
or 021 253 6746
thorold@xtra.co.nz
www.thoroldcountryhouse.co.nz

Double/Twin $195-$250
Single $150 (Full breakfast)
Dinner available by prior arrangement,
special diets catered for
Garden Cottage $250 double,
extra person $50, max 4
Visa MC accepted
Children welcome
2 Queen 2 Twin (4 bdrm)
Bathrooms: 2 Private

Relax in our private, peaceful, quality country home situated on 6 acres just 70 minutes from Auckland Airport. The ideal base to explore the beautiful Coromandel Peninsula. Views extend over the Coromandel Hills and Firth of Thames. Luxury guest rooms open onto wide verandas with private seating areas overlooking park like grounds. The Garden Cottage is a spacious home from home with large lounge, dining room, kitchen, bathroom, BBQ. Tennis court, secluded swimming pool set in subtropical gardens, WiFi, open log fire for cooler nights.

Thames *1 km N of Information Centre*

Ocean View on Thames *B&B Homestay Apartment with Kitchen*

Julie & Steve McLellan
509 Upper Albert Street,
Thames
3500

Tel (07) 868 3588
sjmclellan@xtra.co.nz
http://retreat4u.co.nz

Double/Twin $140-$160
Single $125
(Full breakfast)
Extra persons in apartment $30 each
Visa MC Eftpos accepted
Children welcome
3 Queen 1 Twin (4 bdrm)
Bathrooms: 2 Private

Peace, tranquility, wonderful views and a very warm welcome await you at our attractive two-storey colonial style house, which has panoramic views over the Firth of Thames and is only a ten-minute walk to the town centre and restaurants. Ocean View is a haven in its setting of beautifully landscaped gardens, and with its array of native New Zealand birds. Thames is the perfect location from which to explore the stunning and varied scenery of the Coromandel Peninsula.

Thames - Totara *5 km SE of Thames*
Cotswold Cottage *Luxury B&B Country House*

Graham & Jacqueline Hamlett
46 Maramarahi Road,
Totara, Thames

Tel (07) 868 6306
or mobile 021 113 3463
Fax (07) 868 6202
cotswoldcot@gmail.com
www.cotswoldcottage.co.nz

Double/Twin $130-$195
Single $110-$145
(Full breakfast)
Children under 10 $25
Delicious evening meals $35-$45
Special offer stay 3 nights pay for only 2
Visa MC accepted
Pet free home Children welcome
1 King/Twin 3 Queen 1 Single (4 bdrm)
Bathrooms: 4 Ensuite

Relax and unwind in our lovingly restored 1920's villa just one hour from Auckland and only 3 minutes from historic Thames. This is a wonderful base for travellers touring the Coromandel and surrounding areas. Enjoy the sunny well appointed rooms each with amazing views, tv/radio, coffee/tea, hair dryer, safe and private access. The lounge conservatory, terrace and spa pool offer a choice of places to read, write or simply relax. Generous gourmet breakfasts included and evening meals available. We are passionate about hospitality and Jacqui is a wonderful chef.

Thames *2.5 km SE of Post Office*
Chartré Manor B&B *Luxury B&B Cottage*

Dennis Trebilcock & Pauline Trebilcock-Charteris
306 Grafton Road,
Thames, 3550

Tel (07) 868 3255
or 027 608 2130
welcome@chartremanor.co.nz
www.chartremanor.co.nz

Double/Twin $165-$250
Single $150-$235
(Full breakfast)
Not suitable for children under 12
2 King 2 Queen (4 bdrm)
Bathrooms: 3 Ensuite 2 Private
1 Guest share

Luxury, affordable accommodation in Thames, the capital of the Coromandel Peninsula. Set high above Thames overlooking the firth and township. Magnificent views and sunsets with a native bush backdrop. An ideal base from which to explore the Coromandel Peninsula. Just 90 minutes from Auckland Intl. Airport, Hamilton, Tauranga & Rotorua. Enjoy relaxing on 2.5 acres of pictureque gardens with farm animals, our friendly cat Pippa, sprayfree produce, fresh eggs and neighbouring Llamas. A swimming pool for the summer and log fires in the winter. Guest lounge with Sky TV, DVD, Broadband Internet and special attention to detail to ensure your stay is a happy, memorable experience.

Thames Coast - Te Puru *12 km N of Thames*
Te Puru Coast Bed & Breakfast *B&B Homestay Please add extra tarrif: Twin $105.00*

Bill & Paula Olsen
2A Tatahi Street,
Te Puru,
Thames Coast

Tel (07) 868 2866
Fax (07) 868 2866
tepurucoastbnb@xtra.co.nz
www.tepurucoastbnb.co.nz

Double/Twin $120-$140
Single $100-$100
(Full breakfast)
Children $25 under 12
Dinner $35pp - includes
New Zealand wine or beer
Pet free home
Children welcome
1 Queen 1 Twin 2 Single (2 bdrm)
Bathrooms: 1 Ensuite 1 Private

Welcome to the beautiful Thames Coast. Our modern comfortable home is 80 metres off the main coast road. Guest lounge has TV, books and tea & coffee facilities. You may choose a continental or cooked breakfast and evening meals are on request ($35.00pp) with complimentary New Zealand wine or beer. Our large deck is yours to enjoy or take a 2 minute walk to the beach. A warm welcome greets you on arrival with tea or coffee and homemade cookies.

~

Coromandel *10 km S of Coromandel*
AJ's Homestay *B&B Homestay*
Annette & Ray Hintz
24 Kowhai Drive,
Te Kouma,
RD, Coromandel

Tel (07) 866 7057
or 027 458 1624
Fax (07) 866 7057
rm.aj.hintz@actrix.co.nz

Double/Twin $110-$135
Single $85-$95
(Continental breakfast)
Dinner $35-$40
Visa MC accepted
Children welcome
1 King/Twin 2 Queen
1 Single (3 bdrm)
Bathrooms: 1 Ensuite 1 Family share

AJ's Homestay with panoramic sea views overlooking the Coromandel Harbour, spectacular sunsets. 5 minute walk to a safe swimming beach. Most mornings breakfast is served on the terrace. Our games room has a billiard and table tennis table. Dinner can be arranged. Directions: Thames coast main road (SH25) approximately 50 minutes. At the bottom of the last hill overlooking the Coromandel Harbour. Turn sharp left, at the Te Kouma Road sign. Travel past the boat ramp, next turn left. Kowhai Drive, we are number 24.

Coromandel *3 km S of Coromandel*
Jacaranda Lodge *B&B*

Robin Münch
3195 Tiki Road,
Coromandel, RD 1

Tel (07) 866 8002
or 021 252 6892
Fax (07) 866 8002
info@jacarandalodge.co.nz
www.jacarandalodge.co.nz

Double/Twin $120-$165
Single $70-$130
(Special breakfast)
Visa MC accepted
Pet free home
Not suitable for children
4 Queen 1 Twin 1 Single (6 bdrm)
Bathrooms: 2 Ensuite 1 Private
1 Guest share Spotlessly clean

Robin invites you to share her spacious home set on 6 acres of tranquil country paradise. Located 3km south of Coromandel Town, Jacaranda Lodge provides the perfect escape: relax in one of the guest lounges; stroll around the delightful gardens; experience Coromandel's walks, unique attractions and spectacular coastline. Delicious continental breakfasts include fresh organic produce from Jacaranda's orchard. Large, comfortable bedrooms. Ensuite, private, shared bathrooms. Fully equipped guest kitchen (additional charge may apply). Special dietary needs can be catered for, including kosher. Sleep, eat, enjoy.

Coromandel - Te Kouma *8 km S of Coromandel*
Te Kouma B&B *B&B Separate Suite*

Kurt & Jo Muller
50 Puriri Road,
Te Kouma,
Coromandel

Tel (07) 866 7971
or 021 263 5533
Fax (07) 866 7971
ko_jm_muller@xtra.co.nz

Double/Twin $120-$140
Single $95-$100
(Continental breakfast)
Pet free home
Children welcome
2 Queen 2 Twin (3 bdrm)
Bathrooms: 2 Ensuite 1 Family share
Sorry Showers only - no bath

Our well appointed home has the best views in the area. Kurt speaks German and makes delicious wholemeal breads, served for your breakfast with home preserved fruits and jams. Jo collects pacific seashells and old china. We live in a very tranquil place, abounding with bellbirds, tuis and pigeons, over looking Coromandel Harbour. Fishing trips can be arranged, Coromandel town 10 minutes North. Thames 45 minutes South.

Coromandel *0.5 km S of Coromandel*
The Green House *B&B*

Barb & Tony
505 Tiki Road,
Coromandel

Tel (07) 866 7303
or 0800 473 364
greenhouse@orcon.net.nz
www.greenhousebandb.co.nz

Double/Twin $140-$165
Single $120-$125
(Special breakfast)
Visa MC accepted
Not suitable for children
1 King 1 Queen (2 bdrm)
Bathrooms: 2 new ensuite bathrooms

This relaxed home has very comfortable facilities, lovely views over hills and sea, and is minutes walk to the excellent restaurants of Coromandel Town. Upstairs, the dedicated guest area has a lovely lounge with tea/coffee, fridge, TV, computer, videos, etc. The bedrooms, one with private deck, the other sea views, are separated by the guest lounge. Generous hospitality is offered.

Coromandel *0.5 km E of Coromandel*
Breakaway B&B *B&B Separate Suite Tea/coffee, TV, microwave, fridge*

Michael & Ross
39 Whangapoua Road,
Coromandel

Tel (07) 866 8310
or 027 363 9960
Fax (07) 866 8310
info@breakaway-bb.co.nz
www.breakaway-bb.co.nz

Double/Twin $145
Single $145
(Continental breakfast)
Extra person $25 each
Visa MC accepted
Not suitable for children
Pets welcome
2 Queen 2 Twin (4 bdrm)
Bathrooms: 4 Ensuite 4 Private
Unit 2, twin, large shower room ideal for wheelchair use

Allow time in your travels to stop with us. Michael & Ross invite you to a quiet and relaxing stay in their rural country setting in parklike grounds. Just a 1 minute drive or a 10 minute level walk to Coromandel town which offers an excellent variety of restaurants and cafes. Also a good selection of quality craft shops. A continental breakfast is served in the conservatory overlooking the garden with views of the Coromandel Harbour. The fishing is great !!! Pets are welcome by arrangement.

Kuaotunu *17 km N of Whitianga*
Kaeppeli's *B&B*
Jill Kaeppeli
40 Gray Ave, Kuaotunu,
3592 Whitianga

Tel (07) 866 2445
or 027 656 3442
Fax (07) 866 2445
paradise@kaeppelis.co.nz
www.kaeppelis.co.nz

Double/Twin $130-$190
Single $95-$130
(Full breakfast)
Children negotiable
Dinner $38 by arrangement
Visa MC Eftpos accepted
Children and pets welcome
1 King 2 Single
Bathrooms: 2 Ensuite with ocean views

"Back to Paradise" above the Pacific Ocean. A peaceful, secluded, unique haven with stunning sea, bush and rural views. Relax, unwind, enjoy the natural beauty that surrounds you. Comfortable sunny rooms with private decks and entrances. Panoramic gazebo dining room. Various Dinner options available. Kuaotunu has a choice of clean, safe, white, sandy beaches, kayaking, tennis, bush walks, horse trekking, fishing, golf, arts and crafts. Ideal for exploring the Coromandel. Swiss/ German spoken. Children welcome. Pets to pamper. Our view? Simply the best.

Kuaotunu *16 km N of Whitianga*
@ The Peacheys *B&B Homestay*
Yvonne & Dale Peachey
15 Kawhero Drive,
Kuaotunu
RD 2,
Whitianga

Tel (07) 866 5290
Fax (07) 866 4592
DYPeachey@xtra.co.nz
www.thepeacheys.co.nz

Double/Twin $140
Single $110
(Continental breakfast)
Dinner $35 pp
Visa MC accepted
Not suitable for children
1 King 1 Queen 3 Single (2 bdrm)
Bathrooms: 2 Ensuite

Come & stay awhile to enjoy Kuaotunu, our piece of paradise. We have seven beaches to explore, and ours is only 100 metres from your spacious & comfortable room. We have coastal & forest walks,and close to Coromandel & Whitianga attractions. Experience our incredible night sky & amazing sunsets. Resturants & Cafes are available in Whitianga & Matarangi, or arrange to have dinner with us. (Prior notice essential). Bathrobes, beach towels, refrigerator, tea & coffee available. Barley & Chelsea (the cats) also live here.

Kuaotunu *17 km N of Whitianga*
Drift In B&B *B&B Homestay*
Yvonne & Peppe Thompson
16 Grays Avenue, Kuaotunu,
RD 2, Whitianga

Tel (07) 866 4321
or 027 245 3632
Fax (07) 866 4321
driftin@paradise.net.nz
www.coromandelfun.co.nz/driftin

Double/Twin $125-$125
Single $70-$70
(Full breakfast)
Children negotiable
Dinner main and dessert $30
Visa MC accepted
Children welcome
1 Queen 2 Single (2 bdrm)
Bathrooms: 1 Guest share
with bath and shower

Welcome is assured. This tranquil comfortable modern cedar home is designed to take full advantage of the sun and breathtaking island views by day and moonlit night. An unique beach theme pervades house and garden, small dog in residence. Just a minute stroll to white sand beaches for safe swimming and fossicking. Breakfast is a memorable occasion with sight and sounds of birds and sea complementing an excellent range of home cooking. Drift in, relax and enjoy this unique and special part of New Zealand.

Opito Bay *27 km NE of Whitianga*
At Opito *B&B*
Max & Bev
13 Stewart Place, Opito Bay,
RD 2 Whitianga

Tel (07) 866 0317
or 027 418 5588
Fax (07) 866 0317
max-bev@xtra.co.nz

Double/Twin $120-$150
Single $110
(Full breakfast)
Children $20
Dinner $25 by arrangement
Visa MC accepted
Pet free home
Children welcome
1 Queen (1 bdrm)
Bathrooms: 1 Private
Shower over 'shub' (mini-bath)

A warm kiwi welcome awaits you with complimentary tea & coffee and home baking on the deck. Our clean comfortable B&B offers you your own entrance, bathroom, guest area with sofa-bed, fridge, toaster, electric jug etc. Enjoy soaking in our spa after a swim or walk along Opito's beautiful, safe, white sandy beach, just 2 minutes stroll away. Restaurants at Whitianga or Matarangi or join us for a home cooked dinner or you may choose to self-cater on the BBQ. Laundry facilities available.

Whitianga *1 km S of Whitianga*
Cosy Cat Cottage *B&B Cottage with Kitchen*

Gordon Pearce
41 South Highway (town end),
Whitianga

Tel (07) 866 4488
cosycat@xtra.co.nz
www.cosycat.co.nz

Double/Twin $95-$125
Single $80-$90
(Full breakfast)
Cottage $90-$180
Visa MC accepted
Children welcome
2 Queen 1 Double/Twin
1 Single (3 bdrm)
Bathrooms: 2 Ensuite 1 Private

Welcome to our picturesque 2 storied cottage filled with feline memorabilia! Relax with complimentary tea or coffee served on the veranda or in the guest lounge. Enjoy a good nights rest in comfortable beds and choose a variety of treats from our breakfast blackboard menu. You will probably like to meet Honey the cat or perhaps visit the cat hotel in the garden. A separate cottage is available with queen beds, bathrooms and kitchen. Friendly helpful service is assured - hope to see you soon!

Whitianga - Cooks Beach *17 km N of Tairua*
Mercury Orchard *B&B Cottage with Kitchen*

Heather and Barry Scott
141 Purangi Road,
Cooks Beach,
Whitianga

Tel (07) 866 3119
Fax (07) 866 3115
relax@mercuryorchard.co.nz
www.mercuryorchard.co.nz

Double/Twin $130-$175
Single $120-$140
(Full breakfast)
Children $20
Fig Tree Cottage $175
Paua Bach 175
Visa MC accepted
Children welcome
1 King 2 Queen 2 Single (4 bdrm)
Bathrooms: 3 Ensuite

Paua Bach and Fig Tree Cottage are nestled amongst 5 acres of peaceful country gardens and orchard. Self- contained country style luxury with french doors opening onto your private deck. Crisp cotton bed linen, bathrobes, fresh fruit, flowers and candles. Special to the Bach, an old fashioned outdoor bath. Enjoy a Mercury Orchard full breakfast while listening to the birdsong. Barbeque your evening meal Kiwi style. Hot Water Beach and Cathedral Cove are 7-8 minutes drive. We share our home with a small dog and a cat.

Whitianga *4 km N of Whitianga*
At Parkland Place *Luxury B&B*

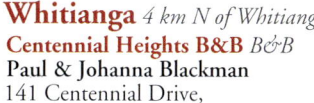

Maria & Guy Clark
14 Parkland Place,
Brophys Beach, Whitianga

Tel (07) 866 4987 or 021 404 923
Fax (07) 866 4946
parklandplace@wave.co.nz
www.atparklandplace.co.nz

Double/Twin $165-$200
(Full breakfast)
Children negotiable
Dinner by arrangement
Visa MC Eftpos accepted
Pet free home
Children welcome
1 King/Twin 4 King
2 Single (5 bdrm)
Bathrooms: 5 Ensuite

Enjoy European hospitality in Whitianga's most luxurious hotel style accommodation. Maria, a ship's chef from Poland and New Zealand husband Guy, a master mariner, will make your stay a memorable experience. Large luxuriously appointed rooms. Magnificent breakfasts. Superb candle-lit dinners or BBQ by arrangement. Sunny picturesque outdoor area with spa pool. Large guest lounge with TV, library, music and refreshments. Situated near the beach and next to reserves and farmland ensures absolute peace and quiet. Privacy and discretion assured. You will not regret coming.

Whitianga *4 km N of Whitianga*
Centennial Heights B&B *B&B*

Paul & Johanna Blackman
141 Centennial Drive,
Whitianga

Tel (07) 866 0279
Fax (07) 866 0276
Blackmanmathis@xtra.co.nz
www.centennialheights.unitrental.com

Double/Twin $150
Single $100
(Continental breakfast provisions)
Children $20
Visa MC Amex accepted
Children welcome
1 King 2 Queen 1 Single (4 bdrm)
Bathrooms: 3 Ensuite 1 Private

Centennial Heights overlooks the sparkling waters of Whitianga Harbour. Paul & Johanna (who speaks fluent German and French) and Mollie our border collie offer warm hospitality in elegant surroundings. Over complimentary pre-dinner drinks we can assist you with information on the areas attractions including fishing, kayaking, tramping, scuba diving, snorkelling, boat cruises and dining out etc. We offer a delicious cooked breakfast which can be enjoyed with spectacular sea views. We look forward to welcoming you and making your stay a pleasant and memorable one.

Whitianga *6 km N of Whitianga*
On The Beach *B&B*

Approved

Gordon and Diana Barnaby
66 State Highway 25,
Simpson's Beach
RD 2
Whitianga, 3592

Tel (07) 866 2433
or 027 245 7496
info@onthebeachwhitianga.co.nz
www.onthebeachwhitianga.co.nz

Double/Twin $120-$180
(Continental breakfast)
Children Up to 12 yrs free
Dinner by request
Visa MC Amex accepted
Children welcome
2 King 1 Queen 1 Single (3 bdrm)
Bathrooms: 3 Ensuite

Diana and Gordon look forward to exceeding your expectations when you choose to stay with them. They have travelled extensively and are aware of what their guests would expect when they are away from home. They look forward to making you welcome and to fulfil you needs.

Hahei *38 km S of Whitianga*

The Church *B&B Cottage No Kitchen Cottage with Kitchen*

Richard Agnew & Karen Blair
87 Beach Road, Hahei,
RD 1, Whitianga

Tel (07) 866 3533 or 0274 596 877
Fax (07) 866 3055
info@thechurchhahei.co.nz
www.thechurchhahei.co.nz

Double/Twin $105-$175
Single $105-$175
(Continental breakfast)
Children $10-$15
Dinner Menu a la carte
Extra Adult $20-$25
Visa MC Eftpos accepted
Children welcome
11 Queen 1 Double/Twin
11 Twin 13 Single (11 bdrm)
Bathrooms: 11 Ensuite

The Church is Hahei's unique accommodation and dining experience. The Church building provides a character dining room/licensed restaurant for delicious evening meals. Wholesome breakfasts in purpose built breakfast room. 11 cosy wooden cottages scattered through delightful bush and gardens offer a range of accommodation and tariffs, with ensuites, fridges, tea and coffee facilities. Some cottages fully self-contained with woodstoves for winter. Small conference facilities. Enjoy the wonders of Cathedral Cove, Hot Water Beach, and the Coromandel Peninsula. Seasonal rates. Smoking outside.

Hahei *0.4 km SW of Hahei*

Hahei B&B *B&B*

Mark Cederman
6 Jackson Place,
Hahei,
RD 1
Whitianga

Tel (07) 866 3730
or 027 499 8879
Fax 07 866 3750
info@haheibandb.co.nz
www.haheibandb.co.nz

Double/Twin $140-$220
(Full breakfast)
Visa MC Eftpos accepted
Children welcome
1 King 3 Queen 3 Single (4 bdrm)
Bathrooms: 2 Ensuite 2 Guest share

A warm welcome awaits you at Hahei Bed & Breakfast. This is a modern, purpose built home with a large swimming pool, beautiful gardens and sun drenched decks. Continental or cooked breakfast served in the privacy of your own rooms, or alfresco on the deck overlooking Hahei and the gardens. Local features and attractions include bush walks, diving and snorkelling in close proximity to digging your own hot pool at Hot Water Beach or walking to picturesque Catherdral Cove.

Hot Water Beach *28 km N of Tairua*
Auntie Dawns Place *Apartment with Kitchen*

Dawn & Joe Nelmes
15 Radar Road,
Hot Water Beach,
Whitianga RD 1

Tel (07) 866 3707
or 021 21 56 300
dawn@auntiedawn.co.nz
www.auntiedawn.co.nz

Double/Twin $100-$135
Single $30-$60
(Continental breakfast)
Visa MC accepted
2 Queen 1 Double/Twin
1 Single (2 bdrm)
Bathrooms: 2 Private

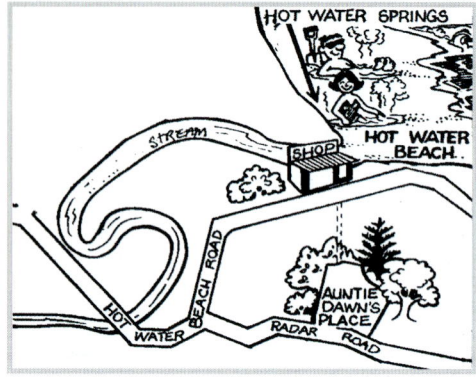

Hot Water Beach is a surfbeach. At low tide hotwater bubbles up in the sand and you dig yourself a "hotpool". Our house is surrounded by huge Pohutukawa trees, 3 minutes walk from hotsprings. We have 6 hens and Joe makes home-brew beer. Each apartment is comfortably furnished with a queen bedroom & spare bed in the living room. Tea, coffee, bread, butter, jam, milk, cereals provided, guests prepare breakfast at preferred time. Directions: turn right into Radar Rd before cafe.

Tairua *45 km E of Thames*
Harbour View Lodge *B&B*

Eve and Alan Roper
179 Main Road,
Tairua

Tel (07) 864 7040
or 027 479 7851
Fax (07) 864 7042
info@harbourviewlodge.co.nz
www.harbourviewlodge.co.nz

Double/Twin $190-$220
Single $160-$190
(Full breakfast)
Visa MC accepted
Not suitable for children
1 King/Twin 2 Queen (3 bdrm)
Bathrooms: 3 Ensuite

Peace & tranquility is yours when you stay in one of our luxury rooms with ensuite. Enjoy the swimming pool and tropical gardens. Start your day with a sumptuous breakfast while you enjoy the breathtaking views of the Tairua Harbour & Paku Mountain. A short stroll each evening to the local restaurants. We can help you plan each day as you experience Hot Water Beach, Cathedral Cove or one of the many other attractions. We have two cats Tommy and Mittens and Louie the cocker spanial waiting to meet you

Whangamata *.2 km N of town centre*
Sandy Rose Bed & Breakfast *B&B*

Shirley & Murray Calman
122 Hetherington Road, (Corner
Hetherington & Rutherford Roads),
Whangamata

Tel (07) 865 6911
sandyrose@whangamata.co.nz
http://sandyrose.whangamata.co.nz

Double/Twin $140
Single $100
(Special breakfast)
Visa MC accepted
Pet free home
Not suitable for children
2 King/Twin 1 Queen
1 Double/Twin (3 bdrm)
Bathrooms: 3 Ensuite

A charming B&B in the Coromandel Peninsula's popular holiday destination, we have 3 tastefully decorated guest bedrooms, all with ensuite bathrooms, comfortable beds and in-room TVs. Complimentary tea & coffee is available in the guest lounge. We are ideally located, close to Whangamata's shops, cafes and restaurants, and an easy stroll to the surf beach, harbour and wharf. Enjoy our extensive special breakfast and use our home as a base to relax and enjoy the natural attractions that Whangamata and area has to offer.

Whangamata *2 km S of Town Centre*
Kotuku *Homestay Cottage with Kitchen Self-contained Studio Bach*

Linda & Peter Bigge
422 Otahu Road,
Whangamata

Tel (07) 865 6128
or 027 358 1227
Fax (07) 865 6128
lindapeter@slingshot.co.nz
www.kotukuhomestay.co.nz

Double/Twin $108-$120
(Full breakfast)
Studio Bach $70-$80
(two nights minimum)
Visa MC Diners accepted
Children welcome
3 Queen (3 bdrm)
Bathrooms: 3 Ensuite

We offer comfortable homestay accommodation in a purpose built home. Rosie, our friendly dog and Elizabeth, the cat, will give you a warm welcome too! Relax in the spacious lounge or private patio; enjoy the Coromandel sunset from our outdoor spa. Kotuku is situated at the quieter end of Whangamata, just a 2 minute stroll to the lovely Otahu Estuary Reserve; ideal for walking, swimming, kayaking or just take a picnic lunch and watch the fascinating shorebirds. Bikes and kayaks are available for your use.

Waihi *1 km S of Waihi*
West Wind Gardens *B&B Homestay*

Josie & Merv Scott
58 Adams Street,
Waihi

Tel (07) 863 7208
westwindgarden@xtra.co.nz
www.athomenz.org.nz

Double/Twin $90
Single $50
(Continental breakfast)
Children $20
Dinner $20
Visa MC accepted
Children welcome
1 Double/Twin 2 Single (2 bdrm)
Bathrooms: 1 Guest share

We offer a friendly restful smoke-free stay in our modern home and garden. Waihi is the gate way to both the Coromandel and the Bay of Plenty with its beautiful beaches. Waihi is a historic town with a vintage railway and a working gold mine discovered 1878 closed 1952. Reopened in 1989 as a open-cast mine.Beach 10 minutes away, beautiful walks, golf courses, trout fishing. Enjoy a home cooked meal or sample our restaurants. Our interests are gardening, dancing and travel.

Waihi *2 km W of Waihi*
Ashtree House *B&B rural plus private unit*

Anne & Bill Ashdown
20 Riflerange Road,
Waihi

Tel (07) 863 6448
or 027 492 8915
Fax (07) 863 6443
ash.tree@clear.net.nz
http://ash.tree@clear.net.nz

Double/Twin $100
Single $50
(Full breakfast)
Children under 10 $10
Dinner $20pp - booking required
Garden Unit $40pp
Children welcome
1 Queen 1 Double/Twin
2 Single (3 bdrm)
Bathrooms: 2 Private 1 Guest share (one in house bathroom)

Modern brick home set on the side of a hill with extensive views and access to trout river. Private guest wing comprising 2 double bedrooms, large private bathroom with shower and bath. Guest lounge with TV, stereo and large selection of New Zealand books. Laundry and separate toilet. 8 acres, large attractive garden and pond area. 1 house dog. Situated 2 minutes to centre of Waihi, complete privacy and quiet guaranteed. Self-contained unit with wheelchair facilities. 5 minutes to beautiful Karangahake Gorge. Middleaged couple, children grown up, one super friendly golden lab, assorted birds hobbies, gardening, reading, talking, and life.

Waihi *0.5 km W of Waihi*
Chez Nous *B&B Homestay*

Sara Parish
41 Seddon Avenue,
Waihi

Tel (07) 863 7538
or 027 644 5562
sarap@slingshot.co.nz

Double/Twin $65
Single $45
(Continental breakfast)
Children $20
Dinner $20pp by arrangement
Visa MC accepted
Children welcome
1 Queen 1 Twin (2 bdrm)
Bathrooms: 1 Guest share

Enjoy a relaxed and friendly atmosphere in a spacious, modern home in an attractive garden setting. Shops and restaurants are within easy walking distance. Discover past and present gold mining activities (tours available), sandy surf beaches, bush walks, 18 hole golf course, art, craft and wine trails. Waihi is an ideal stopover for the traveller who wants to explore the Coromandel Peninsula, Bay of Plenty and Waikato.

Waihi *1 km NE of Waihi*
Dragonfly Garden Bed and Breakfast *B&B*

Bert and Kathy
11 Parry Palm Ave,
Waihi,
2981

Tel (07) 863 9034
or 027 236 1997
wattsdue@paradise.net.nz
www.dragonflygardenbnb.co.nz

Double/Twin $130-$150
Single $90
(Full breakfast)
BBQ, outside garden oven
Not suitable for children
Pets welcome
1 Queen 1 Twin (2 bdrm)
Bathrooms: 2 Ensuite

Enjoy these charming and comfortable detached bedrooms with ensuites which are ideally situated amoungst 1 ½ acres of mature trees and gardens with fishponds. We offer laundry facilities, outdoor garden oven, fireplace and BBQ area. Situated 1 minute from Waihi Centre, 8 minutes from Karangahake george and 15 minutes from the beach. This area offers something for everyone. Your friendly hosts Bert and Kathy and Roco (the Tibetan Terrier) look forward to looking after you.

Waihi Beach *11 km E of Waihi*
Waterfront Homestay *Apartment with Kitchen*

Kay & John Morgan
17 The Esplanade
(off Hinemoa Street),
Waihi Beach

Tel (07) 863 4342
or 021 170 5058
Fax (07) 863 4342
k.morgan@xtra.co.nz

Double/Twin $120
(Continental breakfast)
Self catering breakfast option
Visa MC accepted
Pet free home
Children welcome
1 Queen 3 Single (2 bdrm)
Bathrooms: 1 Private

Waterfront Homestay. Fully self-contained, 2 double bedrooms. Suitable for 2 couples or small family group. Unit is lower floor of family home on waterfront of beautiful uncrowded ocean beach. Walk from front door directly onto sandy beach. Safe ocean swimming, surfcasting, surfing and coastal walks. Restaurant within walking distance or use facilities provided with accommodation. Waterfront Homestay is situated close to popular scenic coastal walks to Orokawa and Homunga Bays. Tariff $120 per couple, bed and breakfast. Hosts John & Kay Morgan.

Waihi Beach *11 km E of Waihi*
Seagulls Bed & Breakfast *B&B*

Marie & Steve Quinlan
8 West Street
(off Pacific Road),
Waihi Beach

Tel (07) 863 4633
or 021 0290 9880
Fax (07) 863 4634
seagullsquinlan@clear.net.nz

Double/Twin $110-$130
Single $95-$100
(Full breakfast)
Children welcome
2 Queen 1 Single (2 bdrm)
Bathrooms: 1 Guest share - large
modern with bath and shower

Relax and unwind at beautiful Waihi Beach - gateway to Coromandel Peninsular, historic Karangahake Gorge, Orokawa/Homunga walkways and Bay of Plenty. Enjoy spectacular panoramic views of main beach (3minutes walk) and Mayor Island. Watch the sunrise, listen to tuis sing in bush on boundary. Modern spacious luxury home with your own TV lounge, tea/coffee facilities, bedrooms all with sea views. Excellent outdoor area, cafes/restaurants RSA closeby, swimming, surfing, fishing, beach and bush walks. Breakfasts include fresh seasonal fruits, homemade preserves, organic produce.

Waihi Beach *12 km N of Katikati*
The Candy's B&B *B&B Cottage with Kitchen*
Gloria & Neil Candy
43 Athenree Road,
Athenree,
Waihi Beach

Tel (07) 863 1159
Fax (07) 863 1196
neilcandy@ihug.co.nz

Double/Twin $130-$135
Single $80-$100
(Continental breakfast)
Dinner $32pp
2 King 2 Twin (3 bdrm)
Bathrooms: 1 Ensuite 1 Private
1 Guest share

Take time out: relax. Our modern home is on three acres, with beautiful harbour views: each room has a privete patio. Walk to Athenree Hotpools, drive 3 minutes to Waihi Surf Beach, 10 minutes south to Katikati, 2 Local Golf Courses, Morton Estate Winery, . 10 minutes north to Waihi Goldmine, walks and excellent restaurants. Neil loves fishing, and Gloria loves crafts. Meals on request. This is paradise and our city pets agree. New 1 bedroom cottage self contained no meals supplied.

Our B&Bs range from homely to luxurious, but you can always be assured of superior hospitality.

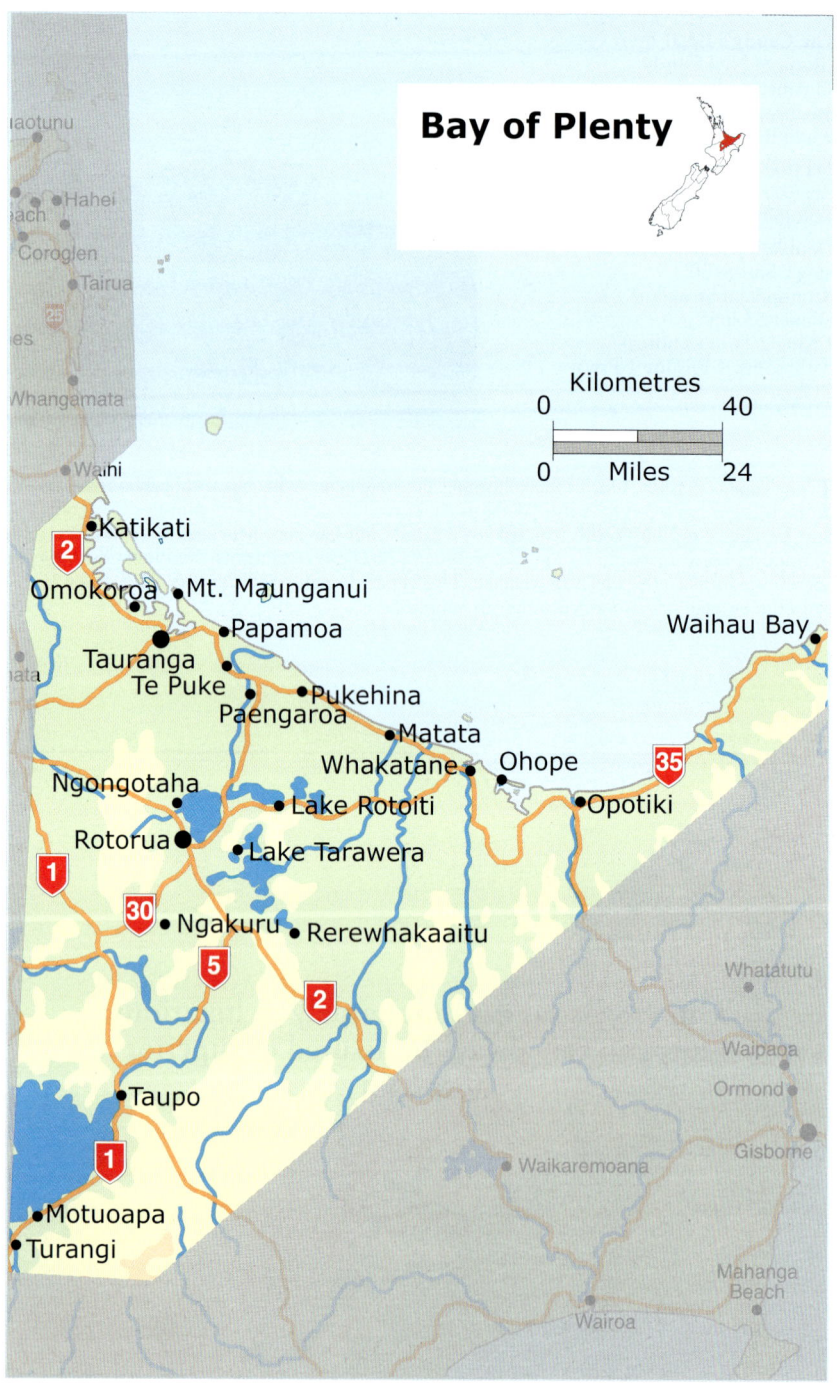

Bay of Plenty

Katikati *8 km N of Katikati*
Cotswold Lodge Countrystay *B&B*
Alison & Des Belsham
183 Ongare Point Road, RD 1, Katikati
Tel (07) 549 2110   Fax (07) 549 2109
relax@cotswold.co.nz
www.cotswold.co.nz

Double/Twin $150-$170 Single $110
(Special breakfast)
Dinner by prior arrangement Visa MC accepted
2 Queen 1 Double/Twin 1 Single (3 bdrm)
Bathrooms: 3 Ensuite

We offer warm kiwi hospitality and a little luxury in our rural home, just 8 mins north of Katikati Mural Town and 15 mins from Waihi Beach. Quality accommodation overlooking kiwifruit and avocado orchards, with views to Kaimai Ranges. Expect to be pampered on arrival with a welcome cuppa and yummy nibbles. Yummy breakfast. We hope you will feel rejuvenated by the time you leave.

All rooms with ensuite bathroom, quality furnishings, hairdryers, bathrobes etc. Evening meals by prior arrangement. Watch the sunset while relaxing in the spa. Petanque in the garden. Short stroll through the orchard and down to the Harbour. Short distance to golf, restaurants, wineries, walking tracks, museum, beaches, fishing, gardens etc. Come and enjoy our piece of paradise. Use us as a base to explore the beautiful Bay of Plenty. We have a friendly Labrador. We look forward to meeting you.

Directions: Just north of Katikati turn east of SH2 into Kauri Point Road. Approx 2.7kms take left hand fork road which is Ongare Point Road and we are 1.8kms on left.

Katikati *3 km N of Katikati*
Aberfeldy *B&B Farmstay*

Mary Anne & Rod Calver
164 Lindemann Road,
RD 1, Katikati

Tel (07) 549 0363
or 0800 309 064
or 027 590 9710
Fax (07) 549 0363
aberfeldy@xtra.co.nz
www.aberfeldy.co.nz

Double/Twin $120
Single $75
(Full breakfast)
Children $40
Dinner by arrangement
We take one party only at a time
Visa MC accepted
Children and pets welcome
1 Queen 1 Twin 1 Single (2 bdrm)
Bathrooms: 1 Private

Home in extensive gardens with private sunny accommodation. The lounge opens onto a patio, and has fridge,microwave, TV, tea and coffee making facilities. 1 party at a time . We farm sheep and cattle. Rod's associated with Kiwifruit and is a Rotarian. Panoramic views of bush-clad hills, farmland and harbour. Activities include farm walks, meeting tame animals especially Piglet & Lucy the Kune Kune pigs. Golf course, horse riding, and beaches nearby.

~

Katikati *9 km N of Katikati*
Panorama Country Lodge *Luxury B&B*
Barbara & Phil McKernon
901 Pacific Coast Highway (SH2),
RD 1,
Katikati

Tel (07) 549 1882
or 0211 655 875
Fax (07) 549 1882
mckernon@xtra.co.nz
www.panoramalodge.co.nz

Double/Twin $170-$200
Single $130-$150
(Special breakfast)
Visa MC accepted
1 King 1 Queen 1 Twin (3 bdrm)
Bathrooms: 1 Ensuite 1 Private

Perfectly situated between beautiful Waihi Beach and Katikati. Nestling in the foothills of the Kaimai Ranges, magnificent ocean views from every room! Relax in spacious and peaceful guest suites, quality furnishings, french doors to swimming pool and terrace, TV, CD, DVD, slippers & robes, coffee & tea, delicious breakfasts, served: in-suite, terrace or dining room. Explore the grounds, orchards, paddocks and meet 'our boys' the alpacas, not forgetting our very friendly dog, Kaimai. Nearby: cafes, wineries, beaches, golf, bushwalks... 'We love it here...so will you!'

Katikati *5 km SE of Katikati*
Tranquility Lodge *B&B Homestay*
Gayle & Capt Reynold Alvins
325 Rea Road,
Katikati
3178

Tel (07) 549 3581
or 027 452 2960
Fax (07) 549 3582
tranquilitylodge@xtra.co.nz
www.tranquilitylodge.co.nz

Double/Twin $150
Single $120
(Special breakfast)
Visa MC accepted
2 King (2 bdrm)
Bathrooms: 2 Ensuite

Nestled in a peaceful valley, warm kiwi hospitality and our friendly Maremma dogs, cats, farmyard pets await you. Take a seat on our large freestanding deck, relax to the tune of birdsong and stream while viewing the Kaimai Ranges, or play a game of Petanque beside our patio area. Each King suite is sumptuously furnished, has its own private entry and deck from which you can enjoy the view of our lifestyle farm and gardens. Bathrobes, slippers, toiletries and hairdryers are supplied in each ensuite.

Katikati *9 km SW of Katikati*
Burr-wood Countrystay *B&B Homestay*
Maureen and Alan Cook
449 Lund Road
RD 2, Katikati
3178

Tel (07) 549 2060
Fax (07) 549 2061
nzjewellery@clear.net.nz

Double/Twin $120-$130
Single $90-$100
(Full breakfast)
Dinner $30 per head
2 courses plus wine
We take one party only at a time
Visa MC accepted
Pet free home
Not suitable for small children
1 Queen 2 Single (2 bdrm)
Bathrooms: 1 Private

Burr-wood is set in a 2 1/2 acre garden and surrounded by native bush. An elevated situation, we overlook to a panorama of land, sea, harbour and islands. Enjoy breakfast which includes homemade bread and jams; complimentary pre-dinner drinks, Dinner is available by arrangement. We are 5 mins from SH2 and within easy reach of Bay of Plenty attractions. We make unique N.Z. Native Timber jewellery. Only one party at a time. Home baking, tea/coffee on arrival. Bathrobes, tea/coffee in rooms. Laundry. Internet for emails.

Omokoroa *13 km N of Tauranga*
Serendipity *B&B Homestay B & B and Homestay*
Sarath and Linda Vidanage
77 Harbour View Road,
Omokoroa,
Tauranga

Tel (07) 548 2044
or 021 999 815 (cell)
sarathv@yahoo.com
www.bnb.co.nz

Double/Twin $125
Single $85
(Full breakfast)
Children $30
Dinner $40
Visa MC accepted
Children welcome
4 Double/Twin (3 bdrm)
Bathrooms: 2 Private
2 bathrooms available

Welcome to our home and garden nestled above spectacular Omokoroa Beach. The beach is a short walk down the steps. Leisurely walking treks take you through the groves and gardens of the peninsula. A beautiful golf course and local hot pools are minutes away. We are a well-traveled couple who have found our paradise. We love to cook and offer a varied cuisine from traditional to exotic. The best of Tauranga and The Bay of Plenty. Free tel. to U.S /Canada,U.K high speed internet.

Omokoroa *17 km N of Tauranga*
Seascape *B&B*
Sue & Geoff Gripton
5 Waterview Terrace,
Omokoroa

Tel (07) 548 1027
or 021 171 1936
grippos@xtra.co.nz
www.seascapenz.com

Double/Twin $110-$120
Single $90
(Full breakfast)
Visa MC accepted
1 Double/Twin 2 Single (2 bdrm)
Bathrooms: 1 Ensuite

Come share our stunning views of Tauranga Harbour and Kaimais. On our doorstep are beaches, walkways, golf, hot pools, boat ramps etc. Just halfway between Tauranga and Katikati, we offer a double room with ensuite and TV, twin room with shared bathroom, both with tea/coffee. Enjoy a cooked or continental breakfast with homemade bread and jams while gazing at view. Only 3 1/2 kilometres from SH2, left at roundabout, 1st right, 1st left into Waterview Terrace. Geoff, Sue and our cat will welcome you.

Tauranga *3 km N of Tauranga Central*
Harbinger House *B&B Homestay*
Helen & Doug Fisher
209 Fraser Street,
Tauranga

Tel (07) 578 8801
or 027 236 8660
or 0274 583 049
Fax (07) 579 4101
d-h.fisher@xtra.co.nz
www.harbinger.co.nz

Double/Twin $90-$110
Single $75-$85
(Continental breakfast)
Children half price
Dinner $35 Visa MC accepted
2 Queen 2 Single (3 bdrm)
Bathrooms: 1 Guest share

Harbinger House provides affordable luxury in the heart of Tauranga, being close to hospital, conference facilities, downtown and a new shopping mall 100 metres away. Our upstairs has been renovated with your comfort in mind, using quality furnishings, linen, bathrobes, fresh flowers, tea and coffee. Laundry facilities are available. The queen rooms have separate vanities and private balconies. Breakfast is continental using fresh local ingredients where possible. Complimentary pick up from public transport depots and off-street parking is provided.

Tauranga *8 km NW of Tauranga*
Oakridge Views *B&B*
Diane & Trevor Hinton
557 Cambridge Road,
Tauriko,
Tauranga

Tel (07) 543 0292
or 027 285 2189
Fax (07) 543 0294
oakridge.views@xtra.co.nz
www.oakridgeviews.co.nz

Double/Twin $110-$135
Single $70-$90
(Full breakfast)
Children under 12 $30
Cooked breakfast $10 extra
Children and pets welcome
1 Queen 1 Twin (2 bdrm)
Bathrooms: 1 Ensuite 1 Private

Welcome to Oakridge Views, where your comfort is our concern. Enjoy our panoramic views of gardens and rolling hills. Relax in our comfortable 1 level home away from home with an acre of gardens. Handy to some of the top restaurants in the bay. Only 10 minutes to downtown Tauranga and over the harbour bridge to Mt Maunganui. Attractions include garden walks, tramping, parks, wineries, beaches, golf courses. Spa pool available. We share our home with our little Bichon Frise, "Penny".

Tauranga - Matua *3 km S of Tauranga*

Aramoana *B&B*

Doreen Anderson
9 Seaway Terrace,
Matua,
Tauranga

Tel (07) 576 3058
or 027 320 0203
Fax (07) 576 3758
andersondem@xtra.co.nz
www.aramoanabnb.co.nz

Double/Twin $120
Single $80
(Full breakfast)
Children $35
Eftpos accepted
Children welcome
1 Queen 1 Twin (2 bdrm)
Bathrooms: 1 Guest share

Relax in comfort by the sea with fabulous views of the harbour and Mt Maunganui. Watch the ships coming and going to the port. Enjoy the lights at night and the moonlight sparkling on the water. Walk along the beach to parks. Dine or shop in nearby Cherrywood village or drive to golf, the nearest course only 4 minutes away. Use Aramoana as your base to explore the bay. Your host has extensive knowledge of the area and will make you very welcome.

～

Tauranga - Whakamarama *15 km N of Tauranga*

Wildhaven Farm *Luxury B&B*

Robert & Bryony Cross
Wildhaven Farm, 257
Whakamarama Road,
RD 6, Tauranga

Tel (07) 552 5484 or 021 0235 1665
Fax (07) 552 5484
roberthhcross@eol.co.nz
http://wildhaven.co.nz

Double/Twin $135 Single $135
(Full breakfast)
Children $15 per child per night
3 course dinner $35 pp by arrangement
Payment by cash/cheque/internet
Children welcome
Non smokers only
1 Double/Twin (1 bdrm)
Bathrooms: 1 Ensuite
Large shower room with heated towel rail and hair dryer

We warmly welcome guests to our little slice of paradise. Our 77 acre working farm has uninterrupted coastal views of Mount Maunganui, north to the Alderman Islands, which you can enjoy from the extensive landscaped gardens and heated swimming pool. We have one large air-conditioned double bedroom, a fold down sofa bed and a cot provides sleeping accommodation for children. Your hosts are, Robert & Bryony and their two children Emma (10) and Freddie (8) and their friendly dog, Hugo.

Mt Maunganui *9 km S of Mt Maunganui*
Pembroke House *B&B*
Cathy & Graham Burgess
12 Santa Fe Key,
Royal Palm Beach,
Papamoa/Mt Maunganui

Tel (07) 572 1000
PembrokeHouse@xtra.co.nz
www.pembrokehouse.co.nz

Double/Twin $100-$110
Single $80
(Full breakfast)
Children $35
Visa MC accepted
2 Queen 1 Twin (3 bdrm)
Bathrooms: 2 Ensuite 1 Private

A modern home. Cross the road to the Ocean Beach, where you can enjoy swimming, surfing and beach walks. Enjoy stunning sea views while dining at breakfast. Near Fashion Island and Palm Beach Shopping Plaza, restaurants and golf courses. Near Mount Maunganui, Tauranga, Rotorua and Whakatane. Separate guest lounge with TV and tea making facilities. Cathy, a schoolteacher, and Graham, semi-retired - your hosts. We are widely travelled and enjoy meeting people. Our home is shared with our Persian cat, Crystal. Unsuitable for pre-schoolers.

Mt Maunganui - Papamoa *9 km SE of Mt Maunganui*
Hesford House *B&B Homestay*
Sally & Derek Hesford
45 Gravatt Road,
Royal Palm Beach,
Papamoa 3118/Mt Maunganui

Tel (07) 572 2825
derek.sally@clear.net.nz
www.hesfordhouse.co.nz

Double/Twin $90-$140
Single $75-$90
(Full breakfast)
Children Negotiable
Visa MC accepted
Pet free home
2 Queen 1 Twin (3 bdrm)
Bathrooms: 1 Ensuite 1 Guest share

We invite you to stay in our tastefully decorated character home. Enjoy panoramic views of the Papamoa Hills together with exquisite sunsets. Opposite is the fabulous Fashion Island with various shops, cafes, popular restaurants, internet cafe and English Pub. Relax in a beautiful garden setting. Complimentary tea/coffee facilities, fridge and TVs in each room. Many attractions including Classic Flyer and museum. A short stroll to our magnificent beach and only 50 minutes drive to Rotorua, Whakatane and Whangamata (Coromandel). Courtesy pickup from public transport.

Mt Maunganui *3 km S of Mt. Maunganui*
Beachside *B&B*

Lorraine & Jim Robertson
21B Oceanbeach Road,
Mt Maunganui

Tel (07) 574 0960
or 021 238 0598
beachside@ihug.co.nz
www.beachsidebnb.co.nz

Double/Twin $100-$140
Single $80-$100
(Full breakfast)
Visa MC accepted
1 King/Twin 2 Queen (3 bdrm)
Bathrooms: 2 Ensuite 1 Private

We are 30 seconds to NZ's most popular beach, but still close to the action and golf courses but far enough away to be quiet. Off-street parking, courtesy transport to/from local airport/buses. Enjoy stunning sea views from our guest lounge while indulging in a generous cooked breakfast plus seasonal fresh fruit salad, home-baked bread & real expresso coffee. We are widely travelled, enjoy meeting and helping our guests. Use our B&B as a base to explore White Island, Rotorua & Coromandel Peninsula.

Te Puke *1 km NW of Te Puke town*
Princess Street Apartment. *B&B Apartment with Kitchen*

The Wilson Family
7 Princess Street,
Te Puke,
3119

Tel (07) 573 9345
Fax (07) 573 9354
ruth_wilson@xtra.co.nz

Double/Twin $90
Single $70
(Continental breakfast provisions)
Children $15 per child
Children welcome
1 King/Twin 2 Twin (2 bdrm)
Bathrooms: 1 Ensuite 1 Private

Fully self contained apartment situated in a quiet cul-de-sac in central Te Puke within walking distance to the township. Enjoy the many restaurants, cafes and shops. The modern apartment, with a full kitchen, laundry facilities, Sky T.V. overlooks a solar heated swimming pool and a tranquil garden setting for your enjoyment. View the many amenities Te Puke has to offer - Kiwifruit Capital of the World, lovely beaches, numerous excellent golf courses nearby, and a 30-40 minute drive from Tauranga, Mount Maunganui, Whakatane and Rotorua.

Te Puke *1.6 km W of Te Puke township*
Lazy Daze Cottage and Homestay *Homestay Cottage with Kitchen*
Quality cottage and homestay
Mel and Sharron Yeates
144 Boucher Ave,
Te Puke,
Bay of Plenty

Tel (07) 573 8188
or 027 271 2188
or 027 626 2926
Fax (07) 573 8188
sharron.yeates@clear.net.nz
www.lazydazecottage.co.nz

Double/Twin $120
Single $100
(Full breakfast provisions)
Children & extra guests $40
Children and pets welcome
2 Queen (2 bdrm)
Bathrooms: 2 Private no bath

Te Puke: Temperate climate. 40 minutes to Rotorua's famous attractions and only 15 minutes to Mt Maunganui, Tauranga. Popular with tourists for many reasons. Golf, fishing, sandy beaches are only 3 of the attractions that make this a great place to visit. We are keen golfers and equipment is available for your use. We have regular visits from grandchildren, your area will be private and quiet. We have 1 small dog.

Te Puke *3.5 km S of Te Puke*
Aotea Villa *B&B Self Contained Bungalow*
Peter & Nanette Miller
246 Te Matai Road,
Te Puke
3188

Tel (07) 573 9433
Fax (07) 573 9433
Millerph@xtra.co.nz
www.aoteavilla.co.nz

Double/Twin $115-$120
Single $90-$95
(Full breakfast)
Children $30 under 13 years
Visa MC accepted
Children and pets welcome
2 Queen 4 Single (3 bdrm)
Bathrooms: 1 Ensuite 1 Guest share
Villa guest share, bungalow has ensuite

Welcome to our relaxing and comfortable 1910 villa situated in the heart of the vibrant Bay of Plenty in pictuesque kiwifruit and avocado countryside. We are minutes from Te Puke, 45 minutes from Whakatane and Rotorua and 20 minutes from Tauranga and Mount Maunganui. Enjoy our spa and swimming pool or relax on our wisteria covered verandahs and view our beautiful sunsets. Laundry and internet facilities. Guest lounge and games room. Stunning local restaurants, excellent golf course close by. Visit our website to findout more.

Pukehina Beach *21 km E of Te Puke*
Homestay on the Beach *Homestay*

Alison & Paul Carter
217 Pukehina Parade,
Pukehina Beach, RD 9, Te Puke

Tel (07) 533 3988 or 027 276 7305
or 027 372 2886
Fax (07) 533 3988
p.a.carter@pukehina-beach.co.nz
www.homestays.net.nz/pukehina.htm

Double/Twin $120-$130 Single $80
(Full breakfast)
Children half price
Dinner $40
Unit $160
Visa MC accepted
Pet free home   Children welcome
2 Double/Twin (2 bdrm)
Bathrooms: 1 Guest share

Welcome to our beachfront home situated on the Pacific Ocean. Guests accommodation is downstairs, which allows complete privacy if desired, includes T.V. Lounge with Coffee/Tea, Fridge, Microwave. A Unit rate is also available. Enjoy magnificent views from your own sundeck, including white Island volcano and occasional visits from Dolphins and Orcas. Te Puke Golf Course 13km away. 30-40 minute drive from Tauranga, Mount Maunganui, Whakatane and Rotorua. Licensed Restaurant/Cafes 2km. Stunning sunrises and sunsets - swimming, walks or relax and enjoy our unique paradise.

Matata *34 km W of Whakatane*
Pohutukawa Beach B&B & Cottage
B&B Farmstay Cottage with Kitchen
Charlotte & Jorg Prinz
693 State Highway 2,
RD 4, Whakatane

Tel (07) 322 2182
Fax (07) 322 2186
joe@prinztours.co.nz
www.beachbnb.co.nz

Double/Twin $120-$140
Single $110
(Continental breakfast)
Dinner $25-$50
Self-contained cottage (sleeps 6) $160-$180
Visa MC accepted
Children welcome
1 King/Twin 2 Queen
1 Double/Twin 1 Twin (4 bdrm)
Bathrooms: 2 Ensuite 1 Private

Awesome Views. Beautiful setting. Interesting hosts. Rural and cosy. Organic farming and gardening. Two ensuite rooms. Self-contained or fully serviced guest house for six people. Relaxing at the pool, sauna and garden. Guided tours on demand. Dinners on request. English and German spoken. You are welcome!

Matata - Pikowai *30 km NW of Whakatane*
Fothergills on Mimiha
S/C Suite with kitchen. Separate fully equipped Cottage.

Bev & Hilton Fothergill
84 Mimiha Road, Pikowai/Matata, Whakatane

Tel (07) 322 2224 or 0274 605 958
or 021 131 5171   Fax (07) 322 2224
bev@fothergills.co.nz www.fothergills.co.nz

Double/Twin $108-$170
Single $100-$125 (Special breakfast)
Children $20 under 13
$30 teens & extra adults
Dinner $50 each, by arrangement
Cottage 2-nights minimum, $320
$750 p.w. double
Visa MC accepted
Children and pets welcome
1 King/Twin 2 Queen 1 Twin (4 bdrm)
Bathrooms: 1 Ensuite 2 Private, 1bathroom in each venue

Our B&B suite is stylish, comfortable, peaceful and quiet. We are friendly, helpful, hospitable hosts. Breakfasts, served in house or garden, are garden-fresh, home-made and delicious. Mimiha Cottage, Qualmark 4 stars, is fully equipped, everything you need for weekend or longer. Stroll in our idyllic garden, play petanque, walk along the unspoilt beach, up the country road or climb the wonderful hills, with our two fox terriers for company. After a busy day, soak in the outdoor spa. Come and enjoy this slice of heaven!

Whakatane *18 km S of Whakatane*
Omataroa Deer Farm *Farmstay*
Jill & John Needham
Paul Road,
RD 2,
Whakatane
3192

Tel (07) 322 8399
Fax (07) 322 8399
jill-needham@xtra.co.nz

Double/Twin $105
Single $80
(Full breakfast)
Children $40
Dinner $25
1 King 1 Queen (2 bdrm)
Bathrooms: 1 Ensuite 1 Private

We invite you to stay with us in our contemporary home which sits high on a hill commanding panoramic views. We farm deer organically and grow hydrangeas for export. You will be the only guest so you have sole use of a quiet private wing. Your evening meal will be venison, lamb or fresh seafood with home-grown vegetables. We dive, fish, tramp, ski, golf and love to travel. Laundry available.

Whakatane *7 km W of Whakatane*

Whakatane Homestay- Leaburn Farm *Homestay Homestay on a dairy farm*
Kathleen & Jim Law
237 Thornton Road, RD 4, Whakatane 3194

Tel (07) 308 7487 or 021 212 1196
Fax (07) 308 7437
kath.law@xtra.co.nz
www.whakatanehomestay.co.nz

Double/Twin $90 Single $60-$65 (Full breakfast)
Dinner $25 - $35 negotiable
Visa MC accepted
Pet free home Pets welcome
1 Queen 2 Single (2 bdrm)
Bathrooms: 1 Guest share

Looking for peace and quiet, or do you want to explore this sunshine coast? If stimulating conversation or a browse in an extensive library is something you enjoy, you are welcome here.

Other guests comments over the 25 years we have been home-hosting, include: *"Fantastic value for money with a very interesting friendly couple"* Alan & Janet..U.K. *"Our first experience of B & B has left a wonderful impression."* David & Terri.NZ .> *"Wish we could be friends for life".* Jim and Pat U.S.A.

As young oldies, we enjoy company, farming tales, travel, business interests, and your choice of topic.

We are handy to the golf course, 7km to thriving Whakatane Township. Special interests of genealogy, Lions Club,and bowls . We have a cafe/restaurant,and gift shop on the property.

Our queen-bedded guest room is adjacent to a spa bathroom, separate shower and toilet, and is shared only with other guests if the twin bedroom is occupied. Be as busy as you like or enjoy restful country atmosphere. Pamper yourselves at our place.

Whakatane *10 km S of Whakatane*
Baker's *B&B Homestay Cottage with Kitchen*

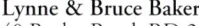

Lynne & Bruce Baker
40 Butler Road, RD 2, Whakatane

Tel (07) 307 0368 or 027 284 6996
Fax (07) 307 0368
bakers@world-net.co.nz
www.bakershomestay.co.nz

Double/Twin $120-$140
Single $90-$110
(Continental breakfast)
Children $20
Dinner $50 by arrangement
(wine included)
Self-contained private cottage available
Visa MC accepted
Children and pets welcome
1 King/Twin 2 Queen 2 Single (4 bdrm)
Bathrooms: 2 Ensuite 1 Private Fully tiled private ensuites

A friendly welcome to our lovely country home nestled amongst mature gardens croquet lawn and Avocado orchard. Enjoy our Swimming or spa pool Choose between our delightful fully self-contained 2 bedroom cottage or be pampered with bed & our special breakfast in our warm spacious home. Cosy guest lounge with comfortable sofas to relax on. Lynne and Bruce are keen outdoor hosts enjoying fishing, surfing, gardening and travel. White Island tours, dolphin watching, deep-sea fishing and diving activities can be arranged for your memorable stay.

Whakatane *1.5 km SE of Whakatane Central*
Crestwood Homestay *Luxury B&B*

Janet & Peter McKechnie
2 Crestwood Rise,
Whakatane,
Bay of Plenty

Tel (07) 308 7554
or 0800 111 449
or 027 624 624 8
Fax (07) 308 7551
pandjmckechnie@xtra.co.nz
www.crestwood-homestay.co.nz

Double/Twin $120-$140
Single $90-$120
(Continental breakfast)
Dinner $40 (wine included)
Visa MC accepted
1 Queen 2 Single (2 bdrm)
Bathrooms: 1 Private 1 Guest share Separate rate for guest sharing facilities

S tyle, comfort,warmth, stunning sea views and five minutes drive to town. Ohope Beach 5kms. Private, quiet self contained upstairs area with spacious rooms, guest lounge, tea/coffee/fridge area and balcony to capture lovely views. Free internet, phone, TV, toiletries, hairdryer and all home comforts. Ideal for four people travelling together Wharf nearby for White Island volcano trips, dolphin watching and fishing charters. Helpful friendly hosts enjoy rugby, fly fishing, coastguard activities, chats around the table and family life.

Ohope Beach *8 km N of Whakatane*
The Rafters *Apartment with Kitchen*

Pat Rafter
261A Pohutukawa Avenue, Ohope Beach

Tel (07) 312 4856
Fax (07) 312 4856
The_Rafters_Ohope@xtra.co.nz
www.wave.co.nz/pages/macaulay/The_
Rafters.htm

Double/Twin $80 Single $75
(Accommodation only)
Children $10
Extra adult $20, limit 1
Children and pets welcome
1 King 1 Single (2 bdrm)
Bathrooms: 1 Ensuite

Breakfast is not supplied, Unit is self-contained. Minimum 2 night stay. Maximum 3 guests. Sea views: White, Whale islands, East Coast. Safe swimming. Many interesting walks. Golf, tennis, bowls, all within minutes.

Licensed Chartered Club Restaurant opposite. Trips to volcanic White Island, fishing, jet boating, diving, swimming with dolphins arranged.

Full cooking facilities; private entrance, sunken garden, BBQ. Complimentary: tea, coffee, biscuits, fruit, newspaper, personal laundry service. Pat's interests are: philosophy, theology, history, English literature, the making of grape wines and all spirits, golf, bowls, music and tramping. I have a friendly weimaraner dog.

Courtesy car available. House trained animals welcomed. 4 restaurants and oyster farm within 5 minutes drive. I look forward to your company and assure you unique hospitality.

Directions: on reaching Ohope Beach turn right, proceed 2km to 261A (beach-side) name "Rafters" on a brick letterbox with illuminated B&B sign.

Ohope Beach *6 km E of Whakatane*
Shiloah *B&B Homestay Cottage with Kitchen*

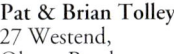

Pat & Brian Tolley
27 Westend,
Ohope Beach

Tel (07) 312 4401
Fax (07) 312 4401

Double/Twin $90-$100
Single $50-$60
(Full breakfast)
Children half price
Dinner $18-25 by arrangement
Self-contained unit available
1 Queen 1 Twin 4 Single (2 bdrm)
Bathrooms: 2 Private bathrooms
in house, 1 Guest share in cottage
- Showers Only

Homestay: paradise on the beach - view White Island and enjoy our hospitality. Facilities available for disabled guests - 5% discount. Well travelled. Also available is a self-catered unit, separate from our B&B, with 1 twin bedroom, 1 single bed and bed settee if required, complete with shower and kitchenette. Tariff; $60 own bedding, extra if supplied. Access to beach across road. Fishing, swimming, surfing, and bush walks.

Ohope Beach *8 km SE of Whakatane*
Oceanspray Homestay *Homestay Apartment with Kitchen*
Cottage with Kitchen

Frances & John Galbraith
283A Pohutukawa Avenue,
Ohope, Bay of Plenty

Tel (07) 312 4112 or 027 286 6824
Fax (07) 312 4192
frances@oceanspray.co.nz
www.oceanspray.co.nz

Double/Twin $150-$190
Single $80-$100
(Full breakfast provisions)
Children negotiable
Visa MC accepted
Children welcome
3 Queen 2 Twin (5 bdrm)
Bathrooms: 1 Ensuite 2 Private
Apartment ensuite & bathroom, Cottage own bathroom

Welcome to our beachfront home. Wonderful sea views from our upstairs decks. Our modern downstairs 3 bedroom apartment is self-contained with own kitchen, lounge, two bathrooms (one ensuite). Adjacent to our house is a 2 bedroom, modern, self-contained cottage. Families welcome. Home comforts - Sky TV, books, videos/DVDs/toys for children. Continental breakfast provisions are supplied into your unit. John's pursuits are kayaking and longline fishing. Frances enjoys entertaining and providing excellent cuisine. Our very sociable cat, Barnaby, will also greet you with a warm welcome.

Ohope *10 km SE of Whakatane*
Moanarua Beach Cottage *Cottage with Kitchen*

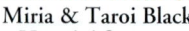

Miria & Taroi Black
2 Hoterini Street,
Ohope

Tel (07) 312 5924
or 021 255 6192
info@moanarua.co.nz
www.moanarua.co.nz

Double/Twin $110-$140
Single $90-$130
(Continental breakfast)
Children 1 baby or small child
Dinner by arrangement
1 King (1 bdrm)
Bathrooms: 1 Ensuite

Naumai, haere mai Miria and Taroi welcome you to a unique cultural experience in a romantic hideaway, a restful retreat nestled between the ocean and the harbour in sunny Ohope. Feel free to use BBQ, luxury spa and expansive decks with views of ocean and harbour. Chat with us about local history and Maori art works that adorn our home, cottage and garden. Kick back, relax in your private fully self-contained cottage or enjoy many local activities. Boat tours and kayaks available for hire.

Ohope Beach *7.5 km E of Whakatane*
Seaview Bed and Breakfast *B&B Homestay*

Lynnette and Ross Nicholson
33 Waterford Avenue,
Waterford Estate, Ohope

Tel (07) 312 6005 or 021 207 3838
Fax (07) 312 6005
r.lnicholson@xtra.co.nz
www.seaviewbb.co.nz

Double/Twin $110-$130
Single $90-$100
(Continental breakfast)
Children by negotiation
Dinner $35pp by arrangement
Visa MC accepted
Children welcome
1 Queen 1 Double/Twin 1 Twin (3 bdrm)
Bathrooms: 1 Guest share plus one extra WC with basin

Relax and enjoy the quiet gated location of Seaview with the lovely Ohope Beach just metres away. From the upstairs deck and diningroom, guests can view White Island and towards Cape Runaway, on clear days.Guests have their own lounge - TV/Video, Tea/Coffee facilities, BBQ, Microwave. Laundry available.Golf Club, Restaurants, Playground are all close by. Lynnette and Ross, who are former farmers, have many interests including Sea/Lake fishing, Reading, Sports, Cooking.We, and a spoilt cat,"Two Bob", will ensure you enjoy your stay at Ohope.

Opotiki *18 km E of Opotiki*
Coral's B&B *B&B Farmstay Cottage with Kitchen*
Coral Parkinson
Morice's Bay,
Highway 35,
RD 1,
Opotiki

Tel (07) 315 8052
or 021 299 9757
coralsb.b@wxc.net.nz

Double/Twin $130
Single $70-$90
(Continental breakfast)
Children $15
Breakfast $10pp by arrangement
Children and pets welcome
2 Queen 2 Single (3 bdrm)
Bathrooms: 1 Private

We provide self-contained accommodation located on our hobby farm. As well as pets and farm animals we collect varied memorabilia. Enjoy the beach and bird life; swim at nearby sandy surf beach. Fish, ramble over the rocks, explore caves. Our 2 storied cottage features lead-light windows, native timbers, large decks look out across the bay and native bush. 3 golf courses within an hours drive; covered parking, home-made bread and preserves. We have a clasic English Daimler car Visit our local Marae.

Opotiki *6 km W of Opotiki*
Coast View *Apartment with Kitchen*
Margaret Green
28 Paerata Ridge Road,
RD 2,
Opotiki

Tel (07) 315 5895
margg@xtra.co.nz

Double/Twin $90-$120
Single $60-$90
(Full breakfast)
Children $40-$60
Children welcome
1 King/Twin (1 bdrm)
Bathrooms: 1 Private

Relax in my bright, comfortable, fully self-contained ground floor unit with separate bedroom. Superb view of the Bay coast and five minutes from the beach. Base yourself here while you enjoy the attractions of this interesting area. I work part time, but I will enjoy meeting you and sharing my attractive home and warm hospitality. I have been an active tramper in this area and now enjoy biking, reading, talking and relaxing. All breakfast ingredients are provided. There are restaurants and take-aways available in Opotiki.

Opotiki *3 km N of Opotiki*
Airlie Lodge *Luxury B&B Luxury Home Stay*

Margaret & John Hunter
99 Beach Road Extension,
Opotiki
3169

Tel (07) 315 8345
or 027 482 5500
airlielodge@xtra.co.nz
www.airlielodge.co.nz

Double/Twin $155-$185
(Full breakfast)
Dinners by arrangement
Eftpos accepted
Pet free home
Not suitable for children
2 King 1 Queen (3 bdrm)
Bathrooms: 2 Ensuite 1 Guest share

The spectacular views from this impressive home takes in panoramic sea and valley scenes, facing out to Whale and White Islands. Your hosts warmly welcome you to Airlie Lodge, and this very special part of the East Coast. Set in lovely garden surroundings on the hill overlooking Opotiki. We make every effort to make your stay memorable and special. Guest accommodation and decor is to a very high standard. Enjoy the luxury of one of the two separate sunny private guest wings in our home.

Opotiki - Waihau Bay *112 km N of Opotiki*
Waihau Bay Homestay *B&B Homestay Apartment with Kitchen*

Noelene & Merv Topia
10942 State highway 35
Waihau Bay, RD 3, Opotiki

Tel (07) 325 3674
or 0800 240 170
n.topia@clear.net.nz
www.waihaubayhomestay.co.nz

Double/Twin $85-$110
Single $55-$75
(Continental breakfast)
Children ¹/₂ price
Dinner $30
Visa MC Eftpos accepted
Children and pets welcome
2 King 1 Queen 2 Twin
2 Single (4 bdrm)
Bathrooms: 3 Ensuite 1 Private
All bathrooms are suitable for disabled

Surrounded by unspoiled beauty we invite you to come and enjoy magnificent views, stunning sunsets, swim, go diving, kayaking (we have kayaks) or just walk along the sandy beach. You are most welcome to join Merv when he checks his craypots each morning and his catches are our cuisine specialty. Fishing trips, horse treks and guided cultural walks are also available. We have 2 self-contained units with disabled facilities, and a double room with ensuite. Our cat Tosca and our small dog Kaykay enjoy making new friends.

Rotorua *4 km SW of Rotorua*

B&B Approved

Hunts Farm *Farmstay*

Maureen & John Hunt
363 Pukehangi Road, Rotorua (Home 1: top photo)
Tel (07) 348 1352 or 027 4863477

Sonya Hunt & Dave Cronshaw
359 Pukehangi Road, Rotorua (Home 2: side photos)
Tel (07) 348 2874 or 027 4863477
sonyahunt@xtra.co.nz
www.bnb.co.nz/hunt.html

Double/Twin $125 Single $80 (Full breakfast)
Children $30 Children welcome
Guest areas have private entrances, lounges with tea/coffee
facilities, and fridges
1 King/Twin 2 Queen 2 Twin 2 Single (4 bdrm)
Bathrooms: 2 Ensuite 1 Guest share

Come and relax in our neighbouring new homes as we help you plan your itinerary and book your local tours. Explore our 150 acre scenic farm running beef and deer. Views of farm, lake, forest and city are uninterrupted panoramic and magical. Guest areas have private entrances, lounges with tea/coffee facilities and fridges.

Home 1 (363) Maureen and John Hunt: Single story ranch style home, private guest wing with TV. Rosie our chief farm helper who lives in her kennel in the garden at 363 replaces our grown family. Two triple rooms each with ensuite and private terrace. 1 Queen with Single and ensuite, 1 King Twin with single and ensuite.

Home 2 (359) Sonya Hunt and Dave Cronshaw: Upstairs private guest wing available to one group at a time only. Well suited for family groups. Enjoy our 12 m swimming pool and our spacious lawns and gardens. At 359 the family includes 2 children and an outdoor cat and dog. 1 Queen with 3 single and ensuite. Complementary high speed wireless internet access available.

Rotorua - Ngakuru *32 km S of Rotorua*
Te Ana Farmstay *Farmstay Cottage No Kitchen*
The Oberer Residence:
Heather Oberer
Poutakataka Road,
Ngakuru, RD 1, Rotorua

Tel (07) 333 2720
or 021 828 151
Fax (07) 333 2720
teanafarmstay@xtra.co.nz
www.teanafarmstay.co.nz

Double/Twin $110-$150
Single $90
(Special breakfast)
Children negotiable
Dinner by prior arrangement
Children welcome
2 Queen 4 Single (4 bdrm)
Bathrooms: 2 Ensuite 1 Family share

Te Ana, The Oberer family sanctuary since 1936, offers peace and tranquility in a spacious rural garden setting affording magnificent views of lake, volcanically-formed hills and lush farmland. Enjoy a leisurely stroll before joining host for a very generous country breakfast. Ideal base from which to explore the Rotorua and Taupo attractions, Waiotapu and Waimungu Thermal Reserves, Waikite Thermal mineral swimming pool and Tamaki Tours Hangi. Families welcomed by Jack, our loyal Jack Russell. Farm tour and fishing rod available.

Rotorua *4 km S of Rotorua*
Serendipity Homestay *B&B Homestay*
Kate & Brian Gore
3 Kerswell Terrace,
Tihi-o-Tonga,
Rotorua

Tel (07) 347 9385
or 027 609 3268
b.gore@clear.net.nz
www.serendipityhomestay.co.nz

Double/Twin $130-$140
Single $80
(Special breakfast)
Children under 12 $35
Dinner $35 by arrangement
Visa MC accepted
Pet free home
Children welcome
1 Queen 2 Single (2 bdrm)
Bathrooms: 1 Private spa bath plus shower

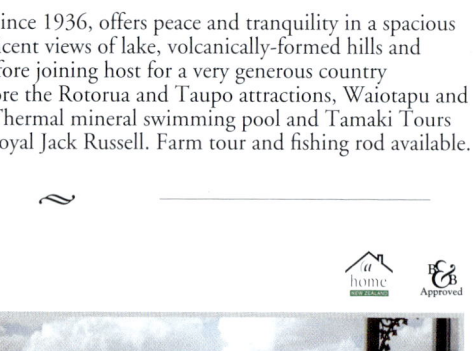

Marvel at unsurpassed views of geysers, city, lakes and beyond. Relax in all day sun, on the deck, in the conservatory or in the privacy of our garden. Indulge in comfort, home-cooked cuisine and the friendly folk who have been enjoying hosting for many years. Our interests are, golf, tramping, travel, the environment, antiques and sharing our extensive local and national knowledge with you. Let us advise you on the 'must see' list while in Rotorua and other highlights of our beautiful country. Welcome!

Rotorua *14 km NE of Rotorua*

Brunswick *Homestay*
Joy & Lin Cathcart
99 Brunswick Drive,
RD 4,
Rotorua 3221

Tel (07) 350 1472
or mob 021 256 5355
Fax (07) 350 1472
joylin@clear.net.nz

Double/Twin $120
Single $75
(Full breakfast)
Visa MC accepted
Pet free home
Not suitable for children
1 King (1 bdrm)
Bathrooms: 1 Private
The bathroom is adjacent to the bedroom

With peaceful surroundings and beautiful views over Lake Rotorua "Brunswick" is 15 mins from Rotorua City centre and 5mins from Rotorua Airport. Having retired from dairy farming Lin now enjoys his golf; Joy plays bridge and gardening is a shared hobby. Our guest room has TV, hot drink facilities, refrigerator and balcony. We are smoke-free and have no pets. After 17 years of hosting and many return guests, a cuppa, Joy's homebaking and a warm welcome await you! Please phone or e-mail for directions.

Rotorua Central *0.5 km S of Post Office*

Tresco Classical Oasis B&B *B&B*
Trinka & Trevor
3 Toko Street, Rotorua

Tel (07) 348 9611
or Freephone 0800 873 726
or 021 355 777
Fax (07) 348 9611
trescorotorua@xtra.co.nz
www.trescorotorua.co.nz

Double/Twin $120-$150
Single $80-$120
(Full breakfast)
Double/Triple $150-$180
Visa MC Eftpos accepted
Pet free home
1 King/Twin 1 King 3 Queen
2 Double/Twin 2 Twin 2 Single (7 bdrm)
Bathrooms: 4 Ensuite 1 Private 2 Guest share

Central location - Just 2 minutes walk to City. 10 minutes walk Polynesian pools and Lake. In a quiet tree-lined street, with gardens, Rotorua's only B&B with authentic Geothermal Hot Pool and thermal central heating. Guests say, " Top marks for full cooked breakfast, cleanliness, friendliness, hospitality, good service and location". We provide Courtesy transport, advice and regional tours. Laundry/drying room. Wireless/Internet. 'Lonely Planet Guide' recommended. We welcome you. [Also New - Fabulous Lake Rotorua Watersedge'Tresco' Cottage and Auckland Waterfront Tresco].

Rotorua *5 km SE of Rotorua*
Walker Homestay & B&B *B&B Homestay Cottage with Kitchen*

Colleen & Isaac Walker
13 Glenfield Road, Owhata, Rotorua

Tel (07) 345 3882
or 021 050 9633
Fax (07) 345 3856
colleen.walker@clear.net.nz

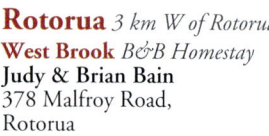

Double/Twin $98-$130
Single $55-$70
(Continental breakfast)
Children half price
Dinner $30 by arrangement
Extra guest $20
Visa MC accepted
Children welcome
1 Queen 1 Double/Twin 1 Twin
1 Single (3 bdrm)
Bathrooms: 1 Ensuite 1 Private Cottage has own bathroom. Room in house - ensuite

2 bedroom cottage in own garden area has lounge, kitchen, bathroom,and laundry. Room in house has ensuite; tea/coffee facilities; microwave; separate entrance and access to hosts living area. Have complete privacy or be one of the family. BBQ available. Colleen is a business administration tutor and Isaac (Ike), a NZ Maori,is a coach driver with a background of farming and paper industry, keen fisherman and golfer. 2 friendly dachshund dogs will welcome you. 24 hours notice for Dinner. Off-road parking.

Rotorua *3 km W of Rotorua*
West Brook *B&B Homestay*

Judy & Brian Bain
378 Malfroy Road,
Rotorua

Tel (07) 347 8073
Fax (07) 347 8073

Double/Twin $90
Single $50
(Continental breakfast)
Children under 12 half price
Dinner $25
Visa MC accepted
Children welcome
4 Single (2 bdrm)
Bathrooms: 1 Family share

Retired farmers with years of hospitality involvement, live 3km from city on western outskirts. Interests include meeting people, farming, international current affairs. Brian a Rotorua Host Lions member, Judy's interest extend to all aspects of homemaking and gardening. Both well appointed comfy guest rooms are equipped with electric blankets. The friendly front door welcome and chatter over the meal table add up to our motto: home away from home. Assistance with sightseeing planning and transport to and from tourist centre available.

Rotorua - Ngongotaha *17 km N of Rotorua*
Clover Downs Estate *B&B Homestay Farmstay*
Lyn & Lloyd Ferris
175 Jackson Road, RD 2, Ngongotaha, Rotorua

Tel (07) 332 2366 , 021 712 866   Fax (07) 332 2367
Reservations@cloverdowns.co.nz
www.accommodationinrotorua.co.nz

Double/Twin $235-$335 Single $220-$330
(Special breakfast)
Children negotiable
Visa MC Diners Amex accepted
Children welcome
3 King/Twin 1 King (4 bdrm)
Bathrooms: 4 Ensuite

Welcome to our fine country Bed & Breakfast accommodation on a deer and ostrich farm, nestled in a peaceful country setting just 15 minutes drive north of Rotorua city.

We can offer a choice of four individually decorated spacious king-size suites each comprising ensuite bathroom, tea/coffee making facilities, refrigerator, telephone, ironing facilities, hairdryer, TV, VCR, stereo & individual outdoor decks. We

serve a leisurely breakfast each morning which, if you desire, is followed by our popular free deer and ostrich farm tour.

Visit our awesome cultural and scenic attractions. Minutes drive from our property you will discover a myriad of things to do and see: stand on active volcanoes, peer into craters, see boiling mud or just soak in a mineral pool. We can advise you on trout fishing at one of the many lakes and rivers in the area, walk cool forest glades or maybe play a round of golf. With days as busy as this you'll be glad to come home to our gracious haven of relaxation. If you wish to go out, Rotorua has some wonderful restaurants and cafes. or you may like to enjoy a Maori hangi and concert. We strive to exceed our guests' expectations through an ineffable blend of warmth, generosity and detail.

Directions: Take State Highway 5 to roundabout. Travel thru Ngongotaha village on Hamurana Road - go over railway line then take third left into Central Road. Turn first right into Jackson Road - Clover Downs Estate is number 175 on left hand side.

Rotorua *12 km NE of Rotorua*
Eucalyptus Tree Country Homestay *B&B Homestay Farmstay*

Manfred & Is Fischer
66 State Highway 33,
RD 4,
Rotorua

Tel (07) 345 5325
or mobile 027 261 6142
Fax (07) 345 5325
euc.countryhome@ihug.co.nz
http://homepages.ihug.co.nz/~euc.
countryhome

Double/Twin $100-$120
Single $70-$80 (Full breakfast)
Dinner $30-40
1 King/Twin 2 Queen
1 Double/Twin (3 bdrm)
Bathrooms: 1 Private 1 Guest share

Welcome to our quiet, smokefree, high quality country home. On our small farm near Lake Rotorua, close to Lake Rotoiti and Okataina, we have calves, sheep, chickens, ducks, rabbits, organic vegetables and fruit trees. Native bush drive to clear trophy trout fishing lakes and bush walks, thermal area, Maori culture, hot pools, whitewater rafting. Our hobbies are trout fishing from boat, fly fishing, ocean fishing with rod, kontiki, hunting and shooting. We lived in the USA, Canada, Indonesia, Mexico and Germany and speak their languages.

Rotorua *4 km E of Rotorua*
Aroden B&B Homestay *B&B Homestay*

Leonie & Paul Kibblewhite
2 Hilton Road,
Lynmore,
Rotorua

Tel (07) 345 6303
or 027 696 4211
Fax (07) 345 6353
aroden@xtra.co.nz

Double/Twin $130-$145
Single $90
(Full breakfast)
Children negotiable
Visa MC accepted
2 Queen (2 bdrm)
Bathrooms: 1 Ensuite 1 Private

A great central location: city 5 minutes, Whakarewarewa Forest adjacent (glow-worms at night!), lakes and thermal nearby. Enjoy Aroden's style, peace and character: 2 lounge areas, well-appointed rooms, comfortable beds and fine linen, modern bathrooms (excellent showers), central heating/open fire, patio, spa and luxuriant garden with native tree collection. Leonie, background in teaching, and Paul, scientist, are fifth generation Kiwi with real knowledge of this remarkable area. And meet Taupo, Paul's delightful guide dog. Breakfast is special - this couple enjoys food! Leonie parle français.

Rotorua - Lake Tarawera *15 km SE of Rotorua*
Lake Tarawera Lake Edge Retreat *B&B Apartment with Kitchen*

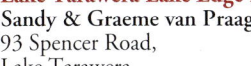

Sandy & Graeme van Praagh
93 Spencer Road,
Lake Tarawera,
RD 5, Rotorua

Tel (07) 362 8080
Fax (07) 362 8060
laketarawera@xtra.co.nz
http://www.laketaraweraescape.co.nz

Double/Twin $110-$130
Single $85
(Breakfast by arrangement)
Children included
Dinner nearby lakeside cafe.
Self-contained $110-130
Visa MC accepted
Children and pets welcome
2 Queen 2 Single (3 bdrm)
Bathrooms: 3 Ensuite

Absolute lake edge with lawn to private jetty & sandy beach in a small rural community. 15 minutes from Rotorua's attractions and central to the surrounding region. Famous for trophy-sized trout, crystal clear water and pristine native bush. Bathe at Hotwater Beach, only accessible by boat(water taxi avail)or walk to The Tarawera Falls,described as one of the best short walks in NZ.Complimentary kayaks or just relax. Dominated by Mt Tarawera, the lake & environs are dramatic in all seasons.

Rotorua - Lake Tarawera *20 km SE of Rotorua*
Lake Tarawera Rheinland Lodge *B&B Homestay*

Gunter & Maria
484 Spencer Road,
RD 5,
Rotorua

Tel (07) 362 8838
Fax (07) 362 8838
tarawera@ihug.co.nz

Double/Twin $120-$150
Single $85-$100
(Special breakfast)
Children half price
Dinner $50
Children welcome
1 King/Twin 1 Queen (2 bdrm)
Bathrooms: 1 Private 1 Family share

Located at the magic Lake Tarawera renowned for its scenery and history we offer warm hospitality with a personal touch. Expect total privacy, magnificent lake views, luxurious and relaxing outdoor whirlpool, spacious bathroom with shower and bath, fitness area, stereo, TV, internet connection, lake beach 5 minutes on foot, sea 45 minutes by car, bush walks, fishing and hunting trips by arrangement, home-made bread, German cuisine on request, organic garden, German/English spoken.

Rotorua Central *1 km S of Rotorua Central*
Innes Cottage *B&B Homestay*

Chris & Gill Innes
18A Wylie Street,
Rotorua Central

Tel 0800 24 30 30
or (07) 349 1839
Fax (07) 349 1890
gill@clican.com
www.innescottage.co.nz

Double/Twin $120-$140
Single $95-$110
(Continental breakfast)
Children POA
Dinner by arrangement
Visa MC accepted
Children welcome
2 Queen 2 Single (3 bdrm)
Bathrooms: 2 Ensuite 1 Private

Centrally situated, within flat walking distance to restaurants and the city, set in a treelined quiet neighborhood only 100 metres from the main road. Close to Te Puia Thermal area and major tourist attractions are easily accessible. After 130 years heritage in the beverage industry we have travelled extensively, have collected a wealth of knowledge and many valuable contacts. Let us assist and advise you on the most popular and "must see" attractions and other highlights of our beautiful country.

Rotorua *10 km N of Rotorua*
Ngongotaha Lakeside Lodge *B&B Apartment with Kitchen*

Lyndsay & Graham Butcher
41 Operiana Street,
Ngongotaha, Rotorua

Tel (07) 357 4020 or 0800 144 020
or 027 385 2807 Fax (07) 357 4020
lake.edge@xtra.co.nz
www.rotorualakesidelodge.co.nz

Double/Twin $170-$230
Single $150-$200 (Full breakfast)
Children over 12 neg
Apartment $250 for two people,
extra people $25 each
Visa MC accepted
1 King/Twin 1 King
1 Queen 2 Single (4 bdrm)
Bathrooms: 3 Ensuite 1 Private
private bathroom in apartment

Arrive to the aroma of home baking and coffee, make yourselves at home in our Award Winning Lakeside Bed & Breakfast.Enjoy stunning panoramic views, fly fishing, bird watching, great food and warm hospitality. Quiet, peaceful, close to major attractions, only ten minutes from town and away from sulphur fumes.Options : B&B - 3 upstairs, well appointed, ensuite bedrooms, share guest lounge/conservatory.Downstairs - luxury, self-contained, fully equipped apartment - sleeps 4.Summer season only.Come, stay awhile, relax and enjoy. We guarantee you a great stay!

Rotorua *10 km SE of Rotorua centre*
Lake Okareka B&B *B&B Homestay Apartment with Kitchen*
Patricia & Ken Scott
10 Okareka Loop Road,
RD 5,
Rotorua

Tel (07) 362 8245
or 0800 652 735
patricia.scott@xtra.co.nz
www.lakeokarekabnb.co.nz

Double/Twin $120-$150
Single $80-$100
(Special breakfast)
Dinner by arrangement
Children welcome
2 Queen 1 Double/Twin
1 Single (3 bdrm)
Bathrooms: 3 Ensuite

A very warm welcome awaits you at tranquil Lake Okareka, one of the most beautiful Lakes in the area. Our modern home captures magnificent Lake views and beyond to Mt Tarawera. Stroll along the waters edge, enjoy the native bush, ferns and birdlife. Use our local knowledge on all nearby hot pools, fishing, scenic, thermal, adventure and cultural activities. Excellent swimming, complimentary kayaks available. Our environment is quiet and peaceful yet only ten minutes from Rotorua. The perfect retreat with space, privacy and home comforts.

Rotorua *1 km N of rotorua*
Robertson House *B&B*
John Ballard
70 Pererika Street,
Rotorua

Tel (07) 343 7559
Fax (07) 343 7559
info@robertsonhouse.co.nz

Double/Twin $150-$170
Single $80-$140
(Continental breakfast)
Extra person $50
1 King/Twin 2 Queen
2 Double/Twin 2 Single (5 bdrm)
Bathrooms: 5 Ensuite

O ur historic home, only 2 minutes drive from city centre, was built by one of Rotoruas forefathers, in 1905. Under the auspices of the Historic Places Trust it has been carefully renovated, retaining its colonial charm. Relax in its warm comfortable atmosphere, or take time out on the verandah and enjoy our old English cottage garden resplendent with colour and fragrance, citrus trees and grape vines. Our friendly hosts are happy to assist with information and bookings for Rotorua's Maori cultural and sightseeing attractions.

Rotorua *2 km N of Rotorua centre*

Rotorua's Legend on the Lake Homestay *B&B Homestay Apartment with Kitchen*

Murray & Heather Watson
33 Haumoana Street, Koutu, Rotorua

Tel (07) 347 1123 or 027 492 7122   Fax (07) 347 1313
muzzandheb@kol.co.nz   www.troutnz.co.nz

Double/Twin $150 Single $150 (Full breakfast)
Children $20   Dinner $45 pp by arrangement
Additional Adults $30/night per person
Visa MC accepted   Pet free home
2 Queen 1 Double/Twin 1 Single (3 bdrm)
Bathrooms: 1 Ensuite 1 Private .

On arrival you will be greeted with our magnificent, quiet and secluded lakes-edge view and a genuine Kiwi welcome. Please join us beside the lake for refreshments as we would love to help you plan your stay by sharing our local knowledge of the area and its many attractions.

Hearing the tranquil lapping of the lake you will find it hard to believe you are only 3 minutes drive from the city centre. You will find your self-contained apartment to have all the comforts of home (washing machine, TV, DVD, video, stereo, oven, microwave and dishwasher). Separate bedroom (queen) and living area/kitchen with ensuite access from both rooms.Free email access.

Our smoke-free apartment ensures a freshness you will enjoy. Breakfast includes fruit, yoghurt, cereal, juice and tea/coffee followed by a cooked breakfast - all this and you can choose the time you would like to have it served. Breakfast is a great time to get to know us and for us to help you make best use of your time in this volcanic thermal paradise.

We are more than happy to assist with local bookings and recommend you sample some of the strong local Maori culture. Murray operates a trout fishing charter business on Lake Rotorua from our Lakeside jetty.Special rates apply.We have both travelled extensively, internationally and throughout New Zealand and enjoy meeting people from all over the world. We have been running homestays for the last 15 years and really know how to make your time here enjoyable and comfortable.

Feel free to sit on the lawn and watch the spectacular sunsets we are lucky enough to enjoy almost every night.We hope you will arrive as our guests and leave as our friends. "Humble luxury here"

Rotorua - Okere Falls - Lake Rotoiti *20 km N of Rotorua*
At The Ferns Bed & Breakfast *B&B Homestay Cottage with Kitchen*

Carol & Bernie Mason
48 Taheke Road,
RD 4, Okere Falls, Rotorua

Tel (07) 362 4087
or 027 251 7932
or 027 4467121
Fax (07) 362 4087
bcmason@xtra.co.nz
www.attheferns.co.nz

Double/Twin $145-$165
Single $145-$165 (Full breakfast)
Dinner $45 each by arrangement
Extra person $20
Breakfast in S/C $15 by request
Visa MC accepted
Children welcome
1 King 1 Queen 1 Single (2 bdrm)
Bathrooms: 1 Ensuite 1 Private

Secluded Okere Falls Lake Rotoiti accommodation, surrounded by tree ferns, bird song,close to shady walks and great trout fishing. If you enjoy peace, quiet and relish the chance to relax and enjoy nature, At The Ferns is the ideal place. Walk to the Lake, Okere Falls, kayak, white water raft or watch the fun. Choose from your own self-contained cottage in the lower garden or have bed & breakfast where the guest room gives you privacy with all the comforts of home.

Rotorua - Lake Rotoiti *20 km NE of Rotorua*
Lakestay Rotoiti *B&B*

Graeme & Raewyn Natusch
173 Tumoana Road,
Lake Rotoiti,
RD 4,
Rotorua

Tel (07) 345 4089
or 027 418 8404
Fax (07) 345 4089
lakestayrotoiti@xtra.co.nz

Double/Twin $120-$150
(Full breakfast)
Dinner $35
Self-contained studio $120-$150
Off season rates May-Oct
Visa MC accepted
2 Queen (2 bdrm)
Bathrooms: 2 Ensuite

Lakestay Rotoiti, a very special destination for the discerning couple or individual travellers both summer and winter with friendly informative hosts and siamese cat. One of just 3 lakefront properties in a beautiful secluded sandy bay surrounded by native bush, forest and stunning lake views from all living and guest bedrooms. Excellent swimming, trout fishing, walking tracks and natural rejuvinating hot baths nearby. Guests enjoy complimentary use of kyaks, dingy, windsurfer and bicycles. Wonderful evening dinner by arrangement. Directions are essential. A truely unique experience.

Rotorua *5 km N of Rotorua*
Tirohangañnui (Big View) *B&B Homestay*

Angela & Tony Thompson
21 Grand vue Road,
Kawaha Point,
Rotorua

Tel (07) 349 4810
or 021 170 3477
Fax (07) 349 4811
a_thompson@clear.net.nz
www.bigview.co.nz

Double/Twin $140-$160
Single $90
(Full breakfast)
Children negotiable
2 Queen (2 bdrm)
Bathrooms: 1 Ensuite 1 Private

Your hosts Angela & Tony invite you to share in the experience, the peace and serenity of Tirohanga-nui (Big View) with its magnificent panoramic lake and city views, only 5 minutes from the city centre and local attractions. We recommend a minimum 2 night stay to allow enough time to discover Rotorua its maori culture, geothermal activity, and beautiful lake and bush walks. Accommodation is offered either self-contained with own entrance and private deck area or in the upstairs bedroom with own private bathroom.

Rotorua *5 km SW of Post Office*
Aria's Farm B&B *B&B Homestay Farmstay Separate Suite*

Kerris & Chris
396 Clayton Road,
Rotorua

Tel 021 753 691
or (07) 348 0790
Fax (07) 348 0863
ariasfarm@xtra.co.nz
www.ariasfarm.com

Double/Twin $99-$130
Single $60-$110 (Full breakfast)
Children 0-3yrs Cot $20, 4-12 yrs $25
Dinner Mains $15 pp,
3-Course (Soup, Mains, Dessert) $30 pp
Laundry full load + dry $10
Visa MC accepted
Pet free home
Children welcome
1 King 3 Queen 1 Twin 3 Single (5 bdrm)
Bathrooms: 1 Ensuite 2 Private 2 Guest share Ensuite or private

Paradise near town - brand new modern lodge on 3 acres with secluded bush & stream, but with city bus right at the front gate! King & Queen beds, ensuite/private bathrooms. Air con & central heating. Unlimited tea/coffee. Laundry, internet, off-street parking. Full breakfast w/fresh eggs, luxury spa after a busy day. Join our fun-loving family with 2 kids, or enjoy your own privacy. Special winter rates, incl semi self-contained 2 bedroom unit.

Rotorua *6 km NW of City*

Affordable Westminster Lodge and Cottage *B&B Farmstay Cottage with Kitchen*

Gillian and Barry Gillette
58A Mountain Road, Rotorua, 3201

Tel (07) 348 4273 or 0800 937864   Fax (07) 348 4205
westminster@slingshot.co.nz   www.westminsterlodge.co.nz

Double/Twin $100-$150 Single $80-$100 (Special breakfast)
Children $20 per child under 14
Fully cooked breakfast for extra $12.00 per person
Visa MC Eftpos accepted   Children welcome
5 Queen 1 Double/Twin 6 Twin 2 Single (8 bdrm)
Bathrooms: 3 Ensuite 3 Private 1 Guest share
Family rooms have bath and shower

Affordable Westminster Lodge and Cottage are English Tudor style homes nestled on the slopes of Mt Ngongotaha overlooking the city of Rotorua. So country, yet only 6 minutes to the city centre. Panoramic views in the day and fairy land at night. We offer superior Bed and Breakfast accommodation in semi self contained units or lodge rooms at affordable prices or you can choose the self catering cottage Children are welcome in our large family rooms. The Lodge is Qualmark 3Star Plus and the Cottage a 4Star.

All rooms have tea and coffee making facilities fridge and microwave Enjoy our delicious special breakfast with fresh fruit salad yoghurt and cereal, hot apple muffins (baked daily) and a freshly laid egg or a scrumptious fully cooked breakfast at a small extra cost.

Experience all the comforts of home in a warm and friendly atmosphere, ensuring your stay in our family home will always be remembered. Breathe in the fresh mountain air and relax in our spa pool that overlooks the city at the end of your busy day. We are a family of eight with five adopted children one still living at home. We have miniature cows friendly sheep, rabbits chickens, and Mrs Pig. Our house pets are a cockatoo Paulie, the cat Socks and Holly and Benji our little dogs. All the animals are friendly and can be hand fed.

Rotorua - The Redwoods *4 km E of Rotorua*

B&B @ The Redwoods *Luxury B&B Homestay*

Vivien & Peter Cooper
3 Awatea Terrace, Lynmore - Rotorua

Tel (07) 345 4499 or 027 270 3594
Fax (07) 345 4499
bnb@theredwoods.co.nz
www.theredwoods.co.nz

Double/Twin $130-$160
Single $130-$160 (Full breakfast)
Single bed available for child to share room
Dinner $35
Host experience in hospitality industry
and silver service
Visa MC accepted
Pet free home Children welcome
Non smokers only
2 Queen 1 Single (2 bdrm)
Bathrooms: 2 Ensuite Excellent shower

Secluded yet central! Two new luxurious ensuite guestrooms with private entrance, guest-only lounge, dining and outdoor living. Decor is simple yet stylish, lounge opens onto courtyard and garden. We live upstairs in a split level home in quiet cul-de-sac; enjoy our company or the privacy of your own space. We combine interaction with discretion. Redwood Forest on your doorstep, city and lakes 5 minutes away with Rotorua's many attractions very accessible. Safe off-street parking. All our guests have enjoyed our personal service and quality recommendations.

Rotorua *5 km SW of Rotorua*

Hillside Homestead B.&B *B&B Homestay*

Lorraine and Jeff Nowland
99 Tihi Road,
Springfield,
Rotorua

Tel (07) 347 9337
or 027 441 1535
Fax (07) 347 9337
hillside.homestead@xtra.co.nz
www.hillsidehomestead.co.nz

Double/Twin $120-$150
Single $120-$130
(Full breakfast)
Visa MC accepted
Pet free home
Not suitable for children
2 Queen 1 Twin (3 bdrm)
Bathrooms: 1 Ensuite 2 Private

You will feel welcome the moment you arrive. Boutique rooms with tea/coffee-making facilities. Refrigerator, telephone, . We have had 17 years as owner-operators of a major tourist attraction, specialising in fragrances, herbs for cooking, restaurant etc. We now enjoy being hosts in our unique homestead, making new friends and sharing our love for music. If in Rotorua for a special occasion we can organize your event . An ideal place to stay where hospitality is guaranteed.

Rotorua - Ngongotaha *12 km N of Rotorua*
Panorama Country Homestay *Luxury B&B Homestay Farmstay*

David Perry & Christine King
144 Fryer Road, Hamurana, RD 2, Rotorua

Tel (07) 332 2618 or 021 610 949
Fax (07) 332 2618
panoramahomestay@xtra.co.nz
http://panoramahomestay.co.nz

Double/Twin $180-$240 Single $115-$135   (Special breakfast)
Dinner By arrangement   Discount for over 2 nights stay
Visa MC accepted
1 King 1 Queen (3 bdrm)
Bathrooms: 2 Ensuite 1 Private
Queen room with private bathroom has large plunge bath.

Aptly named Panorama is your ideal base to stay near Rotorua's many attractions. Take in the magnificent views overlooking Lake Rotorua and legendary Mokoia Island, Mt Tarawera and surrounding country side.

Feel the peace and tranquility as you relax under the stars in the outdoor heated massage spa pool, then curl up in front of the log fire in winter to stay cosy and warm. You may prefer to enjoy an energetic game of tennis on the championship sized court or take in many of the fantastic walks then come home and stretch out on the extra large beds in Panorama's peaceful surrounds for a perfect nights sleep.

The three spacious, luxury bedrooms have private bathrooms/ensuites containing, toiletries, heated towel rails, hairdryers, shaving points and heaters. The large comfortable inner spring beds are warmed with electric blankets, woollen underlays and feather quilts in winter. In the living area, the formal lounge has a native timber, cathedral ceiling, and an open fire where you can relax with a book and listen to soft music.

The large house is centrally heated and wheelchair accessible. Only 15min from Rotorua, Panorama is situated on the northern side of the lake away from the sulphur smells. There is ample room for safe off street parking and helicopter access. Pet lambs and sheep can be fed by hand.

Dave and Chris welcome you to spend a few days at Panorama where hospitality is ensured in their country home. They have lived in Rotorua for many years and have a wealth of knowledge to assist you in enjoying your stay and the local attractions. They would be happy to help you with any bookings you may require.

Rotorua - Rerewhakaaitu *45 km SE of Rotorua*
Ashpit Place *B&B Homestay Farmstay*

Alison & Scott Marshall
815 Ashpit Road,
Rerewhakaaitu,
Rotorua
3073

Tel (07) 366 6709
or 021 117 0317
Fax (07) 366 6710
samarshall@clear.net.nz
www.ashpitplace.co.nz

Double/Twin $190
(Continental breakfast)
Visa MC accepted
1 King/Twin 1 Queen (2 bdrm)
Bathrooms: 2 Ensuite
Spa bath in one suite

Relax and enjoy the panoramic views of Lake Rerewhakaaitu and Mt Tarawera with farming and forestry vistas from the lounge and dining areas. We have some of the best sunsets in the world. The property is in a quiet rural area which is at lakes edge where you can walk at your leisure. We are in between the thermal areas Waiotapu and Waimangu, central to Rotorua and Taupo and on the way to Whirinaki National Park.

Rotorua Central *0.3 km SE of i-Site Centre*
Eaton Hall Bed & Breakfast *B&B Guest House*

Ginni & Alan
1255 Hinemaru Street,
Rotorua, 3010

Tel (07) 347 0366 or
Free Phone 0800 328 664 (NZ only)
Fax (07) 347 0366
eatonhallbnb@xtra.co.nz
www.eatonhallbnb.co.nz

Double/Twin $85-$110
Single $65-$80 (Full breakfast)
Children included in room rate
Additional guests $30 each
Visa MC Eftpos accepted
Pet free home
Children welcome
5 Queen 1 Double/Twin 5 Twin
5 Single (9 bdrm)
Bathrooms: 6 Ensuite 1 Guest share

Eaton Hall is an 85 year old charming historic home right in the very centre of Rotorua Township. We offer a warm, secure, comfortable, quiet & smoke-free accommodation to all discerning travellers. Only a few minutes easy walk to the Polynesian Spa Pools, Museum, Government Gardens, the lovely Lakefront, Restaurants and Cafes, Trading Banks, Rotorua Bus Terminus, Tourism, Information and Travel i-Site Centre. Enjoy a full and yummy breakfast every morning. We'd love you to stay with us during your visit to Rotorua.

Rotorua - Lake Okareka *6 km E of Rotorua*
Lake Okareka Cottage and Loft *Separate Suite Cottage with Kitchen*

Susan and Gregg Brown
4 Millar Road, RD 5,
Lake Okareka, Rotorua 3076

Tel (07) 362 8568
susanbrown@orcon.net.nz
www.lakestay.co.nz

Double/Twin $150-$210
Single $135-$195
(Continental breakfast provisions)
Children $15
Extra adults $20
Visa MC accepted
Pet free home
Children welcome
Non smokers only
1 King 2 Queen (3 bdrm)
Bathrooms: 1 Ensuite 1 Private

Relaxed, tranquil and contemporary accommodation close to Rotorua. The fully self contained cottage opens out onto a patio and garden which overlooks bush and farmland. The cottage contains two Queen Beds, 100% cotton linen, bath, shower, washing machine, drier and kitchen facilities, telephone, LCD TV, SKY TV, DVD and Broadband Access. The loft with king bed also has its own separate access and is intimate but spacious with ensuite, DVD and kitchenette. Our family is made up of Gregg and Susan,and three children, 9, 5 and 2.

Rotorua - Hamurana *20 km N of Rotorua*
Lakeview Heights *B&B Farmstay*

Liz & John Dentice
269 Te Waerenga Road,
Rotorua, 3072

Tel (07) 332 3570
or 021 0224 2513
Fax (07) 332 3570
john-lizdentice@xtra.co.nz
www.lakeviewheightsnz.co.nz

Double/Twin $120-$180
Single $80-$120 (Full breakfast)
Dinner available with prior
arrangement - home cooked using
local produce
Visa MC accepted
Children and pets welcome
3 Queen 2 Single (3 bdrm)
Bathrooms: 1 Ensuite 1 Private 1 Guest share

Our spacious comfortable home has three guest rooms with superb views across the lake to the city and the volcanic Mount Tarawera in the distance. We are bordered by the Te Waerenga Scenic Reserve with native trees,ferns Tuis and Bell birds. John & Liz are well travelled with farming backgrounds and would be delighted to give you a tour of our Arab horses, sheep and calves and Fluff the house cat. Trout fishing can be arranged. 5 minutes to a 9 hole golf course, Kaituna white water rafting, thermal areas and walks to springs

Taupo *3 km E of Central Taupo*
Hill Top Park Homestay *B&B Homestay*

Colleen & Bob Yeoman
61 Puriri Street,
Taupo
3330

Tel (07) 377 0283
Fax (07) 377 4683

Double/Twin $140
Single $80
(Full breakfast)
Children $40
Dinner $40 by arrangement
Children welcome
We take only one party at a time
1 Queen 1 Twin (2 bdrm)
Bathrooms: 1 Ensuite 1 Guest share

Bob and I have enjoyed hosting for many years, our lovely new home in Hill Top Park with beautiful mountains views makes our guests' stay in Taupo very special. All attractions are nearby, golf courses, thermal pools, Huka Falls and fishing. We are retired sheep and cattle farmers, who enjoy travelling and meeting other travellers. Bob excels at golf and is in charge of cooked breakfasts. Home-made jams and marmalade are my specialty. Please phone for directions. Good off street parking

Taupo *1 km S of Taupo*
Pataka House *B&B Homestay Separate Suite*

Raewyn & Neil Alexander
8 Pataka Road,
Taupo

Tel (07) 378 5481
Fax (07) 378 5461
pataka-homestay@xtra.co.nz
www.patakahouse.co.nz

Double/Twin $120
Single $90
(Full breakfast)
Children $30
Separate suite $130
Visa MC accepted
Children welcome
2 Queen 4 Twin (4 bdrm)
Bathrooms: 1 Ensuite 1 Private
1 Guest share both shower & bath

Pataka House is highly recommended for its hospitality. We assure guests that their stay lives up to New Zealand's reputation as being a home away from home. We are easily located just 1 turn off the lake front and up a tree-lined driveway. Our garden room is privately situated, has an appealing decor and extremely popular to young and old alike. Stay for 1 night or stay for more as Lake Taupo will truly be the highlight of your holiday. Mika, a burmese, loves visitors.

Taupo *1 km N of Taupo Central*
Lakeland Homestay *Homestay*
Lesley & Chris
11 Williams Street,
Taupo

Tel (07) 378 1952
or 0274 877 971
Fax (07) 378 1912
lakeland.bb@xtra.co.nz

Double/Twin $130-$140
Single $70
(Continental breakfast)
Visa MC accepted
1 Queen 2 Twin (2 bdrm)
Bathrooms: 1 Ensuite 1 Family share

Nestled in a restful tree-lined street, a mere 6 minutes stroll from the lake's edge and shopping centre Lakeland Homestay is a cheerful and cosy home that enjoys views of the lake and mountains. Keen gardeners, anglers and golfers Chris and Lesley work and play in an adventure oasis. By the way we have two cats, Caddy and Monica.Laundry facilities are available and a courtesy car is available for coach travellers, there is off-street parking. Please phone for directions.

Taupo *14 km NW of Taupo*
Minarapa *B&B Country Stay*
Barbara & Dermot Grainger
620 Oruanui Road,
RD 1,
Taupo

Tel (07) 378 1931
info@minarapa.co.nz
www.minarapa.co.nz

Double/Twin $135-$160
Single $100-$120
(Full breakfast)
Children price on application
Dinner by arrangement
Visa MC accepted
1 King/Twin 2 Queen
2 Twin (4 bdrm)
Bathrooms: 2 Ensuite 1 Private
large rooms with heated towel rails and heater

Wend your way along a wonderful tree-lined drive into rural tranquillity. Minarapa, our extensive country retreat, 12 minutes from Taupo, 45 minutes to Rotorua, is within easy reach of Orakei Korako, Huka Falls and other tourist attractions. Wander here among colourful tree-sheltered gardens, play tennis, billiards, or ball with Toby the dog, visit friendly farm animals or relax in our guest lounge. Retire to spacious, comfortably appointed guest rooms, two with balcony and TV. All offer individual character and tea/coffee facilties.

Taupo *2.5 km S of Taupo*
Fairviews *B&B Homestay*

Brenda Watson-Hughes & Mike Hughes
8 Fairview Terrace,
Taupo
3330

Tel (07) 377 0773
fairviews@reap.org.nz
www.reap.org.nz/~fairviews

Double/Twin $135-$155
Single $115-$135
(Full breakfast)
Visa MC accepted
Pet free home
1 Queen 1 Twin (2 bdrm)
Bathrooms: 1 Ensuite 1 Private

You are invited to stay at our modern homestay situated in a tranquil neighbourhood within walking distance of hot pools, Botanical Gardens and lake. Relax and enjoy Fairviews' gardens. Be as private as you wish or socialise with hosts. Rooms are tastefully decorated and comfortable. Double room is large with private entrance, TV, fridge, tea/coffee facilities, robe and hairdryer. Generous breakfasts provided. Email and laundry are available at small charge. Our regional knowledge is extensive. Interests include theatre, travel, cycling, tramping, antiques/collectables.

Taupo *15 km N of Taupo*
Brackenhurst *B&B Homestay Farmstay Cottage with Kitchen*

Barbara & Ray Graham
801 Oruanui Road,
RD 1, Taupo

Tel (07) 377 6451
or 0274 456 217
Fax (07) 377 6451
rgbg@xtra.co.nz

Double/Twin $110-$150
Single $65
(Full breakfast)
Children $35
Dinner $45
Visa MC accepted
Pet free home
Children and pets welcome
2 Queen 1 Double/Twin
4 Single (4 bdrm)
Bathrooms: 2 Ensuite 2 Private

Brackenhurst is a modern Lockwood home on 14 acres of peaceful countryside with fantails, tuis and bellbirds in the large garden. highland cattle and sheep. A warm welcome with peace and tranquility. . We are half a kilometre from SH1 and close to Huka Falls, geothermal activities, golf courses a days outing to Rotorua, Waitomo Caves or Napier. Private guests wing in the house or separate annex offer away from home comforts. Breakfast to suit, continental style or full English. Dinner available by arrangement.

Taupo *3 km S of Taupo*
Moorhill *B&B Boutique Accommodation*

Liz & Peter Sharland
27 Korimako Road, Taupo 3330,
Tel (07) 377 1069 or 021 300 455
petenlizr@xtra.co.nz   www.moorhill.co.nz
Double/Twin $160-$190 (Full breakfast)
Laundry and Internet at small charge
Visa MC accepted
Pet free home   Not suitable for children
1 King/Twin 1 King 1 Queen (2 bdrm)
Bathrooms: 2 Ensuite

Be assured of a warm welcome at Moorhill, boutique bed and breakfast accommodation at an affordable price. Relax and enjoy our delicious cooked breakfasts, spacious rooms and comfortable beds. Our smoke-free home is set in a large mature garden, a short walk to the Lake, the Botanical Gardens and a few minutes drive to town, excellent restaurants and thermal pools.

The downstairs Magnolia room has a queen sized bed, walk through wardrobe to large luxury ensuite and a sitting area opening onto the garden. Upstairs the spacious Cherry room has super king double or twin bed options, ensuite and views of Lake Taupo. Both well appointed rooms have quality cotton bed linen, duvets, tea making facilities, fridges, heated towel rails, hairdryers and electric blankets. The guest lounge opens onto sunny decks,the perfect place to share travel experiences over a glass of wine. There is ample off-street parking.

Take your time in Taupo, it is an ideal base from which to explore the many attractions including sparkling Huka Falls. World class trout fishing, boating, golf courses, adrenalin pumping activities are all available. The National Park volcanoes provide skiing, mountain walks, including the famous Tongariro Crossing, and are within easy reach. Rotorua and many thermal fields are less than one hours drive whilst Napier and Hawkes Bay vineyards are under two hours. We would be pleased to share our local knowledge, help arrange trips or onward bookings. Peter is a sports fan(atic) whilst Liz dabbles in flower painting and photography. We both enjoy meeting people, gardening, reading, music, good food and wine. We look forward to welcoming you to our home.

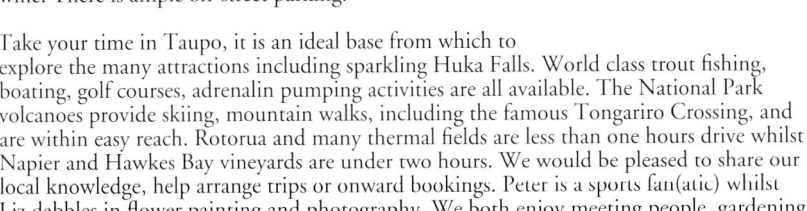

Taupo *15 km N of Taupo*
Maimoa House *B&B Farmstay Apartment with Kitchen New apartment opening soon ask for details*
Margaret & Godfrey Ellis
41 Oak Drive, off Palmer Mill Road,
Taupo
Tel (07) 376 9000
mewestview@xtra.co.nz
www.maimoahomestay.co.nz

Double/Twin $105-$125
Single $75 (Special breakfast)
Children $30
Dinner $30 by arrangement
10% discount for 3 nights or more
Visa MC accepted
Children and pets welcome
1 Queen 1 Double/Twin
1 Twin (3 bdrm)
Bathrooms: 1 Ensuite 1 Guest share
Large Spa bath, seperate shower, toilet

Hello and welcome to our peaceful home with spectacular views over the mountains to the lake. Our spacious new apartment is now available, including our special breakfast. Join us for a 3 course dinner (allergies catered for) with wine. Borrow our tandem or single bikes. We are very happy to arrange on-going recommended B&Bs, local trips & excursions. We have a friendly lab dog, a cat and a few cows. Our interests include church activities travelling and chatting over a glass of wine.

Taupo *1 km N of Town Centre*
Magnifique *B&B Homestay*
Gay & Rex Eden
52 Woodward Street,
Taupo
Tel (07) 378 4915
Fax (07) 378 4915
info@magnifique.co.nz
www.magnifique.co.nz

Double/Twin $140-$155
Single $100-$120
(Special breakfast)
Visa MC accepted
Pet free home
2 Queen 2 Single (3 bdrm)
Bathrooms: 2 Private

We welcome you with refreshments and home-baking while you take in the magnificent sweeping views of town, lake and mountains. You may leave your car and walk just 6 minutes to Taupo's lovely restaurants and shops. Our focus in life is people, so be assured of a warm welcome and the highest standards of comfort and hospitality. Each room has tea making facilities, fridge, TV. We will treat you with our special breakfasts which have not yet failed to delight our guests.

Taupo *1 km N of Taupo*
Fourwinds Bed & Breakfast *B&B Homestay*
Catherine Culling
57 Woodward Street,
Taupo
3330

Tel (07) 376 5350
Fax (07) 376 5360
bnb@fourwindsbedandbreakfast.co.nz
www.fourwindsbedandbreakfast.co.nz

Double/Twin $120-$140
Single $95-$120
(Full breakfast)
Visa MC accepted
Not suitable for children
1 Double/Twin 2 Single (2 bdrm)
Bathrooms: 1 Private
Toilet is separate from bathroom

A warm welcome and a refreshing cup of tea awaits your arrival at Fourwinds. Close to all Taupo attractions and town, with panoramic views of the Lake, Kaimanawa Ranges and mountains. The generous breakfast is served in dining room overlooking the wonderful view. Taupo is an excellent base for day trips to Rotorua, Waitomo, Hawkes Bay and Tongariro National Park. Catherine and Ambee (Cat) enjoy meeting guests from all corners of the world and look forward to you staying with us.

Taupo - Acacia Bay *5 km W of Taupo*
Te Moenga Lodge *B&B Separate Suite*
Brent & Jacque McClellan
60 Te Moenga Park,
Reeves Road, Taupo, 3330

Tel (07) 378 0437
or 027 452 1459
Fax (07) 378 0438
info@temoenga.com
www.temoenga.com

Double/Twin $150-$295
Single $120-$220
(Continental breakfast)
Children 2yrs+ $50 per head
Dinner Local restaurant at end of road
Visa MC Amex Eftpos accepted
Children welcome
3 King/Twin 1 Queen (4 bdrm)
Bathrooms: 4 Ensuite
Chalets have double spa bath

C limb the tree-lined road to the homestead on the hill. Close the door on the everyday and relax so far above the lake it seems you're looking down from the sky. Choose a studio room with ensuite, television, tea/coffee making facilites or a private chalet with king/twin beds, separate lounge, television, spa bath, tea/coffee making facilities. Own the breath-taking view from your chalet for the length of your stay. Brent, Jacque, 3 children and pet boxer dog welcome you to experience Te Moenga Lodge.

Bay of Plenty

Taupo *1 km S of Taupo*
Moselle *B&B Separate Suite Apartment with Kitchen Self Contained*

Grahame & Anne Velvin
3 Te Hepera Street,
Taupo
3330

Tel (07) 377 2922
or 021 254 4511
Fax (07) 377 2290
ragevelvin@xtra.co.nz
http://moselletaupo.com

Double/Twin $180
Single $150
(Full breakfast provisions)
Children welcome
Visa MC Amex accepted
Children and pets welcome
1 King/Twin 1 Queen
2 Single (3 bdrm)
Bathrooms: 3 Ensuite 3 Private 1 spa bath

Moselle has a S/K bed and top quality linen New ensuite,Laundry and fully self contained. Sky TV video and fresh breakfast food supplied daily to your requirements. A four minute drive to the Taupo Golf Club two minutes drive to Thermal Hot Pools & 5 minutes drive to the Taupo Township, walking distance to the Lake. Private parking. 90 minutes to Ski Field.

～

Taupo *13 km N of Taupo*
Bellbird Ridge Alpaca Farm *B&B Farmstay Cottage with Kitchen*

Mark & Leanne Prujean
68 Tangye Road, RD 1, Taupo

Tel (07) 377 1996 or 027 284 1176
or 027 284 1179
Fax (07) 377 1992
info@bellbirdridge.co.nz
www.bellbirdridge.co.nz

Double/Twin $150-$150
Single $130-$130
(Full breakfast provisions)
Children $50 under 12
Dinner by arrangement
3 course $50, 2 course $40, BBQ $30
BYO beverages or purchase from hosts
Visa MC Eftpos accepted
Children and pets welcome
2 Queen 2 Twin (4 bdrm)
Bathrooms: 1 Ensuite 1 Private

Take a break and unwind in our charming and secluded self-contained one bedroom cottage, enjoy our beautiful garden (including 18 hole mini golf course) and friendly alpacas, located only 10 mins from Taupo. The cottage has a separate queen bedroom, kitchen/dining/lounge area & deck with BBQ. Generous breakfast provisions are provided. Also available in a separate guest wing in the homestead, where you would be our only guests, are a queen & 2 twin bedrooms with your own bathroom.

Taupo - Acacia Bay *5 km W of Taupo*
The Loft *B&B*

Jane Redfern and John de Latour
3 Wakeman Road,
Acacia Bay, Taupo

Tel (07) 377 1040
or 027 485 1347
Fax (07) 377 1049
book@theloftnz.com
www.theloftnz.com

Double/Twin $145-$185
Single $100-$120 (Full breakfast)
Children $50-$75
Dinner $30-$45 per person
Washing/internet available -
price on application
Visa MC accepted
Pet free home
Children welcome
3 Queen 3 Single (3 bdrm)
Bathrooms: 3 Ensuite

Situated five minutes from Taupo township and a few minutes walk to the lake and a very good restaurent. The Loft is set in a cottage garden adajacent to a native bush reserve. Hosts Jane & John look forward to your visit. Enjoy a scrumptious breakfast of fresh fruit salad, orange juise, fresly baked crossants , wonderful poached or scrambled eggs with bacon mushrooms and our own delicious tomatoes when in season. Tea and coffee making facilities on landing upstairs.

Taupo *In Huka Falls*
Rive Gauche *B&B Studio unit with mini kitchen*

Lynne Fauchelle
128 Ferndale Way,
Huka Falls,
Taupo

Tel (07) 377 6167
or 021 050 6735
or 027 489 4250
lynnejim4@clear.net.nz
www.rivegauchetaupo.co.nz

Double/Twin $150-$200
Single $140-$160
(Special breakfast)
Pet free home
1 King/Twin 1 King
1 Queen (3 bdrm)
Bathrooms: 3 Ensuite

Welcome to Rive Gauche, our new architecturally-designed home blending contemporary and traditional European design. Situated just off Huka Falls Road and sited to take advantage of views over our 2 1⁄2 acres of garden and vineyard, we are close to Huka Falls, and only 3 minutes from the centre of Taupo. Guests can make the most of the walking and cycle tracks of the Wairakei Tourist Park right on the doorstep, and with the Huka Resort vineyard restaurant only a 4 minute walk.

Turangi *1.5 km E of Turangi Central*
The Andersons *B&B Homestay Cottage with Kitchen*

Betty & Jack Anderson
3 Poto Street,
Turangi

Tel (07) 386 8272
Fax (07) 386 8272
jbanderson@xtra.co.nz
www.superfly.co.nz/
accommodation/andersons

Double/Twin $120
Single $90
(Full breakfast)
Children in cottage only
Cottage (own food) sleeps 2-6
from $95-$105 double
Visa MC accepted
2 Queen 1 Twin (3 bdrm)
Bathrooms: 3 Ensuite

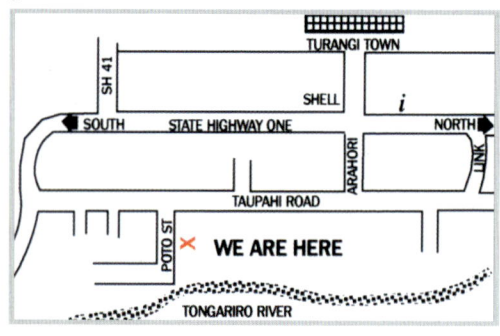

A warm welcome awaits you in our home, in quiet street, beside Tongariro River walkway, handy to restaurants and town and fishing. Arranged transport to Tongariro Crossing and National Park at your door. Lake Taupo and thermal baths 5 minutes drive. Upstairs rooms with balconies, queen beds, ensuites, fridge/jug, separated for privacy by landing. Downstairs twin beds, own entry, bathroom, fridge/jug. Laundry available and lounge to share maps of our volcanic area,or book activities and restaurants. Guest-shy cat. Cottage suitable for families.

Turangi *1 km S of Turangi Information Centre*
Brown Trout House *B&B Homestay*

Bruce & Nita Wilde
11 Kokopu Street,
Turangi
3334

Tel (07) 386 0308
or 027 253 3415
Fax (07) 386 0308
kohinoor@xtra.co.nz
www.browntrouthouse.co.nz

Double/Twin $120
Single $80
(Full breakfast)
Children negotiable
Lunches & dinner by prior arrangement
Visa MC accepted
1 King/Twin 1 Queen
1 Single (3 bdrm)
Bathrooms: 1 Private 1 Family share

W elcome to Brown Trout house overlooking the Tongariro River in Turangi, halfway between Auckland and Wellington. Your comfortable bedroom opens on to the deck. Have refreshments or step out our gate on to the Tongariro River Walkway or in to world famous fishing pools. Bruce is a passionate fisherman willing to share his knowledge. Shuttle pickup for the Tongariro Crossing arranged. Choose walks, golf, skiing or a hot swim 5 mins drive away. Friendly experienced hosts willing to give genuine kiwi hospitality.

Turangi *15 km W of Turangi*
Omori Lake House *Luxury Lodge*
Niel & Raewyn Groombridge
31 Omori Road,
Omori

Tel (07) 386 0420
or 021 667 092
stay@omorilakehouse.co.nz
www.omorilakehouse.co.nz

Double/Twin up to $160
Single up to $140
(Special breakfast)
Dinner by arrangement
Visa MC accepted
Pet free home
Not suitable for children
2 King (2 bdrm)
Bathrooms: 2 Ensuite

Approved

Our new boutique accommodation high above Omori has stunning views across to Taupo. There are two en-suite guest rooms with king beds, tea/coffee facilities and private deck. Raewyn loves to cook and eating well is part of the experience. Enjoy barbeques or meals with kiwi classics Omori on the menu. We are close to a variety of activities including fly-fishing, The Tongariro Alpine crossing, bush walks, thermal pools and ski slopes.

Turangi - Motuoapa *10 km N of Turangi*
Meredith House *B&B Self-contained*
Frances & Ian Meredith
45 Kahotea Drive,
Motuoapa,
RD 2, Turangi

Tel (07) 386 5266
or 0274 406 135
Fax (07) 386 5270
meredith.house@xtra.co.nz

Double/Twin $120
Single $85
(Breakfast by arrangement)
Self-contained $130-160
Visa MC accepted
Children welcome
1 Queen 3 Single (2 bdrm)
Bathrooms: 2 Ensuite

Stop and enjoy this outdoor Paradise. Just off SH1 (B&B Sign). Overlooking Lake Taupo, our 2 storey home offers ground-floor self-contained accommodation with own entrance. Full breakfast on request. Fully equipped kitchen, dining room, lounge. 2 cosy bedrooms (each with TV). Vehicle/boat off-street parking. Minutes to marina and world-renowned lake/river fishing. Beautiful bush walks. 45 minutes to ski fields and Tongariro National Park. Our association with Tongariro/Taupo area spans over 30 years, through work and outdoor pursuits. Welcome to our retreat.

Turangi *54 km S of Taupo*
Founders at Turangi *B&B Homestay*

Peter & Chris Stewart
253 Taupahi Road,
Turangi

Tel (07) 386 8539
Fax (07) 386 8534
chris@founders.co.nz
www.founders.co.nz

Double/Twin $180
Single $120 (Special breakfast)
Visa MC Eftpos accepted
Pet free home
Not suitable for children
2 King/Twin 1 King
3 Queen (4 bdrm)
Bathrooms: 4 Ensuite

Welcome to Turangi and to our New Zealand colonial-style home. Relax and enjoy the unique beauty of the trout fishing capital of the world. Many outdoor activities are available at this place for all seasons, with the Tongariro River, mountains of Tongariro National Park and magnificent Lake Taupo on our doorstep. 4 ensuite bedrooms open on to the veranda. Enjoy breakfast in our sunny dining room or pre-dinner drinks by the fire apres ski in the winter!

Turangi *16 km NW of Turangi*
Wills' Place *B&B*

Jill & Brian Wills
145 Omori Road, Omori

Tel (07) 386 7339
or 027 228 8960
Fax (07) 386 7339
b.g@willsplace.co.nz
www.willsplace.co.nz

Double/Twin $135-$150
Single $100-$120 (Full breakfast)
Children negotiable
Dinner by arrangement
Visa MC accepted
Pet free home
Children welcome
2 Queen 2 Single (2 bdrm)
Bathrooms: 1 Private
Bath with shower over

A lakeside home and superior guest suite with wonderful views. Fishing, boating, swimming, walks. Off the beaten track, yet only 10-15 minutes to shops, restaurants, thermal pools, Tongariro River, rafting, etc. 40 minutes to World Heritage Tongariro National Park. Private suite with two bedrooms, full size bathroom with bath and shower, living area, tea-making facilities, fridge, microwave, television, laundry, email access. Private patio overlooking the lake. Suite yours alone with separate entry and safe parking. Discount for three or more nights.

Turangi *2 km N of Turangi*
At the Tongariro Riverside B & B *B&B Homestay*

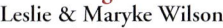

Leslie & Maryke Wilson
72 Herekiekie Street,
Turangi

Tel (07) 386 7447
or 021 074 0749
leslie@bytheriver.co.nz
www.bytheriver.co.nz

Double/Twin $115
Single $100
(Continental breakfast)
Dinner with wine $40 per person,
by arrangement
1 King (1 bdrm)
Bathrooms: 1 Ensuite

Waterfront location with the world famous trout fishing river - the Tongariro - just metres from your king bedroom/ensuite. Wonderful sunsets in a peaceful and tranquil setting. Situated halfway between Auckland and Wellington with secure parking. Experience real Kiwi hospitality. The ideal location for the Tongariro Alpine Crossing -(Shuttles arranged), White Water Rafting and the Skifields. Air-conditioning, Flatscreen TV, Tea/Coffee making facilities, fridge & BBQ. Generous continental breakfast. Mountain Bikes and Fishing equipment are available for hire. Fishing guides arranged. Restaurants a stroll away.

Turangi *0.5 km E of Turangi*
Ika Lodge *B&B Apartment with Kitchen Cottage with Kitchen*

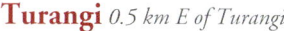

Margaret & Kenneth Toon
155 Taupahi Road,
Turangi
3334

Tel (07) 386 5538
or 027 292 5023
Fax (07) 386 5536
ikalodge@xtra.co.nz
www.ika.co.nz

Double/Twin $125-$150
Single $100-$110
(Breakfast provisions first night)
Dinner on request
Visa MC Diners Amex Eftpos accepted
Children welcome
5 Queen 1 Double/Twin
1 Twin 1 Single (7 bdrm)
Bathrooms: 2 Ensuite 2 Guest share

Ika Lodge offers superior bed and breakfast homestay suites, 2 bedroom apartment and 3 bedroom bungalow on the banks of the Tongariro River and minutes from some of the worlds best trout fishing. A perfect base for the Tongariro National Park ski fields and the famous Tongariro Crossing trek all in a tranquil garden setting.

Gisborne

Waihau Bay

Te Kaha

Maraenui

35

• Anaura Bay

• Tolaga Bay

2

• Waipaoa

Gisborne

2

0   Kilometres   20

0   Miles   12

Anaura Bay *23 km N of Tolaga Bay*
Anaura Beachstay or Willowflat Farmstay B&B *B&B Farmstay Self-contained*
Beachfront Cottage with Kitchen

June & Allan Hall
Anaura Bay, Tolaga Bay,
East Cape 3854, Gisborne

Tel (06) 862 6341
or 021 039 1136
Fax (06) 862 6371
willowflat@xtra.co.nz
www.anaurabeachstay.com

Double $120
Single $70
(Full breakfast)
Children half price
Dinner $25
Rental $120-$200 per night
Children welcome
1 Queen 1 Double/Twin (2 bdrm)
Bathrooms: 1 Family share

Paradise: the best of both worlds. Relax in tranquility on our deck in picturesque Anaura Bay, glorious sunrises, white sand and backdrop of beautiful native bush, fishing, walkways..... OR soak in the spa at our spacious home Willowflat, our sheep, cattle and cropping farm. Tolaga Bay Village, medical centre, takeaways, restaurant, Cashmere Company, hunting, golf, within 12km of Willowflat or 23km of Beachstay. Self-contained option available both venues $120-$200 per night 2 couples, minimum 2 nights.

Tolaga Bay *3 km N of Tolaga Bay*
Papatahi *Homestay Separate Suite*

Nicki & Bruce Jefferd
427 Waiapu Road,
Tolaga Bay

Tel (06) 862 6623
or 021 283 7178
Fax (06) 862 6623
nickibrucej@xtra.co.nz

Double $120
Single $70
(Full breakfast)
Children half price
Dinner $35pp
Children welcome
1 Queen 1 Double/Twin
2 Single (3 bdrm)
Bathrooms: 1 Ensuite 1 Guest share

Papatahi Homestay... easy to find being just 3km north of the Tolaga Bay township, on the Pacific Coast Highway. We have a comfortable, modern, sunny home set in a wonderful garden. Papatahi offers separate accommodation with ensuite. A golf course, fishing charters, the Tolaga Bay Cashmere Co. and several magnificent beaches are all just minutes away. Daily farm activities are often of interest to our guests. Friendly farm pets add to the experience! Great country meals and good wine are a speciality. Inspection will impress!

Gisborne

Waipaoa *20 km N of Gisborne*
The Willows *Farmstay*
Rosemary & Graham Johnson
Waipaoa,
RD 1,
Gisborne

Tel (06) 862 5605
or 027 483 7365
Fax (06) 862 5601

Double $90
Single $50
(Full breakfast)
Children 10% discount
Dinner $30 by arrangement
2 Queen 2 Single (3 bdrm)
Bathrooms: 1 Private 1 Guest share

Our home is situated on a hill amid a park-like garden with some wonderful trees planted by our forefathers. We enjoy the amenities available in the city and also the country life on our 440 acre property involving cattle, sheep, grapes and cropping. We now offer a double bedroom with a private bathroom. The bedroom has its own access so you can enjoy privacy if you so desire. We are situated 20km north of Gisborne on SH2 through the scenic Waioeka Gorge.

Gisborne *0.5 km N of Gisborne Central*
Sea View *B&B Homestay*
Raywyn & Gary Robinson
68 Salisbury Road,
Gisborne

Tel (06) 867 3879
raewyn@regaleggs.co.nz

Double $100
Single $80
(Continental breakfast)
Children welcome
2 Double/Twin 1 Twin
1 Single (3 bdrm)
Bathrooms: 2 Private

Absolute luxury and comfort. Beachfront bed & breakfast. Seaview is situated on the foreshore of Waikanae beach with unsurpassed panoramic views of Young Nicks Head and Poverty Bay. Just 50 metres from front door to golden sand, and warm blue waters. Only 2 minutes drive to the city (easy walking distance) and visitor information centre. Enjoy safe swimming and great surfing. 5 minutes to international golf course and Olympic pool complex. We offer 2 double bedrooms and twin room. 2 private bathrooms. Internet facilities available.

Gisborne *5 km NE of Gisborne*
Beach Stay *B&B*
Peter & Dorothy Rouse
111 Wairere Road,
Wainui Beach,
Gisborne

Tel (06) 868 8111
Fax (06) 868 8162
pete.dot@xtra.co.nz

Double/Twin $90-$110
Single $60 (Full breakfast)
Children $10
Dinner $25 pp
Pets welcome
1 Queen 2 Single (2 bdrm)
Bathrooms: 1 Ensuite 1 Private

We welcome you to our home which is situated right on the beach front at Wainui. The steps from the lawn lead down to the beach, which is renowned for its lovely clean sand, surf, pleasant walking and good swimming. Gisborne can also offer a host of entertainment, including golf on 1 of the finest golf courses, charter fishing trips, wine trails, Eastwood Hill Arboretum etc, or you may wish to relax on the beach for the day.

Gisborne *14 km S of Gisborne*
Fairlight *B&B*
Kay and Don Orchiston
52 Saddler Road,
RD 2,
Gisborne 4072

Tel 06 862 8499
or 027 440 9556
orchiston@clear.net.nz

Double/Twin $120
Single $80
(Full breakfast)
Children by arrangement
Dinner by arrangement
Children and pets welcome
1 King 1 Queen 1 Double/Twin
3 Single (4 bdrm)
Bathrooms: 1 Private
1 shower as well

Our home is situated on a hill with expansive views of the sea, city and rural wine region. We are 14 kms south of the city. Gisborne has beautiful beaches, scenic walks, restaurants and excellent sport facilities. We have 2 friendly sheep dogs and 2 elusive bengal cats. Visitors welcome to experience handling sheep and cattle. Trout fishing and deep sea fishing by prior arrangement.

Taranaki, Wanganui, Ruapehu, Rangitikei

New Plymouth - Brixton *12 km N of New Plymouth*

Loggers Retreat *B&B Cottage with Kitchen*

B&B
Approved

John & Brenda Reumers
42 Richmond Road,
Waitara
4373

Tel (06) 754 3131
or (06) 754 7668
Fax (06) 754 7668
loggersretreat@xtra.co.nz
www.windwand.co.nz/loggersretreat.htm

Double/Twin $130
(Full breakfast provisions)
Pet free home
Not suitable for children
1 Double/Twin (1 bdrm)
Bathrooms: 1 Private
Private outside bath

A rustic character-filled private board and battened 2 storyed cottage. Situated on 6 acres of beautiful rural land, which hosts a hand-built double storyed log house and surrounded by native gardens. Enjoy a wine on the deck or on the bridge over the lake outside your door. This is a family with 3 adult children and a variety of farm animals. All under the watchful gaze of the majestic Mt Taranaki.

New Plymouth *25 km N of New Plymouth*

Cottage by the Sea *Cottage with Kitchen Boutique Cottages with Kitchens*

B&B
Approved

Nancy & Hugh Mills
66 Lower Turangi Road,
RD 43, Waitara

Tel (06) 754 4548
or (06) 754 7915
cottagebythesea@clear.net.nz
www.cottagebythesea.co.nz

Double/Twin $155-$185
Single $145-$175
(Breakfast by arrangement)
Children by arrangement
Extra adults $25 each
Visa MC accepted
Not suitable for children
1 King/Twin 3 Queen
2 Double/Twin (4 bdrm)
Bathrooms: 4 Ensuite
1 ensuite per cottage

COTTAGE
by the sea
TARANAKI NEW ZEALAND

F ind yourself, lose yourself - the choice is yours. Peacefulness and privacy are our specialty - come to unwind or spend that special weekend. Enjoy the everchanging seaviews, discover our tranquil sunken garden, wander down 100 handcrafted steps to the secluded blacksand beach. Two 1-bedroom cottages nestled in their own gardens,and two new boutique, open-plan studios. All have kitchens and ensuites. Minutes from cafes, coastal walks, gardens and Mt Taranaki. Two small poodles may greet you. See our website for photos and details.

New Plymouth *3 km W of CBD*
Vineyard Holiday Flat *B&B Separate Suite*

Shirley & Trevor Knuckey
12 Scott Street,
Moturoa,
New Plymouth

Tel (06) 751 2992
or 027 310 3669
Fax (06) 751 2995
shirley12vineyard@xtra.co.nz

Double/Twin $85
Single $55
(Full breakfast)
Children $20
2 adults, 2 children $120
Visa MC accepted
Children welcome
1 King/Twin 1 Double/Twin
2 Single (1 bdrm)
Bathrooms: 1 Ensuite

Situated in New Plymouth's port-view Moturoa suburb. Enter through hobby vines to the spacious upstairs open-plan studio penthouse; 360 views of harbour, mountains, city; coast north and south. Shoreline pleasures nearby including eateries. Guests may be as self-contained as wished; lock-up garage, separate entrance, mini-kitchen. Private balcony, dining-table, full AV options, phone. Extra bed(s) by arrangement. Ideally situated for exploring Taranaki's attractions, or the perfect R&R retreat. There is a pet cat.

New Plymouth *8 km N of New Plymouth*
Rockvale Homestay *B&B Homestay*

Jeannette & Neil Cowley
97 Manutahi Road,
RD 2,
New Plymouth

Tel (06) 755 0750
or 027 682 1236
Fax (06) 755 0750
rockvale@xtra.co.nz
www.rockvalehomestay.co.nz

Double/Twin $120
Single $90
(Full breakfast)
Children $35 under 12 years
Dinner $30 by arrangement
Visa MC accepted
Children welcome
1 Queen 2 Single (2 bdrm)
Bathrooms: 1 Private

Welcome to our large, country home, surrounded by deer farm, with Mt Egmont as a backdrop. Guests' double room and lounge open onto balcony, with rural views. Relax in spa on deck. Your comfort is our concern. We host 1 guest party at a time. Join us for dinner, in our spacious living area or the deck in summer. We are close to airport, city, beaches, parks and mountain. Six golf courses are within easy drive. We welcome you to our home. Families welcome.

New Plymouth *0.5 km W of New Plymouth*
Airlie House *B&B Apartment with Kitchen*

Gabrielle Masters
161 Powderham Street,
New Pymouth

Tel (06) 757 8866
or 021 472 072
Fax (06) 757 8866
email@airliehouse.co.nz
www.airliehouse.co.nz

Double/Twin up to $145
Single up to $110
(Full breakfast)
Children negotiable
Studio $145 double
Visa MC Eftpos accepted
Children welcome
1 King/Twin 3 Queen 1 Twin
4 Single (5 bdrm)
Bathrooms: 1 Ensuite 3 Private 1 claw bath

Airlie House is a 110 year old character home nestled among mature trees and garden. This beautiful home provides 3 guest bedrooms with ensuites or private bathrooms, plus a studio apartment with its own kitchen and private bathroom. Located in central New Plymouth Airlie House is an easy 5 minute walk from shops, restaurants, the sea front, parks and many other local attractions. All rooms have many amenities available for your comfort, including Sky Digital TV, broadband and wireless internet access.

∽

New Plymouth *5 km W of New Plymouth centre*
Whaler's Rest *B&B*

Maureen & Denis Whiting
86A Barrett Road,
New Plymouth

Tel (06) 751 4272
or 027 328 0268
whalersrest@clear.net.nz
www.whalersrest.co.nz

Double/Twin $100
Single $80
(Full breakfast)
Children $20
Children and pets welcome
1 Double/Twin 1 Twin (2 bdrm)
Bathrooms: 1 Ensuite 1 Private

Large double bedroom with ensuite, and your own deck for drinks, plus twin room with private bathroom. Breakfast, continental or cooked. We are on the gateway to Surf Highway, 10 minutes to Oakura beach and 5 minutes to New Plymouth City featuring the Wind Wand, coastal walkway, Puke Ariki Museum and Pukekura Park. Your hosts Maureen and Denis who love their tennis and garden welcome you. We have a very sociable labrador Stella,and 2 cats, Tuffy and Biscuit. Please phone for bookings and directions.

New Plymouth *0.01 km N of New Plymouth City*
Timata Ora *Luxury B&B*
Carol & Rodney Hall
55 Gover Street,
New Plymouth,
Taranaki

Tel (06) 757 9917
or 0274 523 885
Fax (06) 759 1654
carol_rodney@iconz.co.nz
www.timataora.com

Double/Twin $125-$135
Single $115-$125
(Full breakfast)
Family suite when both
bedrooms used $220
Visa MC Eftpos accepted
4 Queen 1 Twin (5 bdrm)
Bathrooms: 4 Ensuite
All suites each have own bathroom

We warmly welcome guests to our fully refurbished central city home. A 1920s heritage home, Timata Ora offers 4 luxurious queen suites (1 with 4 Poster) each with own bathroom, TV, fridge, hair drier, iron/ironing board, heated towel rails, complimentary beverages and in room treats. The family suite has an additional twin bedroom along with the queen bedroom. Gregarious cat Murphy (the Butler) shares Timata Ora. Breakfast in your suite, dining room, in the conservatory or on the terrace.

~

New Plymouth - Bell Block *9 km SE of New Plymouth*
Hideaway Cottage *Luxury B&B Cottage with Kitchen*
Donald & Robyn Johnson
231 Henwood Road,
New Plymouth,
RD 2

Tel (06) 755 1360
or 027 212 7099
donrobyn@xtra.co.nz
www.hideawaycottage.co.nz

Double/Twin $275
Single $250
(Special breakfast)
Visa MC accepted
Not suitable for children
1 Queen (1 bdrm)
Bathrooms: 1 Ensuite

We look forward to welcomimg youto our little bit of paridise, close to New Plymouth but a world away. Free airport pickup and complimentary wine each night to enjoy by the pool, spa or roaring log fire. A sumptuous breakfast delivered to the cottage with late checkout.Set on 22 acres but handy to the city many golf courses, moutain walks and the sea.

New Plymouth *1 km W of Post Office*

Arcadia Lodge *B&B*

Joanne & Mark Long
52 Young Street,
New Plymouth, 4601

Tel (06) 769 9100
or 0800 ARCADE
Fax (06) 769 9120
arcadialodge@ihug.co.nz
www.arcadialodge.net

Double/Twin $85-$90
(Continental breakfast)
Additional guests $15 per night each
Visa MC Diners
Amex Eftpos accepted
Pet free home
6 Queen 8 Double/Twin
1 Twin 19 Single (18 bdrm)
Bathrooms: 4 Ensuite 1 Private
6 Guest share

Arcadia Lodge has a mix of 18 double, multi-bed and bunk rooms. Each room has a telephone, television, refridgerator and tea and coffee making facilities. Four rooms have ensuites and the rest share modern bathrooms.There are two lounges, with free broadband connection. A continental breakfast is included. Off street parking is provided for 12 cars. Arcadia Lodge is wheelchair friendly. Arcadia Lodge is centrally located within easy walking distance of most of New Plymouth's amenities and the inter-city bus stop.

New Plymouth *2 km NE of Post Office*

The Grange *B&B*

Rachael Nielsen and Alan Clarke
44B Victoria Road,
Brooklands,
New Plymouth

Tel (06) 759 8004
or 027 434 5680
grangebandb@xtra.co.nz

Double/Twin $120-$140
Single $80-$90
(Full breakfast)
Visa MC Diners Amex accepted
Pets welcome
1 King/Twin 2 Queen (3 bdrm)
Bathrooms: 3 Ensuite

Come and stay in our modern award-winning home built with the privacy and comfort of our guests in mind. With unique bush views and a house designed to take full advantage of the sun, our guests can enjoy relaxing in the lounge or the extensive tiled courtyards and listen to the sounds of the native birds. The Grange is centrally heated, security controlled and located adjacent to the renowned Pukekura Park and Bowl of Brooklands. The city is 10 minutes walk.

Stratford *0.5 km N of Stratford*
Stratford Lodge (Stallards) *B&B Homestay Farmstay Guest House*

Billieanne & Corb Stallard
3514 State Highway 3,
Stratford, Northern Boundary

Tel (06) 765 8324
Fax (06) 765 8325
stallardbb@infogen.net.nz
www.stratfordlodge.co.nz

Double/Twin $95
Single $55
(Full breakfast)
Children $20
Visa MC accepted
Pet free home
Children welcome
2 Double/Twin 2 Twin
2 Single (4 bdrm)
Bathrooms: 4 Ensuite 1 Guest share

Graceful"Upstairs Downstairs" comfort. A down to earth gardeners rest Aga cooked or continental breakfast included. Free self-catering kitchen, tea, coffee, biscuits. Homely or private. Own key. Optional separate lounge. Restaurants, taverns, shops nearby. Rooms are antique, romantic with TV, heaters, electric blankets, serviced daily. Gardens, BBQ, row boat, bush bath, river walks. 15 minutes to Mt Egmont ski fields, tramping. Centrally located easy distance to New Plymouth, museums, famous gardens, tourist attractions. Interests include gemstones travel, art. Welcome. AA accredited

Egmont National Park *9 km W of Stratford*
Anderson's Alpine Lodge *Homestay Farmstay*

Berta Anderson
922 Pembroke Rd,
RD 21,
Stratford 4391,
Taranaki

Tel (06) 765 6620
or 0274 412 372
andersonsalpinelodge@xtra.co.nz
www.andersonsalpinelodge.co.nz

Double/Twin $175-$215
Single $175
(Full breakfast)
Visa MC accepted
Pets welcome
1 King/Twin 1 Queen
1 Double/Twin 2 Single (3 bdrm)
Bathrooms: 3 Ensuite

Swiss style lodge rests in 50 acres of native bush capturing majestic views of Mount Egmont/Taranaki. Landscaping includes New Zealand natives,lakes, waterwheel and bushwalks. Three charming rooms with ensuite, one with spa bath. Egmont National Park opposite front gate. 5km to spectacular walking tracks, summit climb (guides available) and skiing. Helicopter rides by request.Trout streams, gardens and museums nearby. 9km to Stratford. Swiss Berta Anderson has lived on the mountain since 1976.

Waitotara - Wanganui *29 km W of Wanganui*
Ashley Park *Farmstay Cottage with Kitchen*
Wendy Pearce
State Highway 3,
Box 36,
Waitotara,
Wanganui

Tel (06) 346 5917
Fax (06) 346 5861
ashley_park@xtra.co.nz
www.ashleypark.co.nz

Double/Twin $100-$140
Single $100
(Full breakfast)
Dinner $30
Visa MC Diners Eftpos accepted
1 Queen 4 Single (3 bdrm)
Bathrooms: 1 Ensuite 1 Guest share

We have a 500 acre sheep and cattle farm and live in a comfortable home, set in an attractive garden with a swimming pool and tennis court. Also in the garden is an antique shop selling Devonshire teas. 100 metres from the house is a 4 acre park and lake, aviaries and a collection of hand fed pet farm animals. We welcome guests to have dinner with us. Self-contained accommodation is available in the park.

Wanganui *2 km NW of Wanganui City centre*
Kembali *B&B Homestay*
Marylyn & Wes Palmer
26 Taranaki Street,
St Johns Hill,
Wanganui

Tel (06) 347 1727
or 027 741 7517
027 244 4347
wespalmer@xtra.co.nz

Double/Twin $100-$115
Single $70-$85
(Full breakfast)
Small charge for laundry facilities
Visa MC accepted
Pet free home
Not suitable for children
1 Queen 1 Twin (2 bdrm)
Bathrooms: 1 Private

Kembali is a modern, centrally heated, sunny home in a quiet street overlooking trees and wetlands. Upstairs guest bedrooms, bathroom and lounge (with TV, fridge, tea/coffee) are for 1 party/groups exclusive use. Retired, no pets, children married, we offer a restful stay. We enjoy meeting people, gardening, travel, reading and have Christian interests. Off-street parking and laundry available. 5 minutes drive to city, heritage buildings, restored paddle steamer, restaurants, museum, art gallery and walks. We look forward to welcoming you.

Wanganui *.5 km N of Wanganui centre*
Braemar House *B&B Guest House*

Clive Rivers
2 Plymouth Street, Wanganui

Tel (06) 348 2301
Fax (06) 348 2301
contact@braemarhouse.co.nz
www.braemarhouse.co.nz

Double/Twin $75-$95
Single $65-$75 (Full breakfast)
Children $10
Dinner $25 by arrangement
Visa MC Eftpos accepted
Pet free home
Children welcome
4 Queen 1 Double/Twin
3 Twin (8 bdrm)
Bathrooms: 4 Guest share
Deluxe sized bath, powerful showers

Welcome to 'Olde Worlde Charm'. This restored historic Homestead, nestled alongside the Wanganui River, has a homely ambience making your stay restful and enjoyable. The graceful entrance leads to eight centrally heated, period-designed bedrooms,drawing room and dining room. Laundry, wireless internet, fully equipped kitchen available. Off-street parking set in beautiful gardens.Close to the city and tourist attractions, The paddle steamer Waimarie passes daily in front of the Homestead. We look forward to you visiting Braemar House.

Wanganui *6 km N of Wanganui*
Arles B&B *B&B Apartment with Kitchen*

Sue & Tom Day
50 Riverbank Road,
RD3, Wanganui, 4573

Tel 06 343 6557
or 021 257 8257
Fax 06 343 6557
sue@arles.co.nz
www.arles.co.nz

Double/Twin $140-$180
Single $120-$150
(Full breakfast)
Children $30-35
Visa MC Diners accepted
Pet free home Children welcome
1 King 2 Queen 1 Double/Twin
2 Twin (6 bdrm)
Bathrooms: 2 Ensuite, 1 Private in
B&B; 1 Private in Apartment

Arles is a charming Edwardian homestead built in the 1880s adjacent to the Whanganui River. We offer affordable luxury to couples and families in the centrally-heated house or 2 bedroom separate modern apartment. All facilities are complimentary and include a fully-equipped kitchen, laundry, broadband/wireless internet, saltwater pool, barbecue and off-road parking. A sumptuous breakfast full of home-made delights starts the day for house guests. We look forward to meeting you.

Taumarunui *5 km NE of Taumarunui*
Matawa Country Home *Farmstay*

Shirley & Allan Jones
213 Taringamotu Road,
Taumarunui

Tel (07) 896 7722
Fax (07) 895 6927
costleyj@farmside.co.nz

Double/Twin $100-$120
Single $70-$80
(Full breakfast)
Children half price
Dinner by arrangement
Children welcome
1 King 1 Twin (2 bdrm)
Bathrooms: 1 Guest share

Our spacious home is situated 5km from the centre of Taumarunui surrounded by a peaceful one acre garden with a native bush backdrop filled with NZ native birds. The bedrooms open on to a large verandah. Laundry available. A stream runs along one boundary of the 80 acre property suitable for walks and summertime swimming. A golf course is located within 2 km, along with guided mountain walks, canoeing, hot pools, scenic flights, skiing, trout fishing and white-water rafting are all within an hours drive.

Taumarunui - Piriaka *10 km S of Taumarunui*
Awarua Lodge *B&B Separate Suite*

Raewyn & Jack Vernon
1063 State Highway 4,
Piriaka,
Taumarunui

Tel (07) 896 8100
or 021 031 5151
Fax (07) 896 8102
info@awarualodge.co.nz
www.awarualodge.co.nz

Double/Twin $180
(Full breakfast)
Suite $350
Visa MC accepted
1 King/Twin 1 King (2 bdrm)
Bathrooms: 1 Private

Awarua Lodge, set in parkland grounds overlooking the Whanganui River, is self-contained guest accommodation offering a suite that sleeps 4. The decor simply commands you to relax. Visit the Whanganui & Tongariro National Parks. Try your hand golfing on Taumarunui's premiere golf course, rated in the top NZ 50. Plan your adventures; tramping, fishing, canoeing, skiing, mountain biking. Watch sheep shearing and the milking of a large NZ dairy herd.

Taumarunui - Owhango *15 km S of Taumarunui*
Fernleaf *B&B Farmstay Cottage No Kitchen*

Carolyn & Melvin Forlong
58 Tunanui Road,
RD 1, Owhango

Tel (07) 895 4847
or 0800 FERNLEAF
0210 275 3847
0210 275 3848
Fax (07) 895 4837
fernleaf.farm@xtra.co.nz

Double/Twin $100-$150
Single $85-$100
(Full breakfast)
Dinner $25
Visa MC Diners Amex accepted
Children welcome
2 Queen 1 Double/Twin
1 Twin (4 bdrm)
Bathrooms: 2 Ensuite 1 Guest share

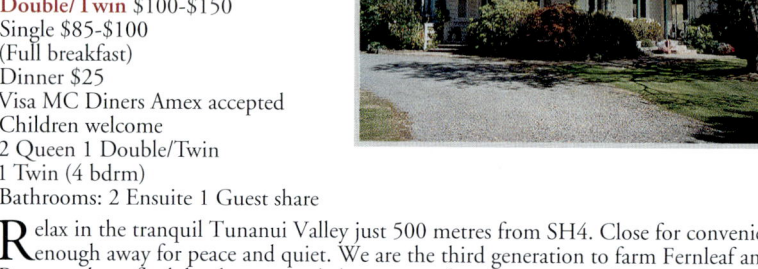

Relax in the tranquil Tunanui Valley just 500 metres from SH4. Close for convenience, far enough away for peace and quiet. We are the third generation to farm Fernleaf and our Romney sheep flock has been recorded every year for ninety years . The views from various vantage point on the farm are awesome, taking in the mountains: Ruapehu, Ngaruahoe, Tongariro and Taranaki. Enjoy our generous country hospitality, wonderful breakfast, a beautiful dalmatian Sally, and friendly cats. Other meals by arrangement. "River Fishing"

Raetihi *0.5 km N of Raetihi*
Log Lodge *Luxury B&B*
Jan & Bob Lamb
5 Ranfurly Terrace,
Raetihi

Tel (06) 385 4135
Fax (06) 385 4835
Lamb.Log-Lodge@Xtra.co.nz

Double/Twin $115
Single $60
(Full breakfast)
Children under 14 $40
Spa $5 per person
Visa MC accepted
1 Queen 1 Double/Twin 4 Single
Bathrooms: 2 Private
We only accept one booking at a time

A unique opportunity to stay in a modern authentic log home sited high on 7 acres on the edge of town. Completely private accommodation, with own bathroom. All sleeping on mezzanine, your own lounge with wood fire, snooker table, TV/video, stereo and dining area, opening onto large verandah, with swimming pool and spa available. Panoramic views of Mts Ruapehu, Ngauruhoe and Tongariro. Tongariro National Park and Turoa Skifield are a half hour scenic drive.

Ohakune *6 km W of Ohakune*
Mitredale *Homestay Farmstay*
Audrey & Diane Pritt
Smiths Road,
RD,
Ohakune

Tel (06) 385 8016
or 027 453 1916
Fax (06) 385 8016
mitredale@ihug.co.nz

Double/Twin $100
Single $60
(Continental breakfast)
Dinner $35pp by arrangement
Visa MC accepted
Pets welcome
1 Double/Twin 2 Single (2 bdrm)
Bathrooms: 1 Family share

We farm sheep, bull beef and run a boarding kennel in a beautiful peaceful valley with magnificent views of Mt Ruapehu. Tongariro National Park for skiing, walking, photography. Excellent 18 hole golf course, great fishing locally. We are members of Ducks Unlimited (a conservation group)and our local wine club. We have 2 labradors. We offer dinner traditional farmhouse (Diane, a cook book author), or breakfast with excellent home-made jams. Take Raetihi Road, at Hotel/BP Service Station corner. 4km to Smiths Road. Last house 2km.

Ohakune *0.9 km SE of Junction*
Dakune Lodge *B&B Ski Lodge*
Nicolas & Tasha Cowell
42 Park Avenue,
Ohakune
4625

Tel (06) 385 8448
Fax (06) 385 8448
info@dakunelodge.co.nz
www.dakunelodge.co.nz

Double/Twin $110-$160
Single $110
(Continental breakfast)
Summer Rate $30 per person
Visa MC Amex Eftpos accepted
2 Queen 5 Double/Twin
11 Single (9 bdrm)
Bathrooms: 3 Guest share

A beautiful wooden Lodge with mountain views in a quiet location, yet near the Junction. Warm comfortable accommodation for singles, couples, families or groups with shared bathrooms. Facilities include sauna, spa,games and drying rooms, in-house massage clinic. Socialise by the log fire in our large friendly lounge. Meals by request. Open all year round - wonderful memories are made here!

Taihape *0.1 km W of Taihape Info Centre*
Korirata Homestay *B&B Homestay*

Patricia & Noel Gilbert
25 Pukeko Street,
Taihape

Tel (06) 388 0315
Fax (06) 388 0315
korirata@xtra.co.nz

Double/Twin $90
Single $55
(Special breakfast)
Children half price under 10
Dinner by arrangement
Visa MC accepted
4 Single (2 bdrm)
Bathrooms: 1 Guest share

B&B
Approved

A warm welcome awaits you at the top of the hill in Taihape, where panoramic views of mountains, ranges and countryside, add to the tranquil surroundings. 3 quarters of an acre is landscaped with shrubs, hydroponics, home-grown vegetables and chrysanthemums in season. Meals, are with hosts, using produce from the garden where possible. Comfortable beds with electric blankets. Rafting, bungy jumping and farm visits can be arranged. 1 hour to Ruapehu, Lake Taupo and 2 and a half hours to Wellington and Rotorua.

**All our B&Bs are non-smoking
unless stated otherwise in the text.**

Taihape/Rangitikei *26 km NE of Taihape*

Tarata Fishaway *Luxury B&B Homestay Farmstay*
Stephen & Trudi Mattock
Mokai Road, RD 3, Taihape

Tel (06) 388 0354 or 027 279 7037
027 227 4986   Fax (06) 388 0954
fishaway@xtra.co.nz   www.tarata.co.nz

Double/Twin $120-$220 Single $60-$110
(Continental breakfast provisions)
Children under 12 half price
Dinner $40 pp by arrangement
Visa MC accepted Children and pets welcome
4 King/Twin 5 Queen 1 Double/Twin 3 Single (9 bdrm)
Bathrooms: 4 Ensuite 1 Guest share spa bath

We are very lucky to have a piece of New Zealand's natural beauty. Tarata is nestled in bush in the remote Mokai Valley where the picturesque Rangitikei River meets the rugged Ruahine Ranges. With the wilderness and unique trout fishing right at our doorstep, it is the perfect environment to bring up our 3 children. Stephen offers guided fishing and rafting trips for all ages. Raft through the gentle crystal clear waters of the magnificent Rangitikei River, visit Middle Earth and a secret waterfall, stunning scenery you will never forget.Our spacious home and our large garden allow guests private space to relax and unwind. Whether it is by the pool on a hot summers day with a good book, soaking in the spa pool after a day on the river or enjoying a cosy winters night in front of our open fire with a glass of wine. Come on a farm tour meeting our many friendly farm pets, experience our nightlife on our free spotlight safari and Tarata is only 6km past the new flying fox and bungy jump.Stay in our Homestead or in Tarata's fully self-contained River Retreats where you can enjoy a spa bath with million dollar views of the river and relax on the large decking amidst native birds and trees. Peace, privacy and tranquillity at its best! We will even deliver a candle light dinner to your door. We think Tarata is truly a magic place and we would love sharing it with you.
Directions: Tarata Fishaway is 26 scenic kilometres from Taihape. Turn off SH1, 6km south of Taihape at the Gravity Canyon Bungy and Ohotu signs. Follow the signs (14km) to the bungy bridge. We are 6 km past here on Mokai Road. Features & Attractions: Trout Fishing and Scenic Rafting, Visit LOTR, 6kms Past Bungy, Flying Fox, Mini Golf (with a difference), swimming pool, spa pools, bush walks, spotlight safaris, camp outs, claybird shooting.

Taihape *1 km S of Taihape*
Llanerchymedd *Luxury B&B Apartment with Kitchen*
Alan & Jan Thomas
10 Dixon Way,
Taihape

Tel (06) 388 0283
or (06) 388 0666
021 127 6211
Fax (06) 388 0683
alajan@xtra.co.nz

Double/Twin $90
(Continental breakfast provisions)
Children $20 per head
Additional guests $20 per head
Children welcome
1 Queen 1 Double/Twin
2 Single (1 bdrm)
Bathrooms: 1 Ensuite

We are a married couple with two children and two cats. LLanerchymedd is a quiet residence, with established gardens. We are two minutes from Taihape and are easily located, 1km south of the town with panoramic views of Mt Ruapehu. A tranquil walk up into the gardens is well rewarded with fantastic views. Take a glass of wine with you and relax in the top gazebo - you will feel on top of the world.

Taihape *32 km E of Taihape*
River Valley Lodge *Adventure Lodge*
Brian & Nicola Megaw
Mangahoata Rd,
Pukeokahu,
Taihape, 4792

Tel (06) 388 1444
or 0800 248 666
Fax (06)388 1859
thelodge@rivervalley.co.nz
www.rivervalley.co.nz

Double/Twin $169-$169
Single $158-$158
(Full breakfast)
Children Please refer to our website
Dinner Please refer to our website
Visa MC Amex Eftpos accepted
Children welcome
6 King/Twin 2 King (8 bdrm)
Bathrooms: 8 Ensuite
All rooms specified have ensuite showers and toilets

River Valley, is an Adventure Lodge. It is a place that is our home, where we have put down deep roots. It is a place where we feel that the spirit in which we do something, is an essential part of any experience. We actively search for ways in which we can offer you, our guests, experiences that are meaningful and personal. Experiences that are creative, where you feel uplifted, where we can share our stories, and you can share yours.

Taihape *1 km S of Taihape*
Lookout Rd B&B *B&B*

Irene and Allistair Verschoor
14 Lookout Road,
Taihape
4720

Tel 06 388 1920
or 027 688 1920
alrene@xtra.co.nz

Double/Twin $99
Single $79
(Continental breakfast)
Dinner by arrangement
1 complimentary glass of wine
with dinner pp
Visa MC accepted
Not suitable for children
1 Queen (1 bdrm)
Bathrooms: 1 Ensuite

Irene and Allistair with Gucci (the dog) and Oscar (the cat) welcome you to our lovely country home with panoramic views, where we invite you to relax and replenish. Not glitzy or intimidating, more comfortable and cosy. Get to know Kiwis on a personal basis. Meals are with hosts using homegrown produce when available. The ensuite has a large double bathtub. A great location 1 hour to Skifields, 1 1/2 hours to Taupo, 2 1/2 hours to Wellington, Rotorua and Hawkes Bay.

Marton *45 km N of Palmerston North*
Rea's Inn *B&B Homestay*

Keith and Lorraine Rea
12 Dunallen Avenue,
Marton

Tel (06) 327 4442
or (027) 479 9589
Fax (06) 327 4442
keithandlorraine@xtra.co.nz

Double/Twin $95
Single $55
(Continental breakfast)
Children half price
Dinner $30
Visa MC accepted
Children welcome
1 Queen 1 Twin (2 bdrm)
Bathrooms: 1 Guest share

We have a warm comfortable home offering hospitality, peace and tranquility. Situated in quiet cul-de-sac with a private garden setting. Guests stay in separate wing of home. Close to Nga Tawa and Huntley Schools. Ideal for weekend retreat or stopover. (Only 2 hours from Wellington Ferry). Your comfort and pleasure are important to us. Clients enjoy our homemade hot bread served at breakfast. Our birman cat likes people too, and we all welcome you to come, relax and enjoy the friendly atmosphere at Rea's Inn.

Taranaki, Wanganui, Ruapehu, Rangitikei

Hawkes Bay

Mahia Peninsula - Mahanga Beach *50 km N of Wairoa*
Reomoana *B&B Apartment with Kitchen Cottage with Kitchen*

Louise Schick
629 Mahanga Road,
RD 8, Mahanga Beach,
Mahia,
Hawkes Bay 4198

Tel (06) 837 5898
Fax (06) 837 5990
reomoana@paradise.net.nz
www.reomoana.co.nz

Double/Twin $120-$150
Single $60
(Continental breakfast)
Children $20
Dinner $35
Visa MC accepted
Children and pets welcome
2 Queen 1 Twin 1 Single (4 bdrm)
Bathrooms: 1 Ensuite 1 Private

"Reomoana" - The voice of the sea. Overlooking the Pacific with breathtaking views this rustic home with handcrafted features combines New Zealand and Hungarian creativity. Situated on a hillside the property is grazed by sheep and cattle, where walks may be enjoyed through QE 2 convenanted native bush. 5mins. walk to 8Kms. of white sandy beach, a recreational paradise for swimming, surfing and fishing. Attractions:- Morere Hot Springs, Paua farm, Marae visits, Golf-course and fishing charters. 6Kms. to Cafe Mahia and Sunset Point Restaurants.

Eskdale *10 km N of Napier*
Cornucopia Lodge *Luxury B&B Cottage with Kitchen*

Melanie Held
361 State Highway 5,
Eskdale,
Napier

Tel (06) 836 6508
or 021 921 211
stay@cornucopia-lodge.com
www.cornucopia-lodge.com

Double/Twin $120-$165
Single $80-$120
(Continental breakfast)
Dinner on request
Visa MC Diners Amex accepted
Children and pets welcome
1 Queen 1 Double/Twin (2 bdrm)
Bathrooms: 2 Ensuite

You will receive a warm welcome from Melanie and the friendly border collies at Cornucopia Lodge. The fully self contained Lodge is situated on three acres of gardens, is tastefully furnished and has two lovely bedrooms each with ensuite. The warm and cosy lounge has an open fireplace and the kitchen is fully equipped.

Hawkes Bay

Bay View - Napier *12 km N of Napier*

Kilbirnie *Homestay*
Jill & John Grant
84 Le Quesne Road, Bay View, Napier

Tel (06) 836 6929
or 027 234 7363
jill.johng@xtra.co.nz
www.bnb.co.nz/kilbirnie.html

Double/Twin $95-$110
(Special breakfast)
Dinner $40pp by arrangement
Visa MC accepted
Not suitable for children
2 Queen (2 bdrm)
Bathrooms: 1 Ensuite 1 Private

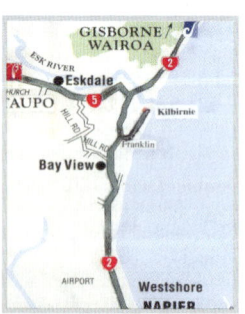

We moved with our dog in 1996 to the quiet end of an unspoiled fishing beach by the Esk River, attracted by the beauty and position away from the traffic, while only 15 minutes of a full range of harbourside restaurants north of Napier.

Kilbirnie is near the Taupo Road intersection with the Pacific Highway to Gisborne, with off-road parking. Upstairs, air-conditioned guest rooms have restful views of the Pacific Ocean one side or vineyards on the other, private bathrooms, excellent showers, abundant hot water, comfortable firm beds and guest lounge with TV tea making and ironing facilities,guests also welcome in family room.

Special breakfast overlooking the ocean is an experience which makes lunch seem superfluous. We are retired farmers with time to share good company, fresh imaginative food and juice, real coffee, an eclectic range of books, who invite you to enjoy our hospitality in modern surroundings. We have 18 years home hosting experience and are non-smokers.

Directions: from Taupo first left after intersection Highways 2 & 5. Franklin Road to Le Quesne, proceed to far end beachfront. From Napier first right after Mobil Station (approx 1km). Prior contact appreciated.

Bay View - Napier *12 km N of Napier*
The Grange *B&B Farmstay & Self-contained Lodge*

Roslyn & Don Bird
263 Hill Road, Eskdale, Hawkes Bay
PO Box 136 Bay View, Hawkes Bay

Tel (06) 836 6666 or 027 28 15738
Fax (06) 836 6456 thefarmstay@xtra.co.nz
www.thefarmstay.com

Farmstay Double/Twin $100-$120 Single $85 (Full breakfast)
LODGE: dbl $140, sgl $100, extra person $30pp, opt breakfast
Dinner $45pp 3 course with wine
Visa MC accepted Children welcome
1 King/Twin 1 King 2 Double/Twin 2 Single (3 bdrm)
Bathrooms: 1 Private 1 Guest share Farmstay guest max 4 share
luxury bathroom, separate toilet

Enjoy genuine kiwi hospitality at our tranquil countryside escape overlooking the picturesque Esk Valley."THE GRANGE"our delightfully modern "FARM-STAY" and superior SELF-CONTAINED "LODGE" offers private,sunny, spacious accommodation in relaxing peaceful surrounds. Breathe in spectacular farm, valley vineyard, coastal and city VIEWS. Feel the comforts of home as we tempt you with fine wine, farm produce, baking, and preserves. We're an outgoing couple who really enjoy the company of guests. Experience our FARM life with Roslyn, Zac (weimaraner farm dog), and Allie(resident cat). Feed sheep(Lilley and Rose etc), cows (especially Snowy), pigs (Bubble and Squeek), chickens, dairy goats (try milking Betsy) or bottle-feeding a lamb (seasonal). Its a winelovers paradise! Don a third generation Hawkes Bay WINEMAKER with more than 30 years experience is passionate about the wine industry and happy to share his knowledge over dinner or help plan your personalized WINERY ADVENTURE. Explore the world's ART DECO Capital NAPIER 12 MINUTES drive away and Hawke's Bay's many regional attractions within 30 minutes. Experience the thrill of MOUNTAIN BIKING at Eskdale mtb park, discover the FISHING waters of the beautiful Esk river or just relax visiting art studios, wineries and rural cafes. We have it all within 5 minutes of home. We are always happy to advise on any tours or special requests as our knowledge, information and contacts throughout Hawkes Bay are invaluable. Unwind on the Deck to the soothing chorus of native birds in the surrounding gardens and trees and at day's end spend time romancing over our wonderful night sky. Email access available. We also offer our Taupo (Kinloch) cottage to those wishing to stay in that area. Share our home or retreat to your "Lodge". "Our Place Is Your Place." 1km off SH5 at Eskdale or 3km off SH2 at Bay View.

Bay View - Napier *10 km N of napier*
Bay Bach *B&B Homestay*
Jill and Iain Angus
117 Rogers Road,
Napier 4104

Tel (06) 836 5141
or 021 105 7512
Fax (06) 836 5141
jill-iain@xtra.co.nz
www.baybach.co.nz

Double/Twin $155
Single $125
(Special breakfast)
Children by arrangement
Dinner $50pp by arrangement
Lunches by arrangement
Visa MC accepted
Children and pets welcome
1 King/Twin 1 King (2 bdrm)
Bathrooms: 2 Ensuite

A warm friendly welcome awaits you at Bay Bach. Our architectural award winning uniquely stylish home has been built with your comfort and relaxation as it's primary goal. The beds and linen are of the highest quality and comfort. You have your own patio, entrance and car park with a two minute stroll to the sea. It's a short drive to our beautiful Art Deco city, Napier. Wineries and restaurants abound Hear the sea and look down the grapes to the hills as you breakfast.

Napier - Westshore *3 km N of Post Office*
Touch th' Tide *B&B Homestay*
Peter and Cheryl Sugden
7 Charles Street,
Westshore,
Napier 4142

Tel Landline (06) 835 7280
Mobile 027 222 9321
Mobile 027 478 9093
suggy@xtra.co.nz

Double/Twin $140-$160
Single $95-$95
(Full breakfast)
Children by arrangement.
Visa MC accepted
Children welcome
2 Queen 2 Single (2 bdrm)
Bathrooms: 1 Private 1 Guest share

W elcome. Enjoy breakfast on the terrace. Watch the yachts, the distant port, people fishing or meandering along the beach reserve. Swim. Walk to the cafes in Ahuriri's historic village or drive a few minutes to the world renowned Art Deco City. Visit the gannet colony, wineries, play golf or walk the estuary with its water sport facilities. We are a retired, well traveled pharmacist and nurse who have lived locally for many years, so can help plan your day. We share our home with you.

Napier *2.5 km W of City*
Logan B & B *B&B Homestay*
Pam & John Thompson
15 Logan Avenue,
Napier
4110

Tel (06) 843 7558
or 027 660 6982
Fax (06) 843 7569
pam.john@xtra.co.nz

Double/Twin $130-$130
Single $110-$110
(Continental breakfast)
1 Queen (1 bdrm)
Bathrooms: 1 Private
Spacious with spa bath & shower
right next to room

We are Art Deco enthusiasts living in an iconic home situated in Napier's renowned Art Deco suburb. A simple 'walk around the block' from our front door enables you to complete much of the 'Marewa Meander' Art Deco tour. Better still, you are just 5 minutes drive from Napier's inner city which is packed with more Art Deco interest, cafes, and shopping. Winery tours are readily available and we have good local knowledge. Excellent off-street parking and pick-up service by arrangement. 2 friendly cats in residence.

Napier *1 km N of Napier*
Spence Bed & Breakfast *B&B Homestay*
Kay & Stewart Spence
17 Cobden Road,
Napier
4110

Tel (06) 835 9454
0800 117 890
Fax (06) 835 9454
ksspence@actrix.gen.nz
www.spencebnb.co.nz

Double/Twin $160-$170
Single $140
(Full breakfast)
Visa MC accepted
Children welcome
1 Queen 1 Single (1 bdrm)
Bathrooms: 1 Ensuite

Welcome to our comfortable near new home. Quiet area, 10-15 minutes walk from Art Deco City centre. Guest suite opens outside to patio, petanque court and colourful garden. Lounge includes double bed settee, TV, kitchenette with tea making facilities, fridge and microwave. Bedroom has queen and single beds, ensuite bathroom. We have hosted for over 10 years and enjoy overseas travel. Able to meet public transport. Directions: port end Marine Parade, Coote Road, right into Thompson Road, left into Cobden Road opposite water tower.

Napier *1.5 km N of Post Office*
A Room with a View *B&B Homestay*

Robert McGregor
9 Milton Terrace,
Napier

Tel (06) 835 7434
or 027 249 2040
Fax (06) 835 1912
roomwithview@xtra.co.nz

Double/Twin $130-$130
Single $100-$100
(Continental breakfast)
Visa MC accepted
1 Queen (1 bdrm)
Bathrooms: 1 Private with bath &
shower, directly oppposite bedroom

After 10 years hosting with my late wife, I'm continuing to enjoy companionship, conversation and laughter with guests. Fourth generation property, 130 year old garden, spacious room, panoramic sea view. 15 minute walk to restaurants at historic Port Ahuriri or our world famous Art Deco city centre. Private bathroom. Free laundry facilities, pick-up service, internet. Off-street parking. Smoke-free inside please. I'm interested in travel, gardening, the arts, and especially local history, as until retirement I was Executive Director of the Art Deco Trust.

Napier *1.2 km N of Napier Central*
Hillcrest *B&B Homestay*

Nancy & Noel Lyons
4 George Street,
Hospital Hill,
Napier

Tel (06) 835 1812
lyons@inhb.co.nz
www.hillcrestnapier.co.nz

Double/Twin $100-$110
Single $80
(Continental breakfast)
Visa MC accepted
Pet free home
Not suitable for children
1 Double/Twin 2 Single (2 bdrm)
Bathrooms: 1 Guest share

If you require quiet accommodation just minutes from the city centre, our comfortable home provides peace in restful surroundings. Relax on wide decks overlooking our garden, or enjoy the spectacular sea views. Explore nearby historic places and the botanical gardens. Your own lounge with tea/coffee making; laundry and off-street parking available. We have travelled extensively and welcome the opportunity of meeting visitors. Our interests are travel, music, bowls and embroidery. We will happily meet you at the travel depots. Holiday home at Mahia Beach available.

Napier *5 km S of Napier*
Snug Harbour *Homestay*
Ruth & Don McLeod
147 Harold Holt Avenue,
Napier

Tel (06) 843 2521
Fax (06) 843 2520
donmcld@clear.net.nz
www.snugharbour.co.nz

Double/Twin $100-$120
Single $70
(Full breakfast)
Dinner $35 by arrangement
Visa MC accepted
Pet free home
1 Queen 1 Twin (2 bdrm)
Bathrooms: 1 Ensuite 1 Family share

Ruth & Don welcome you to their comfortable home with its rural outlook and sunny attractive patio. The garden studio with ensuite and tea making facilities has its own entrance. We are situated on the outskirts of Napier City, the art deco city of the World, and in close proximity to wineries and many other tourist attractions. We both have a background in teaching, with interests in travel, gardening and photography.

~

Napier *1 km N of Napier on hill above city*
The Coachhouse *Cottage with Kitchen*
Jan Chalmers
9 Gladstone Road,
Napier

Tel (06) 835 6126
or 021 251 5847
janchalmers@paradise.net.nz
www.thecoachhouse.co.nz

Double/Twin $100
Single $80 (
Full breakfast provisions)
Children $25 - babies free
$140 for 3, $160 for 4
Visa MC accepted
Children and pets welcome
1 Queen 2 Single (2 bdrm)
Bathrooms: 1 Private

On the hill over-looking a gorgeous Mediterranean garden and sea views, the historic Coach-house is tastefully renovated and totally self-contained. It contains 2 bedrooms, open plan kitchen, dining, living rooms, bathroom and separate toilet. The fridge will be full of a variety of breakfast supplies. TV and radio included and fresh flowers in all rooms. The sunny deck has a table and chairs and gas barbecue. Off-street parking and easy access plus peace and privacy complete the picture.

Hawkes Bay

Napier - Taradale *7.5 km SW of Napier*
'279' Church Road *B&B Homestay*

Sandy Edginton
279 Church Road,
Taradale,
Napier

Tel (06) 844 7814
or 021 447 814
sandy.279@homestaynapier.co.nz
www.homestaynapier.co.nz

Double/Twin $120-$150
Single $90-$100
(Full breakfast)
Dinner by arrangement
Smoking area available
Visa MC accepted
Not suitable for children
1 Queen 1 Double/Twin
1 Single (2 bdrm)
Bathrooms: 1 Guest share Separate toilet

279, an elegant and spacious home set amongst mature trees and gardens, offers excellent hospitality in a relaxed, friendly atmosphere to domestic and international visitors. Located adjacent to Mission Estate and Church Road Wineries, restaurants and craft galleries, 279 is within a short drive of Art Deco Napier, Hastings, golf courses, and tourist activities. I welcome you to 279 and will help make your visit the highlight of your travels.

Napier - Taradale *10 km W of Napier*
Otatara Heights *B&B Apartment with Kitchen*

Sandra & Roy Holderness
57 Churchill Drive,
Taradale,
Napier

Tel (06) 844 8855
Fax (06) 844 8855
sandroy@clear.net.nz

Double/Twin $100
Single $75
(Continental breakfast)
Extra guest $40
1 Queen 1 Double/Twin (1 bdrm)
Bathrooms: 1 Private

Comfortable, quiet apartment in the heart of our foremost wine producing area. Superb day and night views over Napier and local rural scenes. 10 minutes drive to the art deco capital of the world. 2km to Taradale Village. Safe off-street parking. Top quality restaurants and wineries nearby. We are a friendly couple who have enjoyed B&B overseas and like meeting people. Our interests are travel, theatre, good food and wine. Bella, our cat, keeps to herself. Handy to EIT and golf course.

Napier - Marine Parade *0.1 km N of Napier*
Mon Logis *B&B*
Gerard Averous
415 Marine Parade,
PO Box 871,
Napier

Tel (06) 835 2125
or 0274 725 332
Fax (06) 835 8811
monlogis@xtra.co.nz
www.babs.co.nz/monlogis

Double/Twin $160-$220
Single $120-$160
(Full breakfast)
Visa MC Diners Amex accepted
Not suitable for children
2 King/Twin 2 King (4 bdrm)
Bathrooms: 3 Ensuite 1 Private

A little piece of France nestled in the heart of the beautiful wine-growing region of Hawkes Bay. Built as private hotel in 1915, this grand colonial building is a few minutes walk from the city. Now lovingly renovated Mon Logis will cater to a maximum of 8 guests. Downstairs, an informal guest lounge invites relaxation, television viewing or a quiet time reading. Guests can help themselves to coffee/tea and home-made biscuits at any time.

Napier Hill *1 km N of Napier*
Maison Béarnaise *B&B Homestay*
Christine Grouden & Graham Storer
25 France Road,
Bluff Hill,
Napier 4110

Tel (06) 835 4693
or 0800 624 766
Fax (06) 835 4694
chrisgraham@xtra.co.nz
www.maisonbearnaise.co.nz

Double/Twin $160-$180
Single $120-$150
(Full breakfast)
Visa MC accepted
Not suitable for children
2 Queen (2 bdrm)
Bathrooms: 2 Ensuite

Christine, Graham & Brewster (shy cat), welcome you to our attractive, peaceful oasis. Walk to city centre, restaurants, Bluff lookout. Off-street parking, email access, laundry service available. Large bedrooms have views, comfortable beds, electric blankets, and DVD-television. Relax with tea / coffee in your room or guest lounge where newspapers, magazines, books are at your disposal. Delicious breakfasts including home grown and local produce served in dining room or colourful courtyard. Friendly adult retreat. Christine, Napier born, happily shares her wealth of local knowledge.

Napier *0.5 km N of Napier Central*
Seaview Lodge *B&B Homestay*
Catherine & Evert Van Florenstein
5 Seaview Terrace,
Napier

Tel (06) 835 0202
or 021 180 2101
cvulodge@xtra.co.nz
www.aseaviewlodge.co.nz

Double/Twin $140-$160
Single $100-$120
(Continental breakfast)
Visa MC accepted
1 King/Twin 1 King
1 Single (3 bdrm)
Bathrooms: 1 Ensuite 2 Private

Seaview Lodge is a lovingly renovated, spacious late Victorian home. This inner city, beachside bed and breakfast offers a warm welcome and spectacular views. Enjoy breakfast on the lower verandah while watching the waves break on the shore. In the evening relax in the spacious guest lounge or on the upstairs balcony. Situated across the road from the beach, hot pools and conference complex and a three minute stroll to the city centre makes Seaview Lodge an ideal place to explore Napier from.

❀

Napier - Puketapu *25 km W of Napier*
Te Puna Farmstay *Ecostay*
Sarah & Tony
255 Apley Road,
Puketapu
RD 6,
Napier 4021

Tel (06) 844 8753
or 021 165 8306
Fax (06) 844 8753
tonykeele@clear.net.nz
www.farmstaynapier.co.nz

Double/Twin $100-$130
Single $75-$100
(Full breakfast)
Dinner $30 by prior arrangement
Children and pets welcome
1 King/Twin 1 Single (2 bdrm)
Bathrooms: 1 Ensuite 1 Family share

Great excitement. We are completing a lodge on our own hill, from spring 2008 we offer low carbon footprint ECOSTAYS using rainwater and no mains power. You are welcome to our small farm with cattle, sheep, ducks, hens, dogs and indoor cats. Dinner with our own chemical-free seasonal produce and local wines is still available. Just 20 minutes from Napier.

Napier *1 km N of Napier Central*
Villa Vista B&B *B&B*
Tina Roulston & Tim Barker
22A France Road,
Bluff Hill,
Napier

Tel (06) 835 8770
or 027 435 7179
Fax (06) 835 8770
accommodation@villavista.net
www.villavista.net

Double/Twin $145-$160
Single $110-$125
(Special breakfast)
Children negotiable
Visa MC accepted
Children welcome
3 Queen 1 Single (3 bdrm)
Bathrooms: 3 Ensuite

A grand Edwardian villa blessed with fantastic views over the sea to Cape kidnappers from every large and private bedroom. Ensuite, air-conditioning, television, tea/coffee making facilities in each bedroom. Selection of continental and cooked breakfasts are served in the spacious dining room. Amicable children and pets residing. Welcome to Napier.

Napier *3 km S of Napier*
Art Deco Te Awa *B&B*
Kay & Rod Goodspeed
19 Te Awa Avenue,
Napier

Tel (06) 835 1618
or 027 211 0023
Fax (06) 835 3689
kaypat1@xtra.co.nz

Double/Twin $130-$150
(Full breakfast)
Pet free home
1 Queen 1 Double/Twin
1 Twin (3 bdrm)
Bathrooms: 2 Ensuite 1 Private

Art Deco Te Awa is spacious, executive quality accommodation. Ideal for visiting NZ's Art Deco City. Breakfast includes locally grown fresh fruit, home made muesli and preserves. Quality beds with fine linen. Guest rooms include one spacious double room with ensuite bathroom,one queen with ensuite bathroom and one twin with private bathroom, all with heated towelrail, hairdryer and complimentary toiletries. Five minutes to city centre. Ten minutes to airport. Walking distance to the beach and 18 hole golf course. Easy access to Hawke's Bay's wineries.

Hawkes Bay

Just as we have a variety of B&Bs
you will also be offered a variety of breakfasts,
and they will always be generous.

Napier - Hastings *11 km S of Napier - midway Napier/Hastings*
Copperfields *Cottage with Kitchen Apartment with kitchen*

Pam & Richard Marshall
Pakowhai Road, Napier

Tel (06) 876 9710
or 021 212 9631
Fax (06) 876 9710
copperfields@copperfields.co.nz
www.copperfields.co.nz

Double/Twin $100-$130
Single $100-$110
(Continental breakfast provisions)
Children $15   Extra guest $25pp
Dinner $35pp by arrangement
Separate self-contained flat,
weekly rates negotiable
Visa MC accepted
Children and pets welcome
1 King/Twin 1 Double/Twin 3 Single (3 bdrm)
Bathrooms: 2 Private

Welcome to Copperfields lifestyle orchard within 10 minutes of Napier, Hastings, Havelock North and Taradale - central for all tourist attractions. Guests stay in Glen Cottage, spacious two bedroom self-contained cottage attached to our house with private entrance. Large lounge with log fire, fully equipped kitchen/dining. Also private "Church Flat"-unique self-contained accommodation in a historic church and antiques, furniture, craft & art gallery. Family rates negotiable. Dogs welcome (conditions apply). Special 3-course dinner available by prior arrangement.

218

Hastings *14 km NW of Hastings*
Grandvue Country Stay *B&B Homestay*
Dianne & Keith Taylor
Grandvue, 2596 State Highway 50, RD 5 Hastings

Tel (06) 879 6141 or 027 668 0252
Fax (06) 879 6988   homestays@xtra.co.nz
www.bnb.co.nz/grandvuehomestay.html

Double/Twin $95-$120 Single $65 (Full breakfast)
Children negotiable   Dinner $25   Visa MC accepted
Pet free home Children welcome
1 King/Twin 1 Queen (2 bdrm)
Bathrooms: 1 Ensuite 1 Family share

Recently retired and moved from our farm but still the same genuine and caring hospitality. Enjoy with us in a relaxed atmosphere in our extensive private garden the wonderful views over vineyards in the Gimlett Gravels and Ngatarawa area, and to Havelock North hills in the distance. Comfortable beds with firm mattresses make for a good nights sleep (electric blankets for winter warmth). Sit and chat when time allows over a generous breakfast cooked or continental with homemade preserves and goodies - inside or alfresco. Dinner available on request.

Our interests include tramping, bushwalks, gardening, travel and genealogy. Having travelled extensively we do enjoy meeting local and overseas visitors. Let us advise you on all the wonderful things to see and do while in our lovely Hawkes Bay. There are many wineries close by with restaurants, Safari trips to the gannets, Orchard tours, Trout fishing, Golf courses, Panoramic views from Te Mata Peak, Havelock North with boutique shops and cafes and Napier the Art Deco City of the world are just a few.

We can arrange tours for you too, and also advise you on your travel through NZ. After more than 20 years of hosting we have an ever increasing circle of friends with many returning. Please read our guests comments on our B&B Book website. Guests are welcome to use the swimming pool in summer and the tennis court. Dianne is one of a few in NZ who has a certificate in Homestay Management. We look forward to meeting you, and our aim is to make your stay memorable. Arrive as a guest and leave as our friends. Easy access and plenty of parking.

Please let us know
how you enjoyed your B&B experience.
Ask your host for a comment form
or leave a comment on www.bnb.co.nz.

Hastings City *1 km N of Hastings Central*

McConchie Homestay *Homestay*
Barbara & Keila McConchie
115A Frederick Street,
Hastings

Tel (06) 878 4576
barbaramcconchie@xtra.co.nz
www.bnb.co.nz

Double/Twin $100
Single $65
(Full breakfast)
Children $25
Dinner $25 by arrangement
Visa MC accepted
Children welcome
1 Queen 2 Single (2 bdrm)
Bathrooms: 1 Guest share

Enjoy our peaceful garden back section, no traffic noises, yet central to Hastings City. My cats say 'Hi'. Nearby are parks, golf courses, wineries, orchards and the best icecream ever. Short trips take you to spectacular views, Cape Kidnapper's gannet colony, or Napier's art deco, hot pools, or just relaxing and enjoying great hospitality. Directions: from Wellington, arriving Hastings City, turn left into Eastbourne Street, right into Nelson Street, right into Frederick Street, cross Caroline Road. Driveway on right. 115A first house off driveway.

Hastings *3 km S of Hastings*

Raureka *B&B Separate Suite*
Rosemary & Tim Ormond
26 Wellwood Road,
RD 5,
Hastings

Tel (06) 878 9715
or 021 104 5124
Fax (06) 878 9728
r.t.ormond@xtra.co.nz

Double/Twin $120
Single $120
(Continental breakfast provisions)
Cooked breakfast available by request
Visa MC accepted
Pet free home
Not suitable for children
1 Queen (1 bdrm)
Bathrooms: 1 Ensuite

Quietness and privacy are the main ingredients of staying at Raureka. The accommodation is situated separately from the house but close enough for visitors to feel welcome and cared for. Hosts Rosemary and Tim will provide help and advice for planning a successful day around this beautiful region. Fresh flowers, home-baking and complimentary wine are among the many treats ensuring your stay here is a home away from home. Relax by our pool or enjoy a walk amongst our unique 100 year old oak trees.

Havelock North - Hastings *16 km S of Havelock North*

Wharehau *Homestay Farmstay*
Ros Phillips
1604 Middle Road, Havelock North,
RD 11, Hastings 4178

Tel (06) 877 4111
or 021 0271 9215
Fax (06) 877 4115
ros.phillips@xtra.co.nz
www.wharehau.co.nz

Double/Twin $120
Single $60
(Full breakfast)
Children half price
Dinner $30
Beach bach$130-$150
Visa MC accepted
Children welcome
2 Queen 2 Twin 1 Single (4 bdrm)
Bathrooms: 1 Guest share 1 Family share

Wharehau is in the beautiful Tuki Tuki valley -a great base for Hawkes Bay experience. Quarter of an hour travel from Hastings or Havelock North in the midst of Wine Country. Close to golf courses, Splash Planet, gannets and art deco. Or enjoy the peace and space on the farm. Weather permitting a farm 4WD tour is available. Walks available locally. Trout fishing (local guide can be hired) in the Tuki Tuki River. Comfortable beach bach at Kairakau Beach is available for rent.

Havelock North *5 km N of Havelock North*
Totara Stables *B&B Homestay*

Sharon A. Bellaart & John W. Hayes
324 Te Mata - Mangateretere Road,
Havelock North,
RD 2,
Hastings

Tel (06) 877 8882
or 027 486 3910
Fax (06) 877 8891
bookings@totarastables.co.nz
www.totarastables.co.nz

Double/Twin $150-$165
Single $120
(Continental breakfast)
Visa MC accepted
Not suitable for children
1 King/Twin 1 Queen
1 Twin (3 bdrm)
Bathrooms: 1 Ensuite 1 Private

Offering a unique Bed & Breakfast experience in a lovingly restored 1910 villa. Take a peek into the museum of early pioneer farming displayed in the century old stables or marvel at the simplicity of early stationary motors. Feed the hand reared deer, view the classic 1951 Sunbeam Talbot motor car and 1946 Ford Jailbar pickup. We are located in the heart of the Te Mata wine region only minutes from the pictureque village of Havelock North. Non-smoking and not suitable children under 12 years.

Havelock North *3 km S of Havelock North*
Endsleigh Cottages/Muritai *Luxury Cottage with Kitchen Guest House*
3 Self contained cottages and Large Villa

Denis & Margie Hardy
22 Endsleigh Road,
Havelock North

Tel (06) 877 7588
or 0274 443 800
Fax (06) 876 0275
endsleigh.cottages@xtra.co.nz
www.endsleigh.cottages.co.nz
www.muritai.co.nz

Double/Twin $100-$350
Single $100-$250
(Breakfast provisions first night)
Villa $1000 pn-Sleeps 13 comfortably
Visa MC Amex accepted
Pet free home
Children welcome
4 Queen (6 bdrm)
Bathrooms: 3 Ensuite
Cottages 3 baths Muritai 5 bathrooms

From Havelock North take Middle Road south for 3km. Cross intersection with Gilpin & Iona Rds, then left into Endsleigh Road. Cottages on right.Muritai - 68 Duart Road Havelock North.

Havelock North *2 km NE of Havelock North*
'Options' *B&B Homestay*
Rosemary & Graham Duff
92 Simla Avenue,
Havelock North
4130

Tel (06) 877 0257
or 027 653 7270
Fax (06) 877 0257
gr.duff@xtra.co.nz

Double/Twin $130-$150
Single $100-$120
(Full breakfast)
Children negotiable
Dinner by arrangement
Visa MC accepted
Pet free home
1 King 1 Queen 1 Twin
1 Single (3 bdrm)
Bathrooms: 1 Ensuite 1 Private

Options offers: Near Te Mata Peak; Views; 5 minutes to Havelock North village; Wine, gannets and Art Deco all within 30 minutes; Swimming pool and spa; Private sheltered patios; Pet free home; Wireless internet connection; Breakfast inside or outside depending on the weather; Optional evening meal at an additional cost; A home away from home.

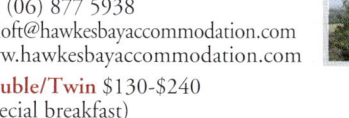

Havelock North *0.5 km S of Havelock North*
The Loft Art Studio and Bed and Breakfast *B&B Homestay*
Iris and John
10 Woodford Heights,
Havelock North
4130

Tel (06) 877 5938
or 021 474 729
027 276 1238
Fax (06) 877 5938
theloft@hawkesbayaccommodation.com
www.hawkesbayaccommodation.com

Double/Twin $130-$240
(Special breakfast)
Dinner in romantic setting by arrangement $45 pp
Visa MC accepted
Pet free home
1 King 1 Queen (2 bdrm)
Bathrooms: 2 Ensuite
King room has spa bath & shower; Queen has shower

Come and be pampered in our paradise. We, Iris and John, 4th generation New Zealanders will welcome you with complimentary refreshments. Our architectural home has many unique features and superb views of Hawke's Bay. Use the courtyard and /or deck.. We will serve you a delicious breakfast. Have a luxurious soak in the spa bath, luxury linen.John is an artist with a house studio to visit. We are close to our best attractions and can advise you on excursions. Cycles available.

Waimarama Beach *34 km SE of Hastings*
Waimarama Bed & Breakfast *B&B Homestay*

Rita & Murray Webb
68 Harper Road,
Waimarama,
Hawkes Bay

Tel (06) 874 6795
Fax (06) 8746 795
rwebb@kol.co.nz

Double/Twin $110
Single $85
(Continental breakfast)
Dinner $25pp
Visa MC accepted
2 Double/Twin (2 bdrm)
Bathrooms: 1 Guest share

Lovely beach for surfing, swimming, diving, boating, fishing etc. Bushwalks and golf course nearby. Situated only 5 minutes walk from beach with lovely views of sea, local park and farmland. Nearest town is Havelock North - 20 minutes drive, with Napier 40 minutes. We have 2 double rooms available and separate toilet and bathroom for guests. Cooked breakfast is offered and dinner is available if required. Please phone for reservations phone (06) 874 6795. No smoking inside please. Pets: 1 cat, 1 dog.

Otane *8 km N of Waipawa*
Ludlow Farmstay *Luxury B&B Farmstay Cottage with Kitchen*

Gwen and Neil White
53 Drumpeel Road, RD 1,
Otane/Waipawa

Tel (06) 856 8348
or 027 441 8354
Fax (06) 856 8348
ludlow.white@xtra.co.nz
www. ludlowfarmstay.co.nz

Double/Twin $150
Single $90
(Full breakfast provisions)
Children $20-$30
Dinner $30 by arrangement
Children welcome
1 King/Twin 1 Queen
1 Double/Twin 2 Twin (3 bdrm)
Bathrooms: 1 Private Shower only

Ludlow is a 560 hectare extensive cropping farm, growing mainly wheat and barley, squash pumpkins, sweetcorn and peas with lamb and beef finishing. Our recently renovated shearers' cottage is situated in private surroundings, 50 metres from main homestead, with full kitchen facilities, laundry, open fire and views over the Drumpeel Valley Farmland, with stock grazing alongside the cottage. Swimming pool and Astrograss tennis court available for guests' use. Farm tour available on request. Expect a warm welcome from Mindy the Jack Russell terrier.

Waipawa *40 km S of Hastings*

Abbotsford Oaks *Luxury B&B*

Nicolette Brasell & Chris Davis
85 Abbotsford Road,
Waipawa,
Central Hawke's Bay

Tel (06) 857 8960
or 027 296 1160
Fax (06) 857 8961
nicolette@abbotsfordoaks.co.nz

Double/Twin $175-$325
Single $140-$280 (Full breakfast)
Dinner by arrangement
Visa MC accepted
1 King 3 Queen (4 bdrm)
Bathrooms: 1 Ensuite 3 Private

Nicolette and Chris warmly welcome you to Abbotsford Oaks. Nestled in picturesque Central Hawkes Bay and surrounded by 3.5 acres of gardens and orchards, Abbotsford Oaks offers a special venue for those wanting a break from their busy lifestyle. Ideal for that restful getaway (as our 2 cats have found), corporate retreat, or as a base to explore the many attractions Hawkes Bay has to offer. Beaches, wineries and art deco/Spanish mission architecture are only 30 minutes away. Golf courses and trout fishing are close by.

Our property was purpose built as a childrens home in the 1920s and has been extensively renovated to provide quality boutique bed & breakfast accommodation. It has spacious rooms most with their own sitting/sun room and private bathroom, with wonderful views of the grounds and countryside. There is also a substantial and elegantly furnished guest lounge with open fire where you can watch TV or just relax. The large dining room also has a comfortable lounge area in which to relax, listen to music or read a book. Breakfast is cooked and continental and can be served in the dining room or the garden. Complimentary coffee, tea and biscuits are available throughout the day. Dinner is available by arrangement.

Waipawa *1 km NE of Waipawa*
Abbot Heights *Luxury B&B*
Jacqui & Charlie Hutchison
6 Parkland Drive,
Waipawa

Tel 027 433 0146
or (06) 857 8585
Fax (06) 857 8580
chipper.c@xtra.co.nz

Double/Twin $150
Single $100
(Continental breakfast)
Not suitable for children
2 Queen (2 bdrm)
Bathrooms: 1 Ensuite 1 Private
Private bathroom has spa bath

Welcome to Parkland Drive! Your relaxed, easy going hosts (and their cat Myrtle) enjoy meeting all new guests at their stunning modern manor set in 12 acres of private gardens. Facilities include a splendid private lounge, luxury goose down duvets, plush bathrobes, top quality linen, spa bath and electric blankets. New gym, indoor heated pool, golf, vineyard, hot-air ballooning, art gallery, theatre, museum, cafes and antique shops are only 5 minutes away. Golden sandy beaches, tramping, hunting and fishing are within 30 minutes.

~

Waipukurau *4.5 km S of Waipukurau*
Pukeora Vineyard Cottage *Cottage with Kitchen*
Kate Norman
Pukeora Estate, 208 Pukeora
Scenic Road (off SH2 south of
Waipukurau), RD 1, Waipukurau

Tel (06) 858 9339
or 021 205 1307
021 701 606
Fax (06) 858 6070
cottage@pukeora.com
www.pukeora.com

Double/Twin $120
Single $90
(Continental breakfast)
Children $25
Visa MC accepted
Children welcome
1 Queen 1 Double/Twin 2 Twin
1 Single (3 bdrm)
Bathrooms: 1 Private

Enjoy exclusive hire of our charming, hilltop cottage which boasts stunning views over the vineyard, river, plains and beyond. The spacious 1920's cottage, with rimu floors, sunny verandah, and open plan lounge/kitchen with log fire, is a private annex to our house. Pukeora Estate, set on 86 acres, is a 5 hectare vineyard, boutique winery and functions venue. Your hosts Kate and Max, with daughters Jessica (age 6) and Marika (age 4), and 3 cats, welcome you. Endless outside space for children. Wine tasting/sales available.

Waipukurau *2 km S of Waipukurau*
Woburn Homestead *Luxury B&B*

Heatha Edwards
216 Hatuma Road,
RD 1,
Waipukurau

Tel (06) 858 9668
or 0274 529 112
heatha.woburnhomestead@xtra.co.nz
www.woburnhomestead.co.nz

Double/Twin $250-$300
Single up to $150
(Special breakfast)
Dinner available by prior arrangement
Visa MC accepted
Not suitable for children
2 Queen 2 Twin (3 bdrm)
Bathrooms: 3 Ensuite

Welcome to Woburn Homestead, an exquisite 7 bedroom home with 6 bathrooms, built in 1893 and listed with the NZ Historic Places Trust.

Heatha and Philip adore sharing their home, and there are 3 tubby Labradors, who relentlessly patrol the grounds for any stray snacks or crumbs!

Hawkes Bay

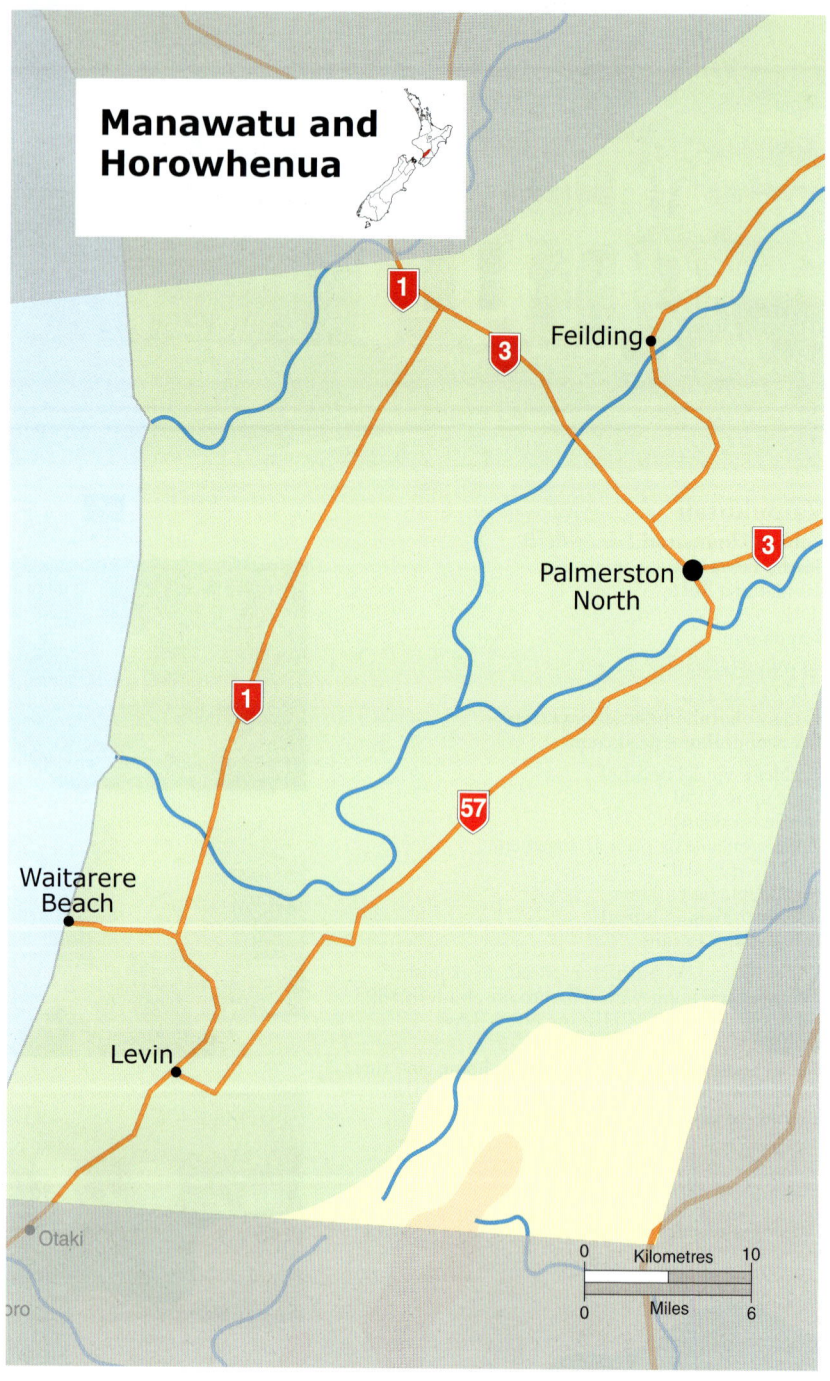

Manawatu and Horowhenua

Feilding

Palmerston North

Waitarere Beach

Levin

Otaki

Kilometres 0 10

Miles 0 6

Feilding *0.25 km N of Feilding Central*
Avoca Homestay *Homestay*

Margaret Hickmott
12 Freyberg Street,
Feilding

Tel (06) 323 4699
margh-avoca@inspire.net.nz

Double/Twin $100
Single $75
(Full breakfast)
Dinner $25 by arrangement
1 Queen 2 Twin (2 bdrm)
Bathrooms: 1 Ensuite 1 Family share

Enjoy a break in friendly Feilding, 13 times winner of New Zealand's Most Beautiful Town Award. You are assured of a warm welcome and an enjoyable stay in a comfortable smoke-free home set in an attractive garden with mature trees and a colourful shrubbery. Off-street parking is provided for your vehicle. The main bedroom has a queen-size bed, ensuite and an outside entrance for your sole use. We are within easy walking distance of the town centre and well situated for the Manfield Park complex.

Feilding *1 km E of Feilding Town Centre*
Feilding Mahoe B&B *B&B Guest House Self contained B&B*

David & Lesley Klue
171 South street,
Feilding
5301

Tel (06) 323 0311
or 027 277 0235
purplepear@xtra.co.nz

Double/Twin $120-$180
Single $70-$100
(Continental breakfast provisions)
Dinner by arrangement
Off street parking
Full Cooking and Laundry Facilities
Eftpos accepted
Children and pets welcome
1 Queen 1 Single (1 bdrm)
Bathrooms: 1 Ensuite

We enjoy our semi rural lifestyle with our three children, small dog, cat, four sheep and pig nestled amongst old native and fruit trees. Your privacy is assured in the guest house, separate from the main house, with views to gardens and a swimming pool. Situated just 1km from Manfield Park, and the town centre - you can enjoy great shopping and cafes, or alternatively, Palmerston North city is only a 15min drive. Welcome to Mahoe, your stay would be our pleasure.

Manawatu Horowhenua

Feilding *5 km W of Feilding*
Minffordd Cottage *Cottage with Kitchen*

Bob and Jenny Phillips
153, Halcombe Road,
RD 5 Feilding, 4775

Tel Mobile 021 331 449
or Land line (06) 323 1182
Fax 06 323 2217
bjphillips@xtra.co.nz
http://minffordd.co.nz

Double/Twin $120
Single $120
(Continental breakfast provisions)
Children $5-$10 depending on age
Alpaca Association of NZ members $110
Visa MC accepted
Pet free home
Children welcome
1 Queen 2 Single (2 bdrm)
Bathrooms: 1 Guest share

Relax in our quiet, rural location, five minutes from Feilding and Manfield Park and 20 minutes from Palmerston North. Feilding has won the Keep New Zealand Beautiful award for 13 years and events include Farmers Market (Friday), tour of the largest lifestock market in the Southern Hemisphere (Fridays), Steam engine trips and all the events at Manfield. The cottage has gas hob, microwave, laundry, fridge freezer, Sky T.V., broadband and ample parking. Continental breakfast provided. Come and see our alpacas and sleep under an alpaca duvet. Bring your horses or alpacas to stay too.

Palmerston North *3 km NW of Palmerston North Centre*
Bradgate *B&B Homestay*

Frances
3 Celtic Court,
Roslyn

Tel (06) 355 5956
Fax (06) 355 5956
vige@value.net.nz

Double/Twin $80
Single $40-$50
(Full breakfast)
Dinner $25
1 Queen 1 Double/Twin
1 Twin (3 bdrm)
Bathrooms: 1 Guest share

Welcome to Bradgate, a four bedroomed brick townhouse located in a quiet cul-de-sac. 33 years ago my husband and I came to New Zealand. We owned a restaurant opposite Virginia Lake Wanganui, after retiring we ran a bed & breakfast overlooking the river. Having shifted to Palmerston North it was time to open up our home again. I have a Labrador named Crunchy. I enjoy playing golf, gardening and meeting people. Close to airport, will pick up if required. Non-smoking house, dinner by arrangement.

Palmerston North *3 km W of Palmerston North*
Andellen *Farmstay Guest House*
Kay and Warren Nitschke
580 Kairanga Bunnythorpe Road,
RD 8, Palmerston North

Tel 027 244 1393
or (06) 355 4155
021 900 228
Fax (06) 355 4155
kw@inspire.net.nz

Double/Twin $110
Single $70
(Continental breakfast provisions)
Children $20 under 12
Dinner $30pp by arrangement
Visa MC accepted
Children and pets welcome
2 Queen 2 Single (3 bdrm)
Bathrooms: 1 Ensuite 1 Private
Spa bath

Enjoy your very own modern three bedroom house with both a private and tranquil setting. Kay, Warren and Libby (12 years) welcome you to 'Andellen', set on 65 acres with lovely native gardens. We offer guests the opportunity to relax in an elegant, tranquil country setting. Accomodation includes private lounge, TV and spa bath. Seasonal farm activities available. Children very welcome. City 3km away. We have a pet cat and dog. Dinner by arrangement. Plenty of parking. Airport 5kms away

Palmerston North *5.5 km E of City Centre*
Clairemont *B&B*
Joy & Dick Archer
10 James Line,
RD 10,
Palmerston North

Tel (06) 357 5508
or 021 063 6951
clairemont@inspire.net.nz

Double/Twin $80
Single $50
(Continental breakfast)
Not suitable for children
1 Double/Twin 1 Twin (2 bdrm)
Bathrooms: 1 Guest share

Welcome to Clairemont. We are a rural spot within the city boundary, plenty of trees and a quite extensive garden. On our 1 1/4 acres we keep a few sheep, silky bantams, and our little dog Toby. We are handy to river walks, golf course, and shops are a few minutes away. We have a cosy, spacious family home we would like to share with you. Our interests are walking, gardening, model engineering and barbershop singing. Good off-street parking. Supper provided.

Manawatu Horowhenua

Palmerston North *13 km E of Palmerston North*
Country Lane Homestay *B&B Homestay*

Fay & Allan Hutchinson
52 Orrs Road,
RD 1 Aokautere,
Palmerston North

Tel (06) 326 8529
or 027 448 5833
Fax (06) 326 9216
countrylane@xtra.co.nz

Double/Twin $100-$140
Single $75-$95
(Full breakfast)
Dinner $25-$30
Not suitable for children
1 King/Twin 1 King 1 Queen
1 Double/Twin 1 Single (3 bdrm)
Bathrooms: 1 Ensuite 2 Private
1 Family share

Luxury country living, short distance from Palmerston North, near Manawatu Gorge, below wind farm. 10km from Pacific College and 2km from Equestrian Centre. Excellent stop over en route to/from Wellington or East Coast. Our home is newly decorated, with antiques in a country traditional style surrounded by our garden. Sawmill on the property, coloured sheep, horses and calves. Manawatu River borders our property. It is our pleasure to provide home-cooked meals with some local produce. Directions: please phone. A brochure with map is available.

Palmerston North *5 km SW of Central Palmerston North*
Udys on Anders *B&B Apartment with Kitchen*

Glenda & Tim Udy
52 Anders Road,
Palmerston North

Tel (06) 354 1722
or 027 440 9299
kiwitim@clear.net.nz
www.udysonanders.co.nz

Double/Twin $130
Single $110
(Full breakfast)
Children $20
Dinner negotiable
Visa MC accepted
Children welcome
1 Queen 1 Double/Twin (1 bdrm)
Bathrooms: 1 Ensuite

We offer superior accommodation. An elegantly furnished self-contained apartment, own lounge and full kitchen. Quiet country location, huge lawn, edge of town, 7 minutes to CBD. Plexipave tennis court, beautiful mediterranean courtyard and large games room for our guests to make use of. Cleanliness, attention to detail and great hospitality are our priorities. We are well travelled and love meeting people. Enjoy your own space or get to know us. So... come, relax, enjoy. Tariff includes full breakfast. Apartment is smoke-free. Dinner by arrangement.

Waitarere Beach *14 km NW of Levin*

Dunes *B&B Homestay*
Robyn & Grant Powell
10 Ngati Huia Place,
Waitarere Beach
5510

Tel (06) 368 6246
or 027 285 3643
sand.dunes@xtra.co.nz
http://waitarere.dunes.googlepages.com

Double/Twin $120
Single $95
(Continental breakfast)
Dinner $30
Visa MC accepted
2 Queen (2 bdrm)
Bathrooms: 2 Ensuite

Robyn & Grant Powell welcome you to our absolute beachfront retreat. Enjoy beach walks and magnificent views of Kapiti and Mounts Taranaki and Ruapehu. We offer 2 queen-size bedrooms with own private entrance and deck areas, ensuites, own living areas with TV, tea/coffee making facilities - continental breakfast provided. Situated 14km north west of Levin, approximately 1 and a half hours from Wellington and 35 minutes from Palmerston North. Laundry facilities, off-street parking, non-smoking. Dinner by arrangement.

Levin *1 km NE of Levin*

Fantails *B&B Cottage with Kitchen Self-contained cottages*
Heather Watson
40 MacArthur Street,
Levin

Tel (06) 368 9011
Fax (06) 368 9279
fantails@xtra.co.nz
www.fantails.co.nz

Double/Twin $130-$160
Single $100-$130
(Special breakfast)
Children negotiable
Dinner by arrangement
Self-contained cottages $110-$150
Visa MC accepted
Children and pets welcome
1 King 2 Queen 1 Twin
4 Single (4 bdrm)
Bathrooms: 3 Ensuite 1 Private

Tranquility, birdsong, native trees. Peaceful, exquisite sanctuary. Pick your own fruit as you wander through 2 acres of botanical gardens. Looking for a retreat? Home baking and certified organic food! Ease the aches of the day away with a sauna or lavender massage bath, the sound of nature enveloping you. Ease back with SKY television before enjoying the comfort of a great night's sleep. Within a five kilometer radius enjoy attractions of the Horowhenua such as golfing, bird trail, tramping and tourist attractions. Laundry available.

Levin *5 km S of Levin*
Ardo Highland Haven *B&B Farmstay*
Malcolm & Rachel Phillips
170 McLeavey Road,
RD 20,
Levin 5570

Tel (06) 368 7080
or 021 50 69 90
Fax (06) 368 7080
info@ardohighlandhaven.co.nz
www.ardohighlandhaven.co.nz

Double/Twin $120-$130
Single $100
(Full breakfast)
Dinner by arrangement
Visa MC accepted
2 Queen 1 Single (3 bdrm)
Bathrooms: 1 Private
We take one booking only at a time

Travelling to or from Wellington? Our country home on 10 acres is easy to find, just 5km south of levin. Our guest rooms are upstairs and very private. Tranquil haven, comfortable beds and full breakfast. We offer refreshments on arrival and dinner by arrangement. Laundry facilities are available. Enjoy our highland cattle and friendly sheep. Mandy, our Australian Terrier will greet you, and Lola, our cat, may put in an appearance! Please take time to read our Guest Reviews. We look forward to meeting you.

Levin *3 km NE of Levin*
Annandale Manor *B&B Farmstay Feijoa Orchard*
Malcolm and Rebecca
108 Arapaepae Road,
SH 57, Levin, 5510

Tel 0800 201 712
or (06) 368 5476
Fax (06) 368 5473
annandalemanor@xtra.co.nz
www.annandalemanor.co.nz

Double/Twin $110-$135
Single $100-$120
(Continental breakfast)
Children 12 and under half price
Dinner Two course $35,
Three Course $55 per person
Cooked Breakfast $10
Spa Pool
Children and pets welcome
1 Queen 1 Double/Twin 1 Twin (3 bdrm)
Bathrooms: 1 Guest share

Look no further you will find it here colonial elegance infused with peace, serenity and abundant hospitality. Prepare to be charmed by the grand old lady that is Annandale Manor. The gardens and orchard with bird song and ambience. You will find activities to energise or slumber to revitalise, with hunting and rafting to beaches and bush walks. Its all here now just waiting for you. The Horowhenua experience that you will not want to miss.

Levin *2 km N of Levin*
Blueberry Art B&B *Luxury B&B Apartments with Kitchen*

Angelika & Josef Kieninger
7 Heatherlea East Road,
Levin

Tel (06) 367 3648
Fax (06) 367 3651
josef.kieninger@xtra.co.nz
www.blueberryart.co.nz

Double/Twin $100-$120
Single $80-$100
(Breakfast by arrangement)
Children welcome by arrangement
Visa MC Eftpos accepted
Children welcome
2 Queen (2 bdrm)
Bathrooms: 2 Ensuite new facilities

Welcome to our Blueberry orchard, relax on 10 acres of park-like grounds. Enjoy the beautiful and friendly alpacas, or join us while working on our art. Angelika is a hat maker and painter and Josef is renowned for his woodblock printing. We enjoy organic vegetables and fruit and produce our own blueberries, nuts, citrus fruit and vegetables.Conveniently located at SH1. Blueberry Art Orchard is the perfect place to stay when traveling to or from Wellington 5 km to Waitarere Beach, tramping and mountain-biking in the Tararuas.

**If you need any information ask your hosts,
they are your own personal travel agent and guide.**

Manawatu
Horowhenua

Wairarapa

Colyton

elding

ewbury

Palmerston
North

Oroua Downs

Tokomaru

Foxton

3

Levin

2

Eketahuna

Otaki

Te Horo

Waikanae

paraumu

kariki

Masterton

Carterton

2

ui

Upper Hutt

eretaunga

53

Martinborough

| 0 | Kilometres | 20 |
| 0 | Miles | 12 |

Eketahuna *45 km N of Masterton*

Brookfields Lodge *B&B Licensed restaurant and separate self catering cottage*

Terry and Corinna Carew
31 Alfredton Road,
Eketahuna, 4900

Tel 06 375 8686
or 021 214 7039
021 145 5947
terry@brookfieldslodge.co.nz
www.brookfieldslodge.co.nz

Double/Twin $120-$140
Single $95-$110
(Full breakfast)
Dinner avaible in the
attached restaurant
Cottage price on application
Visa MC Eftpos accepted
Children welcome
3 Queen (3 bdrm)
Bathrooms: 3 Ensuite
1 bathroom in self catering

Brookfields is ideally situated between Woodville and Masterton providing the discerning traveller with a relaxed friendly place to stay overnight or longer. Originally built as a 3 bedroom villa in 1910, this grand old home has been tastefully restored to provide comfortable en-suite accommodation in the heart of the Tararua District. The emphasis is on good food, cxomfortable surroundings and pleasant company.

≈

Masterton *3 km W of Masterton*

Harefield *B&B Farmstay Cottage with Kitchen*

Marion Ahearn
147 Upper Plain Road,
Masterton

Tel (06) 377 4070
Fax (06) 377 4070

Double/Twin $90
Single $45-$50
(Full breakfast)
Children half price
Self-contained flat for 2 $60
Children welcome
1 Double/Twin 1 Single (1 bdrm)
Bathrooms: 2 Private
1 in flat, 1 private in house

A warm welcome awaits you at Harefield, a small farmlet on the edge of town. A quiet country garden surrounds the cedar house and self-contained flat. The flat has 1 bedroom with double and single beds. 2 divan beds in living area. Self-cater or have breakfast in our warm dining room. Convenient for restaurants, showgrounds, vineyards, schools, tramping. 1.5 hour drive to Picton Ferry. We enjoy meeting people, aviation, travel, reading, art, farming and tramping. Baby facilities available. Smoke-free.

Masterton *10 km W of Masterton*
Tidsfordriv *B&B Homestay*
Glenys Hansen
54 Cootes Road,
Matahiwi, RD 8,
Masterton

Tel (06) 378 9967
Fax (06) 378 9957
ghansen@contact.net.nz

Double/Twin $90-$95
Single $60
(Full breakfast)
Children 1/2 price
Dinner $25 by arrangement
includes pre-dinner drink
Visa MC accepted
Children welcome
1 Queen 2 Single (2 bdrm)
Bathrooms: 1 Private

A warm welcome awaits you at 'Tidsfordriv' - a 64 acre farmlet - seven kilometres off the main bypass route. Enjoy the comforts of a modern home set in parklike surroundings with large gardens & lakes. Bird watch with ease and enjoy the peaceful serenity of this 'Rural Retreat'. Glenys invites you to join her for dinner and enjoy good conversation about gardening, conservation and travel. A friendly Labrador is the outdoor pet. Enjoy visits to Pukaha Mount Bruce Wildlife Centre, and other Wairarapa attractions.

Masterton *1 km E of Masterton*
Mas des Saules *Homestay*
Mary & Steve Blakemore
9A Pokohiwi Road,
Homebush,
Masterton

Tel (06) 377 2577
or (027) 620 8728
Fax (06) 377 2578
mas-des-saules@wise.net.nz

Double/Twin $110
Single $75 (Full breakfast)
Children $40
Dinner $35
Visa MC accepted
Children and pets welcome
2 Queen (2 bdrm)
Bathrooms: 1 Guest share

H idden down a tranquil country lane, discover our authentic French Provencal farmhouse with its landscaped garden, stream, and courtyard. Swimming and trout fishing in nearby river. Our children have departed, leaving us with a cat, small dog, and cattle on our small farm. Guest lounge and bathroom with bath and shower. Open fire and central heating. Enjoy farmhouse cooking with fresh vegetables from our large country garden, barbecues and picnic lunches. We are a well-travelled couple who enjoy helping guests discover the unspoilt Wairarapa.

Masterton *1 km W of Urban Boundary*
Llandaff *B&B Farmstay*
Elizabeth & Robin Dunlop
183 Upper Plain Road Masterton

Tel (06) 378 6628
or 021 359 562
Fax (06) 378 6628
llandaff@xtra.co.nz
www.wairarapa.co.nz/llandaff

Double/Twin $110-$130
Single $70-$100
(Full breakfast)
Children $25
Dinner $30
Children welcome
1 King 2 Queen 1 Double/Twin
1 Twin (5 bdrm)
Bathrooms: 1 Ensuite 3 Guest share
Ensuite shower only

Elegantly restored, the homestead boasts beautiful native NZ timbers throughout, wood panelled rooms, polished floors, old pull-handle toilets, a 'coffin' bath, open fireplaces and cosy woodburning kitchen stove. Explore the historic hayloft and stables, washhouse, dunny, produce shed, gardener's shed, pavilion and dove cote. See the vintage farm machinery. Relax in the majestic garden beneath 120 year old trees, or wander the farm and feed the animals. Bike riding, croquet and petanque are available to guests. Enjoy a cooked breakfast with dinner available on request.

Masterton *2 km E of Masterton*
Apple Source Farmstay *B&B Farmstay*
Mary & Roger Smith
Te Ore Ore,
RD 6,
Masterton

Tel (06) 377 0820
Fax (06) 370 9401
rapukesmith@xtra.co.nz

Double/Twin $110
Single $80 (Full breakfast)
Visa MC accepted
Children welcome
2 Queen 1 Single (2 bdrm)
Bathrooms: 2 Ensuite

A warm welcome awaits you at Apple Source Farm Stay. Our colonial style home is nestled in a woodland garden. The separate guest wing has a lounge and 2 bedrooms each with an ensuite and a laundry service is available. Dinner is available on request and a full breakfast is included in the tarriff.Children are welcome. Our private rural hideaway is only 2kms east of Masterton and we share our home with 2 black cats, Felix and Mister.

Masterton *8 km E of Masterton*
Vista Homestay *B&B Homestay*

Carol and Quenten Hansen
339A Te Ore Ore Settlement Rd,
RD 6,
Masterton

Tel (06) 370 8919
or 027 360 6499
Fax (06) 370 8919
cqhansen@xtra.co.nz

Double/Twin $95
Single $60
(Continental breakfast)
Children $25
Dinner $25 per adult
includes pre-dinner drink
Visa MC accepted
Pet free home
Children welcome
1 Queen 2 Single (2 bdrm)
Bathrooms: 1 Private 1 party per booking

More than just stunning views, Vista Homestay is situated in a tranquil environment where you will be welcomed by the smell of fresh flowers home baking and good coffee. Our modern home and garden are for you to enjoy along with a private spa pool. To make your visit memorable we would love you to join us for dinner.

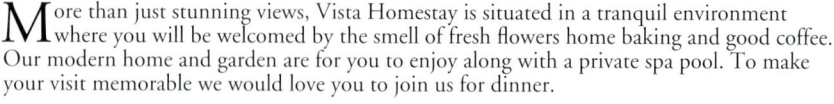

Carterton *1 km N of Carterton*
Homecroft *B&B*

Christine & Neil Stewart
Somerset Road,
RD 2,
Carterton

Tel (06) 379 5959
homecroft@xtra.co.nz

Double/Twin $95-$110
Single $60
(Full breakfast)
Dinner $30pp by arrangement
1 Queen 1 Double/Twin
1 Twin (3 bdrm)
Bathrooms: 1 Ensuite 1 Private

Homecroft is surrounded by our country garden. Handy to the vineyards, crafts, antiques, and golf courses of the Wairarapa. Wellington and the inter-island ferry are 90 minutes away. Guest accommodation is in a separate wing of the house with small lounge, the bedrooms open onto a deck. The double room with ensuite, The Croft, is separate from the house. All bedrooms overlook the garden. A leisurely breakfast at Homecroft is an enjoyable experience. We look forward to making your stay with us happy and relaxing.

Martinborough *0.5 km NW of Martinborough*
Oak House *B&B*
Polly & Chris Buring
45 Kitchener Street,
Martinborough

Tel (06) 306 9198
Fax (06) 306 8198
chrispolly.oakhouse@xtra.co.nz
http://buringswines.co.nz

Double/Twin $120-$130
Single $60
(Special breakfast)
Children by arrangement
Dinner by arrangement
Visa MC accepted
Children welcome
2 Queen 2 Single (3 bdrm)
Bathrooms: 1 Ensuite 1 Guest share

Our characterful 80 year old Californian bungalow offers gracious accommodation. Our spacious lounge provides a relaxed setting for sampling winemaker Chris's wonderful products. Our guest wing has its own entrance, bathroom (large bath and shower) and separate toilet. Our new bedroom has ensuite facilities. Bedrooms enjoy afternoon sun and garden views. Breakfast features fresh croissants, home-preserved local fruits and conserves. Creative cook Polly matches delicious dishes (often local game) with Chris's great wines. Tour our onsite winery with Chris. Meet our multi-talented cats.

Martinborough *1 km W of Martinborough*
The Old Manse *B&B Homestay*
Sandra & John Hargrave
Corner Grey & Roberts Streets,
Martinborough

Tel (06) 306 8599
or 0800 399 229
Fax (06) 306 8540
info@oldmanse.co.nz
www.oldmanse.co.nz

Double/Twin $170-$190
(Full breakfast)
Visa MC Diners
Amex Eftpos accepted
Not suitable for children
5 Queen 1 Twin (6 bdrm)
Bathrooms: 6 Ensuite

In the heart of the wine district, a beautifully restored Presbyterian Manse, built 1876, has been transformed into a boutique homestay. Spacious, relaxed accommodation in a quiet, peaceful setting. 1 twin, 5 queen-size bedrooms all with their own ensuites. All day sun. Off-street parking, open fireplace. Amenities include spa pool, petanque, billiards. Enjoy breakfast or wine overlooking vineyard. Walking distance to Martinborough Square with selection of excellent restaurants. Close to vineyards, antique and craft shops, adventure quad bikes and golf courses. Qualmark 4+

Martinborough *1 km S of Martinbrough Village Square*
The Martinborough Connection *B&B*

David & Lorraine Murray
80 Jellicoe Street,
Martinborough, 5711

Tel (06) 306 9708
or 027 438 1581
Fax (06) 306 9706
martinboroughconnection@xtra.co.nz
www.martinboroughconnection.co.nz

Double/Twin $130-$140
Single $110-$115
(Full breakfast)
Children in room with extra bed $15
Extra adult in room with extra bed $30
Visa MC Eftpos accepted
Pet free home
Children welcome
4 Queen 1 Single (4 bdrm)
Bathrooms: 4 Ensuite

Bed & breakfast accommodation situated within the Martinborough wine village. Originally built in 1889 the property has been fully restored retaining its original character. Open your bedroom door to a sunny verandah & garden. Start the day with a scrumptious breakfast, before visiting Martinboroughs wineries,or Cape Palliser with its spectacular coastline,lighthouse,& furseal colony. Relax at the end of the day in the guest lounge with its open fire or outside in the lovely gardens. We look forward to hosting you.

**All our B&Bs are non-smoking
unless stated otherwise in the text.**

Wellington

Manak

Otaki

Te Horo

Kapiti Island

Waikanae

1

Paraparaumu

Raumati

Kapiti Coast

Pukerua Bay

Plimmerton

2

Paremata

Upper Hutt

1

2

Tawa

Stokes Valley

Johnsonville

Ohariu Valley

See
Wellington City
next page

Lower Hutt

Petone

Aro Valley   Pt. Victoria
Brooklyn   Hataitai
Vogeltown   Mt. Cook
Mornington   Karaka Bay
Melrose   Seatoun
Island Bay   Lyall Bay
Palmer Head
Wellington
International
Airport

Eastbourne

0   Kilometres   10

0   Miles   6

Wellington City

Jonsonville

Khandallah

Ngaio

Wadestown

Interisland
Ferry Terminal

Karori

Wellington
Central

Kelburn

Roseneath

Aro Valley

Mt Victoria

Brooklyn

Mt. Cook

Hataitai

Vogeltown

Seatoun

Island Bay

Wellington
International
Airport

Te Horo *7 km N of Waikanae*

Pateke Lagoons Wetlands *B&B Farmstay Separate Suite*

Peter & Adrienne Dale
152 Te Hapua Road,
Te Horo, RD 1, Kapiti Coast

Tel (06) 364 2222
or 0275 439 661
Fax (06) 364 2214
peterdale@xtra.co.nz
www.pateke-lagoons.co.nz

Double/Twin $195
Single $195
(Special breakfast)
Dinner $65 including wine
Visa MC accepted
Not suitable for children
2 Queen 1 Single (2 bdrm)
Bathrooms: 2 Ensuite
1 Private wheelchair bathroom

Pateke Lagoons overlooks a private 50 acre wetland and waterfowl refuge on the Kapiti Coast. It offers peace and quiet in tranquil rural surroundings. 2 guest rooms, each with ensuite and private courtyard. Large lounge with wildfowl and wetland ecology library. Beautiful views of farmland, sea and wetland. Easy 30 minute walking tracks through native bush and wetland. Fresh seafood is our specialty with garden fresh vegetables. Special breakfast using local products. Close to Ruth Pretty Cooking School. Open wetlands are unsuitable for children.

Waikanae *1 km E of Waikanae*

Country Patch *Apartment with Kitchen Cottage with Kitchen*

Sue & Brian Wilson
18 Kea Street,
Waikanae

Tel (04) 293 5165
or 0274 578 421
027 296 3716
Fax (04) 293 5164
stay@countrypatch.co.nz
www.countrypatch.co.nz

Double/Twin $160-$240
(Full breakfast provisions)
Children $30
Visa MC Eftpos accepted
Children welcome
2 King/Twin 1 Queen
2 Single (3 bdrm)
Bathrooms: 3 Ensuite

Two delightful self-contained accommodation sites. Country patch studio with its own entrance and deck has a queen bed with ensuite and twin beds on the mezzanine floor of the kitchen lounge. Country patch villa has an open fire and a large verandah with magic views. It is wheelchair accessible and the 2 bedrooms (each with ensuite) have king beds that unzip to twin. We warmly invite you to share our patch of the country.

Waikanae Beach *5 km W of Waikanae*

Konini Cottage & Homestead *B&B Separate Suite Cottage with Kitchen*

Maggie & Bob Smith
26 Konini Crescent, Waikanae Beach, Kapiti Coast

Tel (04) 904 6610 or 027 260 6492
Fax (04) 904 6610   konini@paradise.net.nz
www.konini.co.nz

Double/Twin $130-$160 Single $100-$150
(Breakfast by arrangement)
Children $15 under 13yrs. Dinner Cafes/Restaurants within walking
Extra Adult $25 Visa MC Amex accepted Children welcome
2 Queen 2 Single (3 bdrm)
Bathrooms: 1 Ensuite 1 Private

Bob and Maggie welcome you to the haven of KONINI. You can
enjoy a walk or swim at the endless sandy ocean beach, have a
game of golf on the adjoining golf links, or simply sit on the veranda
and enjoy the peace and tranquillity of the large garden. Being only
1 hours drive from the Interisland ferries it is the perfect stop off.
Both the Homestead and the Cottage are of Lockwood solid timber
construction. Bob, a cabinetmaker, has crafted all the furniture.
Maggie has developed the large garden.

THE HOMESTEAD SUITE: A traditional B&B in its own wing of
the main house. The suite comprises Queen bedroom, an adjoining
guests sitting room overlooking the garden & private ensuite
bathroom. Guests may have breakfast(included in tariff) in their
suite or join us in our dining room.

THE COTTAGE: Self contained & situated in the garden.
Tastefully furnished offering a spacious 70 Sq Meters of self-catering
accommodation with fully equipped kitchen. Two bedrooms (one
Queen & one Twin), lounge with cable TV, Shower room, &
laundry facilities. Breakfast can be provided by arrangement.

Directions: Turn off SH1 at traffic lights to the Beach. 4 km to automotive garage. Take
right fork then next right. 1km to Konini Cres.

Waikanae *6 km E of Waikanae*
RiverStone *B&B Cottage with Kitchen*
Paul & Eppie Murton
111 Ngatiawa Road,
Waikanae

Tel (04) 293 1936
riverstone@paradise.net.nz
www.riverstone.co.nz

Double/Twin $130
Single $90
(Full breakfast)
Children $45
Visa MC accepted
1 Queen 1 Twin (2 bdrm)
Bathrooms: 1 Private

Birdsong, the sound of the river and complete privacy. Peace and quiet with a scrumptious breakfast and comfortable accommodation. Riverstone has scenic views a garden with river walks and local pottery and cafe. Waikanae, 5 minutes by car, has cafes, shops, boutiques, Lindale Farm Park, the Southward Car Museum, Nga Manu Bird Sanctuary, golf courses and beautiful beaches. Pick up from train or bus. Laundry facilities. Smoke-free. Internet available.

Waikanae Beach *59 km N of Wellington*
(Helen's) Waikanae Beach B&B *B&B Homestay*
Helen Anderson
115 Tutere Street,
Waikanae Beach,
Kapiti Coast

Tel (04) 902 5829
or 021 259 3396
Fax (04) 902 5840
waikanaebeachbandb@paradise.net.nz
www.waikanaebeachbandb.net

Double/Twin $130-$150
Single $110-$130
(Full breakfast)
Children negotiable
Dinner by arrangement
Visa MC accepted
Pet free home
2 Queen 1 Single (2 bdrm)
Bathrooms: 1 Ensuite 1 Private

Do you need time out to relax and unwind? Then come and experience warm, friendly hospitality by the sea. Drift off to sleep to the sounds of the ocean. Direct access to a sandy, safe swimming beach where you can enjoy long leisurely walks, beautiful sunsets, wonderful views of Kapiti Island, and the Tararua Ranges. All cotton bed linen. Tea-making facilities in guest rooms. Generous breakfasts. Dinner by prior arrangement. Access to laundry. Good restaurants nearby. We look forward to welcoming you, soon.

Waikanae *45 km N of Wellington*
Waimoana *B&B Homestay*

Elizabeth and Bryan Couchman
63 Kakariki Grove,
Waikanae
5036
Kapiti Coast

Tel (04) 293 2005
or 021 0222 0217
relax@waimoana.co.nz
www.waimoana.co.nz

Double/Twin $150
Single $120
(Continental breakfast)
Visa MC accepted
1 Queen (1 bdrm)
Bathrooms: 1 Ensuite

Waimoana was purpose built as a quality homestay. Enjoy majestic sea views over Kapiti from the sundeck or pool. Living rooms radiate from a glass-roofed atrium featuring an indoor swimming pool, garden and waterfall. Our guest room has its own private entrance, parking and ensuite facilities. Local activities include native bush walks, beaches, first-class restaurants and cafes, craft and mosaic shops, bird sanctuaries and golf courses. A warm welcome awaits you from our three sons and cat Tabitha.

Waikanae *1 km E of Waikanae*
Te Rimu B & B *B&B*

Barbara Baylis
11 Hira St,
Waikanae,
5036

Tel (04) 293 2535
or 021 118 9845
bjsmith@ezysurf.co.nz
www.terimu.co.nz

Double/Twin $120-$150
Single $80-$100
(Full breakfast)
Dinner by prior arrangement
Visa MC accepted
Pet free home
Not suitable for children
1 King/Twin 1 Double/Twin (2 bdrm)
Bathrooms: 1 Guest share

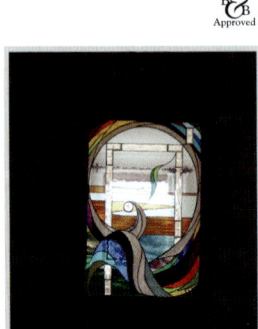

"Welcome to Te Rimu!"

Join me in my beautiful home set among trees, tuis and tranquility on the eastern slopes of the hill in Waikanae.I enjoy good company and good food and will endeavour that you do also. As I work away from home forward bookings would be appreciated, so I can give you great hospitality.

Paraparaumu *41 km N of Wellington*

By the Sea Rosetta Boutique Bed & Breakfast *B&B Separate Suite*

Lorraine & Michael Sherlock
349 Rosetta Road,
Paraparaumu,
Kapiti Coast

Tel (04) 905 9055
or 021 122 0939
Fax (04) 905 9055
rosettahouse@paradise.net.nz
www.rosetta.co.nz

Double/Twin $110-$165
(Full breakfast)
Visa MC accepted
Children welcome
2 Queen 1 Double/Twin (3 bdrm)
Bathrooms: 2 Ensuite 1 Private

Guests rate us 4+star. Highly rated by prominent overseas travel site. Delightful home set in gardens. A few footsteps to magnificent beach, village shops, four excellent restaurants. Champagne room with ensuite tastefully decorated. Garden Suite: two double bedrooms opening out to glass-covered patio-BBQ area, large lounge, bathroom, kitchenette. Suitable 2-4 guests, families. Generous breakfast menu: home-made bread, conserves included in tariff. Flowers, chocolates, chilled spring water in suites. Wireless internet. Off-street parking. Laundry. Newspaper. Very friendly German Shepherd outside and affectionate cat.

Raumati Beach *3 km SW of Paraparaumu*

Sea Haven *B&B Homestay*

Jan & Laurie Bason
325 Rosetta Road,
Raumati Beach,
Paraparaumu

Tel (04) 902 0047
or 021 0279 8803
Fax (04) 902 0045
jan-laurie@paradise.net.nz

Double/Twin $110
Single $95
(Continental breakfast)
Visa MC accepted
Not suitable for children
1 Queen (1 bdrm)
Bathrooms: 1 Private

Welcome to our spacious smoke-free home. Our guest room opens to a small garden, with seating amongst native trees. Private access to the beach. 200-300 metres from village shops, restaurants, swimming pool, bowling green and Marine Gardens. Kapiti Miniature Railway is situated at Marine Gardens with various locomotives running on Sunday afternoons. Golf courses in the area. Laurie, a railway enthusiast, has a miniature locomotive and collection of railway memorabilia. We enjoy overseas travel, and throughout NZ in our Motorhome. One timid cat in residence.

Pukerua Bay *30 km N of Wellington*
Sheena's Homestay *Homestay*

Sheena Taylor
2 Gray Street, Pukerua Bay,
Porirua City 5026

Tel (04) 239 9947
or 027 302 3483
Fax (04) 239 9942
homestay@sheenas.co.nz
www.sheenas.co.nz

Double/Twin $90
Single $50
(Full breakfast)
Children $25
Dinner $15-$25 pp by arrangement
Visa MC Amex Eftpos accepted
Children and pets welcome
1 Double/Twin 1 Twin
1 Single (2 bdrm)
Bathrooms: 1 Family share

Come share our warm, sunny smokefree home with our very friendly cat - Sienna. Relax in the conservatory, enjoy the views. Sheena's a keen woolcrafter - stay 2 nights & have a go at spinning, felting or weave a scarf. Pukerua Bay, home of creative people, has an interesting beach about 15 minutes walk. Frequent trains to Wellington (good bus service) for day trips. Restaurants/cafes 5-15 minutes drive. Most special diets catered for, lunches arranged. Off-street parking; laundry facilities; bike storage; campervan powerpoint; cot/highchair.

Plimmerton *6 km N of Porirua*
Aquavilla Seaside Self-contained B&B *B&B Cottage with Kitchen*

Graham & Carolyn Wallace
16 Steyne Avenue,
Plimmerton, Porirua

Tel (04) 233 1146
or 027 231 0141
aquavilla@paradise.net.nz
www.aquavilla.co.nz

Double/Twin $160-$180
Single $150
(Special breakfast)
Children $50
Dinner $50
Extra adults $50
Visa MC accepted
Children welcome
1 Queen 1 Single (1 bdrm)
Bathrooms: 1 Private

In the gorgeous garden of our seaside villa, your architecturally-designed accommodation features courtyard, kitchenette, barbeque and comfort-plus. Guests love the crisp cotton sheets, flowers,homemade biscuits and artistic touches. Explore Wellington easily by car or rail, or enjoy the forest and beach walks, cafes and restaurants, golfing, galleries, shopping and windsurfing close by. Scrumptious breakfast menu has light or full cooked options: homemade muesli or blueberry pancakes and sweetcorn fritters, etc. Warm and widely-travelled, we're art and nature lovers and very welcoming! Safe parking.

Plimmerton *2 km S of Plimmerton*

SeaStyle *Luxury Apartment with Kitchen*

Chrissy and Jack Lyons
10 Cluny Road,
Plimmerton,
Wellington

Tel (04) 233 9648
or 021 284 0461
Fax (04) 233 9645
bookings@seastyle.co.nz
www.seastyle.co.nz

Double/Twin $120-$150
(Continental breakfast provisions)
Children $30 pp - Max 2
Visa MC accepted
Pet free home
Children welcome
1 Queen 1 Double/Twin (1 bdrm)
Bathrooms: 1 Ensuite

Stay in ,style by the sea in a self contained apartment 1 queen bed, 1 pull out double couch. Fully equipped kitchenette, ensuite, washer/dryer, TV, DVD, phone, off street parking. Just 25 minutes from Wellington City by road/rail. Close to beach, station, shops and restaurants. Directions: Off SH1 at Plimmerton, Steyne Avenue, cross railway to Plimmerton shops, turn left into Beach Road. Follow the beach until you reach Cluny Road. Turn right into Cluny Road, to Number 10, entrance is off Motuhara Road.

Plimmerton *5 km N of Porirua*

Plimmerton Panoramic Bed and Breakfast *B&B*

Keryn and Marissa Martin
11 Corlett Rd,
Plimmerton,
Porirua 5026

Tel (04) 233 1786
or 027 257 7401
keryn.marissa@xtra.co.nz
http://panoramicbnb.com

Double/Twin $130-$140
Single $120
(Continental breakfast)
Children Porta Cot available $25
Cooked breakfast available $15 each
Visa MC accepted
Pet free home
Children welcome
1 King (1 bdrm)
Bathrooms: 1 Ensuite

Our modern home sits on the hill in Plimmerton with stunning panoramic views overlooking Plimmerton Beach, Mana Island, Porirua and Rolling Green Hills typical of New Zealand Country Side. Our view has it all! You can enjoy long walks along the beach, boutique shopping, cafÉ cruising and spa pampering. Your hosts are here to welcome you with warm hospitality and understand the need for a place to retreat and welcome peaceful relaxation at the Plimmerton Panoramic B&B.

Paremata *5 km N of Porirua*
Cottage on the Inlet *Self contained cottage*

Michelle & Mike
300a Paremata Road,
Paremata,
Wellington

Tel (04) 234 1699
or 021 305 342
Fax (04) 234 8817
mdykes@dykesassoc.co.nz
www.cottageontheinlet.co.nz

Double/Twin $160
Single $160
(Breakfast by arrangement)
Extra guests $25 (per night)
Dinner not provided
Children and pets welcome
Non smokers only
1 Queen 2 Single (2 bdrm)
Bathrooms: 1 Private

A re you looking for a private peaceful retreat? Located just north of Wellington on the Pauatahanui Inlet with stunning views of the inlet, marina and out to the coast, the Cottage on the Inlet could be just what you need. This character cottage has recently been fully renovated and is spacious yet cosy whilst still retaining that country cottage feel. Come and enjoy your retreat today.

Tawa *15 km N of Wellington*
Chaplin Homestay *B&B Homestay*

Joy & Bill Chaplin
3 Kiwi Place,
Tawa,
Wellington

Tel (04) 232 5547
or 021 146 5717
021 298 4569
Fax (04) 232 5547
chapta@xtra.co.nz

Double/Twin $90
Single $50
(Continental breakfast)
Dinner by arrangement
Pet free home
Not suitable for children
1 King 1 Double/Twin
1 Single (3 bdrm)
Bathrooms: 1 Private 1 Guest share

Y ou will find No 3 in a quiet cul-de-sac with safe off-street parking 7 minutes by car and rail to Porirua City and 15 minutes to Wellington and the InterIsland Ferry Terminal. Relax in comfort and enjoy good restaurants, close proximity to beaches, tenpin bowling, swimming pool and fine walks. Phone for directions and notification for dinner if required. Laundry facilities available.

Please let us know
how you enjoyed your B&B experience.
Ask your host for a comment form
or leave a comment on www.bnb.co.nz.

Tawa *15 km NW of Wellington CBD*
Perry B&B Homestay *B&B Homestay Homestay B&B*
Jocelyn & David Perry
5 Fyvie Avenue,
Tawa,
Wellington
5028
Tel (04) 232 7664
djperry@actrix.co.nz
Double/Twin $100
Single $60
(Continental breakfast)
Children under 15 $30
Dinner by arrangement
Visa MC accepted
Children welcome
1 Double/Twin 1 Twin
1 Single (3 bdrm)
Bathrooms: 1 Guest share
1 Family share

We are a retired couple. Together with our cat "Boots" we welcome you to stay with us. There is a 5 minute walk to the suburban railway station with a half hourly service into the city (15 minutes) and north to the Kapiti Coast. Alternatively you can drive north to the coast, enjoying sea and rural views before sampling tourist attractions in this area. We are happy to provide transport to and from the Interisland ferry. Laundry facilities available.

Upper Hutt - Te Marua *7.4 km N of Upper Hutt*

Te Marua Homestay *Homestay*

Sheryl & Lloyd Homer
108A Plateau Road,
Te Marua,
Upper Hutt

Tel (04) 526 7851
or 0800 110 851
or 027 450 1679
Fax (04) 526 7866
sheryl.lloyd@clear.net.nz

Double/Twin $100
Single $70
(Continental breakfast)
Dinner $25pp by arrangement
Visa MC Diners Amex accepted
Not suitable for children
1 Queen 1 Double/Twin (2 bdrm)
Bathrooms: 1 Private

Our home is situated in a secluded bush setting. Guests may relax on one of our private decks or read books from our extensive library. For the more energetic there are bush walks, bike trails, trout fishing, swimming and a golf course within walking distance. The guest wing has a kitchenette and television. Lloyd is a landscape photographer with over 30 years experience photographing New Zealand. Sheryl is a teacher. Travel, tramping, skiing, photography, music and meeting people are interests we enjoy.

Upper Hutt *45 km N of Wellington*

Tranquility Homestay *B&B Homestay*

Elaine & Alan
136 Akatarawa Road,
Birchville, Upper Hutt

Tel (04) 526 6948
Free Phone 0800 270 787
027 675 8341
Fax (04) 526 6968
tranquility@xtra.co.nz
www.tranquilityhomestay.co.nz

Double/Twin $90-$120
Single $70-$120
(Continental breakfast)
Children negotiable
Dinner $30 by prior arrangement
Airport pick up
Visa MC Diners Amex accepted
Children and pets welcome
1 King/Twin 1 Queen 1 Double/Twin 1 Single (4 bdrm)
Bathrooms: 2 Ensuite 2 Family share Luxury Queen Ensuite with spa bath, Double has ensuite

Tranquility Homestay. The name says it all. Escape from the stress of city life approx 25 minutes from Wellington off SH2. Close to Upper Hutt - restaurants, cinema, golf, racecourse, leisure centre (swimming), bush walks. We are near the confluence of the Hutt and Akatarawa Rivers which is noted for its fishing. 13km to Staglands. Country setting, relax, listen to NZ tuis, watch the fantails or wood pigeons, or simply relax and read. Comfortable, warm and friendly hospitality.

Lower Hutt *1 km N of Lower Hutt Centre*

Judy & Bob's Place *Homestay*

Judy & Bob Vine
11 Ngaio Crescent,
Woburn,
Lower Hutt

Tel (04) 971 1192
or 021 510 682
or 0274 500 682
Fax (04) 971 6192
bob.vine@paradise.net.nz

Double/Twin $130
Single $65
(Full breakfast)
Dinner $35
Visa MC Diners Amex accepted
Pet free home
1 Queen 2 Single (2 bdrm)
Bathrooms: 1 Private
Limit 1 booking at a time to obviate bathroom sharing

Located in Woburn, a picturesque and quiet central city suburb of Lower Hutt, known for its generous sized houses and beautiful gardens. Within walking distance of the Lower Hutt downtown, 15 minutes drive from central Wellington, its railway station and ferry terminals; airport 25 minutes; 3 minutes walk to Woburn Rail Station. Private lounge and TV. Love to entertain and share hearty Kiwi style cooking with good New Zealand wine. Laundry facilities. Transfer transport available. High speed Internet connections.

Lower Hutt *3 km E of Hutt City*

Casa Bianca *B&B Apartment with Kitchen long term stays available*

Jo & Dave Comparini
10 Damian Grove,
Lower Hutt,
Wellington

Tel (04) 569 7859
or 027 357 4395
Fax (04) 569 7859
casabiancanz@xtra.co.nz
http://Casa Bianca NZ

Double/Twin $95-$120
Single $75-$100
(Continental breakfast provisions)
Longterm stays available
Visa MC accepted
Pet free home
Not suitable for children
1 King 1 Single (1 bdrm)
Bathrooms: 1 Private

Our B&B is close to Hutt City. A short hop to the Open Polytech, Hutt Hospital, and Waterloo station. Wellington is 20 minutes away. We have a lovely self-contained apartment with double bedroom. bathroom, large lounge, fully equipped kitchen, laundry and a single bed in the lounge. Breakfast provisions provided in apartment. Stays long or short term. If you are relocating call us first. Enjoy our special hospitality. Broadband, Safe off-street parking. Not suitable for children. Non smoking please.

Lower Hutt *0.5 km SE of Lower Hutt*
Rose Cottage *B&B Homestay*

Maureen & Gordon Gellen
70A Hautana Street,
Lower Hutt,
Wellington

Tel (04) 566 7755
or 021 481 732
Fax (04) 566 0777
gellen@xtra.co.nz

Double/Twin $110-$125
Single $95-$110
(Full breakfast)
Dinner $35 by arrangement
Visa MC accepted
Not suitable for children
1 King/Twin 1 Queen (2 bdrm)
Bathrooms: 1 Ensuite 1 Family share

Relax in the comfort of our cosy home which is just a 5 minute walk to the Hutt City Centre and 15 minutes to ferries. Originally built in 1910 the house has been fully renovated. Interests,travel,sports and live theatre. As well as TV in guest room there's coffee and tea-making facilities. Breakfast will be served in our dining room at your convenience. Unsuitable for children. We look forward to welcoming you into our smoke-free home which we share with Scuffin our cat.

Lower Hutt - Harbourview *1.5 km W of Lower Hutt*
Harbourcity View B & B *B&B Homestay*

Mary Quayle
14 City View Grove,
Harbourview,
Lower Hutt
5010

Tel (04) 586 0557
or 027 688 3306
harbourcityview@paradise.net.nz

Double/Twin $115-$150
Single $70-$120
(Full breakfast)
Dinner $20 pp. by arrangement
Visa MC accepted
Not suitable for children
1 Single (3 bdrm)
Bathrooms: 1 Ensuite 1 Family share

Welcome to my home situated on the edge of a bush reserve with panoramic views of Wellington harbour and Hutt River. 15-minutes to Ferry, Westpac Stadium and Parliament. 20-minutes to Te Papa, Botanical Gardens and Karori Bird Sanctuary. Hike in the Regional Parks; fish the Hutt River or Golf on nearby courses. At the end of the day relax in secluded bush surrounded garden with a view of the sea. Guest tea/coffee facilities and laundry available. Sightseeing tours arranged, transfers and off street parking.

Lower Hutt *1 km SE of Lower Hutt i-site*

Hallcroft Homestay *B&B*
Lynley Hall
2 Miro Street,
Woburn,
Lower Hutt
5010

Tel (04) 938 1686
or 021 253 4131
lyndavid@paradise.net.nz

Double/Twin $60-$120
Single $60-$60
(Continental breakfast)
Children by arrangement
Cash or NZ cheque only
Children and pets welcome
1 Queen 2 Twin (2 bdrm)
Bathrooms: 1 Guest share

A smoke free, wheelchair accessible home and facilities. Off road parking. One queen bedroom. One twin bedroom. Shared Guest Bathroom. Cot and high chair available. Radio, TV and hairdryers, tea & coffee making facilities in rooms. Continental breakfast 3 mins walk to railway station 20 mins by train to Wellington station. Easy walk to local eating places. One small dog lives inside.

Lower Hutt - Stokes Valley *15 km N of Lower Hutt*

Rambling Brook *Cottage with Kitchen*

Mal & Nina
30 Tawhai Street,
Stokes Valley,
Lower Hutt

Tel (04) 563 8716
malboandnina@yahoo.co.nz

Double/Twin $130-$160
Single $120-$135
(Breakfast by arrangement -
gluten & dairy free available)
Children $35
Short & long term rates
Children welcome
1 Queen 1 Double/Twin (1 bdrm)
Bathrooms: 1 Ensuite

W elcome to Rambling Brook B&B.Come and enjoy our hospitality while relaxing in our private garden beside the stream, with birds singing during the day and the sounds of moreporks and frogs in the evening.We offer a private self contained cottage with off street parking. We have a range of DVD movies to watch and board games to play. 20 minutes to Lower Hutt or Upper Hutt. Close to Golf Course and driving range.Our three cats will also love to meet you.

Eastbourne - York Bay *3 km N of Eastbourne*
Bush House *Homestay*
Belinda Cattermole
12 Waitohu Road,
York Bay,
Eastbourne

Tel (04) 568 5250
or 027 408 9648
Fax (04) 568 5250
belindacat@paradise.net.nz

Double/Twin $100
Single $80
(Special breakfast)
Dinner by arrangement
1 Double/Twin 1 Single (2 bdrm)
Bathrooms: 1 Private 1 Family share

Come and enjoy the peace and tranquility of the Eastern Bays. You will be hosted in a restored 1920's settler cottage nestled amongst native bush and looking towards the Kaikoura mountains of the South Island. My love of cordon-bleu cooking and the pleasures of the table are satisfied through the use of my country kitchen and dining room. Other attractions: A Devon Rex cat. Eastbourne is a small seaside village across the harbour from Wellington City with a range of attractions.

Eastbourne - Days Bay *12 km E of Wellington*
FernTree Hideaway *B&B Apartment with Kitchen*
Robyn & Roger Cooper
7 Huia Road,
Days Bay,
Eastbourne

Tel (04) 562 7692
or 027 616 9826
Fax (04) 562 7690
bnb@ferntree.co.nz
www.ferntree.co.nz

Double/Twin $175-$195
Single $155-$155
(Continental breakfast provisions)
Children $30
Extra adults $47.50.
Visa MC accepted
Children welcome
1 King (1 bdrm)
Bathrooms: 1 Private

Ride our private cable car through native bush to a romantic hideaway in the treetops. Enjoy sparkling harbour views; wake to bellbird song; breakfast on your garden patio; relax with books, TV, DVDs. Open plan lounge/dining/kitchenette, luxury bath/shower, phone, free wireless internet. 200 metres to beach, cafes, bush walks, galleries. Days Bay ferry to Central Wellington (20 minute ride) berths near Te Papa and The Stadium. Inter-island ferry 20 minutes. 'This place is Dreamland - a Kiwi Shangri-la.' Self-catering optional.

Eastbourne - Lowry Bay *14 km N of Wellington*
Lowry Bay Homestay *B&B Homestay*

Pam & Forde Clarke
35 Cheviot Road, Lowry Bay,
Eastbourne, Wellington

Tel (04) 568 4407
or 0508 266 546
Fax (04) 568 4408
homestay@lowrybay.co.nz
www.lowrybay.co.nz

Double/Twin $130-$160
Single $100-$130
(Full breakfast)
Children negotiable
Visa MC Diners Amex accepted
Pet free home
Children welcome
1 King/Twin 1 Queen
1 Single (2 bdrm)
Bathrooms: 1 Private

Warm, restful, peaceful, yet close to Wellington and Hutt Cities, transport, restaurants and art galleries. Play tennis on our court, stroll to the beach, walk in the bush, sail on our 28 foot yacht, or relax under a sun umbrella on the deck. Native birds abound. Our sunny, elegant bedrooms have garden views, TV, tea/coffee and central heating. We share with our 2 grown up daughters, Isabella and Kirsty, interests in sailing, skiing, tennis, ballet and theatre. Laundry. From SH2 follow Petone signs then Eastbourne.

Eastbourne *20 km E of Wellington*
The Anchorage *B&B Homestay*

Bet & Wal Louden
107 Marine Parade,
Eastbourne,
Wellington

Tel (04) 562 8310
or 021 049 5169
or 021 329 993
betandwal@paradise.net.nz

Double/Twin $130
Single $100
(Continental breakfast)
Extra guests $50
Visa MC accepted
Children welcome
Non smokers only
1 Queen 1 Single (2 bdrm)
Bathrooms: 1 Private

Welcome to our waterfront property, wonderful views of Wellington Harbour and city. One minute walk to Eastbourne Village and wharf, supermarket, cafes, restaurants, pub, antique shops and art gallery. We offer for the more adventurous a choice of guided bush walks from an easy 2 hours to a demanding 7 hours (bookings essential; Mon-Friday only), panoramic views of Wellington Harbour, outstanding beech, northern rata and podocarp forests. Coastal walks (mountain bike rides) to Pencarrow Lighthouse. Kayak trips also available. Labrador, Splash on property.

Eastbourne - Mahina Bay *3 km N of Eastbourne Village*
Kanuka Hill Homestead *B&B Separate Suite Self contained with B&B option*

Charles
38 Mahina Rd, Mahina Bay,
Eastbourne, Lower Hutt 5013

Tel (04) 562 6399 or 021 125 6162
Fax (04) 562 6319
charlesb@sunflower.co.nz
kanukahill@sunflower.co.nz
www.sunflower.co.nz

Double/Twin $120-$180
(Full breakfast)
Cooked breakfast or dinner b/a
Single/double rate same
Additional guests $25 per night
Visa MC accepted   Pet free home
1 Queen 1 Double/Twin (1 bdrm)
Bathrooms: 1 Private We take one
party only at a time.

Kanuka Hill Homestead offers secluded accommodation with awesome views high above the harbour from the self contained suite (with cooked-by-the-host-breakfast option). Two rooms, one with a queen sized bed, TV, etc and a sitting room with sofa-bed, TV, DVD, CD player, desk with broadband connection and opening on to a deck.There is also a lovely private bathroom and kitchenette with sink, microwave, toaster, kettle, electric frypan, steamer, cutlery, crockery etcLaundry facilities available.Bush walks, cafes, restaurants, public transport & mini-supermarket nearby.

Wellington - Johnsonville *8 km N of Wellington*
Paparangi Homestay *B&B Homestay*

Joy and Autry Kawana
145 Helston Road,
Johnsonville,
Wellington

Tel (04) 478 1747
or 027 485 6432
autry.joy@xtra.co.nz

Double/Twin $95
Single $60
(Full breakfast)
Dinner with family $20
Children and pets welcome
1 Queen 1 Twin 1 Single (2 bdrm)
Bathrooms: 1 Ensuite 1 Family share

Paparangi Homestay is a restored cottage, over 100 years old and set in over 1 acre of cottage gardens. We are situated 2km from Johnsonville Railway station and shopping centre. We have a friendly dog, 2 cats and hens. Ample off street parking available. Bedrooms have TV/Radio. Autry is a keen hunter and golfer and could arrange a game. Children are welcome. Autry and Joy enjoy the company of other nationalities and our home is your home while you are with us.

Wellington - Johnsonville *8 km N of Wellington*

Cherswud *B&B Homestay*

B&B Approved

David & Marilyn McDonald
121 Helston Road,
Johnsonville, Wellington, 6037

Tel (04) 477 6767 or 021 060 7815
bb@cherswud.com

Double/Twin $110
Single $70
(Special breakfast)
Children $40 up to 12 years
Dinner $30 by prior arrangement
Visa MC accepted
2 Queen (2 bdrm)
Twin beds available if required
Bathrooms: 2 Private

We're delighted to welcome you to Cherswud, our fully-restored 1919 home, with two lounges, conservatory and a sunny deck overlooking a lovely sheltered garden. Both bedrooms are warm and bright with very comfortable beds, electric blankets and feather duvets, and the bookcases are well-stocked. Each room has its own private bathroom, one with a spa bath and massage shower.

We offer warm hospitality with delicious meals, including gluten-free options. Help yourself to tea and coffee in the kitchen at any time. Dinner served with New Zealand wine, although eight restaurants are located within 12 minutes' walk.

Free broadband internet access and free transfer of digital photos from memory sticks/cards to CD.

Twelve minutes from the inter-island ferry and two minutes off SH1 at the Johnsonville exit.

Wellington - Khandallah *7 km N of Wellington*
Clothier Homestay *Homestay*

Sue & Ted Clothier
22 Lohia Street,
Khandallah,
Wellington

Tel (04) 479 1180
or 027 246 6158
Fax (04) 479 2717
sclothier@xtra.co.nz

Double/Twin $110
Single $80
(Continental breakfast)
Not suitable for children
1 Twin (1 bdrm)
Bathrooms: 1 Ensuite

This is a lovely, sunny and warm open plan home with glorious harbour and city views. A quiet easily accessible street just 10 minutes from the city and 5 minutes from the ferry. Close to Khandallah Village where you can make use of the excellent local restaurant, cafe or Monteiths pub. We are a non-smoking household. Another family member is an aristocratic white cat called Dali. We enjoy sharing our home with our guests.

Wellington - Khandallah *7 km N of Wellington*
The Loft in Wellington *B&B Separate Suite*

Phillippa & Simon Plimmer
6 Delhi Crescent,
Khandallah,
Wellington

Tel (04) 938 5015
or 021 448 491
plimmers@paradise.net.nz

Double/Twin $110
Single $90
(Continental breakfast provisions)
Visa MC accepted
Pet free home
Not suitable for children
1 Queen (1 bdrm)
Bathrooms: 1 Ensuite

The Loft in Wellington offers the discerning traveller comfort and style in a beautifully appointed self-contained studio (no cooking facilities). Enjoy complete privacy with your own entrance and new ensuite bathroom. Cable TV, off-street parking, laundry and internet access available. 10 minutes from downtown Wellington. Close to ferry terminal. 300 metres to local train and bus. 15 minutes train ride direct to Westpac Stadium. 500 metres from Khandallah Village and local restaurants. Studio not suitable for pets. We have 3 young children.

Wellington - Ngaio *7 km NW of Wellington*

Ngaio Homestay *B&B Homestay Apartment with Kitchen*

Jennifer & Christopher Timmings
56 Fox Street, Ngaio, Wellington

Tel (04) 479 5325
Fax (04) 479 4325   enquiries@ngaiohomestay.co.nz
www.ngaiohomestay.co.nz

Double/Twin $150-$180 Single $100-$140 (Continental breakfast)
Children negotiable   Dinner $35pp by arrangement
Self-contained $160-$180 double, extra person $45   Visa MC
accepted
1 Queen 1 Double/Twin 2 Twin 3 Single (5 bdrm)
Bathrooms: 3 Ensuite 1 Private
Shower & bath in apartments, shower in ensuite B&B

Welcome to Wonderful Wellington! Share your visit with us and enjoy helpful personal hospitality! Our unusual multi-level open plan character home [built1960] is in the suburb of Ngaio.Guests may leave their car here and take the train to CBD [10 minutes] We are 5 minutes by car to InterIsland Ferry terminal.

Our double room has tea/coffee facilities, quality bedding, tiled ensuite and french doors opening onto a deck and private jungle garden. Breakfast is continental. Evening meals an optional extra.

2 self-contained apartments, 1 queen, 1 twin, adjacent to our property, are comfortable, convenient, tastefully furnished and recently re-decorated. Each apartment also has a couch with a fold-out bed in lounge, fully equipped kitchen, shower, bath, laundry facilities, cable TV, phone and internet [small fee] There is a large garden with trees, birds and views. Perfect for business, holiday or relocating.

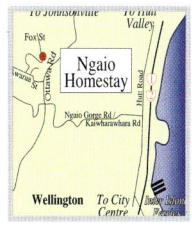

Jennifer plays harp at home and live piano music daily in NZ's top department store.

Compliment from guest: "This is a home where there is beautiful music, art and love."Do come and share! Please phone before 11am or after 3pm or fax or email. Bookings essential.

Wellington - Wadestown *2.5 km NW of Wellington*
The Nikau Palms Bed & Breakfast *B&B*

Diane & Bill Boyd
95 Sar Street,
Wadestown,
Wellington 6012

Tel (04) 499 4513
or 027 674 0644
Fax (04) 499 4517
thenikaupalms@xtra.co.nz
www.thenikaupalms.co.nz

Double/Twin $180-$200
Single $125-$130
(Full breakfast)
Suitable for children 10 and over
Visa MC accepted
2 Queen 1 Single (2 bdrm)
Bathrooms: 2 Ensuite

You are invited to share our spectacular views of Wellington Harbour overlooking the city, Interisland ferry and Westpac Stadium, all within walking distance. Our home is a few minutes drive from Wellington's attractions, Historic Thorndon's restaurants, shops and Heritage Trail and Katherine Mansfield's birthplace. The bedrooms include ensuites, one with private sunroom. Full cooked or continental breakfast provided. Tea and coffee making facilities and refrigerator in bedrooms. Off-street parking provided.

~

Wellington - Wadestown *2 km N of Wellington*
Harbour Lodge Wellington *B&B*

Lou & Chris Bradshaw
200 Barnard Street,
Wadestown,
Wellington

Tel (04) 976 5677
or 021 032 6497
lou@harbourlodgewellington.com
www.harbourlodgewellington.com

Double/Twin $180-$270
(Continental breakfast)
Children negotiable
Visa MC Amex accepted
Children welcome
4 King (4 bdrm)
Bathrooms: 4 Ensuite

Let your stresses be gently lulled away in the luxurious comfort of this beautiful new lodge. Admire the fabulous views of Wellington Harbour from the large sunny deck. Take a spa. Laze in the comfort of a large guest lounge with an open fire and stunning harbour views. All this is only a few minutes drive from central Wellington, ferry terminal or Wellington Stadium. Children of all ages welcome, no pets please.

Wellington - Wadestown *2.3 km N of Central Wellington*
Annaday Homestay *B&B Homestay*

Anne & David Denton
39 Wadestown Road,
Wellington

Tel (04) 499 1827
Fax (04) 472 1190
annaday@tavis.co.nz
www.tavis.co.nz/annaday

Double/Twin $130-$200
Single $90-$150
(Full breakfast)
Children $20-$50
Dinner $20-$35
Sauna $5
Children and pets welcome
2 King/Twin 2 King
2 Queen 2 Twin (5 bdrm)
Bathrooms: 1 Ensuite 1 Private
1 Guest share 1 Family share

Superb views. Excellent facilities. Fast internet. Hospitality adapted to suit you. Start with courtesy pickup, enjoy our free orientation tour of the city, borrow a book, join us for dinner or try the local takeaways or cafes. On the bus route, close to the city, ferries, train & we will take you to the airport. Near stadium & Bowen Hospital. Our dog and grandson stay out of guest areas but make friends if you choose. Discounts/negotiable rates for longer stays and groups.

Wellington - Wadestown *2 km NW of information centre*
Ahu Mairangi *B&B*

James and Helen
128 Weld Street,
Wadestown

Tel landline (04) 473 7157
or freephone 0800 678 031
james' mobile 0274 504 818
james.quinn@xtra.co.nz

Double/Twin $120-$140
Single $100-$110
(Continental breakfast)
Pet free home
1 Queen 1 Double/Twin (2 bdrm)
Bathrooms: 1 Ensuite 1 Private

Welcome to "Ahu Mairangi" Located high up on the hills above Wellington City for awesome views and maximum sun. Our recently modernised home has a large guest bedroom with ensuite which has both bath and shower. Also a second double bedroom with adjoining bath room and separate w.c. Both rooms have peaceful bush views so come and enjoy a relaxing stay in our beautiful city. As we adjoin the town belt there are some great walks for the fitter guests. Dinner optional extra

Wellington - Karori *5 km W of Wellington*

Campbell Homestay *Homestay*
Murray & Elaine Campbell
23 Parkvale Road, Karori 6012, Wellington

Tel (04) 476 6110 or 0274 535 080
Fax (04) 476 6593   ctool@ihug.co.nz

Double/Twin $110 Single $70 (Continental breakfast)
Children half price (under 12) Dinner $35 b/a
Visa MC Eftpos accepted   Children and pets welcome
1 Queen 1 Twin 1 Single (2 bdrm)
Bathrooms: 1 Guest share
Separate toilet, full bathroom/shower next to bedrooms

Welcome to our home right in the village of Karori, but only ten minutes from the central city.Dine with us, or eat out at the local taverns, cafes, enjoy our local village shopping centre,library, Post Office and other amenities all within a few minutes walking distance. As we are on the main bus route, guests,can park their car off street and take the bus into the city. We are happy to pick you up from ferry, train, bus or airport terminals and of course make sure you do not miss your onward connection.We are situated close to the Karori Wildlife Sanctuary, Botanic Gardens and Otari-Wilton's Bush, Cable Car, historic Thorndon's boutique shopping centre and restaurants, Katherine Masefield's birthplace, the Westpac Stadium

"Absolutely Positively Wellington" is a dynamic ever changing compact city making it easy to walk from one place to the next and with simply the most friendly helpful people. Take advantage of Wellington's cultural events: orchestra, ballet, opera, galleries and theatres. Visit our fabulous modern museum Te Papa or take a shuttle ferry across the harbour.

We have two guest bedrooms, 1 Queen and 1 Twin which can also be a single.Guests have the sole use of a separate toilet and a full sized bathroom next door to the bedrooms.Relax and make yourself at home - use our laundry, garden, lounge, email/internet facilities. Meet Charlie our border collie dog. Children of all ages welcome. Our home is perfect for business folk or families relocating as it is so close to all the village amenities and schools.Weekly rates on application Evening meals are an optional extra, $35.00 per person. From the motorway, when coming into Wellington from the north, take the Hawkestone Street/Karori exit off the motorway and follow the signs up past the Botanic gardens, through the tunnel, up the hill past the Marsden shops and down to the Karori village. Turn right at the lights into Parkvale Road (first turn past the Shopping Mall), then turn left down the drive to No 23 where a big welcome awaits you.

Wellington - Karori *5 km W of Wellington City*
Harbour Vista B&B *B&B Homestay*

Gina and Peter Sisson
24 Kilsyth Street,
Wellington
6012

Tel (04) 476 2477
or 021 139 0606
021 059 6645
Fax (04) 476 2479
pgsisson@xtra.co.nz
www.harbourvista.co.nz

Double/Twin $140-$200
(Full breakfast)
Visa MC accepted
Pet free home
Not suitable for children
1 King 1 Queen (2 bdrm)
Bathrooms: 1 Ensuite 1 Private

Welcome to our home situated in a quiet cul-de-sac with awesome views of our suburb, hills and our beautiful harbour! We are 5 to 10 minutes from the Cable Car, Botanical Garden, the Bird Sanctuary and the city. We are widely travelled and enjoy meeting and sharing our home with fellow travellers. Rooms have tea and coffee making facilities, electric blankets, hair dryer and bathrobes. Extremely comfortable beds and a warm welcome awaits you. Internet and laundry service available.

Wellington - Karori *2 km N of the central city*
B&B and Homestay *B&B Homestay Separate Suite*

Judit & Julian Farquhar
15 Nottingham Street,
Wellington
6005

Tel (04) 976 8144
Fax (04) 976 8144
judit.farquhar@gmail.com
http://farquharsbedandbreakfast.
blogspot.com/

Double/Twin $120-$130
Single $80-$90
(Full breakfast provisions)
Children welcome at lower rates
Dinner by arrangement $20-35
Major currencies accepted
Children welcome
1 Queen 2 Single (1 bdrm)
Bathrooms: 1 Private

Welcome to our 100-year-old eco colonial home in the Wellington suburb of Karori with a beautiful mature organic garden, 5 minutes from the central city. We are a well-travelled Hungarian-Kiwi couple with our 7-year-old daughter. There is music, art and technology inside. Good transport and local shops and restaurants. We offer a separate guest-room for 2-3 people with its own WC and washbasin. There is also a self-contained, private apartment with kitchen to accomodate up to 4 people for longer period, by arrangment.

Wellington - Kelburn *1 km W of city centre*
Above Town Bed and Breakfast *B&B*

Maria and Michael Phelan
23 Rimu Road,
Kelburn,
Wellington
6012

Tel (04) 971 5737
abovetownbnb@paradise.net.nz

Double/Twin $140-$170
Single $120-$150
(Full breakfast)
Visa MC accepted
1 King/Twin 1 Double/Twin
(1 bdrm)
Bathrooms: 1 Ensuite

Enjoy our spacious guest room in a quiet street above the city centre. Nearby Wellington's cable car to central city locations and the harbour. Walk to Victoria University and Botanic Gardens. Te Papa, downtown entertainments and Stadium are easily reached. Knowledgeable hosts, Maria and Michael, can provide information to help you explore Wellington. Then relax in your stylish room with sitting area, TV, coffee/tea making, airconditioning and fridge. Double futon for extra guests; quality linen; separate entrance and roadside parking. Friendly pet dog in residence.

Wellington - Aro Valley *2 km SW of Information Centre*
Millie's Bed & Breakfast *B&B Homestay*

Miriam Busby
33 Holloway Road,
Aro Valley, Wellington 6021

Tel (04) 381 2968
or 021 254 7308
Fax (04) 381 2969
miriam.busby@paradise.net.nz
www.milliesbb.co.nz

Double/Twin $130
Single $90
(Full breakfast)
Children $40
Dinner $20 for Colonial cottage cuisine
Children welcome
No credit card facilities,
cash or cheque only
1 Double/Twin 1 Single (2 bdrm)
Bathrooms: 1 Family share,
1 bath & shower available for guests to use.

Named after Millie, the pet cat, at Millie's you awake to the sound of native birdsong. The house is nestled in a bushy valley near the Karori Sanctuary. Situated on a heritage trail, Millie's is close to a bus-stop, Aro Street cafes, restaurants and shops. 20 minutes walk to city. Free off-street parking available. Complimentary breakfast. 1 extra divan bed in kitchen. Deck with BBQ. Dinner, scenic drives, walks & therapeutic art sessions are extra services available.

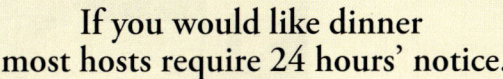

**If you would like dinner
most hosts require 24 hours' notice.**

Wellington - Mt Cook *2 km SE of Wellington*

Apartment One *B&B Homestay*

Jim & Colleen Bargh
1/2 King Street,
Mt Cook,
Wellington

Tel (04) 385 1112
or 027 247 8145
or 027 275 0913
apartmentone@yahoo.co.nz

Double/Twin $130-$140
Single $90-$100
(Full breakfast)
Visa MC accepted
Pet free home
Not suitable for children
2 Queen 1 Single (2 bdrm)
Bathrooms: 2 Ensuite

E xperience apartment living in the city. We moved off the farm into our converted warehouse to try city life. We love its ever-changing beauty and the people are simply the best. Come try it for yourself. Buses depart every few minutes. 2 minutes walk to the Basin Reserve and 10-15 minutes walk to Courtenay Place (Wellington's restaurant, cafe and theatre district). Less than 10 minutes drive to the ferry terminal and airport. We serve a deluxe breakfast to get you through your eventful day.

Wellington - Mt Cook *0.1 km S of Wellington*
Seddon Cottage *Cottage with Kitchen*

Shelley and Richard Steele
63 Nairn Street,
Mount Cook
6011

Tel (04) 382 8916
or 027 292 7335
shelleysteele@hotmail.com
www.seddoncottage.com

Double/Twin $180-$220
(Continental breakfast)
Tariff for longers stays negotiable
Please book by email or telephone
Not suitable for children
Pets welcome
1 Queen 1 Double/Twin (1 bdrm)
Bathrooms: 1 Private
Deep tubbed shower

One bedroom cottage, self contained with queen bed and a double sofa bed. The cottage is light and airy. Provided is a television, laptop with broadband, microwave and expresso coffee maker. A short walk to all of Wellington city's amenities. Lawn tennis available in the summer. We have two teenaged children and a cat. A better alternative to a busy hotel.

Wellington - Mt Victoria *0.5 km E of Courtenay Place*
Austinvilla *B&B Apartment with Kitchen*

Zarli & Mark
11 Austin Street,
Mt Victoria,
Wellington

Tel (04) 385 8334
info@austinvilla.co.nz
www.austinvilla.co.nz

Double/Twin $160-$220
(Continental breakfast)
Visa MC Eftpos accepted
Not suitable for children
2 Queen (2 bdrm)
Bathrooms: 2 Ensuite

Top location: Set amongst beautiful gardens in one of Mt Victoria's elegant turn-of-the-century villas, Austinvilla is within minutes walk of theatres, restaurants, Oriental Bay and Te Papa. Close to public transport and short drive to airport, ferries, and Westpac Stadium.2 self-contained apartments with individual entrances come equipped with queen bed, ensuite (bath and shower), kitchen, living/dining area, cable TV, phone and wireless internet access. Both offer privacy, sun and city views with one having its own patio/garden. Laundry facilities and off-street parking available.

Wellington - Mt Victoria *0.5 km E of Central Wellington*

Villa Vittorio *B&B Homestay*
Annette & Logan Russell
6 Hawker Street, Mt Victoria, Wellington

Tel (04) 801 5761 or 027 432 1267
Fax (04) 801 5762
villa@villavittorio.co.nz
www.villavittorio.co.nz

Double/Twin $195-$220 Single $135 (Full breakfast)
Dinner by arrangement
Visa MC Diners Amex accepted
1 Double/Twin (1 bdrm)
Bathrooms: 1 Private

WELCOME TO VILLA VITTORIO. Centrally located close by Courtenay Place. Short walk to restaurants, theatres, shopping, conference centres, Te Papa Museum, Parliament & Stadium. Guest bedroom with TV, tea & coffee facilities. Adjoining sitting room with balcony overlooking city. Bathroom with show- and bath.

Breakfast served in Italian styled dining room or outside in courtyard. We enjoy having guests, having travelled extensively ourselves. Transport and gourmet dinner by arrangement. Garaging and laundry at small charge. No children or pets.

Directions: phone, fax, email or write.

Wellington - Roseneath *3 km E of Wellington Central*
Harbourview Homestay and B&B *B&B Homestay*

Hilda & Geoff Stedman
125 Te Anau Road,
Roseneath,
Wellington

Tel (04) 386 1043
or 021 0386 351
hildastedman@clear.net.nz
http://nzhomestay.co.nz/
harbourview_homestay

Double/Twin $130-$170
Single $100-$150
(Full breakfast)
Dinner from $40
Visa MC accepted
Children welcome
1 Double/Twin 2 Single (2 bdrm)
Bathrooms: 2 Private

5 minutes drive from Wellington city, 10 minutes drive from the airport and on the No. 14 bus route. The house offers comfortable hospitality and elegance. Each bedroom opens to a wide deck, offering expansive views of Wellington harbour. Pleasantly decorated rooms quality beds and linen, separate guest's bathroom with shower and spa bath. Harbourview is situated in a peaceful setting close to the city, catering for business people, tourists and honeymooners. A surcharge will be added if paying by credit card. The property is not suitable for wheelchair access.

Wellington - Roseneath *2 km E of Central city*
Panorama *B&B*

Peg Mackay
1 Robieson Lane,
Roseneath

Tel (04) 801 8691
or 021 801 869
pegmackay@hotmail.com
www.wellingtonpanorama.co.nz

Double/Twin $140-$170
Single $100-$120
(Continental breakfast)
Children by arrangement
Evening meals by arrangement
Long term rates on application
2 Queen (2 bdrm)
Bathrooms: 1 Private 1 Guest share
1 guest bath

Enjoy the panorama of ships, ferries and tugs and the sun, peace and privacy of our warm modern home above Oriental Bay. You have your own deck and sitting room with TV and refreshments. 5 min walk up to Mt Victoria or 15-20 minute walk down to Oriental Bay, the city, theatres, galleries and Te Papa: the Museum of New Zealand. Taste NZ in the many nearby cafes and restaurants. Ferry/Airport 10 minutes, city 5 minutes drive. AND you can park right at our door!

Wellington - Roseneath *1 km E of Wellington CBD*

Maida Vale *B&B*
Bessie Sutherland
6 Maida Vale Road,
Roseneath,
Wellington

Tel 027 332 1570
or (04) 970 5184
bess.sutherland@clear.net.nz
www.maidavalebnb.co.nz

Double/Twin $150-$180
Single $60
(Continental breakfast)
Children child negotiable
Weekly rates negotiable
Visa MC Amex accepted
Children welcome
1 King 1 Single (2 bdrm)
Bathrooms: 1 Ensuite

Our centrally located home has spectacular views across the harbour to the city centre. The larger room has an ensuite. Both rooms are on the ground floor and have their own entrance (our family lives above). The city centre, restaurants, theatres and museums are a 5 minute drive away or, alternatively, a 20 minute walk along the waterfront. The airport and ferry terminals are 10-15 minutes away. The family will greet you with a warm welcome as will Zoe, the Jack Russell terrier.

Wellington - Roseneath *2 km E of Central City*

Crescent Point *B&B*
Bobbi & John Gibbons
18 The Crescent,
Roseneath,
Wellington 6011

Tel (04) 972 3464
or 027 485 0846
Fax (04) 972 3465
gibbonsjg@paradise.net.nz
www.crescentpoint.co.nz

Double/Twin $140-$180
Single $100
(Full breakfast)
Dinner By Arrangement
Visa MC accepted
Children and pets welcome
2 Queen (2 bdrm)
Bathrooms: 1 Ensuite 1 Private
Ensuite with spa bath

We welcome you to sunny Crescent Point,a spacious modern home with panoramic views overlooking the harbour above Oriental Bay. We offer two bedrooms with ensuites, cable TV. One with kitchenette, own entrance and carpark, the other a spa bath. Take a 5 min bush walk to Oriental Bay beach, then a pleasant 10 min walk to the City entertainment area, with restaurants, theatres and Te Papa. 10-15 min drive to Central City and Ferry. 10 mins to Wellington Airport. There is a cat in residence.

Wellington - Roseneath *1 km N of Wellington CBD*

Roseneath House *B&B*

Linda Forrest
58 Palliser Road,
Roseneath,
Wellington

Tel (04) 384 5501
or 021 1885 846
roseneathhouse@gmail.com
www.roseneathhouse.co.nz

Double/Twin $190
(Full breakfast)
Visa MC accepted
1 King (1 bdrm)
Bathrooms: 1 Ensuite

Roseneath House - located in Wellington's dress circle, is a beautiful old Victorian villa offering breathtaking views over Wellington's stunning harbour and Oriental Bay beach. Walk down the landscaped pathway of native plants or ride the private cable-car. Tucked into the hillside, bathed in all day sun, Roseneath House is surrounded by the city's green belt and walkways to the summit of Mount Victoria. Wander down the hillside and along the picturesque waterfront to all the attractions that Wellington city has to offer. Airport & ferry 15 min. drive away.

Wellington - Hataitai *3 km E of Wellington CBD*

Top O' T'ill *B&B Homestay S/C Studio-Apartment with Kitchen*

Cathryn & Dennis Riley
2 Waitoa Road,
Hataitai,
Wellington 6021

Tel (04) 976 2718
or 0274 716 482
Fax (04) 976 2719
top.o.hill@clear.net.nz
www.topotill-homestay.co.nz

Double/Twin $130-$140
Single $100-$110
(Full breakfast)
S/C $120-$150
Visa MC accepted
Pet free home
Not suitable for children
2 Queen 1 Twin (3 bdrm)
Bathrooms: 2 Ensuite 1 Private

Hataitai - 'breath of the ocean', is a popular eastern suburb midway between the airport and central Wellington. City attractions are 5-10 minutes by bus or car. Our comfortable family home of 60 years is a welcome retreat for guests. The quality studio/apartment is fully equipped - long and short term rates on application. We share a range of cultural interests, have travelled widely, and will help you make the most of your visit to Wellington. Secure wireless internet. Directions: included in web site.

Wellington - Brooklyn (city end) *3 km SW of Wellington City Centre*

Karepa *Homestay*
Ann & Tom Hodgson
56 Karepa Street,
Brooklyn, Wellington

Tel (04) 384 4193
Fax (04) 384 4180
homestay@karepa.info
http://homestay.karepa.info

Double/Twin $135-$165
Single $95-$125
(Full breakfast)
Children by arrangement
Dinner $35 by arrangement
Extra guest $35pp
Visa MC accepted
Children welcome
2 King 1 Double/Twin
1 Single (3 bdrm)
Bathrooms: 2 Ensuite 1 Guest share

S tay at Karepa, our sunny, spacious home overlooking city, harbour and mountains. The secluded rear garden adjoins native bush. Private guest rooms have TV and tea/coffee facilities. City 5 minutes, ferry 10 and airport 15. Residents of 25 years, ex-UK, we have travelled widely, play golf and tennis, and enjoy Wellington's many attractions. Ann gardens and Tom watches from his deckchair. On-site parking. Bus at door. Laundry facilities. Sorry, no smokers or pets. Please phone/fax for directions.

Wellington - Vogeltown (South Mt Cook)
3 km S of Wellington CBD

Finnimore House *B&B Homestay*
Willie & Kathleen Ryan
2 Dransfield Street,
Vogeltown, Wellington

Tel (04) 389 9894
Fax (04) 389 9894
w.f.ryan@xtra.co.nz
www.finnimorehouse.co.nz

Double $100-$130
Twin $110-$140
Single $90-$110
(Full breakfast)
Children $30
Extra person $30   Seaonal rates vary
Visa MC accepted Children welcome
3 Queen 2 Single (3 bdrm)
Bathrooms: 1 Guest share

W elcome to our historical manor 5 minutes drive from downtown Wellington. Your hosts, Willie and Kathleen Ryan, offer warm hospitality, spacious Victorian rooms, a hearty breakfast, and a traditional B&B experience in a welcoming family home with a genuine Irish flavour. Our great location is close to: airport, ferries, restaurants, Basin Reserve, hospital, zoo, Massey University, Hurricanes training ground, National School of Dance and Drama. Secure private parking on-site, convenient public transport. Laundry facilities available (if staying 3 nights). Wellington is yours at Finnimore House.

Wellington - Seatoun *10 km SE of Courtenay Place*
The Admiral's Breakfast B and B Apartment
Luxury B&B Apartment with Kitchen

Karen Cronin and Wren Green
97 Inglis Street,
Seatoun,
Wellington

Tel (04) 934 5913
or 021 345 913
enquiries@admiralsbreakfast.co.nz
www.admiralsbreakfast.co.nz

Double/Twin $185
Single $165
(Full breakfast provisions)
Complimentary champagne gift
basket on arrival.
Visa MC Diners Amex accepted
Not suitable for children
1 Queen (1 bdrm)
Bathrooms: 1 Ensuite

Enjoy the luxury of a spacious apartment in Seatoun. Quiet location, yet only 4 minutes to the airport, 12 min to downtown. Start the day with a breakfast, fit for an admiral. The apartment is completely separate with all the makings for a fine breakfast provided. Check emails via free broadband in your apartment and enjoy breakfast at your leisure. Private courtyard with wonderful harbour views. Excellent restaurants and cafes close by. We welcome travellers for short or longer stays. We are both seasoned travellers.

Wellington - Island Bay *4 km S of Courtenay Place*
Buckley Homestay *B&B Homestay Separate Suite*

Mrs Wilhelmina Muller
51 Buckley Road, Melrose,
Island Bay, Wellington

Tel (04) 934 7151
or 021 112 3445
Fax (04) 934 7152
willy.muller@paradise.net.nz
www.buckleyhomestay.co.nz

Double/Twin $120-$140
Single $110
(Continental breakfast)
Children negotiable
Dinner by arrangement
Visa MC accepted
Pet free home
Children and pets welcome
1 King/Twin 1 Queen 3 Single (3 bdrm)
Bathrooms: 2 Private 1 Family share

Large 2 storey sunny home with spectacular scenery and beautiful views over Wellington. New tastefully decorated, private entrance, 1 bedroom, self-contained suite with private balcony, TV, conservatory. Handy to hospitals. We are interested in food, wine, travel, relaxing and meeting people. Willy is a nurse, enjoys cooking, gardening and speaks Dutch. No pets or children at home. Off-street parking, complimentary refreshments, dinner by arrangement. On bus route. Handy to all tourist attractions, and airport.

Wellington - Island Bay *6 km S of Wellington City Central*

The Lighthouse & The Keep *Self-contained*

Bruce Stokell
326 The Esplanade & 116 The Esplanade,
Island Bay,
Wellington

Tel (04) 472 4177
or 027 442 5555
bruce@thelighthouse.net.nz
www.thelighthouse.net.nz

Double/Twin $180-$200
(Full breakfast provisions)
Visa MC accepted
Not suitable for children
1 Double/Twin (1 bdrm)
Bathrooms: 1 Private

Island Bay - 10 minutes city centre, 10 minutes airport, 20 minutes ferry terminal.

The Lighthouse is on the south coast and has views of the island, fishing boats in the bay, the beach and rocks, the far coastline, the open sea, the shipping and, on a clear day, the South Island. There are local shops and restaurants.

The Lighthouse has a basic kitchen and bathroom on the first floor, the bedroom/sitting room on the middle floor and the lookout on the top. Romantic.

The Keep is a stone tower just 2 minutes from The Lighthouse. It has a lounge/basic kitchen on 1 level and a bed with ensuite on the next level. Also a spa bath in the bedroom. It is very cosy and has excellent views of the sea, especially in a storm. Stairs from the bedroom lead to a hatch which opens on to the roof.

Wellington - Island Bay *3 km S of Courtenay Place*

Ma Maison *B&B Boutique B&B*

Margo Frost
9 Tamar Street, Island Bay, Wellington

Tel (04) 383 4018 or 027 2429 827
Fax (04) 383 4018
bedandbreakfast@paradise.net.nz
www.nzwellingtonhomestay.co.nz

Double/Twin $140
Single $120 (Full breakfast)
 Visa MC accepted
2 Queen (2 bdrm)
Bathrooms: 1 Ensuite 1 Private

Luxury in a warm, comfortable home at a realistic price, our 1920s home is decorated with a French flavour. Drive to door, lovely garden.

The brown guest room has it's own entrance and ensuite, the blue room has private bathroom. Both rooms have queen posturepedic beds and are equipped with everything to make your stay as comfortable as possible.

Island Bay is a popular seaside suburb with excellent local restaurants. We are 8 minutes by car to the city and very handy to great bus service.

A full delicious breakfast is served at a time to suit you. Resident family cat.

Wellington - Island Bay *7 km S of Wellington City Central*

Nature's Touch Guest House *Luxury B&B Separate Suite*

B&B Approved

Maarten & Natsuko Groeneveld

25A Happy Valley Road, Owhiro Bay, Wellington

Tel (04) 383 6977 or 027 559 0966

Fax (04) 383 6977

info@naturestouchguesthouse.com

http://naturestouchguesthouse.com

Double/Twin $85-$160

Single $65-$140 (Full breakfast)

Children up to 12 years old $25

Japanese Dinner $35pp, European Dinner $30pp

Wireles broadband available, bring your own

computer Visa MC accepted

Children welcome

1 King 2 Double/Twin (2 bdrm)

Bathrooms: 1 Private 1 Guest share

Private bath is available for extra $40 p.n.

"Warm welcome & delightful hospitality in beautiful craftman-built home. Spacious, comfortable suite with stunning views. Convenient location. Superb cuisine, both Western & Japanese. A true gem." Margaret, Australia

"Nature's Touch Guest House was the best B&B that we experienced in New Zealand during our trip in March 2008. ...the food was amazing. The breakfasts outdid any other B&B by a long shot, and the Japanese meal was great. Thank-you Natsuko and Maarten for making our vacation memorable with a stay at your home" Don and Julie, Canada

A warm welcome from us and our friendly dog, Lucky! We are nautical themed B&B and just a short stroll to the beach. Only 10 minutes drive to the city, 15 minute drive (almost straight line) to the ferry terminal and the airport driving along the coast. Upper Boat Bedroom (Luxury suite) is for you to enjoy whole of upstairs and elevated views as well as privacy. Enjoy tranquillity.

Wellington - Island Bay *In Wellington*

Island Bay Homestay *Homestay*

Theresa & Jack Stokes
52 High Street, Island Bay, Wellington 6023

Tel (04) 970 3353 or 0800 335 383
Fax (04) 970 3353 tandjstokes@paradise.net.nz
www.wellingtonhomestay.com

Double $90 Single $55 (Full breakfast)
2 Double (2 bdrm)
Bathrooms: 2 Private

We live in a Lockwood house, at the end of High Street in a very private section. Our land goes three quarters of the way up the hill and above that is Town Belt. Wonderful views, overlooking the Cook Strait with its ferries, cargo and fishing boats on the move day and night. We see planes landing or taking off (depending on wind direction) but the airport is round a corner and we get no noise from it.

We only let two of our rooms and each has its own private bathroom, just outside the bedroom door. TV in rooms. A warm, comfortable smoke-free home with warm clean comfortable beds and 2 warm owners who enjoy meeting people. We do our best to provide good, old fashioned Homestay, without charging the earth! We have 2 lovely Moggies. Not suitable for children under 12 years of age.

Directions: from State Highway 1 or 2 take the Aotea Quay turn-off. (From the ferry take the city exit). Follow the main road which bears slightly to the left until you come to a T junction (Oriental Parade). Turn right in to Kent Terrace and get in the right hand lane before going round the Basin Reserve (cricket ground) and in to Adelaide Road. Keep going straight, up the hill and the road becomes The Parade. Keep going until you reach the sea and then turn SHARP right (new guests can easily miss this turn-off) into Beach Street. Left and left again in to High Street and up the private road at the end.

From Wellington Airport: take the rear exit (past the cargo warehouses) and turn right. Follow the coast road for 10 minutes and Beach Street is on the right. For the Navigator we live at - Lat. S.41.20.54 Long E.174.45.54. 14.Full breakfast 7.30am onwards. Regrets we cannot accept bookings from guests arriving from Australia on the midnight arrivals or guests leaving on the 6am departures.

For the Navigator we live at:
Lat. S.41.20.54
Long E.174.45.54. 14

Marlborough

French Pass

Pelorus Sound

Kenepuru Sounds

6

Mahau Sound

Anakiwa

Queen Charlotte Sound

Picton

Koromiko

Rapaura

63

Renwick

Blenheim

1

0 Kilometres 20

0 Miles 12

Picton *1 km E of Picton Central*

Retreat Inn *B&B Homestay*
Alison & Geoff
20 Lincoln Street,
Picton

Tel (03) 573 8160
or 021 143 2224
Fax (03) 573 7799
alisonandgeoff@retreat-inn.co.nz
www.retreat-inn.co.nz

Double/Twin $110-$140
(Special breakfast)
Room rate $110-$140
Not suitable for children
2 Queen 2 Single (3 bdrm)
Bathrooms: 1 Ensuite
1 Private 1 Guest share

Set in peaceful bush surroundings, Retreat Inn Homestay/B&B offers you comfort & rest, with a yummy breakfast! 3 guest bedrooms - one queen (ensuite, bath and shower) with outside access to fern/seating area. Two upstairs rooms, queen and/or twin (private or guest share bathroom) Great for a group of 4. Marlborough province is diverse, unforgettable - come stay 2 or 3 nights and explore what we have to offer. Flat off-street parking. A happy 2 person/2 cat household!

Picton *0.5 km SE of Picton Central*

Grandvue *B&B Homestay Apartment with Kitchen*
Rosalie & Russell Mathews
19 Otago Street,
Picton 7220

Tel (03) 573 8553
or 0800 49 1080
Fax (03) 573 8556
enquiries@grandvuepicton.co.nz
www.grandvuepicton.co.nz

Double/Twin $120-$130
Single $65-$85
(Continental breakfast)
Children $35
Visa MC accepted
Pet free home
Children welcome
2 Queen 1 Twin (3 bdrm)
Bathrooms: 1 Ensuite 1 Family share

On the hills above Picton, Grandvue is a quiet haven in a secluded garden with a grandview. It's a 5 minute walk to the shopping area, restaurants, the waterfront & bushwalks. Russell, retired, enjoys boating, fishing & gardening. Rosalie an enthusiastic patchworker, loves cooking & gardening. Both enjoy meeting people. The accommodation is spacious, warm, quality self-contained with kitchen & ensuite. Other rooms available in our home. Feast on magnificent views from our conservatory while enjoying a wholesome breakfast. Courtesy transport, parking & laundry facilities

Picton *0.25 km SE of Picton*
Rivenhall *B&B Homestay*
Nan & Malcolm Laurenson
118 Wellington Street,
Picton,
Marlborough
7220

Tel (03) 573 7692
rivenhall@kol.co.nz
www.rivenhall.kol.co.nz

Double/Twin $140
Single $100
(Full breakfast)
 Visa MC accepted
Pet free home
Children welcome
1 Queen 1 Double/Twin (2 bdrm)
Bathrooms: 2 Private

Up the rise, on the left, at the top of Wellington Street, is Rivenhall. A gracious home with all the warmth, comfort and charm of days gone by, overlooking the town of Picton with its background of surrounding hills. Yet it is a gentle stroll to the centre of town or the ferry's beyond. Courtesy pick up from the ferry, bus or train. The Marlborough Sounds start at the bottom of our street.

Picton *0.5 km N of Picton*
Echo Lodge *B&B Homestay*
Lyn & Eddie Thoroughgood
5 Rutland Street,
Picton

Tel (03) 573 6367
Fax (03) 573 6387
echolodge@xtra.co.nz

Double/Twin $110-$120
Single $60-$70
(Full breakfast)
Twin $110-120
1 Double/Twin 1 Twin
1 Single (2 bdrm)
Bathrooms: 2 Ensuite

Lyn, Eddie and our little dog Osca welcome you to home-style comfort at Echo Lodge. Starting your day with a smorgasbord style breakfast of home-grown produce and freshly baked bread. A 5 minute stroll into Picton takes you to great restaurants. From our front gate there are lovely bush walks to Bob's Bay, The Snout or Marina. Tea and coffee in your room, ensuite facilities, a sunny patio and log fire for chilly nights ensures your comfort. Courtesy car and off-street parking.

Marlborough

Picton - Kenepuru Sounds *80 km NE of Havelock*
The Nikaus *B&B Farmstay*

Alison & Robin Bowron
86 Manaroa Road,
Waitaria Bay, RD 2,
Picton 7282

Tel (03) 573 4432
or 027 454 4712
Fax (03) 573 4432
info@thenikaus.co.nz
www.thenikaus.co.nz

Double/Twin $130
Single $65
(Full breakfast)
Dinner $30
Visa MC accepted
1 Queen 4 Single (3 bdrm)
Bathrooms: 1 Guest share

The Nikaus sheep & cattle farm is situated in Waitaria Bay, Kenepuru Sound, 2 hours drive from Blenheim or Picton. We offer friendly personal service in our comfortable spacious home. Large gardens contain rhododendrons, roses, Camellia, lilies and perennials, big sloping lawns and views out to sea. House pets Minny (Jack Russel-cross)Honey (Lab)+ 4cats, Other animals include the farm dogs, donkeys, pet wild pigs, turkeys, hens and peacocks. Country meals, home-grown produce. Operators available for fishing trips, launch charters, golf and various walks.

Picton - Queen Charlotte Sounds *16 km W of Picton*
Tanglewood *B&B Homestay Separate Suite Apartment with Kitchen*

Linda & Stephen Hearn
1744 Queen Charlotte Drive,
The Grove, RD 1,
Picton

Tel (03) 574 2080
or 027 481 4388
Fax (03) 574 2044
tanglewood.hearn@xtra.co.nz

Double/Twin $145-$165
Single $95-$120
(Full breakfast)
Dinner $40
Self-contained $195
Visa MC accepted
2 King/Twin 1 Queen
2 Single (4 bdrm)
Bathrooms: 4 Ensuite

Modern architectural home nestled amongst the native ferns overlooking Queen Charlotte Sounds. Enjoy our luxury Super King/Twin ensuite rooms with balcony and views; or a self contained guest wing which includes Queen and two Single beds (with ensuites), lounge, kitchen and sunny balcony/BBQ area. Relax in our jacuzzi surrounded by beautiful native garden and birds or view the glow-worms. Substainal breakfast provided before your day's pursuits, swimming, fishing, kayaking, walking the Queen Charlotte Walkway or exploring Marlborough Wineries. Fifth generation Kiwi hospitality at its best.

Pelorus - Mahau Sound *33 km W of Picton*
Ramona *B&B Homestay*

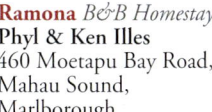

Phyl & Ken Illes
460 Moetapu Bay Road,
Mahau Sound,
Marlborough

Tel (03) 574 2215
or 027 247 6668
Fax (03) 574 2915
illes@clear.net.nz

Double/Twin $120
Single $85
(Continental breakfast)
We can accomodate 3 children
3 course dinner served with local wine
Tea & coffee available in conservatory
Visa MC accepted
Pet free home
Children welcome
2 Double/Twin 2 Twin (2 bdrm)
Bathrooms: 1 Private Hair dryer in bathroom

Our waterfront home on the beautiful Mahau Sound has been designed for you to share. Our guest floor has its own conservatory, here you can view the passing water traffic. Awake to the call of bellbirds and tuis, and after breakfast stroll around our rhododendron garden, or fossick on the beach. In the evening, see our glowworms. Phyl's interests include quilting, gardening and oilpainting. Ken is a retired builder. Visits to local craft studios can be arranged. We host only 1 party at a time.

Picton - Queen Charlotte Sound *11 km W of Picton*
Waterfront Bed & Breakfast *B&B Homestay*

Vicki & David Bendell
Queen Charlotte Drive,
2383 Little Ngakuta Bay,
RD 1,
Picton

Tel (03) 573 8584
or 027 748 4172
waterfront@farmside.co.nz
www.picton.co.nz/waterfront

Double/Twin $185-$185
(Full breakfast)
Dinner with notice $50pp
fresh caught fish/mussel:cheese
platter Diners accepted
Children welcome
1 Queen (1 bdrm)
Bathrooms: 1 Ensuite

Our waterfront accommodation is as close to the water edge as you can get along the scenic route to Nelson. The aptly named ‚ÄúBoatshed‚Äù is a lovely themed room, separate from our cottage, with en-suite and Italian cotton linens. A jetty out front, ideal for fishing or an evening stroll to see the water fluoresce. Join us for a meal on the deck over-looking the Bay. We have a young family and dog and welcome you to stay in a NZ family environment

Picton *3 km NE of Picton*

Michiru *B&B*

Approved

Rosemary & Paul Royer
247B Waikawa Road, Waikawa, Picton
Tel (03) 573 6793   Fax (03) 573 6793
royer@xtra.co.nz
www.picton.co.nz/for/michiru

Double/Twin $160 Single $90 (Special breakfast)
Dinner $50 by arrangement.
Visa MC accepted
Children welcome
1 King 1 Queen 2 Single (3 bdrm)
Bathrooms: 1 Ensuite 2 Private

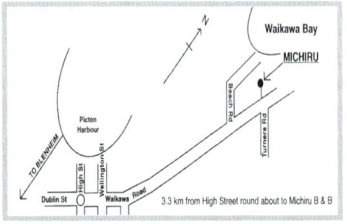

We only have one aim - to give you the finest and most memorable experience that we are able to provide. We overlook Waikawa Bay and the beautiful Queen Charlotte Sounds so you can watch the ferries and cruise ships pass while enjoying breakfast: and all of this is only 3km from Picton town centre.

The bright and sunny rooms are all located on the ground floor with a lovely private guest lounge and garden patio. Guests have the use of laundry facilities. We invite you to join us for Rosemary's delightful 3 course dinners with a glass of wine (by arrangement). We will of course meet or drop you at the ferry terminal, especially if you are walking the Queen Charlotte Track and don't have your

own transport. There is a waterside restaurant and a cafe/bar within 5 minutes walk of the house. You'll love this location!

Walk the Queen Charlotte Track, kayak or sail the Queen Charlotte Sounds, take half or whole day winery tours, daily dolphin watch tours, re-live The Edwin Fox experience (she's the world's ninth oldest ship), visit the fascinating Seahorse World, and finally our favourite place Karaka Point historical site. Superb accommodation for the discerning guests! Our normal check-in time is 4p.m. unless by prior arrangement.

Picton *0.5 km N of Picton Central*
The Gables *B&B Cottage No Kitchen*
Ian & Paula Allen
20 Waikawa Road,
Picton

Tel (03) 573 6772
Fax (03) 573 6772
info@thegables.co.nz
www.thegables.co.nz

Double/Twin $130-$175
Single $100
(Full breakfast)
Children $15
Visa MC accepted
Children and pets welcome
4 Queen 1 Double/Twin
2 Single (5 bdrm)
Bathrooms: 4 Ensuite 1 Private

The Gables is a charming and historic homestead situated close to all of Picton's attractions and amenities. A leisurely amble takes you to the splendid foreshore area, or a selection of restaurants, pubs, shops and supermarkets. Breakfasts at "The Gables" are designed to give you a fulfilling and enjoyable start to an active day. Ian and Paula will make every effort to ensure that their lovely old residence will become your home away from home for the duration of your stay.

Picton *0.5 km E of Picton*
Glengary *B&B*
Glenys & Gary Riggs
5 Seaview Cresent,
Picton

Tel (03) 573 8317
or 027 498 6388
g.riggs@xtra.co.nz
www.glengary.co.nz

Double/Twin $120-$140
Single $70
(Continental breakfast)
Pet free home
Not suitable for children
2 King/Twin 2 Queen (3 bdrm)
Bathrooms: 2 Ensuite 1 Private

Located a short drive from Picton Ferry Terminal and a few minutes walk to the town centre. Inner harbour across the road. Whether you are interested in visiting wineries, fishing, bush walking, cruising, sea kayaking or simply relaxing in idyllic surroundings Glengary Bed & Breakfast is ideally located to explore the Marlborough area. Your friendly hosts will provide you with the best service to ensure your stay in the beautiful Marlborough Sounds is relaxing and enjoyable. Ferry pick up. 2 night stay recemended..

Picton *.25 km SW of Post Office*
Marineland Heritage House B & B *B&B Guest House*
Rosemary Baxter & Peter Broad
28 Waikawa Road,
Picton, 7250

Tel (03) 5736 429
or Freephone: 0800 616 429
Fax (03) 5737 634
marineland@xtra.co.nz
www.marinelandaccom.co.nz

Double/Twin $90-$120
Single $75
(Continental breakfast)
Dinner by arrangement
during winter only
Visa MC Diners Amex Eftpos accepted
Not suitable for children under 13
1 King 1 Queen 5 Double/Twin
3 Twin 1 Single (11 bdrm)
Bathrooms: 5 Ensuite 6 Guest share

Enjoy Marineland Heritage House B & B, built in 1925 for the local Doctor. All downstairs rooms have ensuites, upstairs rooms have shared bathrooms. Rooms have electric blankets & tea/coffee making facilities. A comfortable lounge with Broadband Internet access & TV. Adjacent to the lounge is the breakfast room for our "Picton Breakfast", a wheat & gluten free option is available. We offer a laundry & parking. We are a few minutes walk from town centre & water front.

Picton - Koromiko *5 km S of Picton*
Koromiko Homestead *B&B Self-contained*
Pat & Ian McKinnon
30 Freeths Road,
Koromiko,
Picton

Tel (03) 573 7518
Fax 03) 573 7538
info@koromikohomestead.co.nz
http://koromikohomestead.co.nz

Double/Twin $185-$210
(Full breakfast)
Visa MC accepted
Not suitable for children
2 Queen (2 bdrm)
Bathrooms: 2 Private

Relax in a beautiful rural setting 5km south from Picton, convenient to the Marlborough Sounds and Blenheim vineyards. Quality bed and breakfast accommodation set within extensive gardens on four hectares. Our sunny self-contained guest wing has a lounge, small kitchen, and dining room: all rooms have countryside views. Organic wholefood breakfasts are served alfresco on the garden deck in summer. Hire one of our classic replica two-seater sports cars and tour Marlborough in style. Complimentary transfers to Picton airport or ferry.

Picton- Queen Charlotte Sound - Anakiwa *22 km W of Picton*
Queensview BnB *B&B Separate Suite Apartment with Kitchen*
Ann & John McGuire
259G Anakiwa Road,
Anakiwa - Picton, RD1

Tel (03) 574 2363
or 021 0229 2864
queensview@xtra.co.nz
http://picton.co.nz/queensviewbnb

Double/Twin $145-$180
Single $90-$120
(Full breakfast)
Dinner by arrangement -
BBQ Facilities Available
Local Hotel 6 mins drive
Pet free home
Children welcome
2 Queen 1 Twin (3 bdrm)
Bathrooms: 1 Ensuite 1 Private 1
Guest share Shared bathroom can be booked as Private

Our elevated deck over the top of the Punga trees offers guests arguably some of the best views off the Queen Charltte Sound. The shoreline no more than a 3 min walk. The Queen Charlotte Track (10 mins walk),the holiday town of Picton (30 mins), the marina & mussel town of Havelock (25 mins)and the winery district of Blenheim (40 mins). So if your holiday is walking, swimming, boating, fishing, kayaking or exploring the many wineries then Queensview BnB is the ideal central location.

Picton *0.5 km SE of Picton*
Palm Haven B&B *B&B*

Denise Heaps
15 A Otago Street,
Picton,
7220

Tel (03) 573 5644
or 027 4755 178
Fax (03) 573 5648
palmhaven@xtra.co.nz

Double/Twin $130
Single $85
(Continental breakfast provisions)
Visa MC Eftpos accepted
Pet free home
Not suitable for children
2 Queen 1 Twin 1 Single (3 bdrm)
Bathrooms: 2 Ensuite 1 Private

Palm Haven is a modern purpose built home designed for your comfort and convenience. Overlooking Picton and Mt Freeth, it is just a few minutes walk to the shopping center, cafes, restaurants and waterfront where guided walks, kayaking and a variety of boating, fishing and winery tours are available. Guest rooms, two with ensuites and one with private bathroom, accomadating triple, double or single occupancy all have tea and coffee making facilities, TV and bar fridge. Courtesy pickup from ferry, bus or train is provided.

Blenheim - Rapaura *12 km NW of Blenheim*
Thainstone *Homestay Cottage with Kitchen*

Vivienne & Jim Murray
120 Giffords Road,
RD 3,
Rapaura

Tel (03) 572 8823
Fax (03) 572 8623
thainstone@xtra.co.nz
www.thainstone.co.nz

Double/Twin $140
Single $75
(Full breakfast)
Dinner $45
Self-catering house (sleeps 2-4)
$130-$190, no breakfast
Visa MC Amex accepted
Not suitable for children
1 King 2 Queen 2 Twin (5 bdrm)
Bathrooms: 1 Ensuite 1 Private 1 Guest share

Our large home is surrounded by vineyards and within walking distance of the Wairau River and several wineries. In our home there are 3 upstairs bedrooms and a guest lounge. The self-catering house has 2 bedrooms and is fully equipped for longer stays. The indoor swimming pool is heated during the summer months. We are widely travelled and some interests are bird watching, trout fishing, woodworking and cards. Evening meals, by prior arrangement, are served with Marlborough wines.

Blenheim *1 km W of Blenheim Central*
Beaver B&B *Homestay Cottage with Kitchen*

Jen & Russell Hopkins
60 Beaver Road,
Blenheim

Tel (03) 578 8401
or 021 626 151
Fax (03) 578 8401
rdhopkins@xtra.co.nz
http://marlborough.co.nz/beaver/

Double/Twin $100
Single $60
(Continental breakfast)
Visa MC accepted
Not suitable for children
1 Queen (1 bdrm)
Bathrooms: 1 Ensuite

Our self-contained unit has its own entrance and off-street parking-5 minutes drive from central Blenheim and 10 minutes drive from the wineries and the Aviation Heritage Centre. The bed is queen-size. The mini-kitchen has a microwave, small sink and fridge containing items for a self-serve continental breakfast to have at your leisure. The bathroom has a large bath and a separate shower and toilet. 2 cats live with us and we have bikes for hire.

Blenheim *2.5 km N of Blenheim*
Philmar *B&B Homestay*
Wynnis & Lex Phillips
9 Maple Close,
Springlands,
Blenheim

Tel (03) 577 7788
Fax (03) 577 7788
philmar9@xtra.co.nz

Double/Twin $80-$100
Single $60
(Continental breakfast)
Dinner $20pp by arrangement
2 Queen 1 Twin (3 bdrm)
Bathrooms: 1 Ensuite 1 Guest share

Welcome to our home 2.5 km from the town centre. Guests can join us in our spacious sunny living areas. We both enjoy all sports on TV and our other interests include wood turning, handcrafts and the Lions organisation. Blenheim has many wineries, parks, craft shops, art galleries and golf courses. Not far from Picton, Nelson & Kaikoura whale watching. We share our home with our pets, Lucy-Lu and Louie. Smoking is not encouraged. Just phone to be picked up at airport, bus or train.

Blenheim *2 km S of Blenheim*
Baxter Homestay *B&B Homestay 1 luxury unit w kitchen/dining*

Kathy & Brian Baxter
28 Elisha Drive,
Blenheim

Tel (03) 578 3753
or 021 129 2062
baxterart@xtra.co.nz
www.baxterhomestay.com

Double/Twin $140-$200
(Full breakfast)
Pet free home
Children welcome
No single night bookings
at peak times
1 King/Twin 1 King 1 Queen 1 Single (3 bdrm)
Bathrooms: 3 Ensuite Bath & shower in king/twin ensuite

W arm friendly hospitality awaits you at our sunny, comfortable, modern home. Enjoy magnificent views over Blenheim and nearby vineyards, or explore our terraced gardens, chosen several times for Hunters Garden Marlborough.Adjacent to Wither Hills walking tracks. Studio of renowned N.Z. artist Brian Baxter on site. One luxury self contained unit available. We can arrange visits to wineries, gardens, ski-field, golf courses restaurants etc. Laundry facilities & wireless internet available. Our interests include gardening, music, travel, skiing, sport, art, video production, and meeting people.

Blenheim *2 km N of Blenheim*
The Willows *B&B Homestay*

Millie Amos
6 The Willows,
Springlands,
Blenheim

Tel (03) 577 7853
Fax (03) 577 7853

Double/Twin $112
Single $70
(Continental breakfast)
1 Queen 2 Twin (2 bdrm)
Bathrooms: 1 Private

O nly 2km from the centre of town. The Willows is a spacious and modern home in close proximity to shops, restaurants and wineries. Peaceful location surrounded by lovely gardens. I welcome you to my home, so please phone first.

Blenheim *1 km N of Blenheim Central*

Maxwell House *Homestay*

John and Barbara Ryan
82 Maxwell Road,
Blenheim

Tel (03) 577 7545
Fax (03) 577 7545
mt.olympus@xtra.co.nz

Double/Twin $140
Single $100
(Full breakfast)
Visa MC accepted
Children welcome
1 Queen 1 Twin (2 bdrm)
Bathrooms: 2 Ensuite

Welcome to Marlborough. We invite you to stay at Maxwell House, a grand old Victorian residence. Built in 1880 our home has been elegantly restored and is classified with the Historic Places Trust. Our large guest rooms are individually appointed with ensuite, lounge area, television and tea & coffee making facilities. Breakfast will be a memorable experience, served around the original 1880's kauri table. Set on a large established property Maxwell House is an easy ten minute walk to the town centre. Non-smoking.

Blenheim *30 km S of Picton*

ParkView B&B *B&B*

Geoff & Shirley Cant
30 Solway Drive, Blenheim,
Marlborough

Tel (03) 578-4492 or 0800 78-4492
021 299 1705 or 021 141 7660
Fax (03) 578-4492
parkviewbb@xtra.co.nz
www.parkviewbb.co.nz

Double/Twin $120-$130
Single $95-$100
(Continental breakfast)
Children $45
Cooked breakfast by arrangement
Visa MC accepted
Pet free home Children welcome
3 Queen 1 Single (3 bdrm)
Bathrooms: 1 Ensuite 1 Private 1 Family share Bath & shower in en-suite

ParkView is a modern quality residence in a quiet Blenheim suburb adjacent to Harling Park & Japanese Garden and Wither Hills Farm Park.You can enjoy walking or cycling in Harling Park and the magnificent Wither Hills Farm Park and borrow our cycles and visit some of the many local wineries. Relax on ParkView‚Äôs verandah overlooking the Japanese Garden with a glass of local wine. We offer free of charge:Wireless broadband internet Laundry & BBQComplimentary transfer service to airport, bus, train or restaurant.

Blenheim *0.1 km W of central Blenheim*
Henry Maxwell's B&B *Luxury B&B*

Approved

Diana and Graham Westenra
28 Henry Street,
Blenheim

Tel (03) 578 8086
or 0800 436 796
or 0274 77 4808
Fax (03) 578 8089
graymere@xtra.co.nz
www.henrymaxwells.co.nz

Double/Twin $110-$140
Single $80 (Full breakfast)
Children welcome,
tariff depending on age
Visa MC accepted
3 Queen 2 Twin 3 Single (4 bdrm)
Bathrooms: 2 Ensuite
1 Private 1 Guest share
Bath in the large bathroom

Welcome to Henry Maxwell's Bed & Breakfast and Accommodation. A gracious 75 year old home, under new management. Guests have spacious quiet rooms, 2 with ensuites, 2 share bathroom. Comfortable beds and chairs, TV, tea, coffee, and complimentary port.Breakfast in the unique dining room (maps and charts)is memorable, kitchenette facilities. Guest laundry, wireless, library. 5 minutes stroll to town, restaurants, shops, theatre. Off-street parking.Very suitable for extended stays,conference and wedding parties. Discounts.Outside cat.

Blenheim *7 km N of Blenheim*
Blue Ridge Estate Vineyard Homestay *B&B Homestay*

Approved

Lesley & Brian Avery
50 O'Dwyers Road,
RD 3,
Blenheim

Tel (03) 570 2198
Fax (03) 570 2199
bavery@xtra.co.nz
www.blueridge.co.nz

Double/Twin $200-$245
Single $200-$245
(Full breakfast)
Visa MC accepted
Not suitable for children
2 Queen 2 Twin (3 bdrm)
Bathrooms: 1 Ensuite 2 Private

Set on a 20 acre purpose-designed homestay property, Blue Ridge Estate, 2002 Marlborough Master Builders' "House of the Year", enjoys a rural setting with stunning views across vineyards to the Richmond Range and is close to many of Marlborough's fine wineries, restaurants and gardens. Our home has proven most popular with both international and New Zealand visitors. Come share our home with Bella our friendly young labrador, where comfort and privacy will ensure your Marlborough visit is indeed a memorable one.

Blenheim *9 km NW of Blenheim*
Stonehaven Vineyard Homestay *B&B Homestay*

Paulette & John Hansen
414 Rapaura Road,
RD 3, Blenheim

Tel (03) 572 9730
or 027 682 1120
Fax (03) 572 9730
stay@stonehavenhomestay.co.nz
www.stonehavenhomestay.co.nz

Double/Twin $225-$250
Single $145 (Full breakfast)
Children suitable 10 years and over
Three course gourmet dinner $60pp
wine available
Guest bike hire $30 per day
Visa MC accepted
1 King 1 Queen 1 Twin (3 bdrm)
Bathrooms: 2 Ensuite 1 Private
Twin room private bathroom is downstairs

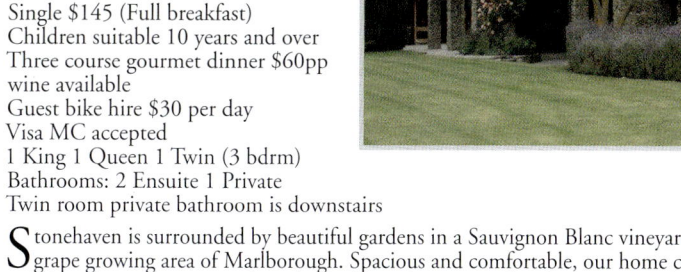

Stonehaven is surrounded by beautiful gardens in a Sauvignon Blanc vineyard in the premium grape growing area of Marlborough. Spacious and comfortable, our home commands exquisite views over vineyards to the Richmond Ranges. Close by are some of NZ's most outstanding wineries. Our delicious breakfasts are often served in the summerhouse overlooking the pool. Dinner is available by arrangement. Wireless internet access available. We have a cat and labrador. We look forward to making your stay as relaxing or as active as you choose.

Blenheim *3 km S of Blenheim*
Redwood Heights *Luxury B&B*

Kathy & Mike Besley
245 Redwood Street,
Blenheim
7201

Tel 0800 733 001
or (03) 578 0143
Fax (03) 578 0143
redwoodheights@xtra.co.nz
www.redwoodheights.co.nz

Double/Twin $115-$175
Single $90
(Full breakfast)
Children by arrangement
Visa MC accepted
Children welcome
1 King 1 Queen 1 Twin (3 bdrm)
Bathrooms: 1 Ensuite 2 Private

Relax in modern, private quality accommodation. Enjoy extensive views and a country atmosphere. Stream Reserve Room is spacious, with ensuite and refreshment making facilities. Separate guest lounge and balcony. Close to wineries, restaurants, 3km to town centre. Adjacent to Wither Hills walkways and bike tracks. A perfect base for day trips to Picton, Marlborough Sounds, Kaikoura or Nelson. 2 friendly cats, kept outside. Wireless, internet available and free laundry. Room pictures and information on website.

Blenheim Central *0.1 km E of Blenheim*

Brickweld House *B&B*

Julie Yonge
5 Weld Street,
Blenheim

Tel (03) 577 9915
or 027 686 5891
info@brickweldhouse.co.nz
www.brickweldhouse.co.nz

Double/Twin $140-$160
Single $70-$100
(Full breakfast)
Dinner by arrangement
Visa MC accepted
Not suitable for children
2 King/Twin 2 Queen (3 bdrm)
Bathrooms: 1 Ensuite
1 Private 1 Guest share

Your sanctuary after discovering the treasures Marlborough has to offer. Enjoy the convenience of a 10 minute stroll to the town centre where you will find many dining options or dine in by arrangement (24 hours notice required). In a peaceful garden setting, relax in the friendly atmosphere; sleep under the luxury of pure silk duvets; breakfast in the garden. Tea and coffee making facilities in rooms; separate guest lounge. Famous wineries just minutes away. Off-street parking. Join me for a glass of world acclaimed Marlborough Sauvignon blanc at the end of your day of adventure. You will also meet Lizzie, my very affectionate cat.

Renwick *10 km W of Blenheim*

Clovelly *B&B Homestay*

Don & Sue Clifford
2A Nelson Place,
Renwick,
Marlborough
7204

Tel (03) 572 9593
or 027 695 1614
Fax (03) 572 7293
clifford@actrix.co.nz
www.clovelly.co.nz

Double/Twin $130
Single $100
(Special breakfast)
Visa MC accepted
Children welcome
1 King/Twin 1 Queen (2 bdrm)
Bathrooms: 2 Private

Our colonial style home is set in lovely private grounds in the heart of vineyard country. We overlook organic orchards and out to the Richmond Range. Complimentary refreshments on arrival. Visit the quaint local English pub - dine in the village or vineyard restaurants. We are close to a number of prestigious vineyards. Complimentary bicycles (including a 1938 vintage tandem!) are available for guests to cycle the vineyards. Don, Sue and our Scottish terriers Chloe and Phoebe and cat Sophie, will welcome you most warmly.

Renwick *10 km W of Blenheim*
Olde Mill House B&B & Bike Hire *B&B Homestay*

Diane Sutton
9 Wilson Street,
Renwick,
Marlborough

Tel (03) 572 8458
or 0800 653 262 (0800 Old BNB)
Fax (03) 572 8458
info@oldemillhouse.co.nz
www.oldemillhouse.co.nz

Double/Twin up to $140
(Continental breakfast)
Children under 12yrs $40
Extra adult in room $70
Visa MC Amex Eftpos accepted
Children welcome
2 King/Twin 1 Queen (3 bdrm)
Bathrooms: 3 Ensuite
Heritage room ensuite with bathtub

Welcome to our elevated character bungalow, refurbished for your comfort whilst retaining its olde world charm. Our property consists of an extensive spa/bbq, garden area for you to relax in and enjoy views to the Richmond Ranges. We provide complimentary cycles for you to enjoy the local wine trail, a complimentary transfer service to local vineyard restaurants for evening dining. We also provide a wireless broadband internet service. We both enjoy gardening, motorcycling and our Border Collie dogs Rosie & Vinnie.

Near French Pass - Pelorus Sounds *110 km NE of Nelson*
Ngaio Bay Eco-homestay and B&B *B&B Homestay*

Jude & Roger Sonneland
Ngaio Bay, French Pass Road,
Pelorus Sounds

Tel (03) 576 5287
Fax (03) 576 5287
welcome@ngaiobay.co.nz
www.ngaiobay.co.nz

Double/Twin $170 Single $125
(Special breakfast)
Children $80 3-12years,
under 2 $30 all inclusive
Dinner $40pp, children 3-12 years $15
Lunch $20pp, picnic $15pp,
$8 per child 3-12 years
Visa MC Eftpos accepted
Children welcome
2 King 3 Single (2 bdrm)
Bathrooms: 2 Private R and D selfcontained, Garden Cottage bathroom in main house

Ngaio Bay, 2 hours scenic drive from Nelson or Blenheim, with private beach, is an authentic Kiwi experience. Near awesome waters of French Pass. The Garden Cottage and Rose & Dolphin are comfortable and private, overlooking beach, garden and bush. A honeymooners favourite. Guests linger at dinner enjoying scrumptious food and good conversation, open fire for cool evenings. Organic vegetable and flower garden and orchard, eco-composting toilets. Swim, walk, boat, relax; your choice.! Private fireheated bath on beach. special. Children welcome. 2 loveable labradors.

Nelson,
Golden Bay

Pakawau

Collingwood

Parapara

Takaka

60

Abel Tasman
National Park

Marahau

Kaiteriteri

Motueka

Motueka Valley

Ruby Bay

Atawhai

Mapua

Upper
Moutere

6 Nelson

Richmond

Wakefield

Brightwater

0   Kilometres   20

0   Miles   12

6

63

65 Murchison

Nelson
Lakes

St Arnaud

Nelson - Atawhai *6 km NE of Nelson*

Mike's B&B *B&B Homestay*
Mike Cooper & Lennane Cooper-Kent
4 Seaton Street,
Nelson

Tel (03) 545 1671
mikecooper@actrix.co.nz
www.bnb.co.nz/hosts/kent

Double/Twin $80-$85
Single $80-$85
(Full breakfast)
Dinner $40 pp with prior notice
Visa MC accepted
2 Queen (2 bdrm)
Bathrooms: 2 Ensuite
Showers in ensuite bathroom

5 minutes NE of Nelson City we welcome you to our comfortable home in a quiet neighbourhood with extensive views out over Tasman Bay to the mountains beyond. Our guests' accommodation is almost self contained and includes ensuite bedrooms, a kitchenette with a fridge/freezer, microwave and complimentary tea and coffee making facilities, a small lounge with TV and part of our collection of books. Laundry facilities and internet access and off street parking are available. Our interests include travel, education, and volunteer work abroad.

Nelson *2 km SW of Central Nelson*

Harbour View Homestay *B&B or House-Let with Kitchen*
Judy Black
11 Fifeshire Crescent,
Nelson

Tel (03) 548 8567
or 027 247 4445
Fax (03) 548 8667
harbourview-homestay@xtra.co.nz

Double/Twin $145-$155
Single $125-$145
(Continental breakfast)
Self-contained house by arrangement
Visa MC accepted
2 Queen 2 Single (3 bdrm)
Bathrooms: 2 Ensuite 1 Private

Harbour View Homestay
Nelson NZ

Our home is above the harbour entrance. Huge windows capture spectacular views of beautiful Tasman Bay, Haulashore Island, Tahunanui Beach, across the sea to Abel Tasman National Park and mountains. Observe from the bedrooms, dining room and decks, ships and pleasure craft cruising by as they enter and leave the harbour. If you can tear yourself away from our magnificent view, within walking distance along the waterfront there are excellent cafes and restaurants. Judy, David and Possum the cat welcome you for a memorable stay.

Nelson *5 km SW of Nelson*

Arapiki *B&B Apartment with Kitchen B&B Self-contained Homestay Units*
Kay & Geoff Gudsell
21 Arapiki Road,
Stoke,
Nelson

Tel (03) 547 3741
bnb@nelsonparadise.co.nz
www.nelsonparadise.co.nz

Double/Twin $90-$120
Single $70-$90
Continental breakfast optional $7.50pp
Visa MC accepted
1 Queen 1 Double/Twin
1 Single (2 bdrm)
Bathrooms: 2 Ensuite

Enjoy a relaxing holiday in the midst of your trip. The 2 quality smoke-free units in our large centrally located home offer comfort, privacy, offstreet parking and Wireless Internet Access. The larger Unit 1 in a private garden setting opens on to a deck with outdoor furniture. It has an electric stove, microwave, TV, auto washing machine and phone. Unit 2 has a balcony with seating to enjoy sea and mountain views. It has a microwave, hotplate, TV and phone. We have two Tonkinese cats.

≈

Nelson *2.5 km S of Nelson*

Sunset Waterfront B&B *B&B Separate Suite*
Bernie Kirk & Louis Balshaw
455 Rock Road,
Nelson

Tel (03) 548 3431
or 0274 363 500
Fax (03) 548 3743
waterfrontnelson@xtra.co.nz

Double/Twin $140-$150
Single $110-$120
(Full breakfast)
Self-catering cottage $180
Visa MC accepted
2 Queen 1 Twin 1 Single (2 bdrm)
Bathrooms: 2 Ensuite

Sunset Waterfront B&B provides wonderful panoramic sea and mountain views of Tasman Bay. Ideally situated to walk to quality seafood restaurants. Stroll along the promenade to enjoy the sunset or take an evening walk along the beach. 10 minutes drive from the airport and bus station. Quiet and secluded location. Freshly brewed coffee and local fresh produce provided. Also freshly picked raspberries and strawberries when in season. No children under 12. Come enjoy our paradise! Parking right up to the house. Cottage available next door.

Nelson *3 km E of Nelson*
Brooklands *B&B Homestay*
Lorraine & Barry Signal
106 Brooklands Road,
Atawhai,
Nelson

Tel (03) 545 1423
Fax (03) 545 1423
barry.lori@xtra.co.nz

Double/Twin $120-$160
Single $75-$100
(Full breakfast)
Children by arrangement
Dinner $50
Visa MC accepted
Pet free home
Children welcome
1 King 1 Queen 1 Double/Twin
1 Twin (3 bdrm)
Bathrooms: 1 Ensuite 1 Guest share spa bath

Spacious, luxurious 4 level home with superb sea views. Spacious well furnished king room on top level. Next level has 2 bedrooms sharing large bathroom with spa bath for 2. 1 bedroom has a private balcony. Spacious indoor/outdoor living areas. We enjoy sports, travel and outdoors. Lorraine makes dolls and bears and enjoys crafts, gardening and cooking. We are close to Nelson's attractions - beaches, crafts, wine trails, national parks, lakes and mountains. We enjoy making new friends. Smoke-free. Courtesy transport available.

Nelson *0.75 km SW of Nelson Central*
Peppertree B&B *B&B Separate Suite*
Richard Savill & Carolyn Sygrove
31 Seymour Avenue,
Nelson

Tel (03) 546 9881
Fax (03) 546 9881
c.sygrove@clear.net.nz

Double/Twin $120
(Continental breakfast)
Children $20
Dinner $30-$40 by arrangement
Extra adult $35
Visa MC accepted
Children welcome
1 Queen 1 Double/Twin
1 Single (1 bdrm)
Bathrooms: 1 Ensuite

Enjoy space and privacy in our heritage villa, only 10 minutes riverside walk from Nelson's city centre. The master bedroom has an ensuite bathroom and walk-in wardrobe. Your private adjoining rooms include a large lounge with double innersprung sofabed, single bed, heat pump, Sky TV, fridge, microwave, kettle etc. Also sunroom with cane setting and private entrance. Email/internet/fax facilities and off-street parking available. Children are welcome. We have 2 daughters aged 14 and 12, and a friendly cat called Chocolate.

Nelson *0.5 km N of Information Centre*
Grampian Villa *B&B*
John & Jo Fitzwater
209 Collingwood Street, 208 Collingwood Street, Nelson

Tel (03) 545 8209
or 021 459 736 (Jo) 021 969 071 (John)
Fax (03) 548 7888
Stay@GrampianVilla.co.nz
http://GrampianVilla.co.nz

Double/Twin $130-$350 Single $130-$350 (Special breakfast)
Children POA Dinner POA
Visa MC Eftpos accepted Pet free home Not suitable for children
2 King/Twin 2 King 3 Queen 1 Single (8 bdrm)
Bathrooms: 8 Ensuite

Located in the tree-lined streets below The Grampians
overlooking Nelson City, historic Grampian Villa & Cottage
are a pleasant 5 minute walk to Nelson's City Centre.

Grampian Villa offers 4 spacious ensuites (3 SuperKing, 1 Queen w/clawfoot bath and shower) each have french doors opening onto the spacious verandahs with views of Nelson City and the sea. Grampian Cottage offers 4 great value-for-money rooms. (1 SuperKing, 2 Queen and 1 Single), all with ensuites.

Grampian Villa Facilities: spacious tiled showers with heated floors and large heated towel rails Wireless DSL internet access

Writing desk in all rooms. TV, DVD, in-house movies etc. available in all bedrooms Complimentary tea/coffee, port, local chocolates, cookies. Enjoy a Latte/Expresso from our professional coffee machine.

Gourmet/Special breakfast changes every day.TV, VCR, CD, DVD, Stereo & SKY available in Lounge Central heating for your comfort We regret that we cannot accommodate children under the age of 12 years or pets.

To check for availability and/or make a reservation please go online to:
http://art.globalavailability.com/guests/guest-main.php?pid=271

Nelson *2 km S of Nelson*
Beach Front B&B *B&B*
Oriel & Peter Phillips
581 Rocks Road,
Nelson

Tel (03) 548 5299
or 021 063 9529
Fax (03) 548 5299
peterp@tasman.net
www.bnb.co.nz

Double/Twin $100-$135
Single $100
(Full breakfast)
Visa MC accepted
Not suitable for children
1 Queen 1 Double/Twin (2 bdrm)
Bathrooms: 1 Ensuite 1 Private

BC&B Approved

Nelson Golden Bay

As recommended by The Rough Guide. Our home is situated overlooking Tahunanui Beach, Haulashore Island and Nelson waterfront-amazing daytime mountain views-magnificent sunsets. Enjoy a wine out on the deck with your hosts. Excellent restaurants and cafes within walking distance, stroll to beach or 5 minute drive to city. Golf course, tennis courts and airport nearby. 1 hour drive to Abel Tasman. Both rooms have ensuite/private facilities, quality beds, electric blankets, fridge, TV, tea & coffee making facilities, heaters, iron and hairdryers. Kiwi Host. House Cat Rufus.

Nelson *0.1 km N of Nelson Information Centre*
Mikonui *B&B*
Elizabeth Osborne
7 Grove Street,
Nelson

Tel (03) 548 3623
bess.osborne@xtra.co.nz

Double/Twin $120
Single $100
(Continental breakfast)
Visa MC accepted
3 Queen (3 bdrm)
Bathrooms: 3 Ensuite

BC&B Approved

100 metres from the Visitor Information Centre in the heart of Nelson City is the Mikonui. This delightful house built in the 1920s, has been the Blair Family home for more than 50-years. The lovely rimu staircase leads to 3 tastefully appointed guest rooms all with ensuites. A delicious continental breakfast is served each morning. Just a short stroll to restaurants, cafes, the cinema and the beautiful Queens Gardens. Come and enjoy the hospitality at the Mikonui, you won't be disappointed. Off-street parking.

Nelson *2 km N of Nelson*
Lamont B&B *B&B*
Pam & Rex Lucas
167A Tahunanui Drive,
Nelson,
New Zealand

Tel (03) 548 5551
or 0274 351 678
Fax (03) 548 5501
rexpam@xtra.co.nz

Double/Twin $125
Single $95 or by arrangement
(Full breakfast)
Children by arrangement
Dinner(2 courses) $30 (24 hrs
notice required)
Visa MC accepted
Children welcome
1 Queen 1 Double/Twin (2 bdrm)
Bathrooms: 1 Private 1 Guest share

We are in a position to offer high standard accommodation having 2 double bedrooms with own toilet and bathroom facilities. Our house is on a private property in Tahunanui Drive opposite the Nelson Surburban Club where it is possible to get an evening meal most nights. A 2 minute drive to Tahuna Beach and 5 minutes to a number of waterfront restaurants gives plenty of variety and choice. We are a few minutes from the airport. Pick-up from airport and bus. 1 cat in residence

---

Nelson *1 km E of Nelson Cathedral*
Te Maunga - **Historic House** *B&B Homestay Apartment with Kitchen*
Anne Kolless
15 Dorothy Annie Way @ 82 Cleveland,
Nelson City

Tel (03) 548 8605
or 021 201 2461
temaungahouse@xtra.co.nz
www.nelsoncityaccommodation.co.nz

Double/Twin $90-$135
Single $75-$90
(Continental breakfast)
Children negotiable
Self-catered $140
Visa MC accepted
Pet free home
Children welcome
1 Queen 2 Double/Twin 1 Twin 1 Single (4 bdrm)
Bathrooms: 2 Private 1 Guest share
showers & tub-shower

Anne welcomes you to her family's 1930's Historic House, a stunning and unique,Arts & Crafts style, native woods example. Mainly as original with modern facilities, Te Maunga sits on a knoll, in rambling gardens, giving commanding views over Nelson, sea and valleys,but only 5 minutes to downtown. Enjoy your special continental style breakfast including local fruits, yoghurts, cheeses , home-made breads, and preserves, or maybe your aperitif, while taking in the amazing views. Self-catered unit next door! NZQA Food safety Cert.

Nelson - Atawhai *7 km N of Nelson*
A Culinary Experience *Luxury B&B Homestay*
Kay & Joe Waller
71 Tresillian Avenue, Atawhai, Nelson

Tel (03) 545 1886 or 0800 891 886 or 027 445 1886
Fax (03) 545 1869
stay@a-culinary-experience.com www.a-culinary-experience.com

Double/Twin $195-$275 Single $180-$260 (Special breakfast)
Not suitable for young children
Join your hosts for a 3-course gourmet dinner
Cooking Classes and Therapeutic Massage can be booked
Visa MC accepted Pets welcome by arrangement
2 King/Twin 2 King (2 bdrm)
Bathrooms: 2 Ensuite

Welcome to our lovely home filled with original art, laughter and fabulous food. Your caring hosts have created a unique boutique accommodation. Joe, a Naturopathic Doctor, provides therapeutic massage. Kay, cookbook author and former cooking school owner, provides delightful dinners or cooking classes.

Let us pamper you! Enjoy gourmet breakfasts: Blueberry Pancakes with glazed bananas, Eggs Benedict, French Crepes. After exploring Nelson's wineries, galleries, restaurants, golfing or hiking/kayaking in Able Tasman Park, indulge in a massage and a soak in the spa.

Choose the quiet, sun-drenched garden or a peaceful patio, sipping a complimentary glass of wine served with yummy appetizers to celebrate sensational sunsets, exquisite bay & mountain views. Read in the sculpture garden and quaff the aroma of fresh herbs, fruit, and organic produce that we grow for our legendary meals. Or sit and chat about boats, art, Rotary, The Red Hat Society, travels and beautiful New Zealand.

Book one of our luxurious rooms: king-size beds, imported linens, heated tile ensuites (bathrooms). Homemade pastries, 24 hour tea facilities, laundry and broadband are next to the guest lounge. With so much to do in the region, a stay of 3 or more nights is recommended. Arrive as guests - leave as friends. (Multi-night discounts available.)

Nelson *1 km E of Nelson Central*
Sussex House Bed & Breakfast *B&B*
Victoria & David Los
238 Bridge Street,
Nelson

Tel (03) 548 9972
Fax (03) 548 9975
reservations@sussex.co.nz
www.sussex.co.nz

Double/Twin $140-$170
Single $110-$140
(Full breakfast)
Visa MC Amex Eftpos accepted
Children welcome
5 Queen 3 Twin 3 Single (5 bdrm)
Bathrooms: 4 Ensuite 1 Private

Experience the peace and charm of the past in our fully restored circa 1880s B&B, one of Nelson's original family homes. Situated beside the beautiful Maitai River, Sussex House has retained all the original character and romantic ambiance of the era. It is only minutes' walk from central Nelson's award-winning restaurants and cafes, the Queens Gardens, Suter Art Gallery and Botanical Hill (The Centre of NZ) and many fine river and bushwalks.

The five sunny bedrooms all have TVs and are spacious and charmingly furnished. All rooms have access to the verandahs and complimentary tea and coffee facilities are provided. Breakfast includes a variety of fresh and preserved fruits, hot croissants and pastries, home-made yoghurts, cheeses and a large variety of cereals, rolls, breads and crumpets. Cooked breakfasts are available.

Other facilities include: wheelchair suite; free email/internet station; fax; courtesy phone; laundry facilities; separate lounge for guest entertaining; complimentary port; tea & coffee facilities; very sociable cat (Riley). We have lived overseas and have travelled extensively. We speak French fluently.

**Ensuite or private bathroom is yours exclusively.
Guest share bathroom is shared with other guests.
Host share bathroom is shared with the family.**

Nelson - Atawhai *5 km N of Nelson on SH6*
Strathaven Lodge *B&B Homestay*
Julie & Hugh Briggs
42 Strathaven Place,
Atawhai,
Nelson

Tel (03) 545 1195
or 027 243 5301
Fax (03) 545 1195
strathavenlodge@xtra.co.nz
www.strathavenlodge.com

Double/Twin $125-$200
Single $100-$125
(Full breakfast)
Children $50
Dinner $40pp
Visa MC Diners accepted
Pet free home
Children welcome
1 King 1 Queen 1 Single (3 bdrm)
Bathrooms: 2 Private

Relax in the terrace spa, enjoy the beautiful sea and mountain views, the spectacular sunsets, listen to the melodious songs of the tuis and bellbirds. Sleep deeply in very comfortable beds, in suites each with private bathrooms, robes, TV's and hairdryers. Bar fridge and tea-making in hall. Savour Hugh's generous breakfasts! Enjoy this slice of paradise! Share your travel experiences with your well travelled hosts, over a complimentary glass of local wine or beer.

Nelson *3 km N of Nelson*
Havenview Homestay *B&B Homestay*

Shirley & Bruce Lauchlan
10 Davies Drive,
Nelson
7010

Tel (03) 546 6045
or 027 420 0737
0800 546 604
havenview@paradise.net.nz
www.havenview.co.nz

Double/Twin $130-$155
(Full breakfast)
Dinner (two course with
a glass of wine) $35 pp
Visa MC accepted
Non smokers only
Smoking area inside
2 Queen (2 bdrm)
Bathrooms: 1 Ensuite 1 Private

Built for the magnificent views, our sunny modern home is on the northern entrance to Nelson, and only three minutes to the city. Relax with a complimentary wine while enjoying panoramic views overlooking the Miyazu Gardens and Tasman Bay. Enjoy dinner with us, or dine at a local restaurant; then relax in our lounge with Sky TV /Internet available. We are well travelled New Zealanders; play golf, and together with our friendly cat, we'll make your stay a pampered experience.

Nelson - Enner Glynn *4 km N of Nelson*
Double View *B&B*

Judy Sisam
142 Panorama Drive,
Enner Glynn
7011

Tel (03) 547 7292
Fax (03) 547 7638
judy@doubleview.co.nz
www.doubleview.co.nz

Double/Twin $160
Single $140
(Special breakfast)
Dinner by prior arrangement
Visa MC Eftpos accepted
Pet free home
1 King 1 Queen (2 bdrm)
Bathrooms: 1 Ensuite
Junior Suite shares ensuite

Double View has spectacular views over Tasman Bay located 5 minutes from Nelson Airport and 10 minutes from Nelson township. The Superior Suite is well appointed with spacious luxury Super King accommodation. The Junior Suite shares ensuite facilities. Guests are welcome to use laundry & small gymnasium. Host Judy previously owned a cooking school and provides a great gourmet selection for breakfast. Dinner available by prior arrangement. Judy welcomes you to Double View to use as your base while exploring the region.

Nelson - Tahunanui *5 km W of nelson*

My Place *B&B*
Jim Chow
87 Parkers Road,
Tahunanui,
Nelson
7011

Tel (03) 539 6369
or 027 710 5572
jchow@kol.co.nz

Double/Twin $110-$125
Single $85-$100
(Full breakfast)
Children by arrangement
Visa MC accepted
Pet free home
Children welcome
1 Queen 1 Double/Twin (2 bdrm)
Bathrooms: 1 Family share

Welcome to my place. Tastefully decorated. Warm hospitality. Quality linen. 8 minutes drive to Nelson CBD. 5 minutes walk to beach. Airport & bus pickup & drop offs. Off street parking. And lots of adventure trips to be had in the Nelson region.

Nelson East *0.7 km E of Cathedral*

Annick House *B&B Separate Suite*
Ann & Nick James
29 Cleveland Terrace,
Nelson
7010

Tel (03) 548 0554
Fax (03) 548 0505
nick.james@xtra.co.nz
www.annickhouse.co.nz

Double/Twin $150-$185
Single $130-$165
(Full breakfast)
Children over 12 are charged full rate
Dinner by arrangement only
Visa MC accepted
Children welcome
2 King/Twin 1 Single (2 bdrm)
Bathrooms: 2 Private

Annick house offers two private self contained studio units in a secluded garden setting five minutes walk to the city centre. Our "Out of Africa" unit is 50sq/m. The "A Touch Oriental" unit is 40sq/m and has a separate lounge. Both are tastefully furnished and have a private entrances and bathrooms. They are equipped with kitchen facilities, cooking essentials and a BBQ. We offer a continental or cooked breakfast tray with fresh fruit in season. Expect a warm friendly welcome from our two Tokinese cats.

Richmond *0.5 km E of Richmond*
Hunterville *Homestay*
Cecile & Alan Strang
30 Hunter Avenue,
Richmond,
Nelson

Tel (03) 544 5852
Fax (03) 544 5852
strangsa@clear.net.nz

Double/Twin $100
Single $70
(Full breakfast)
Children half price
Dinner $30 by arrangement
Children and pets welcome
1 King 1 Twin 1 Single (3 bdrm)
Bathrooms: 1 Private 1 Family share

Experience a family welcome in a real Kiwi home with drinks poolside in summer, or a cuppa and home-made biscuits. Our home is up a short driveway where we enjoy bird-song from surrounding trees. We are enroute to Golden Bay and Able Tasman park but just 15 minutes from Nelson City. We travel frequently so appreciate travellers needs;comfortable beds, laundry, generous breakfasts, dinner with local food and wine. Our interests: music, reading, bridge, our friendly Dalmatian(Coco) and the company of guests.

～

Richmond *1 km E of Richmond*
Antiquarian Guest House *B&B*
Robert & Joanne Souch
12A Surrey Road,
Richmond,
Nelson

Tel (03) 544 0253
or (03) 544 0723
021 417 413
Fax (03) 544 0253
souchebys@clear.net.nz
http://souchebys@clear.net.nz

Double/Twin $95-$125
Single $80 (Full breakfast)
Children $10
Visa MC accepted
Children and pets welcome
1 King 1 Queen 1 Twin (3 bdrm)
Bathrooms: 1 Ensuite 1 Guest share

Bob & Joanne Souch welcome you to their peaceful home only 2 minutes from Richmond (15 minutes drive south of Nelson) - excellent base for exploring National Parks, beaches, arts/crafts, ski fields etc. Relax in the garden, beside the swimming pool or in our large TV/guest lounge. Tea/coffee facilities, home-baking and memorable breakfasts. Our family pet is Gemma (friendly border collie). As local antique shop owners we know the area well.

Richmond *12 km SW of Nelson*
Idesia *B&B*

Jenny & Barry McKee
14 Idesia Grove,
Richmond,
Nelson

Tel (03) 544 0409
or 0800 361 845
Fax (03) 544 0402
idesian@xtra.co.nz
www.idesia.co.nz

Double/Twin $100-$140
(Full breakfast)
Dinner $40 by arrangement
Visa MC accepted
Pet free home
1 King/Twin 1 Queen (2 bdrm)
Bathrooms: 1 Ensuite 1 Private

You are assured of a warm welcome and quality service at Idesia Bed & Breakfast. Our home, elevated for sun and views is in a quiet grove easily accessible from State Highway 6. Breakfast is served with fresh seasonal fruits and a sizzling cooked selection. Join us for dinner, however Richmond's restaurants are close by. We offer broadband wireless network, off-road parking, information/booking Abel Tasman National Park. With our proven B&B experience we aim to give service and hospitality so you enjoy our regions attractions.

~

Brightwater *10 km NW of Richmond*
Westleigh *Homestay Farmstay Separate Suite*

John and Dell
Westleigh,
Waimea West,
Brightwater,
Nelson 7091

Tel (03) 542 3654
westleigh@paradise.net.nz

Double/Twin $$130
Single $100
(Full breakfast)
Dinner 3 course with wine $35pp
Visa MC accepted
Pet free home
1 Queen 1 Double/Twin (2 bdrm)
Bathrooms: 1 Ensuite 1 Guest share

Country home in 27 acres of privacy. House dates from c1860, now updated. 10 minutes to Richmond, golf and beach. Good local restaurants, but most guests eat with us,- more sociable and the food is ok too. A place for RnR, and central to all Nelson attractions. Directions: From Nelson, R6 past Richmond, turn off right at Brightwater, stay on that road c 5K. Westleigh sign prominent lhs. Or phone!

Wakefield *16 km S of Richmond*

Bushwalk B&B & Homestay *B&B Homestay*

Bruce & Sandra Monro
15 Hunt Terrace,
Wakefield,
Nelson
7025

Tel (03) 541 9615
s_bmonro@bushwalk.co.nz
http://bushwalk.co.nz

Double/Twin $120-$160
Single $75-$90
(Full breakfast)
Children by arrangement
3 course dinner by arrangement $40pp
Visa MC accepted
Children welcome
1 King 1 Queen 1 Twin (3 bdrm)
Bathrooms: 1 Ensuite 1 Family share
Ensuite has shower, family share bathroom

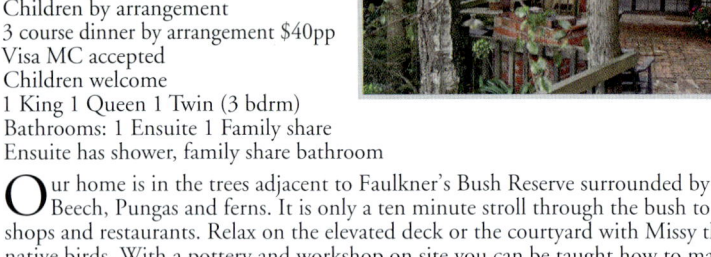

Our home is in the trees adjacent to Faulkner's Bush Reserve surrounded by Totara, Beech, Pungas and ferns. It is only a ten minute stroll through the bush to the local shops and restaurants. Relax on the elevated deck or the courtyard with Missy the cat and the native birds. With a pottery and workshop on site you can be taught how to make a pot on the wheel, with your host, Bruce. Our interests are travel, music, singing, art, golf, pottery and furniture making.

Mapua *30 km W of Nelson*

Hartridge *B&B*

Sue & Dennis Brillard
103 Aranui Road, Mapua, Nelson

Tel (03) 540 2079
or 021 189 7622
Fax (03) 540 2079
stay@hartridge.co.nz
www.hartridge.co.nz

Double/Twin $130-$185
Single $95-$150
(Continental breakfast)
Dinner $45pp
Discounts for 2 nights or more
Seasonal discounts
Visa MC accepted
Not suitable for children
1 King/Twin 1 Queen
1 Double/Twin (3 bdrm)
Bathrooms: 2 Ensuite 1 Private

Delightful, Historic Places listed 1915 home. Midway between Nelson City and fabulous Abel Tasman National Park with its hiking, kayaking or simply cruising. Quiet elevated position in coastal Mapua Village. Antiques, fine arts, mature gardens. Recent upstairs accommodation private and sunny. Every effort made for that vital good night's sleep. Sue's beautifully presented gourmet breakfasts include daily baking, local fruit, great coffee/teas. Private parking, stroll to restaurants, shops, charming wharf area. Beach loop-walk 1hr. Experienced hosts with local knowledge, complimentary extras. Internet broadband.

Mapua *30 km W of Nelson*
Accent House B&B *B&B Bed & Breakfast*

Wayne & Jacqui Rowe
148 Aranui Road,
Mapua Village, Nelson 7005

Tel (03) 540 3442
027 540 3442
Fax (03) 540 3442
info@accentbnb.co.nz
www.accentbnb.co.nz

Double/Twin $185-$230
Single $165-$185 (Full breakfast)
Visa MC Amex Eftpos accepted
Pet free home
Not suitable for children
3 King 1 Twin (4 bdrm)
Bathrooms: 4 Ensuite
Heated white fluffy towels and
heated underfloor tiles.

Welcome to our new award winning home set on 1.5 acres overlooking our lagoon rich with local birdlife and drenched in Tasman Bay sunshine. Stroll to Mapua Village, cafes and local restaurants. Check out the local arts and crafts studios and the many local wineries all within a few minutes drive. Easy drive to Nelson City and Abel Tasman National Park. Private guest entrance, Guest lounge with outdoor access & tea/coffee making facilities, laundry. TV's in all suites and access to our gardens. Directions: From Nelson, Richmond and south - follow State Highway 6 until turn off for SH60 - stay on highway,turn right at Mapua sign into Aranui Road by Mapua school

Mapua *4 km S of Mapua*
Kimeret Place Boutique B&B *Luxury B&B Apartment with Kitchen*
Cottage with Kitchen

Gill & Ian Knight
78 Bronte Road East
(off SH60),
Near Mapua,
Nelson

Tel (03) 540 2727
Fax (03) 540 2726
stay@kimeretplace.co.nz
www.kimeretplace.co.nz

Double/Twin $200-$340
Single $175-$315
(Special breakfast)
2 bedroom cottage $370
Visa MC Diners Eftpos accepted
4 King/Twin (4 bdrm)
Bathrooms: 4 Ensuite

A tranquil coastal setting in the heart of the wine & craft region with stunning views, heated swimming pool and spa. Just 4km to restaurants and 30 minutes to Abel Tasman National Park. A range of accommodation all with ensuite facilities, (2 with spa-baths), TV, DVD, Hi-fi, tea/coffee, fridge, sitting area and views from either balcony or deck. The 2 bedroom cottage also has a kitchenette and dining area. Light meals,laundry and internet are also available. Dog-lovers may wish to meet our golden retriever Alice

Ruby Bay *32 km W of Nelson*
Sandstone House *B&B*

John and Jenny Marchbanks
30 Korepo Road,
Ruby Bay, Nelson

Tel (03) 540 3251 or 027 514 0652
021 248 6778   Fax (03) 540 3251
sandstone@rubybay.net.nz   www.rubybay.net.nz

Double$220   Single $200 (Full breakfast)
Visa MC accepted   Not suitable for children
2 Queen (2 bdrm)
Bathrooms: 2 Ensuite

Welcome to Sandstone House - the ideal place to relax, stay a few days and explore this delightful region. We enjoy a maritime and semi-rural situation, ideally situated midway between Nelson and Motueka. We are handy to all the fine attractions that this region has to offer - National Parks, wineries, award winning restaurants, beaches, arts and crafts, the famous Mapua Wharf and lots lots more. We have 35 years local knowledge and are happy to assist you to make the most of your holiday and can help with any other forward bookings or reservations you may require. We are keen for you to have the best stay and trust you will enjoy our relaxed and homely atmosphere - our place is your place. Feel free to enjoy a drink, snack or a BBQ on either the front deck or the back verandah - depending on the weather, and if its winter time, enjoy some time out by the fire. Feast on the fabulous views anytime. We offer delicious homemade breakfasts with fresh free range eggs, baking, jams and preserves, and other local seasonal produce. Internet and laundry facilities are complimentary, and there is plenty of off street parking available. We hope you have a safe journey and look forward to sharing a "welcome" drink with you when you arrive.

Ruby Bay *20 km W of Nelson*
Broadsea B&B *B&B*
Rae & John Robinson
42 Broadsea Avenue,
Ruby Bay,
Nelson

Tel (03) 540 3511
Fax (03) 540 3511
raer@clear.net.nz

Double/Twin $130-$135
Single $110-$120
(Full breakfast)
Not suitable for children
1 Queen (1 bdrm)
Bathrooms: 1 Ensuite 1 Private

B each front accommodation, with lovely walks on beach and reserve; cafes and tavern close by, as are wineries and restaurants. We are 15 minutes from Richmond and Motueka, 30 minutes from Nelson and the airport. Abel Tasman and Kaiteriteri are within 40 minutes drive. We want our guests to feel at home and have their privacy in a peaceful and private setting. Coffee, tea and old fashioned home-made biscuits available. Our Birman cat Bogart will greet you when you arrive.

Upper Moutere *30 km W of Nelson*
Kotare Estate Boutique Accommodation *Homestay Boutique Accommodation*
Beverley and John Mockett
1270 Moutere Highway,
RD 1 Upper Moutere, 7173

Tel (03) 543 2425
or 027 497 1611
enquiry@kotareestate.co.nz
www.kotareestate.co.nz

Double/Twin $220-$275
(Special breakfast)
Children Under 12 years $80
12 years and over $100
Hosted dinner by arrangement $50
includes local wine Complimentary
afternoon teas and aperitifis
Visa MC accepted Children welcome
1 King 2 Single (1 bdrm)
Bathrooms: 1 Ensuite

B e inspired in the informal elegance and natural beauty of Kotare Estate - a peaceful 15 acres of stunning gardens, bush, orchard and paddocks. Relax in private, spacious and luxurious accommodation - ensuite bathroom, doors to decks and garden, very comfortable king-sized bed. The loft level sleeps two children. See alpacas, black sheep, birds, cattle, haymaking. Enjoy the chemical-free swimming pool; savour home-grown fruit. Within easy access to award-winning wineries, National Parks, artists. Tariff includes scrumptious breakfasts, afternoon teas and aperitifs. Hosted dinners available on request.

Motueka Valley *25 km S of Motueka*
The Kahurangi Brown Trout *B&B Homestay Farmstay*
Apartment with Kitchen

David Davies & Heather Lindsay
2292 Westbank Road,
Pokororo, RD 1, Motueka

Tel (03) 526 8736 or 021 141 0717
Fax (03) 526 8736
enquiries@kbtrout.co.nz
www.kbtrout.co.nz

Double/Twin $150
Single $120 (Full breakfast)
Child in your room $25,
in extra room $100
Dinner $50/head, includes salad,
fresh bread, wine, dessert
Our gardens are 100% organic
Visa MC accepted
Children and pets welcome
2 King/Twin 3 King 3 Single (3 bdrm)
Bathrooms: 3 Ensuite We also have an outdoor wood fired bath

Enjoy the sound of the beautiful Motueka River, which runs past our house. Step across the road for trout fishing, or a refreshing swim. Come "home" for a delicious meal made with our home grown organic fruit and vegies. Comments from last years visitors book say it all: "Everything was fantastic" "Well worth a little detour to find such heaven" "Stayed a week and wish it was longer! Felt like we were part of the family - great hospitality and food and the best breakfasts!!"

Motueka Valley *16 km SW of Motueka*
Waitakiroa Farmstay B & B *B&B Farmstay*

Dianne & Errol Boyes
RD 1,
Westbank Road,
Motueka

Tel (03) 526 8003
waitakiroa@xtra.co.nz
www.riverfarmstay.co.nz

Double/Twin $120 Single $85
(Continental breakfast)
Children under 2 years free
Extra person $25 per night
Guest BBQ facilities available
Children welcome
1 Queen 1 Double/Twin
1 Single (2 bdrm)
Bathrooms: 1 Ensuite

Dianne and Errol welcome you to Waitakiroa Farm-stay. Our 320 acre farm is situated on the banks of the Motueka river, famous for its trout fishing, and in the heart of the beautiful Motueka valley. We are close to Motueka township, stunning Kaiteriteri Beach, 3 national parks, (Nelson Lakes National Park, Abel Tasman National Park, known worldwide for its scenery, and Kahurangi National Park) Come and enjoy a tour of our farm with Errol and experience rural New Zealand life with our family!

Motueka Valley *20 km SW of Motueka*
Vistara Bed and Breakfast *B&B Homestay*

Bruce & Guruvati Dyer
2035 Motueka River Valley,
RD 1 Motueka, 7196

Tel (03) 526 8288
or 021 079 7919
021 079 28008, (03) 548 7284
Fax 03 526 8288
info@vistara.co.nz
www.vistara.co.nz

Double/Twin $95 Single $75
(Continental breakfast)
Children $15
Dinner $25
Visa MC accepted
Children and pets welcome
1 Queen 1 Double/Twin
2 Single (3 bdrm)
Bathrooms: 2 Guest share

We welcome you to Vistara a relaxed peaceful haven situated on our 7 acre property adjacent to the Motueka River. Attractions include great river swimming, native birds and bush, a beautiful garden, mountain scenery and Jess our Jack Russell dog. Bedrooms feature polished floors and charming décor. Guests have their own lounge, tea and coffee facilities and are welcome to use the meditation room. Enjoy a delicious breakfast of home-made preserves, yoghurt, muesli and fresh organic fruit. Meals are organic, vegetarian and lovingly prepared.

Motueka Valley *26 km S of Motueka*
Doone Cottage Country Homestay *B&B Homestay*

Glen & Stan Davenport
2281 Motueka Valley Highway,
Rural District No 1,
Motueka 7196

Tel (03) 526 8740
Fax (03) 526 8740
doone-cottage@xtra.co.nz
www.doonecottage.co.nz

Double/Twin $110-$190
Single $110-$160
(Full breakfast)
Dinner by arrangement
Visa MC accepted
Not suitable for children
2 King/Twin
1 Double/Twin (3 bdrm)
Bathrooms: 3 Ensuite

Charming 130yr old cottage welcoming guests for 25 years. Secluded native flora & flower gardens in mountain setting overlooking Motueka River Valley. 5 Trout rivers - Guiding available. In-house Guestrooms plus Private Garden Chalet. Enjoy countrystyle B & B, homemade breads, preserves, organic vegetables. Sheep, chickens, ducks, donkeys. Weaving/Woolcraft Studio. Short distance Abel Tasman, Kahaurangi, Nelson Lakes. Or just relax & soak up the country atmosphere of yesteryear in this special place. Nelson 45 mins. Picton 2.1/2 hours Westcoast 3 hours.

Motueka *1.4 km E of Motueka*
Williams B&B *B&B Homestay Apartment with Kitchen*

Rebecca & Ian Williams
186 Thorp Street,
Motueka

Tel (03) 528 9385
Fax (03) 528 9385
B&B@motueka-homestay.co.nz
www.motueka-homestay.co.nz

Double/Twin $130
Single $700
(Full breakfast)
Children $20
Dinner by arrangement
Apartment with Kitchen $200
3 Queen 1 Double/Twin
2 Single (4 bdrm)
Bathrooms: 2 Ensuite

We only look expensive. We are 1.4km to Motueka shopping centre and 1.2km to 18 hole golf course. Each bedroom has own ensuite. The guest lounge has tea & coffee making facilities and fridge. Motueka is the stop-over place for visitors to explore Abel Tasman and Kahurangi National Parks. Golden Bay and Kaiteriteri golden sands beach is 10km away. We have a Jack Russell dog. Visa and Mastercard accepted.

Motueka *1 km E of Motueka*
Golf View Chalet *B&B Apartment with Kitchen*

Kathleen & Neil Holder
20A Teece Drive,
Motueka

Tel (03) 528 8353
info@GolfViewChalet.co.nz
www.GolfViewChalet.co.nz

Double/Twin $145-$150
Single $100-$100
(Full breakfast)
Children in B&B $20, in apartment $15
Self-contained apartment
$130 double, extra adult $25
Visa MC accepted
Children welcome
3 Queen 1 Double/Twin
4 Single (4 bdrm)
Bathrooms: 1 Ensuite 2 Private

Welcome to our sunny home with mountain views, adjoining 18 hole golf course, beside the sea. Enjoy our lovely garden setting. Sleep well in comfortable beds. Close to restaurants, National Parks and golden beaches. Central in the Nelson region for day trips. Easy access groundfloor self-cater apartment with carport. Complimentary laundry, tea/coffee making facilities, guest fridge, BBQ. Directions: from High Street (main street), State Highway 60, turn into Tudor Street, left Thorp Street, right Krammer Street, left into Teece Drive.

Motueka *2 km S of Motueka*

Grey Heron - The Italian Organic Homestay *B&B Homestay*

Sandro Lionello & Laura Totis
110 Trewavas Street, Motueka 7120

Tel (03) 528 0472 or 021 0229 3547
Fax (03) 528 0472   sandro@greyheron.co.nz
www.greyheron.co.nz

Double/Twin $100-$130 Single $60-$80 (Continental breakfast)
Dinner $28pp Main + dessert or $40pp typical 3course Italian
dinner Children welcome
3 Queen 1 Single (4 bdrm)
Bathrooms: 1 Ensuite 1 Private 1 Guest share

We are a couple from Northern Italy, much travelled and keen on tramping, mountaineering and motorbiking. We welcome you to our private hideaway and birdwatchers' paradise on the tidal estuary.

Pleasant beach-walks at the door-steps, far enough from the noise of the main road and yet only 5 mins drive to shops and restaurants. Or you can relax here after your exploring day, join us for dinner and taste our italian organic cuisine overlooking a beautiful sunset behind the mountains and enjoying Sandro's huge collection of Jazz records.

The Abel Tasman NP is 25 mins drive; 45 mins drive to the alpine, easy accessible, Kahurangi NP and to Nelson city. The Guest Accommodation includes both ensuite/private and shared-facilities with toilet room and bathroom each separate (4-5 guests max capacity in the shared area). Basic tea-coffee facilities and secure off-street parking.

We serve a generous Continental breakfast including home-made breads and jams, fresh fruit and juice, yogurt and muesli. As keen walkers and mountaineers we can give helpful hints to maximize your exploration of the area. We also offer guided walks thanks to Sandro's experience as geologist and to our interest in the local flora and fauna. Rock-climbing and Italian Language lessons by arrangements.

Water-Taxi ticketing service and Kayak Tours booking service available. We are conveniently located just around the corner from the reliable and well-known "Sea Kayak Company". "Benvenuti tutti gli amici italiani!"

Motueka *10 km S of Motueka*
Motueka River Hills Bed & Breakfast *B&B*

Anthea Garmey & Andrew Claringbold
394 Westbank Road,
RD1,
Motueka

Tel (03) 528 8979
or 027 208 3106
Fax (03) 528 8979
stay@motuekariverhills.co.nz
www.motuekariverhills.co.nz

Double/Twin $130-$150
Single $120
(Full breakfast)
Portacot available for young children
Dinner available by arrangement
Children welcome
1 King/Twin (1 bdrm)
Bathrooms: 1 Ensuite

Motueka River Hills is nestled on the foothills of the Kahurangi National Park above the Motueka River. We have stunning views over rural Motueka, Tasman Bay and out to D'Urville Island. Listen to Morepork while you relax and unwind in the steaming hot outdoor bath. Awake to a gorgeous sunrise and the chorus of native birds. Enjoy a large breakfast with homemade muffins. Andrew is a keen fly fisherman and can provide a guiding service. We share our home with daughter Hannah and cat, Basil.

Motueka *2 km SW of Motueka*
The Queen Vic *B&B Orchardstay*

Clare and Graham Ryder
199 Queen Victoria Street,
Motueka
7120

Tel Landline (03) 528 8963
or Mobile 027 449 9180
0800 307 757
Fax (03) 528 8963
thequeenvic199@gmail.com
http://thequeenvic199.googlepages.com

Double/Twin $120-$135
(Full breakfast)
Visa MC accepted
1 Queen (1 bdrm)
Bathrooms: 1 Ensuite

You will be assured of a warm welcome when you stay at The Queen Vic. Your room, separate from the house and overlooking the orchard is private and spacious with it's own ensuite. Pick fruit fresh off the trees and sample apple juice made from our own granny smith apples. A generous continental or cooked breakfast and delicious home baking is provided and on arrival, a complimentary small bottle of New Zealand wine. ƒOnly 20 mins to the Abel Tasman National Park or beautiful Kaiteriteri beach.

Kaiteriteri *10 km N of Motueka*
Bracken Hill B&B *Luxury B&B*
Grace & Tom Turner
293 Kaiteriteri Road,
RD 2, Motueka

Tel (03) 528 9629
Fax (03) 528 9629
graceturner@xtra.co.nz
www.bnb.co.nz/brackenhillbb.html

Double/Twin $130-$140
Single $100-$110
(Continental breakfast)
Visa MC accepted
Pet free home
Not suitable for children
2 Queen 1 Twin (3 bdrm)
Bathrooms: 3 Private

"Coastal Luxury". Welcome to our tasteful, spacious modern home. Rooms all have sea views over Tasman Bay. Enjoy mountains, native bush, sunrises, sunsets & stars! A viewing sundeck leads to a unique natural rock garden. Guests' TV lounge, laundry facility. Experience Kaiteriteri Beach, Marahau, Kahurangi/Abel Tasman National Parks and Golden Bay.Kayaking,and water taxis. Restaurants close by. Interests: travel & guests will delight in a refreshing breakfast at our peaceful haven. Friendly hosts, Grace & Tom.

Kaiteriteri *12 km N of Motueka*
Bayview *B&B*
Tim Rich
2 Bayview Heights,
Kaiteriteri,
RD 2,
Motueka 7197

Tel (03) 527 8090
or 027 454 5835
Fax (03) 527 8090
book@kaiteriteribandb.co.nz
www.kaiteriteribandb.co.nz

Double/Twin $165-$195
(Full breakfast)
Visa MC accepted
Pet free home
Not suitable for children
1 King/Twin 1 King 1 Twin (2 bdrm)
Bathrooms: 2 Ensuite

Welcome to a piece of paradise. This modern house has huge windows with outstanding sea views overlooking Kaiteriteri Beach out to Abel Tasman National Park. Large, beautifully furnished guest rooms have every convenience you could want. Enjoy delicious home cooked breakfast in the dining room with your host who has an intimate knowledge of the area. Laundry, email and booking facilities for boat trips, walking and kayaking are available. A two day minimum stay in this unique area recommended.

Kaiteriteri *13 km N of Motueka*

Everton B&B *B&B*

Martin & Diane Everton
25 Kotare Place,
Little Kaiteriteri,
RD 2 Motueka

Tel (03) 527 8301
or 021 527 830
Fax (03) 527 8301
everton@xtra.co.nz
www.evertonbandb.co.nz

Double/Twin $140-$160
Single $100-$120
(Continental breakfast)
Wireless Internet
Visa MC accepted
Pet free home
1 King 1 Queen 1 Twin (3 bdrm)
Bathrooms: 1 Ensuite 2 Private

With wonderful sea views we are 2 minutes walk from beautiful Little Kaiteriteri Beach. Continental breakfast may include fresh bread or muffins. Nearby are excellent restaurants for evening dining. Our interests include Rotary, Toastmasters, golf, tennis, music, travel, and boating. The Abel Tasman National Park is right here where you can kayak, walk and water taxi. Martin is licensed to take you on a personalised trip in our boat. We offer email access and wireless internet. We have no pets and are non-smokers.

Kaiteriteri *13 km N of Motueka*

The Haven *Cottage with Kitchen*

Tom & Alison Rowling
Rowling Heights,
RD 2,
Kaiteriteri,
Motueka 7197

Tel (03) 527 8085
Fax (03) 527 8065
thehaven@internet.co.nz
www.thehaven.co.nz

Continental breakfast provisions
Extra couple $50
1 King 2 Twin (2 bdrm)
Bathrooms: 1 Ensuite 1 Private

The Haven - Paradise with a nautical theme. Self-contained 2 bedrooms, Captains Cabin with king-size bed and ensuite, Crews Quarters with 2 large twin beds and private bathroom. Galley kitchen with generous breakfast provisions. 2 decks providing outdoor living. Enjoy relaxed family atmosphere, spectacular views, swimming pool, private bush track to beach. Minimum stay 2 nights, not suitable for small children.

Kaiteriteri *12 km N of Motueka*

Wall Street Accommodation *B&B Separate Suite Apartment with Kitchen*

Dr Hans Brutscher & Fiona Thornton
6 & 8 Wall Street, Kaiteriteri,
RD 2, Motueka 7197

Tel (03) 527 8338
or 021 544 335
or 021 21 66 440
Fax (03) 527 8338
stay@kaiteriteribnb.co.nz
www.kaiteriteribnb.co.nz

Double/Twin $120-$170
Single $110-$150
(Continental breakfast)
Wireless Internet available
Visa MC accepted
Pet free home
Children welcome
3 Queen 1 Twin (4 bdrm)
Bathrooms: 2 Ensuite 1 Private

Two modern stylish homes in a peaceful bush setting, centrally located to explore Abel Tasman National Park, Golden Bay and Nelson environs. Minutes to golden-sanded Kaiteriteri beach, kayak companies and water taxis. Restaurants and store are just a short drive away. We offer 3 Queen rooms and 1 Twin room - choose from B&B, Self-contained or Accommodation only. All rooms have their own courtyard, separate entry, tea/coffee making facilities, TV or DVD. (Kitchenette & full kitchen options available). German & French spoken.

Kaiteriteri *15 km S of Kaiteriteri*

Kaiteriteri Heights *Luxury B&B Separate Suite Apartment with Kitchen*

Mary & Richard Shee
28 Cederman Drive,
Kaiteriteri Heights,
Motueka

Tel 03 527 8662
or 027 229 1698
Fax 03 527 8662
info@KaiteriteriHeights.com
www.kaiteriteriheights.com

Double/Twin $130-$160
Single $110-$110
(Full breakfast)
Dinner b/a using fresh vegetables
from our organic garden
Visa MC Eftpos accepted
Not suitable for children under 12
2 King/Twin 1 Queen
1 Double/Twin 2 Single (2 bdrm)
Bathrooms: 1 Ensuite 1 Private

Kaiteriteri's Premier Bed & Breakfast located in the hills overlooking Tasman Bay and the Riwaka Estuary. On the doorstep of the magnificent Abel Tasman National Park. Take the gentle 5-minute stroll down to Little Kaiteriteri beach, with its golden sands and safe swimming. Full privacy, or interact as part of the family. Shared facilities include the outdoor deck with barbeque area, coffee/tea facilities, spa pool, the main lounge area with TV with Sky.

Kaiteriteri *In Motueka*

Torlesse Heights *B&B Apartment*

Michael & Lorraine
40 Torlesse Drive,
Kaiteriteri,
Motueka

Tel (03) 527 8538
or 021 292 6673
Fax (03) 527 8539
mte@xtra.co.nz
www.kaiteribnb.co.nz

Double/Twin $150-$180
(Continental breakfast)
Non smokers only
1 Queen (1 bdrm)
Bathrooms: 1 Ensuite 1 Private

Our modern home is elevated above the sheltered bays of Kaiteriteri, providing our guests with a unique stepping stone to the outdoor pleasures of this stunning coastline. We offer luxury accommodation with an entry from a private courtyard, superb views of Kaiteriteri Beach and across Tasman Bay to Nelson. From Kaiteriteri Beach you can access the Abel Tasman National Park by either water taxi, launch or Kayak. Our region enables our visitors to experience the arts and crafts and secluded golden sand beaches nearby.

Abel Tasman National Park - Marahau *18 km NW of Motueka*

Abel Tasman Bed & Breakfast *B&B Cottage with Kitchen Motels*

George Bloomfield
Abel Tasman National Park,
Marahau,
Nelson Region

Tel (03) 527 8181
Fax (03) 527 8181
abel.tasman.stables.accom@xtra.co.nz
www.abeltasmanstables.co.nz

Double/Twin $110-$150
Single $80-$100
(Continental breakfast)
Dinner by prior arrangement
Cottage $150 (sleeps 4)
Visa MC accepted
Pet free home Children welcome
3 Queen 2 Double/Twin
4 Single (6 bdrm)
Bathrooms: 5 Ensuite 1 Private
1 Family share Showers

Great views, hospitality, peaceful garden setting are yours at Abel Tasman Stables accommodation. Closest ensuite facility to Abel Tasman National park. Guests comments include: 'I know now that hospitality is not just a word', TH, Germany. 'Wonderful place, friendly hospitality. The best things for really special holidays. We leave a piece of our hearts', P&M, Italy. 'The creme-de-la-creme of our holiday. What a view', MN & JW, England. Homestay bed & breakfast or self-contained options. Cafe close by.

Abel Tasman National Park *17 km NW of Motueka*

Split Apple Rock Homestay *B&B Homestay*

Thelma & Rodger Boys
116 Tokongawa Drive,
Split Apple Rock,
RD 2,
Motueka

Tel (03) 527 8182
splitapplerock@hotmail.com
www.splitapplerock.com

Double/Twin $140-$165
Single $120-$150
(Full breakfast)
Dinner $40 pp by arrangement
Visa MC accepted
Children welcome
1 Queen 1 Twin (2 bdrm)
Bathrooms: 2 Ensuite

Enjoy 180 degree panoramic sea views of Tasman Bay and Abel Tasman National Park. Our Eco-log home rooms have private entrances and decking. We are within walking distance of golden sand beaches, 5 minutes drive to Marahau and the start of Abel Tasman National Park where walking, kayaking, boating, swimming and more are available. 2 cats in residence. Directions: on the Marahau/Kaiteriteri Road take the Tokongawa Drive turn-off, 1.2km up Tokongawa Drive the "Split Apple Rock Homestay" sign is on your right.

Abel Tasman National Park *8 km N of Motueka*

Fraser Highlands *B&B or Cottage with kitchen*

Sue & Jim Fraser
177 Riwaka-Sandy Bay Road,
RD 2, Motueka 7197

Tel (03) 528 8702
or 027 283 8861
fraserhighlands_nz@hotmail.com
www.fraserhighlands.co.nz

Double/Twin $110-$160
Single $90-$140
(Continental breakfast)
Children $10
Dinner $30
Visa MC accepted
Children welcome
3 Queen (3 bdrm)
Bathrooms: 3 Ensuite
Claw foot bathroom on request

Welcome to our unique Scottish home with spectacular panoramic views. The peaceful location has numerous native birds, walking tracks, and large gardens. To add to your comfort we have a spacious lounge with an open fire, and family room. A delicious continental breakfast includes freshly baked home-made breads, muffins, and a variety of fruit. Available on request are - evening meals, guided tours, and a beauty therapist. Within 15 minutes you could be enjoying beaches, restaurants, vineyards, flying, tramping, fishing or Abel Tasman National Park.

Takaka - Patons Rock Beach *10 km W of Takaka*
Patondale *Farmstay Cottage with Kitchen*

Vicki & David James
Patons Rock,
RD 2,
Takaka

Tel (03) 525 8262
or 0800 306 697 (NZ only)
0274 936 891
Fax (03) 525 8262
patondale@xtra.co.nz
www.patonsrockbeachvillas.co.nz

Double/Twin $125-$160
Single $125
(Breakfast provisions first night)
Children $20
Visa MC accepted
Pet free home
Children welcome
4 King 8 Single (8 bdrm)
Bathrooms: 4 Private

Four sunny, spacious, deluxe self-contained units, own attached carports. 2 bedrooms. Peaceful rural setting at the seaward end of our dairy farm yet only a few minutes walk to beautiful Patons Rock Beach. Central location, approx. 5mins to Mussell Inn. Simply the Best. Your Kiwi hosts, David & Vicki invite you to be our guests.

Takaka - Tata Beach *15 km NE of Takaka*
The Devonshires *B&B Homestay*

Brian & Susan Devonshire
32 Tata Heights Drive,
Tata Beach,
RD 1,
Takaka,
Golden Bay

Tel (03) 525 7987
Fax (03) 525 7987
devs@ihug.co.nz

Double/Twin $100
Single $70
(Full breakfast)
Children not suitable
Dinner $25-$30 by arrangement
Visa MC accepted
1 Queen (1 bdrm)
Bathrooms: 1 Ensuite

The Devonshires live at Tata Beach and invite you to enjoy their comfortable home and stroll to the nearby beautiful golden beach. A tranquil base for exploring the truly scenic Golden Bay, the Abel Tasman Walkway, Kahurangi National Park, Farewell Spit, amazing coastal scenery, fishing the rivers or visiting interesting craftspeople. Brian, an educator, wine and American Football buff is a keen fisherman. Susan enjoys crafts, painting, gardening and practising her culinary skills. Charlie Brown and Hermione are the resident cats. Longer visits welcomed.

Takaka *5 km S of Takaka*
Rose Cottage *B&B Cottage with Kitchen*
Margaret & Phil Baker
Hamama Road,
RD 1,
Takaka

Tel (03) 525 9048
Fax (03) 525 9043

Double/Twin $100-$120
Single $80-$100
(Breakfast by arrangement)
Self-contained units $100-$140
Visa MC accepted
3 Queen 6 Single (6 bdrm)
Bathrooms: 4 Private

Rose Cottage, Golden Bay's finest self-contained accommodation, situated in the beautiful Takaka Valley in 2 1/2 acres of garden amoung 300 year old Totara trees. Centrally situated to explore Golden Bays many attractions. Our three units have full kitchens, quality furniture make in Phil's craft workshop, and private sundecks. Our quiet sunny Bed & Breakfast, refurbished 2008, can accommodate up to 4 guests. Enjoy the 12 metre solaheated indoor swimming pool. Enquire about our weekly and monthly rates.

≈

Takaka *5 km N of Takaka*
Matangi Mahana *B&B*
Emma and Diarmuid Brazendale
55 Packard Road,
Takaka
7172

Tel (03) 525 7013
or 027 642 4244
dbrazendale@yahoo.com

Double/Twin $90-$120
(Continental breakfast)
Tariff on request for 3+ nights
or single occupancy
Pet free home
1 Double/Twin (1 bdrm)
Bathrooms: 1 Ensuite

An organic vegetarian / vegan oasis in beautiful Takaka. Matangi Mahaha is a 100 year old villa set in over an acre of gardens, organic orchards and with swimming pool. It has stunning mountain views and is very peaceful. You are welcome to use the swimming pool, or wander through the orchard and pick fruit. The accommodation comprises a large double bedroom with ensuite bathroom and own private lounge. Five minutes from Takaka and Pohara beach. Gateway to Abel Tasman National Park.

Parapara *20 km NW of Takaka*
Hakea Hill House *B&B*

Vic & Liza Eastman
PO Box 35,
Collingwood
7054

Tel (03) 524 8487
Fax (03) 524 8487
vic.eastman@clear.net.nz

Double/Twin $130
Single $90
(Full breakfast)
Children $50
Family dinner by arrangement
Visa MC accepted
Children and pets welcome
2 Queen 6 Single (3 bdrm)
Bathrooms: 2 Guest share
bathtub and shower

Hakea Hill House at Parapara has views from its hilltop of all Golden Bay. The 2 story house is modern and spacious. Two guest rooms have large balconies; the third for children has bunk beds and a cot. American and New Zealand electric outlets are installed. Television, tea or coffee, telephone and broadband lines are available in rooms. Vic is a practising physician with an interest in astronomy. Liza is a quilter and cares for outdoor dogs. Please contact us for reservations and directions.

Collingwood *25 km N of Takaka*
Skara Brae Garden Motels & Bed and Breakfast *B&B Cottage with Kitchen*

Joanne & Pax Northover
7 Elizabeth Street,
Collingwood

Tel (03) 524 8464
Fax (03) 524 8474
skarabrae@xtra.co.nz
www.accommodationcollingwood.co.nz

Double/Twin $130
Single $100
(Continental breakfast)
2 self-contained units $110
Visa MC accepted
2 Queen 1 Double/Twin
1 Twin 2 Single (4 bdrm)
Bathrooms: 1 Ensuite 3 Private

Skara Brae, the original police residence in Collingwood built in 1908, has been tastefully renovated over the years. Our historic home is in a quiet, peaceful garden setting. Join us in the house for bed & breakfast, or our 2 self-contained motel units. Either way you will experience a warm welcoming atmosphere and individual attention. We are a minute away from the excellent Courthouse Cafe and local tavern bistro bar and it is a short stroll to the beach. Farewell Spit trips depart close by.

Collingwood *25 km N of Takaka*

Heron's Rest *B&B Cottage with B&B + cooking facilities*

Maureen & Angus Scotland
23 Gibbs Road,
Collingwood Township,
Golden Bay

Tel (03) 524 8987
Fax (03) 524 8987
be@herons-rest.co.nz
www.herons-rest.co.nz

Double/Twin $100-$120/$85-$90
Single $70-$90
(Special breakfast)
Children Negotiable
Visa MC accepted
1 Queen 1 Double 1 Twin
2 Single (3 bdrm)
Bathrooms: 2 Ensuite
1 Family share bath available

Travelling towards the tip of the South Island, your journey is rewarded by spectacular sea, mountain and estuary views, all visible from Heron's Rest. We're situated between the Abel Tasman and Heaphy Tracks and surrounded by superb sandy beaches, being a short bush-walk (or drive) away from Farewell Spit Tours and Collingwood eateries. Welcoming hosts offer relaxation, comfort and lasting memories served up with home-made and locally-produced foods plus complimentary drinks. Potter's studio, internet, hairdryer, BBQ, laundry available. Directions: Website and Lewis Street signboard along estuary.

Collingwood *25 km N of Takaka*

Horizon Holiday Unit *Holiday Unit*

Shaun & Jenny Solly
54 Excellent Street,
Collingwood

Tel (03) 524 8180
or 027 270 6155
Fax 03 524 8631
jennyozy@xtra.co.nz

Double/Twin $120
Single $80
(Accommodation only)
Children welcome,other bedding
available if more than 2
BBQ available
1 Queen 2 Single (2 bdrm)
Bathrooms: 1 Ensuite

$1,000,000 Views! Ever wondered what it would take to make you get up at sunrise on your hard-earned vacation? We have the answer! A million dollar view from our detached suite in Collingwood. Your hosts Jenny & Shaun offer you detached accommodation to use as your base while you explore the magnificent surroundings. With hunting,fishing walk tracks, guided tours cafes, restaurants only minutes away. We are located just before Collingwood on SH60 our sign (Horizon Holiday Unit) will show you the way.

Pakawau *9 km N of Collingwood*
Twin Waters Lodge *Luxury Lodge*

Trish & Mike Boland
PO Box 33,
Collingwood

Tel (03) 524 8014
Fax (03) 524 8054
twin.waters@xtra.co.nz
www.twinwaters.co.nz

Double/Twin $200-$200
Single $180-$180
(Full breakfast)
Dinner by arrangement
Visa MC accepted
Not suitable for children
1 King/Twin 3 Queen (4 bdrm)
Bathrooms: 4 Ensuite

Nestled harmoniously beside a tidal estuary and just fifty metres from a sandy beach, Twin Waters features curved timber ceilings, panoramic windows and multilevel decks. The elegant interior has ample space for guests to enjoy its charm and tranquility. Waking to tuis singing, breakfasting in the sun, sipping wine on the decks overlooking the estuary, or savouring a delicious dinner, there's sure to be a special moment to remember. Trish and Mike and their feline companions look forward to welcoming you at Twin Waters.

Nelson Lakes - St Arnaud *85 km S of Nelson*
Nelson Lakes Homestay *Homestay*

Gay & Merv Patch
RD 2,
State Highway 63,
Nelson 7072

Tel (03) 521 1191
Fax (03) 521 1191
Home@Tasman.net
www.nelsonlakesaccommodation.co.nz

Double/Twin $125
Single $90
(Full breakfast)
Visa MC accepted
2 King/Twin 1 Queen (2 bdrm)
Bathrooms: 2 Ensuite

Nestled on the sunny slopes of the St Arnaud Mountain Range, Nelson Lakes National Park, our spacious modern home is designed for the comfort and convenience of our guests. Spacious ensuite rooms, with doors opening on to our garden, large comfortable lounge and terrace to relax on at the end of the day and admire the magnificent mountain views. Laundry facilities are available. We have a house cat. Directions: State Highway 63, 4km east of St Arnaud.

Nelson Lakes - Gowan Valley *39 km S of Gowen River*

Braeburn House *B&B Separate Suite*

Lois and Kim Woods
Lake Rotoroa,
RD 3
Murchison 7077

Tel (03) 523 9996
Fax (03) 523 9996
lokim@paradise.net.nz

Double/Twin $200-$300
Single $100-$150
(Breakfast by arrangement)
Dinner bed and breakfast
included in price
Visa MC accepted
Children welcome
1 King 1 Queen 2 Twin (3 bdrm)
Bathrooms: 2 Private

Lake Rotoroa Homestay. Braeburn House is situated 200 metres from Lake Rotoroa in the Nelson Lakes National Park. Enjoy an upstairs private retreat, two bedrooms. TV and bathroom. Or a separate bedroom with its own bathroom. Breakfast, lunch and dinner are served at guests request. A holiday offering bushwalks, boating, kayaks and trout fishing. A large sewing room makes the ideal quilter's retreat with Lois as the resident tutor. Two Burmese cats reside by the fire in a warm comfortable home.

Murchison *0.2 km N of Murchison*

Murchison Lodge *B&B*
Shirley & Merve Bigden
15 Grey Street,
Murchison

Tel (03) 523 9196
or Freephone: 0800 523 9196
info@murchisonlodge.co.nz
www.murchisonlodge.co.nz

Double/Twin $145-$185
Single $115-$160
(Full breakfast)
Children over 12 welcome
Dinner by arrangement
Free wireless broadband
Visa MC accepted
1 King/Twin 2 Queen
1 Twin (4 bdrm)
Bathrooms: 3 Ensuite 1 Private

Warm timber Lodge with comfortable beds and hearty BBQ breakfasts, with our own eggs and fruit. Our four acres support various animals (including a friendly puppy) and accesses the Buller River and its swimming holes. Trees and mountains surround us, yet Murchison‚Äôs cafes are within five minutes walk. Unpack your bags and explore three National Parks; fly-fish, raft or play golf before returning home to a cold beer on the sunny verandah or a wine in front of the log fire. Free wireless broadband.

West Coast

Karamea

67

Carters Beach
Cape Foulwind
Westport
6
Charleston
69
Punakaiki
Reefton
Barrytown
7
Greymouth
Hokitika
Ruatapu

Kilometres
0   60
0   36
Miles

6

Castle Hill Village

Whataroa
Lake Coleridge
Darfield
Franz Josef
Mt Hutt
Methven
Fox Glacier
Staveley
Rakaia

Mount Cook
Ashburton

6

Lake Tekapo
Kimbell
Ealing
Burkes Pass
Fairlie
Geraldine

Reefton *0.1 km S of Reefton Central*
Reef Cottage *B&B and Cafe B&B Cottage with Kitchen*

Susan & Ronnie Standfield
51-55 Broadway,
Reefton

Tel (03) 732 8440
or 0800 770 440
or 027 319 5490
Fax (03) 732 8440
info@reefcottage.co.nz
www.reefcottage.co.nz

Double/Twin $100-$150
Single $95-$135 (Full breakfast)
Dinner By arrangement $10-$35
Visa MC Diners Amex Eftpos accepted
Children welcome
1 King/Twin 1 Queen 2 Double/Twin (4 |
Bathrooms: 2 Ensuite 2 Private
Queen suite has bath

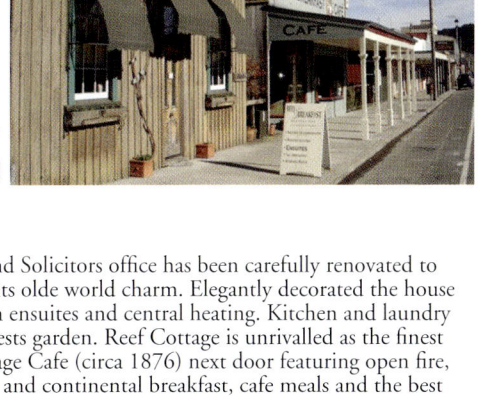

Built in 1887 this former Barrister and Solicitors office has been carefully renovated to add light and space without losing its olde world charm. Elegantly decorated the house features charming character rooms with ensuites and central heating. Kitchen and laundry facilities. Private patio, decking and guests garden. Reef Cottage is unrivalled as the finest accommodation in Reefton. Reef Cottage Cafe (circa 1876) next door featuring open fire, elegant surroundings, homecooked full and continental breakfast, cafe meals and the best espresso coffee in town.

Reefton *.1 km N of Reefton Central*
Quartz Lodge *B&B*

Paddy & Alan Rainey
78 Shiel Street,
Reefton, West Coast

Tel (03) 732 8383
or 0800 302 725
Fax (03) 732 8083
quartz-lodge@xtra.co.nz
www.quartzlodge.co.nz

Double/Twin $90-$130
Single $70-$95
(Full breakfast)
Children $25
Dinner $15-$30
Visa MC accepted
Children and pets welcome
1 King 1 Queen 1 Twin
1 Single (3 bdrm)
Bathrooms: 1 Ensuite 1 Private 1 Guest share

A friendly welcome awaits you when you arrive at Quartz Lodge superior accommodation in the heart of Reefton. Guests only entrance will take you upstairs to rooms with huge picture windows, luxurious beds, quality linen, robes and so much more. Complimentary coffee and a selection of teas are available in your spacious private lounge/dining area. Laundry service and Internet is also available upon request.We pride ourselves on making you feel at home. Quality and comfort says it all!

Karamea *84 km N of Westport*
Beachfront Farmstay B&B *B&B Farmstay*

Dianne & Russell Anderson
3578 Karamea Highway,
RD3, Karamea

Tel (03) 782 6762
or 027 249 8827
Fax (03) 782 6762
farmstay@xtra.co.nz
www.WestCoastBeachAccommodation.
co.nz

Double/Twin $160-$180
Single $140
(Special breakfast)
Children negotiable
Dinner $55
Visa MC accepted
Pet free home Children welcome
1 King 1 Queen (2 bdrm)
Bathrooms: 2 Ensuite

Our dairy farm has 2.5kms of coastline overlooking the wild Tasman Sea, a 2min walk and you will be on a sandy beach usually all to yourself. Relax in elegant rooms with every convenience and privacy. Special farmhouse breakfasts are generous, home preserving, tasty whitebait, bacon and egg dishes. Join us for delicious country cuisine, farm grown meat, fresh fish, organic vegetables, homemade desserts served with NZ wine. Our area offers day walks, unique limestone arches and caves, golf, trout fishing.

Karamea *0.5 km S of Karamea*
Karamea River Motels *Apartment with Kitchen*

Joe, Kay & Justin Beveridge
31 Bridge Street,
RD3,
Karamea

Tel 03 782 6955
or 0800 KARAMEA
Fax 03 782 6944
stay@karameamotels.co.nz
www.karameamotels.co.nz

Double/Twin $100-$160
Single $100-$160
(Continental breakfast)
Children $10 per extra child,
cot and highchair available
Extra adult $20 each
Visa MC Eftpos accepted
Children welcome
1 King/Twin 6 Queen 4 Twin (9 bdrm)
Bathrooms: 7 Private

Karamea River Motels are situated in a rural area with pituresque views. We are only 500m from the township. We have spacious and private villa accommodation suitable for all travellers.

Karamea *92 km N of westport*

Karamea Holiday Homes, Camellia Cottage and Rhodedendron Lodge
Luxury B&B Homestay Separate Suite Apartment with Kitchen Cottage with Kitchen Guest House Self contained boutique deluxe accomodation

Denise Hansen, Holiday Accomodation Managr
3 & 5 Umere Road, Market Cross, Karamea

Tel (03) 786 26641 or 021 770 192
Fax (03) 782 6647
info@karameaholidayhomes.co.nz
www.karameaholidayhomes.co.nz

Double/Twin $99-$280   Single $99-$120
(Continental breakfast provisions)
Children are welcome and catered for
Dinner not included restuarants close
Visa MC Diners Eftpos accepted
Children and pets welcome
Non smokers only
2 King/Twin 3 King 6 Single (4 bdrm)
Bathrooms: 1 Ensuite 2 Private 1 claw foot, 1 family bath, 1 Bush bath.

Camellia Cottage, Max 2 people, king sized oak bed. Claw foot bath, level access shower, character deluxe bathroom, secluded, garden, private bush bath, swing and love seat. Ramped access and fully wheelchair accessible. Rhodedenron Lodge Max 10 people, ideal families/groups, 3 bedroomed large family house. Family bathroom, shower/bath, separate toilet. Fully fenced garden, safe for children and pets. Trampoline, sand pit, swings, hammock. Both places have full kitchen and laundry facilities. Sky TV, DVD/Video, CD/tape player. Broadband internet access, phone. High chair, portacot, pets beds/bowls.

Westport - Cape Foulwind *11 km SW of Westport*

Steeples Cottage, Studio & B&B *Studio B&B, Self Contained cottage with Kitchen*

Pauline & Bruce Cargill
48 Lighthouse Road,
Cape Foulwind, Westport

Tel (03) 789 7876 or 0800 670 708
or 021 663 687
thesteeples@xtra.co.nz
www.holidayhomes.co.nz/westcoast/
foulwind/1005.html

Double/Twin $100 Single $60
(Full breakfast)
Children $20.00
Whitebait meal by arrangement
Self-contained cottage $120
Double Studio B/B $100
Children welcome
4 Queen 1 Single (4 bdrm)
Bathrooms: 3 Ensuite 1 Guest share
1 cottage ensuite studio ensuite and share B/B

Enjoy our peaceful rural accommodation, lovely gardens, magnificent sea views, rugged coastline, beautiful beaches & tranquil sunsets. Great swimming, surfing, fishing kayaking. Walk the popular seal colony walkway, dine at The Bay House Restaurant or friendly Star Tavern. Local attractions includes golf course, Coaltown Museum, jet boating, horse riding, underworld & white water rafting, bush walks unimog trips & Punakaiki National Park. We have a Jack Russell and cat.Laundry and off-street parking.Self Contained Cottage and Queen ensuite studio also available. Whitebait meals by arrangment.Internet available.

Westport *0.02 km N of Westport Central*
Havenlee Homestay *B&B Homestay*
Jan & Ian Stevenson
76 Queen Street,
Westport

Tel (03) 789 8543
or 0800 673 619
Fax (03) 789 8502
info@havenlee.co.nz
www.havenlee.co.nz

Double/Twin $110-$160
Single $100
(Continental breakfast)
Children negotiable
Visa MC accepted
Children welcome
2 Queen (2 bdrm)
Bathrooms: 1 Private 1 Guest share

Peace in Paradise - this is Havenlee: a welcoming, relaxed, spacious, quality homestay where you will feel at home right away. Centrally located, an idyllic base from which to explore the environmental wonderland, share local knowledge or just to take time out. Check out the adventure experiences and local attractions. Soak up the nature, rest and restore body and soul in the peace and quiet of a garden oasis. Generous continental-plus breakfast. Laundry facilities available. Denniston Heritage site is a "must see"

Westport - Cape Foulwind *11 km W of Westport*
Clifftop Homestay B&B *B&B Homestay Separate Suite*
Holiday Home available periodicall
Paddy & Gail Alexander
Clifftop Lane,
Cape Foulwind,
RD 2, Westport

Tel 0800 328 472
or (03) 789 5472
clifftophomestay@yahoo.com

Double/Twin $110-$150
Single $90-$120
(Continental breakfast)
Children $15 under 13yrs,
otehwise $50/$80 for separate room
Cooked breakfast by arrrangement
(whitebait in season) $15pp
Children welcome
1 Queen 1 Double/Twin 1 Single (2 bdrm)
Bathrooms: 1 Private spa bath& shower, separate toilet

We warmly invite fellow travellers to discover the magic of The Cape. Our boutique clifftop B&B offers peace and seclusion with breathtaking views of sea, Steeples and mountains. The private guest wing has a luxurious spa bathroom, and is self contained. Relax on our balcony with complementary refreshments, after exploring stunning beaches, seal colony and lighthouse walkway. Great dining nearby, (Bayhouse Cafe or country pub). Clifftop is the perfect haven. Directions - first right past Star Tavern, right into Clifftop Lane, 2nd house.

Westport - Carters Beach *3 km S of Westport*

Bellaville *B&B Separate Suite*

Marlene & Ross Burrow
No 10 State Highway 67 A,
Carters Beach,
Po Box 157, Westport

Tel (03) 789 8457
or 0800 789 845
or 027 6131 689
bellaville@xtra.co.nz

Double/Twin $100
Single $70
(Full breakfast)
Children $15
Extra adult $20
Pet free home
Children welcome
1 Queen 1 Single (1 bdrm)
Bathrooms: 1 Ensuite 1 Private Spa
Bath With separate shower

Hear the sound of waves pounding our safe swimming beach. Ouiet sunny extra large, studio room, private entrance, parking at door. No steps, no traffic noise. Private ensuite, large bathroom spa bath, shower separate toilet. Ideal family unit. Electric blankets, TV, fridge, tea & coffee and home-baking. Laundry available. Close to all activities, coastal walks, seal colony. 3mins walk to licensed cafe/bar, golf course, playground. Have travelled extensively overseas & in NZ. Don't rush, stay a day or two, you will be glad you did.

~

Westport - Carters Beach *4 km S of Westport*

Carters Beach B&B *B&B*

Sue & John Bennett
Main Road Carters Beach,
On State Highway 67A,
Westport

Tel (03) 789 8056
or 0800 783 566
027 589 8056
cartersbeachaccom@xtra.co.nz
www.bnb.co.nz/cartersbeachbb.html

Double/Twin $100-$120
Single $70-$80
(Continental breakfast)
Pet free home
Children welcome
2 Queen 1 Twin (3 bdrm)
Bathrooms: 1 Ensuite 1 Private

Carters Beach - a lovely relaxed atmosphere, Situated only 4km south of Westport. 3 minute walk to our beach, with fully licenced resturant/cafe and bar. Golf links, world famous seal colony and Bay House Cafe within a few minutes drive. Our rooms are very spacious with TV and tea/coffee making facilities. Own private entrance-ways with sun decks. Laundry facilities available by arrangement. Ideal accommodation for couples travelling together. We look forward to meeting and sharing our local knowledge with you. Cheers, Sue and John Bennett.

Westport - Ngakawau *25 km N of Westport*
Charming Creek B&B *B&B Homestay Beachside*

Gay Sweeney
24 Main Road, Ngakawau

Tel (03) 782 8007
or 027 481 6736
or 0800 to relax (867 3529)
info@bullerbeachstay.co.nz
www.bullerbeachstay.co.nz

Double/Twin $140-$165
Single $130-$150
(Full breakfast)
Children toddlers free
Dinner available see website
Swiss espresso 24 hrs - superb
Visa MC accepted
Children welcome
1 King/Twin 2 Queen (3 bdrm)
Bathrooms: 2 Ensuite

Sleep to the sound of the sea. Behind, the bush-clad high plateau and the spectacular one-day Charming Creek Walk, out front, the Tasman Sea. Try our driftwood-fired hot tub at sunset on the edge of the waves unforgettable! All suites with ensuites, massage showers and private sundecks 24 hr Swiss Espresso machine, wireless internet. Cafes and art closeby - easy day trips to Pancake Rocks, Denniston, and the Oparara Wetlands. Full breakfasts included. Dinner by arrangement. Non-smoking inside.

**Please let us know
how you enjoyed your B&B experience.
Ask your host for a comment form
or leave a comment on www.bnb.co.nz.**

Charleston *17 km S of Westport*
Birds Ferry Lodge and Ferry Man's Cottage
Luxury B&B or Lakeside Cottage
Alison & Andre Gygax
Birds Ferry Road, 8KM North Charleston, just off SHW 6, 17KM
South Westport

Tel 0800 212 207 or 021 337 217
info@birdsferrylodge.co.nz
www.birdsferrylodge.co.nz

Double/Twin $200-$350 Single $200-$350
(Full breakfast)
Cottage suitable for children
Dinner our speciality - be sure to book
Ask about our multi night specials
Visa MC accepted
1 King/Twin 1 King 3 Queen 1 Double/Twin 2 Twin
2 Single (5 bdrm)
Bathrooms: 3 Ensuite 1 Ensuite is purpose built for wheelchair use

Take time out from your journey for a few days, to relax and unwind at Birds Ferry Lodge.
We are located 4-5 hours driving time from The Glaciers, Nelson, Picton and Abel
Tasman. You will enjoy a tranquil spot with views of Mountains, Ocean and native forest.

Guests are often astounded by the remote location yet we are only 15 minutes from "town".
No landline, TV, or clock - just a wealth of peace seclusion and beauty. Lodge guests enjoy
sunsets from the heated spa, privately accessed ensuite guest accommodation, refreshments,
wireless internet, cooked breakfast. 2 friendly in-house Terriers. Dinners by arrangement,
include Quality New Zealand Wines. Home produced vegetables and free-range eggs are
used wherever possible. Homeopathic Massage Therapy also available onsite.

Ferry Man's Cottage enjoys the same views as the Lodge and is situated at the very end
of Birds Ferry Road. Complete privacy, garden bath and all the comforts of Birds Ferry
Lodge with your own kitchen and laundry facility. Sleeps 2-6 Cottage tariff includes quality
breakfast supplies. Close to Seal Colony, numerous short and longer walks, jet boating,
rafting, glow-worm cave tours, cave rafting, Punakaiki's 'pancake rocks'. Easy day trip to
Karamea and Kahurangi National Park.

Punakaiki - Barrytown *27 km N of Greymouth*
Golden Sands Homestay *Homestay*
Sue & Tom Costelloe
4 Golden Sands Road,
Barrytown,
Runanga

Tel (03) 731 1115
Fax (03) 731 1116
goldensands@paradise.net.nz

Double/Twin $95-$105
Single $55
(Continental breakfast)
Children by arrangement
Dinner by arrangement
Visa MC accepted
Children welcome
2 Queen 1 Twin (3 bdrm)
Bathrooms: 1 Ensuite 2 Private

Nestled between the Paparoa Range and Tasman Sea on the corner of Golden Sands Road Barrytown and the Greymouth-Westport Scenic Highway, Golden Sands Homestay offers a friendly atmosphere and comfortable rooms. Handy to Punakaiki, the Pancake Rocks and the Paparoa National Park to the north, with Greymouth a 25 minute drive to the south. As well as stunning views and wonderful sunsets We have internet facilities, a cosy fire in winter and a contented cat. Access and facilities for disabled people.

~

Punakaiki - Barrytown *20 km N of Greymouth*
Kallyhouse *B&B Homestay Apartment with Kitchen*
Kathleen & Alister Schroeder
13 Cargill Road,
Barrytown,
RD 1,
Westland

Tel (03) 731 1006
Fax (03) 731 1106
kallyhouse@xtra.co.nz
www.bnb.co.nz/schroeder.html

Double/Twin $115-$140
Single $75
(Continental breakfast)
Visa MC accepted
Pet free home
Children welcome
3 Queen 1 Twin (4 bdrm)
Bathrooms: 1 Ensuite
1 Guest share 1 Spa Bath

We have a new spacious home on a quiet rear section, a garden setting, native bush backdrop and sea views. We offer a self-contained flat downstairs, with queen room and twin beds in spacious living area. Kitchen, bathroom, washing machine, parking and separate entrance. Also 2 queen rooms upstairs. Breakfast with host. Punakaiki Pancake Rocks and adventure activities in Paparoa National Park, 10-minutes north. Greymouth 20 minutes south. Turn at Allnations Hotel, past 3 houses on left, up lane, house on left. Licensed

Greymouth *0.5 km N of Greymouth Central*
Ardwyn House *Homestay*

Mary Owen
48 Chapel Street,
Greymouth

Tel (03) 768 6107
Fax (03) 768 5177
ardwynhouse@hotmail.com

Double/Twin $85-$90
Single $55
(Full breakfast)
Children half price
Visa MC accepted
Children welcome
2 Queen 3 Single (3 bdrm)
Bathrooms: 1 Guest share

Ardwyn House is 3 minutes walk from the town centre in a quiet garden setting offering sea, river and town views. The house was built in the 1920s and is a fine example of an imposing residence with fine woodwork and leadlight windows, whilst being a comfortable and friendly home. Greymouth's ideally situated for travellers touring the West Coast being central with good choice of restaurants. We offer a courtesy car service to and from local travel centres and also provide off-street parking.

Greymouth *3.5 km S of Greymouth*
Maryglen Homestay *Homestay Bed and Breakfast*

Allison & Glen Palmer
20 Weenink Road,
Karoro, Greymouth

Tel 0800 627 945
or (03) 768 0706
Fax (03) 768 0599
mary@bandb.co.nz
www.bandb.co.nz

Double/Twin $115-$140
Single $90-$125
(Continental breakfast)
Children negotiable
Dinner Snack $20, Full $45
Full dinner (pre-notice)
Visa MC accepted
Children welcome
2 King/Twin 1 Queen 1 Single (3 bdrm)
Bathrooms: 3 Ensuite all private

Large Native ferns and bush surround our hillside home overlooking the sea. Our guests comment- amazing location. The sound of the surf will lull you to sleep. Off the main road, quiet location, 2 rooms have own deck entrance. Amazing sunsets, Complimentary transport available from bus/train. Let us share our wonderful coast with you as we help you plan your days-scenic tours, bush walks, Argo Bike tours, Trans-scenic train (a must), Shantytown History Village, Punakaiki Pancake Rocks. Your home away from home.

Greymouth *6 km S of Greymouth*
Sunsetview *B&B Homestay Apartment with Kitchen*

Russell & Jill Fairhall
335 Main South Road,
Greymouth 7801

Tel (03) 762 6616
Fax (03) 762 6616
sunsetview@xtra.co.nz

Double/Twin $100-$140
Single $90-$120
(Full breakfast)
Children by arrangement
Dinner by arrangement
Lunch by arrangement
Visa MC accepted
Children and pets welcome
2 King/Twin 1 King
1 Queen (4 bdrm)
Bathrooms: 2 Ensuite 1 Private

Jill & Russell welcome you to our sunny modern home with amazing sea and mountain views. We offer well-appointed superior bedrooms. Sky TV in rooms. Home-cooked meals available on request. Outdoor areas, pool and barbecue. Short walk to beach, shop approx 5 to 10 minutes walk Courtesy car available to local resturants, travel centres. Off-street parking. Downstairs apartment has two bedrooms (either can be king double or single beds) bathroom with wardrobe/dressing room. Kitchen with dining/lounge area. Own entrance with undercover parking.

~

Greymouth *5 km S of Greymouth*
Kia Ora Homestay *Homestay*

Ashley & Linda Morley
15 Keith Road,
Paroa, Greymouth

Tel (03) 762 6770
or 027 391 8210
Fax (03) 762 5850
stay@kiaora-homestay.co.nz
www.kiaora-homestay.co.nz

Double/Twin $100-$115
Single $70-$80
(Full breakfast)
Children negotiable
Dinner $40 by arrangement
Visa MC accepted
Children welcome
1 Queen 1 Twin 1 Single (3 bdrm)
Bathrooms: 1 Guest share
1 Family share

Kia Ora ("Greetings, Welcome") Set in very quiet surrounds off main road. The sound of sea and birdsong predominate. A place to relax and unwind. Large lounge, opening onto deck. Enjoy a complimentary beer, seaview and stunning sunsets. 5mins from Town Centre & historic Shantytown. Pickup from Station and Bus. There are many attractions nearby. We've travelled extensively and are able to help with forward planning. We offer you a very warm welcome. Guest comments "Excellent accommodation - best nights sleep since arriving; excellent breakfast"

Greymouth *15 km S of Greymouth*
Chapel Hill *B&B Homestay Farmstay*

Joy & John Ruesink
783 Rutherglen Road,
Paroa,
Greymouth

Tel (03) 762 6662
info@chapelhill.co.nz
www.chapelhill.co.nz

Double/Twin $90-$115
Single up to $90
(Full breakfast)
Dinner $35
Complimentary wine and nibbles
Visa MC accepted
Children welcome
2 King/Twin 1 King
2 Queen (3 bdrm)
Bathrooms: 2 Private 1 Guest share

Touch the ferns out your window! Spectacular architect-designed country stay in a rainforest setting, ONLY 15 minutes south of Greymouth on the Christchurch-Glaciers Highway. Huge logfire for those cooler evenings, free email, big comfy beds with electric blankets. Hearty country breakfasts included. Home-grown food. Dinner, wine, beer available. 40 minutes to Pancake Rocks & Hokitika Gorge, 60 minutes to Arthurs Pass. Non-smoking inside. Pets, farm and wildlife on the property. Unusual multi-level design is unsuitable for toddlers or disabled. Inquire about block or group bookings.

Greymouth *2 km S of Greymouth Post Office*
Jivana Retreat *Luxury B&B Private Chalet*

Sandie
8 Leith Crescent, Greymouth

Tel (03) 768 6102
Fax (03) 768 6108
sandie@jivanaretreat.co.nz
www.JivanaRetreat.co.nz

Double/Twin $135-$145
Single $125
(Special breakfast)
Children negotiable
Dinner $40
Private Chalet $160
Visa MC accepted
Children welcome
Free omfrared sauna
& welcoming snacks
1 King 2 Queen 1 Twin (3 bdrm)
Bathrooms: 1 Ensuite 1 Private 1 Guest share plus bush bath

Jivana Retreat is a serene, affordable, quality haven. Sandie spoils you with a homemade organic breakfast menu of your choice, served indoors in the sunny conservatory, or lush outdoors. Special diets catered for.Fun games, musical instruments, and great library.Pamper yourself with a, massage, reflexology or relaxing yoga session while you stay. Purification/Detox Health programs on request.Beaches, lakes, and rivers are all nearby. A stunning location & tranquil oasis in this mad world! Beautiful hospitality, which refreshes the soul B Jones.

Greymouth - New River *12 km S of Greymouth*
New River Bluegums B & B *B&B Farmstay Cottage with Kitchen*

Sharon & Michael Pugh
985 Main South Road,
New River, Greymouth

Tel (03) 762 6678
or 0274 385 324
or 0276 644 265
Fax (03) 762 6678
mail@bluegumsnz.com
www.bluegumsnz.com

Double/Twin $135-$180
Single $95-$135
(Full breakfast)
Children $25
Dinner by arrangement
Visa MC accepted
1 King 2 Queen 2 Double/Twin
2 Single (3 bdrm)
Bathrooms: 2 Ensuite 1 Private

The Pugh family welcome you to the comfort of their log and stone home on a small farm. The homestead offers a king room with balcony. Two luxurious self-contained cottages, superbly appointed, (double-glazing & heat pumps) overlooking the tennis court. Feed the sheep, cattle or Piggy (Kunekune) and Coco (labrador). 10 min walk to beach & 5 min drive to Shantytown. "Beautiful setting! Delightful home! Your relaxed and welcome manner made us feel like we were somewhere special, we certainly were, thank you!" G&K Guestbook.

Hokitika *2 km N of Hokitika*
Hokitika Heritage Lodge *Luxury B&B Homestay Cottage with Kitchen*

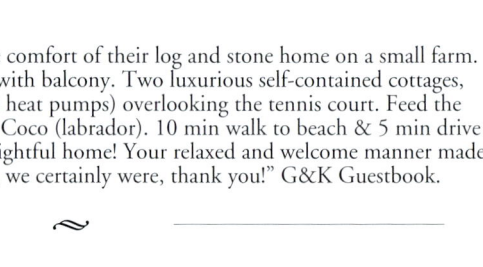

Dianne & Chris Ward
46 Alpine View, Hokitika

Tel (03) 755 7357
or 0800 261 949
or 027 437 1254
Fax (03) 755 7357
hokitikaheritage@xtra.co.nz
www.hokitikaheritagelodge.co.nz

Double/Twin $210-$250
Single $210-$210 (Full breakfast)
Dinner by arrangement
Visa MC accepted
Not suitable for children
Smoking area inside
1 King/Twin 1 King
3 Queen 1 Single (5 bdrm)
Bathrooms: 3 ensuites in Bank House; 1 private in Gatehouse Cottage

NZ hospitality at its best! Our Lodge overlooks Tasman Sea, Hokitika, Southern Alps. Bank House provides full B&B. Three spacious ensuite bedrooms; guest lounge. Historic, stylish decor used throughout the Lodge to reflect NZ history. Gold, Jade and Heritage themed rooms. Gatehouse Cottage is self-catering. Spacious. Includes 2 beautiful bedrooms, private bathroom, lounge, dining and full kitchen. Dianne, (Literacy Teacher) and Chris, (Property Consultant & Rotarian) enjoy chatting with guests over a welcoming drink and home-baking. Broadband Internet, wireless network, television and dinners are available.

Hokitika *3 km S of Hokitika*
Meadowbank *Rural Homestay*
Alison & Tom Muir
Takutai Road,
RD 3,
Hokitika

Tel (03) 755 6723
Fax (03) 755 6723

Double/Twin $90
Single $60
(Full breakfast)
Children half price
Dinner by arrangement
Children welcome
1 Double/Twin 2 Single (2 bdrm)
Bathrooms: 1 Guest share

Tom and Alison welcome you to their lifestyle property, situated just minutes south of Hokitika. Our large home, which we share with 2 cats, is modern, sunny and warm, and has a large garden. Nearby we have the beach, excellent golf-links, Lake Mahinapua, paddleboat, river, and of course Hokitika, with all its attractions. Directions: travel south 2km from south end of Hokitika Bridge on SH6, turn right - 200 metres on right. Northbound traffic - look for sign 1km north of Golf-links and Paddleboat.

~

Hokitika - Upper Kokatahi *28 km E of Hokitika*
Sheridan Farmstay *Farmstay Cottage with Kitchen*
Trish & Terry Sheridan
Middle Branch Road,
Upper Kokatahi
RD 1,
Hokitika

Tel (03) 755 7967
tpsheridan@xtra.co.nz

Double/Twin $120
Single $70
(Full breakfast)
Children negotiable
Dinner $30 by arrangement
Self-contained cottage from $75
Children welcome
1 Queen 2 Double/Twin
3 Twin (6 bdrm)
Bathrooms: 1 Ensuite 2 Guest share 1 Family share

Welcome to our 1000 acre dairy farm at the top of Kokatahi Valley 28km east of Hokitika. Numerous day walks, 3 rivers with trout fishing and kayaking and Lake Kaniere are all minutes away. Share our home with our three lovely cats or stay in our self-contained unit. We enjoy meeting people and love travelling. Terry enjoys current affairs and all sports while Trish is happy in the kitchen or garden. Enjoy dining with us in peaceful surroundings.

Hokitika *7 km E of Hokitika*
Riverside Villa *B&B Homestay*
Margaret & Alan Stevens
185 Woodstock-Rimu Road,
RD 3, Hokitika

Tel (03) 755 6466
or 027 437 1515
enquiries@riversidevilla.co.nz
www.riversidevilla.co.nz

Double/Twin $120-$140
Single $80-$80
(Full breakfast)
Children negotiable
Glow-worm tour after dark
Visa MC accepted
Pet free home
Children welcome
1 Queen 1 Twin (2 bdrm)
Bathrooms: 1 Ensuite 1 Private
Robes provided

Our home is right on the riverbank in the historical goldmining area of Woodstock 7km from Hokitika. With fishing on the boundary, awesome river and mountain views and lovely gardens it's a great place to stay. We are close to the beautiful scenic attractions of the area and centrally placed for day trips to the glaciers or Punakaiki. In the evening, stroll through the bush to our own glow-worm grotto. Great breakfasts and home baking. Popular local restaurants close by for dinner. Warm hospitality assured.

Hokitika *2 km E of Hokitika*
Woodland Glen Lodge *Luxury B&B*
Janette & Laurie Anderson
96 Hau Hau Road,
Blue Spur, Hokitika

Tel (03) 755 5063
or 0800 361 361 (NZ Only)
or 027 201 6126
Fax (03) 755 5063
l.anderson@xtra.co.nz
www.hokitika.net

Double/Twin $180-$220
Single $150-$180
(Full breakfast)
Visa MC Diners Amex
Eftpos accepted
Not suitable for children
5 Queen 2 Twin 2 Single (5 bdrm)
Bathrooms: 3 Ensuite 1 Guest share

Our 6500 square foot lodge is located on 21 acres and is surrounded in native kahikatea trees providing quiet and privacy. A great place for a retreat or time out. Most guests base themselves in Hokitika for visits to the glaciers and Punakaiki, allow 2 nights. We welcome you to Woodland Glen Lodge, we are widely travelled and have many experiences to share with you. Laurie is a retired police officer and commercial pilot, Janette is a health professional with a keen interest in quilting.

Hokitika *1 km N of Hokitika*
Top View B&B *B&B*
Lin & Colin Jackson
24 Whitcombe Terrace,
Hokitika

Tel (03) 755 7060
or 027 381 7206
or 0800 600 503
Fax (03) 755 7060
topview24@clear.net.nz
www.topview.co.nz

Double/Twin $110-$120
Single $80
(Full breakfast)
Children price depending age
Reduced rates for longer stays
Visa MC accepted
Pet free home
Children welcome
2 Queen 2 Twin (3 bdrm)
Bathrooms: 1 Ensuite 1 Guest share Bath and shower in guest share bathroom

We offer you a place to relax with a superb view of mountains, sea and sunsets from the lounge/breakfast room. Colin and Lin are retired farmers with many interests including Lions, Diabetes Societies, outdoor activities. Can provide Whitebait nets, Fishing Rods. We look forward to your company. From the main road north, turn at the Airport sign on Tudor Street, take the next left into Bonar Drive to the top of the hill on to Whitcombe Terrace, turn left.

Hokitika Central *1 km E of Post Office*
Amberlea B & B *B&B*
Sharyn & Butch Symons
146 Gibson Quay,
Hokitika
7810

Tel (03) 755 7346
or 027 697 1130
Fax (03) 755 7349
rpsmsymons@hotmail.com

Double/Twin $120-$140
Single $100-$120
(Full breakfast)
Children welcome - under 5yrs $10,
Under 12yrs $30
Children and pets welcome
3 Queen 1 Twin (4 bdrm)
Bathrooms: 2 Ensuite 1 Guest share
All bathrooms have showers

Sharyn and Butch along with their Bichons and cats invite you to their quiet friendly home situated beside the Hokitika River. Relax in the lovely gardens or watch the sunsets over the Tasman Sea and the Southern Alps. We are a five minute walk from the town centre and all of its tourist attractions, resturants and beach. Visit the Hokitika Gorge. Visit our great greenstone, paua, gold and ruby rock shops or relax at the beach or lakes enjoying the clean air.

Hokitika - Blue Spur *10 km N of Hokitika*
Bushline Retreat Bed and Breakfast *B&B*

Pete and Sue James
4 Humphrey's Gully West,
RD 2,
Hokitika

Tel (03) 755 6603
bushlinebnb@xtra.co.nz
www.bushline.co.nz

Double/Twin $100-$170
Single $80-$120
(Full breakfast)
Children over 5 $25
Children under 5 free
Visa MC accepted
Children welcome
1 King 3 Queen (4 bdrm)
Bathrooms: 2 Ensuite 2 Guest share

Beautiful quiet native bush setting 10 minutes North of Hokitika on the Blue Spur Tourist Drive. Views to the Tasman Sea, bush walks and a spectacular glow worm gully 2 minutes walk from the house. With spacious rooms and living areas, an outdoor spa and kitchen available for the use of guests, Bushline Retreat gives the feeling of true retreat at the end of a day's drive.

Ruatapu *12 km S of Hokitika*
Berwick's Hill *B&B Homestay*

Eileen & Roger Berwick
106 Ruatapu-Ross Road,
State Highway 6,
RD 3, Ruatapu,
Hokitika

Tel (03) 755 7876
Fax (03) 755 7870
berwicks@xtra.co.nz
www.berwicks.co.nz

Double/Twin $100-$130
Single $60-$80
(Full breakfast)
Dinner $40 by arrangement
Visa MC accepted
2 King/Twin 1 Queen (2 bdrm)
Bathrooms: 1 Ensuite 1 Private
Bath in ensuite

Welcome to Berwick's Hill. We offer you a warm and relaxed stay in our comfortable home. Magnificent views of the Tasman Sea and the Southern Alps are seen from the main living areas. Experience the sunsets and sunrises. We are close to Lake Mahinapua, bush walks, the beach and golf course.On our hobby farm we have sheep ,cattle, and one Farm Dog also hens. we share our home with our cat and our house dog.

Whataroa - South Westland *13 km N of Whataroa/10 mins*
Mt Adam Lodge *B&B Homestay Farmstay*

Elsa & Mac MacRae
State Highway 6,
Tetaho,
Whataroa,
South Westland

Tel (03) 753 4030
or 0800 675 137 NZ only
mtadamlodge@paradise.net.nz
www.mountadamlodge.co.nz

Double/Twin $125-$150
Single $105-$115
(Continental breakfast)
Fold-away bed $25extra
Visa MC Eftpos accepted
Children welcome
2 Queen 1 Double/Twin
2 Twin 2 Single (7 bdrm)
Bathrooms: 5 Ensuite 2 Guest share

If you're wanting to escape the crowds in the busy tourist centres then we are an ideal place for you to stay. Just a short 35 minute drive north of Franz Josef Glacier. We are situated on our farm at the foot of Mt Adam surrounded by farmlands and beautiful native bush. Our lodge offers comfortable accommodation and a fully licensed restaurant. You can stroll along the river bank and the farm tracks meeting our variety of animals along the way.

Franz Josef *5 km N of Franz Josef Glacier*
Ribbonwood Retreat *Luxury B&B Cottage with Kitchen*

Julie Wolbers & Jo Crofton
26 Greens Road,
Franz Josef Glacier

Tel (03) 752 0072
ribbon.wood@xtra.co.nz
www.ribbonwood.net.nz

Double/Twin $180-$275
(Full breakfast)
Dinner A variety of restaurants
in Franz Josef village
Visa MC accepted
Not suitable for children
1 King 2 Queen 1 Single (3 bdrm)
Bathrooms: 1 Ensuite
1 Private 1 Family share
Luxurious tiled bathrooms,
private bathroom next to room

Sleep deeply breathing country fresh air! Enjoy views of the forests, glaciers and mountains from your room or cottage with private deck situated in landscaped garden. Ribbonwood Retreat is just minutes from the Franz Josef village and ten minutes drive to the glacier. Jo is a wildlife ranger with extensive knowledge of the local plants and birds and Julie is a school teacher, both trampers and bird enthusiasts. Breakfast specialty is fresh fruit crepes, free range eggs, homemade bread.

Fox Glacier *0.5 km W of Fox Glacier*
The Homestead *B&B Farmstay*
Noeleen & Kevin Williams
PO Box 25, Cook Flat Road, Fox Glacier

Tel (03) 751 0835
Fax (03) 751 0805
foxhomestead@slingshot.co.nz

Double/Twin $140-$180
(Full breakfast)
Cooked breakfast $7pp
Pet free home
Not suitable for children
1 King/Twin 1 King 1 Queen (3 bdrm)
Bathrooms: 2 Ensuite 1 Private

Kevin and Noeleen, welcome you to our 2200 acre beef cattle and sheep farm. Beautiful native bush-clad mountains surround on 3 sides, and we enjoy a view of Mt Cook.

Our spacious 105 year old character home, built for Kevin's grandparents, has fine stained glass windows. The breakfast room overlooks peaceful pastures to the hills, and you are served home-made yoghurt, jams, marmalade, scones etc, with a cooked breakfast if desired.

The guest lounge, with its beautiful wooden panelled ceiling, has an open fire for cool autumn nights.

A rural retreat within walking distance of village facilities, with Matheson (Mirror Lake) and glacier nearby. It is our pleasure to help you with helihikes, helicopter scenic flights and glacier walks.

Unsuitable for small children. Bookings recommended. Smoke-free.

Directions: On Cook Flat Road, fifth house on right, 400 metres back off road before church.

Fox Glacier *20 km S of Franz Josef*
Roaring Billy Homestay *B&B Homestay*

Kathy & Billy
PO Box 16,
21 State Highway 6,
Fox Glacier

Tel (03) 751 0815
Fax (03) 751 0815
billy@xtra.co.nz

Double/Twin $95-$135
Single $90-$135
(Special breakfast)
Visa MC accepted
Not suitable for children
1 King/Twin 1 Double/Twin
1 Twin (2 bdrm)
Bathrooms: 1 Private 1 Guest share

Welcome to the comfort, warmth and hospitality of our 2 storey home. Our livingroom, kitchen, diningroom and veranda are upstairs and lined with local timbers, with 360-degree views of glacier valley, mountains, farms and the township. We're the closest homestay to the glacier and 2 minutes walk to all eating and tourist facilities. We are happy to book your local activities. The bus goes past our home. We offer a special cooked vegetarian breakfast. We have 1 cat, Koko the Tonkinese.

~

Fox Glacier *1 km W of Fox Glacier*
Fox Glacier Homestay *Homestay*

Eunice & Michael Sullivan
64 Cook Flat Road,
Fox Glacier

Tel (03) 751 0817
Fax (03) 751 0817
euni@xtra.co.nz

Double/Twin $90-$120
Single $80-$90
(Continental breakfast)
Children and pets welcome
1 Queen 1 Double/Twin
1 Twin 1 Single (3 bdrm)
Bathrooms: 1 Family share

Eunice and Michael are third generation farming and tourism family. We have 3 grown children, 1 dog (Ruff) and 3 cats (Bushy Tail, Sabrina & Tig). Our grandparents were founders of the Fox Glacier Hotel. We are a couple who enjoy meeting people and would like to share the joys of living in our little paradise (rain and all). Our home is surrounded by a large garden and has views of the mountains and Mt Cook. A 5 minute walk from township.

Fox Glacier *3 km W of Fox Glacier*

Fox Glacier Mountainview B&B *B&B Homestay Cottage with Kitchen*

Karen Simpson (K2)

1 Williams Drive, Fox Glacier, West Coast, South Island.

Tel (03) 751 0770   Fax (03) 751 0774
info@foxglaciermountainview.co.nz
www.foxglaciermountainview.co.nz

Double/Twin $160-$185 Single $160 (Full breakfast)
Children welcome. Portacot available.
TIANZ member. Internet facility available.   TV in all rooms.
Visa MC Eftpos accepted
3 King (3 bdrm)
Bathrooms: 3 Ensuite 1 Private

Welcome to my peaceful hideaway set on 8 acres of pure nature at its best. This modern country home has it all. With wide-open landscape, breathtaking views of Mt Cook and Mt Tasman, and surrounded by bush-clad hills with magnificent reflections on my own special pond.

I have a cosy self-contained cottage (for 2) with basic kitchenette facility and en-suite. Inside my home, are en-suited super king/twin bedrooms, also a super king/twin bedroom with a private bathroom. Three bedrooms have private access. There are two bedrooms, with an adjoining bathroom between, ideal for a family of four.

The area is ecologically diverse, from the West Coast's sub-temperate rain forest, to one of the lowest flowing Glaciers in the Southern Hemisphere at Fox Glacier.

Situated near one of the most photographed mirror lakes in New Zealand (Lake Matheson), and just a short distance further, is access to the wild West Coast (Gillespie's Beach) with long tracks of rugged coastline, which is home to many New Zealand fur seal colonies. From walking adventures to adrenaline activities, I can happily assist enhancing your Glacier experience to the full.

It's truly "a piece of paradise" - I'd like to share the comfort and individual uniqueness with you.

I have travelled extensively in New Zealand as part of my career, gaining a wealth of tourism knowledge, and can help in your travel plans (where to go, or what to do and see) around the rest of our beautiful country
Please check on my website for booking availability, and driving directions.

Fox Glacier *.2 km N of Fox Glacier*
The White Fox B&B *B&B Homestay*

Jane Wellard & Gary Scott
4 State Highway 6,
PO Box 82, Fox Glacier

Tel (03) 751 0717
or 027 306 6759
or 027 738 7452
or (03) 751 0717
Fax (03) 751 0717
thewhitefox@slingshot.co.nz
www.thewhitefoxbandb.co.nz

Double/Twin $140-$170
Single $120-$150
(Continental breakfast)
Children bnegotiable by age
Visa MC accepted
Children and pets welcome
1 Queen 1 Single (1 bdrm)
Bathrooms: 1 Ensuite

Relax & enjoy the warmth & hospitality of a genuine NZ family home. Gary is a 4th generation local & we have considerable knowledge to assist our guests. We offer an easy to find location. Your room has a superior comfort bed, quality linen, electric blankets, TV & modern ensuite. Wake to the aroma of freshly baked bread & enjoy a generous Continental breakfast. We share our sunny home with 2 young daughters Meghan & Isla, Jess the Border Collie & Irish the Tabby Cat.

Take it easy
Don't try to travel too far in one day.

Canterbury

Reefton

Inchbonnie

Kaikoura

Hanmer Springs

7

1

Culverden

Hawarden

Castle Hill Village

73

Amberley

Oxford

Rangiora

Ohoka

Kaiapoi

Darfield

Christchurch, see next page

Mt Hutt

72

Methven

Staveley

Okains Bay

Rakaia

Banks Peninsula

Akaroa

1

Ashburton

Akaroa Harbour

0   Kilometres   40

0   Miles   24

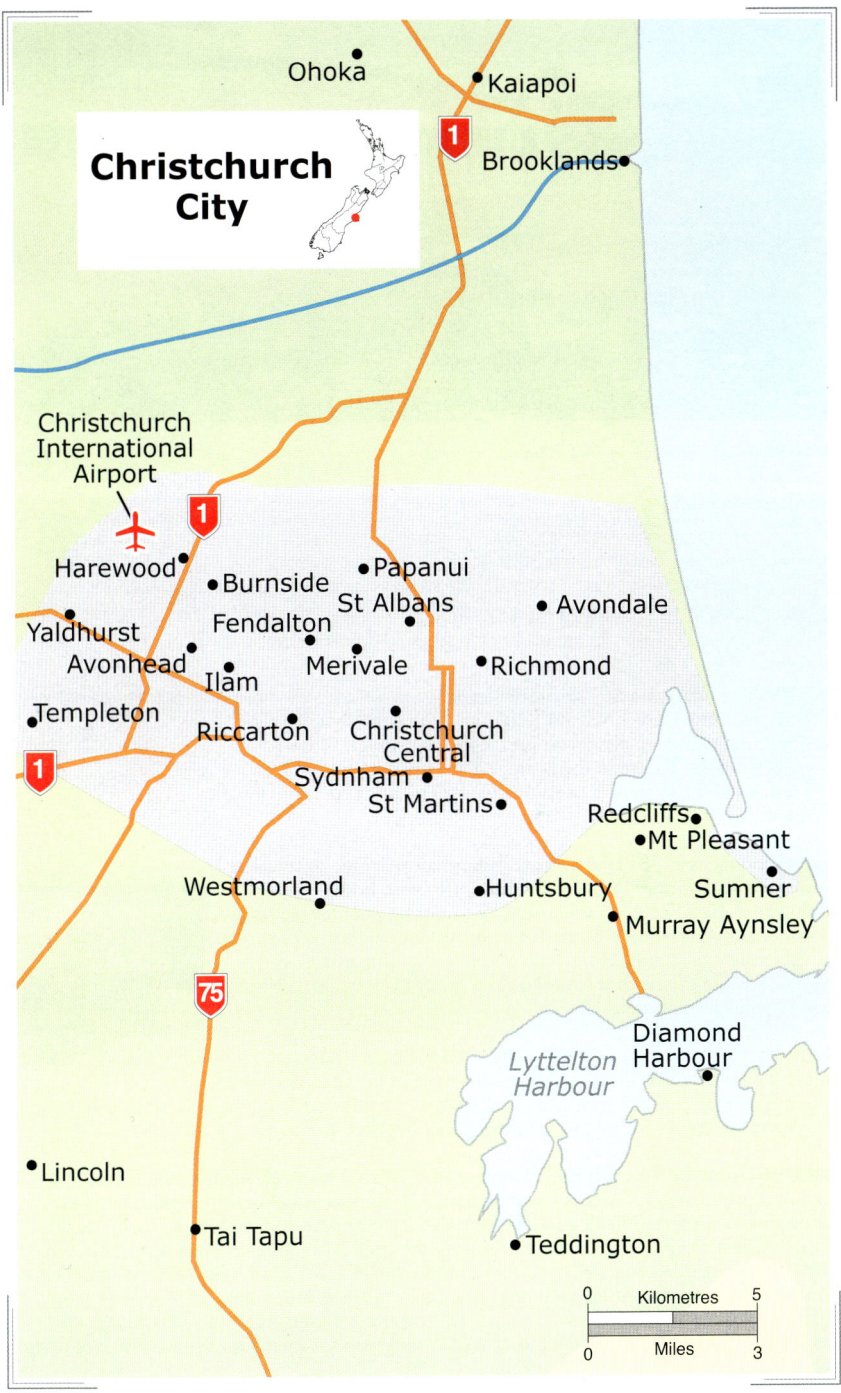

Christchurch City

Ohoka
Kaiapoi
Brooklands

Christchurch International Airport
Harewood
Burnside
Papanui
St Albans
Avondale
Yaldhurst
Fendalton
Avonhead
Merivale
Richmond
Ilam
Templeton
Riccarton
Christchurch Central
Sydnham
St Martins
Redcliffs
Mt Pleasant
Westmorland
Huntsbury
Sumner
Murray Aynsley
Diamond Harbour
Lyttelton Harbour
Lincoln
Tai Tapu
Teddington

0   Kilometres   5
0   Miles   3

Kaikoura *130 km S of Blenheim*

Approved

Bay-View *Homestay*
Margaret Woodill
296 Scarborough Street, Kaikoura
Tel (03) 319 5480 Fax (03) 319 7480
bayviewhomestay@xtra.co.nz   www.bnb.co.nz/bayviewkaikoura.html

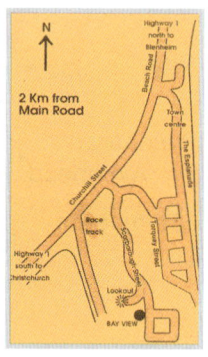

Double/Twin $120 Single $70 (Full breakfast)
Children under 14 $30   Dinner $30   Children and pets welcome
1 Queen 1 Twin 1 Single (3 bdrm)
Bathrooms: 1 Ensuite 1 Private 1 Guest share

Our spacious family home on Kaikoura Peninsula has splendid mountain and sea views and is exceptionally quiet. Only 5 minutes from the Kaikoura township, off the main highway south. The house nestles in an acre of colourful garden and there is plenty of off-street parking.

A guest lounge is available or you are more than welcome to socialise with the host. Laundry facilities and tea/coffee with home-made baking available. There is a solar heated swimming pool for guests use. Traditional breakfast with home-baked bread, muesli, home preserves, available early as required for whale/dolphin watching guests. Enjoy breakfast in the dining area or out on the sunny deck whilst taking in the magnificent mountain view.

We book local activities and happily meet bus or train. Margaret, your friendly host, has lived in the area for most of her life. She has a grown family of 4, and 7 grandchildren. Margaret enjoys gardening, bowls, sewing and choir. She especially enjoys warmly welcoming guests into her home.

"Let Our Home be Your Home". Guests comments: "This B&B is an unforgettable memory for me in NZ 5 weeks travel" (Japan). "Beautiful place, beautiful food, fabulous hospitality, Margaret. Thank you for opening up your home and welcoming us. Be back again" (Wellington). "Thank you for meeting the train and showing us the area. You were highly recommended and we absolutely endorse this" (UK). "Many thanks for your generous hospitality. You and your lovely home are a credit to B&B Homestays" (UK). "The most amazing breakfast in all of New Zealand. The views are amazing too and so is Margaret's hospitality" (Australia). "We felt like family! Thank you for such a lovely visit and wonderful, delicious meals. We thank you a million!" (USA).

Kaikoura - Oaro *22 km S of Kaikoura*
Waitane Homestay *B&B Homestay Cottage with Kitchen*

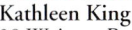

Kathleen King
38 Waitane Road,
Oaro RD 2,
Kaikoura

Tel (03) 319 5494
Fax (03) 319 5524
kathleen.king@xtra.co.nz

Double/Twin $85-$95
Single $50
(Full breakfast)
Children $25
Dinner $25 by arrangement
Visa MC accepted
Children and pets welcome
1 Double/Twin 4 Single (3 bdrm)
Bathrooms: 2 Private

Waitane is 48 acres, close to the sea and looking north to the Kaikoura Peninsula. Enjoy coastal walks to the Haumuri Bluff with bird watching, fossil hunting etc, or drive to Kaikoura along our beautiful rocky coast. This is a mild climate and we grow citrus and sub-tropical fruits, mainly feijoas. Guest room in house has 2 single beds. Self-contained unit has 2 bedrooms, sleeps 4. 1 friendly cat lives here. Join me for dinner - fresh vegies, home preserves and home-made ice cream.

Kaikoura *1 km N of Kaikoura Central*
Bendamere House *B&B*

Kerry & Julie Howden
37 Adelphi Terrace,
Kaikoura

Tel (03) 319 5830
or 0800 107 770
Fax (03) 319 7337
bendamerehouse@xtra.co.nz
www.bendamere.co.nz

Double/Twin $150-$200
Single $130-$170
(Continental breakfast)
Children Negotiable
Visa MC Diners Eftpos accepted
Children welcome
2 King 3 Queen 2 Twin
3 Single (5 bdrm)
Bathrooms: 5 Ensuite

Kaikoura's Bendamere House B&B offers you 5 quality ensuite rooms all with private balconies where you can enjoy the breathtaking ocean and mountain views. Relax in our expansive lawns and rose gardens or take a short stroll into the Kaikoura township .All rooms have sleepyhead beds, silent fridges,heat pumps, tea/coffee/bathrobes and more. Wireless Internet and laundry facilities as well as secure offstreet parking.

Kaikoura *4 km NE of Kaikoura town centre*
The Point *B&B*

Peter & Gwenda Smith
Fyffe Quay,
Kaikoura

Tel (03) 319 5422
Fax (03) 319 7422
pointsmith@xtra.co.nz
www.pointbnb.co.nz

Double/Twin $100-$130
Single $80-$90
(Continental breakfast)
Visa MC accepted
2 Queen (2 bdrm)
Bathrooms: 2 Ensuite

We offer a warm and friendly welcome to our home, which we share with our two daughters Sarah and Kate. Enjoy the quiet, unique location of our farmhouse built in the late 1800's. Our 90 acres of farmland is part of the Kaikoura Peninsula, on the waterfront with spectacular views of the sea and Kaikoura Mountains. Ideally situated for walking around Kaikoura Peninsula and the Seal Colony. Short walk to top Kaikoura restaurants. We run daily Sheep Shearing Shows; have farm dogs and a cat.

Kaikoura *183 km N of Christchurch*
Nikau Lodge *B&B*

John & Lilla Fitzwater
53 Deal Street, Kaikoura (central)

Tel (03) 319 6973
or 021 682 076
or 021 229 9188
or 021 332 076
Fax (03) 319 6973
stay@NikauLodge.com
www.NikauLodge.com

Double/Twin $165-$225
Single $110-$195
(Full breakfast)
Visa MC Eftpos accepted
Pet free home
Not suitable for children
1 King/Twin 5 Queen
1 Single (7 bdrm)
Bathrooms: 6 Ensuite 1 Private

Conveniently located in the heart of Kaikoura close to SH1 with magnificent hilltop views of sea and mountains, Nikau Lodge offers high quality affordable B&B accommodation. 5 minutes walk takes you to Kaikoura's main street where you can enjoy local rock lobster. Relax in the hot-tub or garden with a glass of wine and gaze at the stars and snow-capped mountains. Internet access, Sky/TV, complimentary tea/coffee, in-room TV/movies. We welcome the opportunity to make your stay enjoyable and memorable.

Kaikoura *1 km NW of Kaikoura Central*
Driftwood Villa B&B *B&B Deluxe B&B*

Suzy & Chris Valkhoff
166A Beach Road,
Kaikoura

Tel (03) 319 7116
or 0272 217 675
Fax (03) 319 7116
stayatdriftwoodvilla@xtra.co.nz
www.driftwoodvilla.co.nz

Double/Twin $140-$180
Single $95-$125
(Full breakfast)
Children $10
Full use of kitchen
Visa MC accepted
Children welcome
1 King 3 Queen 1 Twin
4 Single (4 bdrm)
Bathrooms: 4 Ensuite

This one looks good! Many guests before you have found this the ideal place and atmosphere to relax. Guests enjoy the freedom of the whole house while the hosts are unobtrusive and have separate accommodation. Facilities include wireless internet and computer, spacious lounge, Jacuzzi, garden and fully equipped kitchen. Conveniently located opposite Kaikoura Day Spa (www.ibas.co.nz)and a short walk to shops and supermarket. Needless to say that all our rooms are of a good standard and decorated with warmth and style.

Kaikoura *1 km N of Central Kaikoura*
Admiral Creighton B&B *Luxury B&B*

Yvonne & Tony Steadman
191 Beach Road,
Kaikoura

Tel 0800 742 622
or (03) 319 7111
Fax (03) 319 7111
admiral.creighton.b2b@ihug.co.nz
www.admiral-creighton.com

Double/Twin $125-$175
(Full breakfast)
Visa MC Amex accepted
Not suitable for children
1 King/Twin 4 Queen (5 bdrm)
Bathrooms: 3 Ensuite 2 Private

Tops in Service. Best in Value. Superior in Comfort and style. You will love staying at this lovely B&B. On arrival enjoy a complimentary wine or beer as you soak up the magnificent vista of the Seaward Kaikoura Mountains. Continental breakfast, with fully cooked available.Feed the trout, eels and ducks in our stream boundry. Spacious living. Pick up and drop off transport available.Level off street parking. Our Cockatoo Creighton will welcome you warmly. On line booking at www.admiral-creighton.com

Canterbury

Kaikoura *130 km S of Blenheim*

A Rest-n-Kai *B&B*
Carmel Tindall
5 Fyffe Ave,
Kaikoura

Tel (03) 319 7330
cartin@slingshot.co.nz
www.arestnkai.co.nz

Double/Twin $100-$120
Single $40-$65
(Full breakfast)
Children $20
Babies $10
Pet free home
Children welcome
1 Queen 1 Single (2 bdrm)
Bathrooms: 1 Ensuite 1 Family share

Welcome to my home where I offer a Rest-n-Kai. Kai meaning food in Maori. I am a retired nurse and still enjoy caring for people. The home is new and comfortable, with lovely mountain views from the main rooms and external access from the large bedroom. A short walk into the township and other attractions including Whalewatch and Dolphin Encounter. I am happy to assist guests with directions and bookings. Many complimentary comments in visitors book indicate satisfaction with A Rest-n-Kai.

Kaikoura - Mangamaunu *15 km N of Kaikoura*

SurfWatch *B&B Separate Suite Cottage with Kitchen*
Lynn & David Robinson
1137 State Hwy One,
Kaikoura
7340

Tel (03) 319 6611
or 027 616 2903
(03) 319 6658
Fax 03-319-6658
bnb@ofu.co.nz
www.surfwatchbnb.com

Double/Twin $120-$225
Single $120-$225
(Continental breakfast provisions)
Visa MC accepted
Children welcome
1 King 1 Queen 1 Single (2 bdrm)
Bathrooms: 1 Ensuite 1 Private

Kia Ora! The wow factor is here. Five acres of tranquil rural country setting with stunning views overlooking the Pacific Ocean. Quiet and relaxing, melt away the city hustle-bustle in our spacious lawn and gardens. From the OceanView Ensuite you can watch dolphins play while Sharkeys Cottage is nestled in the garden. Both have kitchenettes, private entrances, parking, and are uniquely decorated with local wood and stone. Breakfast at your leisure. Wireless broadband. Lynn, David, Jessica (15) and dogface Layla look forward to meeting you.

Kaikoura *130 km S of Blenheim*

Churchill Park Lodge *B&B Separate Suite*

Gordon & Priscilla Wright
34 Churchill Street, Kaikoura, Marlborough

Tel (03) 319 5526 or 0800 363 690
cplodge@ihug.co.nz
www.churchillparklodge.co.nz

Double/Twin $130 Single $100 (Continental breakfast)
Children by arrangement
Extra guests Add $30 per night
Visa MC accepted
1 Queen 1 Double/Twin 1 Twin (2 bdrm)
Bathrooms: 2 Ensuite

Churchill park lodge is conveniently located in central Kaikoura on SHWY1 (Churchill street) on the hill capturing the magnificent Kaikoura mountain and sea views.

We welcome you to our purpose built, self contained upstair units with ensuite bathrooms (the double ensuite is compact but well appointed). We get many guests comment on how comfy the beds are. The units have T.V., fridge, lounge settee, dining suite, balcony table and chairs, heating and electric blankets with tea and coffee making facilities including plunger coffee. There is also off street parking and a private guest entrance with laundry facilities available. We serve a continental breakfast to your room for you to enjoy at your leisure. We believe the sea and mountain views from your room are unbeatable in Kaikoura.

Our B&B is only 5 minutes walk through Churchill park to the town centre. Where you will find shops, restaurants, cafes, the information centre and beach.

Cilla & Gordon are a down to earth "Kiwi" couple who are keen fishermen. You are welcome to join us on any trips we have planned, checking the lobster pots, catching a fish by boat or surfcasting from the beach. Also the local stream has many brown trout which are very challenging to catch.

We have two friendly dogs (who do not have access to the guest area) "Miss Spanky" a fun Bichon/Tibetan terrier X and "Xena" an aging pointer. We can book local activities or tours, and will happily meet you at the bus or train.

Canterbury

Kaikoura *5 km N of Kaikoura*
Ardara Lodge *B&B Cottage with Kitchen*

Winnie & Phil Hood
233 Schoolhouse Road, RD 1, Kaikoura

Tel (03) 319 5736 or 0800 226 164
ardara@xtra.co.nz
www.ardaralodge.com

Double/Twin $110-$150 Single $110-$140
(Continental breakfast)
Children By arrangement Cottage $165-$250
Visa MC accepted
Children welcome
7 Queen 3 Twin 4 Single (7 bdrm)
Bathrooms: 5 Ensuite 1 Private

After and exhilarating day exploring the natural splendours of Kaikoura unwind in the tranquility of Ardara Lodge.

You will enjoy a relaxed and peaceful stay in a beautiful rural setting near the magnificent Kaikoura mountains. Relax on the decks and enjoy Winnie's colourful garden which complements the panoramic veiw. Enjoy the outdoor hot tub (spa), veiw the Kaikoura mountains by day and the stars by night or read a book in the guest lounge.

The cottage has an upstairs bedroom with a queen and two single beds. Downstairs there is a bedroom with a queen bed, a bathroom with a shower and a lounge, kitchen, dining room. The deck is private with a great veiw of the Mountains. It has been very poplular with groups, families and honeymoon couples. The house has ensuite bathrooms with queen beds, plus a two bedroom unit, all with t.v, fridge, settee and coffee/tea facilities. You have you own private entrance and you are welcome to come and go as you please. We offer laundry facilities, off street parking and a courtesy car from the bus/train. There is an excellent restaurant, Donnegal House, within walking distance.

Phil owns a construction company based in Blenheim and Winnie was an office assistant before purchasing Ardara Lodge. Phil's hobbies are fishing, diving, motor racing, squash and harriers. Winnie's hobbies include gardening, lace making, embroidery and fishing. We like meeting people and look forward to your company.

Directions: Driving North, 4kms from Kaikoura on State Highway 1, turn left into Schoolhouse Road and continue 1.5kms until our sign.

Hanmer Springs *1 km SW of Hanmer Springs*

Albergo Hanmer Lodge & Alpine Villas *Luxury B&B Separate Suite*
Apartment with Kitchen Cottage with Kitchen B&B & Self-contained

Bascha & Beat Blattner
88 Rippingale Road, Hanmer Springs

Toll-Free 0800 342 313 **Ph/fax** (03) 315 7428
albergo@paradise.net.nz   www.albergohanmer.com
Check web for packages

Double/Twin $160-$250 Single $120 (Special breakfast)
Dinner by prior arrangement   Villa $260-$525
Visa MC Diners Amex Eftpos accepted
Pet free home Children welcome
3 King/Twin 1 King 1 Queen 2 Single (4 bdrm)
Bathrooms: 4 Ensuite

BREAKFAST - WELLNESS - CUISINE

Arrive at Albergo to blitz your senses in the fresh n' fun eclectic interiors with whimsical touches. **Dramatic alpine views** from all windows. **Stretch out on super king beds**, with TV/fridge/tea & coffee, and spacious ensuites (great water pressure) - choose the spa one for that bubble bath delight! European comforts for all seasons: u/floor heat, double glaze, aircon. Relax in cosy corners or wander out to the sunken Feng Shui courtyard, with soothing waterfall & fragrant lavenders galore. **Privacy & all day sun:** 2 minutes from Hot Pools, shops & cafes, or via new scenic walkway. **Ask about pamper package delights, fishing & hunting.**

Your dedicated hosts have spent 9 years refining the Albergo experience by creating the stand alone Alpine Villa, with self-catering options. The awesome cinema & DVD library compliments the superb American king bedroom with large ensuite, boasting 'wow' views from the high panorama window, while you shower! Slip on a fluffy bathrobe, wander out to the split-level courtyard with private Jacuzzi and soak up Hanmer's starry night skies.

We are passionate about breakfasts! Served at a time to suit you, **Albergo's renowned 3-course breakfast** offers over 10 choices: Creative fruit platters or Swiss Birchermuesli, followed by the wafting smell of the famous **homemade bread, & fine Italian coffee.**This perfect fusion of NZ & Swiss cuisine features: Salmon Eggs Benedict, French fluffy omelets, wafer-thin crepes, 'Albergo Egg Nests' or 'Full NZ', with crispy bacon. Fondue dinners by prior arrangement.

'Best breakfasts ever and Gold award for porridge' Sheila Bennett, NYC. *'Loved the milk jug containing cow - the decor and food was divine'* Charlotte, UK. *'Your quirky decors are a feast for the eyes, what an accommodation experience'* Gavin & Kerrie, Brisbane

DIRECTIONS: At junction before main village, 300m past Caltex Garage, take Argelins Rd (Centre branch), take 2nd road left Rippingale Rd. Albergo Hanmer is 800m down on the left (Sign at drive entrance).

Hanmer Springs *0.1 km E of in Hanmer village*

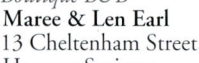

Cheltenham House *Luxury B&B Cottage No Kitchen*
Boutique B&B
Maree & Len Earl
13 Cheltenham Street,
Hanmer Springs

Tel (03) 315 7545
Fax (03) 315 7645
enquiries@cheltenham.co.nz
www.cheltenham.co.nz

Double/Twin $200-$240
Single $170-$210
(Special breakfast)
Children by arrangement
Extra person $40
Visa MC Diners Eftpos accepted
Children and pets welcome
2 King/Twin 5 Queen
1 Single (6 bdrm)
Bathrooms: 5 Ensuite 1 Private

Located on a quiet street, 200 metres from the Thermal Pools, restaurants & forest walks, we renovated this gracious 1930's home with the guests' comfort paramount. The four spacious, sunny suites in the house and two cottage suites in the park-like garden, are centrally heated. Enjoy breakfast of your choice served in your own suite and complimentary wine in the billiard room in the evening. Star-gaze, while soaking in the garden spa. Together with our sociable siamese & labrador, we look forward to meeting you.

Hanmer Springs *130 km N of Christchurch*

Cheshire House *Luxury B&B*
Jan & Chris Ottley
164C Hanmer Springs Road,
Highway 7A,
Hanmer Springs

Tel (03) 315 5100
or 0800 337 332
janandchris@xtra.co.nz

Double/Twin $150-$170
Single $120-$140
(Full breakfast)
Visa MC Eftpos accepted
Pet free home
Children welcome
2 Queen 1 Twin (3 bdrm)
Bathrooms: 3 Ensuite

Cheshire House is conveniently located two minutes drive from Hanmer Springs township. Come and be spoilt with our English hospitality, and then relax in one of our three beautifully furnished ensuite bedrooms, with your own private guest entrance and stunning mountain views. Jan & Chris will ensure that you have a memorable stay and breakfast in Hanmer Springs. There are many activities for you to enjoy if you wish.Then Experience Hanmer Springs delightful thermal pools and then relax, by indulging your health,body,and,mind.

Hanmer Springs *005 km N of village centre*
Hanmer View *Luxury B&B*

Margaux & Paul Delamain
8 Oregon Heights,
Hanmer Springs
7334

Tel (03) 315 7947
or 027 431 9620
Fax (03) 315 7947
hanmerview@xtra.co.nz
www.hanmerview.co.nz

Double/Twin $170-$200
Single $140-$170
(Full breakfast)
Visa MC accepted
Not suitable for children
1 King/Twin 2 Queen (3 bdrm)

Hanmer View adjoining the forest and Conical Hill walkway enjoys stunning panoramic views of the village and Hanmer Basin. Enjoy a tranquil stay in air-conditioned ensuited rooms with views and balcony. Margaux and Paul with their cats and dog have pleasure in welcoming you and ensuring you have an enjoyable stay at Hanmer View. We are happy to facilitate your choice and enjoyment of the activities Hanmer Springs and its environs offer. Stroll to the village centre and pools. Special packages and wireless internet available.

Culverden *3 km S of Culverden*
Ballindalloch *Farmstay*

Diane & Dougal Norrie
Longplantation Road,
Culverden RD 2,
North Canterbury 7392

Tel (03) 315 8220
or 027 437 3184
Fax (03) 315 8220
norrie@amuri.net

Double/Twin $130
Single $80
(Full breakfast)
Children $35
Dinner $35 by arrangement
Children welcome
1 Queen 2 Single (2 bdrm)
Bathrooms: 1 Guest share

Welcome to "Ballindalloch" a family farming enterprise with 3 family members farming on their own behalf on 4,000 acre irrigated farms, now milking 2,500 cows. We are just over 1 hour north of Christchurch, half an hour to Hanmer Springs, 1 1/2 hours to Kaikoura Whale Watch. Culverden is situated between 2 excellent fishing rivers. Having travelled extensively overseas we appreciate relaxing in a homely atmosphere - this we extend to our guests. We look forward to welcoming you to our home.

Hawarden *2 km N of Hawarden*

The Dutch Station *Countrystay: Luxury B&B-room and self-contained apartment*
Rein Bakker / Gertruud Steltenpool
135 Bentleys Road,
RD 1, Hawarden 7385

Tel (03) 314 2200
or 021 261 3461
info@thedutchstation.co.nz
www.thedutchstation.co.nz

Double/Twin $120-$200
Single $70-$85
(Full breakfast)
Children please contact us first
Dinner by arrangement
See our website for further
information and arrangements
Children and pets welcome
1 King 1 Queen 2 Single (3 bdrm)
Bathrooms: 1 Ensuite 1 Private
sliding showers; ensuite with bath and bidet

Our vision is: to be the most caring host in a carefree environment. Beautiful views on the Southern Alps, peaceful surroundings, luxury accommodation, careful hosts and free Dutch Golf on our own course, which is unique in the Southern Hemisphere. What else do you want? The self-contained unit includes 2 bedrooms, bathroom, fully equipped kitchen and living with satellite TV. The B&B-room contains a cooler, coffee/tea facilities and TV. Infrared sauna and Internet facilities available. The cat is called Scuff and the dog Storm.

~

Amberley *1 km S of Amberley*

Bredon Downs *B&B Homestay*
Bob & Veronica Lucy
Bredon Downs,
Withdrawn

Tel *Withdrawn*

Double/Twin *Withdrawn*

Our drive goes off SH1 and so we are conveniently en route to and from the Interisland Ferry, just 48km north of Christchurch and 100km south of the Kaikoura whales, and within easy reach of Hanmer Springs. The house is surrounded by an English style garden with swimming pool, and close to the Waipara wineries, beach and attractive golf course. We have travelled extensively and lived overseas, and now share our lives with a newfoundland, 3 geriatric donkeys and Barney the cat!

Amberley *45 km N of Christchurch*

Amber Cottage Bed & Breakfast *B&B Homestay*

Elizabeth Perkins
23 Teviot View Place,
Amberley
7410

Tel (03) 314 7077
or 021 140 6330
Fax (03) 314 7030
ambercottage@xtra.co.nz

Double/Twin $110-$130
Single $80-$90
(Full breakfast)
Children under 12 half price
Dinner $30 by arrangement
Visa MC accepted
Pet free home
Children welcome
1 Queen 1 Twin (2 bdrm)
Bathrooms: 2 Ensuite

Enjoy a warm comfortable stay at Amber Cottage set on half an acre of gardens and orchard in a quiet street. I enjoy cooking, gardening and take pleasure in sharing home-grown produce. Having enjoyed friendly hospitality on travels overseas I look forward to returning it. Amberley is situated close to the beach, golf course the vineyards and wineries of Waipara. Turn into Amberley Beach Road, then right into Teviotview Place.

Rangiora *2 km E of Rangiora*

Coldstream House *Luxury B&B Farmstay Cottage No Kitchen*

Willemina and Rupert Ward
11 Coldstream Road,
Rangiora
8254

Tel (03) 310 6006
or 021 039 6016
Fax (03) 310 6007
willeminaward@hotmail.com
www.coldstreamhouse.co.nz

Double/Twin $120-$140
Single $100-$120
(Full breakfast)
Our second casual bedroom is great for 2 children
Dinner not offered but cafes and restaurants nearby
Children welcome
1 Queen 1 Double/Twin (2 bdrm)
Bathrooms: 1 Ensuite 1 Family share ensuite
spacious bathroom with shower

Coldstream House is an original Canterbury Homestead. Willemina and Rupert Ward and their three children offer a very friendly welcome. The "Copper Cottage" guest cottage is 130 years old and has a pretty country bedroom with ensuite and private verandah with farm view. Coldstream has a beautiful living and dining room for guests use overlooking 130 year old tranquil formal gardens and tenniscourt surrounded by beautiful trees and a wild flower garden. We have a second casual bedroom which is great for kids.

Rangiora - Fernside *5 km W of Rangiora*
Petes Farm Stay B&B *B&B Farmstay*

Gaye & Peter Hurst
45 Mairaki Road,
Rangiora
RD 1, 7471

Tel (03) 313 5180
or 027 221 8989
Fax (03) 313 5182
petesfarm@xtra.co.nz
http://petesfarm.co.nz

Double/Twin $120-$140
Single $80-$100
(Continental breakfast)
Children half price
Dinner $40 per person.
Visa MC accepted
Children welcome
1 King/Twin 1 Queen
1 Double/Twin 2 Single (3 bdrm)
Bathrooms: 2 Private

Welcome to Pete's Farm B&B. We are situated 25 minutes from Christchurch Airport & City. Also just seconds off Inland Scenic Route 72. See a sheep shearing and dog demo. Relax in our new home and experience first hand the quietness and great views we get from every room in the house.

Oxford *60 km W of Christchurch*
Country Life *B&B Apartment with Kitchen*

Helen Dunn
137 High Street,
Oxford,
North Canterbury
7430

Tel (03) 312 4167

Double/Twin $90
Single $50
(Full breakfast)
Dinner $20 by arrangement
Children and pets welcome
4 Twin (2 bdrm)
Bathrooms: 1 Ensuite 1 Family share

Country life has been operating since 1987, the house is 80 years old and has a spacious garden, warm and sunny. Helen enjoys meeting people from far and wide - whether overseas visitors or those wanting a peaceful break away from Christchurch - all are welcomed at Country Life. High Street is left off the Main Road. Sign outside the gate.

Oxford *54 km W of Christchurch Airport*

Hielan' House *B&B Homestay Countrystay*

Shirley & John Farrell
74 Bush Road,
Oxford,
North Canterbury

Tel (03) 312 4382
or 0800 279 382 (freephone)
or 0274 359 435
Fax (03) 312 4382
hielanhouse@ihug.co.nz
www.hielanhouse.co.nz

Double/Twin $150-$160
Single $120-$130 (Full breakfast)
Children price on application
Dinner by arrangement
Visa MC accepted
Children and pets welcome
1 King/Twin 1 Queen 1 Twin 1 Single (2 bdrm)
Bathrooms: 2 Ensuite

Quality upstairs guest rooms with relaxing areas, ensuites, separate entrance. TV, tea/coffee facilities, fridges, hairdryers, bathrobes, slippers. Complimentary laundry, internet, sauna, spa, outdoor swimming pool, golf clubs to use. Safe parking. Enjoy John's breakfasts, dinners with home-grown meat/vegetables. Relax, unwind on 6 acres in peaceful, rural Oxford or stay longer and make us your base for day trips to Arthurs Pass, Hamner, Akaroa. Situated 3 mins from Inland Scenic Route 72, via Bay/Bush Roads. We enjoy meeting people and look forward to spoiling you.

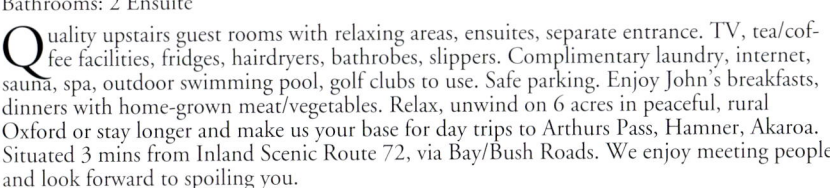

Ohoka *6 km W of Kaiapoi*

Oakhampton Lodge *B&B*

Angus & Jackie Watson
24 Keetly Place,
Ohoka,
Kaiapoi RD 2, 7692

Tel (03) 312 6413
or 021 502 313
Fax (03) 312 6314
info@oakhampton.co.nz
www.oakhampton.co.nz

Double/Twin $150-$180
(Full breakfast)
Not suitable for young children
Dinner $35 available on request
Visa MC accepted
Non smokers only
1 King 1 Queen 1 Twin (2 bdrm)
Bathrooms: 2 Ensuite

Set amongst 4 acres of lawns, mature trees and herbaceous borders, Oakhampton Lodge is the perfect place to unwind and experience a slice of country life. Ideal for weekend stays or as a stopover while travelling around New Zealand. Heading north from Christchurch on the Northern Motorway (SH1) take second Kaiapoi/Ohoka turnoff over Waimakariri River, follow signs to Ohoka. Keetly Place is 6 kms along Mill Rd, on right, just before Ohoka Hall and Service Station. No 24 is on your right.

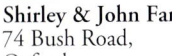

Kaiapoi - Mandeville *20 km N of Christchurch*
Ohoka Meadows B&B / Gatehouse Cottage *B&B Farmstay*
Cottage with Kitchen

Mary and Graeme Chisnall
49 Ohoka Meadows Drive,
RD 2, Kaiapoi
7692

Tel (03) 313 1781
or 0274 311 979
ohokameadows@xtra.co.nz
www.ohokameadows.co.nz

Double/Twin $120-$150
Single $100
(Full breakfast)
Child price on application
Dinner by arrangement
Children welcome
1 King 1 Queen 1 Twin (2 bdrm)
Bathrooms: 3 Ensuite

Graeme and Mary welcome you into their home.Enjoy privacy and peace while staying in modern B&B rooms with your own facilities, our luxurious fully equipped Gatehouse Cottage with full kitchen or enquire about our apartment in the Christchurch city. Take Chester and Devon, the alpacas for a walk or feed the other animals. Enjoy 4 acres of landscaped grounds and admire the mountains. Only 22 kms to Christchurch International Airport and Shopping Malls. Our interests include model engineers, jetboating, teaching and entertaining guests.

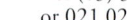

Christchurch - Brooklands *15 km N of Christchurch Centre*
ātaahua *B&B Cottage No Kitchen Romantic accommodation*

Julie & Mura Anderson
96 Harbour Road,
Brooklands,
Christchurch

Tel (03) 329 8382
or 021 0226 2513
enquiries@ataahuachristchurch.co.nz
www.ataahuachristchurch.co.nz

Double/Twin $140-$250
Single $120
(Full breakfast)
Children discuss
Good restaurants handy
or bring picnic/BBQ available
Visa MC Diners accepted
Pets welcome
2 Queen 1 Double/Twin (3 bdrm)
Bathrooms: 3 Ensuite
Spa in Te Moemoea

Stay at ātaahua - te whare manaaki tangata (Maori for Beautiful - the house that cares for people) - an easy drive from airport, shopping malls and city centre. More than just a bed for the night - a unique holiday experience. Delightfully romantic accomodation to suit all budgets. Friendly hosts including Tane our newfoundland dog are happy to share our Maori art collection. Walk in the wildlife reserve alongside the lagoon or relax on our wharf.

All our B&Bs are non-smoking unless stated otherwise in the text.

Christchurch - Harewood *7.5 km N of Christchurch Centre*

St James B&B *Luxury B&B*
Margaret & David Frankish
125 Waimakariri Road, Harewood,
Christchurch 8005

Tel (03) 359 6259 or 027 455 3554
027 432 0996
Fax (03) 359 6299
dj.frankish@xtra.co.nz
www.stjamesbnb.com

Double/Twin $120-$160
Single $75-$90 (Full breakfast)
Children $40
Visa MC accepted
Children welcome
1 King 1 Queen 1 Single (2 bdrm)
Bathrooms: 1 Ensuite 1 Private

Located 5 minutes from Christchurch Airport, 10 minutes from city. Begin/ end your South Island trip in our warm, modern home with its tranquil garden setting, and the horses who share our 3 acre property. Our lovely guest rooms include private lounges, ensuite bathroom and private spa/bathroom upstairs. Rooms have tea/coffee facilities and TV. Internet access is available. Our beautiful spoodle collects the daily newspaper. Close by are golf courses, excellent restaurants, shopping, Wildlife Reserve, McLeans Island Recreation Area and Antarctic Centre.

Christchurch - Harewood *4 km N of Central Post Office*

Belmont on Harewood *B&B Homestay*

Approved

Alan and Jan Taylor
37 Harewood Road,
Papanui,
Christchurch
8053

Tel (03) 354 6890 or (021) 479 920
Fax (03) 354 6895
janalltd@paradise.net.nz
www.belmontbnb.co.nz

Double/Twin $120-$250
Single $110-$220
(Full breakfast)
Children under 12 yrs in parents room $25
Dinner by request or in 1 of 15 quality eateries or restaurants within 4 min walk
Visa MC accepted
Children welcome
1 Twin Super King suite. 3 Queen (3 bdrm)
Bathrooms: 2 Ensuite 1 Private 1 Guest share/fully disabled bathroom facility

Our Edwardian home is wheelchair friendly and located by car, about 7 minutes from the airport and 10 minutes from the city centre. For your business or holiday needs, for your arrival and departures, we are perfectly located. Excellent shopping facilities at the Northlands Mall include movie theatres and a wide choice of restaurants and eateries and all are within a 3 to 5 minute walk from our home. A bus service to the city, airport, and the city's other major shopping malls, is at our gate. We have off-street parking and offer a free courteousy airport pickup.

We have a cat and dog. The quality of your stay is important to us. Please let us know if you have any special requests. Our home is centrally heated throughout. Features from this circa 1900 era include native Rimu timbers, tiled fire places, leadlight windows, 3-metre high ceilings, ornate plaster archway, ceiling roses and cornices. Our rooms are warm, enjoying the morning sun and over look our formal gardens. Bedrooms are served by either ensuites, a lovely marble tiled guest bathroom with modern facilities and a heated tile floor or alternatively a fully compliant disabled bathroom.

Christchurch - Yaldhurst *8 km W of Christchurch Central*
Gladsome Lodge *B&B Homestay*
Stuart & Sue Barr
314 Yaldhurst Road,
Russley, Christchurch 8042

Tel (03) 342 7414
or 0800 222 617
or 021 278 6982
Fax (03) 342 3414
sue@gladsomelodge.com
www.gladsomelodge.com

Double/Twin $100-$130
Single $95-$110
(Continental breakfast)
Children 0-5 free, 5-12 $20
Dinner $25 by arrangement
Cooked breakfast available
Visa MC Diners Amex accepted
Children welcome
3 Queen 1 Double/Twin 1 Twin 2 Single (5 bdrm)
Bathrooms: 2 Ensuite 3 Guest share One

Located close to airport with easy access to key attractions. Be assured of professional, attentive hosting in a friendly environment. Enjoy our tennis court, swimming pool or sauna. Guest internet access available. We are able to accommodate couples travelling together. Have knowledge of Maori history and culture. Our house is centrally heated. On bus route to city. On route to ski fields and West Coast Highway.Outside friendly dog. Hosts Sue and Stuart, New Zealanders who have travelled and have a wide variety of interests.

Christchurch - Yaldhurst *12 km W of Christchurch*
Miners Arms Alpaca Farmstay B+B *B&B Farmstay Separate Suite*
Lorna and Steve Tanner
441 Old West Coast Road,
RD6, Christchurch

Tel (03) 342 5827
or 021 050 4060
Fax (03) 342 5826
lorna@minersarms.co.nz
www.minersarms.co.nz

Double/Twin $130-$150
Single $90-$100
(Full breakfast)
Extra adults $40
Visa MC accepted
1 Queen 1 Double/Twin
1 Single (2 bdrm)
Bathrooms: 1 Private
with bath and shower

Enjoy the best of both worlds and a warm welcome only 10 minutes from the airport and close to the city in our superior, private first floor guest suite, surrounded by 10 acres of paddocks, woodland, orchard. Sleeping 1-5, it has well-equipped lounge with bed-settee, 2 bedrooms, bathroom , balcony.Broadband available.A wonderful base for your Christchurch/ Canterbury holiday.See the sights by day, then relax or meet our alpacas, sheep, chickens, ducks and Maremma sheepdogs. Near restaurants/wineries, golf, zoo, river walks, fishing, one hour ski-fields.

Canterbury

Christchurch - Avonhead *10 km W of Christchurch Central*
Russley 302 *B&B*

Helen & Ron Duckworth
302 Russley Road,
Avonhead, Christchurch 8042

Tel (03) 358 6510
or 021 662 016
Fax (03) 358 6470
haduck@ducksonrussley.co.nz
www.ducksonrussley.co.nz

Double/Twin $120-$150
Single $80-$120
(Full breakfast)
Evening meal served (with
local wines) by arrangement
Complimentary airport transfers
day or night
Visa MC accepted
1 King 1 Queen 1 Twin 1 Single (4 bdrm)
Bathrooms: 1 Ensuite 2 Private

Located on main north/south highway near Christchurch airport Russley 302 provides complimentary airport transfers and excellent hospitality for guests arriving and departing the "garden city". All guest rooms are very attractively furnished, and comfortable. Each double room is well equipped with private bathroom, tea/coffee facilities, refrigerator, television, electric blanket, clock/radio, hair dryer. Email/fax facilities available if required. Dinner is available by prior arrangement. Our "garden city" has much to offer and is an ideal location for daily excursions to Canterbury's hinterland.

Christchurch - Burnside *8 km NW of Christchurch*
Burnside Bed & Breakfast *B&B*

Elaine & Neil Roberts
31 O'Connor Place,
Burnside,
Christchurch
8005

Tel (03) 358 7671
Fax (03) 358 7761
elaine.neil.roberts@xtra.co.nz

Double/Twin $90-$110
Single $65-$70
(Continental breakfast)
Pet free home
Children welcome
1 Queen 1 Twin (2 bdrm)
Bathrooms: 1 Guest share

Welcome to our comfortable, modern home in quiet street, 5 minutes from the airport and 15 minutes to the city centre. Relax in the garden with tea or coffee and freshly baked muffins. Enjoy a generous continental breakfast with home-baking and preserves. Free broadband internet, laundry facilities and off-street parking available. Private bathroom facilities arranged with prior booking at $110.00. Our interests include sport, gardening, reading,travel and local history. We enjoy sharing our home with guests and look forward to meeting you.

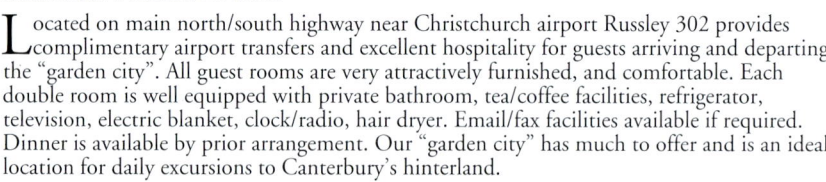

Christchurch - Burnside *7 km W of Christchurch*
Stableford Airport B&B *B&B*

Margaret & Tony Spowart
2 Stableford Green,
Burnside,
Christchurch
8053

Tel (03) 358 3264
or 021 883 804
stableford@xtra.co.nz
www.stableford.co.nz

Double/Twin $140
Single $130
(Full breakfast)
Visa MC accepted
2 Queen 1 Twin (3 bdrm)
Bathrooms: 2 Ensuite 1 Private

Welcome to Stableford, the closest B&B to the Christchurch Airport, making it ideal for arriving or departing visitors. City bus-stop at door. We are situated adjacent to the prestigious Russley Golf Club. Let us know if you require a tee booking at the Russley Golf Course. Stableford is new, clean and comfortable with a separate guest lounge. Good restaurants nearby or dinner by arrangement. Our interests are travel, sport, music, & antiques.

Christchurch - Burnside *8 km NW of City Centre*
Blossom Tree Homestay *B&B Homestay*

Lorna Watson
29 O'Connor Place,
Burnside,
Christchurch 8053

Tel (03) 358 2635
Fax (03) 358 2665
blossomtree@xtra.co.nz

Double/Twin $100-$120
Single $60-$80
(Continental breakfast)
Children $20
Children welcome
1 Queen 1 Double/Twin
2 Single (3 bdrm)
Bathrooms: 2 Private 1 Guest share

Located 5 minutes from Christchurch Airport, free transfer to and from airport, car hire depots very close, 15 minutes from City Centre. Good bus services closeby. Russley Golf Course and a variety of excellent restaurants and cafes nearby. Modern 7 year old home, along with it's owners, Lorna & Lyndsay and lovely cat Emma, welcomes bed & breakfast guests. Enjoy lovely surroundings and a generous continental breakfast. Off-street parking and laundry facilities available. We look forward to welcoming you.

Christchurch - Ilam *7.5 km NW of Christchurch*
Anne & Tony Fogarty Homestay *Homestay*

Anne & Tony Fogarty
7 Westmont Street,
Ilam,
Christchurch
8041

Tel (03) 358 2762
Fax (03) 358 2767
tony.fogarty@xtra.co.nz

Double/Twin $100
Single $60
(Continental breakfast)
Dinner $30 by arrangement
Visa MC accepted
4 Single (2 bdrm)
Bathrooms: 1 Guest share
1 Family share

Our home is in the beautiful suburb of Ilam, only minutes from Canterbury University and Canterbury University College of Education. Close to Christchurch Airport (7 minutes by car) and the railway station (10 minutes). A bus stop to the central city, with its many attractions is 50 metres from our home. Willing to arrange transport from airport or train.Excellent local information. Guests are welcome to use our laundry. Complimentary tea and coffee at any time. Stay with us and get value for money.

~

Christchurch - Papanui *5 km E of Christchurch Airport*
Heatherston Boutiqe Bed and Breakfast *Luxury B&B*

Jan and Murray Binnie
46 Searells Road,
Christchurch
8052

Tel (03) 355 3239
or 027 418 8961
Fax (03) 355 3259
enquiries@heatherston.co.nz
www.heatherston.co.nz

Double/Twin $120-$150
Single $120
(Full breakfast)
Not suitable for children
2 King/Twin 1 Queen
1 Single (3 bdrm)
Bathrooms: 3 Ensuite

Comfortable, convenient and quiet. A superbly situated, purpose-built, modern house with every convenience, only ten minutes from the Airport, and ten minutes from Central Christchurch. Heatherston has a sunny guests' kitchenette/lounge, bedrooms with comfortable beds, refreshment facilities, and television. Ensuites have heated towel rails, hairdryers and toiletries. Heatherston is close to shops and restaurants, and is conveniently located for sight-seeing in the city, or travelling to wineries, walking tracks, golf courses, and skifields. Heatherston is the perfect tranquil retreat!

Christchurch - Fendalton *5.0 km NW of Christchurch city centre*
Glenveagh B&B *B&B*

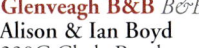

Alison & Ian Boyd
230C Clyde Road,
Fendalton,
Christchurch

Tel (03) 351 4407
or 0800 000 107
Fax (03) 351 4406
boyd45@xtra.co.nz
www.glenveagh.co.nz

Double/Twin $120-$190
Single $120-$150
(Continental breakfast)
Children by arrangement
Visa MC Eftpos accepted
1 King/Twin 1 Queen
1 Twin 2 Single (3 bdrm)
Bathrooms: 1 Ensuite 1 Private

Ian & Alison welcome you to our beautiful home in a quiet area of Fendalton, Christchurch. Just off airport,city road. We have three guest rooms, upstairs and downstairs a lounge, courtyard. Tralee: King/twin/triple with ensuite and TV. Erigal: Twin with private bathroom and TV. Galway: Queen with private bathroom and TV. Restaurants within walking distance. Off-street parking. Courtesy car from airport, bus, train. Five minutes by car to central city, bus at gate. Continental breakfast. No smoking inside. Look forward to your company.

Christchurch - Riccarton *6 km E of Christchurch Central*
Sunrise *B&B Homestay Guest House*

Ella and Kamal
9 Main South Road,
Upper Riccarton, Christchurch

Tel (03) 981 3807 or 0800 526 924
or 0274 808 955
Fax (03) 981 3809
stay@sunrisebnb.co.nz
www.sunrisebnb.co.nz

Double/Twin $65-$75
Single $55-$60
(Breakfast by arrangement)
Children negotiable
Family room sleeps three $90
Visa MC accepted
Children welcome
2 Queen 4 Twin 1 Single (5 bdrm)
Bathrooms: 2 Guest share

www.sunrisebnb.co.nz
stay@sunrisebnb.co.nz

Sunrise BnB welcomes you to the Garden City. We are a caring, comfortable and affordable accommodation with room only options. Walking distance to University, shopping areas, 24x7 super market and internet cafe. Sunrise has a homely atmosphere and offers warm sunny rooms, independent kitchen, lounge, laundry, parking. We have courtesy pick up from airport, rail, and bus (by arrangement) and offer excellent weekly and long term rates. Your hosts: Ella, Kamal & family including Gypsy,our affectionate German Shepherd. We look forward to see you soon.

Christchurch - Riccarton *6 km W of City centre*
Thistle Guest House *B&B Guest House*

John and Alison Goodfellow
21 Main South Road,
Church Corner, Upper Riccarton,
Christchurch, 8042

Tel (03) 348 1499
or 0800 93 21 21
Fax (03) 348 1577
stay@thistleguesthouse.co.nz
www.thistleguesthouse.co.nz

Double/Twin $86-$96
Single $55-$78
(Continental breakfast)
Visa MC Amex Eftpos accepted
Children welcome
1 King 4 Queen 3 Twin
4 Single (10 bdrm)
Bathrooms: 1 Ensuite 3 Guest share

A small friendly guest house offering quality homestyle accommodation. 10 private bedrooms with fridge, tea/coffee facilities and wireless internet access for laptops. Fully equipped guest kitchen, lounge, off-street parking and attractive garden. Laundry facilities and guest telephone also available. Handy to Canterbury University and College of Education and two minutes walk to shops, restaurants and supermarket. On good bus route to city (15 minutes) and 10 minutes drive from airport. Courtesy pick-up by arrangement. Weekly rates and tariffs excluding breakfast also available.

∼

Christchurch - Merivale *2 km N of Christchurch*
Leinster B&B *B&B Homestay*

Kay and Brian Smith
34B Leinster Road,
Merivale,
Christchurch

Tel (03) 355 6176
or 027 433 0771
Fax (03) 355 6176
brian.kay@xtra.co.nz

Double/Twin $150-$175
Single $120 (Full breakfast)
Children negotiable
Visa MC accepted
Children welcome
1 Queen 1 Double/Twin
1 Single (2 bdrm)
Bathrooms: 1 Ensuite 1 Private

At Leinster Bed & Breakfast we pride ourselves on creating a relaxed friendly atmosphere in our modern sunny home. Only 5 minutes to city centre (art gallery, museum, botanical gardens, Cathedral Square, casino, town hall etc), 10 minutes from the airport. For evening dining convenience there are excellent restaurants just a leisurely stroll away at Merivale Village. Laundry, email, fax and off-street parking facilities makes us your home away from home. Bedrooms have TV, electric blankets, heaters, tea/coffee. Well behaved puss & pooch in residence.

Christchurch - Merivale *3 km N of Christchurch*

Melrose *B&B*

Elaine & David Baxter
39 Holly Road,
Merivale,
Christchurch

Tel (03) 355 1929
or 027 647 5564
Fax (03) 355 1927
BaxterMelrose@xtra.co.nz
www.melrose-bb.co.nz

Double/Twin $120-$140
Single $80 (Full breakfast)
Children $30
Visa MC accepted
Children welcome
3 Queen (3 bdrm)
Bathrooms: 1 Ensuite 1 Private
2 Guest share

A warm welcome awaits you at Melrose, a charming character home (1910) located in a small quiet street, just off Papanui Road only minutes away from the city and all the shops, restaurants and cafes of Merivale. Our house is spacious, we offer large rooms with tea & coffee making facilities and a private dining room/lounge. We have many interests and having travelled extensively, are keen to accommodate your needs. Our family comprises 2 daughters and a boxer, Milly. Off-street parking. Children are welcome.

Christchurch - St Albans *3 km N of Christchurch City*

Severn Street B&B *B&B*

Tina & Peter Reynolds
15 Severn Street,
St Albans,
Christchurch
8001

Tel (03) 960 3185
or 027 332 5219
Fax (03) 960 3186
tina.reynolds@paradise.net.nz

Double/Twin $125
Single $90
(Full breakfast)
Children $35
Visa MC accepted
Children welcome
2 King/Twin 2 Queen (3 bdrm)
Bathrooms: 1 Ensuite 2 Private

Severn Street B&B is a warm character home in a tree lined street, 5 minutes drive from town, and close to the bus route. Facilities include; large warm bedrooms, guest kitchen, cot, highchair, fax/email, off-street parking, hot spa, tea and coffee, courtesy pick up, Deutsche Sprache. Peter and I and are well travelled New Zealanders. Peter is an English language teacher, and I am a retired Occupational Therapist.

Canterbury

Christchurch - Richmond *2 km E of CBD*

Avon Grove Villa Bed & Breakfast *B&B*

Approved

Janice and Ian Cundall
273 River Road,
Christchurch,
8013

Tel 03 381 7099
or 027 442 3076
enquiries@avongrovevilla.co.nz
www.avongrovevilla.co.nz

Double/Twin $140-$160
(Full breakfast)
Visa MC accepted
Children welcome
2 Queen (2 bdrm)
Bathrooms: 2 Ensuite

Situated beside the Avon River this 1900's Avon Grove Villa welcomes you to Christchurch City. There are several restaurants and shops within a ten minute walk. Two large, comfortably appointed, double guest rooms, each with the original fireplace and large bay windows, are available. Each room has an ensuite, TV, and tea and coffee facilities. A full cooked breakfast is served daily. Avon Grove Villa is owned by Janice and Ian Cundall. They have two adult children.

Our B&Bs range from homely to luxurious, but you can always be assured of superior hospitality.

~

Christchurch - Avondale *8 km NE of Christchurch Central*

Hulverstone Lodge *B&B*

Diane & Ian Ross
18 Hulverstone Drive, Avondale, Christchurch

Tel (03) 388 6505 or 0800 388 650 (NZ only)
Fax (03) 388 6025
hulverstone@caverock.net.nz
www.hulverstonelodge.co.nz

Double/Twin $120-$160 Single $100-$120
(Full breakfast)
Triple (queen + single) $200.00
Visa MC accepted
Pet free home Not suitable for children
3 King/Twin 1 Queen 1 Single (4 bdrm)
Bathrooms: 2 Ensuite 1 Private 1 Guest share 1 Family share

Gracing the bank of the Avon River in a quiet suburb, yet only 10 minutes from the city centre, stands picturesque Hulverstone Lodge. From our charming guest rooms watch the sun rise over the river, catch glimpses of the Southern Alps or enjoy views of the Port Hills. Delightful riverside walks pass the door. A pleasant stroll along the riverbank leads to New Brighton with its restaurants, sandy Pacific Ocean beach and pier. Numerous golf courses and the QEII Leisure Complex are close at hand.

Located just off Christchurch's Ring Road system, Hulverstone Lodge offers easy access to all major tourist attractions, while frequent buses provide convenient transport to the city. An ideal base for holidays year-round, Hulverstone Lodge is only a couple of hours from quaint Akaroa, Hanmer Springs' thermal pools, Kaikoura's Whalewatch, and several ski fields.

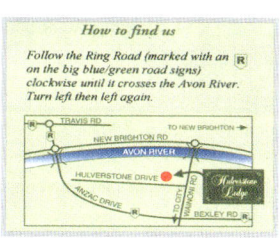

You are guaranteed warm hospitality and quality accommodation at Hulverstone Lodge. All our rooms are decorated with fresh flowers from our garden. A delicious breakfast, either cooked or continental, is included in the tariff. We also offer: - complimentary pick up; - king, queen or twin beds;- 'francais parle', Deutsch gesprochen. Come and experience the ambience of Hulverstone Lodge.

Windsor Hotel
BED & BREAKFAST

Christchurch City *.5 km NW of Christchurch CBD*
B&B Hotel *B&B Hotel*
Carol Healey & Don Evans
52 Armagh Street, Christchurch 8013

Tel (03) 366 1503 or 0800 366 1503   Fax (03) 366 9796
reservations@windsorhotel.co.nz   www.windsorhotel.co.nz

Double/Twin $140 Single $98 (Full breakfast)
Triple $180, Quad/Family $200
Visa MC Diners Amex Eftpos accepted
12 Double/Twin 18 Twin 10 Single (40 bdrm)
Bathrooms: 24 Guest share

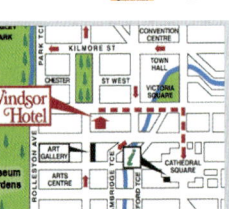

Looking for Bed & Breakfast in Christchurch, then try The Windsor. Built at the turn of the century this inner city residence is located on the Tourist Tram Route and is within 5-10 minutes walk of the city centre, restaurants, convention centre, casino, galleries, museum and botanical gardens. Guests are greeted on arrival by our pet dachshund, Miss Winnie and shown around our charming colonial style home. Often described as traditional, this family operated bed & breakfast hotel prides itself on the standard of accommodation that it offers. The warm and comfortable bedrooms are all decorated with a small posy of flowers and a watercolour by local artist Denise McCulloch.

The shared bathroom facilities have been conveniently appointed with bathrobes provided, giving warmth and comfort in the bed & breakfast tradition. Such things as "hotties" and "brollies" add charm to the style of accommodation offered, as does our 1928 Studebaker sedan.

Our generous morning breakfast (included in the tariff) offers fruit juice, fresh fruits, yogurt and cereals followed by bacon and eggs, sausages, tomatoes, toast and marmalade, and is served in the dining room each morning between 6.30 and 9.00. The 24 hour complimentary tea & coffee making facilities allow guests to use them at their own convenience. "Supper" (tea, coffee and biscuits) is served each evening in the lounge at 9.00.

As part of our service the hotel offers "Free" broadband internet / wireless access, coin operated laundry, luggage lift, off-street parking and bicycle and baggage storage.

QUOTE THIS BOOK FOR 10% DISCOUNT

Christchurch City *0.8 km N of Christchurch Cathedral Square*
Home Lea B&B *B&B Homestay*

Pauline & Gerald Oliver
195 Bealey Avenue,
Christchurch

Tel (03) 379 9977
or 0800 355 321
Fax (03) 379 4099
homelea@xtra.co.nz
www.homelea.co.nz

Double/Twin $145-$190
Single $95-$135
(Special breakfast)
Children negotiable
Dinner by arrangement
Extra adult $35
Visa MC Amex Eftpos accepted
Children welcome
1 King 2 Queen 4 Single (4 bdrm)
Bathrooms: 2 Ensuite 2 Private

Home Lea offers the traveller a comfortable and enjoyable stay. Built in the early 1900s, Home Lea has the charm and character of a large New Zealand home of that era: rimu panelling, leadlight windows, and a large lounge with a log fire. Off-street parking. Wireless/broadband internet available for guests. Special diets catered for. Pauline and Gerald are happy to share their knowledge of local attractions and their special interests are travel, sailing and music.

Christchurch City *1.2 km N of Christchurch Central*
Eliza's Manor on Bealey *Luxury B&B*

Ann Zwimpfer & Harold Williams
82 Bealey Avenue,
City Central, Christchurch

Tel (03) 366 8584
or 0800 366 859
Fax (03) 366 4946
info@elizas.co.nz
www.elizas.co.nz

Double/Twin $185-$295
Single $165-$275
(Special breakfast)
Visa MC Diners Amex
Eftpos accepted
Pet free home
Not suitable for children
4 King 4 Queen 1 Single (8 bdrm)
Bathrooms: 8 Ensuite
Large tiled walk in showers

Eliza's is a beautifully restored Victorian mansion, built in 1861. The original architecture includes a magnificent staircase in the foyer, lead light windows and wood panelling. The tariff includes a full continental and cooked breakfast. It is a short drive from the airport and a 15 minute level walk to the Arts centre, botanical gardens, art gallery, museum, city centre, golf course and restaurants. Free parking and internet access is available to guests. We are a day trip to Hanmer Springs, Akaroa, and Kaikoura.

Christchurch City *1 km N of Christchurch Central*

The Devon B&B *B&B*
Sandra & Benjamin Humphrey
69 Armagh Street,
Christchurch

Tel (03) 366 0398
Fax (03) 366 0392
stay@thedevon.co.nz
www.thedevon.co.nz

Double/Twin $145-$180
Single $98-$145
(Full breakfast)
Children under 15 years $30
Extra adults $40
Visa MC Diners Amex
Eftpos accepted
6 Queen 3 Twin 2 Single (11 bdrm)
Bathrooms: 6 Ensuite 1 Private
4 Guest share

The Devon is a personal guest house located in the heart of beautiful Christchurch City, which offers elegance and comfort in the style of an olde worlde English manor. Just 5 minutes walk to Christchurch Cathedral, Town Hall, and Convention Centre, casino, museum, art gallery, hospital and botanical gardens in Hagley Park. TV lounge, tea & coffee making facilities. Off-street parking. Free broadband internet/wireless access and luggage storage.

Christchurch City *1 km E of Centre*

The Chester *B&B*
Jennifer & Jan van den Berg
Suite 3,
173 Chester Street East,
Christchurch City

Tel (03) 366 5777
or 021 365 495
Fax (03) 365 6314
thechester@clear.net.nz
www.thechester.com

Double/Twin $110-$135
Single $95-$110
(Continental breakfast)
Visa MC accepted
Pet free home
Not suitable for children
1 King/Twin 1 Single (2 bdrm)
Bathrooms: 2 Ensuite

The Chester B&B Apt 3,situated in the historic Old Wards Brewery Building, dates back to the 1850's. Now converted into elegant apartments, this unique suite offers all modern comforts and amenities in close walking distance of the city centre, restaurants, banks, town hall, arts centre, casino & convention centre. Perfect for holiday or business. Your hosts Jan & Jennifer van den Berg will ensure your stay is comfortable and memorable. Car Rentals,Theatre & concert bookings can be arranged on request.

Christchurch City *.5 km SW of Information Centre*
Slingerland Green Stay *B&B*

Catherine Slingerland
25 Cambridge Terrace,
Christchurch 8013

Tel (03) 379 7632
Fax (03) 379 7632
caseo@xtra.co.nz
www.slingerland.co.nz

Double/Twin $120
Single $100
(Special breakfast)
Children $20
Extra person $20,
Breakfast - Lacto-ovo Vegeterian
Children and pets welcome
Non smokers only
1 Queen 1 Double/Twin 1 Single
(2 bdrm)
Bathrooms: 1 Ensuite 1 Family share

Relax in front of the picture window in the sunny & spacious lounge, watch the ducks swimming in the Avon River and people embarking on a punt ride through the Botanic Gardens. Many other attractions are within a short walk: The Canterbury Museum, Arts Centre, Tramway & Cathedral Square. Start your day with a healthy vegetarian breakfast of a fresh fruit smoothie, a variety of cereals and breads, plus a hot "English breakfast".

❧

Christchurch - Templeton *3 km S of Hornby*
Cedarview Farm Homestay B&B *B&B Homestay Farmstay*

Carol & Terrance White
33 Barters Road,
Templeton RD 5, Christchurch

Tel (03) 349 7491
or 0274 335-335
Fax (03) 349 7755
cedarviewfarm@xtra.co.nz
www.cedarviewhomestay.com

Double/Twin $135-$190
Single $125-$140 (Full breakfast)
Family room options,
please ask for rates giving childs ages
High quality accomodation
in a very convenient location
Visa MC accepted
Pet free home
Children welcome
1 King 1 Queen 2 Single (3 bdrm)
Bathrooms: 1 Ensuite 1 Private

Cedarview Farm Homestay B+B is ideally situated for visitors to Christchurch. Our modern smoke free home is close to the Airport, highways, shopping, bars, restaurants. An easy 15-20 minute drive into the central city. Our rooms are bright, well appointed and have lovely views out over our small farm where we keep cattle, sheep, hens, a farm cat called Alfie and Labrador called Ruby. We moved to New Zealand from the UK in 1986. Our lifestyle is quiet and relaxed. Enquiries are welcome. See you soon.

Christchurch - Sydenham *1.5 km S of Christchurch City Square*

Designer Cottage, Villa & Designer 55 *B&B Homestay*
Cottage with Kitchen

B&B
Approved

Chet Wah
53 Hastings Street West, Sydenham, Christchurch City

Tel 0800 161 619 or (03) 377 8088
or 021 210 5282 Fax (03) 377 8099
stay@designercottage.co.nz
www.designercottage.co.nz

Double/Twin $80-$200 Single $60-$120
(Continental breakfast)
$100-$350 for six people for the whole house
Visa MC accepted
Pet free home
4 Queen 1 Double/Twin 1 Twin 1 Single (7 bdrm)
Bathrooms: 2 Ensuite 3 Guest share 1 Family share

Designer Cottage, Villa & Designer 55 are charming places to stay. Just off Colombo Street situated in peaceful surroundings, and within 20 minutes walk to the city centre or 2 minute walk to shops and restaurants.

We offer a variety of rooms, which are all tastefully decorated, including share facilities, private room with ensuite and a self-contained cottage. Seasonal, corporate & long stay rates apply. Wireless Broadband available. There is off-street parking and free pick up from city centre on arrival (by arrangement only).

Once settled in you will be welcomed with a 'mean' cup of coffee or tea by the friendly host.Your friendly host, Chet, has an honors degree in Landscape Architecture and is passionate about traditional buildings and his landscaping ideas. Designer Cottage is one of his finest collections of the charms of yesterday and all guests are welcome to view the concepts of 'Designer Village 'and hear his stories about these cottages.

Please let us know
how you enjoyed your B&B experience.
Ask your host for a comment form
or leave a comment on www.bnb.co.nz.

Christchurch - St Martins *3 km S of Christchurch City Centre*

Kleynbos B&B *B&B Separate Suite Apartment with Kitchen*

Gerda De Kleyne & Hans van den Bos
59 Ngaio Street,
Christchurch

Tel (03) 332 2896
KLEYNBOS@xtra.co.nz
www.kleynbos.co.nz

Double/Twin $80-$100
Single $50-$75
(Continental breakfast)
Children are welcome,
cot available
Apartment $100-$130
Visa MC accepted
2 Queen 2 Double/Twin
2 Single (4 bdrm)
Bathrooms: 2 Ensuite
1 Private 1 Guest share

Quality accommodation with a personal touch, since 1991. 3km to city centre, in an easy to find, friendly, tree-lined street. Your large ensuite rooms are $100 with microwave, fridge and jug. A computer is available to keep in contact with friends and family. A self-catering option is available in the apartment, sleeps 5 for $100-$130. The children are 19 and 16 years old. Directions; SH74 Barbadoes Street, Waltham Road, Wilsons Road, right into Gamblins Road, first left is Ngaio Street.

Christchurch - Westmorland *7 km SW of Christchurch*
Slippers *Luxury B&B*

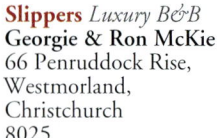

Georgie & Ron McKie
66 Penruddock Rise,
Westmorland,
Christchurch
8025

Tel (03) 339 6170
Fax (03) 339 6170
mckiepic@paradise.net.nz
www.slippersbnb.co.nz

Double/Twin $190
Single $120
(Full breakfast)
Dinner $50 per person,
including fine wine
Visa MC accepted
Not suitable for children
1 King/Twin 1 Single (2 bdrm)
Bathrooms: 1 Private

Pure wool slippers await you when you arrive at Slippers. Enjoy stunning views of the Alps, Canterbury Plains and the city. Your suite of rooms includes two bedrooms, lounge, private bathroom, private entrances and secluded balcony area. Special diets catered for. Home baking, fruit bowl, tea and plunger coffee always available. Off street parking. City bus at gate. Photographers, use our darkroom and digital facilities. Allow us and our two cats to help you to get the most from your Christchurch stay. Check our website.

Christchurch - Westmorland *7 km SW of Cathedral Square*
Sportmans Lodge *B&B*

Phil & Pauline Wilson
6 Ennerdale Row,
Westmortland,
Christchurch
8025

Tel (03) 339 8633
Fax (03) 339 8632
sportsmanlodge@xtra.co.nz

Double/Twin $150-$180
Single $100-$130
(Continental breakfast)
Visa MC accepted
3 King/Twin (3 bdrm)
Bathrooms: 3 Ensuite

The Sportsman's Lodge was purpose built in 1997, for the outdoor sportsmen and women in mind, and is a private large modern home in a very quiet, well established area with off-street parking. The lodge offers three private super-king-twin guestrooms upstairs. The guest lounge provides panoramic views of the Southern Alps and Canterbury plains, while the living and dining rooms feature great city views at night. Town is only 10 minutes away, 5 minutes to mall, 10 minutes to train and 20 minutes to airport.

Christchurch - Huntsbury *4 km S of Christchurch Central*

Andaview B&B *Luxury B&B*

Anne & Keith Clark
18 Woodlau Rise,
Huntsbury,
Christchurch
8022

Tel (03) 332 5522
Fax (03) 332 5592
andaview@xtra.co.nz
www.andaview.co.nz

Double/Twin $170-$230
Single $150-$175
(Full breakfast)
Visa MC Eftpos accepted
Pet free home
Not suitable for children
1 King/Twin 1 King (2 bdrm)
Bathrooms: 1 Ensuite 1 Private
Double Spabath

Experience genuine Kiwi hospitality only 10 minutes from the city centre. Suites are designed with executives and the discerning traveller in mind. Our guest rooms have spectacular views and amenities to satisfy your every need. Relax in our guest lounge with a New Zealand wine and watch the sun set behind the mountains. We offer free Hi-speed internet access and complimentary airport/rail pick up or drop off.

Christchurch - Murray Aynsley *4 km SE of City Centre*
Information

Pool House *B&B Separate Suite*

Jill and Richard Entwistle
57 Aynsley Terrace,
Murray Aynsley,
Christchurch, 8022

Tel (03) 337 0380
or 021 131 6441
entwistle@slingshot.co.nz

Double/Twin $135
Single $95
(Continental breakfast)
Children by arrangement
Visa MC accepted
Children welcome
Non smokers only
1 King/Twin (1 bdrm)
Bathrooms: 1 Ensuite

The Pool House offers quiet and comfortable, private self-contained accommodation with separate living and sleeping areas, bathroom en-suite. Ample self-serve continental breakfast provided. Children by arrangement, on a sofa-bed. Outdoor swimming pool. Hansen Park and the Heathcote River offering gentle riverside walks and a children's playground. Central Christchurch and the Port of Lyttelton are 10 minutes by bus or by car. Local sandy beaches are 10-15 minutes by car.

Christchurch - Redcliffs *10 km E of Cathedral Square*
Pegasus Bay View *B&B Separate Suite*

Denise & Bernie Lock
121A Moncks Spur Road,
Redcliffs,
Christchurch

Tel (03) 384 2923
or 021 254 2888
pegasusbay@slingshot.co.nz
www.pegasusbayview.co.nz

Double/Twin $140-$150
Single $110-$120
(Continental breakfast)
Visa MC accepted
1 Queen 1 Double/Twin (2 bdrm)
Bathrooms: 1 Private

Enjoy spectacular views over the South Pacific and across the city to the Southern Alps from our modern home. Your private guest suite has its own entrance and is tastefully furnished, with spacious bedroom, TV lounge (which can converted to a second double bedroom for additional family/friends) and private bathroom. Relax over a delicious breakfast, served outside on warm days, while enjoying the stunning panorama. Close to beach and restaurants and just 15 minutes drive from Christchurch City centre. We offer wireless broadband access.

Christchurch - Mt Pleasant *9 km E of Cathedral Square*
A Nest on Mount Pleasant *B&B Apartment with Kitchen*

Kathryn & Kai Tovgaard
24 Toledo Place,
Mount Pleasant,
Christchurch 8081

Tel (03) 384 9485
or 027 203 0637
Fax (03) 384 8385
thenestonMP@xtra.co.nz
www.anestbnb.co.nz

Double/Twin $95-$120
Single $85-$110
(Full breakfast)
Children discounted
Visa MC Diners Amex accepted
Pet free home
Children welcome
2 Queen 2 Twin (3 bdrm)
Bathrooms: 1 Ensuite 1 Private

Unique fully self-contained home , yet with all the service and warm hospitality of a homestay. This is the promise of The Nest. The Nest is situated in one of Christchurch's most loved hill suburbs with views of our estuary, sea and mountains beyond. Tranquil and secure, with garage parking, TV,DVD, stereo, and BBQ. Very close to Christchurch's best beaches with excellent cafes and restaurants, Ferrymead Historic Park, Lyttelton Harbour, Tamaki Heritage Village and hillside walks with breathtaking views to the Southern Alps.

Christchurch - Mt Pleasant *8 km E of Christchurch*

Mt Pleasant Bed & Breakfast *B&B Separate Suite with full-size private kitchen*

Nicola & Paul Kristiansen
14 Hobday Lane, Mt Pleasant, Christchurch

Tel (03) 384 9220
Fax (03) 384 9235
Kristiansen@xtra.co.nz
http://mtpleasantbandb.co.nz

Double/Twin $110
(Continental breakfast)
Big size lounge.
Private Kitchen.
Visa MC accepted
Pet free home
Children welcome
1 Queen (1 bdrm)
Bathrooms: 1 Ensuite Private sauna holds six

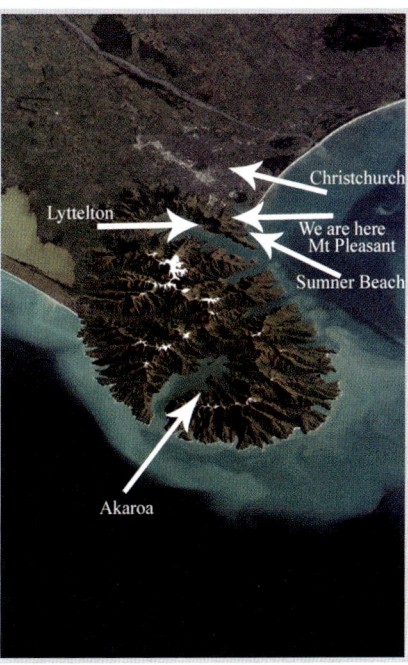

This unique home offers a friendly and relaxed stay in your private suite. Enjoy your spacious and comfortable queen bedroom, ensuite bathroom with vintage cast-iron bath (such bliss our guests tell us!)

Sitting room with private entrance leading to deck and sauna. Own kitchen facilities. Explore the huge rambling garden facinating with waterwheel, plentiful trees and abundant bird life.

Conveniently situated 15 minutes from city, 10 minutes to popular Sumner Beach, 5 minutes to windsurfing, gondola, walking and bike tracks. You'll love it!

Christchurch - Sumner *12 km E of Cathedral Square*

Villa Alexandra *B&B Apartment with Kitchen*
Self Contained Beach Front Apartment.

Wendy & Bob Perry
1 Kinsey Terrace,
Christchurch
8081

Tel (03) 326 6291
Fax (03) 326 6096
villa_alexandra@xtra.co.nz
www.villaalexandra.co.nz

Double/Twin $120-$135
Single $80-$90
(Full breakfast)
Children under 12 $15
Apartment $150 p/n
Children welcome
1 Queen 1 Double/Twin
1 Twin (3 bdrm)
Bathrooms: 2 Ensuite 1 Private

Enjoy the warmest hospitality in our spacious turn of the century villa overlooking Sumner Bay. Our home retains the graciousness of a bygone era while offering all modern comforts. In winter enjoy open fires, cosy farmhouse kitchen and on sunny days the verandah and turret. Spectacular sea views from Sumner to the Kaikouras. We enjoy food, wine, music, gardening, tramping, travel. 5 minutes walk to beach; off-street parking; laundry. Also self-contained beach front apartment, 2 double bedrooms, $150 per night, minimum 3 nights.

Christchurch - Sumner Beach *12 km E of Cathedral Square*

Cave Rock Bed & Breakfast *B&B*

Gayle & Norm Eade
16 Esplanade, Sumner, Christchurch

Tel (03) 326 6844
or 027 436 0212
Fax (03) 326 5600
eade@chch.planet.org.nz
www.caverockguesthouse.co.nz

Double/Twin $140-$150
Single $105-$115
(Continental breakfast provisions)
Children $20
Corporate Rates available
Visa MC Eftpos accepted
Pet free home
Children welcome
3 Queen 1 Double/Twin (4 bdrm)
Bathrooms: 4 Ensuite
One with spa bath ensuite

The Cave Rock B&B - Sumner's ultimate Beachfront accommodation opposite Sumner's Cave Rock. Hosts Gayle & Norm Eade enjoy meeting people from overseas and within NZ. Large spacious double rooms with sea views, TV, heating and ensuite bathrooms, can sleep up to 4. Kitchen facilities. Sumner - the ideal holiday location, 15 minutes from Ch.Ch City, excellent bus service - cafe/bars, shops, cinema, within walking distance. Hill and cliff walks close by, safe sandy beach across the road. We have a friendly dalmatian dog.

Christchurch - Sumner *13 km E of Christchurch Cathedral Square*

Abbott House Sumner Bed & Breakfast *Self-contained suite with kitchen, & self-contained studio*

Janet & Chris Abbott
104 Nayland Street,
Sumner, Christchurch

Tel (03) 326 6111 or 0800 020 654
or 021 654 344
Fax (03) 326 7034
info@abbotthouse.co.nz
www.abbotthouse.co.nz

Double/Twin $120-$140
Single $100-$120
(Breakfast provisions first night)
Children $10 per extra child
per night (Max $30pw)
Weekly discounts
Visa MC accepted
Children welcome
3 King/Twin (3 bdrm)
Bathrooms: 1 Ensuite 1 Private

Your hosts, Chris and Janet Abbott welcome you to our historic restored 1870s villa in Christchurch's unique seaside village. Our home is one block from the beach, and an easy ten-minute walk along the beach to Sumner's many cafÈs, restaurants, boutique shops and cinema. Both suite and studio have king-sized beds, own kitchen areas, TV, DVD and internet access. Off-street parking. Laundry facilities. Home-baked bread.Wonderful base for many walks, mountain biking and road biking.

Christchurch - Sumner *15 km E of Cathedral Square*

Scarborough-Heights *Luxury B&B*
Barbara and Brian Hanlon
21 Godley Drive,
Scarborough, Christchurch 8081

Tel (03) 326 7060
or 027 229 7312
Fax (03) 326 7061
stay@scarborough-heights.co.nz
www.scarborough-heights.co.nz

Double/Twin $180
Single $120
(Full breakfast)
Children $50 (5-12years)
Dinner $50 by arrangement
Visa MC accepted
Children welcome
1 King 1 Queen 3 Single (2 bdrm)
Bathrooms: 1 Ensuite 1 Private
Private bathroom has bath and shower.

Scarborough-Heights is a large, modern architecturally designed home set in an award winning garden, high on Scarborough Hill and offering luxurious bed & breakfast accommodation. All rooms offer spectacular views of the Southern Alps, Christchurch City and South Pacific Ocean. We provide friendly hospitality in peaceful, quiet surroundings yet are only 20 minutes from the city centre and 5 minutes from the trendy and popular seaside village of Sumner with its many cafes, specialty shops and cinema. We share our home with two cats.

Christchurch - Sumner *13 km E of Cathedral Square*

Tiromoana Luxury B&B Guests' kitchen facilities

Helen Mackay & Brian Lamb
89 Richmond Hill Road,
Sumner, Christchurch

Tel (03) 326 6209
or 021 070 3777
Fax (03) 326 6208
relax@tiromoana.co.nz
www.tiromoana.co.nz

Double/Twin $140-$150
Single $90-$135
(Full breakfast)
Children $20
Visa MC accepted
Children welcome
1 King/Twin 1 King 1 Queen
1 Double/Twin (3 bdrm)
Bathrooms: 1 Ensuite 1 Private
Plus bath outside under the stars!

Tiromoana was built in 1904 in a spectacular position overlooking the beach. A perfect spot to relax, wander the garden, have a bath outside under the stars and sleep to the sound of the sea. The atmosphere is friendly, relaxed and informal, providing guests' lounge and kitchen facilities, and a fresh and generous breakfast. Laundry facilities available. Sumner is 15 minutes from the city, within easy walking of village cafes, movie theatres, specialty shops and the beach. We look forward to welcoming you.

Lincoln *20 km S of Christcurch*

Hazelview B&B Apartment with Kitchen

Diane & Rick Fraser
1153/2 Springs Road,
Lincoln
7647

Tel (03) 325 3362
enquiry@hazelview.co.nz
www.hazelview.co.nz

Double/Twin $130
Single $110
(Continental breakfast provisions)
Children using existing
kingsize bed in lounge
10% discount three or more nights
Visa MC accepted
1 King 1 Double/Twin (1 bdrm)
Bathrooms: 1 Ensuite

In a totally private rural setting Hazelview nut orchard is only a short drive from the city and airport. The upstairs apartment has one luxury bedroom with finest linen, ensuite bathroom (spa bath and separate shower), spacious lounge, TV & VCR, guest library, kitchen facilities and extra bed. Restaurants, wineries, golf, Lincoln Village and University are all nearby. Coffees, teas and nibbles included. Be assured of a warm welcome and memorable stay. Two cats and two young adults at home.

Lincoln-Tia Tapu *20 km SE of Christchurch*
Fantail Lodge on Greenpark *Country B&B*
Pamela & Doug Hueston
164 River Road,
Tai Tapu-Lincoln,
Christchurch RD 2
7672

Tel (03) 325 7572
or 027 433 7706
or 027 425 7007
riversidegpk@xtra.co.nz
www.phototours.co.nz

Double/Twin $100-$130
Single $90-$110
(Continental breakfast)
Visa MC accepted
1 King 1 Double/Twin (2 bdrm)
Bathrooms: 1 Ensuite 2 Family share

Located on River Road meandering along the Halswell River. Artist Pamela and Photographer Doug share the comfort of their elegant and spacious home, landscaped grounds, in tranquil country surroundings, views of the Alps, sunsets, nestled in our 10 acre farmlet, farming cattle and sheep. Native birds: Fantails and Pukekos often frequent our garden. Pick-up from Airport, (25km.) by arrangement.Near Lincoln University 5km Local award winning winerys- restaurants within 5-12 km.We also offer guided Banks Peninsula Tours and other Photography Tours

Lyttelton *9 km E of Christchurch*
The Rookery *B&B Homestay*
Angus & Rene Macpherson
9 Ross Terrace,
Lyttelton
8082

Tel (03) 328 8038
rooks@amma.co.nz
http://therookery.co.nz

Double/Twin $131-$148
Single $84
(Full breakfast)
2 Queen 1 Single (3 bdrm)
Bathrooms: 1 Ensuite
1 Family share

The Rookery is one of Lyttelton's oldest cottages with delightful panoramic views over the harbour. To capture the character of the Victorian era we as designers have paid particular attention to the colours and finishes that ensure our visitors' enjoyment during their stay. Rooms are double glazed with underfloor heating and electric blankets. Only 15 minutes from the Garden City we are ideally located for exploring the Banks Peninsula. Angus, Rene and our two cats Cleopatra and Caesar offer you a warm and friendly welcome.

Governors Bay *13 km SE of Christchurch*

Tintagel House *B&B*

Niare and Alister Scoble
22, Zephyr Terrace,
Governors Bay,
RD 1, Lyttelton
Christchurch,
Canterbury 8971

Tel (03) 329 9580
or 021 058 2075
tintagelhouse@xtra.co.nz
http://tintagelhouse.co.nz

Double/Twin $140-$180
Single $80-$90
(Full breakfast)
Children by arrangement
Cash or cheque only
Not suitable for children
Pets welcome
1 King 1 Queen 1 Twin (2 bdrm)
Bathrooms: 1 Ensuite 1 Private

Set in a tranquil garden' Tintagel House', which was built in 1964, over looks the top end of Lyttelton harbour. We came to live here in 2005 after spending 6 years in the UK, where Niare ran a B&B in our National Trust House, at Lanhydrock in Cornwall, supported by the animals Jolee (white retriever) Cinnamon and Dolly-Pepper, (Cats). Our day begins and ends with the song of bellbirds. A ten minute walk down to the Jetty passes the local Pub and Cafe.

~

Teddington - Lyttelton Harbour *20 km S of Christchurch*

Bergli Hill Farmstay *Farmstay*

Rowena & Max Dorfliger
265 Charteris Bay Road,
Teddington, RD 1 Lyttelton

Tel (03) 329 9118
or 027 482 9410
Fax (03) 329 9118
bergli@ihug.co.nz
www.vmacgill.net/bergli

Double/Twin $125-$150
Single $85-$110
(Full breakfast)
Dinner from $35 by arrangement
Visa MC accepted
Children and pets welcome
1 King/Twin 1 Queen
1 Double/Twin 3 Twin
9 Single (3 bdrm)
Bathrooms: 2 Ensuite 1 Family share

Lyttelton Harbour and the Port Hills create a dynamic panorama you can enjoy from our custom-built log house. Rowena speaks Japanese (but is a Kiwi) and Max speaks German. We are both self-employed and enjoy sharing woolcrafts from our sheep and alpacas,or a sail on Max's yacht. Our pet cats,cows and calves welcome guests enthusiastically. Whether relaxing on the veranda at Max's hand-crafted table or sipping wine in the spa bath, we are sure you will make good memories.

Please let your hosts know if you have to cancel
they will have spent time preparing for you.

Diamond Harbour *25 km E of Christchurch*
The Old Exchange *B&B*
Jill & Graeme Martin
2 Waipapa Avenue,
Diamond Harbour,
Christchurch

Tel (03) 329 4275
or 027 482 6014
martingj@xtra.co.nz
www.bankspeninsulaholidayhomes.co.nz

Double/Twin $110
Single $70
(Continental breakfast)
Children by arrangement
Dinner within strolling distance
from Godley House Restaurant
2 Queen (2 bdrm)
Bathrooms: 2 Ensuite
Large shower with toilet and basin

The Old Exchange guest accommodation is quaint and full of charm and character, with inner harbour views. The two newly renovated warm and comfortable bedrooms are housed in what was once the old Telephone Exchange and Post Office for Diamond Harbour. Five minute walk to Diamond Harbour beach or Jetty where one can catch a ten minute ferry ride across the harbour to Lyttelton. Guest Comment - 'Fantastic place - the best so far in NZ and in our top list for B&Bs worldwide - thanks so much'.

Banks Peninsula - Okains Bay *18 km N of Akaroa*

Kawatea *Farmstay*
Judy & Kerry Thacker
1048 Okains Bay Road, Okains Bay, Banks Peninsula

Tel (03) 304 8621 Fax (03) 304 8621 kawatea@xtra.co.nz
www.kawateafarmstay.co.nz

Double/Twin $120-$155 Single $80-$155 (Full breakfast)
Children by arrangement   Dinner $35   Visa MC accepted
3 Queen 2 Single (3 bdrm)
Bathrooms: 1 Ensuite 1 Private 1 Guest share Bath, Shower,
Separate Toilet

Experience the grace and charm of yesteryear, while
enjoying the fine food and wine of NZ today. Revel
in the peace of countrylife, but still be close to sights and
activities. Welcome to Kawatea, an historic homestead set
in spacious gardens, and surrounded by land farmed by our
Irish ancestors since the 1850s. Built in 1900 from native
timbers, the carefully renovated house features stained glass
windows and handcrafted furniture.

Linger over your choice of breakfast in the conservatory. Join
us in the evening for creative country fare and seafood from
the Bay whilst sharing experiences with fellow travellers.

Explore our 1400 acre farm and feed the pet sheep. Enjoy
Okains Bay's unspoilt swimming beach, observe the
birdlife on the estuary, or walk along the scenic coastline to
secluded bays and a seal colony with excellent photographic
opportunities. Learn about Maori culture and the life of
early settlers at the acclaimed Okains Bay Museum.

Visit Akaroa with its French influence and galleries. Sample
local wines and watch traditional cheese making. Golf,
kayak, take a cruise or swim with the rare Hector Dolphins.

We have been hosting since 1988, and offer thoughtful
personal attention and friendly hospitality in a relaxed
atmosphere. Directions: Take Highway 75 from Christchurch through Duvauchelle.
Turn left at signpost marked Okains Bay. Kawatea is 11km on right.

Akaroa - Barry's Bay *12 km W of Akaroa*

Rosslyn Estate *B&B Homestay Farmstay*
Ross, Lynette, Kirsty (16) & Matt (14) Curry
Barry's Bay, RD 2, Akaroa

Tel (03) 304 5804 or 027 237 8609
Fax (03) 304 5804
rosslyn@akaroanz.co.nz

Double/Twin $130-$150 Single $120 (Full breakfast)
Children negotiable
Dinner $45pp
1 night stay $150, 2 or more nights $130 per/night
Visa MC accepted
2 Queen (2 bdrm)
Bathrooms: 2 Ensuite

Rosslyn is a large historic homestead built in the 1860's of native timbers milled on the property, set on a working dairy farm amid the rolling hills of Banks Peninsula over looking the serene Akaroa Harbour.

Our family home of four generations situated within informal gardens offers the tranquillity of farm life, while our entrance is conveniently situated on the main road between Christchurch and 12km before Akaroa, allowing you to explore this intriguing volcanic peninsula with ease. While with us you will have a large ground floor bedroom, firm queen bed, ensuite bathroom, antiques, central heating and screened windows for your comfort. A spa room, and laundry are also available at no charge.

Breakfast ranges from fresh fruit to full cooked. We take pride in offering quality home grown and prepared produce and preserves, served at the family table in the farm style kitchen.

We have been privilaged to share our lifesyle with guests since 1987, in that time we have enjoyed some amazing experiences, fantastic dinner conversations and long breakfasts, we trust we can enhance your trip as well with local knowledge and a slice of a kiwi family, which includes our pets.

We look forward to welcoming you with a refreshing tea, coffee or cool drink served with home baking.

Directions: State Highway 75, Rosslyn Estate sign behind picket fence (left travelling to Akaroa) in Barry's Bay. The house is set 400m from the entrance.

Akaroa - Paua Bay *12 km E of Akaroa*
Paua Bay Farmstay *B&B Farmstay*

Murray & Sue Johns
Postal: C/- 113 Beach Road, Akaroa, Banks Peninsula

Tel (03) 304 8511 or 021 133 8194
Fax (03) 304 8511
info@pauabay.com
www.pauabay.com

Double/Twin $120-$140 (Full breakfast)
Dinner $40 Children welcome
1 Queen 1 Twin (2 bdrm)
Bathrooms: 1 Ensuite 1 Guest share

Time spent at Paua Bay is a truely unique experience. Not only will you be able to enjoy the wonderful surroundings but also you will join a traditional NZ farming family sharing their daily endeavors.

Set in a private bay our 900 acre sheep, cattle & deer farm is surrounded by spectacular coastline, native bush & streams. You are spoilt for choice, walk to the beach, enjoy seals and extensive birdlife, join in seasonal farm activities.

The farmhouse is surrounded by a wonderful garden and around each corner in the path is a new surprise, a secluded moonlight bath.....a hammock....a sculpture. The guest room has wooden floors, a clawfoot bath, fresh flowers and from the queensize bed you can watch the sun rise out of the South Pacific.

In the evening take the opportunity to enjoy the company of our 6th generation farming family. Share a generous meal of fresh farm produce with relaxed conversation around the large kitchen table. New Zealand wines & beers are included.

The nearby historic French settlement of Akaroa offers guests world renouned harbour cruises and its Hector dolphins. Quiet wanderings exploring this village allows guests time to reflect on days gone by.

Akaroa *5 km N of Akaroa*
LeLievre Farmstay *Homestay Farmstay*
Hanne & Paul LeLievre
Box 4 Akaroa,
154 Takamatua Valley Road,
Banks Peninsula

Tel (03) 304 7255
Fax (03) 304 7255
Double.L@Xtra.co.nz
www.sealtours.co.nz

Double/Twin $140
Single $90
(Full breakfast)
Dinner $35
Children welcome
1 Queen 1 Double/Twin
1 Single (2 bdrm)
Bathrooms: 2 Ensuite

Our home is situated 1.5km up Takamatua Valley and 5km from Akaroa. We farm sheep, cattle deer and usually have a menagerie of orphaned pets etc. Our interests include golf and bridge. We invite you to enjoy some good old fashioned country hospitality. A trip to the Akaroa Seal Colony, which featured on the TV programmes A Flying Visit, Totally Wild and The Great Outdoors, is a must do. Safari includes a scenic drive, through, a working farm, with the farmer.

Akaroa *80 km SE of Christchurch*
The Maples *B&B*
Lesley & Peter Keppel
158 Rue Jolie,
Akaroa

Tel (03) 304 8767
Fax (03) 304 8767
maplesakaroa@xtra.co.nz
www.themaplesakaroa.co.nz

Double/Twin $140-$150
Single $100
(Full breakfast)
Visa MC accepted
3 Queen 1 Single (3 bdrm)
Bathrooms: 3 Ensuite

The Maples is a charming historic 2 storey home built in 1877. It is situated in a delightful garden setting, 3 minutes walk from the cafes and waterfront. We offer 2 queen bedrooms with ensuites upstairs and a separate garden room with a queen and single bed also ensuite. You can relax in the separate guests' lounge where tea and coffee is available. Our delicious continental and cooked breakfasts include freshly baked croissants and home made jams.

Akaroa *80 km SE of Christchurch*
Wilderness House *Luxury B&B*
Jim & Liz Coubrough
42 Rue Grehan,
Akaroa

Tel (03) 304 7517
or 021 669 381
Fax (03) 304 7518
info@wildernesshouse.co.nz
www.wildernesshouse.co.nz

Double/Twin $275
Single $275
(Full breakfast)
Dinner by special arrangement
Visa MC Eftpos accepted
Not suitable for children
1 King/Twin 3 Queen (4 bdrm)
Bathrooms: 3 Ensuite 1 Private

Treat yourself to a memorable experience in one of Akaroa's gracious historic homes. Built in 1878 our home is set in a one acre garden including a petite vineyard. Rooms have wireless internet, harbour/valley views and feature gorgeous linen, garden flowers, a selection of teas, coffee and home-baking. Linger over our special breakfasts. Secluded and private we are just a short stroll to the village. Join us for a glass of our wine each evening. Unwind, relax and enjoy! Resident cat George.

Akaroa Harbour - French Farm *70 km SE of Christchurch*
Bantry Lodge *B&B Cottage with Kitchen*
Dolina Barker
French Farm,
RD 2,
Akaroa

Tel (03) 304 5161
or 027 313 2406
Fax (03) 304 5162
barker.d@xtra.co.nz
www.bantrylodge.co.nz

Double/Twin $130-$150
(Full breakfast)
Dinner $40 by arrangement
Self-contained cottage sleeps 4
Visa MC Diners Amex accepted
Children and pets welcome
2 Queen 2 Double/Twin (3 bdrm)
Bathrooms: 2 Private 1 Guest share

This historic home has views across Akaroa Harbour 50 metres away. Groundfloor queen room has french doors to verandah and sea views, private bath. Upstairs queen room with balcony overlooks harbour , private bath. Coffee, tea facilities provided with home-baking. The comfortable sitting room is for relaxing or joining me for a drink. Full breakfast is served in the elegant dining room. Tranquillity and space. A self-contained cottage sleeps 4. Linen, breakfast ingredients supplied. 1 shy cat.

Akaroa *80 km SE of Christchurch*

Mulberry House *B&B Homestay Cottage with Kitchen Guest House*

Anne Craig & Jack Clark
9 William Street, Akaroa 8161,

Tel (03) 304 7778 or 021 610456
Fax (03) 304 7778
anneandjacknz@yahoo.com
www.mulberryhouse.co.nz

Double/Twin $125-$165 Single $90 (Special breakfast)
$10 surcharge 1 night stay
Children welcome
3 King 1 Queen 1 Twin 4 Single (7 bdrm)
Bathrooms: 2 Ensuite 1 Private 2 Guest share

Experience the very best in homestyle accommodation and delight in the setting of Mulberry House, which accommodates up to thirteen guests. All rooms are beautifully decorated and feature quality beds and fine linen. There is a choice of double rooms, with or without ensuite, and a twin room which will delight children.

The romantic poolside summerhouse has its own kitchen, ensuite and garden to provide total privacy if desired. We also have a beautifully furnished,self contained cottage with full kitchen.

Breakfasts are a specialty and feature a choice of American, European, English, and New Zealand styles. Champagne breakfasts and other meals by arrangement. Meals can be served outside in the summer months overlooking the pool.

Your hosts: Well travelled and semi retired Anne Craig and Jack Clark offer unparalleled hospitality. Fussy about food, both Anne and Jack love to cook: Anne preserves and bakes, and Jack adds his American expertise to breakfasts of pancakes, waffles, omelettes, fresh fruits, and delicious coffee from the espresso machine.

Guest Comments - Desmond Balmer (LondonGuardian/Observer Travel) recommends Mulberry House as amongst New Zealand's Top Twenty. Featured on Sydney's channel 7 "Ernie Dingo's Getaway" as "the place to stay "in Akoroa. Featured in Autumn 2000 European "Wining and Dining.

Akaroa *80 km SE of Christchurch*
La Belle Villa *B&B*

Alice & Paul Hewitson
113 Rue Jolie,
Akaroa

Tel (03) 304 7084
or 021 045 9156
Fax (03) 304 7084
bookings@labellevilla.co.nz
www.labellevilla.co.nz

Double/Twin $140-$160
Single $120-$140
(Special breakfast)
Visa MC accepted
Children welcome
1 King/Twin 2 King
1 Queen (4 bdrm)
Bathrooms: 4 Ensuite

A warm welcome awaits you. Relax in the surroundings of a bygone era and appreciate the antiques in our much photographed historic villa. Built in the 1870's La belle Villa is set in beautiful, mature grounds,with a trickling stream, it offers indoor/outdoor living including seperate guest lounge. Our special alfresco breakfast which includes fresh local produce, homebaking and espresso coffee has won universal praise. Located in close proximity to restaurants, shops and cinema makes us the ideal place to stay in Akaroa.

Akaroa *80 km SE of Christchurch*
Aka-View *B&B*

Lib & Ben Hutchinson
5 Langlois Lane,
Akaroa
7542

Tel (03) 304 8008
or 027 459 6042
Fax (03) 304 8008
aka-view@xtra.co.nz
www.aka-view.co.nz

Double/Twin $165-$180
Single $125-$135
(Full breakfast)
Visa MC accepted
Pet free home
3 Queen 1 Twin (4 bdrm)
Bathrooms: 1 Ensuite 2 Private

A ka-View is a puurpose built Mediterranean styled Bed & Breakfast. The upper level features two queen suites, one twin, private guest study, separate tea /coffee facilites, all with unsurpassed harbour views. In addition, guests may choose to use the formal lounge, with cosy fire, stylish but comfortable furnishings. A romantic option is our lower level garden studio-private coutyard, sunny, queen with ensuite, lounge, TV, full tea/coffee making facilities. Enjoy a continental or cooked breakfast in the kitchen or delivered to your garden studio.

Akaroa
L'Abri of Takamatua *B&B Cottage with Kitchen*

Jane Cook
7 Takamatua Bay Road,
Akaroa,
Christchurch

Tel (03) 304 7833
or 027 202 8521
janee_cook@hotmail.com

Double/Twin $250
(Special breakfast)
Dinner $60pp
Cottage $195
Visa MC accepted
Pets welcome
3 Queen
Bathrooms: 2 Ensuite 1 Private

L'Abri sits about the beautiful Takamatua Bay, just minutes from Akaroa. It offers luxury bed & breakfast accommodation in a new, architecturally designed home. The two guestrooms/ensuites have their own access to extensive decks. The cottage, in garden provides self-contained privacy amid productive organic gardens. Enjoy fresh flowers and gourmet breakfast of locally sourced food. Dine in by prior arrangement or eat out in one of Akaroa's famous restaurants. Jane's menagerie includes a cat named Daisy, three outdoor cockatiels and hens.

Highcountry Canterbury - Castle Hiii *33 km W of Springfield*
The Burn Alpine B&B *B&B Homestay*

Bob Edge & Phil Stephenson
11 Torlesse Place,
Castle Hill Village, Canterbury

Tel (03) 318 7559
Fax (03) 318 7558
theburn@xtra.co.nz
www.theburn.co.nz

Double/Twin up to $160
Single $80-$90
(Continental breakfast)
Children under 13 half price
Dinner home cooked dining $35 pp
Dinner, Bed & Breakfast $115 pp
Visa MC accepted
Children welcome
3 Queen 1 Twin (4 bdrm)
Bathrooms: 2 Guest share
Two bathrooms with showering facilites and seperate toilets

1 hour west of Christchurch, a carefree atmosphere prevails at The Burn. Nestled in the heart of the Southern Alps, it's arguably New Zealand's highest B&B. We designed and built our alpine lodge to maximise mountain vistas. Centered in the mystic Castlehill Basin, surrounded by native forest, this is a fantastic place to return after a days activity or just kick back and relax on the sunny deck. A host of outdoor sports include ski/snowboarding, hiking, mountain biking, and flyfishing. Professional flyfishing guiding available.

Canterbury

Darfield *4 km W of Darfield*
The Oaks Historic Homestead *B&B Homestay*

Madeleine de Jong
State Highway 73,
Corner of Clintons Road,
Darfield

Tel (03) 318 7232
or 027 241 3999
Fax (03) 318 7236
theoaks@quicksilver.net.nz
www.theoakshomestead.co.nz

Double/Twin $175-$275
Single $150 (Full breakfast)
Dinner $47.50 pp on request
Visa MC Eftpos accepted
Children and pets welcome
3 Queen 1 Single (4 bdrm)
Bathrooms: 1 Ensuite 2 Private

One of Canterbury's oldest homesteads, restored to its former glory. Located amidst stunning scenery of the Southern Alps to the Westcoast, with ski fields, golf courses and tourist attractions on its doorstep. The Oaks features: guest rooms with ensuite/private bathrooms, a guest dining and living room featuring stunning open fires, a traditional large homestead kitchen, beautiful verandas for outdoor entertaining. Children welcome. Pets on request. Your Host Madeleine speaks 5 languages and is a keen cook. Wherever possible I try to use fresh organic produce.

Mt Hutt - Methven *6.4 km E of Methven*
Pagey's Farmstay *B&B Farmstay Kitchen - new*

Shirley & Gene Pagey
663 Methven-Chertsey Road,
RD 12 Rakaia

Tel (03) 302 1713
Fax (03) 302 1714
pageysfarmstay@wave.co.nz
www.tourism.net.nz

Double/Twin $120
Single $90
(Full breakfast)
Children under 12 half price
Dinner $30pp
Spa pool
Pet free home
Children welcome
1 King 1 Queen 4 Single (3 bdrm)
Bathrooms: 2 Private new - large showers

Enjoy hospitality and freedom in our lovely expansive home with new kitchen, bathrooms, large redorated bedrooms with luxurious beds, set amidst aged oak trees and large rose garden. Watch our 47" TV . Enjoy a pre-dinner drink, wine, crystal clear mountain water and home-grown cuisine. Star gaze in our luxurious massaging spa. Surrounding activities include breathtaking bush walks, 2 superior golf courses, ballooning and skiing. Short notice is our speciality. Directions from Methven town centre, turn down Methven Chertsey Road, 6km signposted.

Mt Hutt - Methven *11 km W of Methven*

Glenview Farmstay *B&B Farmstay Cottage No Kitchen*

Helen & Mike Johnstone
142 Hart Road, Methven,

Tel (03) 302 8620 Fax (03) 302 8620
helenmikejohnstone@yahoo.com

Double/Twin $110 Single $80 (Full breakfast)
Children $25
Dinner $25
Children welcome
2 Queen 2 Double/Twin 1 Twin 2 Single (5 bdrm)
Bathrooms: 1 Ensuite 1 Guest share Ensuite in unit

Glenview Farmstay is situated at the base of Mt Hutt Ski Field, with the house designed to look at the mountains and down the Canterbury Plains to the Port Hills.

We farm cattle and sheep on our 1200 acre farm. We have several working farm dogs and a very friendly cat and a pet dog.

There is a peaceful unit in the garden which is suitable for a couple or a family. It has two bedrooms, one with 1 queen bed and the other with 1 double and 1 single bed, ensuite, TV, tea & coffee facilities and wonderful views. The rooms in the house have separate access, good heating and are non-smoking. Dinner by arrangement. Free farm tours on request.

Methven is only 10 minutes away and we are very close to good fishing, golf, ballooning, horse treking, bush walks and jet boating. Free transfers to local walkways. One hour from Christchurch and we are on the way to Queenstown along Highway 72.

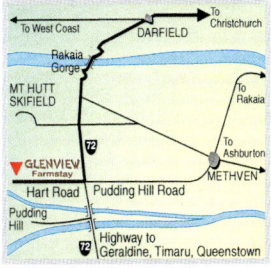

Mt Hutt - Methven *4 km NW of Methven - Mt Hutt Village*

Green Gables Deer Farm *B&B Farmstay*

Irene & Mike Harris
185 Waimarama Road, Methven-Mt Hutt Village,
Postal No. 12, Rakaia

Tel (03) 302 8308 or New Zealand (0800 466 093)
Fax (03) 302 8309
greengables@xtra.co.nz   www.nzfarmstay.com

Double/Twin $140-$180 Single $110-$140
(Special breakfast)
Children $55   Dinner $50 pp by arrangement
Visa MC accepted   Children welcome
2 King 2 Twin (3 bdrm)
Bathrooms: 2 Ensuite 1 Private

Set in tranquil surroundings at the foot of Mt.Hutt, Green Gables Deer Farm is within easy reach of Christchurch (1hr), Kaikoura for Whale Watching and Dolphins (3hrs), Mt.Cook (3.5hrs) and Queenstown (approx 5.5hrs).

Our stylish rooms have all the comforts you will require with your own private entrance opening out onto the garden with a backdrop of graceful deer wandering in the paddocks and the ever changing colours of the mountain views. There is plenty of room to stroll, maybe feed the pet deer and meet our friendly dogs or just relax and unwind.

Start your evening meal with a complimentary pre-dinner drink and enjoy the fresh local produce used in our home cooked meals and desserts.

ACTIVITIES:- Try out the many summer and winter activities close by - Golf courses at Methven and Terrace Downs (club & cart hire available), Fishing, Hot Air ballooning, Jet Boating, Skiing, 4WD Scenic Tours (available by arrangement), Horse Trekking, Scenic Flights, Ecotours and Alpine Rhododrendon Walks to name but a few. There are even trips to "Eldoras" the Lord of the Rings film site at Mt.Sunday

LOCATION:- Situated on S/H77 4kms N/W Methven. From Inland Scenic-Route 72 turn into S/H77 travel 5kms Green Gables Deer Farm is on the right.

Staveley - Mt Somers *20 km SW of Methven*
Korobahn Lodge *B&B Homestay*
Caroline & John Lartice
Burgess Road,
Staveley

Tel (03) 303 0828
carolinel@slingshot.co.nz
www.korobahnlodge.co.nz

Double/Twin $150-$180
Single $110-$130
(Full breakfast)
Dinner $55 3 courses with
wine or beer, by arrangement
Visa MC accepted
Children welcome
2 Queen 1 Twin (3 bdrm)
Bathrooms: 3 Ensuite

Welcome to our unique North American barn style homestead. Korobahn is tucked into the foot of Mt Somers and stands in several acres of gardens, surrounded by farmland. The property has been totally refurbished, and offers high quality accommodation and comfort. Korobahn Lodge is on Inland Scenic Highway 72, approximatly 110 kilometres southwest of Christchurch Airport and on the way to Mt Cook and Queenstown. Local activites include bush walking, horse treks, Lord of the Rings film site, jet boating, fishing, in season skating and skiing.

Staveley - Mt Somers *110 km SW of Christchurch*
Alpine Views Farmstay and B&B *B&B Homestay Farmstay*
Anna & Ken McNally
28 Symes Road, RD1, Ashburton

Tel (03) 303 0800
or (027) 303 0700
anna@alpineviews.co.nz
http://alpineviews.co.nz

Double/Twin $120-$150
Single $80
(Full breakfast)
Children welcome - pet animals to feed!
Dinner available on request $40
Caravan sites available $20/night
Visa MC accepted
Children and pets welcome
2 Queen 1 Twin (3 bdrm)
Bathrooms: 2 Ensuite

Alpine Views is nestled under Mt Somers where walking tracks and ice skating are popular, and only 15 minutes from the Mt Hutt Ski area. Three acres of park-like gardens with mature trees and panoramic views of the Southern Alps. We offer warm comfortable, quality accommodation and food. Part of a 60acre farm with a variety of animals with working dogs. Situated on Scenic Highway 72, one hour drive from Christchurch Airport, on route to Mt Cook and Queenstown destinations.

Rakaia *50 km S of Christchurch*
St Ita's Guesthouse *B&B Guest House*

Miriam & Ken Cutforth
11 Barrhill/Methven Road,
Rakaia Township, Canterbury

Tel (03) 302 7546
or 027 488 8673
Fax (03) 302 7564
stitas@xtra.co.nz
www.stitas.co.nz

Double/Twin $130
Single $80
(Full breakfast)
Children $30
Dinner $30pp
Visa MC accepted
Children welcome
2 Queen 1 Double/Twin
4 Single (4 bdrm)
Bathrooms: 3 Ensuite 1 Private with bath

Relax in our elegant and comfortable historic former convent, 600 metres from SH1 in small town New Zealand. Excellent base for exploring Ashburton District. Excellent first and last stop from Christchurch International Airport. Three bedrooms have ensuites and garden views. The fourth the Chapel has a private bathroom. Walking distance to local shops, great cafes, crafts and winery. Close to golf and salmon fishing, 30 minutes to skiing, jet boating. Dinner by arrangement. Full breakfasts. Share the open fire with our two moggies.

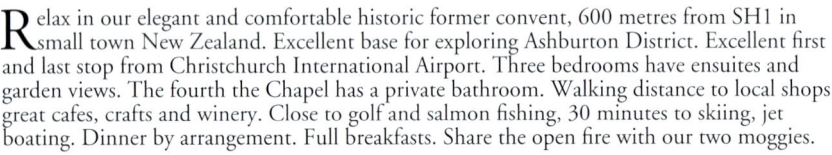

Ashburton *90 km S of Christchurch*
Weir Homestay *B&B Homestay*

Pat & Dave Weir
35 Leeston Street,
Ashburton Central

Tel (03) 308 3534
pndweir@clear.net.nz

Double/Twin $100
Single $50
(Breakfast by arrangement)
Dinner $25
Visa MC accepted
1 Double/Twin 3 Single (2 bdrm)
Bathrooms: 1 Ensuite 1 Guest share
1 Family share

Our comfortable home is situated in a quiet street with the added pleasure of looking onto a rural scene. We are 10-15 minutes walk from town. Guest rooms have comfortable beds with electric blankets. We welcome the opportunity to meet and greet visitors and wish to make your stay a happy one. Your hosts are retired but active, hobbies general/varied from meeting people to walking etc. Request visitors no smoking inside home. Off-street parking.

Ashburton *1 km N of Ashburton Info Centre*
Carradale Manor *B&B Homestay*
Karen & Jim McIntyre
93 Pages Road, Allenton, Ashburton

Tel (03) 308 6577 Fax (03) 308 6548
jkmcintyre@xtra.co.nz
www.ashburton.co.nz/carradale

Double/Twin $120-$140 Single $80 (Full breakfast)
Children under 12 half price Dinner $40 by arrangement
Visa MC accepted
2 King/Twin 1 Queen (3 bdrm)
Bathrooms: 1 Ensuite 1 Private

We are one hour from Christchurch International Airport. Our sunny spacious home, which is just off State Highway One in Ashburton, is situated in a beautiful, large and sheltered garden by a stream, where you can enjoy peace and tranquility.After offering hospitality for 16 years on Carradale Farm, we have now retired from Carradale Farm in the country to Carradale Manor in the town where we will continue to operate with those same high standards.

We offer either a fully cooked breakfast, or continental breakfast, served with delicious home made jams and preserves.For your convenience tea/coffee making facilities, and electric blankets are for use in all rooms. Internet access available.

As we have both travelled extensively in New Zealand, Australia, United Kingdom, Europe, North America, Zimbabwe, South Africa, Vietnam and Singapore, we would like to offer hospitality to fellow travellers. Our hobbies include meeting people, travel, reading, photography, gardening, sewing, cake decorating, rugby, cricket, Jim belongs to the Masonic Lodge and Karen is involved in Community Affairs including Probus.

For young children we have a cot and highchair available.Our resident cat 'Lady Jane' is on hand to comfort you.

CARRADALE MANOR, "WHERE PEOPLE COME AS STRANGERS AND LEAVE AS FRIENDS"

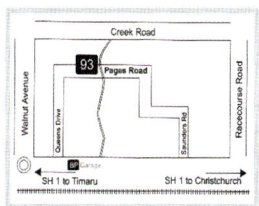

Ashburton *7 km SE of Ashburton*
Lake Hood Homestay B&B *B&B*

Eric and Eleanor Weir
14 Witney Lane,
Lake Hood,
Ashburton

Tel (03) 302 6914
Fax (03) 302 6914
enquiries@lakehoodhomestay.co.nz
www.lakehoodhomestay.co.nz

Double/Twin $130-$150
(Full breakfast)
Visa MC accepted
Pet free home
Not suitable for children
1 King/Twin 1 Queen (2 bdrm)
Bathrooms: 2 Ensuite

Lake Hood Homestay B&B is located on the canal network adjoining Lake Hood, 7km from Ashburton. Lake Hood is home to a variety of water sports and popular for swimming, jogging, walking, fishing or just generally relaxing. Our homestay comprises two modern studio suites each featuring: separate entrance, King or Queen bed (twin by arrangement), private en-suite, television, tea/coffee making, door to patio and canal-side garden. Delicious country-style breakfast included. Free use of kayaks, bicycles. Sailing, fishing by arrangement. See www.lakehoodhomestay.co.nz

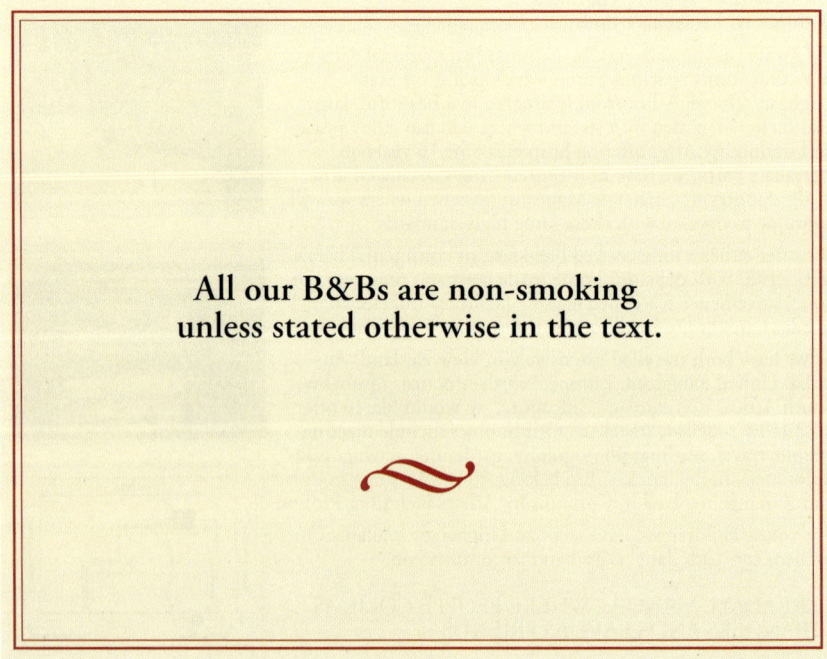

**All our B&Bs are non-smoking
unless stated otherwise in the text.**

South Canterbury & North Otago

Geraldine *0.5 km S of Geraldine*
Victoria Villa *B&B Cottage with Kitchen*

Leigh & Jerry Basinger
55 Cox Street, Geraldine 7930

Tel (03) 693 8605
or 0800 537 533
027 482 1842
Fax (03) 693 8605
gtbasinger@yahoo.com

Double/Twin $100-$125
Single $80-$100
(Full breakfast)
Children $10-$15
Dinner by arrangement
Detached studio unit
Visa MC Amex accepted
3 Queen 2 Double/Twin
2 Single (4 bdrm)
Bathrooms: 3 Ensuite 1 Private

Welcome to our historical villa, completely refurbished - spacious bedrooms with ensuites or private bathroom. Off-street parking, private entrance and lounge. Molded ceilings, native woods. Also, separate studio with ensuite and light cooking area; ideal for family. On Highway 79 to Mt Cook and Queenstown. 7 minutes walk to Geraldine Village which has boutique movie theatre, fine restaurants, sports pub,world class glass blower, boutique shops, 2 golf courses. Adjacent to domain. Personality pet dog and cat. Your hosts will assist to make your stay enjoyable.

≈

Geraldine *0.2 km S of Geraldine*
Lilymay *B&B*

Lois & Les Gillum
29 Cox Street,
Geraldine

Tel (03) 693 8838
or 0800 545 9629
lilymay@xtra.co.nz

Double/Twin $95-$100
Single $70-$75
(Full breakfast)
Children $20 - $25
Visa MC accepted
Children welcome
2 Queen 1 Double/Twin
3 Twin 3 Single (3 bdrm)
Bathrooms: 2 Guest share

Closest B&B to village shops, restaurants & cafes. A charming character home set in a large colourful garden. A friendly, warm welcome is assurred with tea/coffee and Lois' home-baked cookies. Ample off-street parking and separate guest entrance. Teas, coffee, etc. available at all times in the guest lounge with cosy open fire. We are on the main road to Mt Cook, the Southern Lakes and mountains. The ideal stopover from Christchurch (137 km).

Geraldine *3 km N of Geraldine*
Rivendell *B&B Homestay Apartment with Kitchen*

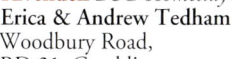

Erica & Andrew Tedham
Woodbury Road,
RD 21, Geraldine

Tel (03) 693 8559
or 021 264 1520
rivendellnz@xtra.co.nz
www.rivendellnz.co.nz

Double/Twin $100-$130
Single $85-$95
(Full breakfast)
Self-contained studio unit
with kitchen $100
Not suitable for children
Pets welcome
1 Queen 1 Double/Twin
1 Single (3 bdrm)
Bathrooms: 2 Ensuite 1 Family share
Rose Room has bath and shower

Set in over 3 acres, Rivendell is a traditional New Zealand villa and has beautiful secluded gardens that can be enjoyed relaxing on the large verandah or in the heated spa pool. Our home provides all modern facilities including central heating, internet and laundry. The delightful village of Geraldine with its numerous cafes, restaurants, shops and cinema is only 5 minutes drive. We offer you a truly warm welcome together with our friendly dogs & animals.

Geraldine *1.5 km W of town centre*
The Downs B&B *Luxury B&B*

Alycen & Myron Cournane
5 Ribbonwood Road,
The Downs, RD 21,
Geraldine

Tel (03) 693 7388
or 021 675 249
Fax (03) 693 7388
info@thedowns.co.nz
www.thedowns.co.nz

Double/Twin $200-$220
Single $150-$150
(Full breakfast)
Visa MC Diners Amex accepted
Children welcome
3 Queen 1 Twin (4 bdrm)
Bathrooms: 3 Ensuite 1 Private
Bathrooms have heaters,hairdryers &
quality toiletries.

South Canterbury
North Otago

Alycen, Myron & Max (the cat) opened this new business early in 2005. The house dates from the 70s but since then has undergone some major alterations.The upper level is now totally for guest use. There are 3 high quality ensuite guest rooms (1 with extra bedroom if required). Free guest laundry. Guestlounge/breakfast room with open bar, tea, coffee etc. Step from the lounge onto the balcony and down to the large lawn and gardens. Enjoy the peace and quiet!

Geraldine *0.5 km S of Geraldine*
Forest View *B&B*
Denese Roy
128 Talbot Street, Geraldine

Tel (03) 693 9928
or 0800 572 740
Fax (03) 693 9928
forest.view@xtra.co.nz

Double/Twin $65-$120
Single $45-$80 (Special breakfast)
Children negotiable, roll way, crib,
high chair available
Dinner $40 by arrangement -
special 3-4 course with wine.
Sleep-out $45-$65,
with continental breakfast
Visa MC accepted Pet free home
Children and pets welcome
1 King 1 Queen 1 Double/Twin
2 Twin 1 Single (5 bdrm)
Bathrooms: 1 Ensuite 1 Private 1 Guest share hair dryers, heaters, shampoo etc provided.

"More than just a night's lodging", come experience elegant hospitality. Forest View's original owner is back from California and ready to pamper you. Enjoy complimenary afternoon tea in the award winning gardens. Take a 5 minute stroll to the charming english like village, or short forest walks. A scrumptious 3 course gourmet breakfast with memorable entrees. Choose from french toast, pancakes, omelets and more. Common guest book comment: "Best breakfast in NZ." Internet,laundry & guest lounge.

Winchester *16 km N of Timaru*
Stonybanks *B&B*
Chris & Andrew Lush
Stonybanks
32 Harrisons Rd,
Winchester,
South Canterbury

Tel (03) 615 8385
or 027 661 5888
thegrange@ihug.co.nz

Double/Twin $110
Single $75
(Full breakfast)
Pet free home
Children welcome
2 Queen 2 Single (4 bdrm)
Bathrooms: 1 Ensuite 1 Private
1 Guest share

"Stonybanks" is a comfortable, well appointed home set in 6 acres of beautiful grounds. We are just off Highway 1 in the village of Winchester, moments from Highway 79 to Mt Cook, Queenstown and Southern Lakes. The area is renowned for its world class salmon and trout fishing. We are within easy driving distance of restaurants, pubs and cafes, and are happy to share our knowledge of the south island with you. We are 200m north of the Winchester village on Harrison Road.

Timaru - Seadown *4.8 km N of Timaru*
Country Homestay *Homestay*

Margaret & Ross Paterson
491 Seadown Road,
Seadown,
RD 3,
Timaru

Tel (03) 688 2468
or 021 213 7434
Fax (03) 688 2468

Double/Twin $90
Single $60
(Full breakfast)
Children half price
Dinner $25
Visa MC Diners Amex accepted
1 Double/Twin 2 Single (3 bdrm)
Bathrooms: 1 Guest share

Our homestay is approximately 10 minutes north of Timaru, situated 4.8km on Seadown Road off State Highway 1 at Washdyke - third house on left past Pharlap Statue. We have hosted on our farm for 11 years - now retired and have a country farmlet with some farm animals, with views of farmland and mountains. Day trips to Mt Cook, Hydro Lakes and ski fields, fishing, golf course few minutes away. Laundry facilities available. Interests are farming, gardening, spinning, embroidery and overseas travel.

Timaru Central *1 km W of timaru*
Jones Homestay *Homestay*

Margaret & Nevis Jones
16 Selwyn Street,
Timaru

Tel (03) 688 1400
Fax (03) 688 1400
nevisjones@xtra.co.nz

Double/Twin $120
Single $70
(Full breakfast)
Children half price
Visa MC accepted
2 Double/Twin 1 Twin
(3 bdrm)
Bathrooms: 2 Ensuite 1 Guest share

Welcome to our spacious character brick home built in the 1920s and situated in a beautiful garden with a grass tennis court. A secluded property with off-street parking and views of the surrounding sea and mountains. Centrally situated, only 5 minutes from the beach and town with an excellent choice of cafes and restaurants. On arrival tea is served on our sunny verandah. Hosts have lived and worked extensively overseas, namely South Africa, UK and the Middle East, and enjoy music, theatre, tennis and golf.

South Canterbury
North Otago

Timaru *8 km W of Timaru*
Berrillo *Luxury B&B Homestay*
Owen & Liz Berrill
32 Gladstone Road,
RD 4,
Timaru

Tel (03) 686 1688
or 021 295 2451
Fax 03 686 1678
oberrill@xtra.co.nz
www.berrillo.co.nz

Double/Twin $145
Single $100 (Full breakfast)
Children $45
Dinner $40 pp by arrangement
Visa MC accepted
1 Queen 2 Twin (2 bdrm)
Bathrooms: 2 Ensuite with power
shower, hair driers, heated towel rails

A Touch of Tuscany in Timaru. A warm welcome awaits you and we offer a complimentary glass of wine on the terrace overlooking stunning views of Mt Cook. Our award winning Home of the Year 2000 is nestled in an olive grove. We have a purpose-built guest wing with separate antique furnished lounge, Sky TV, tea/coffee making facilities. Sit and chat with us or just relax and enjoy the peace. We enjoy golf, art and music. Golf courses nearby, skifields 1 hour away. Resident labrador.

~

Timaru Central *0.1 km W of Central Timaru*
Sefton Homestay Bed & Breakfast *B&B Homestay*
Trish & John Blunden
32 Sefton Street,
Seaview,
Timaru

Tel (03) 688 0017
or 027 473 7366
or 027 470 0000
Fax (03) 688 0042
trish@seftonhomestay.co.nz
www.seftonhomestay.co.nz

Double/Twin $125
Single $110
(Full breakfast)
Children $^1/_2$ Price
Visa MC accepted
Children welcome
1 King/Twin 1 Queen
1 Double/Twin (3 bdrm)
Bathrooms: 1 Ensuite 1 Private

Relax in our superbly appointed and spacious 2 storey character brick home with sweeping views from the mountains to the sea. Refurbished with the feel of yesteryear, but with ambience and style you will love. All our children have left home with the exception of our labrador Ollie who enjoys meeting people as we do. A genuine 5 minute walk to the nearest restaurants

Timaru - Pleasant Point *17 km W of Timaru*
Longview Bed & Breakfast *B&B Farmstay*

Anita & Alan Blakemore
86 Longview Road,
Pleasant Point,
Timaru
7983

Tel (03) 614 7766
or 027 308 5078
longview86@xtra.co.nz
www.longviewfarmstay.co.nz

Double/Twin $130-$140
Single $80-$100
(Full breakfast)
Children Up to $40
Dinner by prior arrangement $40
Visa MC accepted
Children welcome
2 Queen 1 Twin (3 bdrm)
Bathrooms: 1 Guest share

Combine tranquility and stunning panoramic mountain views with the convenience of being 2 hrs drive from Christchurch and Mt Cook. Longview is situated on 25 acres, 2 kms from Pleasant Point. Wander through the olive grove, see our farm animals or relax in our private guest lounge. Join us for a chat and meet Becky, our Cocker Spaniel. Local attractions include Maori rock art, steam train, 18-hole golf course and 3 major ski fields. A choice of cafes and restaurants can be found nearby.

Timaru *1 km S of Information centre*
Blueberry Cottage *B&B Homestay*

Barbara & Rodger Baird
72A High Street,
Timaru

Tel (03) 684 3115
or 027 636 4301
Fax (03) 684 3172
relax@blueberrycottage.co.nz
www.blueberrycottage.co.nz

Double/Twin $95-$100
Single $70-$75
(Continental breakfast)
Children negotiable
Visa MC accepted
Pet free home
1 King/Twin 1 King
1 Double/Twin (2 bdrm)
Bathrooms: 1 Guest share
Bath and wet shower

Our delightfully upgraded 1950's brick home offers comfort and spectacular views of the ocean and inland to Mt Cook. The tastefully furnished rooms have television and separate patios. Handy to hospital, gardens & beach. Walking distance to shops, cafe/bars, or eating place of your choice. Day trips to lakes, skiing in winter, Mt Cook, fishing rivers, bush walks and towns nearby. Our interests can be detected by our nautical theme, the vintage car in the garage and our choice of music. "Relaxation at its best".

Timaru *1 km N of Post Office*
Nelson Heights B&B *B&B*

Claire & Lindsay
12 Nelson Terrace,
Timaru,
South Canterbury

Tel (03) 688 6646
or 027 274 3318
Fax (03) 688 6646
claire.lindsay@xtra.co.nz
www.nelsonheights.co.nz

Double/Twin $160-$170
Single $140 (Full breakfast)
Visa MC Diners Amex Eftpos accepted
1 King/Twin 3 King (4 bdrm)
Bathrooms: 4 Ensuite One with Spa Bath

A warm welcome to our 1920's villa. Nelson Heights is centrally situated to Caroline Bay, Restaurants, CBD and shopping. The guest lounge features SKY, DVD, Internet, Tea/Coffee facilities. Our balcony views the Bay and Port and a must to enjoy breakfast alfresco. Complimentary transport, golf on champion course, laundry facilities. Beautifully appointed bedrooms, Flat screen TV's, Internet and modern ensuite's all designed to cater for your comfort, satisfaction and enjoyment. Our 20 years in the hospitality industry ensures that your needs are catered for.

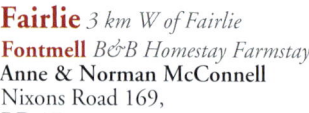

Fairlie *3 km W of Fairlie*
Fontmell *B&B Homestay Farmstay*

Anne & Norman McConnell
Nixons Road 169,
RD 17,
Fairlie

Tel (03) 685 8379
Fax (03) 685 8379

Double/Twin $100-$120
Single $65 (Full breakfast)
Children $35
Dinner $25
Cottage $190
2 King/Twin 1 Queen
1 Double/Twin 2 Twin
1 Single (4 bdrm)
Bathrooms: 1 Private 1 Guest share

Our farm consists of 400 acres producing lambs, cattle and deer. The house is situated in a large English style garden with many mature trees in a tranquil setting. In the area are 2 ski fields, golf courses, walkways and scenic drives. Informative farm tours available. Our interests include golf, gardening and music. New fully self contained 3 bedroom cottage with panoramic views of the Fairlie Basin. Directions: Nixons Road 1km West of Town Centre, Fontmell 2km up Nixons Road.

Fairlie - Kimbell *8 km W of Fairlie*
Rivendell Lodge *B&B Homestay Countrystay*

Joan Gill
15 Stanton Road, Kimbell,
RD 17, Fairlie

Tel (03) 685 8833
or 027 4819 189
Fax (03) 685 8825
info@rivendell-lodge.co.nz
www.rivendell-lodge.co.nz

Double/Twin $120-$150
Single $80-$95
(Full breakfast)
Children negotiable
Dinner $45 per person
Visa MC accepted
Pet free home
Children welcome
3 Queen 1 Double/Twin
2 Single (4 bdrm)
Bathrooms: 2 Ensuite 2 Private separate spa bath available

Quality country comfort and hospitality offered in a peaceful historic village on the Christchurch-Queenstown route. Joan is a well-travelled writer, passionate about mountains, literature and local history. I enjoy cooking and gardening and delight in sharing home grown produce. Take time out for fishing, skiing, walking, golf or water sports. Relax in the garden, complete with stream, or come with us to some of our favourite places. Complimentary refreshments on arrival. Laundry facilities available.

Lake Tekapo *40 km W of Fairlie*
Freda Du Faur House *B&B Homestay*

Dawn & Barry Clark
1 Esther Hope Street,
Lake Tekapo

Tel (03) 680 6513
dawntek@xtra.co.nz
www.fredadufaur.co.nz

Double/Twin $150-$170
Single $100-$110
(Continental breakfast,
or cooked on request)
Visa MC accepted
1 Queen 1 Double/Twin 2 Single (3 bdrm)
Bathrooms: 2 Ensuite 1 Private

Experience tranquillity and a touch of mountain magic. A warm and friendly welcome. Comfortable home, mountain and lake views. Rimu panelling, heart timber furniture, attractive decor, blending with the McKenzie Country. Bedrooms in private wing overlooking garden, two opening onto balcony. Refreshments on patio surrounded by roses or view ever changing panorama from lounge. Walkways nearby. Mt Cook one hour away. Views of skifield. Five minutes to shops and restaurants. Call for Directions. Happy hour 6-7. Our new Persian kitten called Bella welcomes you.

Lake Tekapo *43 km W of Fairlie*

Creel House *B&B*
Grant & Rosemary Brown
36 Murray Place,
Lake Tekapo

Tel (03) 680 6516
Fax (03) 680 6659
creelhouse.l.tek@xtra.co.nz
www.laketekapoflyfishing.co.nz

Double/Twin $155-$165
Single $95
(Continental breakfast)
Off-season tariff $130 double/twin
Visa MC accepted
Children welcome
2 Queen 1 Twin 2 Single (3 bdrm)
Bathrooms: 1 Ensuite 2 Private
1 private with bath

Built by Grant, our three storied home with expansive balconies offers panoramic views of the Southern Alps, Mt John, Lake Tekapo and surrounding mountains. All rooms are spacious and comfortable, with guest lounge and separate guest entrance. A NZ native garden adds an attractive feature. Restaurants in township. Our younger daughter, 18 yrs , is living with us on the ground floor with two cats, thus separate from our guest accommodation. Grant is a professional flyfishing guide (NZPFGA) and offers guided tours.

Lake Pukaki - Mt Cook *7 km N of Twizel*

Rhoborough Downs, Pukaki *Homestay*
Roberta Preston
State Highway 8
Tekapo/Twizel

Tel (03) 435 0509
or 027 621 7941
ra.preston@xtra.co.nz

Double/Twin $130
Single $70
(Continental breakfast)
Children $50
Visa MC accepted
1 Double/Twin 1 Twin
1 Single (3 bdrm)
Bathrooms: 1 Guest share
Seperate toilets

A quiet place to stop, halfway between Christchurch and Queenstown or Christchurch and Dunedin via Waitaki Valley. 40 minutes to Mt Cook. The 10,000 acre property has been in the family 89 years. Merino sheep graze to 6000 feet, hereford cattle. Views of the southern sky. The homestead is set in tranquil gardens. Afternoon tea/drinks served on the veranda. We have a black lab.? Twizel has a bank, doctor, shops and several restaurants. Please phone for bookings and directions. Cot available.

Lake Pukaki *27 km W of Lake Tekapo*

Tasman Downs Station *Farmstay*

Linda & Bruce Hayman
Lake Pukaki,
Lake Tekapo
7945

Tel (03) 680 6841
Fax (03) 680 6851
samjane@xtra.co.nz

Double/Twin $120-$130
Single $85-$100
(Full breakfast)
Dinner $45 pp by arrangement
1 Queen 1 Twin (2 bdrm)
Bathrooms: 1 Private 1 Guest share

" A place of unsurpassed beauty" located on the shores of Lake Pukaki, magnificent views of the lake, Mount Cook and Southern Alps. Our local stone home blends in with the natural peaceful surroundings. This high country station has been in our family since 1914 and runs mainly Angus cattle. Bruce an ex-RAF pilot and Linda enjoy sharing their knowledge of farming with guests. An opportunity to experience true farm life with friendly hosts, dinner by arrangement. Meet our good natured corgi.

Twizel - Mt Cook *2 km W of Twizel Info Centre*

Artemis B&B *B&B Homestay*

Jan & Bob Wilson
33 North West Arch,
Twizel

Tel (03) 435 0388
Fax (03) 435 0377
artemistwizel@paradise.net.nz

Double/Twin $125
Single $105
(Special breakfast)
Visa MC Eftpos accepted
Pet free home
Not suitable for children
2 Queen 1 Single (2 bdrm)
Bathrooms: 1 Ensuite 1 Private

Jan and Bob welcome you to the magnificent Mackenzie Basin and the Mount Cook National Park. Our modern home, which is situated on a hectare of land, has stunning mountain views along with space and tranquility. We are a short drive to Mount Cook National Park and a three minutes drive to restaurants. There is a guest sitting room with a balcony and tea/coffee making facilities. We look forward to sharing our home with you and are happy to discuss your New Zealand itineraries and sightseeing.

Twizel - Mt Cook *0.5 km S of Twizel*
Hunters House and Hunters Cottage Self Contained
B&B Cottage with Kitchen
Anne & Matt Hunter
58 Tekapo Drive,
Twizel

Tel (03) 435 0038
Fax (03) 435 0038
annehunter@xtra.co.nz

Double/Twin $160
Single $110
(Full breakfast)
Visa MC accepted
Not suitable for children
2 King/Twin (2 bdrm)
Bathrooms: 2 Ensuite

Hunters House is architecturally designed for guests and features every comfort in a warm welcoming environment. It overlooks the native tussocks and trees of the Green Belt on the township boundary with the mountains as a backdrop. All rooms are tastefully decorated with all facilities and french doors opening to the peaceful outdoors sited for the sun and views. We also have a self contained cottage fully equiped with all home comforts and same views Situated in its own private setting. "Cead Mile Failte"

Twizel - Mt Cook *1 km N of Twizel*
Pinegrove *B&B Cottage with Kitchen 2 Cottages with kitchens*
Al & Joh Ingram
29 North West Arch,
Twizel

Tel (03) 435 0430
or 021 464 726
aljohpinegrove@xtra.co.nz

Double/Twin $140-$160
Single $100
(Special breakfast)
Children $10-$25
Visa MC Eftpos accepted
Children welcome
2 Queen 1 Double/Twin
2 Single (2 bdrm)
Bathrooms: 2 Private
Walk in showers

Rest a while in the beautiful Mackenzie District with its mountains and lakes. We are only 45 mins from Mt Cook and 2 mins drive to near by restaurants. We welcome you to our sunny cottages situated in an extensive garden with fishpond and tranquil areas to sit in. The cottages are fitted with modern conveniences with your comfort in mind. You can indulge in home baked goodies from the breakfast hamper. We look forward to meeting you and welcoming you to our haven.

Twizel *0.2 km S of Central Twizel*
Aoraki Lodge *B&B*
Ian & Sandy Darwin
32 Mackenzie Drive,
Twizel

Tel (03) 435 0300
Fax (03) 435 0305
ian.sandy@xtra.co.nz
www.aorakilodge.co.nz

Double/Twin $150-$170
Single $100-$120
(Full breakfast)
Not suitable for children
Walking distance to restaurants
and other facilites
60 kilometres to Mt Cook
Visa MC Eftpos accepted
4 Queen (4 bdrm)
Bathrooms: 4 Ensuite

Relax in the informal atmosphere of our Lodge set amongst a rambling "country-style" garden. Aoraki Lodge located in the centre of Twizel at 32 Mackenzie Drive, is a short walk to local restaurants, clubs and facilities, yet offers complete privacy. Ian & Sandy Darwin welcome you and will suggest on what to "see" and "do" in this beautiful part of the world. Ian, a member of the NZPFG Association, is well known for fly fishing guiding his clients in the local area. If you prefer close proximity to town with total privacy, relaxation and a casual atmosphere with friendly hosts then a stay at Aoraki Lodge is for you.

Twizel - Mount Cook *30 km N of Twizel*
Gladstone Cottage *Cottage with Kitchen*
Peter & Margaret Hands
32 North West Arch,
Twizel,
7944

Tel (03) 435 0527
info@gladstonecottage.co.nz
www.gladstonecottage.co.nz

Double/Twin $140-$200
Single $100
(Continental breakfast)
Visa MC Eftpos accepted
Pet free home
1 Queen 2 Single (2 bdrm)
Bathrooms: 1 Guest share

We are suitated in the beautiful Mackenzie Basin and are 45 minutes driving time from Mount Cook. We look forward to welcoming you to our new fully self contained cottage built on a six acre block of land that is shared with our own home. There are a good selection of restaurants and cafes within a 2 minute drive or 15 minute walk. Please visit our website for more photographs, information and directions at www.gladstonecottage.co.nz

South Canterbury
North Otago

Twizel *160 km W of Timaru*
Heartland Lodge *Homestay Apartment with Kitchen*

Mary and Jim Powell
19 North West Arch,
Twizel,
8773

Tel (03) 435 0008
heartlandlodge@xtra.co.nz
www.heartland-lodge.co.nz

Double/Twin $140-$240
Single $140-$200
(Full breakfast)
Dinner provided with
24hrs prior notice
Visa MC Eftpos accepted
Children and pets welcome
3 King 1 Queen 4 Single (3 bdrm)
Bathrooms: 3 Large ensuite
bathroms with spa baths

Heartland Lodge is a purpose built homestay forty minutes from the Aoraki Mount Cook World Heritage Park. Large guest rooms feature full size ensuite bathrooms with spa baths. We are minutes from the Twizel town centre and its services and restaurants. Mary and Jim are a fund of local knowledge and will help you plan activities and further travel. Dinner is available, made from fresh, local produce and special diets can be catered for.

Lindis Pass *17 km W of Omarama*
Dunstan Downs *Farmstay*

Tim & Geva Innes
Dunstan Downs,
Omarama
9448

Tel (03) 438 9862
Fax (03) 438 9517
tim.innes@xtra.co.nz

Double/Twin up to $260
Single up to $130
(Full breakfast provisions)
Children half price under 12
Tarrif includes dinner bed & breakfast
GST will be added to all tariffs
Visa MC accepted
Children and pets welcome
1 Queen 2 Twin 1 Single (3 bdrm)
Bathrooms: 1 Ensuite 1 Guest share 1 Family share

Dunstan Downs is a merino sheep and cattle station in the heart of the South Island high country. Our home is full of country warmth, you are welcome to join us for dinner (wine served) or bed and breakfast. The surrounding mountains and valleys are an adventure playground, tramping, mountain biking, fishing,farming activities or lazing around soaking up the peace and tranquillity.No pets inside.

Please let us know
how you enjoyed your B&B experience.
Ask your host for a comment form
or leave a comment on www.bnb.co.nz.

Kurow *60 km W of Oamaru*

Glenmac Farmstay *Farmstay Campervan facilities*

Approved

Kaye & Keith Dennison
RD 7K, Oamaru

Tel (03) 436 0200
Fax (03) 436 0202
glenmac@farmstaynewzealand.co.nz
www.farmstaynewzealand.co.nz

Double/Twin $90-$110
Single $45-$55
(Full breakfast)
Children under 13 half price
Dinner $25
Self-contained price on application
Visa MC accepted
Children and pets welcome
1 Queen 2 Double/Twin
2 Twin (5 bdrm)
Bathrooms: 1 Ensuite 1 Guest share 1 Family share

South Canterbury
North Otago

Peaceful location. Enjoy home-cooked meals, a comfortable bed, relax and be treated as one of the family. Explore our 4000 acre high country farm. See merino sheep and beef cattle. On farm enjoy horse riding, take a 4 wheel drive farm tour, walk some of our many tracks. Nearby fly and spinner fishing (guide available), mountain biking, golf or explore the Fossil Trail. Directions: At end of Gards Road which is 10km east of Kurow on right or 13km west of Duntroon on left.

Oamaru - Waianakarua *27 km S of Oamaru*
Glen Dendron *B&B Farmstay*
Anne & John Mackay
284 Breakneck Road, Waianakarua, R D 90, Oamaru

Tel (03) 439 5288 or 021 615 227
Fax (03) 439 5288
anne.john.mackay@xtra.co.nz
www.glenhomestays.co.nz

Double/Twin $135-$165
Single $110-$130 (Full breakfast)
Children $50 Dinner $40 with wine
Visa MC accepted Pet free home Children welcome
2 King/Twin 2 Queen (4 bdrm)
Bathrooms: 2 Ensuite 1 Guest share Spa bath

Award Winning Homestay.Enjoy tranquility and beauty when you stay in our stylish modern home, spectacularly sited on a hilltop overlooking the picturesque Waianakarua River and surrounded by 5 acres of landscaped garden.

After a sumptuous farm-cooked breakfast, feed the sheep and alpacas. Then take a stroll through the forest, native bush complete with waterfalls and birds or beside the river. Play a round on our private golf course. Later, watch the seals and penguins on a beach nearby. Then, complete a perfect day with our gourmet 3 course dinner with fine NZ wine before snuggling down for a peaceful sleep in the fresh country air.

After a lifetime spent in farming and forestry we relish the opportunity to share our home and semi-retired lifestyle with guests. Our adult family lives overseas so we travel frequently and have a great interest in other countries and cultures. We are very keen gardeners, read widely and enjoy antiques. Anne is a floral designer and John is a tree connoisseur.

An overnight stay is not enough to do justice to this lovely area - with so much to see, why not stay awhile!We can plan customised itineraries of the area's many attractions. Oamaru's historic architecture. Garden, heritage and fossil trails. Beaches, fishing, seals and penguins. Famous Moeraki Boulders and other interesting geological features.Use us as a base for day visits to Oamaru, Dunedin, Waitaki Valley and Mt Cook. Christchurch International Airport - 3.5 hours.We dont mind short notice!

Oamaru *3 km S of Oamaru, just off SH1*
Springbank *B&B Apartment with Kitchen*

Joan & Stan Taylor
60 Weston Road,
Oamaru

Tel (03) 434 6602
or 027 403 5410
Fax (03) 434 6602
joan-t@clear.net.nz

Double/Twin $110
Single $75
(Continental breakfast)
Children $10
Visa MC accepted
Pet free home
Children welcome
1 King/Twin
1 Double/Twin (1 bdrm)
Bathrooms: 1 Private
Bathroom has bath and shower

We look forward to sharing our retirement haven with visitors from overseas and New Zealand. Our modern home and separate guest flat are set in a peaceful and private large garden. Feed the goldfish.Our guest flat is sunny, warm, spacious and comfortable. We enjoy helping visitors discover our district's best kept secrets! Penguins, gardens, Moeraki Boulders, beaches, pool, fishing and golf. Our interests are travel, gardening, grandchildren. Stan's are Lions and following sports. Joan's all handcrafts, patchwork, floral design.

~

Oamaru *1.3 km N of Oamaru Centre*
Highway House Boutique B&B *B&B Homestay*

Stephanie & Norman Slater
43 Lynn Street,
(Cnr Thames Highway & Lynn St),
Meadowbank, Oamaru

Tel (03) 437 1066
or 0800 003 319
Fax (03) 437 1066
highwayhouse@netspeed.net.nz
www.highwayhouse.co.nz

Double/Twin $140-$165
Single $120-$145
(Full breakfast)
Children negotiable
Visa MC Amex accepted
Pet free home
Children welcome
2 King 1 Twin (3 bdrm)
Bathrooms: 1 Ensuite 1 Guest share 1 Family share large-size showers

Our character residence on Thames Highway, (1.3km north of town centre), has been entirely refurbished to the highest standard. We provide a full cooked breakfast and other refreshments as required. We can assist with tours of historic Oamaru or visits to the nature sites. Our courtesy car can collect or take you to nearby dining establishments. If you appreciate a quality ambiance and particular assistance from Stephanie and Norman who have travelled widely overseas, Highway House will be ideal for you. French also spoken.

Oamaru *2 km N of Oamaru Central*
Coral Sea Cottage & Ocean View Apartments *B&B Cottage with Kitchen*

Apartments with some cooking facilities
Nicola & Peter Mountain
Ocean View, 34 Harlech Street,
Oamaru

Tel (03) 437 1422
or 021 659 757
or 021 042 6997
Fax (03) 437 1427
nmountain@xtra.co.nz

Double/Twin $145
Single $90
(Full breakfast provisions)
Children 5-16 $25
Visa MC accepted
Children and pets welcome
4 King/Twin 2 Queen
1 Single (7 bdrm)
Bathrooms: 2 Ensuite 2 Private Ensuite is shower room, private has bath and shower

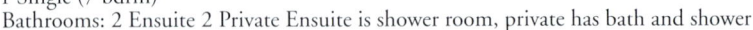

Relax on a peaceful hillside in our cosy cottage with secluded grounds or in self-contained apartments in our home overlooking the Pacific. All well equipped, most with Sky TV. Cot, high chair available. Enjoy wonderful views, pet farm animals and our son's art gallery. Resident dogs and cats! Near local shops, restaurants. 2km to historic town centre, art galleries, famous blue penguin colony. We look forward to welcoming you and offering help with planning your visit to our area. "Best stay we had." (European Guest)

Oamaru *0.5 km W of Oamaru centre*
Homestay Oamaru *B&B Homestay*
Doug Bell
14 Warren Street,
Oamaru

Tel (03) 434 1454
or 027 408 2860
homestayoamaru@paradise.net.nz
www.bellview.co.nz

Double/Twin $75-$95
Single $45-$60
(Full breakfast)
Dinner $25
Pet free home
Not suitable for children
2 Queen 1 Double/Twin (3 bdrm)
Bathrooms: 2 Ensuite 1 Family share

Sweeping views over the town and harbour. Warm, spacious and comfortable accommodation for the travelling enthusiast, with books, maps, atlases and guides for you perusal. Quiet, private site, close to town centre. (see map on website). Off-street parking. Southern scenic walkway access at property boundary. Some of the area's attractions include sea and river fishing, historic architecture, unique geological features and eco-tourism. Host has detailed local knowledge. Site unsuitable for young children or pets.

Oamaru - Airedale *8 km NW of Oamaru*
Seadowns Farmstay *Farmstay*
Lynne & Colin Gibson
1D RD Oamaru, North Otago,
Rapid No 217 Rosebery Road,
Airedale, Oamaru

Tel (03) 434 9479
or 021 188 9865
Fax (03) 434 9499
Seadowns@farmside.co.nz
www.seadowns.co.nz

Double/Twin $135-$160
Single $75
(Continental breakfast)
Children $40
Evening meal available by
arrangement $35 per person
Children and pets welcome
2 Double/Twin 1 Twin (3 bdrm)
Bathrooms: 1 Guest share 1 Family share

Seadowns is an intensive breeding property of 1100 acres of rolling hill country, with hereford, romney and dorset downs studs. The homestead built in 1939 is a relaxing home set in a peaceful country garden with coastal views. We have a fox terrier and cat. Complimentry farm tour. View or participate in shearing and farm activities. Historic sites on the property include: Oamaru stone quarrying site, limestone cliffs, lobster catching. Experience penguin colonies, historic Oamaru precinct, with 19th century architecture, Moeraki Boulders and salmon fishing. Preferred method of payment is cash, due to unreliable internet connection.

Oamaru *8 km S of Oamaru*
Ranui Retreat Bed and Breakfast/Homestay *B&B Homestay*
Sheryl Laraman and Family
27 Woolshed Road,
Totara,
Oamaru,
8D RD

Tel (03) 439 5241
ranui_retreat@actrix.gen.nz
www.ranui-retreat.co.nz

Double/Twin $125-$160
Single $100
(Full breakfast)
Children negotiable
Dinner 25 pp
Visa MC accepted
Children and pets welcome
2 Queen (2 bdrm)
Bathrooms: 1 Ensuite 1 Private

Welcome to Ranui Retreat. We are close to historic Oamaru and the main highway to Dunedin. Views of Otago rural landscape stretching to the Kakanui Mountains enhance the rural sense of this five acre property of mature oak, elm and ash trees. There is birdsong aplenty. Character rooms include rich, handmade quilts which add to the relaxed ambience. Join the family for the evening or you may like to retire to other spaces with music and a good book from our library selection.

Oamaru *0.5 km S of Oamaru*
Federation House Homestay Inn B&B *B&B Homestay*

Rodger McCaw
60 Tyne Street,
Oamaru
9400

Tel (03) 434 9537
or 021 0246 2418
Fax (03) 434 9537
info@federationhouse.co.nz
www.federationhouse.co.nz

Double/Twin $100-$150
Single $60-$100
(Full breakfast)
Dinner by arrangement
Off Season Rates - special discount
from May until October
Visa MC accepted
Pet free home
Children welcome
3 King/Twin 2 Twin (5 bdrm)
Bathrooms: 3 Ensuite 1 Guest share 1 Family share

A large two storied Heritage House with a commanding site in the exclusive suburb of Cape Wanbrow. So very close to Oamaru's Historic Precinct, Harbour and Penguin Colony with views from rooms. Enjoy an era of magnificent building of Australasian Federation architecture.

~

Palmerston *2 km S of Palmerston*
Mount Royal B&B *B&B*

Jo & Trevor Studholme
Mount Royal,
RD 1
(Just off SH1),
Palmerston,
Otago

Tel (03) 465 1884
or 021 876 880
Fax (03) 465 1440
mt.royal.bandb@clear.net.nz

Double/Twin up to $130
(Full breakfast)
Private sitting room
Pet free home
Not suitable for children
1 King 1 Twin (2 bdrm)
Bathrooms: 1 Private

O ur 1930s homestead situated in a quiet rural setting 400m from State Highway 1 and 1km south of Palmerston, the gateway to Central Otago goldfields. As hosts, we enjoy making you welcome and would like you to stay to visit the Moeraki Boulders and coastal walkways, before heading central, perhaps following the gold trail: The Macraes Gold Mine is thought to be the largest open-cast mine in the Southern Hemisphere (tours by appointment).

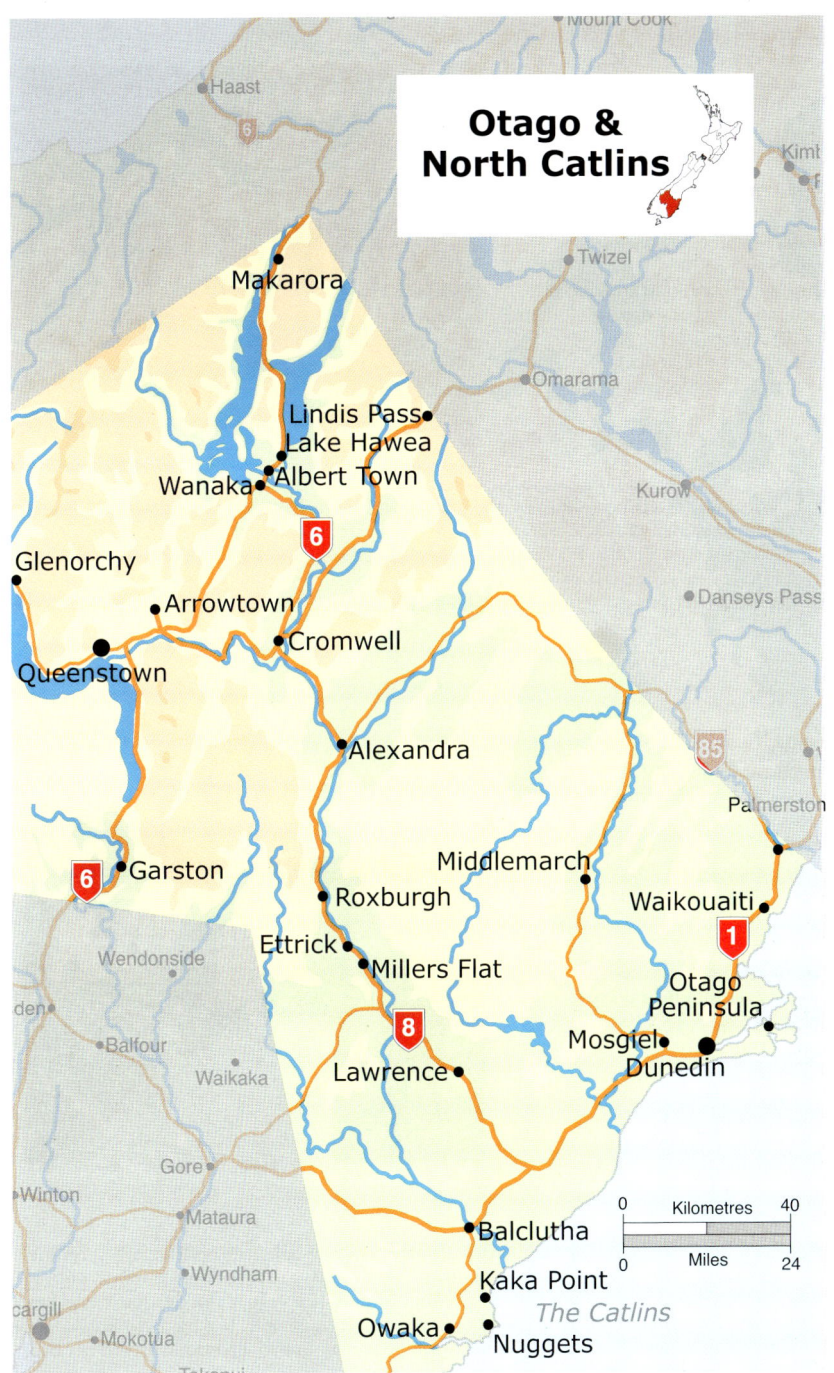

Otago & North Catlins

Haast
Mount Cook
Kimb
Twizel
Makarora
Omarama
Lindis Pass
Lake Hawea
Kurow
Wanaka
Albert Town
6
Danseys Pass
Glenorchy
Arrowtown
Queenstown
Cromwell
Alexandra
85
Palmerston
6
Garston
Middlemarch
Waikouaiti
Wendonside
Roxburgh
1
Balfour
Ettrick
Millers Flat
Otago Peninsula
den
8
Mosgiel
Waikaka
Lawrence
Dunedin
Gore
Winton
Mataura
Wyndham
Balclutha
cargill
Kaka Point
The Catlins
Mokotua
Owaka
Nuggets

Kilometres 0 — 40
Miles 0 — 24

Otago
North Catlins

Makarora *65 km N of Wanaka*
Makarora Homestead *B&B Cottage with Kitchen*

Kenna Fraser & Rick McLachlan
53 Rata Road,
Makarora

Tel (03) 443 1532
Fax (03) 443 1525
info@makarora.com
www.makarora.com

Double/Twin $125-$145
Single $100-$120
(Continental breakfast provisions)
Restaurant is walking distance (500 m)
Visa MC accepted
Children and pets welcome
7 Queen 1 Double/Twin
7 Twin (8 bdrm)
Bathrooms: 3 Ensuite 3 Guest share

Makarora Homestead offers a secluded retreat in the midst of the Southern Alps & is perfect for travellers looking for the peace & tranquility of the mountains. We offer a self-contained studio with kitchenette, ensuite & private balcony OR 2 detached bedrooms each with ensuite, tea/coffee making facilities & shared sundeck. Nestled at the edge of the native forest with panoramic views of the mountains & surrounding wapiti deer farm. Hand feed our tame deer Nigel, "retired" pony Dudley & various friendly sheep.

~

Wanaka *1 km S of Wanaka*
Berryfarm Homestay *B&B Homestay Separate Suite Guest lounge*

Annette & Bob Menlove
83 Orchard Road,
Wanaka, Central Otago

Tel (03) 443 4248
or 021 494 149
021 344 016
Fax (03) 443 4249
bobannette@menlove.net
www.berryfarmhomestay.co.nz

Double/Twin $150-$170
Single $150
(Full breakfast)
Visa MC accepted
Children welcome
1 King/Twin 1 Double/Twin
1 Twin (3 bdrm)
Bathrooms: 2 Ensuite 1 Private
Spa and Bath

We are a Berryfarm growing raspberries, strawberries boysenberries and tomatoes, on the outskirts of Wanaka just 3 mins into town. Very close to very good restaurants, golf course, ski fields and fishing. We have just retired from a sheep cattle and deer farm and have been hosting for a number of years. We both enjoy meeting people. We have two cats and a labrador dog. We have a separate guest area with your own lounge bedrooms have their own TV very quiet and private.

Wanaka *0.4 km E of Centre Wanaka*
Lake Wanaka Homestay *B&B Homestay*
Gailie & Peter Cooke
85 Warren Street,
Wanaka

Tel (03) 443 7995
or 0800 443 799
Fax (03) 443 7945
wanakahomestay@xtra.co.nz
www.lakewanakahomestay.co.nz

Double/Twin $130-$140
Single $90-$100
(Full breakfast)
Visa MC accepted
Not suitable for children
2 Double/Twin (2 bdrm)
Bathrooms: 1 Guest share
Great Shower

Welcome to our home. Relax and enjoy breathtaking views of lake and mountains, just 5 minutes walk to shops, restaurants, lake. Peter, keen fly fisherman, is happy to show guests where to find the big ones. Complimentary tea, coffee, home-made cookies during your stay. Warm home, cooked breakfast, comfortable beds, electric blankets, bedroom heaters, We have shared our home with guests for many years, making wonderful friendships. We both enjoy meeting people, fishing, golf, skiing, walking, gardening. Kate, our labrador dog is everyone's friend.

Wanaka *3 km N of Wanaka Shops*
Beacon Point *B&B Homestay Apartment with Kitchen*
Diana & Dan Pinckney
302 Beacon Point Road,
PO Box 6, Lake Wanaka

Tel (03) 443 1253
or 0272 460 222
0274 354 847
Fax (03) 443 1254
dan.di@lakewanaka.co.nz
www.beaconpoint.co.nz

Double/Twin up to $120
Single up to $90
(Continental breakfast)
Children $30
Dinner $40
Rolla Beds
Pet free home Children welcome
1 Queen 1 Twin (2 bdrm)
Bathrooms: 1 Ensuite

Beacon Point B&B has an acre of lawn and garden for your enjoyment. Leads to a walking track to the village around the edge of the lake. Private spacious studio with ensuite, queen and single beds (2 rooms), kitchen, TV,DVD, sundeck and BBQ. Studio equipped with every need for perfect stay. We enjoy planning your days with you. Our intrests include farming, forestry, fly fishing, real estate, boating, gardening and grandchildren. Turn right at lake - Lakeside Road - then to Beacon Point Road 302.

Otago
North Catlins

Wanaka *10 km N of Wanaka*

The Stone Cottage *B&B Apartment with Kitchen*

Belinda Wilson
Wanaka, RD 2, Central Otago

Tel (03) 443 1878
Fax (03) 443 1276
stonecottage@xtra.co.nz
www.stonecottage.co.nz

Double/Twin $260-$290
Single $240
(Full breakfast provisions)
Children half price under 12 years
Dinner $65-70
Visa MC accepted
1 King 1 Queen 2 Single (2 bdrm)
Bathrooms: 1 Ensuite 1 Private

5 0 years ago, a spectacular garden was created at Dublin Bay on the tranquil shores of Lake Wanaka. Its beauty still blooms today against a backdrop of the majestic Southern Alps.

Accommodation is private, comfortable and elegantly decorated.

The Stone Cottage offers 2 self-contained loft apartments with breathtaking views over lake Wanaka to snow clad alps beyond. Featuring your own bathroom, bedroom, kitchen, living room and balcony. Television, DVD, Video, CD player, fax, email & wireless internet available. Private entrance.

Enjoy breakfast at leisure, made from fresh ingredients from your well stocked fully equipped kitchen, Pre-dinner drinks, delicious 3 course dinner and NZ wines or a gourmet picnic hamper is available by arrangement.

Walk along the beach just 4 minutes from The Stone Cottage or wander in the enchanting garden. Guests can experience trout fishing, nature walks, golf, boating, horse riding, wine tasting and ski fields nearby. Only 10 minutes from Wanaka, this is the perfect retreat for those who value privacy and the unique beauty of this area. Relax in the magic atmosphere at The Stone Cottage and awake to the dawn bird chorus of native bellbirds and fantails.

Wanaka *1.3 km S of Wanaka*
Harpers *B&B Homestay*
Jo & Ian Harper
95 McDougall Street,
Wanaka

Tel (03) 443 8894
Fax (03) 443 8834
harpers@xtra.co.nz
www.harpers.co.nz

Double/Twin $140
Single $100
(Continental breakfast)
Visa MC accepted
1 King/Twin 2 Single (2 bdrm)
Bathrooms: 1 Ensuite 1 Private
Bath and Shower with twin room

We take pride in offering a friendly, comfortable home. Share breakfast and awesome lake and mountain views with us. Also explore our extensive garden, which provides a tranquil environment for relaxing. We offer a drink and muffins on your arrival. This is a smoke-free home. Recent guests' comments: "Wonderful welcoming homestay."Friendly hosts, excellent breakfasts. "Wonderful hospitality, fantastic breakfast." "Excellent hosts, breakfasts to die for." "Very comfortable. Great hosts. Top spot." "Wonderful views. The muffins and pancakes do live up to expectations." "A home from home."

Wanaka *4 km S of Wanaka*
Stonehaven *Homestay*
Deirdre & Dennis
Maxwell Road,
RD 2,
Wanaka

Tel (03) 443 9516
Fax (03) 443 9513
moghul@xtra.co.nz
www.stonehaven.co.nz

Double/Twin $125
Single $95
(Full breakfast)
Children $20 negotiable
Portacots and highchairs available
Visa MC accepted
Children and pets welcome
2 Queen 2 Single (2 bdrm)
Bathrooms: 1 Ensuite 1 Private

Our home is set in two acres about five minutes drive from Wanaka. All beds have electric blankets. Tea and coffee is freely available. We have extensive views of surrounding mountains. Children are welcome and child care by arrangement. Our nearby tree collection has an accent on autumn colour. Local walks a speciality. Organic fruit both in season and preserved. We have a small dog and a cat. No smoking inside please. Please phone for directions.

Wanaka *0.2 km E of Wanaka Central*

Te Wanaka Lodge *B&B Guest House Ski Lodge/Chalet in Winter*

Graeme & Andy Oxley, Lynne Graham
23 Brownston Street, Wanaka

Tel (03) 443 9224
or Free Call 0800 WANAKA (926252)
Fax (03) 443 9246
tewanakalodge@xtra.co.nz
www.tewanaka.co.nz

Double/Twin $159-$230
Single $149-$185 (Full breakfast)
Garden cottage room $230 ($250 for 3 persons)
Visa MC Amex Eftpos accepted
9 Queen 4 Twin (13 bdrm)
Bathrooms: 13 Ensuite

Owned & run by outdoor enthusiasts, the lodge is a place for active people who want to get out & explore our picturesque town and locale. Get good advice from your hosts about all the local walks and great things to do. Te Wanaka enjoys a reputation as a relaxed, fun and friendly place to stay.

After an adventurous day exploring our mountains, lake & streams, guests can soak in the private garden hot tub/spa, sit back in one of our comfy lounges or enjoy the sun in our pretty courtyard garden.

- All bedrooms with ensuite and private balcony
- LCD Flat Screen TV (5 Channels Sky) - Delicious full cooked breakfast included - Vegetarian, gluten & dairy free breakfast options available
- Guest Lounges with Log Fire & Library - Wireless & High Speed internet available - House Bar specialising in local beers and wines - In-house therapeutic massage - Mountain Bike Hire
- Luggage storage - Laundry service - Gear drying room (Ski & other)

Wanaka *2 km NW of Wanaka Central*
Lake Wanaka Home Hosting *B&B Homestay*

Joyce & Lex Turnbull
19 Bill's Way,
Wanaka

Tel (03) 443 9060
Fax (03) 443 1626
lex.joy@xtra.co.nz
www.lakewanakahomehosting.co.nz

Double/Twin $110-$160
Single $75
(Full breakfast)
Children under 10 years $25
Dinner $40
Visa MC accepted
Pet free home
Children welcome
1 King/Twin 1 Double/Twin
1 Twin (3 bdrm)
Bathrooms: 2 Private

We welcome visitors to Wanaka, enjoy sharing our natural surroundings with others. We have a large peaceful home where our guests can experience not only the austerity of the lake and mountains around them, but also experience the ambience of Wanaka itself. Guest room with super king bed has adjoining TV lounge with TV, tea & coffee facilities, private bathroom. Good laundry facilities. We wish your stay in Wanaka will be a very happy one. Directions: please ring for directions. We enjoy your company.

Wanaka *2.3 km NW of Wanaka Centre*
Peak-Sportchalet *B&B Apartment with Kitchen 1 or 2-bedroom Chalet fully self-contained*

Alex & Christine Schafer
36 Hunter Crescent,
Wanaka 9305

Tel (03) 443 6990
stay@peak-sportchalet.co.nz
www.Peak-Sportchalet.co.nz

Double/Twin $110-$170
Single $90-$110
(Special breakfast)
Visa MC accepted
Pet free home
Children welcome
1 King 1 Queen 1 Twin (3 bdrm)
Bathrooms: 2 Ensuite 1 Private
underfloor-heating (Chalet);
hairdryer; high quality showers

Welcome at Peak-Sportchalet - your Qualmark 4 Star accommodation in Wanaka. Experience ambience and hospitality in our 3 guest suites and selfcontained Chalet. All are individually designed and appointed with fine furniture, ensuite or private bathrooms, TV, DVD and Sound System. Sliding doors open onto private sundecks with great mountain views. Awake refreshed after a relaxing nights sleep on our prime quality mattresses and duvets. Start your day healthy with our memorable breakfast-buffet. We also cater for special diets. Broadband/Wireless

**Otago
North Catlins**

Wanaka - Albert Town *6 km N of Wanaka*

Riversong *B&B Homestay*

Ann & Ian Horrax
5 Wicklow Terrace,
Albert Town, RD 2, Wanaka

Tel (03) 443 8567
or 021 113 6397
Fax (03) 443 8564
info@riversongwanaka.co.nz
www.riversongwanaka.co.nz

Double/Twin $150-$170
Single $110
(Full breakfast)
Children $25
Dinner $55pp by arrangement
Visa MC accepted
Children welcome
1 King/Twin 1 Queen
1 Single (3 bdrm)
Bathrooms: 1 Ensuite 1 Private

Riversong is 5 minutes from Wanaka Township, at Albert Town, on the banks of the majestic Clutha River. At our secluded haven all rooms have river and mountain views, with immediate access to the river. Ann's background is healthcare and Ian's law. We invite you to share the comforts and privacy of our home and garden and Ian's knowledge of the region's fishing and guidance service. We aim to provide a memorable and comfortable stay. We have 2 outside lab dogs. Wireless/broadband available.

Wanaka *0.5 km N of Wanaka*

Criffel Peak View *B&B Apartment with Kitchen*

Caroline Holland
98 Hedditch Street,
Wanaka

Tel (03) 443 5511
Fax (03) 443 5521
stay@criffelpeakview.co.nz
www.criffelpeakview.co.nz

Double/Twin $150-$160
Single $120 (Full breakfast)
Apartment from $200 for 4 people
Visa MC accepted
Children welcome
2 King/Twin 1 King 2 Queen (3 bdrm)
Bathrooms: 2 Ensuite 2 Private

A cosy modern cottage situated in a quiet cul-de-sac, just a short walk from the lake and town. Great mountain views, large sunny deck, friendly young hosts and a crazy cat called Splodge. Our 3 guest rooms look out towards the Criffel Range and are equipped with super king or queen sized beds and TVs. The guest lounge has Wireless Internet, guest computer, tea/coffee making and variety of reading material. Our apartment is perfect for larger groups and families.

Wanaka *2.4 km E of Wanaka*
The Cedars *B&B Homestay*
Mary & Graham Dowdall
7 Riverbank Road, RD 2,
Wanaka 9382, Central Otago

Tel (03) 443 1544
or 021 1208 960
Fax (03) 443 1580
thecedarswanaka@xtra.co.nz
www.thecedars.co.nz

Double/Twin $195-$225
Single $150-$185
(Full breakfast)
Dinner by arrangement
with 24 hours notice
Visa MC accepted
Children are very welcome
2 Queen 1 Single (2 bdrm)
Bathrooms: 1 Ensuite
1 Private with Spa Bath

Cead Mile Failte - One hundred thousand welcomes. A warm Irish/Kiwi welcome awaits you at The Cedars, by Mary, Graham, Rough Collie Nessa and cat Cara. Our stone home on 11 acres has panoramic mountain views, expansive gardens, guest lounge with large open fire. Nearby attractions include The Maze, Warbirds Museum, golf, ski fields, walking tracks, paragliding, lakes and rivers for water pursuits: shops and restaurants. Full breakfast is served with fresh and home-made produce. We offer evening meals or BBQ by prior arrangement.

Wanaka *2.5 km W of Wanaka*
Wanaka Jewel *Luxury B&B Homestay Separate Suite*
Pam & Bruce Mayo
7 Foxglove Heights,
Far Horizon Park,
Lake Wanaka

Tel (03) 443 5636
or 027 285 6234
or (03) 443 2722
Fax (03) 443 2723
wanakajewel@xtra.co.nz
www.bnb.co.nz/wanakajewel.html

Double/Twin $185-$225
Single $170-$210
(Full breakfast)
Visa MC accepted
Not suitable for children
2 Queen (2 bdrm)
Bathrooms: 1 Ensuite 1 Private
two persons spa bath

Welcome to Wanaka Jewel - a stay in paradise. 3 minutes from township. Wanaka Jewel is a newly built luxury home with purpose built bed & breakfast suites set on 1 acre surrounded by magestic mountains and superb lake views, close to town. Own private entrance. These suites are beautifully appointed with quality linen. Complimentary pool, spa, tennis courts, gymnasium, BBQ, pitch and putting green available to guests. Complimentary tea, coffee anytime, sumptious breakfast. Be assured of a warm welcome and a memorable stay.

Wanaka *5 km N of Wanaka*
Ferryman's Cottage *B&B Homestay*
Marie Lewis & Bryan Lloyd
4 Arklow Street,
Albert Town,
RD 2,
Wanaka

Tel (03) 443 4147
or 021 144 7513
Fax (03) 443 4147
ferrymanscottage@xtra.co.nz
www.ferrymanscottage.co.nz

Double/Twin $160-$175
Single $105-$125
(Full breakfast)
Visa MC accepted
2 Queen (2 bdrm)
Bathrooms: 1 Ensuite 1 Private

Ferryman's is our lovingly restored historic cottage, located 5 minutes from Wanaka, on the banks of the Clutha River (famous for fishing). The warmth, peace and tranquility of our home, has been created for you to enjoy. A unique garden fresh breakfast experience from Marie's kitchen awaits you. Laze in our cottage garden. Stroll, 1 minute to fish, or walk riverside tracks.Bryan, lawyer by day, laidback host by night, Marie, (foodie, teacher), and our cat, Indy, invite you to our corner of Paradise.

Wanaka *1 km S of Wanaka Central*
Oak Tree Bed & Breakfast *B&B Homestay*
Sharlene & Ray Mulqueen
4 Little Oak Common,
Wanaka
9305

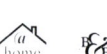

Tel (03) 443 9106
Fax (03) 443 9109
r.s.mulqueen@xtra.co.nz
www.oaktreewanaka.com

Double/Twin $130-$160
(Continental breakfast)
Visa MC accepted
Pet free home
2 King (2 bdrm)
Bathrooms: 1 Ensuite 1 Private

Bed & Breakfast accommodation with spectacular mountain views, and friendly relaxed hospitality. Situated in a quiet cul-de-sac, we are within easy walking distance or a 2 minute drive to town. Our home is comfortable, modern and spacious and warm. A delicious breakfast is served in the dining area, while watching the morning sun over the beautiful Southern Alps. Free email and laundry. Off-street Parking.

Wanaka *12 km E of Wanaka*
Kanuka Lodge *B&B*

Heather & Graeme Halliday
110 Shortcut Road,
SH 8A,
Luggate,
RD2,
Wanaka

Tel (03) 443 7448
halldday@es.co.nz

Double/Twin $90-$120
Single $70-$90
(Full breakfast)
Children $20
Visa MC accepted
Children and pets welcome
1 Queen 1 Double/Twin
1 Single (3 bdrm)
Bathrooms: 1 Guest share

Our home is near the Clutha river, 10 minutes drive from Wanaka. It features NZ art and books. We welcome you with a glass of fine NZ wine. At breakfast you must try the Central Otago apricots and Heather's wildflower honey. You can admire the alpine landscape with geologist, photographer and fisherman Graeme, and plan your exploration of Wanaka. We have friendly cats and horses. Heather, originally from Bath in England, gives rides in her vintage buggies and grows the exotic spice saffron.

Wanaka *0.2 km E of Wanaka Central*
Renmore House *B&B*

Rosie and Blair Burridge
44 Upton Street,
Wanaka
9305

Tel (03) 443 6566
or 027 434 2075
Fax (03) 443 6567
info@renmorehouse.co.nz
www.renmore-house.co.nz

Double/Twin $190-$220
Single $170-$190
(Full breakfast)
Visa MC Eftpos accepted
Children welcome
3 King/Twin (3 bdrm)
Bathrooms: 3 Ensuite

Blair, Rosie and Sophie the cat extend a warm welcome to Renmore House a luxury, purpose built B&B just 2 minutes walk from Wanaka village and very convenient to most Wanaka activities. We are committed to ensuring your every comfort and privacy in our home including assistance with travel,mountain bikes, wireless internet, laundry facilities, guest lounge and a scrumptious breakfast menu. Sounds of springfed creeks running through our garden create a peaceful ambiance for guests wishing to barbeque or just relax with a book.

Wanaka *2 km N of Post Office*
Greystones B/B *B&B Boutique*
Dorothy & Ian McDonald
219 Beacon Point Road,
Wanaka

Tel (03) 443 6362
or 027 343 8885
Fax (03) 443 6062
iandorothy@xtra.co.nz

Double/Twin $140-$150
Single $100
(Full breakfast)
Pet free home
Children welcome
1 Queen 1 Twin (2 bdrm)
Bathrooms: 1 Private 1 Family share

Dorothy & Ian extend a very warm & friendly welcome to Greystones. An interesting boutique home with art, furniture, and sound surround music. With a sumptious breakfast and pre-dinner drinks. A casual stroll to lake and town. We come from a farming background and both enjoy Golf & bridge - only too happy to have a game of either! and we also tend a very interesting garden. We take pleasure in sharing our home and hope to make your stay comfortable & memorable.

Wanaka *0.8 km SE of Wanaka shops*
Golfside B&B *B&B*
Lynda and David Doolan
56 Golf Course Road,
Wanaka
9305

Tel (03) 443 4581
or 021 236 0882
ddoolan@hotmail.com
www.golfsidebandb.co.nz

Double/Twin $140-$180
(Full breakfast)
Visa MC accepted
2 King 1 Twin (2 bdrm)
Bathrooms: 2 Ensuite

Golfside, Wanaka's only B&B accommodation overlooking the golf course with fantastic views towards the lake and mountains. 10 minute walk to town, 2 minute drive. Purpose built in 2005 with a separate wing to the family home. Each room has its own private access with ample parking. Feel at home in a modern, quality room that includes tea/coffee making, fridge, LCD TV/DVD choose from our up to date DVD selection or browse your emails on our laptop. Friendly hosts originally from the U.K.

Lake Wanaka *1 km N of Post Office*
Black Peak Lodge *B&B Homestay*
Helen and David Rule
38 Kings Drive, Wanaka

Tel (03) 443 4078 or Mobile 027 457 3539
Fax (03) 443 4038
hellbell@xtra.co.nz
www.blackpeaklodge.co.nz

Double/Twin $180-$220 Single $160-$180 (Full breakfast)
Children gladly welcomed Visa MC accepted
2 King/Twin 2 Queen (3 bdrm)
Bathrooms: 1 Ensuite 2 Private

Welcome to Black Peak Lodge. Unwind in comfort.... in winter by the log fire, in summer on the open deck in awe of the spectacular view. Relax in the lounge, indulging in fine wines and mouthwatering appetizers whilst listening to music of your choice. Recharge and recuperate in the spa amidst the tranquil ambiance that is ....Black Peak Lodge. Join us in our recreational activities: biking, fishing, boating, water skiing, walking or enjoying time with our gorgeous Golden Retriever, Rosa Bella.

Drift off to sleep under fine bed linens, subtle lighting and the most divine pillows in your charming room. All rooms ensure top of the line comfort for you. Each offers lush spa robes, television, DVD, C.D. player, phone and Internet port, along with extra touches that will make your stay unforgettable.

Awake to the tantalizing aroma of great food and fresh coffee. Indulge yourself in the breakfast room, on the deck whilst basking in the sun or in the haven of your own room.

Guest Services: Tea and coffee making facilities; Extensive CD and DVD library; Outstanding mountain views; Ski storage and drying facilities; Internet and full business facilities; Restaurant, child minding and activities reservation service.

Wanaka *2.7 km N of Wanaka Central*
Missy's B&B *B&B Farmstay Complete with calves and sheep*

Michael & Carolyn-Anne Thompson
RD 1,
158 Cardrona Valley Road,
Wanaka

Tel (03) 443 9208
or 027 479 9474
Fax (03) 443 9208
stay@missyswanaka.co.nz
http://mssysbandb.co.nz

Double/Twin $135
Single $80
(Full breakfast)
Dinner $30 a couple
Visa MC accepted
Children welcome
1 Queen (1 bdrm)
Bathrooms: 1 Private spa pool and heated pool

Michael, Missy, Nike (friendly dog) extend a warm welcome to all guests. Our house on 10 acres is 2.7 kms from centre of Wanaka on Cardrona Valley Road, 20kms to nearest ski field (1km to nearest restuarant/pub). 2 queen beds, electric blankets, spa pool, heated swimming pool), full breakfast. Dinner available 24 hrs notice ($15each). Guest lounge , sky TV. Discount if your stay is longer than one night.

Wanaka *3 km NW of Wanaka*
Davidsons *Luxury B&B*

Susan and Charlie Davidson
49 Peak View Ridge, Wanaka

Tel (03) 443 7139
or 027 220 5024
ibdavidsonnz@hotmail.com
www.wanakalodge.co.nz

Double/Twin $150-$200
Single $150-$175
(Full breakfast)
Children welcome
Dinner Fine dining or basic
eat with us options available
Dryng room & spa
Children welcome
1 King/Twin 1 King
1 Queen (3 bdrm)
Bathrooms: 1 Private 1 Guest share
Upstairs rooms provide a lower cost shared bathroom option

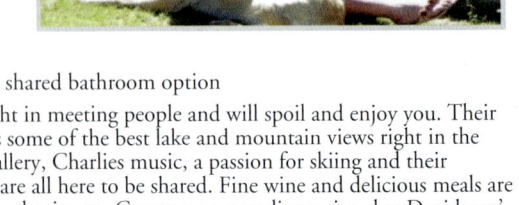

Susan and Charlie Davidson delight in meeting people and will spoil and enjoy you. Their modern spacious stone home has some of the best lake and mountain views right in the township of Wanaka. Susan's Art gallery, Charlies music, a passion for skiing and their beautiful friendly Labradour Sandy are all here to be shared. Fine wine and delicious meals are available as well as the massage spa and privacy - Guests are never disappointed at Davidsons'.

Lake Wanaka *2 km NW of Wanaka*
Wanaka Alpine Lodge *B&B Cottage with Kitchen*

Murray & Lynette Christie
Albert Town,
Hawea H/Way,
Rapid 114,
Wanaka 2RD

Tel (03) 443 2450
or 027 346 3194
Fax (03) 443 6262
muz.lyn@xtra.co.nz

Double/Twin $150-$165
Single $100-$120
(Full breakfast)
Dinner by arrangement
Visa MC Eftpos accepted
Pet free home
Children welcome
1 King 2 Queen 1 Twin (4 bdrm)
Bathrooms: 5 Ensuite

Hosts Murray and Lynette extend to you a warm welcome to their new B&B situated 3 minute's drive from Lake Wanaka on the West Coast Highway. Rooms have ensuites, air conditioning, TV, tea/coffee facilities and guest laundry. Share a cooked breakfast served al fresco courtyard style or in the warmth of the breakfast room. Check in/out by arrangement. Hosts Murray and Lynette Christie.

Cromwell *1 km S of live in Cromwell*
Stuart's Homestay *B&B Homestay*

Elaine & Ian Stuart
5 Mansor Court,
Cromwell

Tel (03) 445 3636
Fax (03) 445 3617
ian.elaine@xtra.co.nz

Double/Twin $110-$130
Single $70-$80
(Full breakfast)
Dinner $25-$35 by arrangement
Visa MC accepted
Pet free home
Children welcome
2 Queen 2 Single (3 bdrm)
Bathrooms: 1 Ensuite 1 Guest share

Welcome to our home which is situated within walking distance to most of Cromwell's amenities. We are semi-retired Southland farmers who have been hosting for over 15 years. Cromwell is a quiet and relaxed town with historic gold diggings, vineyards, orchards, trout fishing, boating, walks, close to ski fields. 45 minutes to Wanaka or Queenstown. Share dinner with us or just bed & breakfast. Tea and coffee, home-made cookies available. We enjoy sharing our home and garden with visitors and a friendly stay is assured.

**Otago
North Catlins**

Cromwell *1 km N of Cromwell*
Cottage Gardens *B&B Homestay detached twin studio*
Jill & Colin McColl
80 Neplusultra Street,
Cromwell,
Central Otago

Tel (03) 445 0628
Fax (03) 445 0628
cottage.gardens@ihug.co.nz
www.cromwellbedandbreakfast.co.nz

Double/Twin $100-$110
Single $55-$75
(Continental breakfast)
Dinner $25pp by prior arrangment
Visa MC accepted
Not suitable for children
2 Twin 1 Single (3 bdrm)
Bathrooms: 1 Ensuite 2 Private

Hospitality is our speciality. For 14 years we have welcomed travellers many returning. Enjoy our semidetached twin studio with adjacent garden. The upstairs twin room has private bathroom, tv, teamaking. Our home is built using local stone and timbers and over looks 18 hole Golf course. Cromwell, surrounded by orchards and vineyards has excellent sporting facilities. Members of Lions International and Woolcrafters. Retired orchardists and pre-school teacher. Bluebelle, a feline with attitude Queenstown, Wanaka 45 minutes, Fiordland, Te Anau 2.5 hours drive.Free laundry. Welcome.

Cromwell *5 km N of Cromwell*
Lake Dunstan Lodge *Homestay*
Judy & Bill Thornbury
Northburn,
RD 3,
Cromwell

Tel (03) 445 1107
or 027 431 1415
Fax (03) 445 3062
william.t@xtra.co.nz
www.lakedunstanlodge.co.nz

Double/Twin $110-$130
Single $80 (Full breakfast)
Children negotiable
Dinner $25-35 by arrangement
Visa MC accepted
Children welcome
2 Queen 3 Single (3 bdrm)
Bathrooms: 2 Ensuite 1 Guest share

Friendly hospitality awaits you at our home privately situated beside Lake Dunstan. We are ex-Southland farmers and have a cat Ollie. Our interests include Lions, fishing, boating, gardening and crafts. Bedrooms have attached balconies, fridge, tea and coffee facilities. Guests share our living areas, spa pool and laundry. Local attractions: orchards, vineyards, gold diggings, fishing, boating, walks, 4 ski fields nearby. Enjoy dinner with us or just relax in the peaceful surroundings. No smoking indoors please. Directions: 5km north of Cromwell Bridge on SH8.

Cromwell *50 km E of Queenstown*
Cherry Tree Homestay *B&B Homestay*
Adrienne and Stuart Heal
87 Inniscort Street,
Cromwell
9310

Tel (03) 445 4094
or 027 235 8820
heals@xtra.co.nz

Double/Twin $130-$150
(Full breakfast)
Dinner encouraged to join us
Price negotiable
Not suitable for children
1 Queen 1 Double/Twin
1 Twin (3 bdrm)
Bathrooms: 2 Ensuite

Come stay with us at our B&B, Its name derived from our old cherry tree. Food, wine, golf, mountain air and bikes. There's plenty to do: wonderful hikes. History, vineyards, orchards and lakes. Over dinner and chat, we'll soon become good mates. Phoebe, our spaniel, she lives outdoors. Lively and friendly, she isn't a bore!!! We escaped from the city three-years ago. We really love life - wouldn't you know. Young, fit, "retired"- we've changed our pace. Come stay with us, put a smile on your face.

Arrowtown *0.5 km SW of Arrowtown*
Jopp Inn *Luxury B&B Separate Suite*
Bev & Jim Feehly
80 Cotter Avenue,
Arrowtown
9302

Tel (03) 442 1131
or 021 267 8758
021 148 4573
Fax 03 442 1131
jimandbev@arrowtown-jopp-inn.co.nz
www.arrowtown-jopp-inn.co.nz

Double/Twin $150
Single $120
(Continental breakfast provisions)
Pet free home
Not suitable for children
1 King/Twin (1 bdrm)
Bathrooms: 1 Private

Otago
North Catlins

Our luxurious new fully self contained apartment, close to skifields, golfcourses and wineries has superb views over the Wakatipu Basin to the surrounding mountains. The centrally heated apartment has it's own entrance, bedroom, lounge with TV and DVD, kitchenette, and bathroom with hairdryer and robes. A speciality continental breakfast hamper is provided. Off street parking. Ten minutes easy walk to the town centre. 20 minutes drive to Queenstown. Bev and Jim have travelled widely and Jim's family have lived in Arrowtown for over 140 years.

Arrowtown *3 km S of Arrowtown*
Peony Gardens *B&B Apartment with Kitchen*

Ian & Margaret Chamberlain
231 Lake Hayes Road,
RD1,
Queenstown

Tel (03) 442 1280
or 0274 361 661
Fax (03) 442 1210
ijchamberlain@xtra.co.nz

Double/Twin $140
Single $120
(Continental breakfast)
Pet free home
Children welcome
1 Queen 1 Double/Twin
2 Twin (2 bdrm)
Bathrooms: 1 Guest share

Our garden was the original Peony Gardens situated at Lake Hayes, between Queenstown and Historic Arrowtown. The self-contained flat has two bedrooms, full kitchen facilities, heat pump, and opens onto a balcony which looks over to the lake and our garden. A short walk will take you to the edge of the lake with wonderful views of the mountains. Easy access to four Ski Fields and four very scenic Golf Courses. We enjoy meeting people, will do all we can to make your stay memorable.

Arrowtown *20 km SE of Queenstown*
Arrowtown Heights B&B *Luxury B&B*

Rae & Winston Wallace
6 May Lane,
Arrowtown

Tel (03) 442 1726
or 027 279 1552
info@arrowtownheights.com
www.arrowtownheights.com

Double/Twin $140-$180
Single $120
(Full breakfast)
Visa MC accepted
Pet free home
1King/Twin 1 Queen (2 bdrm)
Bathrooms: 1 Ensuite 1 Private

You are always sure of a welcome at Arrowtown Heights. Our contemporary home provides spacious and luxurious accommodation in a separate wing designed especially for guests. Step out of your bedroom to sit and relax in the garden, enjoy the panoramic views or the luxury of the outdoor spa. Join us for coffee and a chat. We are happy to assist or direct you to a wide range of local sights and activities. We look forward to your visit.

Arrowtown *4 km W of Arrowtown*
Willowby Downs *B&B Homestay Farmstay*

Pam & David Mcnay
792 Malaghans Road,
R D 1,
Queenstown

Tel (03) 442 1714
or 027 222 0964
Fax (03) 4421887
willowbydowns@xtra.co.nz
www.willowbydowns.co.nz

Double/Twin $150
Single $100
(Full breakfast)
Children neg
Visa MC accepted
Children and pets welcome
2 Queen 1 Twin 2 Single (3 bdrm)
Bathrooms: 2 Ensuite 1 Guest share

With Pam & David you are assured of a warm and friendly welcome, ex hoteliers they are passionate and practiced in the art of southern hospitality. With tea and coffee on your arrival you can relax in this warm and sunny home environment."Willowby Downs" has lovely well appointed guest rooms, electric blankets, T.V, laundry options available with guests welcome to the internet, fax and Telephone facilities. Pam & David are able to arrange any extra tour or special events you may require.

Arrowtown *20 km N of Queenstown*
Arrowtown Alpine View Bed & Breakfast *B&B*

Murray & Eunice
421 Slopehill Road,
Arrowtown

Tel (03) 442 4843
or 021 051 7307
Fax (03) 442 4843
mande@xtra.co.nz

Double/Twin $170
Single $120
(Full breakfast)
Dinner by arrangement
Pet free home
Not suitable for children
Non smokers only
2 King/Twin 3 Queen (3 bdrm)
Bathrooms: 1 Private

Situated on one acre in rural Arrowtown, 5kms from historic Arrowtown gold mining village. Wonderful mountain vistas of Coronet Peak and Remarkables. Very tranquil and relaxing in a homely atmosphere with tennis court, spa, access to computer (internet) and Sky TV. Three upstairs bedrooms- two with balconies. Only 10mins from International Airport (Queenstown)- can arrange pickup. Close to world class golf courses- Millbrook & Michael Hill, ski fields - Coronet Peak & Remarkables, lake walks, wine tours, bungy jumps and a host of other activities.

Arrowtown *1 km N of Arrowtown*
Ella's B&B *B&B*

Joyce & Brian Egerton
119 Cotter Ave,
Arrowtown

Tel (03) 442 0266
or 021 071 1313

Double/Twin $140
Single $100
(Continental breakfast)
Children $20
2 King/Twin (2 bdrm)
Bathrooms: 2 Ensuite

A warm and friendly welcome awaits, when you come to stay at Ella's B&B. Spacious rooms each with their own ensuites and doors onto a sunny balcony. A continental breakfast served either in the dining room or out on the deck. Enjoy the views over Tobins track, the hills above the Arrow River. Your hosts Joyce & Brian await your company at Ella's B&B in beautiful Arrowtown.

~

Arrowtown - Queenstown *4 km W of Arrowtown*
Willowbrook *B&B Apartment with Kitchen Cottage with Kitchen*

Trish & Tony White
Malaghan Road,
RD 1,
Queenstown

Tel (03) 442 1773
or (027) 451 6739
Fax (03) 442 1780
info@willowbrook.net.nz
www.willowbrook.net.nz

Double/Twin $160-$185
Single $130-$150
(Continental breakfast)
Cottage $325 (4 persons)
Visa MC Diners Amex accepted
2 King 2 Queen 3 Twin (7 bdrm)
Bathrooms: 5 Ensuite 1 Private

Willowbrook offers both B&B and self-catering accommodation in an idyllic rural setting below Coronet Peak. Only 15 minutes from Queenstown and 5 minutes from Millbrook Resort and historic Arrowtown, we are close to skifields and golf courses. Our accommodation comprises The Main House (B&B); The Cottage (self-catering) and The Barn (self-catering). All have Sky TV, wireless broadband and own barbeque. The large garden contains a tennis court, luxurious spa pool and some very sociable sheep. Trish & Tony are knowledgeable, friendly and love what they do.

Arrowtown - Queenstown *14 km N of Arrowtown*
Crown View *B&B Farmstay*

Caroll & Reg Fraser
457 Littles Road,
Dalefield, Queenstown 9371

Tel (03) 442 9411
or 0274 495 156
0274 767 576
Fax (03) 442 9411
info@crownview.co.nz
www.crownview.co.nz

Double/Twin $165-$190
(Full breakfast)
Dinner by arrangement
Barbeque available
Visa MC accepted
Children welcome
3 King (3 bdrm)
Bathrooms: 1 Ensuite 2 Private
Rose Room has spa bath in private bathroom

Peaceful, relaxing rural setting. Fantastic views of Remarkable mountains and Crown Range. 15 minutes from either Queenstown and Arrowtown. 3 double bedrooms two with super king-size beds, 1 with king. Rooms have tea & coffee facilities, & TVs. Relax with us and enjoy our rural lifestyle, (a home away from home) along with our west highland dog, Archie, sheep, cows (Issie & Bella) Alpacas (Oscar & Jimmie) and lots of chickens. Come as a guest leave as a friend.

Arrowtown - Queenstown *12 km NE of Queenstown*
The Ferry Bed & Breakfast (circa 1872) *B&B Cottage with Kitchen*

Glenys & Kevin Reynolds
92 Spence Road, Lower Shotover,
Queenstown, 9300

Tel (03) 442 2194
or 0800 111 804
027 235 6104   Fax (03) 442 2190
info@ferry.co.nz
www.ferry.co.nz

Double/Twin $195-$235
Single $195-$235 (Full breakfast)
Children under 12 free
Whole House Deals -
contact for further information
Visa MC accepted
Children welcome
1 King 1 Double/Twin 1 Twin (3 bdrm)
Bathrooms: 1 Ensuite 1 Private
Dbl with ensuite, or dbl/family
with private bathroom

Unique Historic B&B formerly a popular hotel for over 100 years. Kevin has traced the hotel's history back to 1868 - photo's display this throughout. Glenys enjoys helping you to make the most of your stay in Queenstown offering advice & information. Kevin loves to talk Fly Fishing & can supply local information, Buckley our friendly English Springer likes to walk you along our beautiful track by the river. Situated in a delightful rural area, the perfect place to relax after a busy day.

Queenstown *0.3 km S of Queenstown Central*

The Stable *B&B Homestay*
Isobel & Gordon McIntyre
17 Brisbane Street, Queenstown 9197

Tel (03) 442 9251
Fax (03) 442 8293   gimac@queenstown.co.nz
www.thestablebb.co.nz

Double/Twin $200-$220 Single $160 (Full breakfast)
Visa MC accepted
Pet free home Not suitable for children
1 King 1 Double/Twin 2 Single (2 bdrm)
Bathrooms: 1 Ensuite 1 Private

A 135 year old stone stable, converted for guest accommodation, and listed by the New Zealand Historic Places Trust, shares a private courtyard with our home.

The Garden Room is in the house, providing convenience and comfort with lake and mountain views. Our home is in a quiet cul-de-sac and set in a garden abundant with rhododendrons and native birds. It is less than 100 metres from the beach where a small boat and canoe are available for guests' use. The famous Kelvin Heights Golf Course is close and tennis courts, bowling greens and ice skating rink are in the adjacent park. All tourist facilities, shops and restaurants are within easy walking distance, less than 5 minutes stroll on well lit footpaths. Both rooms are well heated with views of garden, lake or mountains. Tea and coffee making facilities are available at all times.

Guests share our spacious living areas and have free use of our library and laundry. A courtesy car is available to and from the bus depots. We can advise about and are booking agents for all sightseeing tours. Do allow an extra day or two for all the activities in the Queenstown region. No smoking indoors.

Your hosts, with a farming background, have bred Welsh ponies and now enjoy weaving, cooking, gardening, sailing and the outdoors. We have an interest in a successful vineyard and enjoy drinking and talking about wine. We enjoy meeting people and have travelled extensively overseas.

Directions: Follow State Highway 6A (Frankton Road) to where it veers right at the Millenium Hotel. Continue straight ahead. Brisbane Street (no exit) is second on left. Phone if necessary.

Queenstown *1.5 km NE of Queenstown Central*
Birchall House *B&B*
Joan & John Blomfield
118 Panorama Terrace,
Larchwood Heights,
Queenstown

Tel (03) 442 9985
Fax (03) 442 9980
birchall.house@xtra.co.nz
www.zqn.co.nz/birchall

Double/Twin $160-$180
Single $125-$145
(Continental breakfast)
Children $50
Visa MC accepted
Pet free home
Children welcome
1 Queen 2 Twin (2 bdrm)
Bathrooms: 2 Ensuite

Welcome to our Queenstown home, purpose built for guests in a beautiful setting. Birchall House enjoys a magnificent 200 degree view of lake and mountains within walking distance of town. Guest accommodation is spacious, private, separate entrances, centrally heated, electric blankets, smoke-free. Continental or cooked breakfast available. From Frankton Road, turn up Hensman Road, left into Sunset Lane. Or, Frankton Road, turn up Suburb Street, right into Panorama Terrace. Access via Hensman & Sunset Lane. Off-street parking. Visit our website: www.zqn.co.nz/birchall.

Queenstown *0.5 km N of Queenstown Central*
Anna's Cottage & Rose Suite *Cottage with Kitchen Suite with kitchen*
Myrna & Ken Sangster
67 Thompson Street,
Queenstown

Tel (03) 442 8994
or 027 693 3025
Fax (03) 441 8994
annas.rose@xtra.co.nz

Double/Twin $125-$155
Single $95
(Breakfast by arrangement)
Extra adult $50
Visa MC Eftpos accepted
Children welcome
1 King/Twin 1 Queen (2 bdrm)
Bathrooms: 2 Ensuite

A warm welcome to Anne's Cottage and Rose Suite. The cottage has fully equipped kitchen, living room, T.V., new ensuite, hairdryer, washing machine, superking bed. Quality towels and linen. Rose Suite attached to the end of our home, self-contained with small kitchen, queen bed with new ensuite, T.V., washing machine. Both serviced daily. Enjoy the peaceful mountain views. Private drive and parking at the Cottage. A few minutes from central Queenstown. Breakfast available at extra charge.

Queenstown *0.8 km NW of Central Queenstown*
Coronet View Apartments & B&B
Guest House Private B&B - Hotel
Neil Dempsey
30 Huff Street, Queenstown 9300

Tel (03) 442 6766 or 0800 89 6766
Fax (03) 442 6767
stay@coronetview.com
www.coronetview.com

Double/Twin $165-$250 Single $145-$230
(Includes continental breakfast)
Children $30 Extra Adult $40
Apartments from $200-$800 (with Kitchenetts & Kitchens)
Visa MC Eftpos accepted Children welcome
3 King/Twin 6 King 1 Queen (10 bdrm)
Bathrooms: 9 Ensuite 1 Private

Centrally located just ten minutes walk from town, Coronet View enjoys superb views of Coronet Peak, The Remarkables and Lake Wakatipu.

Beautifully appointed rooms offer every comfort in either hosted accommodation or private apartments. Coronet View offers luxurious guest rooms either B&B or fully self-contained private apartments.

Guest common areas occasionally shared with gorgeous persian cats include elevated and spacious dining and living areas, outdoor decks, a sunny conservatory, outdoor barbeque, pool and jacuzzi area and computers with internet access.

Bed & Breakfast - A home away from home with true kiwi hospitality. Most rooms feature super king beds with lovely quilts, sheepskin electric blankets, tiled ensuites etc.

Your hosts are knowledgeable local people who can recommend and book your activities at no extra cost.

Apartments on site Queenstown. 1-6 bedroomed ensuited apartments. Most configurations feature ensuites, super king beds, generous living areas, fully equipped kitchens and laundries.

Queenstown *0.5 km NE of Town Centre*

Delfshaven *Homestay*

Irene Mertz
11 Salmond Place
(off Kent Street),
Queenstown

Tel (03) 441 1447
irenemertz@xtra.co.nz

Double/Twin $200
Single $150
(Special breakfast)
Visa MC accepted
Pet free home
Not suitable for children
1 Queen (1 bdrm)
Bathrooms: 1 Private

Nestled on the lower Commonage, close to town, in a quiet street, is my warm, modern 2-storied home, offering great hospitality, magnificent views in all rooms over lake, mountains, and township. The comfortable guest suite has both bath and shower. TV and teamaking facilitie and opens to the views and garden. It is a 5 minute downhill walk to the town. I am a retired teacher, widely travelled, enjoy good food and wine, love art, music, and meeting people. My piano waits to be played.

≈

Queenstown *1.2 km N of Queenstown*

Campbells on Earnslaw *B&B*
Aderianne & Bevan Campbell
9 Earnslaw Terrace,
Queenstown

Tel (03) 442 7783
Fax (03) 442 7784
stay@campbells.net.nz
www.campbells.net.nz

Double/Twin $175
Single $135
(Continental breakfast)
Extra person $50
Children welcome
1 Queen 2 Single (2 bdrm)
Bathrooms: 1 Private

We look forward to welcoming you to our home, which has 180 degree spectacular panoramic views of lake, mountains and golf course. Guests own private living room with balcony, TV, fridge, toast, tea & coffee making facilities. Ideal for 2 couples or family, only 1 party at a time. Experienced hosts we can advise and arrange your sightseeing and activities. From Frankton Road turn up Suburb Street, right into Panorama Terrace, right into Earnslaw Terrace. We are only a 10 minute stroll into town centre.

Queenstown *3 km NE of Queenstown centre*

Larch Hill B&B/Homestay *B&B Homestay Apartment with Kitchen*

Lesley & Chris Marlow
16 Panners Way, Queenstown

Tel (03) 442 4811 or 027 339 6483
Fax (03) 441 8882   info@larchhill.com
www.larchhill.com

Double/Twin $135-$190 Single $115 (Special breakfast)
Apartment (sleeps 4) $210-$290
Visa MC Amex accepted Children welcome
2 King 1 Queen 1 Twin 2 Single (4 bdrm)
Bathrooms: 2 Ensuite 2 Private
All rooms have ensuite or private bathroom

We offer you a warm welcome to Larch Hill B&B in beautiful Queenstown, purpose built on an elevated site overlooking Lake Wakatipu.

As featured in 'National Geographic Traveler Magazine' 2006 and Cathay Pacific's 'Discovery' Magazine, all rooms in our comfortable and relaxing homestay have spectacular lake and mountain views, with tea/coffee making facilities. A restful theme flows through the bedrooms into the dining room with its library, opening onto a sunny courtyard surrounded by cottage gardens.

We are just 3 minutes' drive from the centre of Queenstown and within walking distance of the lake. Public transport passes our street regularly. Breakfasts are generous with homemade bread, freshly baked croissants and pastries, fresh fruit salad, yoghurt, and freshly ground, percolated coffee. Our self-contained apartment is ideal for families or small groups. We can provide pre-arranged complimentary pickups from Queenstown airport. Feel free to use our local knowledge to help plan your itinerary. We are booking agents for Queenstown tours and activities. We have no pets and are non-smokers, but guests are welcome to smoke outdoors. Fax, email and wireless internet facilities available.

Directions: from Frankton drive 2.5 kms on State Highway 6A (Frankton Road) towards Queenstown. Turn into Goldfield Heights at Sherwood Manor. Second left is Panners Way. Larch Hill B&B is No. 16 at the end of the accessway, 1/2 way down Panners Way on the left.

Queenstown *2 km N of Queenstown*
Lake Vista Bed & Breakfast *Luxury B&B*
Lucille & Graeme Simpson
62 Hensman Road, Queenstown

Tel (03) 441 8838
Fax (03) 441 8938
bookings@lakevista.co.nz
www.lakevista.co.nz

Double/Twin $175-$240
Single $120-$185
(Full breakfast)
Children welcome
Dinner by arrangement
Wireless internet available
Visa MC Eftpos accepted
Pet free home
Children welcome
1 King/Twin 2 Queen
2 Twin 1 Single (3 bdrm)
Bathrooms: 1 Ensuite 1 Guest share

Set high on Queenstown hill, a major feature of Lake Vista is our encompassing views over Lake Wakatipu to the Remarkables mountain range. You can even enjoy the view lying in bed - imagine that! We offer wireless internet for your laptop or use our guest computer. All rooms have their own mini-bars, security boxes, TV, hair dryers, underfloor heating, electric blankets, heated towel-rails, radio/alarms and tea/coffee facilities. Gourmet breakfasts complete the package. Be pampered with the personal attention of your hosts, Lucille & Graeme.

Queenstown *1.40 km SE of Queenstown*
"Kemnay" *B&B*
Heather & Fraser Ronald
57 Panorama Terrace,
Queenstown

Tel 03 442 6270
hfronald@xtra.co.nz

Double/Twin $130-$140
Single $100
(Full breakfast)
Children by arrangement
1 Queen 1 Twin (2 bdrm)
Bathrooms: 1 Private
Bath & Shower

Heather and Fraser warmly welcome you to their Queenstown Home. Wonderful views of lake and mountains, also overlooks golf course. Queen bed, plus twin, private bathroom. Small comfortable seating area with tea and coffee making facilities. One party at a time. Off street parking. 1.4km from town centre.Directions: Approaching Queenstown along Frankton Road, turn right into Hensman Road, then first turn left inot Panorama Tce.

Queenstown *14.5 km SE of Queenstown*
Bayswater *B&B*
Marie and Angus Buchanan
4 Cedar Drive,
Kelvin Heights,
Queenstown, 9300

Tel (03) 441 2336
or Mobile 027 424 1890
vinnetta@kol.co.nz

Double/Twin $140-$155
Single $90-$110
(Continental breakfast)
2 King/Twin 1 Queen (2 bdrm)
Bathrooms: 2 Ensuite

W e would like to welcome you to our warm sunny Kelvin Heights home, with spectacular lake and mountain views. Our rooms have comfortable beds, electric blankets, heaters and own television. Tea/coffee facilities available. We are a 15 minute senic drive to downtown Queenstown. 1/2 hour drive to either Coronet or Remarkables ski fields, 2 minute walk to the beach and amazing walking tracks. A 5 minute drive to the spectacular Kelvin Heights Golf course and less than 1/2 hour to the Arrowtown and Milbrook courses

≈

Glenorchy *48 km N of Queenstown*
Glenorchy Lake House *B&B*
Toni and John Glover
13 Mull Street,
Glenorchy, 9350

Tel (03) 442 7084
Fax (03) 442 7086
info@glenorchylakehouse.co.nz
www.glenorchylakehouse.co.nz

Double/Twin $245-$400
Single $220-$375 (Full breakfast)
Kinloch Lodge boat collects guests for dinner at 6:00 pm
Sister hotel to Kinloch Lodge
Visa MC accepted
Pet free home
Children welcome when family has sole occupancy
1 King/Twin 1 King (2 bdrm)
Bathrooms: 1 Ensuite 1 Private Luxury
Bathrooms with separate bath /shower

G lenorchy Lake House fronts Lake Wakatipu in the heart of Glenorchy . 360 degree views, rooms designed for ultimate comfort and a therapeutic massaging spa await in this natural heaven ñ very close to Paradise, the Routeburn track and the Mt Aspiring National Park World Heritage area. Guests enjoy the comforts of the Lake house to themselves, with staff slipping in to do breakfast in the morning, to clean and tidy and to ensure a fresh baking is laid for afternoon tea.

Garston *50 km S of Queenstown*
Menlove Homestay *B&B Homestay Separate Suite*
Bev & Matt Menlove
17 Blackmore Road,
PO Box 39,
Garston 9750

Tel (03) 248 8516
mattmenlove@xtra.co.nz

Double/Twin $90
Single $50
(Continental breakfast)
Dinner $25 by arrangement
1 Double/Twin 1 Single (1 bdrm)
Bathrooms: 1 Ensuite

We are organic gardeners and our other interests include lawn bowls, sailing, gliding and alternative energy. Garston is New Zealand's most inland village with the Mataura River (famous for its fly fishing) flowing through the valley, surrounded by the Hector Range and the Eyre Mountains. A fishing guide is available with advance notice. For day trips, Garston is central to Queenstown, Te Anau, Milford Sound or Invercargill. We look forward to meeting you.

Garston *50 km S of Queenstown*
Naylor House *Cottage with Kitchen*
John and Avis McIver
33 Naylor Road,
Garston,
Southland

Tel (03) 248 8809
or 027 653 6110
Fax (03) 248 8809
naylorhouse@slingshot.co.nz
www.naylorhouse.co.nz

Double/Twin $150
(Breakfast by arrangement)
Dinner by arrangement
Visa MC accepted
Pet free home
Children welcome
1 King/Twin 1 Queen
2 Twin (3 bdrm)
Bathrooms: 1 Private

Welcome to Historic Naylor House situated in the heart of the beautiful and tranquil Garston Valley. Garston is Central to Queenstown, Te Anau, Milford Sound and Invercargill. The Mataura River which is famed for its fly fishing is on our doorstep. We look forward to sharing all our local knowledge and our beautiful location with you.

Alexandra *3.5 km N of Alexandra*
Duart *B&B Homestay*
Mary & Keith McLean
Bruce's Hill Lane,
356 Manuherikia Road,
RD 3, Alexandra, 9393

Tel (03) 448 9190 or 027 316 3569
Fax (03) 448 9190
duart.homestay@xtra.co.nz
www.duarthomestay.co.nz

Double/Twin $110-$110
Single $90-$90
(Continental breakfast)
Children negotiable
Dinner $25 by arrangement
Visa MC accepted
Pet free home
Children and pets welcome
1 Double/Twin 1 Twin 1 Single (3 bdrm)
Bathrooms: 1 Ensuite 1 Guest share En suite downstairs; private, guest share upstairs.

Your accredited Kiwi Hosts, Mary and Keith, welcome you to our secluded home, 5 minutes from Alexandra. Your privacy is assured, but we enjoy company and conversation if that is your wish. Relish the spectacular views from our extensive stone terraced garden, or relax in the sitting room, library or verandahs. Revel in the myriad activities and experiences Alexandra offers; e.g. the climate, Rail Trail, award winning vineyards, galleries, mountain biking, kayaking etc. Laundry, Sky TV. Complimentary tea, coffee, biscuits, fruit, pre-dinner drink and nibbles.

Roxburgh - Ettrick *17 km SW of Ettrick*
Wilden Station Homestead *B&B Homestay Farmstay*
Sarah & Peter Adam
Wilden School Road,
Wilden,
West Otago

Tel (03) 204 8115
Fax (03) 204 8116
wildenstation@farmside.co.nz

Double/Twin $180
Single $120
(Special breakfast)
Children $20
Dinner $45
Visa MC accepted
Children welcome
2 Queen 2 Single (3 bdrm)
Bathrooms: 1 Ensuite 1 Private

Experience high-country farm life with us, our two boys and two cats. Watch our dogs work the sheep. Stroll through trees to a small lake, explore our historic farm buildings, fish the Pomahaka River, tour the property, or simply relax in our gracious homestead. Enjoy superb meals prepared by your internationally experienced chef/ hostess (all by prior arrangement). Unwind in our tranquil surroundings about 2 hours from Dunedin, Queenstown, Wanaka. Families most welcome. Please telephone for directions.

Roxburgh - Millers Flat *16 km S of Roxburgh*
Quince Cottage *B&B Cottage No Kitchen*

Wendy Gunn & Cally Johnstone
Rapid No 1581,
Teviot Road,
Millers Flat

Tel (03) 446 6889
thequince@clear.net.nz
www.quincecottage.co.nz

Double/Twin $220
Single $125
(Special breakfast)
Dinner $65pp
Visa MC accepted
1 Queen
Bathrooms: 1 Ensuite

Q uince Cottage - half way between Dunedin and Queenstown/Wanaka or a destination in itself. The Cottage is set apart from the house surrounded by a big open garden dotted with trees, and lawn stretching into the distance. It is open plan with a dining table, TV, CD player, fridge, air-con and heating. Meals are served in the main house, however if you wish to dine in the cottage we are happy to deliver your meals. Dinner is $65 pp - 3 courses and complimentary Central Otago wine.

Middlemarch *4 km SW of Middlemarch*
'The Farm' *Homestay Farmstay*

Lynley & Glynne Smith
Farm Road, RD 2,
Middlemarch

Tel (03) 464 3610
or 027 4362423
or 021 224 3004
Fax (03) 464 3612
glynley@xtra.co.nz
www.thefarm-homestay.com

Double/Twin $110
Single $75 (Full breakfast)
Dinner $35pp
Children and pets welcome
1 King 1 Twin (2 bdrm)
Bathrooms: 1 Guest share Spa available outside

O ur charming old stone house and gardens are set amoust mature oaks, with the spectacular Rock and Pillar Range as a backdrop. Lynley & Glynne welcome you to their peaceful relaxed haven which includes a 200 acre farm, sheep, cattle, horses, 2 family cats & a Jack Russell dog. From high country farming background, interested in horses, hunting and a tranquil lifestyle. On the Central Otago Rail Trail, 1 hour from Dunedin, this is a convenient and hospitable stop for exploring this picturesque area. Guests can be picked up from Dunedin airport with their bikes, over night and then can be delivered to Clyde - cost $100 for each trip.

Lawrence *30 km N of Balclutha*
The Ark *B&B*

Frieda Betman
8 Harrington Place
(Main Road),
Lawrence

Tel (03) 485 9328
the.ark@xtra.co.nz
www.theark.co.nz

Double/Twin $100
Single $50
(Full breakfast)
Children $15
2 Double/Twin 1 Twin
1 Single (4 bdrm)
Bathrooms: 1 Family share

My home is on the main road near the picnic ground with its avenue of poplars. The house is 100 years old, has character, charm and a lived in feeling. It's home to Ambrose & Pumpkin, my cats and Holly, a miniature Foxie. Guestrooms are restful with fresh flowers, fruit, and breakfast includes hot bread, croissants, home-made jams. Free-range eggs. There is a lovely peaceful atmosphere in our early gold mining town. Approx. 45 minutes to Dunedin airport, just over an hour to Dunedin.

~

Waikouaiti *40 km N of Dunedin*
Boutique Bed & Breakfast *B&B Farmstay Separate Suite*

Barbara & John Morgan
107 Jefferis Road,
Waikouaiti,
RD 2
Nr Palmerston

Tel (03) 465 7239
or 027 224 8212
021 161 0243
Fax (03) 465 7239
info@boutiquebedandbreakfast.co.nz
www.boutiquebedandbreakfast.co.nz

Double/Twin $120-$180
Single $100-$120
(Full breakfast)
Visa MC accepted
3 Queen 1 Double/Twin (3 bdrm)
Bathrooms: 3 Ensuite

Enjoy a tranquil garden setting on a deer park. Our unique guest rooms are purpose built and designed for your comfort and pleasure. After a delicious breakfast, experience John's deer tour with dogs George and Mildred. Central location, from which to explore beautiful coastal Otago and only 30 minutes from Dunedin

Dunedin *2 km W of Dunedin*

Magnolia House *B&B*

Joan & George Sutherland
18 Grendon Street,
Maori Hill,
Dunedin
9010

Tel (03) 467 5999
Fax (03) 467 5999
mrsuth@xtra.co.nz

Double/Twin $130
Single $100
(Special breakfast)
Not suitable for children
1 Queen 1 Double/Twin
2 Single (3 bdrm)
Bathrooms: 1 Private 1 Family share

O ur quiet turn-of-the-century villa sits in broad, flower-bordered lawns backed by native bush with beautiful, tuneful birds. All rooms have electric heating, comfortable beds with electric blanket, and antiques, while the queen room has an adjoining balcony. Close by is Moana Pool, the glorious Edwardian house Olveston, and Otago Golf Course. Our special breakfast will set you up for the day. We have a courtesy car, and two burmese cats. It is not suitable for children or smokers.

Dunedin *7 km NE of Dunedin*

Harbourside B&B *B&B Homestay*

Shirley & Don Parsons
6 Kiwi Street,
St Leonards, Dunedin

Tel (03) 471 0690
Fax (03) 471 0063
harboursidebb@xtra.co.nz

Double/Twin $85-$100
Single $70-$100
(Full breakfast)
Children $20
Dinner $30
Visa MC accepted
Pet free home
Children welcome
1 King/Twin 2 Queen
3 Single (3 bdrm)
Bathrooms: 1 Ensuite 1 Guest share

W e are situated in a quiet suburb overlooking Otago Harbour and surrounding hills. Within easy reach of all local attractions. Lovely garden or harbour views from all rooms. Children very welcome. Directions: drive into city on one-way system watch for Highway 88 sign follow Anzac Avenue onto Ravensbourne Road. Continue approx 5km to St Leonards turn left at Playcentre opposite Boatshed into Pukeko Street then left into Kaka Road, straight ahead to Kiwi Street turn left into Number 6.

Dunedin *0.1 km N of Dunedin Central*
Albatross Inn *B&B*
Glynis Rees
770 George Street, Dunedin

Tel (03) 477 2727 or 0800 441 441
Fax (03) 477 2108 albatross.inn@xtra.co.nz
www.albatross.inn.co.nz

Double/Twin $110-$160 Single $95-$110
(Special breakfast)
Children $15 Visa MC Diners Amex Eftpos accepted
Pet free home Children welcome
3 King 4 Queen 2 Double/Twin 5 Single (8 bdrm)
Bathrooms: 8 Ensuite

Welcome to Dunedin and Albatross Inn! Our beautiful late Victorian house is ideally located on the main street close to the university, gardens, museum, shops and restaurants.

Our attractive rooms have ensuite/private bathrooms, telephone, TV, radio, central heating, tea/coffee, warm duvets and electric blankets on modern beds. Firm beds upon request. Quiet rooms at rear of house. Several rooms have kitchenette and fridge.

Enjoy our sumptious breakfast in our cosy breakfast room. We serve freshly baked bread and muffins, fresh fruit salad, yoghurt, juices, cereals, teas, freshly brewed coffee. We are happy to recommend and book tours for you. All wildlife tours pick up and drop off here. We can recommend many great places to eat, most just a short walk down George Street. Nearby laundry, non-smoking, cot and highchair.

Some comments from our visitors Book! The right balance of everything location, breakfast and lovely room. Delightfully different. Absolutely fantastic as always. Home away from Home. A touch of Class, lovely home beautifully presented. Perfecto!

Homepage: www.albatross.inn.co.nz. Winter special $90 Double - special conditions apply. Complimentary e-mail and wireless internet.

Dunedin *1 km W of Dunedin*

Highbrae Guesthouse *B&B Guest House wireless internet availability*

Fienie & Stephen Clark
376 High Street, Dunedin

Tel (03) 479 2070
or 027 4328 470
Fax (03) 479 2100
highbrae@xtra.co.nz
www.highbrae.co.nz

Double/Twin $100-$140
Single $80-$100
(Continental breakfast)
Children $25 if sharing
room with parents
Cooked breakfast extra
Visa MC Amex accepted
Pet free home
Children welcome
1 King 2 Queen 1 Twin 1 Single (4 bdrm)
Bathrooms: 1 Private 1 Guest share 1 Family share

Experience a taste of early Dunedin. This heritage home was built on the High Street in 1908 to provide first class accommodation to its residents. Today it is still an impressive home with spectacular views of the city and harbour. The upstairs guest rooms and self contained unit are carefully restored to preserve their character for visitors, who delight in the many features in the home. Wireless internet is available and a courtesy van can meet you at the bus or train if required.

Dunedin *1 km W of Dunedin*

Grandview *Luxury B&B Guest House*

Steve Scott
360 High Street, Dunedin 9001

Tel (03) 474 9472
or 021 101 9857
0800 749 472
Fax (03) 474 9473
nzgrandview@msn.com
www.grandview.co.nz

Double/Twin $100-$195
Single $80-$145
(Continental breakfast)
Children or extra person $25
Visa MC Diners Amex Eftpos accepted
Children welcome
1 King 3 Queen 1 Double/Twin
1 Twin 4 Single (7 bdrm)
Bathrooms: 2 Ensuite
1 Private 2 Guest share

Grandview is centrally located! The casino, restaurants, shops, cafes and bars are only a short stroll away! Relax in luxury in this charming 1901 heritage listed Edwardian mansion. Featuring magnificent panoramic views from our viewing platforms and spa area. Television, videos, free internet, free laundry facilities and scrumptious continental breakfasts are all a complimentary part of the Grandview experience. Rooms to suit all budgets! From comfortable standard rooms to our luxury trendy spa suites for your pleasure!

Otago
North Catlins

Dunedin *10 km SW of Dunedin*
Grant's Farm *B&B Apartment with Kitchen*

Approved

Tom and Jeanette Grant
151 Old Brighton Road,
Fairfield RD 1,
Dunedin 9076

Tel (03) 488 0336
Fax 03 488 0364
grantsfarm@xtra.co.nz
www.visit-dunedin.co.nz/grantsfarm.html

Double/Twin $110-$140
Single $90-$110
(Continental breakfast)
Children by arrangement
Dinner not supplied
Visa MC accepted
Pet free home
1 Queen 1 Double/Twin
1 Single (2 bdrm)
Bathrooms: 1 Ensuite

Our typical NZ woolshed on 20ha is now a unique home with private fully self contained guest accommodation complete with woodfire. Situated on the Kaikorai Estuary we have heaps of bird life sheep and cattle and also an airstrip with biplanes. We are in a peaceful rural setting with wonderful views, only 15 minutes from Dunedin Airport and 8 minutes to either Dunedin or Mosgiel. Excellent restaurants and miles of beach walks are minutes away. 1 loving outdoor cat. Guests wish they could stay longer!

Dunedin - North East Valley *3 km NE of Dunedin*
Bygone Era Bed & Breakfast *Luxury B&B*

Approved

Angela and Jasper (the cat)
396 North Road,
North East Valley,
Dunedin, 9010

Tel (03) 473 8572
or 021 106 8878
Fax (03) 473 8572
enquiries@atouchofelegance.co.nz
www.atouchofelegance.co.nz

Double/Twin $145-$195
Single $130-$180
(Full breakfast)
Visa MC Eftpos accepted
Not suitable for children
3 Queen (3 bdrm)
Bathrooms: 1 Ensuite
1 Guest share

Situated eight minutes from the city centre, Bygone Era is close to all amenities and a perfect base from which to experience the many attractions Otago has to offer. The 1905 home retains many of its original architectural features. Guest accommodation is provided with luxury in mind and includes 1000 thread-count linen, luxury feather & down underlays, pillows and duvets. A sumptuous cafe style breakfast is included and will most likely include silver table service. Your hosts are Angela and Jasper (the cat).

Dunedin *0.5 km SW of Dunedin*
Deacons Court *B&B*

B&B
Approved

Jill McDonald & Roger Whitworth
342 High Street,
Dunedin
9016

Tel (03) 477 9053
or 0800 268 252
Fax (03) 477 9058
info@deaconscourt.com

Double/Twin $100-$160
Single $80-$120
(Full breakfast)
Children $20-$50
Visa MC Eftpos accepted
Children welcome
2 King/Twin 2 King
1 Queen 3 Single (4 bdrm)
Bathrooms: 2 Ensuite 1 Private

Deacons Court is a charming superior spacious Victorian villa 1km walking distance from the city centre and is on the city's heritage building register. We are only 500m from cafes, bars and some of Dunedin's unique attractions and offer you friendly but unobtrusive hospitality in a quiet secure haven. Guests can relax in our delightful rose garden and spacious conservatory. Our extra large bedrooms , have ensuite or private bathrooms, TV and comfortable seating. Complimentary broadband, 24 hour tea or coffee, and free parking available.

Otago Peninsula - Broad Bay *16 km E of Dunedin*
Chy-an-Dowr *B&B*

B&B
Approved

Susan & Herman van Velthoven
687 Portobello Road,
Broad Bay, Dunedin

Tel (03) 478 0306
or 021 036 5190
or 021 156 0715
Fax (03) 478 0306
hermanvv@xtra.co.nz
www.chy-an-dowr.co.nz

Double/Twin $195-$250
(Special breakfast)
Visa MC accepted
Pet free home
Not suitable for children
1 King 1 Queen 1 Single (2 bdrm)
Bathrooms: 1 Ensuite with shower
1 Private with bath and shower.

Chy-an-Dowr (House by the Water), quality boutique accommodation located midway on scenic Otago Peninsula. Our character 1920's home with its harbourside location has panoramic views and is situated across the road from a small beach and enroute to the albatross and penguin colonies. The upstairs guest area is spacious and private with a sunroom and two comfortable suites with bathrobes, tea/coffee, TV, fridge. Enjoy a delicious breakfast at your leisure. Originally from Holland, we enjoy welcoming people and sharing our wonderful location with them.

Otago
North Catlins

Otago Peninsula - Broad Bay *16 km E of Dunedin*
Broad Bay White House *B&B Homestay*

Chris & Margaret Marshall
11 Clearwater Street,
Broad Bay,
Dunedin

Tel (03) 478 1160
Fax (03) 478 1159
broadbaywhitehouse@paradise.net.nz
www.broadbaywhitehouse.co.nz

Double/Twin $150-$195
Single $140-$165
(Full breakfast)
Visa MC Amex accepted
Pet free home
3 Queen 1 Single (3 bdrm)
Bathrooms: 2 Ensuite 1 Private
Showers only in bathrooms

Looking for peace and quiet, privacy, panoramic views over the harbour, superb meals with silver service? Look no further. We are a tranquil semi-rural hideaway located on the Otago Peninsula. Handy to albatross, penguin and seal colonies. All bedrooms enjoy spacious decks and panoramic views over the harbour. House is centrally heated throughout. Relax and wander through gardens and enjoy the abundant bird life. Have fun with a game of petanque (no experience required).

Otago Peninsula - Macandrew Bay *11 km E of Dunedin*
Mac Bay Retreat *B&B Cottage with Kitchen*

Jeff & Helen Hall
38 Bayne Terrace,
Macandrew Bay,
Dunedin
9014

Tel (03) 476 1475
Fax (03) 476 1975
jhall9@ihug.co.nz
www.macandrewbay.co.nz/macbayretreat

Double/Twin $125
Single $110
(Continental breakfast)
Extra people $25pp
Visa MC accepted
1 King 1 Double/Twin (1 bdrm)
Bathrooms: 1 Ensuite

Mac Bay Retreat - Otago Peninsula. Welcome to your private self-contained smoke-free retreat, 15 minutes from Dunedin centre on the Otago Peninsula. Relax with the spectacular view overlooking the harbour from Dunedin City to Port Chalmers. Your cosy retreat is separate from the host's house and gives you a choice of either a super king or double bed plus an ensuite, modern kitchen and TV. Suitable for 1 couple, possibly 2 couples, travelling together. Only minutes from Dunedin's most popular attractions.

Otago Peninsula - Portobello *20 km NE of Dunedin*
Peninsula B&B *B&B*

Toni & Stephen Swabey
4 Allans Beach Road,
Portobello,
Dunedin

Tel 0800 478 090
or (03) 478 0909
027 634 3661
Fax (03) 478 0909
toni@peninsula.co.nz
www.peninsula.co.nz

Double/Twin $145-$195
Single $120-$140
(Full breakfast)
Children POA
Free wireless broadband internet
Visa MC accepted
Children welcome
1 King/Twin 1 King 2 Queen 1 Single (4 bdrm)
Bathrooms: 2 Ensuite 1 Guest share

Come and relax in the elegant and romantic Victorian ambience of our beautiful 1880s villa. Situated in peaceful gardens, enjoy wonderful views of the harbour from your ensuite room. Relish your delicious cooked breakfast in the morning, with home baking. Catch up with our complimentary newspaper and make yourself at home with tea/coffee making facilities. Keep in touch with home with our free wireless broadband internet. We are ideally located for wildlife and scenic attractions and just a minute's walk from Portobello's two restaurants.

Otago Peninsula - Portobello *20 km NE of Dunedin*
Captain Eady's Lookout *B&B Homestay*

Richard & Ana Good
2 Moss Street,
Portobello,
Dunedin 9014

Tel (03) 478 0537
or 021 478 785
capteady@earthlight.co.nz
www.capteady.co.nz

Double/Twin $160-$195
Single $150-$185
(Special breakfast)
Children negotiable
Dinner $40 by prior arrangement
Twin Room $100-120
Visa MC accepted
Children welcome
2 Queen 1 Twin (3 bdrm)
Bathrooms: 2 Ensuite 1 Family share

Captain Eady's Lookout is a delightful bed and breakfast on the water's edge. This character house, built early last century by Captain Eady, a ferry master, stands on a small bluff overlooking Otago Harbour. One bedroom opens onto a secluded garden, one overlooks the harbour. You may have a special breakfast in our conservatory whilst taking in the splendid harbour views. The house has many antiques and on the walls are paintings by local artists. You may sample the large jazz collection. Cats in residence.

**Otago
North Catlins**

Otago Peninsula - Pukehiki *12 km E of Dunedin City*
Patton's Hill B&B Homestay *B&B Homestay Farmstay*
Ray and Beatrice Hall
Rapid 974 Highcliff Road,
Dunedin
RD 2

Tel (03) 476 1007
or 027 436 3663
Fax (03) 476 1007
rbhall@ihug.co.nz

Double/Twin $100-$120
Single $80-$100
(Full breakfast)
Children negotiable
Pet free home
Children welcome
1 Queen 1 Twin (2 bdrm)
Bathrooms: 1 Guest share

We welcome you to stay in our modern home situated on a 30 acre farm originally settled in the 1800s. Share with us country living on the beautiful Otage Peninsula. We are situated close to Dunedin and all Peninsula attractions, including Larnach Castle, Albatoss, Seal and Penguin colonies. Enjoy magnificent harbour and ocean views. Guest rooms are equipped with heating and electric blankets. Off street parking is provided for your convenience.

Otago Peninsula - Portobello *20 km NE of Dunedin*
McAuley Glen Bed & Breakfast *Luxury B&B Homestay*
Mary & Pat Curtin
13 McAuley Road,
Portobello,
Dunedin

Tel (03) 478 0724
or 021 237 1919
Fax (03) 478 0724
maryandpat@clear.net.nz

Double/Twin $195-$220
Single $165-$195 (Full breakfast)
Children under 10 negotiable
Dinner by arrangement
Visa MC accepted
Children welcome
2 Queen 1 Twin (3 bdrm)
Bathrooms: 2 Ensuite
Spacious,walk in shower, heated tile floor

Magical rural setting, romantic, private, peacfull, 3/4 acre of beautiful gardens with bird song. 5min walk to restaurants, hotel & dairy. 20min drive to Albatross, Penguin & Seal colonies. Suites have: Separate patio garden entrances, TV,CD,DVD, quality furnishings/fittings luxury bedding/bathrobes, Mini kitchen: micro wave,fridge, tea/coffee/baking/ chocolates. Complimentery ale/wine, sauna & outdoor jacuzzi spa included. Room service, laundry & internet available. Mary & Pat operate Scenic & Wildlife Tours - sea kayaking & mountain biking. We look forward to sharing our piece of paradise with you.

Otago Peninsula - Broad Bay *15 km N of Dunedin*
Fantail Lodge *2 self-contained cottages with Kitchens*

Vic and Tessa Mills
682 Portobello Road,
Broad Bay,
Dunedin

Tel (03) 478 0110
or 0274 156 222
fantail.lodge@xtra.co.nz

Double/Twin $150-$150
Single $100-$120
(Accommodation only)
Extra adults or children $20 each
Continental Provisions extra
Visa MC accepted
Pet free home
Children welcome
1 Queen 1 Double/Twin
2 Single (3 bdrm)
One ensuite in each cottage.

Peacefully situated on the beautiful Otago Peninsula, close to beaches, seals, penguins and albatrosses, our lush, harbourside garden contains two, delightfully rustic, self -contained cottages. Fantail Cottage has double bed accommodation with two singles on a mezzanine. Bellbird offers a queen bed and an exclusive spa pool. Both are equipped for self catering or continental breakfast hampers by arrangement. Free use of kayaks. An ideal base for touring and a great location for a romantic getaway.

Mosgiel *2 km SW of Mosgiel*
The Trees *B&B*

Jenny Blackgrove & Rex Moore
70 Main South Road,
East Taieri,
Mosgiel 9024

Tel (03) 489 4837
or 021 0244 2839
Fax (03) 477 1479
rex.moore@clear.net.nz

Double/Twin $120
Single $75
(Full breakfast)
Dinner $45 by prior arrangement
Visa MC accepted
Not suitable for children
1 King 1 Twin (2 bdrm)
Bathrooms: 1 Guest share
Shower and separate bath

Welcome to our quiet, semirural home set on an acre of lawns and trees. We are 15km SW of Dunedin, half-way between Dunedin and the airport. There are 3 golf courses in close proximity. Resident animals are 2 cats and a border collie dog named Dougal. Rex enjoys flying light aircraft and sailing, Jenny is a Cordon Bleu trained cook and besides cooking, Jenny's interests include gardening and reading. We both have travelled extensively. Facilities include off-street parking and make yourself tea, coffee & juice.

Otago
North Catlins

Mosgiel *1 km N of Mosgiel*

Marg's Manor *Homestay*
Margaret
103 Main South Road,
East Taieri,
Mosgiel,
Dunedin

Tel (03) 489 2030
Fax (03) 489 2030
msscott@xtra.co.nz

Double/Twin $110-$125
Single $85-$95
(Continental breakfast)
Dinner $30 by arrangement
Full breakfast by arrangement
Not suitable for children
1 Queen (1 bdrm)
Bathrooms: 1 Ensuite

Haere Mai, welcome to my sunny cottage home situated halfway between Dunedin Airport and Dunedin city, with rural views over the Taieri Plains. Enjoy your own entrance and outdoor table just beside room, or relax up in the back garden spaces amongst the vegetables and herbs that I enjoy cooking with. Dinner and cooked breakfast by arrangement, off street parking available. I enjoy travelling, teach early childhood and I am 5th generation for local knowledge. Resident cat called Fluff.

Balclutha *4 km N of Balclutha/Catlins*

Lesmahagow *Luxury B&B Boutique*
Noel & Kate O'Malley
Main Road,
Benhar, RD 2,
Balclutha

Tel (03) 418 2507
or 0800 301 224 (NZ only)
027 457 8465
lesmahagow@xtra.co.nz
www.lesmahagow.co.nz

Double/Twin $140-$150
(Full breakfast)
Dinner $35
Lunches on request
Visa MC Eftpos accepted
Children welcome
2 Queen 2 Double/Twin
1 Single (3 bdrm)
Bathrooms: 2 Private 1 Guest share

Lesmahagow offers excellent accommodation in an historic homestead and garden setting. Centrally situated, discerning travellers can make Lesmahagow their base to explore the Catlins region, Dunedin and the Otago Penninsula or the historic goldfields of Lawrence. Centrally heated, with delightful bedrooms and gorgeous bathrooms, you can be sure of wonderful hospitality and a truly memorable stay. Evening meals are our speciality and our breakfasts will satisfy all taste buds! Come and discover this hidden paradise! You will love the experience.

If you would like dinner most hosts require 24 hours' notice.

Kaka Point - The Catlins *21 km S of Balclutha*

Rata Cottage *B&B Cottage with Kitchen*

B&B Approved

Jean Schreuder
31 Rata Street,
Kaka Point,
South Otago
Tel (03) 412 8779

Double/Twin $80
Single $75
(Continental breakfast)
Extra person $15
Children welcome
1 Twin (1 bdrm)
Bathrooms: 1 Ensuite

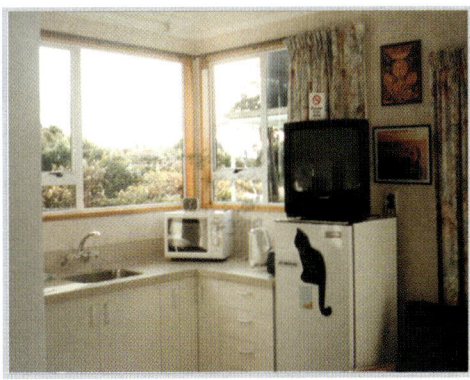

A fully self-contained sunny bed & breakfast unit in a tranquil bush garden setting, with sea view, bell birds and tuis. Bedroom with twin beds, plus double divan in lounge. Wheelchair facilities. 5 minutes from a beautiful sandy beach for swimming or long walks. Next door to scenic reserve and bush walks. You can have breakfast in the garden with the birds if you wish. Non-smoking. Laundry facilities available. Cooking facilities.

Otago North Catlins

Kaka Point - The Catlins *20 km NE of Owaka*

Nugget Lodge *Apartment with Kitchen*

Pauline & Willy Simpson
367 The Nuggets Road,
RD1
Balclutha,
9271

Tel (03) 412 8783
Fax (03) 412 8784
lighthouse@nuggetlodge.co.nz
www.nuggetlodge.co.nz

Double/Twin $160
(Breakfast by arrangement)
Extra guest $25-00
Visa MC accepted
Pet free home
Not suitable for children
1 King 1 Queen 1 Single (2 bdrm)
Bathrooms: 2 Ensuite

A small intimate business catering for the eco-traveller. Two modern, private, fully self contained and centrally heated units. Absolutely on the water's edge over looking the Pacific Ocean. Discover the enchantment of The Catlins with its magnificent unspoilt scenery. Bush walks, penguins, sealions, seals and a bird watchers' paradise. After a day exploring The Catlins sit on your private verandah and sip a glass of wine. One day is not enough to experience the beauty of this area. Restaurants nearby.

Owaka - The Catlins *15 km S of Owaka*

Greenwood Farmstay *B&B Farmstay Separate Suite*
Self-contained Beach Cottage - sleeps 8

Helen-May & Alan Burgess
739 Purakaunui Falls Road,
Owaka, South Otago

Tel (03) 415 8259
or 027 438 4538
Fax (03) 415 8259
greenwoodfarm@xtra.co.nz
www.greenwoodfarmstay.co.nz

Double/Twin $140-$150
Single $120 (Full breakfast)
Children $90
Dinner $40 per person (3 course)
Self-contained cottage $90 double
Extra person $15
Children welcome
2 Queen 1 Twin (3 bdrm)
Bathrooms: 1 Ensuite 1 Private 1 Guest share
1 Family share 2 bathrooms at Beach Cottage

Welcome ... Within walking distance to beautiful Purakaunui Falls. Alan enjoys taking people around our sheep, cattle and deer farm and you may stand on the cliffs where the movie "Narnia" was filmed. We enjoy evening dining with our guests. Our home offers warm, very comfortable accommodation. One guest bedroom with ensuite and day-room opens to the large garden. A private bathroom services other guest rooms. Email/phone for directions. Ask about our self-contained cottage at Papatowai Beach.

Owaka *6 km N of Owaka*

Hillview *B&B Farmstay Cottage with Kitchen*

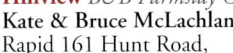

Kate & Bruce McLachlan
Rapid 161 Hunt Road,
Katea, RD 2,
Owaka,
South Otago

Tel (03) 415 8457
or 027 433 4759
Fax (03) 415 8457
hillviewcatlins@xtra.co.nz

Double/Twin $105-$120
Single $60
(Continental breakfast)
Children $40
Dinner from $30, bookings essential
Visa MC accepted
Children and pets welcome
2 Queen 4 Single (4 bdrm)
Bathrooms: 2 Guest share

Our sheep and cattle grazing property is situated 15 minutes from Nugget Point, 10 minutes from Cannibal Bay. Relax in our cosy private cottage set in a large developing garden, or enjoy the relaxed atmosphere of our home. Our pets usually live outside. Bruce enjoys working with horses, training sheepdogs and often works on another local farm. Kate is a school librarian who enjoys reading, gardening, and handcrafts. We enjoy our grandchildren and meeting people. Breakfast with us or in private. Phone evenings.

Owaka - The Catlins *1 km N of Owaka*

J T's Catlins B&B *B&B Homestay*

John & Thelma Turnbull
2885 Main Road,
Owaka

Tel (03) 415 8127
or 027 649 7693
Fax (03) 415 8129
jtowaka@ihug.co.nz
www.jtscatlinsbnb.co.nz

Double/Twin up to $120
Single up to $80
(Full breakfast)
Dinner by arrangement
Children welcome
1 Queen 1 Twin (2 bdrm)
Bathrooms: 1 Guest share
Toilet, shower & bathroom,
3 seperate rooms

Welcome to our warm and comfortable home on the Southern Scenic Route, situated on a 25 acre farmlet, surrounded by colourful, peaceful gardens with splendid unspoilt views. Located in the heart of the Catlins, renowned for its wildlife and spectacular scenery, we are within walking distance of Owaka Township with its restaurants, museum and other amenities. Our guests are encouraged to dine with us for the evening meal when we enjoy quality local food and wine. We look forward to meeting you. Travel safely.

**Otago
North Catlins**

Southland, South Catlins & Stewart Island

Te Anau - Manapouri *20 km E of Manapouri*

Crown Lea *Farmstay*
Florence & John Pine
310 Gillespie Road,
RD 1,
Te Anau

Tel (03) 249 8598
or 021 1680 299
Fax (03) 249 8598
crownlea@xtra.co.nz
www.crown-lea.com

Double/Twin $180
Single $180
(Full breakfast)
Dinner $40
1 Queen 1 Twin (3 bdrm)
Bathrooms: 1 Ensuite 2 Private

Our 900 acre sheep, cattle and deer farm offers a farm tour after 6pm, and views of Lake Manapouri, Fiordland mountains, and Te Anau Basin. Day trips to Doubtful and Milford Sounds, visits to Te Anau, glowworm caves, or hikes on the walking tracks in Fiordland all within easy reach. Having travelled in South Africa, UK, Europe, USA, Canada, Hong Kong and Singapore, we and Harriet the cat look forward to welcoming you to and sharing our home with you.

Te Anau - Manapouri *20 km S of Te Anau*

The Cottage *B&B Homestay*
Don & Joy MacDuff
Waiau Street,
Te Anau - Manapouri

Tel (03) 249 6838
or 021 138 6110
don.joymacduff@xtra.co.nz
www.thecottagefiordland.co.nz

Double/Twin $135-$165
(Special breakfast)
The $135 double is
booking directly with us
Not suitable for children
2 Queen (2 bdrm)
Bathrooms: 2 Ensuite

Gateway to Doubtful Sound & Fiordland. Doubtful Sound Boat only a 2minute walk. Our comfortable home with cottage/decor is a combination of Old/World charm and kiwi ingenuity. Located in tranquil bush setting with lovely mountain & water views. Tea/coffee/fridge in each room.Your own private outdoor area. Excellent breakfasts. Enjoy our social hour most/evenings. We, with Millie (Dog) extend to you a warm Kiwi welcome. Directions/Pass Store and ManapouriMotors on left, continue down to PearlHarbour and we are on the bend on Rt behind the bushes.

Southland
South Catlins

Te Anau *5 km S of Te Anau*
Kepler Cottage *B&B Homestay*
Jan & Jeff Ludemann
William Stephen Road,
Te Anau

Tel (03) 249 7185
or 027 431 4076
Fax (03) 249 7186
kepler@teanau.co.nz
www.fiordlandaccommodation.co.nz

Double/Twin $150-$200
(Full breakfast)
Visa MC Diners accepted
1 Queen 3 Single (2 bdrm)
Bathrooms: 1 Ensuite 1 Private

Jeff, an aircraft engineer and Jan, who works from home as a marketing consultant, welcome you to their small farmlet on the edge of Fiordland, just 5 minutes drive from Te Anau. Relax outdoors in the garden and enjoy the peace and comfort of our rural location between visiting Milford or Doubtful Sounds, or walking one of the many nearby tracks. Our family includes Kimba our siamese cat and Ronni our cairn terrier. We can advise tours and sightseeing and make bookings where needed.

~

Te Anau *1 km N of Te Anau Centre*
Shakespeare House *B&B Separate Suite*
Marg, Jeff, Kylie & Ray
10 Dusky Street, Te Anau
PO Box 32, Te Anau

Tel (03) 249 7349
or 0800 249 349
Fax (03) 249 7629
marg.shakespeare.house@xtra.co.nz
www.shakespearehouse.co.nz

Double/Twin $100-$130
Single $90-$110
(Full breakfast)
Children $5-$15
Self-contained, 2 bedrooms - sleeps 5
Visa MC Eftpos accepted
Pet free home
Children welcome
8 King 4 Single (8 bdrm)
Bathrooms: 8 Ensuite No Baths

Shakespeare House is a well established Bed & Breakfast, where we keep a home atmosphere with personal service. We are situated in a quiet residential area yet are within walking distance of shops, lake and restaurants. Our rooms are ground floor and have the choice of king, queen or twin beds. Each room has private facilities, TV, tea/coffee making. Tariff includes continental or delicious cooked breakfast. Guest laundry available, internet and payphone facilities on site. Winter rates May to September.

Te Anau *2 km E of Te Anau*
Rose 'n' Reel *B&B Farmstay Cottage with Kitchen*

Lyn & Lex Lawrence
Ben Loch Lane,
RD 2,
Te Anau

Tel (03) 249 7582
or 027 4545 723
Fax (03) 249 7582
rosenreel@xtra.co.nz
www.rosenreel.co.nz

Double/Twin $100-$120
Single $75-$90
(Continental breakfast)
Visa MC accepted
2 Queen 1 Double/Twin
1 Single (3 bdrm)
Bathrooms: 1 Private 1 Guest share

Genuine Kiwi hospitality in a magic setting 5 minutes from Te Anau. Hand feed tame fallow deer, meet our friendly cat Ben and dog Meg. Sit on the veranda of our fully self-contained cabin and enjoy watching deer with a lake and mountain view. The 2 room cabin has cooking facilities, fridge, microwave, TV, 1 queen, 1 double plus bathroom. Our 2 storey home is set in an extensive garden. 2 guest bedrooms. Lex is a fishing guide, I love to garden. Directions: please phone.

Te Anau *1.5 km N of Te Anau*
The Croft *B&B Farmstay Cottage with Kitchen*

Jane & Ross McEwan
153 Te Anau Milford Sound Road,
RD 1,
Te Anau

Tel (03) 249 7393
or 027 682 0061
Fax (03) 249 7393
jane@thecroft.co.nz
www.thecroft.co.nz

Double/Twin $150-$175
(Continental breakfast)
Extra person $25
Visa MC accepted
2 Queen 1 Single (2 bdrm)
Bathrooms: 2 Ensuite

Warm hospitality and quality accommodation are guaranteed at The Croft, a lifestyle farm near Te Anau. Our 2 modern self-contained cottages are set in private gardens and enjoy magnificent lake and mountain views. Timber ceilings, large ensuite bathrooms, window seats and elegant furnishings are highlights. Microwaves, fridges, sinks, TVs, DVDs and CD mini systems. Enjoy breakfast with Jane & Ross or served in your cottage. Pets include Dolly the sheep, Mac the Jack Russell, Kitty and Jerry. Lake and river access from our farm.

Te Anau *1 km N of Te Anau Central*
Cosy Kiwi *B&B Guest House*
Eleanor & Derek Cook
186 Milford Road, Te Anau 9600

Tel (03) 249 7475
or 0800 249 700
Fax (03) 249 8471
info@cosykiwi.com
www.cosykiwi.com

Double/Twin $150-$165
Single $135-$150
(Special breakfast)
Children $40
Triple $175-$190
Visa MC Eftpos accepted
Children welcome
4 King 3 Queen 4 Twin
5 Single (7 bdrm)
Bathrooms: 7 Ensuite

Eleanor & Derek welcome you to our Bed & Breakfast (30 years experience in hospitality industry). Privacy with comfort, quiet spacious ensuited bedrooms, quality beds, individual heating and television. Breakfast buffet of home-made breads, jams, fresh fruits, dessert fruits, yoghurt, brewed coffee, special teas,plus mouthwatering pancakes with maple syrup or ham and cheese. Two minute walk to shops and restaurants, bookings arranged for all tours, pick-up at gate. Guest lounge with internet access, laundry, off-street parking and luggage storage.

Te Anau *5 km E of Te Anau*
Stonewall B&B *Apartment with Kitchen*
Nicky Harrison & Jim Huntington
36 Kakapo Road,
RD 2,
Te Anau

Tel (03) 249 8686
Fax (03) 249 8686
info@stonewallfiordland.co.nz
www.stonewallfiordland.co.nz

Double/Twin $150
(Continental breakfast provisions)
Children negotiable
Children welcome
1 Queen (1 bdrm)
Bathrooms: 1 Ensuite

Come up the driveway past the pond and dry stonewalls to our self-contained guest studio, sited at our home amidst our deer farm in Kakapo Road, only 5 kms out of Te Anau. You have your own private accommodation, including ensuite bathroom and kitchen. Your courtyard over looks our organic vegetable garden to the mountains of Fiordland. Enjoy the peaceful environment and home produce as we do.

Te Anau *1 km N of Town Te Anau*
Te Anau Lodge *Luxury B&B*
Matt Dagger & Chloe Marsden
52 Howden Street,
Te Anau

Tel (03) 249 7477
Fax (03) 249 7487
info@teanaulodge.co.nz
www.teanaulodge.com

Double/Twin $200-$350
Single $170-$270
(Full breakfast)
Visa MC Eftpos accepted
Children welcome
3 King/Twin 3 King 4 Queen 3 Twin 7 Single (7 bdrm)
Bathrooms: 7 Ensuite 1 Private
(7 Bathrooms in total, 2 with spa baths)

Experience the genuine warmth of traditional hospitality in the relaxed and peaceful environment of our 1936 relocated former convent. Set on 2.7 hectares with breathtaking lake and mountain views, Te Anau Lodge has been lovingly restored maintaining its original and delightful charm, with modern facilities. Enjoy our famous cooked breakfasts in the Chapel, spend your evenings relaxing in our library or having a drink in our sunny courtyard. Complimentary laundry facilities, luggage storage and high speed wireless internet access. A unique and special accommodation experience.

Te Anau - Manapouri *8 km S of Manapouri*
Connemara Cottage *B&B Farmstay Cottage with Kitchen*
Bev & Murray Hagen
415 Weir Road,
Manapouri,
Te Anau

Tel (03) 249 9399
or 027 292 3651
hagen@farmside.co.nz

Double/Twin $130-$160
(Full breakfast provisions)
Children by arrangement
1 Queen 1 Double/Twin (1 bdrm)
Bathrooms: 1 Ensuite

Yours exclusively, cosy self-contained cottage in a tranquil garden setting with magnificent mountain views. The bedroom has a queen bed while the lounge has a very comfortable double foldout sofabed. Relax and enjoy breakfast in the privacy of your cottage. Manapouri,'The Gateway to Doubtful Sound' is 5mins from our 750acre Deer, Sheep, and Cattle Farm, which bounds two fishing rivers. Murray's interests include Microlights, while Bev enjoys gardening, bowls crafts etc. We and Angel (cat) welcome you. Farm Tour inclusive when time permits.

**Southland
South Catlins**

Te Anau *0.4 km N of Te Anau Centre*
Antler Lodge *B&B Cottage with Kitchen*

Helen & Chris Whyte
44 Matai Street,
Te Anau

Tel (03) 249 8188
Fax (03) 249 8188
antler.lodge@xtra.co.nz
www.antlerlodgeteanau.co.nz

Double/Twin $130-$155
(Continental breakfast provisions)
Visa MC accepted
1 King 2 Queen (3 bdrm)
Bathrooms: 3 Ensuite

Helen and Chris invite you to enjoy their comfortable bed & breakfast accommodation. Situated in a quiet residential area close to shops, restaurants and within walking distance of the lake. We offer 3 spacious self contained units, each with a private ensuite. The 2 cottages each have kitchen facilities, tv, electric heating and comfortable furnishings. Our third unit is an upstairs suite with private entrance and sunroom dining area. Continental breakfast provisions are provided in this unit. This suite has beautiful mountain views.

Te Anau *1 km S of Central Te Anau*
Cat's Whiskers *B&B*

Anne Marie & Lindsay Bernstone
2 Lakefront Drive,
Te Anau
9600

Tel (03) 249 8112
Fax (03) 249 8112
bookings@catswhiskers.co.nz
www.catswhiskers.co.nz

Double/Twin $165-$195
Single $130-$150
(Full breakfast)
Children $30
Visa MC accepted
Children welcome
2 King 2 Queen 4 Single (4 bdrm)
Bathrooms: 4 Ensuite

Our peaceful lakefront home is a comfortable villa with 4 guest rooms all with ensuite bathrooms. Relax while you take in stunning views of Lake Te Anau. Meet fellow guests for a cooked or continental breakfast in our dining room. Opposite Department of Conservation Visitor Centre. Our cat and small Maltese dog live with us. King, Queen or Twin beds. Fast internet access. TV, fridges, tea and coffee making facilities. Booking service for local trips. Off street parking. Guest laundry and short term luggage storage.

Te Anau *5 km N of Te Anau*
Lochvista B&B *B&B*
Viv Nicholson
454 State Highway 94,
Te Anau

Tel (03) 249 7273
Fax (03) 249 7278
lochvista@xtra.co.nz
www.lochvista.co.nz

Double/Twin $160-$190
Single $150-$160
(Continental breakfast)
Full breakfast by arrangement $15pp
1 King 1 Queen 1 Twin (2 bdrm)
Bathrooms: 2 Ensuite

Welcome to Fiordland. Lochvista is situated on Te Anau Milford Highway 5km from the town centre, overlooking Lake Te Anau and Murchison mountains. 2 rooms one with queen bed and one with king/twin with ensuite, tea/coffee making facilities, fridge, TV & hairdryer. French doors onto the patio where you can sit and take in spectacular views. Fiordland has a great deal to offer and I am more than happy to help guests with any booking to make their stay more relaxing. A cat called Mischief.

Te Anau *.2 km W of central Te Anau*
House of Wood *B&B Homestay*
Merle & Cliff Buchanan
44 Moana Crescent,
Te Anau

Tel (03) 249 8404
or (021)158 6686
Fax (03) 249 7676
houseofwood@xtra.co.nz
www.houseofwood.co.nz

Double/Twin $125-$140
Single $100-$120 (Full breakfast)
Children Cost by arrangement
Dinner 3 course dinner with drinks usually served
Visa MC Eftpos accepted
Pet free home
Children welcome
2 King/Twin 1 King 3 Queen (4 bdrm)
Bathrooms: 3 Ensuite 1 Private
1 room with private bath. Separate shower & toilet

A warm welcome is assured when you arrive at our home. We really enjoy meeting guests from overseas (and locals). Our house is a unique architecturally designed home of native and exotic timber. Sit at the outdoor tables and enjoy the beautiful views. Our interests are boating, fishing, golf, rowing, gardening. We can help you plan your activities and book trips, with pick up at door. We are 2 minutes walk from town 5 minutes to Lake. Dinner by arrangement. Check-in after 2pm please.

Southland South Catlins

Mossburn *25 km S of Mossburn*
Turner Farmstay *Farmstay*
Joyce & Murray Turner
RD 1,
Otautau,
Southland

Tel (03) 225 7602
Fax (03) 225 7602
murray.joyce@farmside.co.nz
www.innz.co.nz/host/e/etalcreek.html

Double/Twin $100
Single $70
(Full breakfast)
Children under 12 $25
Dinner $35
1 Queen 4 Single (3 bdrm)
Bathrooms: 1 Private 1 Guest share

Our modern home on 301 hectares, farming sheep, is situated half-way between Invercargill and Te Anau, which can be reached in 1 hour. We enjoy meeting people, will provide quality accommodation, farm-fresh food in a welcoming friendly atmosphere. You can join in farm activities, farm tour or just relax. The Aparima River is adjacent to the property. Murray is a keen fly fisherman. Guiding & advice available. Pet Bichon Frise. Evening meal on request. Directions please phone/fax. 24 hours notice to avoid disappointment.

Mossburn *15 km SW of Mossburn*
Pembroke Farmstay *B&B Farmstay Cottage with Kitchen*
Liz and David Thomas
154 Dunrobin Valley Rd,
Mossburn,
RD 2,
Lumsden 9792

Tel (03) 248 6330
or 027 248 6329
027 390 5634
davt@woosh.co.nz
www.pembrokefarmstay.co.nz

Double/Twin $95-$95
Single $90-$90
(Full breakfast)
Children $15 per child under 12
Dinner $25 for two course meal
Children welcome
1 Double/Twin (1 bdrm)
Bathrooms: 1 Private

Liz and David welcome you to their 5000 acre sheep and cattle high country farm, in the scenic Dunrobin Valley. Join us as we go about our farm activities, if you wish. Watch our sheep dogs work. The Aparima river has good trout fishing and is 5 minutes walk from the cottage. The self contained cottage is private and very comfortable. We have pet sheep, ponies and horses. Farm fresh eggs and bacon are part of the breakfast menu, with us in the homestead.

Lumsden *12 km S of Lumsden*
Chartlea Park Farmstay *B&B Farmstay Historical*
Ken & Trish MacKenzie
1 Chartlea Park Road, Balfour, 9779

Tel (03) 201 6442
or 027 285 5121
027 285 5150
Fax (03) 201 6442
ken.trish.mack@xtra.co.nz
www.chartleaparkfarmstay.co.nz

Double/Twin $145
Single $85
(Full breakfast)
Children $45
Dinner $40pp 2 course NZ with wine
Visa MC accepted
Children welcome
4 King/Twin 1 Queen (3 bdrm)
Bathrooms: 1 Guest share 1 Family share
Bedrooms have own washstand facilities

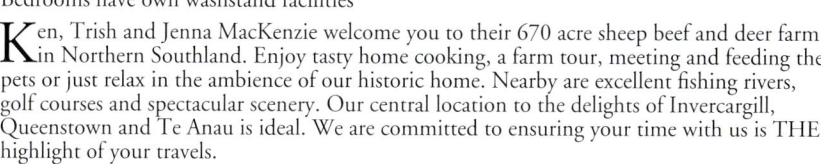

Ken, Trish and Jenna MacKenzie welcome you to their 670 acre sheep beef and deer farm in Northern Southland. Enjoy tasty home cooking, a farm tour, meeting and feeding the pets or just relax in the ambience of our historic home. Nearby are excellent fishing rivers, golf courses and spectacular scenery. Our central location to the delights of Invercargill, Queenstown and Te Anau is ideal. We are committed to ensuring your time with us is THE highlight of your travels.

Balfour *3 km N of Balfour*
Hillcrest *Homestay Farmstay*
Liz & Ritchie Clark
206 Old Balfour Road,
RD 1,
Balfour

Tel (03) 201 6165
Fax (03) 201 6165
clarkrl@xtra.co.nz
www.bnb.co.nz/hillcrestbalfour.html

Double/Twin $120-$150
Single $120-$150
(Full breakfast)
Dinner $40pp
Visa MC accepted
Children welcome
2 King/Twin 1 Single (2 bdrm)
Bathrooms: 1 Private 1 Family share

Welcome to our 650 acre sheep and deer farm, 3km from State Highway 94. Relax in our garden, enjoy a farm tour with mountain views or a game of tennis. Trout fishing in the Mataura, Oreti and Waikaia Rivers. Fishing guide can be arranged with notice. Enjoy a relaxing dinner with fine food, wine and conversation. Cooked breakfast is served and enjoy fresh baked bread, yoghurt, muesli, jams and preserves. Interests include handcrafts, tennis, photography and fishing. We have 2 cats. Directions: please phone.

Southland
South Catlins

Gore *1 km N of Gore*
Connor Homestay *Homestay*
Dawn & David Connor
29 Aotea Crescent,
Gore,
Southland

Tel (03) 208 3598
or 0800 372 484
027 669 1362
Fax (03) 208 3598
ddconnor@esi.co.nz
www.bnb.co.nz/connororchids.html

Double/Twin $100-$110
Single $80 (Full breakfast)
Dinner by arrangement
Visa MC accepted
1 King/Twin 1 Queen
1 Twin (2 bdrm)
Bathrooms: 1 Private 1 Guest share

Dawn & David invite you to enjoy quality accommodation in their modern home, situated in a quiet residential area overlooking the Hokonui Hills & farmland, close to golf course, driving range, bush walks and good fishing rivers including Mataura, well known for its brown trout. Fishing guide or advise available. We enjoy meeting people and sharing travel experiences. Laundry facilities available. Smoke-free accommodation. Please phone for directions.

Gore *3 km NW of Gore*
Hokonui Homestay *Luxury B&B Rural Lifestyle*
Brian & Shona McLennan
258 Reaby Road,
RD 4,
Gore

Tel (03) 208 4890
or 027 568 4835
Fax (03) 208 4890
bssm@sld.quik.co.nz
www.bnb.co.nz/hokonuihomestay.html

Double/Twin $100-$120
Single $80-$90
(Full breakfast)
Children negotiable
Dinner by arrangement
Visa MC accepted
Children welcome
1 King 1 Queen 1 Twin (3 bdrm)
Bathrooms: 2 Ensuite 1 Private

Brian & Shona provide a private, spacious, modern new home on a 12 acre lifestyle property with spectacular views. Private upstairs unit, underfloor heating and full size snooker table. Close to the Mataura River, 18 hole Golf Course and Native Bush Walks. A perfect base for sightseeing Southland and attending the NZ Gold Guitar Awards, Waimumu Fieldays and the Hokonui Fashion Awards. Interests - golf, fishing, dog trialing, music and wine tasting. Horse and Dog facilities available. Phone for directions.

Fortrose - The Catlins *50 km SE of Invercargill*
Greenbush *B&B Farmstay*

Ann & Donald McKenzie
298 Fortrose - Otara Road,
Fortrose, RD 5,
Invercargill

Tel (03) 246 9506
or 021 395 196
Fax (03) 246 9505
info@greenbush.co.nz
www.greenbush.co.nz

Double/Twin $160-$200
Single $120-$150
(Full breakfast)
Children negotiable
Dinner $50 by arrangement
Visa MC accepted
Pet free home
1 King 1 Queen 2 Single (3 bdrm)
Bathrooms: 3 Ensuite

Greenbush Bed & Breakfast is ideally located off the Southern Scenic Route from Fortrose. Within 30 minutes drive from Greenbush you can enjoy Curio Bay, Waipapa Point and Slope Point,the southern most point of the South island. Greenbush is nestled in 2 acres of garden. You will wake to the song of birds and magnificent views of green rolling countryside. Enjoy our beach.We would appreciate it if guests arrived after 4 p.m Directions:- at Fortrose take Coastal Route drive 4km.

Invercargill *5 km N of Invercargill city*
Glenroy Park Homestay *B&B Homestay*

Margaret & Alan Thomson
23 Glenroy Park Drive,
Invercargill

Tel (03) 215 8464
or 027 376 2228
Fax (03) 215 8464
home_hosp@actrix.co.nz
www.bnb.co.nz/glenroypark.html

Double/Twin $110-$120
Single $75-$85
(Full breakfast)
Children $12 up to 12 years
Dinner $35 3 course
Children welcome
1 Queen 1 Twin 1 Single (3 bdrm)
Bathrooms: 1 Private 1 Guest share
Heated tile floors

Exclusively yours, in a quiet retreat near restaurants and parks. Be our special guests and share an evening of relaxation and friendship. Our interests are golfing, meeting people, travel and cooking. We look forward to your visit. Invercargill is the gateway to Queenstown, Fiordland, Catlins and Stewart Island. Directions: from Queenstown turn left at second lights (Bainfield Road), take first left, third house on left. From Dunedin turn right at second set of lights (Queens Drive), travel to end, turn left, first street right, third house left.

**Southland
South Catlins**

Invercargill *5 km W of Invercargill*
The Oak Door *B&B*

Lisa & Bill Stuart
22 Taiepa Road,
Otatara,
RD 9,
Invercargill 9879

Tel (03) 213 0633
Fax (03) 213 0633
blstuart@xtra.co.nz

Double/Twin $100
Single $80
(Full breakfast)
Children POA
Pet free home
Non smokers only
2 Queen 2 Twin (3 bdrm)
Bathrooms: 2 Guest share

Bill (Kiwi) & Lisa (Canadian) welcome you to their warm, self-built, unique home. Enjoy attractive gardens and native bush setting; minutes from: Invercargill CBD, Scenic route amenities, airport. Coffee/tea awaits you on arrival at The Oak Door. Guests comment on a warm comfortable visit, where beds, breakfast and hospitality are quality plus! A Warm Welcome! (Nonsmoking/no pet). Directions: Drive past the airport entrance. Take first left (Marama Avenue South). Take first right Taiepa Road second drive on right (#22).

Invercargill *3 km N of Invercargill City Centre*
Gimblett Place *B&B*

Alex & Eileen Henderson
122 Gimblett Place,
Kildare,
Invercargill

Tel (03) 215 6888
Fax (03) 215 6888
the_grove@xtra.co.nz
www.bnb.co.nz/hosts/gimblettplace

Double/Twin $95
Single $65
(Full breakfast)
Children negotiable
Dinner by arrangement
Visa MC accepted
Pet free home
1 Queen 2 Single (2 bdrm)
Bathrooms: 1 Guest share

Eileen & Alex are experienced hosts who are ex-farmers and offer comfortable accommodation in a quiet cul-de-sac close to city amenities, golf, parks, restaurants. We are pleased to assist with local and tourist information and can guide if required (ie Catlins). Alex is a vintage car and machinery enthusiast and can arrange good viewing. Close to famous trout fishing rivers. Directions: find Queens Drive, Gimblett Street is first left north of Thomsons Bush, fourth right into Gimblett Place (cul-de-sac)

Invercargill - Waianiwa *18 km W of Invercargill*

Annfield Flowers *B&B Homestay*
Margaret & Mike Cockeram
126 Argyle-Otahuti Road,
Waianiwa,
RD 4,
Invercargill 9874

Tel (03) 235 2690
or 021 385 134
Fax (03) 235 2745
annfield@woosh.co.nz

Double/Twin $110-$120
(Full breakfast)
Dinner $20 to $30
Visa MC accepted
1 King/Twin 1 Double/Twin
(2 bdrm)
Bathrooms: 1 Ensuite

We are 1km from the Southern Scenic Route (signposted Waianiwa/Drummond. Annfield has modern facilities but retains 1860's character. Our sunny guest room opens into the garden. We only host one party at a time. We are semi-retired, and keep coloured sheep and alpacas. We enjoy meeting people and sharing dinner or a light meal, including our own produce. Our dog, Meg, will greet you and she and two cats have limited access to the house. Complimentary laundry facilities.

Invercargill *10 km E of Invercargill on Southern Scenic Rte*

Long Acres Farmstay *Farmstay Self-contained & B&B*
Helen & Graeme Spain
Waimatua, RD 11, Invercargill

Tel (03) 216 4470
or 027 228 1308
Fax (03) 216 4470
longacres@woosh.co.nz
www.longacres.co.nz

Double/Twin $120-$150
Single $100-$120
(Full breakfast)
Children negotiable Dinner $45
Self-contained $160-$200
Visa MC accepted
Children welcome
2 Queen 1 Double/Twin 1 Twin (4 bdrm)
Bathrooms: 1 Queen Ensuite 1
Queen Private 1 Double guests share

Enjoy Southland Hospitality at our 1300acre Sheep and Dairy farm, with amazing bush/bird walk. Free Farm Tour. 30minutes to Bluff. Stewart Island a great day trip. Ideal stopover for Catlins, Te Anau,Queenstown and Dunedin. We offer a quality farmstay retreat. Home cooked meals available. Guest Comments "Great Hospitality" A peaceful relaxed farmstay for the length of time you choose. Directions from Invercargill,east on Southern Scenic Route approximately 10kms or 15minutes. Look for Long Acres Farmstay Sign on left.

**Southland
South Catlins**

Invercargill *4 km N of Invercargill Central*
Stoneleigh Homestay *B&B Homestay*

Joan & Neville Milne
15 Stoneleigh Lane,
Invercargill

Tel (03) 215 8921
joan@stoneleighhomestay.co.nz
www.stoneleighhomestay.co.nz

Double/Twin $110-$125
Single $80-$90
(Full breakfast)
Dinner $35
Visa MC accepted
Pet free home
1 Queen 3 Single (3 bdrm)
Bathrooms: 1 Private 1 Guest share

We welcome guests to share our modern home in a quiet lane 5 minutes from the main centre, and just off the main road to TeAnau and Queenstown. We have underfloor heating, electric blankets and guests have their own TV. We are keen golfers and members of the Invercargill club, a championship course rated in the top 10 in N.Z. Our interests are golf, travel, gardening, cooking, wine and meeting people. Enjoy our hospitality, share an evening meal with us. Pick ups can be arranged.

Invercargill *6 km NE of Invercargill*
The Manor *B&B Homestay*

Pat & Frank Forde
9 Drysdale Road,
Myross Bush, RD 2, Invercargill

Tel (03) 230 4788
or 027 667 0904
Fax (03) 230 4788
the.manor@xtra.co.nz
www.manorbb.co.nz

Double/Twin $110-$150
Single $70-$85
(Full breakfast)
Children negotiable
Dinner By arrangement
Visa MC accepted
Pet free home Children welcome
3 Queen 2 Single (3 bdrm)
Bathrooms: 1 Ensuite 1 Private 1 Guest share one

Relax, enjoy our warm, comfortable home, underfloor-heating, a sheltered garden setting, 10 acre farmlet (sheep, lambs, horses, hens). Private guest area, television, refrigerator, tea/coffee making facilities. We are retired farmers, golfers, enjoy gardening, harness racing, travel, meeting people. Pleasant outdoor areas, meals of fresh home-grown produce, cooked/ continental breakfasts. Courtesy pick up. A stop on your way to Stewart Island, Southern Scenic Route, Queenstown or Te Anau. We would enjoy having you stay with us. 5 minutes drive north east Invercargill along State Highway 1.

Invercargill *0.01 km NW of Invercargill City Centre*
Victoria Railway Hotel *Hotel*

Trudy & Eian Read
3 Leven Street, off Picadilly Lane,
Invercargill

Tel (03) 218 1281
Fax (03) 218 1283
vrhotel@xtra.co.nz
www.vrhotel.info

Double/Twin $145-$160
Single $117-$130
(Full breakfast)
Children $15
Dinner Mains $26-$32 pp Breakfast
- $10-$20 pp
Visa MC Diners Amex Eftpos accepted
5 Queen 4 Double/Twin
2 Twin (11 bdrm)
Bathrooms: 11 Ensuite 2 Guest share

Come and enjoy old world charm and southern hospitality in a boutique hotel in the heart of the city. This Invercargill Landmark built in 1896 is a Class 1 heritage building. Architecturally designed upgrade completed May 2004. City Council Environment Award recipient May 2007. Variety of accommodation options including Executive and VIP, plus two Ground floor Accessible units. Come relax in our lounge bar before dining in and enjoy traditional home cooked meals and a selection of fine NZ wines and local Invercargill Beers.

Invercargill *15 km N of Invercargill*
Tudor Park Country Stay and Garden *B&B Homestay Country Stay*
Garden & Beach House

Joyce & John Robins
RD 6, Invercargill, 9876

Tel (03) 221 7150
or 027 431 0031
Fax (03) 221 7150
tudorparksouth@hotmail.com
www.tudorpark.co.nz

Double/Twin $140-$220
Single $100-$130 (Full breakfast)
Dinner by arrangement from $45
Cottage at Riverton $150 a night,
minimum 2 nights
Visa MC accepted
Children welcome with
parent supervision
1 King/Twin 3 Queen
1 Twin (5 bdrm)
Bathrooms: 2 Ensuite 1 Private 1 Guest share in cottage

Tudor Park has been tastefully decorated and furnished with antiques and quality linens. All rooms have their own facilities and garden views. Guests privacy is respected whilst enjoying quality accommodation with friendly persoalised service. You are welcome to relax, enjoy the large garden, animals & attractions of the area. We enjoy travel, overseas & in NZ, walking & people. We also have a house 20mtres from the beach at Riverton. Please enquire.

Southland
South Catlins

Invercargill - Otatara *5 km W of Invercargii*
Otatara Golf Stay *B&B Homestay*

Suzanne Forbes
39 Aicken Road,
Otatara,
RD 9,
Invercargill 9051

Tel 03 213 1418
or 027 252 6807
Fax 03 213 1448
suzanne.forbes@xtra.co.nz

Double/Twin $90-$120
Single $80-$100
(Full breakfast)
Pets welcome
2 Queen 1 Double/Twin (3 bdrm)
Bathrooms: 1 Ensuite 1 Family share

We have been in farming all our lives now having a change. Otatara Golf Stay offers you peace & privacy in comfortable accommodation. Stunning garden walk, just unravel & relax have a wine after a busy day.

Bluff *25 km S of Invercargill*
The Lazy Fish *Separate Suite Cottage with Kitchen*

Robyn & Roy Horwell
35 Burrows Street, Bluff, 9814

Tel (03) 212 7245
or 021 211 7424
Fax (03) 212 8868
horwell@thelazyfish.co.nz
www.thelazyfish.co.nz

Double/Twin $100-$120
(Breakfast by arrangement)
Continental breakfast $8.50pp
Children welcome
2 Double/Twin (2 bdrm)
Bathrooms: 2 Ensuite

Very homely fully self-contained unit attached to our home, in a peacefull garden setting. Sleeps 4, double bed in bedroom and sofa bed in lounge. Also double bedroom attached to house, tea & coffee making facilities and microwave. Sunny shelterd courtyard. Friendly labrador in residence. Gateway to Stewart Island and Southern Scenic Route. Take a break and absorb our Coastal and native bush walks, maritime museum, restaurants and supermarket all within walking distance. 5 minutes walk to Stewart Island ferry. Continental breakfast by arrangement.

Riverton *45 km W of Invercargill*

Reo Moana *B&B*

Jean Broomfield
192 Rocks Highway,
Riverton,
Southland

Tel (03) 234 9044
Fax (03) 234 9047
alanb@orcon.net.nz

Double/Twin $150
Single $100
(Full breakfast)
Children negotiable
Pet free home
Children welcome
1 King 1 Twin (2 bdrm)
Bathrooms: 2 Ensuite
Excellent Showers & heated tile floors

Reo Moana overlooks a beautiful secluded swimming and surfing beach with extended views to the open sea beyond, and northward to the mountains and hills of Southland. Tastefully decorated, the warm and spacious guest rooms each have ensuite bathrooms and sea views. Your host Jean has many years experience in the tourism industry. I welcome you to Riverton, on the Southern Scenic Route and just 45 minutes from Tuatapere and the Humpridge track.

Stewart Island *1 km S of Oban*

Glendaruel Bed & Breakfast *B&B*

Raylene & Ronnie Waddell
38 Golden Bay Road,
Oban,
Stewart Island

Tel (03) 219 1092
Fax (03) 219 1092
r.r.waddell@xtra.co.nz
www.glendaruel.co.nz

Double/Twin $200
Single $100-$150
(Full breakfast)
Children by arrangement
Dinner $40 by arrangement
Visa MC accepted
1 King/Twin 1 Queen
1 Single (3 bdrm)
Bathrooms: 3 Ensuite

Peaceful bush setting, 10 minutes walk from village, 3 minutes from Golden Bay on beautiful Paterson Inlet. Handy for water taxis, kayak hire, sandy beaches and bush walks. Large guest lounge and three balconies with bush and sea views. Colourful garden - bird lovers' paradise. Central heating. Courtesy transfers. Advice and assistance with local activities. We have travelled widely and love welcoming guests from around the world. Our friendly Cairn Terrier, Douglas, helps us provide traditional Scottish and Kiwi hospitality. "A Hundred Thousand Welcomes!"

Southland
South Catlins

Stewart Island *0.2 km W of Oban township*
Sails Ashore & Kowhai Lane B&B *Luxury B&B*
Apartment with Kitchen Holiday Home & Self-catering Flat
Iris and Peter Tait
11 View Street & 6 Kowhai Lane, Stewart Island

Tel (03) 219 1151 or 0800 783 9278 (0800 Stewart)
Fax (03) 219 1151
tait@sailsashore.co.nz
www.sailsashore.co.nz

Double/Twin $150-$405 (Breakfast by arrangement)
Restaurants nearby for dinner
Please Note Photos are of Sails Ashore
Visa MC Eftpos accepted
Pet free home Not suitable for children
3 King/Twin 1 Queen 2 Single (2 bdrm)
Bathrooms: 6 Ensuite

Sails Ashore is everything discerning guests would expect from a Qualmark 4 Star plus hosted boutique accommodation. Kowhai Lane Holiday home is 4 star self catering and available on either a room or whole of house basis. Both are situated within 4 or 5 minutes stroll of the village centre and overlook the harbour.

All rooms are fully ensuite and centrally heated. Facilities include an extensive library of books and local interest DVDs to enjoy on lazy evenings. Both are an ideal base from which to explore the magic of Stewart Island.

Hosts Iris and Peter have over 70 years combined Island life. Peter was one time Forest Ranger in Charge of Stewart Island and Iris a foundation Trustee of Ulva.

Both places are **packaged** with a Sails guided exploration of Ulva Island Open Sanctuary. We also offer road tours exploring Island life from days of early Maori up to the present. Tours are run on demand to suit both guests and weather on the day with a maximum party size of 6 per guide. The Ulva Island walk is added to the first night tariff at both Sails Ashore & Kowwhai Lane.

Index

A

Abel Tasman 324-325
Acacia Bay 179, 181
Ahipara 11
Airedale 431
Akaroa 399-405
Albany 73
Albert Town 440
Alexandra 462
Alfriston 94
Amberley 366-367
Anakiwa 289
Anaura Bay 187
Aro Valley 268
Arrowtown 449-453
Ashburton 410-412
Atawhai 299, 305, 307
Auckland 78-94
Auckland Airport 91-92
Avondale 381
Avonhead 374

B

Balclutha 474
Balfour 487
Banks Peninsula 398
Barry's Bay 399
Barrytown 340
Bayly's Beach 37
Bayswater 75
Bay View 208-210
Bell Block 194
Bethells Beach 68
Blenheim 290-296
Blue Spur 348
Bluff 494
Bream Bay 46
Brightwater 311
Brixton 191
Broad Bay 469, 470, 473
Brooklands 370
Brooklyn 275
Burnside 374, 375

C

Cambridge 108-110
Cape Foulwind 335-336
Cape Karikari 9
Carters Beach 337
Carterton 240
Castle Hill 405
Charleston 339
Christchurch 370-394
Clevedon 95
Coatesville 73
Collingwood 328, 329
Cooks Beach 128
Coopers Beach 10
Coromandel 123-125
Cromwell 447-449
Culverden 365

D

Darfield 406
Dargaville 36-38
Days Bay 258
Devonport 75-77
Diamond Harbour 397
Drury 97
Dunedin 465-469

E

Eastbourne 258-260
Egmont National Park 196
Eketahuna 237
Ellerslie 87
Enner Glynn 308
Eskdale 207
Ettrick 462

F

Fairlie 420, 421
Feilding 229-230
Fendalton 377
Fernside 368
Fortrose 489
Fox Glacier 350-353
Franz Josef 349
French Farm 402

French Pass 297

G

Garston 461
Geraldine 414-416
Gisborne 188-189
Glenbervie 44
Glenorchy 460
Gore 488
Governors Bay 396
Gowan Valley 331
Greenhithe 74
Grey Lynn 85
Greymouth 341-344

H

Hahei 131
Hamilton 101-107
Hamurana 173
Hanmer Springs 363-365
Harbourview 256
Harewood 371, 372
Hastings 219-221
Hataitai 274
Havelock North 221-223
Hawarden 366
Herne Bay 78
Hillsborough 91
Hobsonville 68
Hokitika 344-348
Hot Water Beach 132
Houhora 9
Howick 90
Huntly 100
Huntsbury 389

I

Ilam 376
Invercargill 489-494
Island Bay 276-280

J

Johnsonville 260-261

K

Kaiapoi 370
Kaiaua 95
Kaikoura 356-362
Kaitaia 10
Kaiteriteri 321-324
Kaiwaka 49
Kaka Point 475-476
Karamea 334-335
Karangahake 117
Karori 266, 267
Katikati 139-141
Kelburn 268
Kenepuru Sounds 284
Kerikeri 11-13
Khandallah 262
Kimbell 421
Kohukohu 33
Koromiko 289
Kuaotunu 126-127
Kumeu 67
Kurow 427

L

Lake Okareka 173
Lake Pukaki 422-423
Lake Rotoiti 167
Lake Tarawera 163
Lake Tekapo 421-422
Lake Wanaka 445, 447
Lawrence 464
Levin 233-235
Lincoln 394-395
Lindis Pass 426
Lower Hutt 255-257
Lowry Bay 259
Lumsden 487
Lyttelton 395
Lyttelton Harbour 396

M

Macandrew Bay 470
Mahanga Beach 207
Mahau Sound 285
Mahia Peninsula 207

Mahina Bay 260
Makarora 434
Manapouri 479, 483
Mandeville 370
Mangamaunu 360
Mangawhai Heads 52
Mangere 92
Mangere Bridge 91
Manukau 93
Manurewa 94
Mapua 312-313
Marahau 324
Martinborough 241-242
Marton 205
Masterton 237-240
Matakana 59
Matakohe 39
Matangi 107
Matata 148-149
Matauwhi Bay 24
Matua 144
Merivale 378-379
Methven 406-408
Middlemarch 463
Millers Flat 463
Miranda 96
Mission Bay 88
Mosgiel 473-474
Mossburn 486
Motueka 318-320
Motueka Valley 316-317
Motuoapa 183
Mount Cook 425
Mount Tiger 44
Mt Cook 269, 270, 275,
       422, 423, 424
Mt Eden 86
Mt Hutt 406-408
Mt Maunganui 145-146
Mt Pleasant 390, 391
Mt Somers 409
Mt Victoria 270-271
Murchison 331
Murray Aynsley 389

N

Napier 208-218
Napier - Hastings 218
Nelson 299-309
Nelson Lakes 330-331
Newmarket 85
New Plymouth 191-195
New River 344
Ngaio 263
Ngakawau 338
Ngakuru 158
Ngongotaha 161-171
North East Valley 468
North Shore 72

O

Oamaru 428-432
Oaro 357
Ohakune 201
Ohaupo 102, 104
Ohoka 369
Ohope 154
Ohope Beach 152-154
Okahu Bay 87
Okaihau 12
Okains Bay 398
Okere Falls 167
Okiato 27, 30
Okura 72
Omapere 34-35
Omokoroa 142
Onerahi 42
Opito Bay 127
Opononi 33-34
Opotiki 155-156
Opua 21-23
Orakei 87
Orewa 62-63
Otago Peninsula 469-473
Otane 224
Otatara 494
Otorohanga 112
Owaka 476-477
Owhango 200
Oxford 368-369

P

Paeroa 117
Paihia 14-23
Pakaraka 32
Pakawau 330
Palmerston 432
Palmerston North 230-232
Pamapuria 10
Papakura 96
Papamoa 145
Papanui 376
Paparoa 39, 40
Parapara 328
Paraparaumu 249
Paremata 252
Parnell 82
Patons Rock Beach 326
Paua Bay 400
Pelorus 285
Pelorus Sounds 297
Picton 282-290
-Piha 71
Pikowai 149
Pio Pio 115
Piriaka 199
Pleasant Point 419
Plimmerton 250, 251
Ponsonby 79, 80, 81
Portobello 472
Puhoi 60, 61
Pukehiki 472
Pukehina Beach 148
Pukerua Bay 250
Puketapu 216
Punakaiki 340

Q

Queen Charlotte Sounds 284-285, 289
Queenstown 452-460

R

Raetihi 200
Raglan 100
Rakaia 410

Ramarama 98
Rangiora 367-368
Rangitikei 203
Ranui 70
Rapaura 290
Raumati Beach 249
Red Beach 63
Redcliffs 390
Reefton 333
Remuera 82-85
Renwick 296-297
Rerewhakaaitu 172
Riccarton 377, 378
Richmond 310-311, 380
Riverhead 73
Riverton 495
Roseneath 272, 273, 274
Rotorua 157-173
Roxburgh 462-463
Ruakaka 46-47
Ruatapu 348
Ruby Bay 314-315
Russell 24-31

S

Sandspit 55-58
Seadown 417
Seatoun 276
Silverdale 64, 66
Snells Beach 60
St Albans 379
St Arnaud 330
Staveley 409
Stewart Island 495-496
St Heliers 89
St Martins 387
Stokes Valley 257
Stratford 196
Sumner 392-394
Sumner Beach 392
Swanson 69
Sydenham 386

T

Tahunanui 309
Taihape 202-205
Taiharuru 43
Tairua 132
Takaka 326-327
Tamahere 103
Tangowahine 38
Taradale 214, 218
Tata Beach 326
Taumarunui 199-200
Taupo 174-181
Tauranga 143-144
Tawa 252-253
Te Anau 479-485
Te Awamutu 111
Teddington 396
Te Hana 53
Te Horo 245
Te Kouma 124
Te Kuiti 114
Te Marua 254
Templeton 385
Te Pahu 106
Te Puke 146-147
Te Puru 123
Te Wahapu 26, 29
Thames 117-123
The Catlins 475-477, 489
The Redwoods 170
Tia Tapu 395
Timaru 417-420
Tirau 110
Titirangi 90
Tolaga Bay 187
Totara 122
Turangi 182-185
Twizel 423-426

U

Upper Hutt 254
Upper Kokatahi 345
Upper Moutere 315

V

Vogeltown 275

W

Wadestown 264-265
Waianakarua 428
Waianiwa 491
Waihau Bay 156
Waiheke Island 78
Waihi 134, 135
Waihi Beach 136, 137
Waikanae 245-248
Waikanae Beach 246-247
Waikouaiti 464
Waimarama Beach 224
Wainui 64
Waipaoa 188
Waipawa 225-226
Waipu Cove 47-49
Waipukurau 226-227
Waitakere Ranges 69
Waitarere Beach 233
Waitoki 66
Waitomo Caves 113
Waitomo District 112-115
Waitotara 197
Waiwera 62
Wakefield 312
Wanaka 434-446
Wanganui 197, 198
Warkworth 54-60
Wellington 260-280
Wellsford 53, 54
Westmorland 388
Westport 335-338
Westshore 210
Whakamarama 144
Whakatane 149-151
Whangamata 133
Whangaparaoa 64-66
Whangarei 40-45
Whangarei Heads 45
Whataroa 349
Whatawhata 106

Whatuwhiwhi 9
Whitianga 128-130
Winchester 416

Y

Yaldhurst 373
York Bay 258

The New Zealand
Bed & Breakfast
Book

Please help us to keep our standards high

To help maintain the high reputation of **The New Zealand Bed & Breakfast Book** we ask for your comments about your stay.
You can simply stick a stamp on this form or save all your comment forms and return them in an envelope.

Alternatively, leave your comment at our website
www.bnb.co.nz

Name of Host or B&B_____

Address _____

_____

Considering things such as breakfast, meals, beds, cleanliness, hospitality and value for money, what is your overall satisfaction rating, with 1 being the lowest and 10 being the highest rating?

1   2   3   4   5   6   7   8   9   10

Do you have any comments?

We may display your comments on our website. The rating will be confidential and will be kept for administration purposes.
Fill in your details to go into our regular prize draws!
Your details will not be passed on to anyone else. If you do not have email we suggest you use a friend's email address.

Your name   _____

Your Town/city
and country   _____

Email   _____

Please Post this form to:
The New Zealand B&B Book,
PO Box 6843, Wellington, New Zealand

501

Place stamp
here or send
forms in one
envelope

Moonshine Press
PO Box 6843
Wellington
New Zealand